Luddens' *Adult* Guide to Colleges and Universities

LaVerne L. Ludden, Ed.D.
Marsha Ludden, M.A.

Park Avenue

An imprint of JIST Works, Inc.

Luddens' Adult Guide to Colleges and Universities
© 1997 by LaVerne L. Ludden, Ed.D., and Marsha Ludden, M.A.

Other Books by These Authors
Back to School: A College Guide for Adults
Mind Your Own Business!
Franchise Opportunities Handbook
Effective Communication Skills
Job Savvy
You Can Bank on It!
Checking & Savings Accounts
Consumer Loans & Credit Cards

Published by Park Avenue Productions
An imprint of JIST Works, Inc.
720 N. Park Avenue
Indianapolis, IN 46202-3431
Phone: 317-264-3720   Fax: 317-264-3709
E-mail: JISTWorks@AOL.com or jistinfo@in.net

Cover Design by Brad Luther

Ludden, LaVerne, 1949-
    [Adult guide to colleges and universities]
    Luddens' adult guide to colleges and universities / LaVerne L.
Ludden, Marsha Ludden.
      p. cm.
    ISBN 1-57112-076-9
    1. Adult education—United States—Handbooks, manuals, etc.
    2. Continuing education—United States—Handbooks, manuals, etc.
    3. Universities and colleges—United States—Directories.
    I. Ludden, Marsha. II. Title
    LC5251.L83 1997
    374'.973—dc20   96-34855
                            CIP

Printed in the United States of America

99 98 97 96   5 4 3 2 1

We have been careful to provide accurate information throughout this book, but it is possible that errors and omissions have been introduced. Please consider this in making any important decisions. Trust your own judgment above all else and in all things.

ISBN: 1-57112-076-9

Table of Contents

Introduction

uddens' Adult Guide to Colleges and Universities provides you with information on nearly 500 adult-friendly colleges and universities. More than 2,500 two-year, four-year, and graduate degree programs are represented. Every one of these colleges is an accredited and respected institution. Classroom-based programs in this guide can be found in all 50 states, the District of Columbia, and Puerto Rico. In addition, a large number of nontraditional programs are listed. These include guided study, correspondence, televised, videotaped, and computer-based courses. You will not find a more comprehensive guide to nontraditional-and traditional-degree programs for adults.

This book is a valuable reference guide if you're thinking about returning to college for either an undergraduate or graduate degree. The colleges listed provide programs that make it far more convenient for adults to pursue a degree than has ever been possible. It is now possible to take college classes in many cities at work sites, high schools, shopping malls, and other accessible locations. You can speed up the process of earning a degree by getting credit for life experience and exams. Programs are offered at night, on weekends, weekly, monthly, through week-long seminars, and in almost every other format imaginable. If you can't get to the class, let it come to you through television or computer. This guide will help you identify several colleges that can meet your special needs and concerns.

Chapter 1 gives advice and information about going back to school, gleaned from a companion book by Dr. LaVerne L. Ludden—*Back to School: A College Guide for Adults* (Indianapolis: JIST Works, Inc., Park Avenue, 1996). You'll find suggestions for overcoming many of the doubts that adults face when contemplating a return to school. It describes the academic world and what every adult student should know about pursuing a college degree. The chapter also introduces you to nontraditional degree programs and explains how they work. Most important, you'll discover practical information that can help you get started and succeed in college.

Chapter 2 focuses on how to identify, evaluate, and select a college that best meets your needs. Our goal is to help you find a college that is not only reputable, convenient, and adult-friendly but also most likely to ensure your achievement of a degree. Going to college is only the first step in advancing your career. The ultimate goal is graduation. Discovering the college that will help you accomplish this goal is a vital step and should be given careful attention and time. Reading through this chapter will make you a wiser consumer of educational services.

The bulk of this book is devoted to a listing of detailed information on nearly 500 colleges and universities. Traditional college guides provide information about traditional degrees, dorm life, social activities, and athletics. This guide contains data on nontraditional degrees, concentrations or majors available, extended classroom sites, admissions requirements for nontraditional students, exams for credit, credit for life experience, services for adult students, and much more data of particular interest to adult students. This guide will help you identify and understand the many degree programs available in formats designed for adult students. Enough data is included on each college to help you determine which ones you want to contact for further information.

Information for this guide was obtained through surveys distributed to each institution in the book. Most of the colleges responded to a survey distributed in the first quarter of 1996. Some institutions not responding to this survey had responded to an earlier one distributed in 1995—they are marked in the guide with an asterisk (*) after their name. Institutions that submitted a response to either survey were included, providing readers with the largest possible collection of adult-friendly degree programs. To avoid distorting or misinterpreting information, we have tried to retain the original wording used by college officials when answering questions in the survey.

Many readers will be aware of colleges that are adult-friendly but are not included in this guide. This is not due to a lack of effort on our part. We have sent out four questionnaires during the past year to more than 1,000 colleges and universities. Some well-known institutions that are key providers of adult higher education chose not to respond. We are not sure of the reasons for this, but can only speculate that they feel too busy or do not think it is worth their time.

Keep in mind that institutions that responded to the survey did so because they are interested in serving adult students and want as many adults as possible to know about their programs. We think this demonstrates a positive attitude toward adult students and that any of these institutions would be a good choice for an adult considering the pursuit of a college degree.

We are interested in hearing from our readers. Let us know what you think about this guide. Is there more information you would like to have about colleges? What parts of the book are most useful to you? What would you like to see changed? Did this book help you get started on a degree? Future editions of this guide can be made more useful with feedback from readers. We welcome your thoughts and concerns. Contact us through our publisher.

Chapter 1

Going Back to College

Returning to college is a challenge being accepted by millions of adults throughout the United States. For some, seeking a college degree has been a lifelong dream. Perhaps circumstances in their lives prevented their attending college in their earlier days. Some may have started a degree but never completed it. Others may not have been disciplined enough right after high school to be academically successful in college. Dropping out of school was a solution to their problem. Now as adults, earning a college degree has become a driving force. Some adult students are fulfilling a promise to parents to get a degree. Others are setting an example for their own children. Difficulty in getting promotions or even jobs motivates some adults to return to college and get a degree.

If you are an adult who has decided to return to college, you need to consider potential obstacles to your educational success. Adult students often share common concerns and doubts. Before making a decision to go back to college, review the challenges listed in this chapter and the suggestions for successfully surmounting them.

Do I Belong in College?

In the past, college has been thought of as the gathering place of the young. Customarily, students have been encouraged to enter college as soon as they completed high school. While this is the norm in our society, it may not be in the student's best interest. Often young students, lacking maturity and self-discipline, find plenty of time to socialize but little time for serious academic work. Even serious students may have difficulty applying their theoretical learning to real-life situations when they enter the workplace.

While colleges still recruit high school graduates, adults students have increasingly become an important part of their student bodies. Statistics indicate that at the end of this decade at least 50 percent of undergraduate and graduate students will be over 25 years of age, and many will be 35 years and older. Colleges find adult students to be more focused, better prepared, and more independent in their studies. Adults can expect to perform as well as or even better than they would have as traditional students.

Colleges recognize that adults belong in their classrooms. Colleges and universities are changing class hours, curricula, methods of class registration, and location of classes to meet the needs of adult students. Students today can take classes by correspondence, video, television, and computer. Classes are offered at locations more convenient to adults: in businesses, local high schools, and shopping malls. Some colleges have established special offices that specifically aid adult students in their college experience.

So do you—an adult—belong in college? The answer is yes. A college education today is definitely for adults. You have the ability to learn. You will find a large percentage of adults among the student body. You can find a college that meets your needs as an adult.

What If My Grades Aren't Good Enough?

Adult students often lack confidence in their learning abilities now because they are looking back at their youthful performance. Perhaps you didn't have great grades in high school and chose not to attend college, or maybe you dropped out of college because of poor grades. Before you decide that you can't be academically successful, recall what you were like at that time. How mature were you? Was your social life more important than academics? Did you have difficulty adjusting to a large university? Did you have conflicts with teachers? Did you have problems focusing and completing work on time? Were you experiencing some emotional, physical, or financial problems? Often our life situations affect our concentration and ability to make the grade.

You should also consider the skills you have developed in your work. Many of those skills will help you in the classroom. Do you speak to groups? Do you write reports? Do you participate in group meetings? Do you organize your work? Do you take notes at meetings? Do you participate in training activities? Do you study problems and find solutions? These skills help make you a better student and increase your potential for success in college.

Adults are often afraid of college math and foreign language requirements. They may not have used geometry or algebra for years. They may never have taken a foreign language at all. Don't be overly concerned about these course requirements; there are many ways that colleges help adults address these issues. Many colleges offer free tutoring to students needing help in math. Depending on your major area of study, a foreign language may not even be required, and usually only college-level algebra is required to meet the math requirements. However, as the global economy grows, many businesses are encouraging their employees to become skilled in foreign languages. This skill might be a benefit in finding a job or advancing, and again tutoring may be available.

Matching a program and school to your needs and academic preferences is important to your success. If you dropped out of a large university, a small college may be the place for you. On the other hand, perhaps you find a large university more appealing. Schools offering a structured program may be helpful to you. Perhaps you want more independent courses to meet your needs. Taking time to select an appropriate college will have a direct effect on how well you do.

Is That Degree Really Going to Help Me?

For many adults, graduation day is the fulfillment of a goal set long ago. On graduation day, the pride of accomplishment, the attainment of a goal, and the increased sense of self-worth cannot be measured. The confidence earning a degree instills will be an important asset in your future endeavors.

Your degree has more tangible outcomes as well. As technology increases, businesses require more education. Fewer jobs require only a high school education. New jobs with higher wages require education beyond high school. White-collar jobs in many large companies are being eliminated. Managers tend to keep employees or promote those employees with the most education. Nearly 27 percent of the workforce now has a college degree. Higher education is becoming almost a necessity rather than an option to remain competitive in today's workforce.

Higher education also means higher earnings. In 1996, the U.S. Census Bureau reported that the mean monthly earnings for high school graduates in 1993 were $1,080, compared to $2,339 for college graduates. Individuals with advanced degrees earn $3,331, while those with professional degrees earn $5,067. Another important fact contained in this report is that the difference in monthly earnings for four-year college graduates was 99 percent greater than high school graduates in 1983, but the figure in 1993 was 117 percent—an increase of 18 percent. Of course, earnings are greatly affected by your major. College graduates with degrees in engineering earn an average of $3,189 compared to $1,699 for graduates with degrees in education.

Reports from the U.S. Department of Labor indicate that college graduates have a lower unemployment rate. This means that over a lifetime, they make more money than high school graduates or graduates with a vocational certificate. Of course, circumstances may affect the financial benefits of a college education. You may know a college graduate who is unemployed or who makes less money than you do. You may even be supervising a college graduate. These statistics are averages and vary from one part of the country to another or from one person to another. However, for many people, a college degree helps them achieve a more satisfying life both personally and financially.

How Long Will It Take?

For many adults the time needed to complete a degree has been a hindrance to returning to school. Some adults complete their degrees in 3 years. Others may work on their degrees for 10 or 12 years. To get a perspective on the time needed, consider that no matter how long it takes to gain a degree, you will be better off when it is completed. Getting started is essential. When you put off starting a degree program, you are only prolonging the time required to complete your degree. Even a small start is progress toward your goal.

Many colleges and universities offer ways of speeding up the process of earning a degree. Accelerated degree programs allow you to complete courses in a 5- to 7-week period—a semester is normally 15 to 18 weeks long. Accelerated programs are offered at many colleges throughout the United States. There are also a large number of colleges that allow students to earn credits through testing programs. By successfully completing these tests, students can earn as many as 30 semester hours, or one year of college credit. Some colleges allow even more hours to be accumulated through testing programs. Prior learning assessment evaluates a student's life experiences—work, volunteer service, training, and other relevant experiences—and awards college credit for it. You may already have experiences that can be translated into college credits. More complete information about speeding up the process can be found in *Back to School: A College Guide for Adults.*

No one can tell you exactly how long it will take to complete a college degree. Everyone is different. You need to evaluate your situation and set your goals. Keep in mind that it may be possible to finish a degree program much sooner than you think.

How Do I Balance Family, Work, and School?

Returning to college is not easy, but managing your time to include work on a college degree is possible for anyone. Remember that millions of adults throughout the country are doing it. Returning to college requires you to set priorities. Your relationships with your employer and your family may change temporarily.

Returning to college will affect your relationship with your employer. For this reason, you need to talk to your employer about your goal. Find out how a degree will affect your career with your current employer. You need support from supervisors and coworkers to provide flexibility in your work schedule. Flexibility is needed because there are likely to be situations when you need to take time off work to complete course assignments. You can help make up for this by basing class projects and assignments on tasks that will benefit your employer. Just knowing that your employer supports your efforts will help you as you pursue your degree.

Returning to college also affects your family. Talk to your spouse and children about the time limits you will experience. Discuss ways you can share household chores. Help your children understand that you will need quiet times to study. Your children need to understand that you may not always be available for every family activity. Help your children understand that this temporary sacrifice will lead to a college degree that will benefit the entire family. Parents returning to college often discover that their children's study habits improve when their children see them studying.

You may need to alter some priorities in your social activities. Volunteer work, social and recreational activities, and even additional work assignments may have to be limited or even eliminated until you finish your degree. Only you can decide if these sacrifices are best for you. Keep in mind that these changes are temporary.

You may reduce the stress of college requirements by choosing a college program that is structured for an adult's needs. A degree program that allows flexibility in completing course requirements may be right for you. If traveling is a part of your work, obtaining a degree from one of the innovative programs that don't require classroom attendance is another possibility.

Keep in mind your goal and the reasons for reaching it. Set a time to complete your degree. Work hard to meet that deadline. Knowing that an end is coming will make balancing family, work, and college much easier.

How Will I Pay for My Education?

A college education is somewhat expensive; however, it is an investment that results in a potential increase in income. Furthermore, it is an investment with a definite payoff, as evidenced by the previously cited statistics on the earnings of college graduates.

There are ways to reduce the cost of a college education. Attending a community college to earn a two-year associate degree is one way to save money and increase your value in the workplace at the same time. Tuition at community colleges is usually much less than at four-year colleges. By earning an associate degree, you may be able to increase your income before you complete a bachelor's degree. (An associate degree may also be earned at a four-year college.)

Adult students can qualify for financial aid. It is not necessary to be a "full-time" student to receive aid. Tuition assistance through employers is often available to employees. This benefit is so important to some adults that they may change employers to gain this assistance. By offering this benefit, an employer shows how much the company values education.

Adults have assets that traditional students don't. Loans such as home-equity loans or short-term loans are feasible options for adults. Often adults have credit card limits high enough to charge books and tuition for a semester. Just like any other purchase you make, if you want a college education, you will find a way to finance your purchase.

How Far Do I Have to Go?

You may be surprised to find that you do not need to travel very far to find an "adult-friendly" college. As colleges have become more competitive in recruiting adult students, they have made class locations more convenient. Instead of your traveling to a college campus, the campus may come to you. The purpose of this guide is to help you locate the colleges near you.

Many colleges have established extension class sites. Business offices, public school buildings, industrial plants, and community centers are among the locations that colleges may use. A faculty member from the main campus may travel to the class location, or the college may hire a qualified individual from the community. Courses may be taught using interactive television. The instructor is viewed live from the main campus by students at the remote site. The instructor and the class may both see and hear each other by television. Using TV, a class on the main campus and several remote classes may be taught at the same time. Interactive television is only one form of distance education or distance learning.

Correspondence degrees are another form of distance education. Often public universities offer correspondence degrees at a lower tuition rate for residents of their state. A student's location offers no problems in taking this type of course. For adult students, correspondence courses offer more control and flexibility in the course work.

Technology—television, videotapes, and computers—are changing the meaning of correspondence degrees. These programs are especially useful for students who live in remote areas or who must travel extensively because of their work. As technology increases, more innovative programs will be available.

What Is the Difference Between a College and a University?

Businesses and other institutions sometimes use the terms "college" or "university" very casually. For example, McDonald's Hamburger University is a training program used by that company. You need to understand the various types of institutions of higher education and what is meant by *college* or *university*.

A *college* is defined as an institution that grants degrees to students who can demonstrate mastery of knowledge considered appropriate for the degree awarded. In this book, college is used in a generic sense—applying to all institutions of higher education that award degrees.

Community colleges and *junior colleges* usually offer college-level courses that lead to a two-year associate degree. Some privately owned junior colleges do not offer degrees but prepare students to enter a four-year institution at the junior level. Community colleges are often funded by state governments.

Adult students find community colleges attractive for several reasons. The philosophy of education at community colleges focuses on preparing students for particular careers. Faculty members often have work experience in their teaching areas. Class schedules and the college's location are often convenient for adult students. Because they are not involved in research and hire fewer doctoral faculty, tuition is cheaper.

Community colleges almost always provide an atmosphere that is adult-friendly. The philosophy of community colleges makes it easier for an adult to attend and earn an associate degree. Because this approach is common among community colleges, we have chosen not to include them in this guide. Rather, we recommend that you investigate local community colleges—when it is appropriate for your needs—as possible choices for an associate degree.

Four-year liberal arts colleges emphasize a well-rounded education with less concentration on preparing for a specific career. Students usually major in a field such as English, literature, mathematics, the arts, and life sciences. Most liberal arts colleges are private institutions. Many are associated with churches. Attending a liberal arts college can be expensive.

At first thought, such a college may seem an unwise choice for a career-minded adult. However, when asked about the type of education they prefer, a significant number of business leaders said a liberal arts degree. Many four-year liberal arts colleges have been providing innovative, nontraditional degree programs for working adults. These programs are within career areas such as business or nursing, or may be a liberal arts degree. Some are now offering master's degrees in areas such as education and business.

Four-year colleges graduate most of their students with bachelor's degrees in professional areas such as engineering, nursing, and business. Many liberal arts colleges also offer these types of degrees. The differences between the two are becoming less obvious.

Most four-year colleges are private. Tuition is more than at most state institutions. Faculty at these schools often have connections with professionals in their field of specialty, resulting in graduates having an advantage when seeking employment. Many of these colleges have reputations for producing outstanding, well-prepared professionals in particular fields.

Universities traditionally award graduate degrees. A comprehensive university offers bachelor's, master's, professional, and doctoral degrees in a variety of areas. Some offer only master's degrees or have a limited number of doctoral degrees. In recent years, many four-year colleges have changed their names from college to university to avoid being confused with junior and community colleges.

Most universities are state-supported, since providing graduate education is expensive. Research is given top priority at the university. Teaching undergraduate students is often assigned to teaching assistants, who are graduate students rather than university faculty.

The advantages of universities often include a highly useful library system, a wide variety of degree programs, and a quality graduate degree for a lower cost. Universities have high name recognition, which can help students when they are seeking employment. Graduate students may study with experts in their chosen field. However, universities have been reluctant to initiate programs directed at adults.

What Is Accreditation?

The U.S. Department of Education recognizes accrediting bodies that can confer accreditation on colleges and universities. The accrediting bodies—while recognized by the federal government—are independent agencies. The accredited colleges and universities are members of the accrediting agency. Accreditation is a self-policing system, which protects the public and ensures that each college maintains established educational standards including those the institution determines for itself.

The regional accrediting bodies are the most highly respected. The United States has been divided into six regions. Each body provides the accreditation for the colleges within its region. Colleges must request accreditation within the region of its state. The following are the six regions and their accrediting bodies.

Middle States Association of Colleges and Schools	Delaware, District of Columbia, Maryland, New Jersey, New York, Pennsylvania, Puerto Rico, Virgin Islands
New England Association of Schools and Colleges	Connecticut, Maine, Massachusetts, New Hampshire, Rhode Island, Vermont
North Central Association of Colleges and Schools	Arizona, Arkansas, Colorado, Illinois, Indiana, Iowa, Kansas, Michigan, Minnesota, Missouri, Nebraska, New Mexico, North Dakota, Ohio, Oklahoma, South Dakota, West Virginia, Wisconsin, Wyoming
Northwest Association of Schools and Colleges	Alaska, Idaho, Montana, Nevada, Oregon, Utah, Washington

Southern Association of Colleges and Schools	Alabama, Florida, Georgia, Kentucky, Louisiana, Mississippi, North Carolina, South Carolina, Tennessee, Texas, Virginia
Western Association	California, Hawaii, American Samoa, Guam, Commonwealth of the Northern Marianas, and the Trust Territory of the Pacific Islands

Colleges must also be approved for operation by statewide agencies for higher education, which are concerned with protecting citizens from fraudulent institutions. The name used for these agencies varies from state to state. Usually the name includes the word "commission" or "regents." Some state agencies use the evaluations of the regional accrediting bodies to determine the status of a college. Others use their own standards of evaluation. In this case, an institution might be accredited by the state without being accredited by a regional body. Students would not qualify for federal financial aid but could qualify for state financial aid.

If the regional body is thought to be unable to evaluate a college's mission, philosophy, and structure, the institution may seek accreditation from a different accrediting body. The Distance Education and Training Council oversees many nontraditional colleges. This body may accredit home study schools granting associate, bachelor's, and master's degrees, including innovative programs using videos, television, and computer technology. It is involved in a most exciting area of adult education.

A new college striving for credibility will apply for accreditation. Once it has satisfied basic requirements, it can be granted preaccreditation status but must wait until it graduates its first class of students. After its first graduation, the college is reviewed again before full accreditation is granted. An accredited institution is normally reviewed about every ten years to be sure it continues to meet its educational goals. It is also possible for a college to be fully accredited, but be required to obtain accreditation for a new degree it is adding.

What's So Important about Accreditation?

Accreditation is important to students for several reasons. Accreditation is used in obtaining financial aid for students. Only colleges and universities accredited by a body recognized by the U.S. Department of Education qualify to offer their students federal financial aid. Employers who offer tuition reimbursement usually pay only for courses taken at an accredited college. Some employers, especially larger corporations, do not accept degrees from nonaccredited colleges.

An accredited college will not accept the transfer of credits from a nonaccredited school. If you plan to go to an accredited graduate school, you must have a bachelor's or master's degree from an accredited school.

Accreditation is a consumer's guide to quality education. It assures students that the college is meeting the educational standards that it has set for itself.

You may decide to attend a nonaccredited college. The program may be innovative. The location and class schedule may be perfect for your lifestyle. Often innovative programs are scrutinized more closely than traditional programs. Some colleges may lack only a graduating class to gain accreditation. Students in this situation can be confident that their degrees will be recognized as being granted by an accredited college. Perhaps you want to be one of the pioneers in that first graduating class.

What Kind of Degree Should I Get?

Gaining a degree is the ultimate goal of most college students. By granting the degree, the college recognizes that the student has learned about a variety of subjects and has specialized knowledge about certain subjects. Earning a degree shows others that the student set a goal and reached it. The degree represents the learning that has taken place in an individual's life.

Colleges offer several different types of degrees. The length of time needed to complete each one varies. College degrees are offered at the undergraduate and graduate levels. Both the associate degree and the bachelor's degree are undergraduate degrees. An associate degree may be earned in two years of full-time college work. Typically, four years of full-time college work are needed to complete a bachelor's degree. It is not necessary to complete an associate degree before earning a bachelor's degree. However, the credits earned in gaining an associate degree may be used to obtain a bachelor's degree.

A bachelor's degree is usually one of the entrance requirements of a graduate program. Graduate degrees include master's degrees and doctoral degrees. Some master's degrees are called terminal. This means that no higher degree is offered in that field. An example is the Master of Library Science. Other master's programs are preparation for doctoral work. Doctoral degrees may be earned in an academic area—normally a Ph.D. or Ed.D.—or in a professional field. A doctoral degree is required in professions such as medicine, law, or dentistry.

How Do Degrees Differ?

Associate degrees are offered at technical schools, junior colleges, and community colleges as well as four-year colleges. Most associate degrees may be earned in two years of full-time classes—about 60 semester hours or 90 quarter hours. Some associate degrees require three years of class work. Many associate degrees are directly connected to an occupation—such as dental hygiene, early childhood education, or electronic technology.

Basically, an associate degree is equivalent to the freshman and sophomore years of college. However, you have a diploma as well as those college credits when you have finished. Since getting any kind of degree is an ego booster, many adults find this degree attractive. An associate degree may be a financial booster as well. According to the U.S. Department of Labor, workers with an associate degree earn a yearly average of $5,000 more than high school graduates. Many students transfer their credits to a four-year college and earn a bachelor's degree.

When most people think of a college degree, they think of a bachelor's degree. At a traditional college, a bachelor's degree requires four or even five years of full-time classes—about 120 semester hours or 180 quarter hours. The most common bachelor's degrees are the Bachelor of Arts (B.A. or A.B.) and the Bachelor of Science (B.S.). The difference between these depends on the college. You should ask a college advisor to explain your college's explanation. Several other bachelor's degrees may be available, such as Bachelor of Fine Arts (B.F.A.), Bachelor of Business Administration (B.B.A.), and Bachelor of Science in Nursing (B.S.N.).

Master's degrees may prepare students for particular professions or be a step toward earning a doctoral degree. Most academic master's degrees require one year of course work—about 33 semester hours or 45 quarter hours. Sometimes a written thesis is also required. Academic master's degrees include the Master of Arts (M.A.) and the Master of Science (M.S.). Professional master's degrees may require one and a half or two years of course work—45 to 60 semester hours, or 75 to 90 quarter hours. Examples of professional master's degrees are Master of Business Administration (M.B.A.), Master of Library Science (M.L.S.), Master of Public Administration (M.P.A.), and Master of Public Health (M.P.H.).

Since master's students have proved their academic skills by obtaining a bachelor's degree, educators have been more inclined to take a nontraditional approach with master's degree programs. Market competition and student demands create pressure on universities to meet the needs of adult students seeking master's degrees since almost 80 percent of all graduate students are over 25. Many nontraditional master's degree programs are available.

Professional degrees usually require three years of academic studies, with a doctoral degree awarded at the completion. Normally a bachelor's degree is required but a master's degree is not. This degree prepares the individual for a particular profession. The Juris Doctorate (J.D.) to practice law, the Doctor of Medicine (M.D.), Doctor of Veterinary Medicine (D.V.M.), and Doctor of Ministry (D.Min.) are all professional degrees.

The requirements for the various professional degrees are controlled by professional organizations and state agencies. Licensing requirements make offering this degree in a nontraditional way very difficult. Therefore, of all the degree programs, the professional degrees are the least accommodating for adult students. The Doctor of Ministry is the one exception.

The doctorate is the highest academic degree awarded. The Doctor of Philosophy (Ph.D.) has traditionally emphasized research and mastering a foreign language to use in this research. However, in recent years the difference between it and the Doctor of Education (Ed.D.) has become less obvious. The requirements vary with the university. Other doctoral degrees include the Doctor of Business Administration (D.B.A.) and the Doctor of Public Administration (D.P.A.).

Traditionally a doctorate requires a master's degree and three years of additional studies. Students must complete course work, write a dissertation based on their own research, and be evaluated by a committee of faculty members using both written and oral comprehensive exams. In some cases a student with a bachelor's degree may earn both a master's degree and the doctorate at the same time.

Universities often award honorary doctorates to persons who have contributed to the institution through monetary means or their individual accomplishments. Honorary doctorates are not earned through academic work.

Nontraditional accredited doctoral programs are now offered by various institutions. However, traditional universities are sometimes reluctant to recognize the quality of these degrees. If you plan to teach at the university level, having a degree that is recognized by the academic community is important. This fact should be included in your decision to enter a nontraditional doctoral program.

What Is a Major?

If you are seeking an associate or bachelor's degree, you will be asked to choose a major area of study. Approximately one-fourth to one-half of your course work will be in this area of study. You may also be asked to have a minor area of study. The minor requires about one-half the number of credits needed for a major. Since not all majors and minors require the same number of credits, your choice will affect the number of hours you must study.

Your major will affect your eligibility for some graduate programs. For example, if you want to enter a graduate program in an area such as chemistry, mathematics, or psychology, your bachelor's degree major will need to be in that area of study.

Your major will affect the type of jobs you are considered qualified to perform. For example, an employer is not likely to hire an accountant who does not have a bachelor's degree with a major in accounting. Furthermore, the degree may be required for state certification for an occupation.

The courses required to complete a major are normally determined by a vote of the faculty in that particular department of the college. For example, the professors in the chemistry department set requirements for all chemistry majors. This would include chemistry courses, related courses in areas such as physics and mathematics, and a core of general education courses required by the university. This curriculum will then be followed by all chemistry majors in selecting classes.

Selecting a major early in your academic career is helpful in completing your degree in a timely manner. As you schedule your courses, you will be able to follow the departmental curriculum and not take unnecessary courses. Often students who have declared their majors are given priority in registering for classes in their major area. When you have selected your major, you will be assigned an academic advisor from your major department. This advisor will help you select courses to meet degree requirements. Usually this advisor has a clearer understanding of departmental policies than a general advisor assigned when you first enter college.

What Is a Traditional Program?

Certain assumptions can be made about the way a traditional college program is structured. Basically, traditional students live on the college campus and attend classroom lectures led by an instructor. The college is a small learning community where students live and work together seeking knowledge. In some schools, dormitory directors plan activities outside the classroom to encourage student participation in active learning.

The courses are offered in an academic year divided into either semesters— 15 to 18 weeks long—or quarters—11 to 12 weeks. Courses are assigned a certain number of credits based on the amount of time a student attends class meetings held by a college instructor. For example, a class meeting 45 hours during a semester earns 3 semester credit hours. (Each credit hour is equal to 15 hours in the classroom.) Classes usually meet either 50 minutes three days a week or 75 minutes two days a week.

Traditional colleges and universities assume that their students are recent high school graduates attending classes full-time while living on campus. These students move through the degree program pursuing courses full-time. These assumptions affect the way the institution functions. Courses are normally offered between 7 A.M. and 4 P.M. Courses meet two, three, or sometimes four times a week. Faculty office and administrative office hours are usually between 8:00 A.M. and 5:00 P.M. This means that registration, advising, career advising and placement, and the bookstore are usually limited to these times.

Traditional college faculty and administrators assume that credit for learning is earned by students when they attend classes structured by the institution and conducted by an instructor. Strict guidelines are set for the transfer of credits accumulated by students at other colleges. Normally courses are transferred if they have been completed within a recent time period, come from an accredited college, and are equivalent to a course offered at the college.

In most colleges, 25 to 33 percent of a student's course work comes from general or liberal education courses. These courses are chosen by the faculty and administration as important for all students graduating from their institution.

Faculty at traditional schools have strong academic credentials. Doctoral degrees are common. Faculty members are expected to earn tenure—a lifelong guarantee of a job. Tenure is earned by conducting research, teaching, and providing service to the university and the community. Faculty also have an important role in setting school policies.

How Do I Enroll in a Traditional Program?

The admissions office is the first place you must contact to enroll in a college or university. Each school has a formal admissions procedure with specific dates for submitting your application and notification of acceptance. Your high school transcript with courses and grades or proof of completion of a GED must be sent to the college. Many colleges require that the applicant receive an acceptable score on either the SAT (Scholastic Aptitude Test) or the ACT (American College Test). A written essay may also be requested. All of this paperwork must be completed by the application date.

After you have been accepted as a student, you may register for classes and begin working on your degree. An advisor will meet with you to plan the classes you will take for the term. A curriculum guide for your major will help you know what courses are required for graduation. A recommended schedule for the entire degree program will tell you what courses are prerequisites—courses that must be completed before you are allowed to register for other courses. The guide also tells you how many elective courses you may take. Knowing your major lets you plan your course schedule more effectively and efficiently.

You will register for courses one term at a time. Most schools offer several registration times, such as early registration, advanced registration, preregistration, open registration, and late registration. A course schedule or listing is usually available a few weeks before the first registration date. It shows the days, times, locations, and instructors of various classes. Using this information, you must decide when you can take your classes. You have to avoid conflicts of classes that meet on the same days and at the same hours. The locations of the classes must be considered to allow sufficient time for you to get from one class to another. You may prefer a particular instructor for a course, and this further restricts your choice of courses.

A college advisor must approve your schedule. Then your schedule must be entered in the college computer system to verify that all the classes are open. Depending on the college system, you may have to take your schedule to the registrar's office, the advisor may enter it, or you may register by phone or computer on your own. Sometimes a class is closed. This means that the class limit has been reached. If this happens, you may schedule the same class at a different time. If you are unable to get the class, you will have to return to your advisor for approval for a different course, which adds time to your registration process. (Sometimes if a class is full, an instructor will allow a student with a good reason to schedule the class; however, some instructors are adamant about limiting the number of students in their classes.)

Registering early is an excellent idea. Obviously courses at the most popular times and with outstanding professors will be filled quickly. Some students avoid early registration because tuition payment may also be required earlier. If you find yourself in this situation, you will need to decide which is more important to you—the cash or the schedule you desire.

Registration is followed by payment at the bursar's office. Usually you will receive a bill from the bursar's office when you register early. Open and late registrations require immediate payment at the bursar's office. To do this, you will probably stand in a long line, thus increasing your registration time. If you fail to pay your bill, your registration will probably be canceled and your name removed from the class lists.

Registration tasks may also include obtaining a photograph ID card to be used for admission to sporting activities, concerts, and the library. You may need a parking permit from the campus security office to post in your car when you are on campus.

How Should I Prepare for Classes?

You will need to have books and materials for each of your classes. Your next stop is the bookstore. If more than one bookstore is available, it is wise to compare prices. Bookstores may be run by the university, outsourced to a private firm paying the university to operate on campus, or be a private store located near the campus. Each bookstore will have a record of the books and materials required for each course. If you have financial aid that can be used to buy books, you will need to find out how the bookstore handles purchases made in this way.

What If I Need to Change My Schedule?

Once the term has begun, you may discover that you have conflicts and cannot take a particular class, or you may want to add a class to your schedule. To drop a class, you may not need the approval of your advisor. Usually you will receive a full refund if a course is dropped during the first week of classes. The longer you wait to drop a course, the more tuition will be forfeited. If you want to add a class, do it as soon as possible. Waiting may mean that you miss the introduction to the course and get behind in assignments.

How Will I Know I'm Making Progress?

After you have selected your major (usually during the sophomore year), you will meet with your advisor from time to time to review your progress. When you have academic questions, contact your advisor. At the beginning of your final term, you may be required to notify the registrar's office of your intention to graduate. The application may be sent to you, or there may be a general announcement in the class schedule booklet. This form allows the registrar's office to verify your records and confirm your eligibility for graduation. That office will notify you concerning your graduation status. Throughout your college experience you should be aware of taking the required courses and maintaining a certain grade point average to avoid an unpleasant surprise when you believe you have completed your degree.

What Is a College Catalog?

Colleges and universities have different procedures and policies. A college's catalog states all of its policies and procedures and the requirements necessary to complete each degree. The catalog is considered a contract between the school and you. Generally, you will need to meet the requirements stated in the catalog in use at the time of your enrollment. You may be allowed to change to a different catalog during your college experience if it offers you more flexibility. More restrictive policies cannot be applied retroactively.

It is important to understand the catalog. Read it and discuss unclear items with other students, faculty, or advisors. Remember that the faculty's and administration's interpretation will be the final authority. If you are unclear about a particular statement, ask for a written clarification to avoid misunderstandings. Keep this documentation as proof of what you were told. Many students have needed this type of proof in problem situations.

What's a Nontraditional Degree Program?

Nontraditional programs assume that college-level learning can take place in various situations and places. Learning does not have to be conducted on the college campus with residential students. Classes may be offered in blocks of three or four hours one day or evening a week, or for two or three days over a weekend. The course of study may be structured through an agreement between the instructor and the student(s). The learning may even be self-directed without an instructor's presence.

Nontraditional programs recognize that adult students have different needs and responsibilities than traditional students. Adults are viewed as customers with needs to be met. In response, the institution offers classes at times appropriate for working adults. Administration offices are open at convenient hours. Books and materials may be distributed in class. Students are billed for them. Telephone, fax, computer, and mail registration may be available. Registration may not even be necessary in some programs that are structured with predetermined courses in which classes are conducted in a lock-step fashion.

Classes may be held in shopping malls, work sites, office complexes, and other locations convenient for adults. Video, television, and computer learning offer students the opportunity to access courses at work or even in their homes.

Nontraditional degree programs are more willing than traditional programs to transfer college credits regardless of when they were earned. Many programs grant credit to adults for their life experiences that are equivalent to college learning. Exams may be given to test the adult's knowledge of a certain college course. The Council for the Advancement of Experiential Learning (CAEL) has promoted many programs acknowledging learning by adults through their experiences outside the classroom. The learning portfolio is one example: It is a written compilation of an adult's learning experiences that are comparable to college-level learning.

General education requirements in these programs are usually much broader than in traditional programs. Rather than a specific course requirement, the student may choose a course from that field of study. Often there is no foreign language requirement, and the mathematics requirements are limited. For some adults the general education requirements may be met through exams or prior learning portfolios.

The faculty are usually individuals with advanced degrees but are employed in nonacademic jobs typically related to the courses they teach. Although they may have a master's degree rather than a doctorate, their practical experiences make their teaching more current and relevant than traditional faculty. Courses tend to deal with practical issues rather than theory and research.

Can I Find a Nontraditional/ Traditional Degree Program?

Some colleges have modified their traditional degree programs to meet the needs of adults. By simply changing a few procedures, colleges can make attendance more convenient for adults. Recognizing that SAT and ACT scores sometimes fail to evaluate accurately the potential for an adult's academic success in college, some colleges may not require adult students to take these tests. Credit may be given for credits earned at other institutions and for prior learning—usually confirmed through examinations. Classes are held on week nights after 5 P.M. and on weekends. Scheduling for general education courses and courses for majors popular with adults is made more convenient. Registration may be done over the telephone, with a computer, or at hours convenient to adults. Some courses are available in outlying communities, allowing adults to attend class without driving to campus.

What Is a Learning Contract?

A learning contract is a legally binding agreement between a student and the school. It may also be called a study contract, a study plan, or a degree plan. For the student, the contract states the goals to be achieved and the plans to accomplish them. For the school, the contract states what will be done when the student reaches these goals. Usually this means the school grants the student a stated amount of credit or a degree when the contract is completed.

A learning contract is stated very specifically. A simple learning contract consists of the following:

- The educational goals the student expects to achieve

- A description of the methods used to achieve these goals

- A stated method of evaluating the learning that is taking place

- An explanation of the way any problems and disagreements will be resolved

The contract should include a clause calling for binding arbitration by an impartial third party to settle any disputes about the work. This is both an excellent and legal way to avoid misunderstandings about what work is expected to earn the credit or degree.

What Are the Advantages?

A learning contract allows you to take an active part in your learning. You share in deciding what materials and topics will be studied, how you will study, and how your learning will be evaluated. The learning process may be traditional or innovative, depending on the contract. It is an individualized way of approaching learning.

Flexibility is very much a part of a learning contract. The contract may begin at any time and be completed at any time. No connection with semesters or quarters is needed. The learning contract offers a clear understanding of what must be done to reach the goal.

You can't be asked to do more than the contract states, but you also can't do less.

How Is a Learning Contract Established?

A learning contract may be initiated by either a faculty member or the student. It may be written for an entire degree program or for portions of the degree program. Some schools have different contracts for each subject area within the degree program.

Since the learning contract is individualized, you should expect to do some negotiating in establishing it. You may meet with advisors to review your prior learning experiences, determine your learning needs and goals, and develop a plan to reach your goals. Once your goals are set, a committee of faculty members and administrators may meet to approve your contract. Although administrators try to be consistent, one student may receive more credit than another for the same amount of work.

When a final agreement is reached, an actual contract is completed. To receive the set amount of credit or to graduate, you must meet the contract goals.

What Is an Accelerated Degree Program?

Accelerated degree programs for adults are offered by many small—600 to 3,000 students—liberal art colleges. Students in this type of program are usually over the ages of 23 to 30 and have significant work experience.

Students in an accelerated program are usually required to have at least 60 credit hours of previous college-level credit. Depending on the particular program, credit may be granted for transferred college credit, examinations, and prior learning assessments. Learning methods and class scheduling are geared to working adults. Class work focuses on the real world in which adults function.

Most accelerated programs offer professional majors in areas such as business, counseling, nursing, and education. Some programs require students to have a certain number of years of work experience in their major area. The definition of work experience may vary from school to school.

An adult may be admitted to the degree program at any time throughout the year. When a group of 18 to 22 students has been admitted to the program at one location, a class is formed. Course work then begins. This group of students remains together throughout the completion of their degree.

Each class takes one course at a time. These five- to six-week courses meet either one night a week or on the weekend for four hours. When a course is completed, the class moves on to the next course with very few breaks in the process. The outside work required compares to a semester or quarter course in a traditional program. A degree may be completed within 16 to 22 months.

What Are the Advantages?

An accelerated degree program allows you to earn a degree in a shorter time than a traditional program. The sequence of courses does require a commitment to a grueling schedule for several months.

Since the course work is often more practical than in a traditional program, adults find that they can apply their learning on the job. Teamwork and making class presentations, both part of the business world, are used in many accelerated classrooms. Students may be required to be a part of a three- or four-member study group. This group works together in completing major assignments and often makes group presentations in class. In addition, they operate as a support group, encouraging each member to complete the degree program.

The scheduling of classes in the evenings and on weekends is geared to a working adult's schedule. While accelerated programs may be offered on campus, some schools have established centers in cities where students may register and attend classes in their local communities. Sometimes a class meets at a business location, with the employer providing the classroom space. Books and other needed materials are provided at the class meeting site.

What Is a Virtual Campus?

Several state universities and some private colleges offer a unique program that can be called *a virtual campus*. Although a physical campus does not exist, an administrative office is maintained. The college itself offers no classes, but it does provide a way for students to accumulate college credit and earn degrees.

Credits are earned by a combination of college credits, prior learning assessment, examinations, military service school courses, and correspondence courses. Students may take courses from any accredited institution of higher education and transfer the credits to the college. Credits earned through correspondence courses at an accredited institution are accepted. Some schools accept noncollegiate courses offered by the military, business, professional groups, government, and nonprofit agencies. Such programs, which have been previously evaluated, may be taken with the knowledge that the college will grant credit. Examinations like CLEP, ACT, DANTES, and GRE are other ways to earn credit. Guided study courses—individualized study guided by a mentor—may also be acceptable. Students may submit their prior learning assessments to be evaluated for credit.

What Are the Advantages?

The virtual campus is especially useful to individuals who are forced to relocate frequently. Many students in this situation have accumulated many credit hours but have never been able to graduate. They are the victims of policies that require a minimum number of credits from that institution in order to graduate.

The virtual campus offers a variety of majors for students seeking bachelor's degrees. With the help of an advisor, students may set up an individualized plan of study. The program establishes the courses that must be completed and how the courses will be completed. With so many different ways of earning credit, the student may choose from a wide variety of learning opportunities.

What Is Distance Education?

Distance education uses available technology to instruct students in a variety of places outside the walls of the college. Correspondence courses, first offered in the mid-1800s, were the original form of distance education. This simple use of printed technology was upgraded in the 1930s with the first application of electronic technology. Radio broadcasts devoted to learning made instruction available to students throughout the world.

Today modern technologies make a college education available to students even in remote parts of the world. Audiotapes, videotapes, telephone lines, television, and computers are used in a variety of ways to teach students. Using these methods, individuals and groups can be reached.

Printed text, audiotape, and videotape programs are commonly used to provide courses to individuals. Lectures are sometimes recorded as supplements to the textbooks and other reading materials used. Many colleges and universities offer correspondence courses, but fewer schools offer students the opportunity to earn a complete degree using only correspondence courses. Computer-assisted instruction (CAI) is used by some colleges to deliver courses. Using the telephone, students have access to advisors and instructors to complete course work. A few institutions offer degree programs using videotaped lessons. One drawback to using any of these methods is the lack of interaction between the student and the instructor, and with other students.

More interaction takes place through computer-based degree programs. A student's work or home computer is linked by telephone to a computer at the college. This method is more group-oriented because the course is taken in conjunction with a campus class. Messages can be sent by computer to the instructor and other students. Course assignments are logged into the computer. Interactive computer conferencing is a key part of this program. New developments are currently taking place as the Internet and other online services offer adults the potential to get a degree via personal computer.

Some colleges provide degree programs through televised courses. Interactive video programs are another delivery method used by some schools. On-campus classes are broadcast live to outlying classes. An audio link allows students to hear and speak to the instructor. An interactive video link allows the college to duplicate the classroom in several locations at one time. Often a business place or local high school is set up with the necessary equipment to provide the class. Sometimes a course facilitator is present to help students with questions and problems that can't be resolved remotely.

What Are the Advantages?

Distance education allows students to learn no matter where they live. Earning a degree is now possible even for individuals in the most remote parts of the world. When traveling to campus is time-consuming and expensive, the convenience of learning at a local high school or business is a great advantage. For the homebound, distance education can open a whole new world of learning.

Using a computer or video recorder allows students to set their own classroom hours. The college computer is available to students 24 hours a day, every day of the week. Even televised courses can be videotaped when the broadcast time doesn't fit the student's schedule.

So How Do I Sign Up?

Because many adults are now attending colleges, most college admissions officers have experience working with adult students. An admissions officer should be able to answer your questions about how to enroll and start your degree.

Talk to people at work or to friends who have returned to college. Find out how they dealt with some of the problems you anticipate. Talk to them about any degrees or colleges you are considering. Ask if any particular person was especially helpful. The guidance you get from these experienced adult students is priceless, so use it.

Using this guide, you can explore a variety of colleges and innovative educational programs. Use it to find the program that is best for you. If you are interested in learning more about financing your education, accelerating your degree, and coping with family, work, and school, *Back to School: A College Guide for Adults* provides answers to these questions and many more.

Chapter 2

Selecting a College

hoosing a college is an important decision, and this chapter provides the information you need to make a good decision. Not every college is a good "fit" for every individual. Your personal situation will affect your college choice. You should consider several colleges and the degree programs they offer before you make this major decision. Remember, you are not limited to colleges and universities in your vicinity. Consider colleges with extended campuses in your community, universities with distance learning programs, and independent study programs.

The college you choose may make a difference in your ability and willingness to complete your degree. While advice from others is certainly an excellent way of gaining information about a school, you are the one making the decision. It should be based on your personal situation and the issues you will face as an adult student. Knowing what you expect from your educational experience will give you some additional guidance in making your choice.

This book contains information on nearly 500 colleges and universities that offer a wide variety of adult degree programs using innovative programs and teaching methods. Use this information to broaden your possible choices.

To help you make your decision, this chapter offers some criteria you may want to use in choosing the college that is right for you. It also describes how you can use the information about colleges and universities in this book.

College Status and Reputation

The status and reputation of a college are important but not the most critical factors in selecting a college. When you seek employment or a promotion, your work record and experience will probably have as great an influence as the reputation of your alma mater. However, if you are competing with a person of equal experience and ability, the status of your alma mater might be important.

Begin the process of evaluating an institution's reputation by finding out what it has to say about itself. The address, phone number, fax number, e-mail, and Internet Web address are provided—when available—for each institution. You should contact the college and ask for the college catalog and any promotional literature related to the degree programs in which you're interested.

Accreditation is the way colleges and universities review one another academically. The highest level of accreditation is awarded by the six regional accrediting bodies listed in Chapter 1. Many accrediting agencies have a professional focus. For example, the Accrediting Board for Engineering and Technology (ABET) provides accreditation for engineering and technology degrees. Employers sometimes consider a degree more valuable if it is conferred by a college accredited both regionally and professionally.

In some cases, a college may decide that a regional accrediting body doesn't have a sufficient understanding of the college's degree programs to know how to evaluate them. An institution may seek out accreditation from a national body recognized by the U.S. Department of Education. All of the colleges and universities in this guide have been accredited by a body recognized by the U.S. Department of Education. The following are some of the national accrediting bodies listed by institutions in this guide:

- Accrediting Association of Bible Colleges (AABC). This body accredits Bible colleges and institutions offering undergraduate programs.

- Distance Education and Training Council (DETC). This body accredits home study programs including associate, bachelor's, and master's degrees.

- Association of Theological Schools in the United States and Canada (ATSUSC). This body accredits institutions offering graduate professional education for ministry and graduate-level study of theology.

Ask college officials about accreditation of both the institution and its professional degrees to obtain a better understanding of their importance.

Colleges and universities receiving state funding may be better known to employers and the general public. State-funded institutions almost always receive their accreditation through the regional bodies and do not always stress it the way private institutions do. This is because a state college or university has a level of recognition resulting from its state support. Many employers have a high level of confidence in graduates from certain state-supported institutions. However, there are definitely strengths within private colleges. Almost 70 percent of all students enrolled in graduate programs received their undergraduate degrees from private colleges. Because the quality of education at private colleges varies—and is not subject to review and control by state legislatures—you should check a college's reputation before you make a decision.

Colleges and universities are reviewed in several books and magazines each year. As you read these reviews, remember that the information given is a general evaluation. It is not being reviewed from the adult student's perspective. Also, the criteria are subjective and may not be the same criteria that you would use to evaluate an institution. Networking is another way to evaluate a school's reputation. Talk to friends, peers, and coworkers. Find out what they know about the college and its graduates. Check with the human resources department at your workplace about a college's reputation.

Understanding Adult Learning Styles

Find a college that recognizes the difference between traditional college students and adult learners. Adult educators have developed several theories and concepts about the needs of adult learners. These ideas may be used to evaluate your college choices.

Obviously, adults are more mature. Look for a college that has established degree programs, rules, and regulations that recognize this maturity. Faculty should treat adults with respect and recognize their work experience as a positive contribution in the classroom. Find out if topics and projects from your job can be integrated into the classroom. Sometimes the students in the class have more practical experience in a particular course than the instructor. The contribution to class discussion and projects by other students may greatly enhance your learning experience.

Adults are problem-solvers. They value practical knowledge that can be applied to their lives right now. Find out if the college uses adjunct faculty who are practitioners in their particular field. Look for a school that encourages its faculty to present theory and research in such a way that it can be applied to practical projects and activities in the workplace and the community.

Adults want to play an active role in their learning. Look for an atmosphere that allows student participation in decision making in the classroom. Techniques used to accomplish this include learning contracts, choice of class assignments, selection of class topics, flexibility in meeting course requirements, and self-paced activities. Adults expect to understand clearly what the instructor requires to get a good grade in the course. A *syllabus* is a paper describing the course, learning objectives, class outlines, required texts and supplemental reading materials, other course materials, assignments, guidelines for grading, office hours and contact information for the instructor, and related course information. Ask the college for a sample course syllabus to see how complete it is.

Teachers of adults should understand that mature learners tend to have better study habits than younger students. The maturity and work experiences of adult students help them to be more disciplined. Because they are often applying their learning in their work, they are motivated to learn. They have job skills such as writing, reading, math, and computer work that transfer readily to the classroom. These students should be taught and evaluated at their level of maturity.

Limiting Disruption to Your Career

If you have already established a career, you may not want to disrupt it. Your financial responsibilities may make it necessary for you to continue working full-time and at the same earning level. Relocating to obtain a degree may not be practical. If you do not want to relocate, three possibilities are available. Find a local college that offers courses during times that fit your work schedule. Find a college the operates in another city but offers courses in your community. Or pursue a degree through some type of distance education program.

Ideally, working adults want to avoid interference between work and college. Time is a factor that must be considered. No one gets more than 24 hours to use in one day. Job promotions are obtained through extra work hours and extra effort. If you're spending time on classes and study, you don't have much extra time for work. Expecting a job promotion while you are attending school is not realistic. You should focus on earning a degree that will increase your opportunities for a promotion after graduation.

Your current job requirements will greatly affect your ability to attend class. What are your work hours? Is there any flexibility in those hours? Do you travel extensively? Are there times during the year when your workload is increased?

Look for a college that offers courses in time slots that allow you to attend class without significantly disrupting your work schedule. Find out whether you can complete your degree in this time frame. Ask advisors and other students how difficult it is to register for these courses. If a required course is offered only one semester during the year, the class may be filled before you can register for it. This could mean a delay in earning your degree, which costs you both time and money. People who travel extensively have a hard time attending classes regularly. If you are in this situation, a degree through a distance education program might meet your needs.

Some schools require campus residency for a short time. Using vacation time or other authorized time off allows adults to meet this requirement; however, it does limit vacation times while you are working on the degree. You may need to discuss this with your family.

Nearly all working adults have experienced times when their jobs required more time and attention than usual. When work and school conflict, attending class and completing course work on time may not be possible. Find out whether faculty members are flexible in accepting course work later if you're caught in a stressful situation. Find out if class attendance is mandatory, and whether absence affects the course grade.

For many working adults, distance education is a practical way to get a degree. Since you set the pace of completing the course, schoolwork can be delayed if your job becomes too demanding. However, delaying the schoolwork too long will mean taking longer to complete the degree. The faster you complete the degree, the sooner you can concentrate on your career.

Looking for colleges that allow you many options to speed up your degree-completion program may be important to you. Look for colleges that accept credit through examinations and for prior learning experience and have liberal acceptance of transfer credits and accelerated courses.

Getting the Degree You Want

Your career plans will definitely affect your degree program selection. In some cases—for example, in business management—you may have a choice of major areas of study in obtaining a degree. Other degrees—such as elementary education—may be limited and even require specific courses in the major area. Typically, careers requiring a license or certification are more restrictive.

Before you select a degree program, decide on your career objectives. Find out how your degree will help you reach those objectives. If you are planning to use your degree to advance in your current job situation, find out what degree programs are valued in your workplace. If you are changing careers, the *Occupational Outlook Handbook* (published by the U.S. Department of Labor and reprinted by JIST) is a source of information about various majors and related job opportunities.

Obviously if you are interested in a specific major leading to a degree, you will want a school that offers that degree. Remember, however, that you want a degree program that offers required courses at times or in a format that fits you as an adult student. Some colleges may have the degree you want, but no courses scheduled when you can attend. Internships may be required to complete the degree. Find out if this can be done through your current employer. Specifically ask your advisor if this program is practical for an adult student.

A general studies degree is offered by many colleges, often through distance education. Technically it is not a major but a degree program description. Most general studies programs require a student to take three or four courses from several major fields. This requirement offers students a liberal education with a broad perspective. If your career goal doesn't have specific academic requirements, a general studies degree may be your choice. However, if your goal is a professional field with specific academic qualifications, this degree won't meet your needs. Employers have difficulty matching this degree with particular job requirements, since it doesn't have a major area of study.

Many colleges offer adult degree programs with majors in business areas. If you want a business degree, you will probably have several college choices. Other degrees are offered on a more limited basis.

Consider Your Personal Learning Style

Your personal learning style should be a critical factor in determining which college program is right for you. Degree programs are structured in different ways. Not every program works for everyone. Use the following information to determine your learning style.

Independent learning requires discipline in the use of time, the ability to stay on-task, and extra effort to plan the course of study. Because a course of study often has lengthy deadlines, it is easy to procrastinate when completing assignments. Correspondence courses typically require the greatest amount of independence and discipline. Distance education programs using television and computers are usually more structured. Independent learning offers students flexibility in the learning schedule and makes students primarily responsible for their learning. Interaction with other class members and instructors is limited.

Answer the following questions to assess your ability to study independently. The more questions you answer yes, the more likely you are to succeed in an independent learning program.

1. Do you prefer to have flexibility in your learning schedule?

2. Do you like having primary responsibility for your learning?

3. Are you task-oriented?

4. Do you practice effective time management?

5. Do you feel comfortable conducting your studies with limited interaction with instructors?

6. Are you disciplined in the use of time?

7. Are you willing to expend the effort needed to plan your learning activities?

Interactive learning involves group discussions and projects as well as interaction between the instructor and students. For some students, social interaction is necessary to learning. Social interaction and peer support motivate some people to reach their goals. Classroom-based education uses social interaction to the greatest extent. Interactive distance learning using television, radio, or the telephone allows some personal interaction, but not to the same extent.

Answer the following questions to determine the importance of interactive learning to you. The more questions you answer yes, the more important social interaction is to your learning experience.

1. Do you learn from class discussion?

2. Do you prefer group homework assignments to personal assignments?

3. Are you more motivated by social interaction?

4. Do you enjoy small group discussions and tasks?

5. Do you frequently talk with instructors about topics presented in class?

6. Do you frequently ask the instructor's guidance about assignments?

7. Do you find yourself energized by social interaction with other students in and out of class?

Visual learning emphasizes writing and reading. Visual learners use books as information sources, find note-taking reinforcing, and understand concepts through demonstrations and videos. About 70 to 80 percent of the population are visual learners. All college programs use some visual learning. Classroom-based programs using reading and writing are effective for visual learners. Correspondence courses offer another effective mode of learning for visual learners.

To determine whether you are a visual learner, answer the following questions. The more positive answers you have, the more likely it is that you are a visual learner.

1. Do you learn better by reading than by having someone explain a concept to you?

2. Do you learn better from seeing a demonstration than from hearing someone describe a process to you?

3. Does watching someone role model a task help you learn better?

4. Do you remember concepts you read in a book better than those you hear in a lecture?

5. Do you prefer to review lecture material from notes than from a tape?

6. Do you find information from a video easier to learn than what you hear in a lecture?

Auditory learning uses classroom lectures, audio tapes, and discussion groups. Conversations with other students or an instructor are useful to the auditory learner. Classroom programs involving lectures and discussions are effective for auditory learners. Distance education programs that are interactive work well for auditory learners. The more affirmative answers you have to the following questions, the more likely it is that you are an auditory learner.

1. Do you learn better from a lecture than from reading course materials?

2. Are you able to learn more from listening to tapes than from using other methods of learning?

3. Do you learn better through small group discussions?

4. Do conversations with instructors and other students help you learn more than reading books and other materials?

5. Would you rather prepare for exams by reviewing tapes of lectures instead of studying notes and other written materials?

Experiential learning is learning through actual experience. Practicums, internships, and cooperative learning opportunities are useful for experiential learners. Actually giving speeches, demonstrations, and presentations are helpful. Role playing, laboratory activities, and community and work activities are some other methods used in this type of program. Colleges that recognize experiential learning give credit for courses that center on community and work activities. Such courses may be offered in a classroom-based program or through guided study courses. Experiential learners should seek out colleges that give the largest number of credits through these kinds of learning activities. Assess your tendency to be an experiential learner by the number of yes answers you have to the following questions.

1. Do you learn more by doing a task than by reading or listening?

2. Are learning activities implemented through work assignments highly effective for you?

3. Is a role-playing exercise an effective way for you to learn new material?

4. Do you learn more from simulations and games than from other teaching methods?

5. Does preparing and giving class presentations and demonstrations help you learn better than other methods?

6. Are laboratory activities more helpful for learning than classroom lectures?

Technological learning is the ability to learn using a variety of modern technologies, including television, videos, and computers. Using technology is easier and more comfortable for some people than others. Technological learners should look for colleges that use computer-based education programs, multimedia software, computer bulletin boards, and computer conferencing. Programs based on television and videos are effective, whereas computers have the advantage of being interactive. Technological learners will find that these programs will improve their learning. Answer the following questions to determine if you are a technological learner.

1. Do you enjoy working with computers?

2. Do you find that computer-based education programs are positive learning tools?

3. Do you feel comfortable using bulletin board systems or the Internet?

4. Do you learn better through multimedia software than by reading or listening to others?

5. Do you enjoy engaging in computer conferencing?

6. Are video and television presentations a good way for you to learn?

You may have found that you fit into more than one learning style. You are not unusual. Most people use more than one learning style. You may have discovered one preferred learning style, with one or more others supporting it. Use the information you have gained to select a degree program that offers you the opportunity to learn using your preferred learning style(s).

Finding the Right Degree Program

Based on the previous sections, there are four important issues you should consider when you select a college:

- Matching your career goals with a major or concentration of study

- Finding a college that fits your personal learning style

- Identifying a college that uses adult teaching methods

- Discovering a college that limits the disruption to your career and lifestyle

As an adult, you are capable of deciding on a degree program that meets your particular needs. These needs may be met in a traditional program. However, you should consider other types of programs, too. Each college description in this guide provides information that will help you begin evaluating the factors that are relevant to you.

Degrees and Majors

Each description contains a listing of all degrees and majors offered by the institution. In the third column of that listing is the format used to deliver the degree program. Several formats may be specified for each degree. The following table explains the format codes:

Code	Type of Format
E	Evening/Weekend Classes
A	Accelerated courses
T	Televised to extension sites
TH	Televised to students' homes
V	Videotaped courses
C	Correspondence courses
CT	Computer-based courses (including online)
S	Self-designed, independent study

Extension Sites

Each description also lists cities where the college has extension sites. Note that we have listed only those extension sites where all courses needed to complete a degree are offered. Many institutions have extension sites that offer only a limited number and type of courses. This service is also a convenience to students, but we felt it would be more useful to list only those sites where all courses for a degree are provided.

Requirements

The question of campus residency is also important for many adults. A campus residency requirement means that the institution expects you to attend a specific number of courses at the main campus. For some institutions, residency is expanded to mean attending courses at an extension site. In a few cases, residency may be limited to an intense workshop for a week or two weeks each year at the main campus. The guide provides information about residency to help you better understand a college's graduation requirements.

Admissions requirements are another factor to consider when you choose a college. For acceptance into an adult degree program, there are four or five typical admissions requirements. One is completion of high school (or GED) for undergraduate degrees. Graduate degree programs require completion of a bachelor's degree—usually from an accredited college.

Another typical requirement is that you must be an adult. Sometimes this is defined by age, normally 23 to 25—in rare cases 30. Work experience is another way of defining an adult. Usually three to six years of full-time work experience meets this requirement. In some cases, only work experience in a professional or managerial position is accepted. Some colleges have both age and work experience requirements. Documentation by resume may be needed as proof of an applicant's work experience.

Some colleges may require a minimum performance on an entrance exam. Traditional students usually must meet a minimum score requirement on either the SAT or ACT. A college that understands adult students usually doesn't have this requirement. Such exams are not valid predictors of success for adult students. An exam that measures writing ability is more common and is usually developed and evaluated by the college. Such exams typically are used not to exclude students from the program but, rather, to indicate those whose writing skills need improvement. Students who do poorly may be required to follow a specific sequence of English courses to improve their English skills. A similar approach may be taken with mathematics exams if a degree program has several courses that require basic math abilities.

If you have some prior college credits, you must arrange for transcripts to be sent from the institutions you've attended. Many colleges require that applicants have a minimum GPA of 2.0. However, most schools realize that the grades you received as a traditional student are not an accurate indicator of your ability to complete course work successfully as an adult. If your GPA is less than 2.0, many colleges will work with you. You may be admitted to a degree program on probation. Be sure you understand all of the conditions placed on your probation.

This guide lists information about admissions requirements. There are separate sections for undergraduate and graduate degree requirements. In addition, the requirements for graduation are included to give you more information that's important in selecting a college.

Fees, Tuition, Costs

Finding a college that fits your budget is another consideration in choosing a degree program. Getting the best quality education for the most reasonable price is important. Tuition is usually stated as the cost per credit hour; however, simply comparing tuition rates of different schools is not always accurate.

Another simple approach is multiplying the number of hours required for a degree by the tuition rate per credit hour. The estimated cost of books, class materials, and fees should be added to calculate the total cost. Usually tuition and fees increase by 3 to 7 percent each year. These increases should be included in figuring the gross cost.

The net cost is even more accurate. Several other factors need to be considered. First, think about the number of courses you need to complete the degree. Sometimes it is possible to reduce the number of courses required, thereby reducing the amount of tuition you pay. There are four methods for reducing course hours:

1. **Gain credit through exams.** The cost of earning credit through exams is usually much less than tuition. Colleges that allow unlimited exam credits offer the best opportunity to lower the cost of a degree.

2. **Gain portfolio credits.** Normally colleges charge a minimal amount for assessing prior learning experience and granting portfolio credits. The more credits you earn this way, the lower the cost of your degree.

3. **Gain credit by transferring credits.** Many colleges accept transfer credits. The more transfer hours accepted, the lower the cost of your degree.

4. **Accumulate other credits.** Other methods of accumulating credits also reduce the total cost for completing a degree.

You should also consider the opportunity costs of a degree—job promotions, raises, and general increases in earnings that are delayed while you are completing your degree. Finding a degree program that can be completed as quickly as possible may be important to you financially.

This guide contains information you can use to make a preliminary assessment of the costs of a given college. Tuition, books, and miscellaneous costs are shown.

Maximum Hours Awarded For

Each description also lists which exams—if any—the college uses for granting credit, along with the maximum number of credits allowed for each. Information is also included about credits awarded for prior learning experience, including the maximum number of credits allowed.

Financial Aid/Status

Financial aid is another way to reduce the cost of a college degree. It's important to find a college that offers the same consideration for financial assistance to both adult and traditional students. Most institutions place priority on providing scholarships to traditional students. A few offer scholarships to adult students. Many adult students receive financial reimbursement from an employer. Usually the employer doesn't make the payment until the course is successfully completed. If this is your situation, you will want to find a school that offers deferred tuition payment. Many institutions offer this service.

It is also possible to get financial assistance from state and federal sources. State and federal governments determine the maximum amount of aid available to you, but the college determines the specific amount awarded. Remember that grants don't have to be repaid, but loans do. Full-time students can receive higher amounts of financial aid, so you may want to identify colleges that structure courses to help working adults qualify as full-time students. This is one advantage of accelerated degree programs.

The guide lists scholarships the university awards to adults, describing the type, amount, and eligibility requirements of those scholarships. The percentage of adult students receiving aid is also listed. Be aware that some colleges may interpret this question in a way that includes students receiving tuition assistance from employers. There is also information about the school's definition of a full-time student—that is, one who qualifies for federal and state grants and loans.

Features and Services

Colleges should recognize that adult students need different services than traditional students. The convenience of these services can help you avoid some frustrating moments as you pursue your degree.

The way you register for classes is an important consideration. Registration is the process of enrolling for courses. You must select the days and times that the courses will be taken. Registration should be convenient for adults. Look for colleges that allow registration by telephone, computer, fax, or mail. If you select a college with an established sequence of courses, registration will not be required.

Academic advising is another factor associated with registration. Some colleges require students to talk to an academic advisor before registering for classes each term. Finding a convenient time to meet with an advisor may not be possible. This requirement also implies that you are not mature enough to plan your own educational program. Certainly you should expect to have access to an advisor when you need one, but requiring it is unfair to adult students. Academic advisors should have office hours that are convenient to adult students. It is wise to talk with an advisor at the beginning of your degree program and as you approach graduation to confirm that you are meeting all requirements.

Having easy access to the course is important. Parking becomes an issue for classroom-based programs. Many colleges require that students register their cars if they are parking on campus. Registering your car requires time and usually costs money. Find out the distance of the parking lot or garage from your classrooms. Usually satellite campus locations offer more convenient parking without car registration. For distance education programs, find out how you will obtain course materials, how you will submit assignments, and how you will be evaluated. Correspondence courses sometimes require students to take tests at specific places and times. Ask about the ease of accessing computer bulletin boards and viewing television courses.

Look for a college that is sensitive to adults and their concerns. Policies and procedures should reflect an understanding of adult students. College staff should treat you as a valued customer and provide high-quality service. Office hours should be set for times that suit a working adult's schedule.

There should be areas throughout the campus for off-campus students to study. In addition, student lounges with tables and vending machines should be available. Classroom buildings should also provide access to vending machines. Students should be allowed to take food and drinks to class. This is especially important when classes meet at meal times. Look for a college cafeteria that has hours and services for nontraditional students. A well-lit campus is important for students attending evening classes. Look for good campus security. Find out how to contact campus security in an emergency.

Having access to a bookstore with convenient hours for working adults is important. Some programs—especially those with classes held off-campus—provide books directly to the classroom.

Access to the library and its services is also important. Most college libraries are open at hours that fit a working adult's schedule. When classes are held at remote locations, students may find it difficult to get to the library. Some libraries offer a remote computer link that allows off-campus students to use the card catalog and journal databases. Interlibrary loans allow students to borrow materials from nearby libraries. Look for colleges where the library staff will copy and mail journal and magazine articles to students in remote areas. If you plan to get a degree through a distance education program, identify libraries that have the resources you will need to complete your degree. You may have access to a local college library. Often states have policies that allow any state resident to use the library services of state-supported colleges and universities.

You should also investigate the career center. You may not feel that you need this service; however, with downsizing and reengineering, it is wise to know what the career center can offer you. Most career centers are geared to helping traditional students find entry-level jobs. This is not what an adult student needs. Look for services you can use. The trend is to put a career placement officer in a particular school. For example, a school of business might offer career assistance. This gives the career staff a better understanding of the skills a graduate has to offer. Determine if the services of the career center are available to students at remote class sites and to those graduating from distance education programs.

A Caveat about the Data

This book should be used only as a general guide that offers a snapshot in time. Many colleges are modifying and improving the services they provide adult students. The answers given at the time of the survey may no longer be accurate. For example, new extension sites or degree programs may have been added or admissions requirements may have changed. Another point to consider is that, no matter how hard we try to be accurate, some mistakes may creep into the data. If we were to achieve 99.9 percent accuracy, there is the possibility of approximately 50 errors.

What should you do to protect yourself against the possibility of inaccurate data? Check with the college and request specific information about its degree programs for adults. If you are interested in a college's program, arrange a meeting with an admissions official from the school. This guide is designed to help you begin the process of identifying potential colleges; you must continue to collect and refine your understanding of the information.

Comparing Colleges

Unfortunately the perfect college does not exist. You are not going to find a college that meets *all* of your needs. The following worksheet should help you narrow your choices and make comparisons among colleges. The most important step is to get started and not put off advancing your career. Make your selection and go for it!

College Selection Worksheet

Write the names of the colleges at the top of the worksheet. The criteria used for selecting a college are listed on the left side of the page. Rate each criterion for a college on the basis of 5 (excellent) to 1 (poor). The final score for each college can be used as a rough guide in determining the one that is most appropriate for you.

	College 1	College 2	College 3
Potential disruption of career			
Acknowledges lifestyle and family concerns			
Positive atmosphere for adult learning			
Good reputation of college			
Good reputation of degree program			
Has a degree program that meets my goals			
Has a degree program with good potential			
College expenses are affordable			
Meets my personal learning style			
Reasonable admissions requirements			
Registration procedures are simple			
Advising is readily available			
Ease of access to classrooms is convenient			
There is sufficient space for parking			
Ease of access to services is convenient			
College is sensitive to adult concerns & needs			
Campus facilities are designed for adults			
Campus offices have hours for adults			
Staff treat adults as customers			
Books and materials are easily obtained			
Library services accommodate adult needs			
Career center meets needs of working adults			
Total Score:			

Directory of Colleges and Universities

Adelphi University

University College ◆ **Garden City, NY 11530**

Phone: (516) 877-3448 ◆ Fax: (516) 877-3429

E-mail: katopes@adlibv.adelphi.edu
Web address: http://www.adelphi.edu

Founded: 1896

Accredited by: Middle States

Enrollment: 8,000 ◆ Adult students: 800

University status: Private, Nonprofit

Degree	Concentration/Major	Format
B.S.	Management & Communications	E,A
B.A.	Social Science	E,A
B.A.	Humanistic Studies	E,A
B.A.	Fine Arts	E,A
B.A.	Elementary/Secondary Education	E,A

Campus Extension Site

Huntington, NY

Requirements

Residency requirement: All courses necessary for graduation are offered at our Huntington campus. Undergraduate admissions requirements: We require a formal application, including an essay indicating motivation. Graduation requirements (undergraduate): 120 total credits to include major credits as well as 28 credits in required courses.

Fees, Tuition, Costs

Undergraduate application fee: $35
Undergraduate tuition: $375/credit
hour
Undergraduate cost of books: $100/semester

Financial Aid/Status

Scholarship programs for adults: Amounts vary depending on student's financial need and number of credits taken. Full-time status: 12 credits, but some state aid is available for students taking 4 credits/semester. Percentage of adult students receiving financial aid: 100 percent.

Maximum Hours Awarded For

CLEP: Yes
Prior learning portfolio: Yes

Features and Services

1. Is it possible to purchase books during hours most adult students attend classes? **Yes.**

2. Are the institution's administrative offices open during hours adult students attend class? **Yes.**

3. What is the registration and payment process for adult students? **Credit card, cash, etc. Registration is on-site or mail-in.**

4. What is the process for advising adult students? **Each student has his or her own academic advisor.**

5. What career and placement services are available to adult students? **Career Service Center available to adult students.**

6. What characteristics of the institution's adult degree programs are most appealing to students? **All courses carry four credits; most meet once a week; personal attention to students.**

Albertus Magnus College

700 Prospect Street ◆ **New Haven, CT 06511**
Phone: (203) 773-8536 ◆ Toll-free phone: (800) 578-9160
Fax: (203) 773-3117

Founded: 1925

Accredited by: New England

Enrollment: 935 ◆ Adult students: 470

University status: Private, Church, Roman Catholic Church

Degree	Concentration/Major	Format
B.S.	Business Administration/ New Dimensions Program	A
B.A.	All majors	E
B.S.	All majors	E
A.A.	All majors	E
M.A.L.S.	Master of Arts Liberal Studies	E

Campus Extension Sites

New Haven, CT
Fairfield, CT

Requirements

Residency requirement: No. Undergraduate admissions requirements: 16 units required for admission, 4 English, 3 math, 2 science, 2 lab, 2 foreign language, 2 social studies, 2 history, 1 elective. Graduate admissions requirements: For the M.A.L.S.—only proof of a bachelor's degree; no specific entrance exams or tests. Graduation requirements (undergraduate): 60 credits for A.A.; 120 credits for B.A. Graduation requirements (graduate): Successful completion of 30 credits; M.A.L.S.

Fees, Tuition, Costs

Undergraduate application fee: $35
Graduate application fee: $35
Undergraduate tuition: $12,350/year/45 credits
Graduate tuition: $288.33/credit
Undergraduate cost of books: $75-$200
Graduate cost of books: $50-$100
Other costs: Travel expenses to and from home

Financial Aid/Status

Full-time status: Students enrolled in 4 classes; 12 credits or more

Maximum Hours Awarded For

CLEP: Yes

Features and Services

1. Is it possible to purchase books during hours most adult students attend classes? **Yes.**

2. How do students taking extended classes access library resources? **Must have student I.D. number/card.**

3. What is the registration and payment process for adult students? **Register at Continuing Education office on campus. Payment due at the Business office on campus.**

4. What is the process for advising adult students? **Continuing Education director advises students.**

5. What characteristics of the institution's adult degree programs are most appealing to students? **Flexibility and breadth of course offerings make getting a degree much easier.**

Albright College

P.O. Box 15234 ◆ Reading, PA 19612
Phone: (610) 921-7516 ◆ Fax: (610) 921-7560

Founded: 1856

Accredited by: Middle States

Enrollment: 1,200 ◆ Adult students: 312

University status: Private, Church, United Methodist Church

Degree	Concentration/Major	Format
B.S.	Business Administration	E
B.S.	Accounting	E
B.S.	Computer Science	E
B.A./B.S.	Psychology	E
M.B.A.	Through Saint Joseph's University of Philadelphia	E

Requirements

Residency requirement: Yes. Undergraduate admissions requirements: File transcripts from high school and any other colleges attended. Complete 12 course units from two or more departments including general studies with 2.0 average. Complete degree application.
Graduate admissions requirements: Application, B.A., official transcripts, scores on Graduate Management Admission Test, two letters of recommendation. Foreign students: English as a Foreign Language, document of financial support.

Fees, Tuition, Costs

Undergraduate application fee: $15
Graduate application fee: $30
Undergraduate tuition: $640/course unit
Graduate tuition: $420/semester hour
Undergraduate cost of books: $75/book

Financial Aid/Status

Full-time status: Three course units/semester

Maximum Hours Awarded For

CLEP: Yes
Other exams: Yes

Features and Services

1. Is it possible to purchase books during hours most adult students attend classes? **Yes.**

2. Are the institution's administrative offices open during hours adult students attend class? **Yes.**

3. What is the registration and payment process for adult students? Mail-VISA, MC, or employee reimbursement In person. **By mail—credit card only.**

4. What is the process for advising adult students? **Available 6:30 A.M.-7:00 P.M. Explains degree requirements; helps with course choice.**

5. What career and placement services are available to adult students? **Evening resume writing workshops; job openings posted; testing available during day.**

6. What characteristics of the institution's adult degree programs are most appealing to students? **Albright is known for high-quality education; one-to-one service. Acts as satellite campus for M.B.A. St. Joseph's University, Philadelphia.**

Alfred Adler Institute of Minnesota

1001 W. Highway 7 ◆ Suite 344 ◆ Hopkins, MN 55305
Phone: (612) 988-4170 ◆ Fax: (612) 988-4171

Founded: 1969

Accredited by: North Central

Enrollment: 300 ◆ Adult students: 100 percent

University status: Nonprofit

Degree	Concentration/Major	Format
M.A.	Adlerian Counseling and Psychotherapy	E
Post M.A.	Adlerian Psychotherapy	E

Requirements

Residency requirement: Students must attend classes on campus. Graduate admissions requirements: 18 quarter credits in psychology and related field; minimum GPA 3.0.
Graduation requirements (graduate): Students must have a minimum of 60 credits and complete a practical internship.

Fees, Tuition, Costs

Graduate application fee: $50
Graduate tuition: $410/credit
Graduate cost of books: $50/class

Financial Aid/Status

Scholarship programs for adults: Scholarships are available.
Full-time status: This is a part-time program.
Percentage of adult students receiving financial aid: 50 percent.

Features and Services

1. Is it possible to purchase books during hours most adult students attend classes? **Yes.**

2. Are the institution's administrative offices open during hours adult students attend class? **Yes.**

3. How do students taking extended classes access library resources? **A library is available on-site.**

4. What is the registration and payment process for adult students? Registration is done quarterly. Registration may be mailed. **Payment plans are available.**

5. What is the process for advising adult students? New students receive advising. **Advising is ongoing and by appointment.**

6. What career and placement services are available to adult students? **Students are helped in resume development and critique, interviewing skills, and general job search skills.**

7. What characteristics of the institution's adult degree programs are most appealing to students? **Month-to-month class format; hands-on internship.**

Allentown College
of St. Francis de Sales

2755 Station Avenue ◆ Center Valley, PA 18034
Phone: (610) 282-1100 ◆ Fax: (610) 282-2850
Web address: http://www.allencol.edu

Founded: 1964

Accredited by: Middle States

Enrollment: 2,350 ◆ Adult students: 1,250

University status: Nonprofit, Church, Roman Catholic Church

Degree	Concentration/Major	Format
B.S.	Accounting and Business	A,E
B.A.	Management	A,E
B.A.	Psychology	A,E
B.S.	Marketing	A,E
B.S.	Computer Science	A,E
B.S.	Finance	A,E
B.A.	Human Science	A,E
B.A.	Business Communication	A,E
B.A.	English	E
M.B.A.	Accounting, Management, Marketing	E,S
M.I.S.	Information Science	E
M.S.N.	Nursing	E
M.Ed.	Secondary/History/English/Math	E

Campus Extension Site

Easton, PA

Requirements

Residency requirement: Must complete 20 courses at campus Undergraduate admissions requirements: Open Graduate admissions requirements: Two courses with grade of C or better (B for graduate school) Graduation requirements (undergraduate): 40 courses including major

Graduation requirements (graduate): 12 graduate courses

Fees, Tuition, Costs

Undergraduate application fee: $30
Graduate application fee: $30
Undergraduate tuition: $660/ course
Graduate tuition: Variable
Undergraduate cost of books: $300-$600
Graduate cost of books: $400
Other costs: Transportation

Financial Aid/Status

Full-time status: 12 hours/ semester—undergraduate; 9 hours/ semester—graduate
Percentage of adult students receiving financial aid: 75 percent

Maximum Hours Awarded For

CLEP: 24
DANTES: 18
Other exams: 6
Prior learning portfolio: Yes

Features and Services

1. Is it possible to purchase books during hours most adult students attend classes? **Yes.**

2. Are the institution's administrative offices open during hours adult students attend class? **Yes.**

3. What is the registration and payment process for adult students? **Deferred payment allowed if reimbursed by employer or if student receives financial aid.**

4. What is the process for advising adult students? **Program coordinator does advising.**

5. What career and placement services are available to adult students? **Same as for traditional students; full-time office.**

6. What characteristics of the institution's adult degree programs are most appealing to students? **6-8 week sessions.**

American Schools of Professional Psychology*

220 South State Street ◆ Chicago, IL 60604
Phone: (312) 922-1025 ◆ Toll-free phone: (800) 742-0743
Fax: (312) 922-1730

Founded: 1976

Accredited by: North Central Association

Enrollment: 848

Features and Services

1. Is it possible to purchase books during hours most adult students attend classes? **Yes**

2. Are the institution's administrative offices open during hours adult students attend class? **Yes**

Degree	Concentration/Major	Format
Psy.D.	Doctorate-Clinical Psychology	E
M.A.	Clinical Psychology	E
M.A.	Professional Counseling	E

Requirements

Residency requirement: Yes
Graduate admissions requirements: Baccalaureate or advanced degree from accredited institution; minimum GPA 3.25 (4.0); undergraduate course work in psychology

Fees, Tuition, Costs

Graduate application fee: $55
Graduate tuition: $357/credit hour

Financial Aid/Status

Full-time status: Nine credit hours/trimester

Responded to 1995 survey only.

The American University*

Nebraska Hall
4400 Massachusetts Ave., N.W. ◆ **Washington, DC 20016**
Phone: (202) 885-3964 ◆ Fax: (202) 885-3991
Web address: http://www.american.edu

Founded: 1893

Accredited by: Middle States

Enrollment: 11,708 ◆ Adult students: 3,860

University status: Private

Maximum Hours Awarded For

CLEP: Yes
PEP: Yes
DANTES: Yes
Prior learning portfolio: 30

Features and Services

1. Is it possible to purchase books during hours most adult students attend classes? **Yes.**

2. Are the institution's administrative offices open during hours adult students attend class? **Yes.**

3. What is the process for advising adult students? **Academic advising is provided through the Office of Return To School Program. Advisors admits students to the program, assist in identifying appropriate areas of expertise, evaluate transferable credits, and help students identify an academic degree program.**

4. What characteristics of the institution's adult degree programs are most appealing to students? **Ability to earn credit for experiential learning, attend weekend master's programs, and enter any traditional major in addition to special programs.**

Degree	Concentration/Major	Format
B.A.	Liberal Studies	E
B.A.	Assessment of Prior Experiential Learning Special program leading to bachelor's degree, which enables adults to earn college credit	E,A
B.A.	Most Majors	E
M.A./M.S.	Most Programs	E
M.A.	Communication: Public Communication	E,A
M.A.	Communication: Journalism and Publications	E,A
M.S.	Computer Science (Artificial Intelligence)	E,A
M.S.	Information Systems	E,A
M.S.	Human Resources Development	E,A
M.P.A.	Key Executive Program	E,A
Ph.D./Ed.D.	Most Programs	E

Requirements

Residency requirement: The special programs listed allow students to attend concentrated classes during the weekend.
Undergraduate admissions requirements: APEL program is for adults who graduated from high school eight or more years ago. Have sufficient life experience to earn 6-30 semester hours of credit, and have had a five-year break from academic studies prior to admission. See Admissions Office for admissions requirements for other undergraduate degrees.
Graduate admissions requirements: Vary by program.

Fees, Tuition, Costs

Undergraduate application fee: $45
Graduate application fee: $50
Undergraduate tuition: $531/credit
Graduate tuition: $571/credit

Financial Aid/Status

Full-time status: 12-17 semester hours for undergraduates; 9 semester hours for graduate students

American University of Puerto Rico

P.O. Box 2037 ◆ Bayamon, PR 00960-2037
Phone: (809) 798-2040 ◆ Fax: (809) 785-7377

Founded: 1963

Accredited by: Middle State

Enrollment: 3,000

University status: Private

Degree	Concentration/Major	Format
B.B.A.	Marketing, Accounting, Purchasing Management	E
B.B.A.	Management, Human Resources	E
B.S.S.	Word Processing	E
B.A.	Communication	E

Campus Extension Sites

Bayamon, PR
Manati, PR

Requirements

Residency requirement: Yes
Undergraduate admissions requirements: Official high school transcript, CEEB or SAT, vaccination

Fees, Tuition, Costs

Undergraduate application fee: $15
Undergraduate tuition: $3,000/year
Undergraduate cost of books: $400

Financial Aid/Status

Scholarship programs for adults: Same as for other students
Full-time status: Minimum of 12 credits

Maximum Hours Awarded For

CLEP: 6
DANTES: 6

Features and Services

1. Is it possible to purchase books during hours most adult students attend classes? **Yes.**

2. Are the institution's administrative offices open during hours adult students attend class? **Yes.**

3. How do students taking extended classes access library resources? **Open until 9:00 P.M.**

4. What is the registration and payment process for adult students? **Same payment plan as for all other students.**

5. What is the process for advising adult students? **A counselor is available at night as well as on Saturday.**

6. What career and placement services are available to adult students? **Same as for other students.**

Anderson University

1100 E. 5th Street ◆ **Anderson, IN 46012**
Phone: (317) 641-4251 ◆ Toll-free phone: (800) 428-6414
Fax: (317) 641-3851
E-mail: abeverly@anderson.edu

Founded: 1917

Accredited by: North Central

Enrollment: 1,920 ◆ Adult students: 305

University status: Nonprofit, Church, Church of God (Anderson)

Degree	Concentration/Major	Format
A.A.	Business	E
A.A.	General Studies	E
A.A.	Criminal Justice	E

Requirements

Undergraduate admissions requirements: Admission form, official transcript from high school or any attendance at college, one reference form
Graduation requirements (undergraduate): 124 credit hours

Fees, Tuition, Costs

Undergraduate application fee: $20
Undergraduate tuition: $193/hour for age 25+
Undergraduate cost of books: $300/semester
Other costs: $100 technology fee/semester for computer use for students taking 6 hours or more

Financial Aid/Status

Full-time status: 12 credit hours or more
Percentage of adult students receiving financial aid: 70 percent

Maximum Hours Awarded For

Other exams: 8

Features and Services

1. Is it possible to purchase books during hours most adult students attend classes? **No.**

2. Are the institution's administrative offices open during hours adult students attend class? **No.**

3. How do students taking extended classes access library resources? **Open evening and weekend hours.**

4. What is the registration and payment process for adult students? **Students over 25 register and pay for classes at the Adult Education office, hours 8-7 M-Th, 8-5 F.**

5. What is the process for advising adult students? **Student declaring major sets schedule with major advisor. Undeclared students are advised by Adult Education.**

6. What career and placement services are available to adult students? **Workshops on resume writing, interview skills. Some companies recruit on campus.**

7. What characteristics of the institution's adult degree programs are most appealing to students? **Reduced tuition rate; encouragement and support from Adult Education staff.**

Assemblies of God Theological Seminary

1445 Booneville Avenue ◆ **Springfield, MO 65802**

Phone: (417) 862-3344 ◆ Toll-free phone: (800) 467-AGTS
Fax: (417) 864-7165 ◆ E-mail: gkellner@affil.ag.org

Founded: 1971

Accredited by: North Central

University status: Private, Church, Assemblies of God

Degree	Concentration/Major	Format
M.Div.	Master of Divinity (In-service Track)	E,A,C
M.A.	Christian Ministries—Biblical Studies	E,A,C
M.A.	Christian Ministries—Church Studies	E,A,C
M.A.	Christian Ministries—Missions	E,A,C

Campus Extension Sites

Phoenixville, PA
Kirkland, WA
Lakeland, FL
Dunn, NC
Waxahachie, TX
Minneapolis, MN

Requirements

Residency requirement: Students must attend one-week accelerated sessions each semester. Visits to extension sites occur midway through course work. 1/6 program may be by correspondence. M.Div. candidates must visit main campus. Graduate admissions requirements: Bachelor's with a 2.5 GPA, one course each (grade at least C) in philosophy, psychology, social science. Application, photo, official transcript, two personal/ministerial references, Christian profession of faith.
Graduation requirements (graduate): M.A. and M.Div., completion of all course work, plus an Analytical Reflection paper.

Fees, Tuition, Costs

Graduate application fee: $35
Graduate tuition: $210/credit, any format
Graduate cost of books: $60/semester
Other costs: Travel to extension centers

Financial Aid/Status

Scholarship programs for adults: Need-based tuition discount for Assemblies of God ministers and lay persons
Full-time status: Nine semester hours/semester

Maximum Hours Awarded For

CLEP: Yes
Other exams: Yes
Prior learning portfolio: Yes

Features and Services

1. How do students taking extended classes access library resources? **Open during on-site visits. Materials available by phone, mail, fax, e-mail, or interlibrary loans.**

2. What is the registration and payment process for adult students? **Preregistration available. Register on-site first day of extension session. Correspondence use of prepared forms.**

3. What is the process for advising adult students? **Assigned advisor and student meet at one-week orientation. Mentoring by phone and correspondence.**

4. What career and placement services are available to adult students? **The seminary works closely with the denomination in placing graduates.**

5. What characteristics of the institution's adult degree programs are most appealing to students? **Students don't have to relocate. Flexibility through format variations. On-site visits and mentoring develop sense of community.**

Atlantic College

P.O. Box 3918 ◆ Guaynabo, PR 00970-3918
Phone: (787) 720-1022 ◆ Fax: (787) 720-1092

Founded: 1981

Accredited by: Accrediting Council

Enrollment: 329

Adult students: 100 percent

University status: Private, Nonprofit

Degree	Concentration/Major	Format
B.B.A.	General Administration	E
B.B.A.	Accounting	E
B.B.A.	Marketing	E
B.S.S.	Secretarial Sciences	E
B.A.	Graphic Arts	E

Requirements

Residency requirement: Students must attend classes on campus. Undergraduate admissions requirements: Students must submit a high school diploma or GED, a skill test, and an application.
Graduation requirements (undergraduate): Graduates must complete the program with a 2.0 GPA.

Fees, Tuition, Costs

Undergraduate application fee: $30
Other costs: Laboratory fees

Financial Aid/Status

Scholarship programs for adults: No scholarships available
Full-time status: 12 credits
Percentage of adult students receiving financial aid: 29 percent

Features and Services

1. Is it possible to purchase books during hours most adult students attend classes? **No.**

2. Are the institution's administrative offices open during hours adult students attend class? **Yes.**

3. What is the registration and payment process for adult students? **Registration is processed by computer.**

4. What is the process for advising adult students? **Advising is done individually on a voluntary basis.**

5. What career and placement services are available to adult students? **Students are given assistance in finding work.**

6. What characteristics of the institution's adult degree programs are most appealing to students? **Blending of theory and practice.**

Atlantic Union College

Box 1000 ◆ **South Lancaster, MA 01561**
Phone: (508) 368-2300 ◆ Toll-free phone: (800) 282-2030
Fax: (508) 368-2015 ◆ E-mail: ibothwell@atlanticuc.edu
Web address: http://www.atlanticuc.edu

Founded: 1882

Accredited by: New England

Enrollment: 600 ◆ Adult students: 118

University status: Private, Church, Seventh-Day Adventist

Degree	Concentration/Major	Format
B.A./B.S.	Art	S
B.S.	Behavioral Science	S
B.A.	Business Administration	S
B.A.	Communication	S
B.S.	Computer Science	S
B.S.	Elementary or Early Childhood Education	S
B.A.	English	S
B.A.	History	S
B.S.	Interior Design	S
B.A.	Modern Languages	S
B.S.	Human Movement	S
B.S.	Psychology	S
B.A.	Religion/Theology/Personal Ministries	S
B.A.	General or Interdisciplinary Studies	S

Requirements

Residency requirement: Attendance at 8-10 day seminars in January and July is required. Undergraduate admissions requirements: 25 or older; high school diploma or equivalent (including 5 GCE passes or GED certificate—no subtest score below 50), may be admitted on provisional basis. Non-English speaking score 550 on TOEFL. Graduation requirements (undergraduate): Unit's work in liberal arts: humanities, social science, science, mathematics, religion; two or three units in major area; at least two final units not prior learning credit from Adult Degree Program.

Fees, Tuition, Costs

Undergraduate application fee: $15
Undergraduate tuition: $3,190/semester
Undergraduate cost of books: $200
Other costs: Costs of seminar attendance in January and July and travel costs

Financial Aid/Status

Full-time status: Enrolled for a unit (15-18 semester hours) during each six-month period (January-July, July-January)

Percentage of adult students receiving financial aid: 50 percent

Maximum Hours Awarded For

CLEP: 64
PEP: 64
DANTES: 64
Other exams: Yes
Prior learning portfolio: Yes

Features and Services

1. Is it possible to purchase books during hours most adult students attend classes? **Yes.**

2. Are the institution's administrative offices open during hours adult students attend class? **Yes.**

3. How do students taking extended classes access library resources? **Students use libraries near their own homes.**

4. What is the registration and payment process for adult students? **Students register during January and July seminars. Payment at registration. Credit cards accepted.**

5. What is the process for advising adult students? **Advising through interviews, phone, and mail before seminars and through conferences during seminars.**

6. What career and placement services are available to adult students? **The college's career placement office is available to adult students.**

7. What characteristics of the institution's adult degree programs are most appealing to students? **The ability to pursue a wide range of degrees while living and working at home. The favorable faculty-student ratio.**

Auburn University Graduate Outreach Program

202 Ramsay Hall ◆ Auburn University, AL 36849
Phone: (334) 844-5300 ◆ Fax: (334) 844-2519
E-mail: jcbrandt@eng.auburn.edu
Web address: http://www.auburn.edu
Program's Web address:
http://www.eng.auburn.edu/department/eop/eophome.html/

Founded: 1856

Accredited by: Southern Association

Enrollment: 22,000 ◆ Adult students: 430

University status: Nonprofit, Public

Degree	Concentration/Major	Format
M.B.A.	Business	V
M.A.E.	Aerospace Engineering	V
M.S.	Aerospace Engineering	V
Ph.D.	Aerospace Engineering	V
M.Ch.E.	Chemical Engineering	V
M.S.	Chemical Engineering	V
Ph.D.	Chemical Engineering	V
M.C.E.	Civil Engineering	V
M.S.	Civil Engineering	V
Ph.D.	Civil Engineering	V
M.C.S.E.	Computer Science	V
M.S.	Computer Science	V
Ph.D.	Computer Science	V
M.I.E.	Industrial Engineering	V
M.S.	Industrial Engineering	V
Ph.D.	Industrial Engineering	V
M.Mtl.	Materials Engineering	V
M.S.	Materials Engineering	V
Ph.D.	Materials Engineering	V
M.M.E.	Mechanical Engineering	V
M.S.	Mechanical Engineering	V
Ph.D.	Mechanical Engineering	V
M.E.E.	Electrical Engineering	V
M.S.	Electrical Engineering	V

Campus Extension Sites

Throughout U.S.

Requirements

Residency requirement: Not all degrees require time on campus. M.E. and M.B.A. require one or two days for oral exam; M.S. for oral defense of thesis; Ph.D. requires three consecutive quarters of residency.

Graduate admissions requirements: Completed application; two transcripts from each institution attended; three letters of recommendation from instructors and/or supervisors; GRE/GMAT scores.

Graduation requirements (graduate): Engineering: 45-48 quarter hours; on-campus comprehensive oral exam. M.B.A.: 67-87 quarter hours; three to five days on campus for case analysis.

Fees, Tuition, Costs

Graduate application fee: $25
Graduate tuition: $202/credit hour
Graduate cost of books: $30-$120
Other costs: $130 registration fee; $20 graduation fee; additional charges for shipping and handling videos, depending on student's location

Financial Aid/Status

Scholarship programs for adults: Scholarships are based on departmental availability. Percentage of adult students receiving financial aid: 90 percent.

Features and Services

1. Is it possible to purchase books during hours most adult students attend classes? **Yes.**

2. Are the institution's administrative offices open during hours adult students attend class? **Yes.**

3. How do students taking extended access library resources? **Students may use student I.D. on campus or make library material loans.**

4. What is the registration and payment process for adult

students? **Registration by Graduate Outreach office. Bills are sent from Bursar's office as fees are listed.**

5. What is the process for advising adult students? **Students are assigned an advisor within their individual departments.**

6. What career and placement services are available to adult students? **Alumni Placement Services are available.**

7. What characteristics of the institution's adult degree programs are most appealing to students? **The convenience of viewing classes by**

video ensures students of never missing a class because of work or travel schedule.

Audrey Cohen College*

345 Hudson Street ◆ New York, NY 10014

Phone: (212)989-2002 ◆ Toll-free phone: (800)-33-THINK

Fax: (212)924-4396

Founded: 1964

Accredited by: Middle States

Enrollment: 1,150 ◆ Adult students: 1,150

University status: Private

Degree	Concentration/Major	Format
B.A.	Human Services	E
B.A.	Business Management	E
M.A.	Administration	E

Requirements

Residency requirement: Bachelor's degrees can be completed in two years and eight months while working full-time. Undergraduate admissions requirements: Students are accepted on current ability and skills. Also, students must schedule a personal interview, file an application, take an admissions exam with essay, and submit two letters of reference. Graduate admissions requirements:

An earned bachelor's degree from an accredited institution, a personal interview, two written essays, an approved work site, and two letters of reference.

Fees, Tuition, Costs

Undergraduate application fee: $20
Graduate application fee: $30
Undergraduate tuition: $245/credit
Graduate tuition: $283/credit

Financial Aid/Status

Full-time status: 16 credits/semester
Percentage of adult students receiving financial aid: 80 percent

Maximum Hours Awarded For

Other exams: 32
Prior learning portfolio: 32

Features and Services

1. Is it possible to purchase books during hours most adult students attend classes? **Yes.**

2. Are the institution's administrative offices open during hours adult students attend class? **Yes.**

3. What characteristics of the institution's adult degree programs are most appealing to students? **Day, evening, or evening weekend classes, individualized learning, accelerated degree programs are available. Students apply classroom theory to internships or their place of employment.**

Augustana College

2001 South Summit Avenue ◆ Sioux Falls, SD 57197
Phone: (605) 336-5516 ◆ Toll-free phone: (800) 727-2844
Fax: (605) 336-5518 ◆ E-mail: mbailey@inst.augie.edu
Web address: http://www.augie.edu

Founded: 1835

Accredited by: North Central

Enrollment: 1,800 ◆ Adult students: 450

University status: Private, Church,
Evangelical Lutheran Church of America

Degree	Concentration/Major	Format
B.A.	In all 46 majors, 38 minors and 14 preprofessional programs	E
M.A.	Selected Studies, Teaching, Secondary Education, Special Education	E
M.S.	Nursing, Communication Disorders	E

Requirements

Residency requirement: Yes
Undergraduate admissions requirements: Be 24 or older; application; high school transcript or documentation of GED; one recommendation form concerning applicant's academic preparation and character
Graduate admissions requirements: Completed 9 graduate hours; complete one course in major area; B average in degree course work; filed graduate course plan; demonstrate ability to meet degree requirements
Graduation requirements (undergraduate): 130 credit hours including core courses and a two-course graduation requirement in religion; grade point minimum 2.0; file graduation and diploma form

Graduation requirements (graduate): 32 credit hours; grade point minimum 3.0; written English proficiency; 23 hours at Augustana (8 hours in residency); complete degree in seven years; graduate paper; written and oral exams

Fees, Tuition, Costs

Undergraduate application fee: $25
Graduate application fee: $50
Undergraduate tuition: $190/credit hour
Graduate tuition: $220/credit hour
Undergraduate cost of books: $200
Graduate cost of books: $200
Other costs: Full-time students only—$130 activity fee

Financial Aid/Status

Scholarship programs for adults: Adults qualify for most scholarships. Several endowed scholarships especially for adults are available.
Full-time status: Any student taking 10 credit hours or more.
Percentage of adult students receiving financial aid: 95 percent.

Maximum Hours Awarded For

CLEP: 88
Other exams: 12
Prior learning portfolio: Yes
Additional information: Transfer credits

Features and Services

1. Is it possible to purchase books during hours most adult students attend classes? **Yes.**

2. Are the institution's administrative offices open during hours adult students attend class? **Yes.**

3. What is the registration and payment process for adult students? **Same as that for traditional students. Pay by mail, at business office, or by phone using credit card.**

4. What is the process for advising adult students? **Nontraditional advisor available. Assigned advisor through major department.**

5. What career and placement services are available to adult students? **Career Center used by traditional students.**

Aurora University

347 South Gladstone ◆ Aurora, IL 60506

Phone: (708) 896-1975 ◆ Web address: http://www.aurora.edu

Founded: 1893

Accredited by: North Central

Enrollment: 2,000 ◆ Adult students: 1,400

University status: Private

Degree	Concentration/Major	Format
B.A.	Accounting	E
B.A./B.S.	Business Administration	E
B.A.	Communication	E
B.A./B.S.	Computer Science	E
B.A.	Criminal Justice	E
B.A./B.S.	Economics	E
B.A./B.S.	Finance	E
B.A.	Industrial Management	E
B.A./B.S.	Management	E
B.A./B.S.	Marketing	E
B.A.	Psychology	E
B.A.	Sociology	E
B.S.	Professional Studies	E,A
B.S.N.	Nursing	E
M.A.T.	Teaching	E

Campus Extension Sites

Waukegan, IL
Chicago, IL
New Berlin, WI

Requirements

Residency requirement: Students may attend classes on the Aurora campus or at the extended campus sites.
Undergraduate admissions requirements: Adult students are considered individually. Transfer students should have at least 2.0 GPA on 4.0 scale.
Graduate admissions requirements: 2.75 GPA on 4.0 scale; bachelor's degree; other specific requirements depending on graduate program.
Graduation requirements (undergraduate): 120 semester hours with 2.0 GPA on 4.0 scale.
Graduation requirements (graduate): GPA of 3.0 on 4.0 scale. Requirements vary by graduate program.

Fees, Tuition, Costs

Undergraduate application fee: $25
Graduate application fee: $25
Undergraduate tuition: $376/semester hour
Graduate tuition: $376/semester hour
Undergraduate cost of books: $60/course
Graduate cost of books: $60/course

Financial Aid/Status

Scholarship programs for adults: Transfer scholarships are available to full-time transfer students with 3.0-4.0 GPA. May receive up to $3500/year.
Full-time status: 9 semester hours/term.

Maximum Hours Awarded For

CLEP: 30
PEP: 27
DANTES: Yes
Other exams: Yes
Prior learning portfolio: 60
Additional information: Life Experience Assessment Program—30 credit hours

Features and Services

1. Is it possible to purchase books during hours most adult students attend classes? **Yes.**

2. Are the institution's administrative offices open during hours adult students attend class? **Yes.**

3. What is the registration and payment process for adult students? **Deferred payment and payment plans are available.**

4. What is the process for advising adult students? **Advisors are available both day and evening hours.**

5. What career and placement services are available to adult students? **Workshops, seminars, career fair, job bulletin, and individual services available to all students.**

6. What characteristics of the institution's adult degree programs are most appealing to students? **Convenient schedules and location; deferred payment; specific programs available.**

Averett College

420 W. Main St. ◆ Danville, VA 24541
Phone: (804)791-5650 ◆ Toll-free phone: (800)448-5233
Fax: (804)791-5898 ◆ E-mail: alice0@averett.edu
Web address: http://www.averett.edu

Founded: 1859

Accredited by: Southern Association

Enrollment: 2,600 ◆ Adult students: 1,700

University status: Private, Church,
Baptist General Board of Virginia

Degree	Concentration/Major	Format
B.B.A.	Business Administration	E,T,A
M.B.A.	Business Administration	E,T,A
All college degrees except education		E,C,V,S.

Campus Extension Sites

Vienna, VA
Norfolk, VA
Richmond, VA
Hampton, VA
Roanoke, VA
Newport News, VA
Lynchburg, VA
Other Virginia locations

Requirements

Undergraduate admissions requirements: 22 years of age, two years of work experience, high school or equivalent diploma, three references, 2.00 GPA for transfer students
Graduate admissions requirements: 23 years of age, BA from an accredited college or university, three years of work experience, 3.00 GPA
Graduation requirements (undergraduate): 123 credits with a 2.00 GPA

Graduation requirements (graduate): 36 credits with a 3.00 GPA

Fees, Tuition, Costs

Undergraduate application fee: $25
Graduate application fee: $25
Undergraduate tuition: $9,065
Graduate tuition: $10,845
Undergraduate cost of books: $1,200
Graduate cost of books: $1,200

Financial Aid/Status

Full-time status: 12 credits/semester
Percentage of adult students receiving financial aid: 80 percent

Maximum Hours Awarded For

CLEP: Yes
DANTES: Yes
Other exams: Yes
Prior learning portfolio: Yes

Features and Services

1. Is it possible to purchase books during hours most adult students attend classes? **Yes.**

2. Are the institution's administrative offices open during hours adult students attend class? **Yes.**

3. How do students taking extended classes access library resources? **800 number, modem computer connection to campus library, agreements with other libraries.**

4. What is the registration and payment process for adult students? **Special payment arrangements may be made.**

5. What is the process for advising adult students? **Professional advising staff and faculty advising.**

6. What career and placement services are available to adult students? **Career counselor available to all students.**

7. What characteristics of the institution's adult degree programs are most appealing to students? **Acceleration, learning model suited to adults, faculty with academic certification and business experience, grad students receive computers.**

Baker University

6600 College Blvd., Suite 340 ◆ School of Professional and
Graduate Studies ◆ **Overland Park, KS 66211**
Phone: (913) 491-4432 ◆ Toll-free phone: (800) 955-7747
Fax: (913) 491-0470 ◆ Web address: http://www.bakeru.edu

Founded: 1858

Accredited by: North Central

Enrollment: 2,000 ◆ Adult students: 1,000

University status: Private, Church, United Methodist Church

Financial Aid/Status

Full-time status: Full-time students earn at least 12 hours in 15 weeks. Percentage of adult students receiving financial aid: 40 percent.

Maximum Hours Awarded For

CLEP: Yes
PEP: Yes
DANTES: Yes
Other exams: Yes
Prior learning portfolio: Yes

Degree	Concentration/Major	Format
B.B.A.	Business Administration	E,A
B.S.M.	Management	E,A
M.S.M.	Management	E,A
M.B.A.	Business Administration	E,A
M.L.A.	Liberal Arts	E
M.A.E.D.	Education	E

Features and Services

1. Is it possible to purchase books during hours most adult students attend classes? **Yes.**

2. How do students taking extended classes access library resources? **Students use area libraries.**

3. What is the registration and payment process for adult students? **Drop off payment on the way to class or mail in. Books and materials are delivered to the site.**

4. What is the process for advising adult students? **Student services office advise by appointment or telephone.**

5. What career and placement services are available to adult students? **Students may use main campus placement office. Available jobs are posted at off-campus sites.**

6. What characteristics of the institution's adult degree programs are most appealing to students? **Classes meet one night a week; lock-step program.**

Campus Extension Sites

Overland Park, KS
Topeka, KS

Requirements

Residency requirement: Students are not required to attend classes on the main campus.
Undergraduate admissions requirements: Adult students must be 23 or older with two years of work experience. Two letters of recommendation are required. Graduate admissions requirements: Students must be 25 or older with three years of work experience. They must have a bachelor's degree from a regionally accredited institution. Two letters of recommendation are required. Graduation requirements (undergraduate): 124 credit hours; GPA = 2.5 or above; complete B.B.A. or B.S.M. program courses. Graduation requirements (graduate): Complete degree credits; GPA = 3.0 or above All credits must be completed within six years.

Fees, Tuition, Costs

Undergraduate application fee: $20
Graduate application fee: $20
Undergraduate tuition: $225/credit hour
Graduate tuition: $265/credit hour
Undergraduate cost of books: $1,360
Graduate cost of Books: $1,600
Other costs: Laptop computers for students in business programs, with the option to purchase the computer at the conclusion of the program—usually for less than $500

Ball State University

Carmichael Hall 200 ◆ Muncie, IN 47306

Phone: (317) 285-1581 ◆ Toll-free phone: (800) 872-0369

Fax: (317) 285-5795 ◆ E-mail: oojkdanglade@bsu.edu

Web address: http://www.bsu.edu

Founded: 1918

Accredited by: North Central

Enrollment: 19,500 ◆ Adult students: 6825

University status: Public

Degree	Concentration/Major	Format
M.B.A.	Business Administration	T
B.S.	Nursing (for RNs)	T
M.S.	Computer Science (being developed)	T, CT
B.S.	General Arts	T
A.A.	General Arts	T,C
M.A.E.	Elementary Education (being developed)	T
M.A.E.	Special Education (being developed)	T
M.A.	Executive Development for Public Service (being developed)	T
	Endorsement/Gifted and Talented (Graduate—being developed)	T
M.A./M.S.	75 degrees	E
D.Ed.	Adult Education	E
D.Ed.	Educational Administration	E
D.Ed.	Special Education	E
D.Ed.	Elementary Education	E
Ph.D.	Educational Psychology	E
Ph.D.	Counseling Psychology	E
Ph.D.	English	E
Ed.S.	Curriculum	E
Ed.S.	Educational Administration	E
D.A.	Music	E

Campus Extension Sites

Indianapolis, IN
Fort Wayne, IN
LaPorte, IN

Requirements

Residency requirement: Students are not required to attend on-campus classes for the M.B.A., Nursing, A.A.s, B.S. in General Arts or Computer Science. Graduate education degrees will require one or two classes. Undergraduate admissions requirements: Admissions application, official high school transcript or GED certificate, official transcript from any colleges attended. Some students over 23 may be required to take the SAT or ACT.

Graduate admissions requirements: Bachelor's from an accredited college with acceptable academic performance. Must meet departmental standards. Graduation requirements (undergraduate): 126 semester hours for most degrees. Graduation requirements (graduate): 30 semester hours.

Fees, Tuition, Costs

Undergraduate application fee: $15
Graduate application fee: $15
Undergraduate tuition: $98/hour
Graduate tuition: $104/hour
Undergraduate cost of books: $45
Graduate cost of books: $60
Other costs: Computer support for some courses, requiring either the purchase of hardware and software or access to them by other means

Financial Aid/Status

Full-time status: 12 semester hours
Percentage of adult students receiving financial aid: 25 percent

Maximum Hours Awarded For

CLEP: 18
DANTES: 15
Other exams: 62
Prior learning portfolio: 62

Features and Services

1. Is it possible to purchase books during hours most adult students attend classes? **Yes.**

2. How do students taking extended classes access library resources? **On campus weekends and evenings; use Internet connection or any state-supported area library.**

3. What is the registration and payment process for adult students? **On-campus registration as for traditional students. Off-campus registration by mail or phone. Bills mailed from Bursar.**

4. What is the process for advising adult students? **All have campus advisor. Advisors travel to off-campus sites. May phone Continuing Education office.**

5. What career and placement services are available to adult students? **Career Services office offers the Home Page on the WWW and automated phone services.**

6. What characteristics of the institution's adult degree programs are most appealing to students? **Evening classes. "Reflex" office serves nontraditional students' interests/needs.**

Barat College*

700 East Westleigh Road ◆ Office of Adult Admission
Lake Forest, IL 60045
Phone: (708) 295-4260 ◆ Fax: (708) 615-5000

Founded: 1858

Accredited by: North Central

Enrollment: 730 ◆ Adult students: 329

University status: Private, Nonsectarian

Maximum Hours Awarded For

CLEP: 18
PEP: 33
Prior learning portfolio: 18

Degree	Concentration/Major	Format
B.A.	Management and Business Department	E
B.A.	Computer Information Systems	E
B.A.	Communication Arts	E
B.A.	Elementary Education	E
B.A.	Learning Disabilities	E
B.A.	Secondary Education	E
B.A.	Dance	E

Requirements

Residency requirement: Yes
Undergraduate admissions requirements: Completed application form, official transcripts from all colleges attended, high school transcript and standardized tests, two recommendations from a professor and employer

Fees, Tuition, Costs

Undergraduate application fee: $20
Undergraduate tuition: $10,560/year

Financial Aid/Status

Full-time status: Enrollment in four or more classes/term

Bard College
Annandale-on-Hudson, NY 12504
Phone: (914) 758-7508 ◆ Fax: (914) 758-5801
E-mail: becker@bard.edu ◆ Web address: http://www.bard.edu

Founded: 1860

Accredited by: Middle States

Enrollment: 1,000 ◆ Adult students: 75

University status: Nonprofit

Degree	Concentration/Major	Format
B.A.	Social Science	E
B.A.	Arts	E
B.A.	Languages and Literature	E
B.A.	Natural Science and Mathematics	E
B.S.	Natural Science and Mathematics	E
B.P.S.	Natural Science and Mathematics	

Requirements

Residency requirement: Bard College has no extended campus locations. Students are required to attend classes on the campus. Undergraduate admissions requirements: 24 years of age or over, application form, two letters of recommendation from former teachers/employers, official transcripts of all undergraduate work.
Graduation requirements (undergraduate): 124 hours (64 hours at Bard), minimum of 40 credits outside major, 2 semesters of First-Year Seminar, 1 course from each distribution area and quantitative course, complete senior project.

Fees, Tuition, Costs

Undergraduate application fee: $40
Undergraduate tuition: $250/credit hour
Undergraduate cost of books: $200-$300 for full-time students

Financial Aid/Status

Full-time status: 12 credit hours
Percentage of adult students receiving financial aid: 80 percent

Maximum Hours Awarded For

Prior learning portfolio: 60
Additional information: Life experience credits: 30

Features and Services

1. Is it possible to purchase books during hours most adult students attend classes? **Yes.**

2. Are the institution's administrative offices open during hours adult students attend class? **Yes.**

3. What is the registration and payment process for adult students? **Evening registration and payment by mail. Day classes register with professor and pay before classes begin.**

4. What is the process for advising adult students? **A faculty advisor is assigned on student's acceptance into the Continuing Studies Program.**

5. What career and placement services are available to adult students? **The services of the Career Development Office are available to adult students.**

6. What characteristics of the institution's adult degree programs are most appealing to students? **Smaller classes; more personalized curriculum; availability of professors for tutorials.**

Barry University*

11425 N.E. 2nd Avenue ◆ **Miami Shores, FL 33161**
Phone: (305) 899-3318 ◆ Toll-free phone: (800) 945-2279
Fax: (305) 899-3346
Web address: http://www.barry.edu

Founded: 1940

Accredited by: Southern Association

Enrollment: 7,500 ◆ Adult students: 2,000

University status: Nonprofit, Church, Roman Catholic Church

Features and Services

1. Is it possible to purchase books during hours most adult students attend classes? **Yes.**

2. What characteristics of the institution's adult degree programs are most appealing to students? **Credit awarded for college-level learning from work experience (portfolio); four 10-week terms/year.**

Degree	Concentration/Major	Format
B.P.S.	Business	E,A
B.P.S.	Personal Financial Planning	E,A
B.P.S.	Health Services Administration	E,A
B.P.S.	Human Resource Management	E,A
B.P.S.	Management Information Systems	E,A
B.P.S.	Public Administration	E,A
B.P.S.	Telecommunications	E,A
B.P.S.	Behavioral Sciences	E,A
B.P.S.	Humanities	E,A
B.L.S.	Humanities	E,A
B.L.S.	Legal Studies	E,A
B.L.S.	Social Sciences	E,A

Requirements

Residency requirement: No
Undergraduate admissions requirements: Interview with an academic advisor/director, submit an application, provide transcripts of college course work or, if fewer than 12 credits have been earned, provide proof of high school graduation/GED, and achieve a 2.0+ in all previous college work

Fees, Tuition, Costs

Undergraduate application fee: $30
Undergraduate tuition: $178/credit

Financial Aid/Status

Full-time status: 12 credits/term
Percentage of adult students receiving financial aid: 40 percent

Maximum Hours Awarded For

Prior learning portfolio: Yes

Bartlesville Wesleyan College*

2201 Silver Lake Road ◆ **Bartlesville, OK 74006**
Phone: (918)335-6259 ◆ Toll-free phone: (800)375-4647
Fax: (918)335-6244

Founded: 1910

Accredited by: North Central

Enrollment: 508 ◆ Adult students: 95

University status: Nonprofit, Church, Wesleyan Church

Degree	Concentration/Major	Format
B.S.	Management of Human Resources	E,A

Requirements

Residency requirement: No
Undergraduate admissions
requirements: Must have 64 hours
or A.A. degree from accredited
college and be 25 years

Fees, Tuition, Costs

Undergraduate application fee:
$100
Undergraduate tuition: $180/credit

Financial Aid/Status

Percentage of adult students
receiving financial aid: 55 percent

Maximum Hours Awarded For

CLEP: 36
DANTES: 36
Prior learning portfolio: 22

Features and Services

1. What characteristics of the institution's adult degree programs are most appealing to students? **Shortened time, convenient location, one night a week.**

Beaver College

450 S. Eaton Road ◆ **Glenside, PA 19038**
Phone: (215) 572-2921 ◆ Toll-free phone: (800) 776-BEAVER
Fax: (215) 572-2156 ◆ E-mail: admiss@beaver.edu
Program's Web address: http://www.beaver.edu

Founded: 1853

Accredited by: Middle States

Enrollment: 1,500 ◆ Adult students: 33

University status: Nonprofit, Church, Presbyterian Church, U.S.A.

Degree	Concentration/Major	Format
B.S.	Accounting	E
B.A./B.S.	Business Administration	E
B.A.	Corporate Communications	E
B.A./B.S.	Computer Science	E
B.A.	English	E
B.A.	Health Administration	E
B.A.	Liberal Studies	E
B.S.	Management	E
B.S.	Management Information Systems	E
B.S.	Marketing	E
B.S.	Human Resources Administration	E

Requirements

Residency requirement: Yes
Undergraduate admissions requirements: Application, official transcripts from postsecondary schools attended, meet with Director of Weekend College Graduate admissions requirements: Bachelor's degree from accredited college, application, two official transcripts, three letters of recommendation; one from professor/employer

Fees, Tuition, Costs

Undergraduate application fee: $30
Graduate application fee: $35

Undergraduate tuition: $260/credit hour
Graduate tuition: $315/credit hour

Financial Aid/Status

Scholarship programs for adults: Scholarships are available for adult students who are full-time.
Full-time status: 12 credit hours.

Maximum Hours Awarded For

CLEP: Yes
Other exams: Yes

Features and Services

1. Is it possible to purchase books during hours most adult students attend classes? **Yes.**

2. Are the institution's administrative offices open during hours adult students attend class? **Yes.**

3. What is the registration and payment process for adult students? **Deferred payment available. Through Employee Reimbursement Agreement all or part of tuition paid.**

4. What is the process for advising adult students? **Each student has a faculty advisor and support of Continuing Education staff.**

5. What career and placement services are available to adult students? **Career Services department available to adult students.**

6. What characteristics of the institution's adult degree programs are most appealing to students? **Personalized service.**

Bellarmine College

2001 Newburg Road ◆ **Louisville, KY 40205-0671**
Phone: (502) 452-8155 ◆ Toll-free phone: (800) 274-4723
Fax: (502) 452-8203

Founded: 1950

Accredited by: Southern Association

Enrollment: 2,300 ◆ Adult students: 1,150

University status: Private, Church, Roman Catholic Church

Degree	Concentration/Major	Format
B.S.	Computer Information Systems	E
B.S.	Management Information Systems	E
B.A.	Psychology	E
B.A.	Communications	E
B.A.	Liberal Studies	E
B.S.	Nursing (for RNs only)	E
B.A.	Accounting	E
B.A.	Business Administration	E
B.A.	Economics	E
M.A.	Liberal Studies	E
M.S.	Nursing	E
M.A.	Business Administration	E
M.A.	Teaching	E
M.A.	Education	E

Campus Extension Site

Ashland, KY

Requirements

Residency requirement: We send Bellarmine faculty to Ashland for all M.S.N. courses.
Undergraduate admissions requirements: 23 or older, five years from high school graduation; application, high school transcript or GED, college transcripts, one page describing goals. Contact college for more details.
Graduate admissions requirements: Graduate application form, official transcripts of all undergraduate and graduate credits from all accredited institutions.

Graduation requirements (undergraduate): 126 semester hours, GPA of 2.0, 24 semester hours in upper-level courses, course requirements for major, 36 hours at Bellarmine College with 12 hours in major, complete General Education Requirements.
Graduation requirements (graduate): 3.0 GPA, requirements vary with degree.

Fees, Tuition, Costs

Undergraduate application fee: $25
Graduate application fee: $25
Undergraduate tuition: $280/credit hour
Graduate tuition: $305/credit hour
Undergraduate cost of books: $100/2 courses

Graduate cost of books: $100/2 courses
Other costs: Nominal costs—lab fees ($25)

Financial Aid/Status

Scholarship programs for adults: Some available for M.B.A. and graduate education programs
Full-time status: 12 hours/semester

Maximum Hours Awarded For

CLEP: Yes
DANTES: Yes
Other exams: Yes
Prior learning portfolio: 12
Additional information: Maximum of 30 hours from any combination

Features and Services

1. Is it possible to purchase books during hours most adult students attend classes? **Yes.**

2. Are the institution's administrative offices open during hours adult students attend class? **Yes.**

3. How do students taking extended classes access library resources? **Students may dial a toll-free number and speak with our librarian.**

4. What is the registration and payment process for adult students? **Registration by phone/evening hours. Payment by mail/phone. Credit cards, reimbursement, other plans.**

5. What is the process for advising adult students? **Adults are responsible to seek advice from their department of study or Continuing Education.**

6. What career and placement services are available to adult students? **Students may register with Career Services.**

7. What characteristics of the institution's adult degree programs are most appealing to students? **Availability of degree programs in the** evening, condensed courses in the summer, small class size, access to professors outside class.

Belmont Abbey College

100 Belmont-Mt. Holly Road ◆ **Belmont, NC 28012**
Phone: (704) 825-6671 ◆ Fax: (704) 825-6658

Founded: 1876

Accredited by: Southern Association

Enrollment: 800 ◆ Adult students: 45

University status: Private, Church, Roman Catholic Church

Maximum Hours Awarded For

CLEP: 30
PEP: 30
DANTES: 30
Other exams: Varies
Prior learning portfolio: 30

Features and Services

1. Is it possible to purchase books during hours most adult students attend classes? **Yes.**

2. Are the institution's administrative offices open during hours adult students attend class? **Yes.**

3. What is the registration and payment process for adult students? **Registration and payment are separate from traditional students.**

4. What is the process for advising adult students? **Adult students are assigned an advisor throughout their college program.**

5. What career and placement services are available to adult students? **Same as for traditional students.**

6. What characteristics of the institution's adult degree programs are most appealing to students? **Accelerated courses, personal service, flexibility, tuition deferment.**

Degree	Concentration/Major	Format
B.A.	Business Administration	E,A
B.A.	Accounting	E,A
B.S.	Computer Information Services	E,A
B.A.	Liberal Studies	E,A
B.A.	Elementary Education	E
B.A.	Economics	E,A
M.S.	Accounting	E
M.B.A.	International Business	E

Requirements

Residency requirement: Yes
Undergraduate admissions requirements: High school graduate and 22 years of age or older
Graduate admissions requirements: Graduate of four-year institution of higher education, G.R.E. or G.M.A.T.
Graduation requirements (undergraduate): 120 credit hours, 30 credit hours in major, minimum of 30 credit hours taken at Belmont Abbey College
Graduation requirements (graduate): 30 credit hours, 12 hours in core courses

Fees, Tuition, Costs

Undergraduate application fee: $20
Graduate application fee: $20
Undergraduate tuition: $219/credit hour
Graduate tuition: $250/credit hour
Undergraduate cost of books: $200
Graduate cost of books: $200

Financial Aid/Status

Scholarship programs for adults: North Carolina grant, partial need scholarships
Full-time status: 12 credit hours/semester
Percentage of adult students receiving financial aid: 35 percent

Bemidji State University

1500 Birchmont Drive N.E. ◆ **Bemidji, MN 56601-2699**
Phone: (218) 755-2068 ◆ Toll-free phone: (800) 475-2001
Fax: (218) 755-4048 ◆ E-mail: egersich@vaxl.bemidji.msus.edu
Web address: http://bsuweb.bemidji.msus.edu/~cel/home.html

Founded: 1919

Accredited by: North Central

Enrollment: 4,800

University status: Public

Degree	Concentration/Major	Format
A.A.	Liberal Studies	C,CT
A.S.	Criminal Justice	C,CT
B.S.	Criminal Justice	C,CT
B.A.	History	C
B.S.	Elementary Education	E,T
B.S.	Business Administration	E
B.S.	Vocational Education	E,T,C
B.S.	Nursing	E,T
B.A.	Industrial Technology	E,T,CT
B.A.	Social Studies	C
B.S.	Applied Psychology—Human Services	E,C
M.S.	Curriculum and Instruction	E,T

Campus Extension Sites

Hibbing, MN
Minneapolis/St. Paul, MN

Requirements

Residency requirement: The nursing major requires 17 quarter credits on-campus attendance. Other majors do not have this requirement.
Undergraduate admissions requirements: Applicants must rank in upper half of high school graduating class, or score 21 or above on the ACT, or successfully complete GED with composite score of 50 or better.
Graduate admissions requirements: Applicants must have a baccalaureate degree from accredited or approved international college or university and a minimum cumulative GPA of 2.75 (A = 4.0). Some programs require a higher GPA.
Graduation requirements (undergraduate): Graduation requires 192 quarter credits with an overall 2.0 GPA and 2.25-2.50 GPA in major program.
Graduation requirements (graduate): The graduate program requires completing one-half of the course work at the "600 level," satisfying a competency area requirement, completing a research project, and passing oral and written exams.

Fees, Tuition, Costs

Undergraduate application fee: $20
Graduate application fee: $20
Undergraduate tuition: $52.50-$63.60
Graduate tuition: $82.40-$94.35
Undergraduate cost of books: $65/course
Graduate cost of books: $65/course
Other costs: Computer and software

Financial Aid/Status

Full-time status: 12 credits/quarter
Percentage of adult students receiving financial aid: 42 percent

Maximum Hours Awarded For

CLEP: 40
DANTES: No limit
Other exams: Yes
Prior learning portfolio: No limit

Features and Services

1. Is it possible to purchase books during hours most adult students attend classes? **Yes.**

2. Are the institution's administrative offices open during hours adult students attend class? **Yes.**

3. How do students taking extended classes access library resources? **Students may visit the campus library or use local libraries. Computer access is available.**

4. What is the registration and payment process for adult students? **Registration may be done by phone. The fee statement is mailed to students.**

5. What is the process for advising adult students? **Advising is done by the faculty and designated support staff.**

6. What career and placement services are available to adult students? **Career and placement services are** provided by the Student Services Center.

7. What characteristics of the institution's adult degree programs are most appealing to students? **Flexibility and access.**

Berean University of the Assemblies of God

1445 Booneville Avenue ◆ **Springfield, MO 65802**
Phone: (417) 862-2781 ◆ Toll-free phone: (800) 443-1083
Fax: (417) 862-5318 ◆ E-mail: jnicholson@affil.ag.org
Web address: http://www.woodtech.com/Berean

Founded: 1948

Accredited by: Distance Education

Enrollment: 7,000 ◆ Adult students: 100 percent

University status: Nonprofit, Church, Assemblies of God Church

Degree	Concentration/Major	Format
B.A.	Bible/Theology	C
B.A.	Pastoral Ministries	C
B.A.	Christian Education	C
B.A.	Christian Counseling	C
M.A.	Christian Counseling	C,V
M.A.	Biblical Studies	C
M.A.	Ministerial Studies	C

Requirements

Residency requirement: Programs are offered in a distance education (independent study) format and can be completed without coming to campus. Christian Counseling (M.A.) requires three separate one-week practicums in Akron, Ohio. Undergraduate admissions requirements: Application checklist and official high school diploma or GED. Graduate admissions requirements: An accredited undergraduate degree with a minimum GPA of 2.5, three reference forms, all official college transcripts, 500-word essay. Graduation requirements (undergraduate): Complete 128 semester credit hours including 30 credits of Bible. Cumulative GPA of C (2.0) must be maintained. Graduation requirements (graduate): Complete 36 to 42 semester credit hours with an overall GPA of 2.5.

Fees, Tuition, Costs

Undergraduate application fee: $25
Graduate application fee: $35
Undergraduate tuition: $69/credit hour

Graduate tuition: $129/credit hour
Undergraduate cost of books: $25-$50/course
Graduate cost of books: $100-$150/course

Financial Aid/Status

Scholarship programs for adults: A new program of small direct scholarships is available. Ministerial and family discounts are offered. Full-time status: 12 credit hours/semester for full-time college level; 6 to 9 credit hours for graduate level. Percentage of adult students receiving financial aid: 5 percent.

Maximum Hours Awarded For

CLEP: 32
DANTES: 32
Other exams: 32
Prior learning portfolio: 32
Additional information: A maximum of 32 advanced-standing credits allowed

Features and Services

1. Are the institution's administrative offices open during hours adult students attend class? **Yes.**

2. How do students taking extended classes access library resources? **Students use libraries in their local areas.**

3. What is the registration and payment process for adult students? **Payment must be made prior to shipping of courses. Payment may be made using cash or credit cards.**

4. What is the process for advising adult students? **Advising is available by phone, fax, and e-mail from qualified representatives on each level.**

5. What characteristics of the institution's adult degree programs are most appealing to students? **They can stay home to obtain their degrees. They can study whenever they want and at their own pace.**

Bethel College

1001 W. McKinley Avenue ◆ **Mishawaka, IN 46545**

Phone: (219) 257-3350 ◆ Toll-free phone: (800) 422-4251

Fax: (219) 257-3357

Founded: 1947

Accredited by: North Central

Enrollment: 1,352 ◆ Adult students: 550

University status: Private, Church, Missionary Church

Degree	Concentration/Major	Format
A.A.	American Sign Language	E
A.A.	Business Management	E
A.A.	Early Childhood Education	E
A.A.	Writing	E
A.A.	Liberal Studies	E
B.A.	Liberal Studies	E
A.A.	Social Science	E
B.A.	Social Science	E
B.A.	American Sign Language/Interpreting	E
B.A.	Bible and Ministry	E
B.A.	Human Services	E
B.A./B.S.	Organizational Management	E,A
B.S.	Accounting	E
B.S.	Business Administration	E
B.S.	Computer Information System Mgt.	E,A
B.S.N.	Nursing Degree Completion	E
M.Min.	Church Ministry	E
M.B.A.	Business Administration	E

Campus Extension Site

Donaldson, IN

Requirements

Residency requirement: Off-campus classes are held at Ancilla College. Students are not required to attend classes at Bethel College.

Undergraduate admissions requirements: High school graduate, satisfactory test scores. Graduate admissions requirements: Bachelor's degree, satisfactory test scores, minimum undergraduate GPA, prerequisite courses, satisfactory oral and written skills. Graduation requirements (undergraduate): Meet general studies and major course requirements, 124 hours minimum, 2.0 GPA, residency, account paid. Graduation requirements (graduate): Meet course requirements, 2.5 GPA, residency, account paid, M.Min.-33 hours, M.B.A.-36 hours.

Fees, Tuition, Costs

Undergraduate application fee: $25
Graduate application fee: $25
Undergraduate tuition: $4,875/semester
Graduate tuition: $300/semester hour
Undergraduate cost of books: $75/course
Graduate cost of books: $90/course
Other costs: Computer for Computer Information System major; uniforms for nursing

Financial Aid/Status

Scholarship programs for adults: Tuition reduction grants ($100/semester) for first 18 hours, part-time students only; federal and state grants and federal loans available

Full-time status: Undergraduate—12 semester hours; graduate—9 semester hours
Percentage of adult students receiving financial aid: 90 percent

Maximum Hours Awarded For

CLEP: open
PEP: open
DANTES: open
Other exams: open
Prior learning portfolio: 30

Features and Services

1. Is it possible to purchase books during hours most adult students attend classes? **Yes.**

2. How do students taking extended classes access library resources? **Use on-site library, computer online to home campus library resources.**

3. What is the registration and payment process for adult students? **Rolling registration; billing at start of semester.**

4. What is the process for advising adult students? **Each student assigned an adult program counselor or faculty advisor, depending on the program.**

5. What career and placement services are available to adult students? **Full availability of services to all current students and alumni.**

6. What characteristics of the institution's adult degree programs are most appealing to students? **Courses adults need are offered at convenient time, affordable cost, accelerated courses, personal attention by caring staff.**

Bethel College*

300 E. 27th St. ◆ N. Newton, KS 62117
Phone: (316) 283-2500 ◆ Toll-free phone: (800) 522-1887
Fax: (316) 284-5286 ◆ Web address: http://www.bethelks.edu

Founded: 1887

Accredited by: North Central

Enrollment: 645

University status: Private, Church, Mennonite

Degree	Concentration/Major	Format
BA	Nursing	V

Requirements

Residency requirement: Yes
Undergraduate admissions requirements: Application, high school and any college transcripts, recommendation(s)

Fees, Tuition, Costs

Undergraduate tuition: $8,540/yr

Financial Aid/Status

Full-time status: 12 credit hours
Percentage of adult students receiving financial aid: 97 percent

Maximum Hours Awarded For

CLEP: 15

Features and Services

1. Is it possible to purchase books during hours most adult students attend classes? **Yes.**

2. Are the institution's administrative offices open during hours adult students attend class? **Yes.**

3. What characteristics of the institution's adult degree programs are most appealing to students? **Small classes.**

Birmingham Southern College

B.S.C. Box 549066 ◆ Birmingham, AL 35254
Phone: (205) 226-4804 ◆ Toll-free phone: (800) 523-5793
Fax: (205) 226-4843 ◆ E-mail: jhand@bsc.edu
Web address: http://www.bsc.edu
Program's Web address: http://www.bsc.edu

Founded: 1856

Accredited by: Southern Association

Enrollment: 1,562 ◆ Adult students: 30 percent

University status: Private, Church, United Methodist Church

Degree	Concentration/Major	Format
B.S.	Business Administration/Finance, Management, Marketing	A,E
B.S.	Accounting	A,E
B.S.	Health Care Management (HCM)	A,E
B.A.	Human Resource Management (HRM)	A,E
B.S.	Education/K-6	A,E
M.Ac.	Accounting (noncertification)	A,E
M.P.P.M.	Private Management	A,E

Requirements

Residency requirement: This is a resident program.
Undergraduate admissions requirements: Freshman must have high school diploma with C average in academic subjects or acceptable GED. Transfer students submit all transcripts from previous schools, C average on accepted courses.
Graduate admissions requirements: Acceptable scores on GRE, GMAT, or MAT; submission of transcripts from all previous schools, two letters of recommendation, and acceptance by Admissions Committee after interview.
Graduation requirements (undergraduate): 36 course units; one unit = 4 semester hours/6 quarter hours; C average in all courses.
Graduation requirements (graduate): B average in all courses (no more than two C's); M.P.P.M.—16 course units; M.Ac.—10 course units.

Fees, Tuition, Costs

Undergraduate application fee: $25
Graduate application fee: $25
Undergraduate tuition: $640/course
Graduate tuition: $1,220/course
Undergraduate cost of books: $75/course
Graduate cost of books: $100/course
Other costs: $6.00 activity fee/course; $5.00 parking sticker/year

Financial Aid/Status

Scholarship programs for adults: Two scholarships are provided by the Alumni Council for two courses per year for two students receiving no other financial aid.
Full-time status: Students taking two courses (units)/term.
Percentage of adult students receiving financial aid: 87 percent.

Maximum Hours Awarded For

CLEP: 16 units
Other exams: 16 units
Prior learning portfolio: 16 units

Features and Services

1. How do students taking extended classes access library resources? **The library is open till midnight from Sunday to Thursday. It is open on Saturday and Sunday.**

2. What is the registration and payment process for adult students? **Mail-in registration is available. Credit cards are accepted.**

3. What is the process for advising adult students? **Interview prior to admission, an academic plan is made, advisor approves courses, mentors, phone.**

4. What career and placement services are available to adult students? **A full-time career counselor is available for after-hours appointments if required.**

5. What characteristics of the institution's adult degree programs are most appealing to students? **Excellent program, small classes, personal attention, all courses offered in evening on predictable two-year cycle; may finish in four years.**

Bluefield College

3000 College Drive ◆ **Bluefield, VA 24605**
Phone: (540) 326-4231 ◆ Toll-free phone: (800) 872-0176
Fax: (540) 326-4288

Founded: 1922

Accredited by: Southern Association

Enrollment: 700+ ◆ Adult students: 160

University status: Nonprofit, Church, Baptist Church

Degree	Concentration/Major	Format
B.S./B.A.	Organizational Management and Development	E,A
B.A.	Christian Ministry	E,A

Campus Extension Sites

Blacksburg, VA
Marion, VA
Clifton Forge, VA
Roanoke, VA
Dublin, VA
Salem, VA
Richlands, VA
Wytheville, VA

Requirements

Residency requirement: Students do not have to attend classes on the main campus.
Undergraduate admissions requirements: Students must be 25 or older and have 54 prior college credits with a GPA of at least 2.0.

Fees, Tuition, Costs

Undergraduate application fee: $15
Undergraduate tuition: $8,400
Undergraduate cost of books: $900
Other costs: $100 confirmation; $200 student activity fee

Financial Aid/Status

Scholarship programs for adults: $200 and $500 Academic Dean's Scholarships are available. These are based on need.
Full-time status: A student taking 12 or more hours/semester is considered a full-time student.
Percentage of adult students receiving financial aid: 80 percent.

Maximum Hours Awarded For

CLEP: 30
DANTES: 30
Prior learning portfolio: 30

Features and Services

1. Is it possible to purchase books during hours most adult students attend classes? **Yes.**

2. How do students taking extended classes access library resources? **Students use interlibrary loan at the Bluefield campus or through cooperative library arrangements.**

3. What is the registration and payment process for adult students? **Register through counselor. Financial aid, tuition reimbursement, 50 percent paid with tuition payment plan.**

4. What is the process for advising adult students? **Students are advised through the admissions counselor.**

5. What characteristics of the institution's adult degree programs are most appealing to students? **An accelerated baccalaureate program.**

Bluffton College*
Office of Continuing Studies
280 W. College Avenue ◆ **Bluffton, OH 45817**
Phone: (419) 358-3311 ◆ Fax: (419) 358-3232

Founded: 1899

Accredited by: North Central

Enrollment: 900

University status: Private, Church,
General Conference Mennonite Church

Features and Services

1. What characteristics of the institution's adult degree programs are most appealing to students? **Accelerated schedule, classes one night/week, mixture of full-time faculty and academically qualified practitioners teaching in the program, responsive to student input, delivery of text books and business office correspondence to classroom.**

Degree	Concentration/Major	Format
B.A.	Organizational Management	E,A
B.A.	Business Administration	E,A
B.A.	Accounting	E,A
B.A.	Early Childhood Education	E,A
B.A.	Social Work	E,A
B.A.	Criminal Justice	E,A

Requirements

Undergraduate admissions requirements: Bachelor's—at least 60-90 hours of transferable college credit; must be 25 years of age or older; must be employed full-time; must demonstrate minimum proficiency in writing skills. 2+2 associate degree; contact registration for further details.

Fees, Tuition, Costs

Undergraduate application fee: $20
Undergraduate tuition: $250/credit hour

Financial Aid/Status

Full-time status: 12 semester hours

Boise State University

BSU-Division of Continuing Education
1910 University Drive ◆ **Boise, ID 83725**
Phone: (208) 385-4457 ◆ Toll-free phone: (800) 824-7017
Fax: (208) 385-3467 ◆ E-mail: jofenne@micron.net
Program's Web address: http://www-cot.idbsu.edu/~/pt/

Founded: 1932

Accredited by: Northwest Association

Enrollment: 16,000

University status: Public

Degree	Concentration/Major	Format
M.S.	Instructional and Performance Technology	CT

Requirements

Residency requirement: The M.S. degree is a totally nonresident program. Students receive instruction using computer conferencing.
Graduate admissions requirements: undergraduate degree, application, access to a computer system, official college transcripts, essay (one to two pages), resume, MAT scores.
Graduation requirements (graduate): B in all courses meeting requirements for M.S., 36 credit hours including required core courses and electives.

Fees, Tuition, Costs

Graduate application fee: $20
Graduate tuition: $315/credit (36 credits)
Graduate cost of books: $100 average/course
Other costs: A personal computer; and IPT software, costing approximately $45

Financial Aid/Status

Full-time status: 8 credit hours
Percentage of adult students receiving financial aid: 8 percent

Maximum Hours Awarded For

DANTES: Yes

Features and Services

1. Is it possible to purchase books during hours most adult students attend classes? **Students can order books online or through toll-free number.**

2. Are the institution's administrative offices open during hours adult students attend class? **Yes.**

3. How do students taking extended classes access library resources? **Students may access the library online.**

4. What is the registration and payment process for adult students? **Registration is conducted online. Payment with credit card, voucher from organization, payment in full.**

5. What is the process for advising adult students? **Assigned advisor at enrollment. Discussions are conducted by phone and online.**

6. What career and placement services are available to adult students? **Students are full-time professionals. Many have used online job announcement service to advance.**

7. What characteristics of the institution's adult degree programs are most appealing to students? **The convenience of earning a degree from home or office and the incredible network of their professional peers.**

Boston College*

Chestnut Hill, MA 02117

Phone: (617) 552-3900 ◆ Fax: (617) 552-3199
Web address: http://www.infoeagle.bs.edu

Founded: 1863

Accredited by: New England

Enrollment: 14,500 ◆ Adult students: 1,500

University status: Private, Church, Roman Catholic Church

Features and Services

1. Is it possible to purchase books during hours most adult students attend classes? **Yes.**

2. Are the institution's administrative offices open during hours adult students attend class? **Yes.**

3. What characteristics of the institution's adult degree programs are most appealing to students? **Atmosphere.**

Degree	Concentration/Major	Format
B.A.	Liberal Arts (all majors)	E

Requirements

Residency requirement: Yes
Undergraduate admissions requirements: Graduation from high school or GED

Fees, Tuition, Costs

Undergraduate application fee: $40
Undergraduate tuition: $407/credit

Financial Aid/Status

Full-time status: 12 credits

Bradley University

1501 W. Bradley Avenue ◆ **Peoria, IL 61625**
Phone: (309) 677-2523 ◆ Fax: (309) 677-3321
E-mail: cepd@bradley.bradley.edu
Web address: http://www.bradley.edu
Program's Web address: http://www.bradley.edu/bucepd/

Founded: 1895

Accredited by: North Central

Enrollment: 5,973 ◆ Adult students: 1,866

University status: Private

Degree	Concentration/Major	Format
M.S.E.E.	Electrical Engineering	V
M.S.M.E.	Mechanical Systems or Energy Science/ThermoScience	V

Requirements

Residency requirement: Students use videos for learning. Attendance on campus is not required. Graduate admissions requirements: Students must reside in Illinois; have an appropriate undergraduate degree; and submit official transcripts of all course work, two letters of recommendation, application, and sometimes a GRE score.

Fees, Tuition, Costs

Graduate tuition: $310/semester hour

Financial Aid/Status

Scholarship programs for adults: Scholarships are not available for off-campus programs.
Full-time status: A full-time student is enrolled in 12 or more semester hours.

Maximum Hours Awarded For

CLEP: 60
Other exams: Yes

Features and Services

1. How do students taking extended classes access library resources? **Services are available through the division of Continuing Education and Professional Development.**

2. What is the registration and payment process for adult students? **Registration and tuition are handled by Continuing Education. Deferred payment is available.**

3. What is the process for advising adult students? **Faculty advisors will meet in person or use the phone or e-mail.**

4. What career and placement services are available to adult students? **Adults may use the Smith Career Center.**

5. What characteristics of the institution's adult degree programs are most appealing to students? **The videotape format is well suited for master's degree programs in engineering.**

Briar Cliff College*

3303 Rebecca Street ◆ Sioux City, IA 51104
Phone: (712) 279-1629 ◆ Toll-free phone: (800) 662-3303
Fax: (712) 279-1698
Web address: http://www.briar-cliff.edu

Founded: 1930

Accredited by: North Central

Enrollment: 1,158 ◆ Adult students: 380

University status: Private, Church, Roman Catholic Church

Degree	Concentration/Major	Format
B.A.	Business Administration	E
B.A.	Human Resource Management	E
B.A.	Accounting	E
B.S.N.	Nursing	E

Requirements

Residency requirement: Yes
Undergraduate admissions
requirements: High school diploma
or GED

Fees, Tuition, Costs

Undergraduate application fee: $20
Undergraduate tuition: $222/credit

Financial Aid/Status

Full-time status: 8 semester credits/
term
Percentage of adult students
receiving financial aid: 95 percent

Maximum Hours Awarded For

CLEP: 12
PEP: 15
DANTES: 15
Other exams: 15
Prior learning portfolio: 15

Features and Services

1. Is it possible to purchase books during hours most adult students attend classes? **Yes.**

2. What characteristics of the institution's adult degree programs are most appealing to students? **Flexibility, location, and costs.**

Bryant College

1150 Douglas Pike ◆ Smithfield, RI 02917
Phone: (401) 232-6100 ◆ Toll-free phone: (800) 622-7001
Fax: (401) 232-6741 ◆ E-mail: admissions@bryant.edu
Web address http://www.bryant.educ/

Founded: 1863

Accredited by: New England

Enrollment: 3,610 ◆ Adult students: 1,276

University status: Private, Nonsectarian

Degree	Concentration/Major	Format
A.S.	General Business Administration	E
B.S.B.A.	Accounting	E
B.S.B.A.	Applied Actuarial Math	E
B.S.B.A.	Computer Information Systems	E
B.S.B.A.	Finance	E
B.S.B.A.	Management	E
B.S.B.A.	Marketing	E
B.A.	Communications	E
B.A.	Economics	E
B.A.	English	E
B.A.	History	E
M.S.A.	Accounting	E
M.B.A.	Several concentrations	E
M.S.T.	Taxation	E

Requirements

Residency requirement: Students must attend classes on campus.
Undergraduate admissions requirements: Students must file application, submit an official high school transcript or official copy of GED, official college transcript, if any.
Graduate admissions requirements: Students must file a signed application form and essay, two letters of recommendation, official transcripts of all colleges attended, GMAT scores, TOEFL courses (international students).
Graduation requirements (undergraduate): B.S.B.A. and B.A.—121 credits consisting of liberal arts core, liberal arts distribution, business core, major/minor electives; 61 credits being lower division requirements.
Graduation requirements (graduate): 3.0 final GPA; complete 33 to 61 credits determined by undergraduate degree and/or prior course work; complete requirements within six years.

Fees, Tuition, Costs

Undergraduate application fee: $35
Graduate application fee: $50
Undergraduate tuition: $13,900 full-time; $450/3 credit
Graduate tuition: $820/course; M.B.A., M.S.A.—$1,190/course

M.S.T.
Undergraduate cost of books: $50-$60/course
Graduate cost of books: $50-$60/course

Financial Aid/Status

Scholarship programs for adults: Students enrolled full-time may file annual FAFSA to qualify. No part-time scholarships are available.
Full-time status: Full-time students must take 12 credits or 4 classes each semester.
Percentage of adult students receiving financial aid: 1 percent.

Maximum Hours Awarded For

CLEP: Yes
DANTES: Yes
Other exams: Yes
Prior learning portfolio: Yes
Additional information: Maximum of 30 credits from tests and credit for prior learning

Features and Services

1. How do students taking extended classes access library resources? **Same as traditional students. Library catalog may be accessed through the Internet; limited WWW page.**

2. What is the registration and payment process for adult students? **Early registration and preregistration in person. Mail in and fax: no payment; Late registration: payment.**

3, What is the process for advising adult students? **Academic advisors have day and evening hours for registering, plus Saturday hours for admissions.**

4. What career and placement services are available to adult

students? **Counseling, career development course, workshops, special programs, internships, "shadowing" program.**

5. What characteristics of the institution's adult degree programs are most appealing to students? **Degrees enhance student's career;** day, evening, and weekend classes; taught by accredited faculty; balance of professional and liberal arts.

Burlington College*

95 North Avenue ◆ **Burlington, VT 05401**
Phone: (802) 862-9616 ◆ Toll-free phone: (800) 862-9616
Fax: (802) 658-007

Founded: 1972

Accredited by: New England

Enrollment: 200 ◆ Adult students: 25

University status: Private, Nonprofit

Features and Services

1. Is it possible to purchase books during hours most adult students attend classes? **Yes.**

2. Are the institution's administrative offices open during hours adult students attend class? **Yes.**

3. What characteristics of the institution's adult degree programs are most appealing to students? **Flexible, challenging, individualized, low residency, frequent contact, independent study.**

Degree	Concentration/Major	Format
B.A.	Psychology	S
B.A.	Transpersonal Psychology	S
B.A.	Humanities	S
B.A.	Writing and Literature	S
B.A.	Human Services	S
B.A.	Individualized Major	S

Requirements

Residency requirement: Courses are delivered through a four-day residential retreat, followed by a semester of self-study. Undergraduate admissions requirements: 45 college credits.

Financial Aid/Status

Full-time status: 12 credits/ semester
Percentage of adult students receiving financial aid: 88 percent

Fees, Tuition, Costs

Undergraduate application fee: $50
Undergraduate tuition: $3,150 for full-time students

Cabrini College

610 King of Prussia Road ◆ **Radnor, PA 19087-3698**
Phone: (610) 902-8500 ◆ Fax: (610) 902-8522

Founded: 1957

Accredited by: Middle States

Enrollment: 1,475

Degree	Concentration/Major	Format
B.A.	Organizational Management	A,E
B.A.	Professional Communication	A,E

Requirements

Residency requirement: Students do not have to attend classes on campus.
Undergraduate admissions requirements: Complete application, official transcripts from high school and other colleges.
Graduate admissions requirements: Completion of all undergraduate studies with an overall average of B.
Graduation requirements (undergraduate): Completion of 123 credit hours with GPA 2.0; 45 hours must be completed at Cabrini; core curriculum and major requirements met; financial obligations fulfilled.

Fees, Tuition, Costs

Undergraduate application fee: $25
Undergraduate tuition: $218/credit hour
Undergraduate cost of books: $400

Financial Aid/Status

Scholarship programs for adults: No scholarships are available.

Maximum Hours Awarded For

CLEP: Yes
PEP: Yes
DANTES: Yes
Other exams: Yes
Prior learning portfolio: Yes

Features and Services

1. Is it possible to purchase books during hours most adult students attend classes? **Yes.**

2. What is the registration and payment process for adult students? **Registration is handled through the Continuing Education department. Payment is made at registration.**

3. What is the process for advising adult students? **Students make an appointment with an advisor prior to first registration.**

4. What characteristics of the institution's adult degree programs are most appealing to students? **Accelerated program; evening classes; adult environment conducive to interaction with other adult students.**

Caldwell College

9 Ryerson Avenue ◆ Caldwell, NJ 07045
Phone: (201) 288-4424 ◆ Fax: (201) 403-8042
E-mail: caldwellce@aol.com

Founded: 1939

Accredited by: Middle States

Enrollment: 1,800 ◆ Adult students: 850

University status: Private, Church, Roman Catholic Church

Degree	Concentration/Major	Format
B.S.	Business Administration	E,C
B.A.	Communications	E,C
B.A.	English	E,C
B.A.	Education	E,C
B.A.	History	E,C
B.A.	Mathematics	E,C
B.A.	Psychology	E,C
B.A.	Religious Studies	E,C
B.A.	Social Studies	E,C
B.A.	Sociology	E,C
B.A.	Criminal Justice	E,C
B.S.	Computer Science	E,C

Requirements

Residency requirement: Students are not required to attend classes on campus. This is a guided independent study program. Undergraduate admissions requirements: Students in the on-campus program must have a high school diploma or GED. Students in the external degree program must have 12 transferable credit hours.
Graduation requirements (undergraduate): 122 credit hours and pass a comprehensive examination.

Fees, Tuition, Costs

Undergraduate application fee: $25
Undergaduate tuition: $240/credit

Financial Aid/Status

Scholarship programs for adults: Scholarships are not available.
Full-time status: A full-time student takes 12 or more credit hours.

Maximum Hours Awarded For

CLEP: Yes
PEP: Yes
DANTES: Yes
Prior learning portfolio: 18

Features and Services

1. Is it possible to purchase books during hours most adult students attend classes? **Yes.**

2. Are the institution's administrative offices open during hours adult students attend class? **Yes.**

3. What is the registration and payment process for adult students? **By mail or fax or in person.**

4. What is the process for advising adult students? **Professional advisors are assigned to each student.**

5. What career and placement services are available to adult students? **Students may use the Career Planning office.**

6. What characteristics of the institution's adult degree programs are most appealing to students? **Location, personal attention, safe campus, moderate tuition.**

California Baptist College

8432 Magnolia Avenue ◆ **Riverside, CA 92504**
Phone: (909) 689-5771 ◆ Toll-free phone: (800) 782-3382
Fax: (909) 351-1808 ◆ E-mail: admissions@cbc.edu

Founded: 1950

Accredited by: Western Association

Enrollment: 1,200 ◆ Adult students: 40

University status: Private, Church, Southern Baptist

Degree	Concentration/Major	Format
B.S.	Business Administration	E,A
B.S.	Information Systems/ Systems Engineering	E,A
B.S.	Political Science/ Public Administration	E,A
B.S.	Psychology	E,A
B.A.	Liberal Studies	E,A
B.A.	Philosophy (Great Works "reading" program)	E,A
B.A.	Christian Ministry/Fine Arts	E,A
B.S.	Physical Education/Science	E,A
B.S.	Communication Arts/ Computer Illustration	E,A
M.S.	Counseling Psychology/MFCC	E,A
M.S./M.A.	Education	E,A
M.B.A.	Business Administration	E,A

Campus Extension Sites

Fort Irwin, CA
Riverside, CA
San Bernardino, CA
Barstow, CA
Hesperia, CA

Requirements

Residency requirement: Students do not have to attend classes on the main campus.
Undergraduate admissions requirements: Students in the evening college must have 24 semester hours of postsecondary credit or its equivalent and have a minimum cumulative GPA of 2.0 in all postsecondary courses.
Graduate admissions requirements: General requirements: Accredited undergraduate degree with 2.75 GPA; some prerequisite courses; other requirements depend on the degree sought.
Graduation requirements (undergraduate): Students must complete 124 semester hours with the proper number of core, elective, and general education courses.
Graduation requirements (graduate): Graduate requirements vary depending on the major. Students must complete the prescribed number of courses and credit hours.

Fees, Tuition, Costs

Undergraduate application fee: $30
Graduate application fee: $40
Undergraduate tuition: $300/ semester credit hour
Graduate tuition: $249/semester credit hour
Undergraduate cost of books: $260
Graduate cost of books: $600

Financial Aid/Status

Scholarship programs for adults: Armed Forces Support Scholarship, $4,000 for active duty military or DOD civilian; government employee, $2,000; recruitment scholarship, $2,000 for bringing two or more individuals into the program.
Full-time status: Full-time students are enrolled in 12 semester hours (undergraduate) and 9 semester hours (graduate).
Percentage of adult students receiving financial aid: 99 percent.

Maximum Hours Awarded For

CLEP: 30
PEP: 30
DANTES: 30
Other exams: 30
Prior learning portfolio: 30
Additional information: Any combination of these credits not exceeding 45 units

Features and Services

1. Is it possible to purchase books during hours most adult students attend classes? **Yes.**

2. Are the institution's administrative offices open during hours adult students attend class? **Yes.**

3. How do students taking extended classes access library resources? **Students use local libraries. Online** searches available through "faxing" requests to main campus.

4. What is the registration and payment process for adult students? **Registration and all other paperwork are processed by the Program Advisor located on-site.**

5. What is the process for advising adult students? **Students are assigned personal program advisors,** who guide them through the program.

6. What career and placement services are available to adult students? **Full placement and counseling services are available on campus.**

7. What characteristics of the institution's adult degree programs are most appealing to students? **The 16-month delivery time, evening courses, and some weekend classes.**

California Institute of Integral Studies

765 Ashbury Street ◆ San Francisco, CA 94117
Phone: (415) 753-6100

Founded: 1973

Accredited by: Western Association

Enrollment: 1,100

University status: Nonprofit

already completed toward a bachelor's degree.
Graduate admissions requirements: General requirements include the completion of a bachelor's degree with a cumulative GPA of 3.0.

Fees, Tuition, Costs

Undergraduate application fee: $60
Graduate application fee: $60

Degree	Concentration/Major	Format
B.A.	Bachelor's Completion Program	E
Ph.D.	Learning and Change in Human Systems	C,T
Ph.D.	Traditional Knowledge	C,T

Requirements

Residency requirement: The Bachelor's Completion Program meets on weekends on the campus. Ph.D. students meet for two brief periods of intensive study on campus.
Undergraduate admissions requirements: Applicants must have 74 units of academic work

California Polytechnic State University

Jespersen Hall, Cal Poly ◆ San Luis Obispo, CA 93407
Phone: (805) 756-2053 ◆ Fax: (805) 756-5933
E-mail: cebarnes@calpoly.edu
Web address: http://www.calpoly.edu
Program's Web address: http://www.calpoly.edu/eups

Founded: 1901

Accredited by: Western Association

Enrollment: 15,000

University status: Public

Degree	Concentration/Major	Format
M.B.A.	Business Administration	E
M.A.	Education	E

Requirements

Residency requirement: Students must attend classes on campus. Undergraduate admissions requirements: 25 years or older; high school diploma, GED, or California High School Proficiency Exam; C average in any college courses in last five years; assessment of English and math skills. Graduate admissions requirements: Bachelor's degree with average GPA 2.5, meet standards and exams for desired degree program, application, official transcripts from all schools attended. Graduation requirements (undergraduate): Complete required credit units for major; 2.0 GPA; complete U.S.C.P., General Education and Breadth, Graduation Writing, Senior Project, and academic residence requirements; evaluation for graduation.

Graduation requirements (graduate): Final evaluation; GPA 3.0; demonstrate competency in writing skills.

Fees, Tuition, Costs

Undergraduate application fee: $55
Graduate application fee: $55
Undergraduate tuition: 0-6 units/$497, 6+/$747
Graduate tuition: 0-6 units/$513, 6+/$777
Undergraduate cost of books: Varies
Graduate cost of books: Varies
Other costs: Facility fee, laboratory fee, parking fee

Financial Aid/Status

Scholarship programs for adults: Scholarships are given to students regardless of age.
Full-time status: Full-time undergraduate students take 12 units/quarter. Graduate students take 8 units/quarter.

Features and Services

1. How do students taking extended classes access library resources? **Students are issued library cards through Extended Education.**

2. What is the registration and payment process for adult students? **Students register and pay for classes through Extended Education.**

3. What is the process for advising adult students? **Students advised by College in which they are enrolled. University services are available to adults.**

4. What career and placement services are available to adult students? **Students enrolled in regular academic courses may use these services.**

5. What characteristics of the institution's adult degree programs are most appealing to students? **Modular programming, weekend schedule, late afternoon classes for teachers.**

California School of Professional Psychology

2749 Hyde Street ◆ San Francisco, CA 94109
Phone: (415) 346-4500 ◆ Toll-free phone: (800) 457-1273
Fax: (415) 931-8322 ◆ E-mail: mullenp@class.org
Program's Web address: http://www.webcom.com/cspp

Founded: 1969

Accredited by: Western Association

Enrollment: 2,350

University status: Private

Degree	Concentration/Major	Format
M.O.B., M.S.	Organizational Behavior	E
Ph.D.	Organizational Psychology Alameda Campus	E
Psy.D.	Organizational Consultation Alameda Campus	E

Campus Extension Sites

Fresno, CA
Alameda, CA
Los Angeles, CA
San Diego, CA

Requirements

Residency requirement: Students must attend some classes on campus.
Graduate admissions requirements: Accredited bachelor's degree with 3.0 GPA; complete prerequisite courses; application including essay, recommendations, interview.
Graduation requirements (graduate): Master's of Organizational Behavior degree—4 required MOB courses, 15 electives, 21 required course units.

Fees, Tuition, Costs

Graduate application fee: $65
Graduate tuition: $15,700/year
Graduate cost of books: $1,300/year
Other costs: Computers for students

Financial Aid/Status

Scholarship programs for adults: Scholarships and loans are available for full-time and moderated degree-seeking students.

Features and Services

1. What characteristics of the institution's adult degree programs are most appealing to students? **Evening classes for M.O.B.**

California State University, Bakersfield

9001 Stockdale Highway ◆ Bakersfield, CA 93311-1099
Phone: (805) 664-3396 ◆ Toll-free phone: (800) 788-2782
Fax: (805) 664-2447
E-mail: torr@csubak.edu
Web address: http://www.csubak.edu/
Program's Web address: http://www.csubak.edu/extuniversity/home_page.html

Founded: 1970

Accredited by: Western Association

Enrollment: 1,500 ◆ Adult students: 90 percent

University status: Public

Degree	Concentration/Major	Format
B.A.	Liberal Studies Multiple Subject Waiver	E
B.A.	Economics—Applied Economics	E
B.S.	Business Administration—General	E
M.B.A.	Business Administration	E
M.S.A.	Science Administration	E
M.A.	Education—Curriculum and Instruction	E
M.A.	Education—Education Administration	E
M.A.	Education—Special Education (Learning Handicapped)	E

Campus Extension Sites

Lancaster, CA
Edwards AFB, CA
China Lake NAWC
Ridgecrest, CA
Tulare, CA

Requirements

Residency requirement: Students may attend classes on campus, but it is not a requirement.
Undergraduate admissions requirements: Students are required to complete lower-division course work through the community college in their area and submit an application and transcripts.
Graduate admissions requirements: Students must have a bachelor's degree with 2.5 GPA in last 90 quarter units, and be admitted by the institution and a master's program.
Graduation requirements (undergraduate): Students must complete 186 quarter units including general education requirements; GPA above 2.0.
Graduation requirements (graduate): Students must complete 45 quarter units with GPA above 3.0.

Fees, Tuition, Costs

Undergraduate application fee: $55
Graduate application fee: $55
Undergraduate tuition: $85-$135/quarter unit
Graduate tuition: $90-$135/quarter unit
Undergraduate cost of books: $60/course
Graduate cost of books: $80/course
Other costs: Access to a computer in conducting research through distance learning technology with the main library

Financial Aid/Status

Scholarship programs for adults: Because these are resident programs, students are eligible to apply for scholarships from the main campus.
Full-time status: Undergraduates—12 quarter hours/term (3 courses); graduate—9 quarter hours/term (3 courses).
Percentage of adult students receiving financial aid: 10 percent.

Maximum Hours Awarded For

CLEP: Yes
PEP: Yes
DANTES: 36
Other exams: 20
Prior learning portfolio: 20
Additional information: Possible earning of up to 45 quarter units for passing externally developed tests.

Features and Services

1. Is it possible to purchase books during hours most adult students attend classes? **Yes.**

2. Are the institution's administrative offices open during hours adult students attend class? **Partially.**

3. How do students taking extended classes access library resources? **Students may use computer link to main campus library.**

4. What is the registration and payment process for adult students? **Students submit registration with (1) payment in full, (2) deferred payment option, or (3) financial aid.**

5. What is the process for advising adult students? **Students meet with an advisor once each quarter at the distance site.**

6. What career and placement services are available to adult students? **Placement service is not available at remote sites. Internships are offered for undergraduates.**

7. What characteristics of the institution's adult degree programs are most appealing to students? **Convenience and quality of instruction.**

California State University, Chico*

Center for Regional and Continuing Education
Chico, CA 95929
Phone: (916) 898-6105 ◆ Fax: (916) 898-6105
Web address: http://www.csuchico.edu

Founded: 1887

Accredited by: Western Association

Enrollment: 12,000

University status: Public

Features and Services

1. What characteristics of the institution's adult degree programs are most appealing to students? **Students attending off-campus learning centers can order books by phone, using a major credit card.**

Degree	Concentration/Major	Format
B.S.	Social Science	V
B.S.	Sociology	V
B.S.	Liberal Studies	V

Requirements

Undergraduate admissions requirements: For admissions information, write to CSU—Chico, Chico, CA 95929-00720.

Financial Aid/Status

Full-time status: 12 semester units or more

Fees, Tuition, Costs

Undergraduate application fee: $55
Undergraduate tuition: $670/6 units

California State University, Dominguez Hills

SAC II 12126
1000 E. Victoria Street ◆ **Carson, CA 90747**
Phone: (310) 516-3743 ◆ Fax: (310) 516-4399
E-mail: huxonline@dhvx20.csudh.edu
Web address: http://orca.csudh.edu
Program's Web address: http://orca.csudh.edu/~hux/index.html

Founded: 1961

Accredited by: Western Association

Enrollment: 2,000

University status: Public

Features and Services

1. How do students taking extended classes access library resources? **Students are given a HUX library card.**

2. What is the registration and payment process for adult students? **Payment and registration mailed. Payment by check, money order, or credit card. Cash is not accepted.**

3. What characteristics of the institution's adult degree programs are most appealing to students? **Totally correspondence.**

Degree	Concentration/Major	Format
M.A.	Humanities (Art, History, Literature, Music, Philosophy, Theater)	C/CT

Requirements

Residency requirement: Courses are conducted through correspondence and online. Attending class on campus is not required.
Graduate admissions requirements: Bachelor's degree from an accredited institution, GPA 3.0 in last 60 semester/90 quarter units, application, two official transcripts from previous schools, and intellectual autobiography.
Graduation requirements (graduate): Student must file a Graduation Application with $35 fee, successful completion of the Advancement for Candidacy Exam, GPA of 3.0.

Fees, Tuition, Costs

Graduate application fee: $55
Graduate tuition: $120/semester unit
Graduate cost of books: $50/ quarter

Financial Aid/Status

Scholarship programs for adults: No scholarships are available.
Full-time status: Students taking eight units/quarter are full-time.
Additional information: Students may transfer nine semester units from an accredited institution if taken in last five years.

California State University, Sacramento

6000 J Street ◆ **Sacramento, CA 95819**
Phone: (916) 278-6780 ◆ Fax: (916) 278-7842
Web address: http://www.csus.edu

Founded: 1947

Accredited by: Western Association

Enrollment: 23,000

University status: Public

Degree	Concentration/Major	Format
M.S.	Accountancy	E
M.A.	Anthropology	E
M.B.A.	Business Administration	E
M.S.	Counseling	E
M.S.	Counseling—Career Counseling Option	E
M.A.	Education—Early Childhood	E
M.A.	Education—Special Education	E
M.A.	French	E
M.A.	Liberal Arts	E

Most of the university's degrees offer enough evening sections to obtain a degree.

Requirements

Residency requirement: Relatively few of our courses are offered off campus or through nonclassroom settings (e.g., video).
Undergraduate admissions requirements: At junior level (56 semester hours) the emphasis is on a 2.0 GPA and four basic general courses in speech, composition, logic, and math. At freshman level, emphasis on test scores and college prep courses.
Graduate admissions requirements: The criteria vary with each school and department. Requirements may include bachelor's in same field or equivalent, GPA 2.5-3.0, recommendations, testing.

Graduation requirements (undergraduate): 124-140 total units, of which 51 are in General Education including a writing exam, 2.0 GPA.

Fees, Tuition, Costs

Undergraduate application fee: $55
Graduate application fee: $55
Undergraduate tuition: $700/0-6 units; $1,000/7 or more units
Graduate tuition: $700/0-6 units; $1,000/7 or more units
Undergraduate cost of books: $200-$300
Graduate cost of books: $200-$300
Other costs: Art supplies, lab fees, parking fees

Financial Aid/Status

Scholarship programs for adults: List of scholarships available at Re-entry Office.
Full-time status: Full-time students take 12 semester hours.

Maximum Hours Awarded For

DANTES: Yes
Other exams: Yes
Prior learning portfolio: 6
Additional information: Advanced Placement Exams

Features and Services

1. Is it possible to purchase books during hours most adult students attend classes? **Yes.**

2. Are the institution's administrative offices open during hours adult students attend class? **No.**

3. What is the registration and payment process for adult students? **Registration is done through a computer over the phone. Payment may be mailed or in person.**

4. What is the process for advising adult students? **Re-entry office sees people over 25. Advising includes academic, career, and financial.**

5. What career and placement services are available to adult students? **Available to current students and include counseling, workshops, computer-based programs, others.**

6. What characteristics of the institution's adult degree programs are most appealing to students? **Evening hours, friendly, small office environment, comprehensive services.**

Calumet College of St. Joseph

2400 New York Avenue ◆ **Whiting, IN 46394**
Phone: (219) 473-4228
Toll-free for Chicago Area: (312) 721-0202
Fax: (219) 473-4259

Founded: 1951

Accredited by: North Central

Enrollment: 1,200

Adult students: 67

University status: Private, Church, Roman Catholic Church

Degree	Concentration/Major	Format
B.S.	Management	A
B.S.	Accounting	E
B.S.	Addictionology	E
B.S.	Biology	E
B.A.	Communication Arts	E
B.S.	Communication Information Systems	E
B.S.	Criminal Justice	E
B.S. in Ed	Elementary Education	E
B.A.	English	E
B.A.	Fine Arts	E
B.S.	General Studies	E

BA/BS 33 majors plus associate. 2/3 courses offered evening/weekend.

Campus Extension Sites

Munster, IN
Merrillville, IN
Chesterton, IN

Requirements

Residency requirement: Students may take last two years of bachelor's at extended campus. On-campus attendance for video-assisted courses. Undergraduate admissions requirements: Official transcript of high school diploma or GED, admission application, transcript of any postsecondary education, successful completion of Admissions Assessment. Graduation requirements (under-graduate): Students must have 124 credit hours and meet all degree requirements.

Fees, Tuition, Costs

Undergraduate application fee: $25
Undergraduate tuition: $170/hour
Undergraduate cost of books: $280/semester
Other costs: Organizational Management (degree completion)—$2,600/semester tuition, lab fees, activity fees, graduation fee of $50

Financial Aid/Status

Scholarship programs for adults: LESS award given to students 55 or over; 50 percent tuition remission. Other scholarships are available.
Full-time status: Full-time students take 12 credit hours.
Percentage of adult students receiving financial aid: 80 percent.

Maximum Hours Awarded For

CLEP: Yes
DANTES: Yes
Other exams: Yes
Prior learning portfolio: Yes

Features and Services

1. Is it possible to purchase books during hours most adult students attend classes? **Yes.**

2. Are the institution's administrative offices open during hours adult students attend class? **Yes.**

3. How do students taking extended classes access library resources? **The library is open weekends and evenings.**

4. What is the registration and payment process for adult students? **All registrations (early, regular, late) have evening hours. Payment plans are available.**

5. What is the process for advising adult students? **Academic advising during evening hours is available.**

6. What career and placement services are available to adult students? **The career placement center offers evening hours by appointment and has job fairs.**

7. What characteristics of the institution's adult degree programs are most appealing to students? **Accelerated program, convenient locations.**

Calvin College

1801 E. Beltline, S.E. ◆ **Grand Rapids, MI 49546**
Phone: (616) 957-6555 ◆ Fax: (616) 957-8551
E-mail: roel@calvin.edu
Web address: http://www.calvin.edu

Founded: 1876

Accredited by: North Central

Enrollment: 3,900 ◆ Adult students: 2 percent

University status: Private, Church, Christian Reformed Church

Degree	Concentration/Major	Format
B.A.	Organizational Leadership	E,A

Requirements

Residency requirement: Students attend classes on the main campus. Undergraduate admissions requirements: 24 or older, two years of work experience, 53 semester hours of transferable (C- or better) credits, GPA 2.0 (four-year school) or 2.5 (two-year school), application form and letter, able to do research project. Graduation requirements (undergraduate): 120 semester hours with 39 semester hours in the major and a liberal arts core of about 35 semester hours.

Fees, Tuition, Costs

Undergraduate tuition: $9,420/39-hour major
Undergraduate cost of books: $600 (included in tuition)

Financial Aid/Status

Scholarship programs for adults: An Alumni Scholarship of $500 is available. Need-based assistance of under $500/student is offered. Full-time status: Students taking three courses/semester are full-time.
Percentage of adult students receiving financial aid: 25 percent.

Maximum Hours Awarded For

CLEP: 16
PEP: 16
DANTES: 16
Other exams: 16
Prior learning portfolio: 16

Features and Services

1. Is it possible to purchase books during hours most adult students attend classes? **Yes.**

2. Are the institution's administrative offices open during hours adult students attend class? **Yes.**

3. How do students taking extended classes access library resources? **The library is available every evening. The card catalog can be accessed by modem.**

4. What is the registration and payment process for adult students? **Registration and payment are done by mail through the CAP and Financial Services offices.**

5. What is the process for advising adult students? **Advising is handled by the CAP office staff personally one-to-one.**

6. What career and placement services are available to adult students? **All placement services are available.**

7. What characteristics of the institution's adult degree programs are most appealing to students? **High availability of courses and professors, Christian perspective, supportive CAP staff.**

Cambridge College

1000 Massachusetts Avenue ◆ **Cambridge, MA 02138**
Phone: (617) 868-1000 ◆ Toll-free phone: (800) 877-4723
Fax: (617) 349-3545

Founded: 1971

Accredited by: Northeastern Association

Enrollment: 1,501 ◆ Adult students: 100 percent

University status: Private

Full-time status: Undergraduate full-time students must take 12 semester credits; graduate students take 8 credits.
Percentage of adult students receiving financial aid: 80 percent.

Maximum Hours Awarded For

CLEP: Yes
PEP: Yes
DANTES: Yes
Other exams: Yes
Prior learning portfolio: Yes

Degree	Concentration/Major	Format
B.A.	Psychology	E
B.A.	Educational Psychology	E
B.A.	Family and Community Systems	E
B.A.	Organizational Psychology	E
B.A.	Elementary Certification	E/Day
M.E.D.	Education	E
M.E.D.	Counseling	E
M.M.D.	Management	E

Features and Services

1. Is it possible to purchase books during hours most adult students attend classes? **Yes.**

2. Are the institution's administrative offices open during hours adult students attend class? **Yes.**

3. How do students taking extended classes access library resources? **Use Harvard University and other university libraries through ProQuest in the learning center.**

4. What is the registration and payment process for adult students? **Students may pay in full at registration, use payment plan, or receive financial aid.**

5. What is the process for advising adult students? **Biweekly meetings of an assigned learning seminar (undergraduate) or professional seminar (graduate).**

Campus Extension Site

Springfield, MA

Requirements

Residency requirement: Students must attend classes on campus.
Undergraduate admissions requirements: Application, resume, high school/GED, personal statement, writing sample, letter of recommendation, college records, five years of work experience after high school graduation.
Graduate admissions requirements: Application, B.A./B.S. records, resume, writing sample, personal statement, letter of recommendation, five years of work experience.
Graduation requirements (undergraduate): Students must have 120 credit hours including required courses.
Graduation requirements (graduate): The number of credits required varies with the major. Required courses for each major must be taken.

Fees, Tuition, Costs

Undergraduate application fee: $30
Graduate application fee: $30
Undergraduate tuition: $250/credit
Graduate tuition: $315/credit
Undergraduate cost of books: $500
Graduate cost of books: $800
Other costs: Library fees, graduation fee, testing fees

Financial Aid/Status

Scholarship programs for adults: Students are required to file all federal financial aid forms.

6. What career and placement services are available to adult students? **We do not have a** **placement office. Ninety percent of students are full-time employees.**

7. What characteristics of the institution's adult degree programs are most appealing to students? **Our education programs.**

Campbell University

P.O. Box 1135 ◆ Buies Creek, NC 27506
Phone: (910) 893-1275 ◆ Toll-free phone: (800) 334-4111
Fax: (910) 893-1274 ◆ Web address: http://www.campbell.edu

Founded: 1887

Accredited by: Southern Association

Enrollment: 6,800 ◆ Adult students: 33 percent

University status: Private, Church, N.C. Baptist

Degree	Concentration/Major	Format
A.A.	General Education/History/Government/Business/Economics/CIS	E,A
B.A.S.	Applied Science	E,A,S
B.B.A.	General/Accounting/CIS	E,A
B.H.S.	Health Careers	E,A,S
B.S.	Economics/Government/History/Psychology	E,A
M.A./M.Ed.	Counseling—School and Community	E
M.B.A.	General	E,A

Campus Extension Sites

Undergraduate classes at:
Camp Lejeune Campus, Jacksonville, NC
Ft. Bragg Campus, Fayetteville, NC
Pope AFB Campus, Fayetteville, NC
The Raleigh Center, Raleigh, NC
Graduate classes at:
Fayetteville,NC
Goldsboro, NC
Rocky Mt., NC
Jacksonville, NC
Raleigh, NC

Requirements

Residency requirement: Students in the graduate counseling programs are required to attend on-campus classes.
Undergraduate admissions requirements: High school diploma or equivalent.
Graduate admissions requirements: Bachelor's degree with required courses, minimum GPA, admissions test.
Graduation requirements (undergraduate): 128 semester hours of credit with 2.0 GPA and completion of course requirements.
Graduation requirements (graduate): 30-48 semester hours of credit, 3.0 GPA, within prescribed time period.

Fees, Tuition, Costs

Undergraduate application fee: None
Graduate application fee: $15-$25
Undergraduate tuition: $92-$100/semester hour
Graduate tuition: $155-$165/semester hour

Financial Aid/Status

Full-time status: Full-time students must take 12 semester credit hours.

Maximum Hours Awarded For

CLEP: Yes
PEP: Yes
DANTES: Yes
Prior learning portfolio: Military
Additional information: Maximum 64 semester hours from nontraditional programs

Features and Services

1. Is it possible to purchase books during hours most adult students attend classes? **Yes.**

2. How do students taking extended classes access library resources? **Students have access to libraries near off-campus sites and the campus library.**

3. What is the registration and payment process for adult students? **On-site payment during registration; payment acceptable by cash, check, credit card, or time payment.**

4. What is the process for advising adult students? **Full-service academic advising is available on-site.**

5. What career and placement services are available to adult students? **Placement service is available on the main campus.**

6. What characteristics of the institution's adult degree programs are most appealing to students? **Quality programs, cost, convenience, accelerated terms, adult fellow students.**

Campbellsville College*

200 West College Street ◆ **Campbellsville, KY 42718**
Phone: (502) 465-8158 ◆ Fax: (502) 789-5020
Web address: http://www.campbellsvil.edu

Founded: 1906

Accredited by: Southern Association

Enrollment: 1,260 ◆ Adult students: 100

University status: Private, Church, Southern Baptist

Features and Services

1. Is it possible to purchase books during hours most adult students attend classes? **Yes.**

2. What characteristics of the institution's adult degree programs are most appealing to students? **At least 25 percent of the classes must be taken on the campus.**

Degree	Concentration/Major	Format
A.S.	Business Administration	E
B.S.	Organizational Administration	E,A
M.A.	Education Curriculum and Instruction	E
B.S.	Christian Ministries	
	During the day in Louisville, KY	

Requirements

Residency requirement: Yes
Undergraduate admissions requirements: High school diploma, ACT
Graduate admissions requirements: Possess BA/BS, 2.75 GPA, prefer a teaching certificate

Financial Aid/Status

Full-time status: 12 credit hours/ semester

Cardinal Stritch College*

6801 N. Yates Road ◆ Milwaukee, WI 53217
Phone: (414) 352-5400 ◆ Toll-free phone: (800) 347-8822
Fax: (414) 351-0257

Founded: 1937

Accredited by: North Central

Enrollment: 5,100 ◆ Adult students: 2,250

University status: Private, Church, Roman Catholic Church

Features and Services

1. Is it possible to purchase books during hours most adult students attend classes? **Yes.**

2. What characteristics of the institution's adult degree programs are most appealing to students? **Accelerated format. Most major courses are completed on same night of the week with same group of students, with instructor changing every five to six weeks.**

Degree	Concentration/Major	Format
A.B.	Business	E,A
B.S.	Business Management	E,A
B.S.	Business Administration	E,A
M.B.	Business Administration	E,CT,A
M.B.	Management	E

Requirements

Undergraduate admissions requirements: Application form and fee of $20, present high school diploma or equivalency diploma, rank in upper 50 percent of high school class, possess GPA equal to a C average, rank in top 50 percent nationally on college entrance exams, and a 840 SAT or 20 ACT score

Financial Aid/Status

Full-time status: In accordance with financial aid standards
Percentage of adult students receiving financial aid: 32 percent

Fees, Tuition, Costs

Undergraduate application fee: $20
Graduate application fee: $20
Undergraduate tuition: $165/credit
Graduate tuition: $260/credit

Caribbean University

P.O. Box 493 ◆ **Bayamon, PR 00960-493**
Phone: (809) 780-0070 ◆ Fax: (809) 785-0101

Founded: 1969

Accredited by: Middle States

Enrollment: 3,000 ◆ Adult students: 42 percent

University status: Nonprofit

Degree	Concentration/Major	Format
A.S.	Computer Programming	E
A.S.E.	Drafting	E
A.S.	Business Administration	E
A.S.S.	Secretarial Science	E
B.S.	Analysis and Design	E
B.S.E.	Civil and Industrial Engineering	E
B.S.S.	Secretarial Science	E
B.B.A	Business Administration	E
B.S.	Computer Programming	E
B.S.	Pre-Medical	E
B.A.E.	Secondary Education	E
B.A.E.	Elementary Education	E
B.A.	Social Work	E
B.A.	Criminal Justice	E
B.S.N.	Nursing	E

Campus Extension Sites

Carolina, PR
Vega Baja, PR
Ponce, PR

Requirements

Residency requirement: Every student has to attend class at one of the campuses.
Undergraduate admissions requirements: High school diploma or equivalent, file an admissions application and official transcripts.
Graduate admissions requirements: Bachelor's degree, official transcripts, admissions application, testing.
Graduation requirements (undergraduate): Students must complete 133 credits with a 2.4 general course minimum grade point, and complete an internship.
Graduation requirements (graduate): Students must complete 40 credits with a 3.0 GPA, and complete an internship.

Fees, Tuition, Costs

Undergraduate application fee: $15
Graduate application fee: $15
Undergraduate tuition: $90/credit
Graduate tuition: $110/credit
Undergraduate cost of books: $360
Graduate cost of books: $600
Other costs: Lab fees, construction, extra hours

Financial Aid/Status

Percentage of adult students receiving financial aid: 82 percent

Maximum Hours Awarded For

CLEP: Yes
DANTES: Yes

Features and Services

1. Is it possible to purchase books during hours most adult students attend classes? **Yes.**

2. Are the institution's administrative offices open during hours adult students attend class? **Yes.**

3. How do students taking extended classes access library resources? **The library is open Monday to Saturday.**

4. What is the registration and payment process for adult students? **Students select courses and go to registrar's office.**

5. What is the process for advising adult students? **Students are advised by the department heads.**

Carlow College

3333 Fifth Avenue ◆ **Pittsburgh, PA 15213**

Phone: (412) 578-6092 ◆ Toll-free phone: (800) 333-CARLOW

Fax: (412) 578-6321

Founded: 1929

Accredited by: Middle States

Enrollment: 2,225 ◆ Adult students: 1,690

University status: Private, Church, Roman Catholic Church

Degree	Concentration/Major	Format
B.A.	Business/Communication	E,A
B.A.	Communication	E,A
B.A.	Liberal Studies	E,A
B.A.	Professional Writing/Business or English	E,A
B.A.	Psychology	E,A
B.S.	Accounting	E,A
B.S.	Business Management	E,A
B.S.	Health Science	E,A
B.S.	Information Management	E,A
B.S.	Medical Marketing	E,A
B.S.N.	R.N. to B.S.N.—Completion program for R.N.s	E,A
M.S.	Professional Leadership in Health Service Education, Management for Nonprofit Organizations, or Training and Development	E,A
M.Ed.	Early Childhood Education, Early Childhood Supervision, Educational Leadership (with Montessori, principal, and gifted education certification)	E
M.S.N.	Home Health Advanced Practice Nursing (Family Nurse Practitioner) Home Health Case Management/Administration, Gerontological Case Management/Administration, Gerontological Advanced Practice Nursing, Family Home Health Nurse Practitioner Certification	E

Campus Extension Sites

Beaver, PA
Cranberry, PA
Greensburg, PA

Requirements

Residency requirement: Students must meet 32 credits residency requirement for baccalaureate programs.

Undergraduate admissions requirements: Application, personal statement, reference, interview, official transcripts, Pennsylvania nursing license (nurses); CAP students—21 or older, 30 college credits, two years of work experience, commitment.

Graduate admissions requirements: Official transcripts of all college credits, GPA 3.0, three professional recommendations, experience in setting appropriate to degree, interview, other requirements of different programs.

Graduation requirements (undergraduate): Students must complete 120 credits (125 for nursing majors) and meet all general and major course requirements.

Graduation requirements (graduate): Graduate students must meet varied requirements depending on the major.

Fees, Tuition, Costs

Undergraduate application fee: $20
Graduate application fee: $35
Undergraduate tuition: $314/credit—C.E. students
Graduate tuition: $334/credit
Other costs: Support service fee ($18/credit—undergraduate; $22/credit—graduate), lab fees, parking permit, supplemental tuition for nursing courses

Financial Aid/Status

Scholarship programs for adults: Continuing education students are eligible for financial aid if they meet the requirements. Students are encouraged to take advantage of tuition reimbursement programs through their employers.
Full-time status: Full-time students must be registered for 12 credits or more in a semester.

Maximum Hours Awarded For

CLEP: 30
Other exams: Yes

Prior learning portfolio: 30
Additional information: Maximum of 30 credits for CLEP or prior learning or combination of both

Features and Services

1. Is it possible to purchase books during hours most adult students attend classes? **Yes.**

2. Are the institution's administrative offices open during hours adult students attend class? **Yes.**

3. How do students taking extended classes access library resources? **Students access the library by computer from off-campus sites and use area libraries by agreement.**

4. What is the registration and payment process for adult students? **Register through advisor, forms to C.E. office. Pay by credit card, payment plan, reimbursement.**

5. What is the process for advising adult students? **All matriculated students are assigned faculty advisors.**

6. What career and placement services are available to adult students? **The Career Services Office offers career planning and job placement to all students.**

7. What characteristics of the institution's adult degree programs are most appealing to students? **Options/flexibility in times/locations of classes, choice of majors, accelerated programs, support for and sensitivity to adult students.**

Carroll College

1601 North Benton Avenue ◆ Helena, MT 59625
Phone: (406) 447-4384 ◆ Toll-free phone: (800) 992-3648
Fax: (406) 447-4533 ◆ E-mail: enroll@carroll.edu
Web address: http://www.carroll.edu

Founded: 1909

Accredited by: Northwest Association

Enrollment: 1,412 ◆ Adult students: 24 percent

University status: Private, Church, Roman Catholic Church

Fees, Tuition, Costs
Undergraduate application fee: $25
Undergraduate tuition: $10,574/yr
Undergraduate cost of books: $450

Financial Aid/Status
Scholarship programs for adults: Scholarships for adult students vary.
Full-time status: Full-time students must take 12 credits or more.

Maximum Hours Awarded For
CLEP: Yes
Other exams: Yes

Features and Services

1. Is it possible to purchase books during hours most adult students attend classes? **No.**

2. Are the institution's administrative offices open during hours adult students attend class? **No.**

3. How do students taking extended classes access library resources? **The library is open till 12:00 A.M. during the week.**

Degree   Concentration/Major   Format

The college did not provide a list of majors or the type of format used that would be convenient for adult students.

Requirements
Residency requirement: All students must complete one year in residence.
Undergraduate admissions requirements: Complete application includ-ing essay, high school and/or college transcripts, test scores (ACT, SAT, or ASSET), letter of recommendation. Graduation requirements (under-graduate): 122 semester hours, completion of General Liberal Arts requirements; department requirements vary.

4. What is the registration and payment process for adult students? **Same as for traditional students.**

5. What career and placement services are available to adult students? **Nontraditional** students use the same placement services that traditional students use.

Carson-Newman College

P.O. Box 72025 ◆ Jefferson City, TN 37760
Phone: (423) 471-3413 ◆ Toll-free phone: (800) 678-9061
Fax: (423) 471-3502
E-mail: jshannon@cncadm.cn.edu
Web address: http://www.cn.edu

Founded: 1851

Accredited by: Southern Association

Enrollment: 2,201 ◆ Adult students: 15 percent

University status: Private, Church, Southern Baptist

Degree	Concentration/Major	Format
B.S.	Business Administration	E
B.A.	General Studies	E

Requirements

Residency requirement: Students are not required to attend classes on the main campus, but they must have 32 semester hours from Carson-Newman through either on- or off-campus programs.
Undergraduate admissions requirements: High school diploma or GED.
Graduate admissions requirements: Bachelor's degree with 3.0 GPA.
Graduation requirements (undergraduate): Students must complete 128 semester hours, 32 hours in residence, 36 hours of courses at the 300-400 level, 60 hours from a four-year college.
Graduation requirements (graduate):

Graduate students must complete 42 hours of credit with a maximum of 9 hours of transferred credit.

Fees, Tuition, Costs

Undergraduate application fee: $25
Graduate application fee: $25
Undergraduate tuition: $365/day; $130/night
Graduate tuition: $160/hour
Undergraduate cost of books: $250/year
Graduate cost of books: $300/year
Other costs: $100/semester for computer network fee

Financial Aid/Status

Scholarship programs for adults: Adult students may apply for scholarships including the Academic Scholarship and the Presidential Scholarship. Other financial aid is available.
Full-time status: Full-time students must be registered for 12 credit hours/semester.
Percentage of adult students receiving financial aid: 75 percent.

Maximum Hours Awarded For

CLEP: Yes
PEP: Yes
DANTES: Yes
Other exams: Yes
Prior learning portfolio: Yes

Features and Services

1. Is it possible to purchase books during hours most adult students attend classes? **Yes.**

2. Are the institution's administrative offices open during hours adult students attend class? **Yes.**

3. How do students taking extended classes access library resources? **The library is open for extended hours. It may be accessed by computer network.**

4. What is the registration and payment process for adult students? **Payment may be made by bank cards, check, or cash.**

5. What is the process for advising adult students? **Students are assigned an academic advisor through**

the department of their interest.

6. What career and placement services are available to adult students? **Students may use** the placement center for career planning and job placement.

7. What characteristics of the institution's adult degree programs are most appealing to students? **Personal service, available by phone any time, one-stop shopping approach.**

Carthage College

2001 Alford Park Drive ◆ **Kenosha, WI 53140**
Phone: (414) 551-6300 ◆ Toll-free phone: (800) 551-5343
Fax: (414) 551-5704 ◆ E-mail: spsinfo@cns.carthage.edu
Web address: http://www.carthage.edu/

Founded: 1847

Accredited by: North Central

Enrollment: 2,200 ◆ Adult students: 25 percent

University status: Private, Church,
Evangelical Lutheran Church of America

Degree	Concentration/Major	Format
B.A.	Business Administration	E,A
B.A.	Marketing	E
B.A.	Accounting	E
B.A.	Social Work	E
B.A.	Elementary Education	E
M.A.	Education	E

Requirements

Residency requirement: All classes are held on campus.
Undergraduate admissions requirements: Students must submit a completed application form, official transcripts (high school transcript needed if student has fewer than eight transferable college credits).
Graduate admissions requirements: Bachelor's degree, acceptable GPA, working in educational profession.

Student must submit application, personal statement, valid teaching license, MAT scores, three recommendations, interview, transcripts.
Graduation requirements (undergraduate): Students must complete 138 credit hours, 32 hours at Carthage; have a minimum GPA of 2.0; and participate in commencement.
Graduation requirements (graduate): The program of study

must be approved. Graduate students complete 36 credit hours (24 credits in concentration area with B), complete thesis or comprehensive exam, and make oral defense.

Fees, Tuition, Costs

Undergraduate application fee: $10
Graduate application fee: $25
Undergraduate tuition: $145-$195/credit hour
Graduate tuition: $205/credit hour
Undergraduate cost of books: $50-$100/class
Graduate cost of books: $50-$100/class
Other costs: Computer labs available on campus

Financial Aid/Status

Scholarship programs for adults: No scholarships are provided.
Full-time status: Full-time students are enrolled in 12 or more hours/semester.
Percentage of adult students receiving financial aid: 43 percent.

Maximum Hours Awarded For

CLEP: 32
DANTES: 32
Other exams: 32
Additional information: 28 credits maximum for correspondence; 32 credit maximum for all exam credit

Features and Services

1. Is it possible to purchase books during hours most

adult students attend classes? **Yes.**

2. Are the institution's administrative offices open during hours adult students attend class? **Yes.**

3. How do students taking extended classes access library resources? **The library may be accessed by the campus online network.**

4. What is the registration and payment process for adult students? **Registration by mail, phone, fax, e-mail.**

Payment by check, credit card, or student loan.

5. What career and placement services are available to adult students? **The Career Center is open 8 A.M.-8 P.M., Monday-Thursday; 8 A.M.-4:30 P.M., Friday.**

Cedar Crest College*

100 College Dr. ◆ **Allentown, PA 18104**

Phone: (610) 437-4471 ◆ Toll-free phone: (800) 360-1222

Fax: (610) 740-3786

Founded: 1867

Accredited by: Middle States

Enrollment: 1,765 ◆ Adult students: 900

University status: Private, Church, United Church of Christ

Features and Services

1. Is it possible to purchase books during hours most adult students attend classes? **Yes.**

2. Are the institution's administrative offices open during hours adult students attend class? **Yes.**

3. What characteristics of the institution's adult degree programs are most appealing to students? **User-friendly staff and faculty.**

Degree	Concentration/Major	Format
All degrees are open to adults.		E

Requirements

Residency requirement: Yes
Undergraduate admissions requirements: Interview and college transcripts, high school diploma or GED recipient

Fees, Tuition, Costs

Undergraduate tuition: Day/$408; Evening/$216

Financial Aid/Status

Full-time status: 12 credits or more
Percentage of adult students receiving financial aid: 30 percent

Maximum Hours Awarded For

CLEP: Yes
Other exams: Yes
Prior learning portfolio: 12
Additional information: Credit for PONSI-evaluated corporate training

Centenary College

400 Jefferson Street ◆ **Hackettstown, NJ 07840**
Phone: (908) 852-4696 ◆ Toll-free phone: (800) 236-8679
Fax: (908) 852-3454

Founded: 1867

Accredited by: Middle States

Enrollment: 944 ◆ Adult students: 50 percent

University status: Private, Church, United Methodist Church

Degree	Concentration/Major	Format
A.A.	Liberal Arts	E
B.S.	Accounting	E
B.S.	Business Administration/Marketing	E
B.S.	Business Administration/Management	E
B.S.	Business Administration/ Global Business	E
B.S.	Business Administration/ Computer Information Systems	E
B.A.	American Culture	E
B.A.	English	E
B.A.	Individualized Studies	E
B.A.	International Studies	E
B.A.	Mathematics/Applied or Pure Math	E
B.A.	History/American Studies or East Asian Studies	E
B.A.	Political Science/American or International Politics	E
B.A.	Psychology	E
B.A.	English, Elementary Education	E
B.A.	English, Secondary Education	E
B.A.	History, Elementary Education	E
B.A.	History, Secondary Education	E
B.A.	Math, Elementary Education	E
B.A.	Math, Secondary Education	E
B.A.	Psychology, Elementary Education	E
B.A.	Individualized Studies, Elementary Education	E

Requirements

Residency requirement: Students must complete the final 32 credits of their degree at Centenary.

Undergraduate admissions requirements: High school diploma or equivalent, official transcripts from high school or any college attended, SAT, ACT, or TOEFL scores; essay and recommendations are optional.
Graduate admissions requirements: Bachelor's degree, 2.8 GPA or above, personal interview, two letters of recommendation.
Graduation requirements (undergraduate): 128 credits (Bachelor's); 64 credits (Associate), GPA 2.0, complete core requirements, final 32 hours must be earned at Centenary.
Graduation requirements (graduate): 33 credits, GPA 3.0 or better.

Fees, Tuition, Costs

Undergraduate application fee: $25
Graduate application fee: $30
Undergraduate tuition: $12,400/ year; $230/credit
Graduate tuition: $230/credit
Undergraduate cost of books: $75/ class
Graduate cost of books: $100/class

Financial Aid/Status

Scholarship programs for adults: Scholarships are available for full-time students.
Full-time status: Students taking 12 credit hours/semester are full-time students.
Percentage of adult students receiving financial aid: 72 percent.

Maximum Hours Awarded For

CLEP: Yes
PEP: Yes
DANTES: Yes
Prior learning portfolio: 64

Features and Services

1. Is it possible to purchase books during hours most adult students attend classes? **Yes.**

2. Are the institution's administrative offices open during hours adult students attend class? **Yes.**

3. What is the registration and payment process for adult students? **Register at Registrar or Admissions; no appointment needed. Half of tuition paid at registration.**

4. What is the process for advising adult students? **Advising during day by appointment only. This is one-on-one with faculty in major several times during the year.**

6. What career and placement services are available to adult students? **Students may use** the Career Development Office on campus.

7. What characteristics of the institution's adult degree programs are most appealing to students? **Life Learning credit, evening courses, B.A.—individualized studies, CLEP.**

Centenary College of Louisiana

2911 Centenary Blvd. ◆ **Shreveport, LA 71104**
Phone: (318) 869-5131 ◆ Toll-free phone: (800) 234-4448
Fax: (318) 869-5026 ◆ E-mail: dgwin@beta.centenary.edu
Web address: http://www.centenary.edu

Founded: 1825

Accredited by: Southern Association

Enrollment: 1,016 ◆ Adult students: 20 percent

University status: Private, Church, United Methodist Church

Degree   Concentration/Major   Format

The college did not specify any particular majors offered in a format convenient to adult students.

Requirements

Residency requirement: Students must attend classes on campus.
Undergraduate admissions requirements: High school diploma or GED, personal interview, application, official transcripts from high school and colleges attended, SAT or ACT scores, recommendations.
Graduate admissions requirements: Undergraduate degree, certification (Education degree programs only).

Graduation requirements (undergraduate): 124 credit hours.

Fees, Tuition, Costs

Undergraduate application fee: $30
Undergraduate tuition: $10,400/year
Graduate tuition: $300/Education; $600/MBA
Undergraduate cost of books: $650/year
Graduate cost of books: $300

Financial Aid/Status

Scholarship programs for adults: Scholarships are available for full-time students.
Full-time status: Full-time students take 12 credit hours/semester.

Maximum Hours Awarded For

CLEP: Yes

Features and Services

1. Is it possible to purchase books during hours most adult students attend classes? **Yes.**

2. What is the process for advising adult students? **Students are assigned an academic advisor.**

3. What career and placement services are available to adult students? **All placement services are available to students.**

Central Michigan University College of Extended Learning

Rowe Hall Room 128 ◆ **Mount Pleasant, MI 48859**
Phone: (517) 774-7813 ◆ Toll-free phone: (800) 950-1144
Fax: (517) 774-2461 ◆ E-mail: louis.j.wilson@cmich.edu
Web address: http://www.cmich.edu
Program's Web address: http://www.cel.cmich.edu

Founded: 1892

Accredited by: North Central

Enrollment: 29,000 ◆ Adult students: 13,000

University status: Public

Degree	Concentration/Major	Format
B.S.	Administration	E,A,T,C
B.S.	Guest Services	E,A,T,C
B.S.	Industrial	E,A,T,C
B.S.	Organization	E,A,T,C
B.S.	Service Sector	E,A,T,C
B.S.	Community Development	E,A,T,C
B.S.	Community Services	E,A,T,C
B.S.	Health Services	E,A,T,C
B.S.	Public Administration	E,A,T,C
B.S.	Recreation	E,A,T,C
B.A.A.	Administration	E,A,T,C
B.A.A.	Allied Health	E,A,T,C
B.A.A.	Economics	E,A,T,C
B.A.A.	Industrial Technology	E,A,T,C
B.A.A.	Communication	E,A,T,C
B.A.A.	Public Administration	E,A,T,C
B.A.A.	Psychology	E,A,T,C
M.S.A.	General Administration	E,A,T
M.S.A.	Human Resources Administration	E,A,T
M.S.A.	Health Services Administration	E,A,T
M.S.A.	Public Administration	E,A,T
M.S.A.	International Administration	E,A,T
M.S.A.	Software Engineering Administration	E,A,T
M.A.	Education/Instruction	E,A,T
M.A.	Adult Education	E,A,T
M.A.	Administration	E,A,T
M.A.	Special Education	E,A,T
M.A.	Humanities	E,A,T

Campus Extension Sites

Etobicoke, Ontario
Great Falls, MT
Edmonton, AB
Guadalajara, Mexico
Winnipeg, MB
Detroit, MI
Memphis, TN
Grand Rapids, MI
Saginaw, MI
Traverse City, MI
Dayton, OH
Kansas City, MO
Atlanta, GA
Washington, DC
Honolulu, HI
Richmond, VA
Ft. Polk Center, LA
Ft. Leavenworth, KS
Jacksonville, FL
Andrews AFB, MD
Offut AFB, NE
McGuire AFB, NJ
Fort Hamilton, NY
Fort Bragg, NC
Grand Forks AFB, ND
Minot AFB, ND

Requirements

Residency requirement: No on-campus residency is required.
Undergraduate admissions requirements: High school completion or course work at regionally accredited institution, application.
Graduate admissions requirements: Completed bachelor's degree from a regionally accredited institution and a cumulative grade point average of 2.5 or higher, application, official transcripts.
Graduation requirements (undergraduate): B.S. and B.A.A. degrees contain required courses and 124 credit hours for completion. Various courses are required depending on the major.
Graduation requirements (graduate): M.S.A. requires 36 semester credit hours; M.A.—33

credits. Each degree has core courses and other requirements depending on the area of concentration.

Fees, Tuition, Costs

Undergraduate application fee: $50
Graduate application fee: $50
Undergraduate tuition: $145/credit hour
Graduate tuition: $195/credit hour
Undergraduate cost of books: $60
Graduate cost of books: $60

Financial Aid/Status

Scholarship programs for adults: Adult students may apply for scholarships. Financial help is available for adults through various means; 33 percent receive tuition assistance from their employers.
Full-time status: Undergraduates enroll for 12 credit hours/semester (6 hours/term); graduate students enroll for 9 hours.
Percentage of adult students receiving financial aid: 8 percent.

Maximum Hours Awarded For

CLEP: 64
PEP: 3
DANTES: 7
Prior learning portfolio: 60
Additional information: Advance placement exams—39

Features and Services

1. Is it possible to purchase books during hours most adult students attend classes? Yes.

2. Are the institution's administrative offices open during hours adult students attend class? **Yes.**

3. How do students taking extended classes access library resources? **CMU has an award-winning home delivery library service, accessed through a toll-free phone number or a personal computer modem with 24-hour delivery turnaround policy.**

4. What is the registration and payment process for adult students? **Registration and payment can be done at class, program center office, by mail, or by phone.**

5. What is the process for advising adult students? **Advising is done at the class site, in person by appointment, and by toll-free phone anytime.**

6. What career and placement services are available to adult students? **Career Services/ Resource Center provides complete services from resumes to job placement bulletins.**

7. What characteristics of the institution's adult degree programs are most appealing to students? **Programs have time- and money-saving benefits: weekend class format, convenient locations, home delivery library, and on-site advising.**

Central Missouri State University
403 Humphreys ◆ Warrensburg, MO 64093
Phone: (816) 543-4672 ◆ Toll-free phone: (800) SAY-CMSU
Fax: (816) 543-8333
Web address: http://www.cmusuvmb.cmsu

Founded: 1871

Accredited by: North Central

Enrollment: 11,000 ◆ Adult students: 25 percent

University status: Public

Degree	Concentration/Major	Format
B.S.	Accounting	E
B.S.	Computer Information Systems	E
B.S.	Management	E
M.B.A.	Business Administration	E
M.S.	Industrial Safety	E,T
M.A.	Criminal Justice	T
M.S.	Education	E

Campus Extension Sites

Kansas City, MO
St. Louis, MO
Alburque, NM
St. Joseph, MO

Requirements

Residency requirement: Some programs of study require students to attend on-campus classes. Others do not.
Undergraduate admissions requirements: ACT-20; upper half of high school class.
Graduate admissions requirements: The requirements vary depending on the degree.
Graduation requirements (undergraduate): The requirements vary depending on the degree.
Graduation requirements (graduate): The requirements vary depending on the degree.

Fees, Tuition, Costs

Undergraduate application fee: $25
Graduate application fee: $25
Undergraduate tuition: $82/on-campus credit hour; $97/off-campus credit hour
Graduate tuition: $123/credit hour
Undergraduate cost of books: $250/year
Graduate cost of books: Varies by degree
Other costs: Lab fees

Financial Aid/Status

Scholarship programs for adults: Vary greatly. Students should contact our graduate office.
Full-time status: Undergraduate full-time is 12 hours; graduate is 9 hours.

Features and Services

1. Is it possible to purchase books during hours most adult students attend classes? **Yes.**

2. Are the institution's administrative offices open during hours adult students attend class? **Yes.**

3. How do students taking extended classes access library resources? **Students may use libraries in their areas through interlibrary agreements.**

4. What is the registration and payment process for adult students? **Registration and payment can be done in person or by phone, fax, or mail.**

5. What is the process for advising adult students? **On-site advising is available for most off-campus degrees.**

6. What career and placement services are available to adult students? **A full-service career center is offered.**

7. What characteristics of the institution's adult degree programs are most appealing to students? **Convenient times and locations. Books can be ordered by phone and sent directly to the students.**

Chadron State College

1000 Main Street ◆ Chadron, NE 69337
Phone: (308) 432-6461 ◆ Fax: (308) 432-6229
E-mail: cwright@cscl.csc.edu
Web address: http://www.csc.edu

Founded: 1911

Accredited by: North Central

Enrollment: 3,206

University status: Public

Maximum Hours Awarded For

CLEP: 27
Other exams: Yes
Prior learning portfolio: 40

Features and Services

1. How do students taking extended classes access library resources? **The library is open until 11:00 P.M.**

2. What is the registration and payment process for adult students? **Registration and payment are the same for all students.**

3. What is the process for advising adult students? **Advising is the same for all students.**

4. What career and placement services are available to adult students? **The Career Resource Library, NCIS, and career counseling are available.**

Degree   Concentration/Major   Format

Preprofessional, undergraduate, and graduate degrees offered. The university did not specify which degrees were in a format convenient for adult students.

Requirements

Residency requirement: Students are not required to attend classes on campus.
Undergraduate admissions requirements: Application, ACT or SAT not required if high school graduate five or more years prior to application, official high school/college transcripts, health form.
Graduate admissions requirements: Application, prerequisites, GRE, GMAT, essay, and other tests, complete 12 graduate credits (3.0 GPA), meet department requirements.
Graduation requirements (undergraduate): Formal application, meet GPA (2.0-2.5), 30 semester hours from Chadron, pass exit assessments, 125 semester hours completed, meet department requirements, participate in commencement.
Graduation requirements (graduate): Application, meet requirements of residence, teaching or other experiences, time limit, examinations, and any other requirements, GPA-3.0.

Fees, Tuition, Costs

Undergraduate application fee: $10
Graduate application fee: $10
Undergraduate tuition: $52.50/resident/credit
Graduate tuition: $66/resident/credit
Undergraduate cost of books: $600/year
Graduate cost of books: $600/year

Financial Aid/Status

Scholarship programs for adults: No scholarships are offered.
Full-time status: Full-time undergraduates are enrolled in 12 hours/semester; graduate students, 9 hours.

Chaminade University of Honolulu

3140 Waialae Avenue ◆ Honolulu, HI 96816-1578
Phone: (808) 735-4755 ◆ Fax: (808) 735-4766

Founded: 1955

Accredited by: Western Association

Enrollment: 2,000 ◆ Adult students: 1,300

University status: Private, Church, Roman Catholic Church

Degree	Concentration/Major	Format
A.A.	Liberal Arts	E,A
A.A.	Management	E,A
A.S.	Criminal Justice	E,A
A.S.	Early Childhood Education	E,A
B.A.	Business Administration	E,A
B.A.	English	E,A
B.A.	Historical and Political Studies	E,A
B.A.	Psychology	E,A
B.A.	Social Studies	E,A
B.B.A.	Accounting	E,A
B.B.A.	Management	E,A
B.S.	Criminal Justice	E,A
B.S.	Secondary Edcuation	E,A

Campus Extension Sites

Schofield Barracks, HI
Fort Shafter, HI
Tripler Army Medical Center, HI
Barbers Point Naval Air Station, HI
Pearl Harbor Naval Base, HI
Marine Corps Base Keneohe Bay, HI

Requirements

Residency requirement: Students are not required to attend classes on the main campus.
Undergraduate admissions requirements: Application, official transcripts from high school or any college attended, recommendation, medical/health requirements.
Graduate admissions requirements: The requirements for graduate students depend on the degree.
Graduation requirements (undergraduate): Associate degree—60 credits; bachelor's degree—124 credit hours, including core courses, major area of study, and electives.
Graduation requirements (graduate): Each degree has its own requirements for graduation.

Fees, Tuition, Costs

Undergraduate application fee: $50
Graduate application fee: $50
Undergraduate tuition: LD $78/credit; UD $106/credit
Graduate tuition: $265/credit
Undergraduate cost of books: $50/class
Graduate cost of books: $80/class

Financial Aid/Status

Full-time status: 9 credit hours
Percentage of adult students receiving financial aid: 90 percent

Maximum Hours Awarded For

CLEP: 30
DANTES: 30
Other exams: 60
Prior learning portfolio: 60
Additional information: CLEP/DANTES—total of 30 from both; Exam/Portfolio—total of 60 from both

Features and Services

1. Is it possible to purchase books during hours most adult students attend classes? **Yes.**

2. How do students taking extended classes access library resources? **Military and public libraries at sites, and the university library are open evenings and weekends.**

3. What is the registration and payment process for adult students? **Students register for evening classes at any site. Payment can be made at any site.**

4. What is the process for advising adult students? **Academic advising is available at all off-campus sites.**

5. What career and placement services are available to adult students? **All evening students may use the university career and placement services.**

6. What characteristics of the institution's adult degree programs are most appealing to students? **Convenience, flexibility, cost.**

Champlain College

163 S. Willard Street ◆ **Burlington, VT 05402-0670**
Phone: (802) 860-2727 ◆ Toll-free phone: (800) 570-5858
Fax: (802) 860-2775 ◆ E-mail: conant@champlain.edu
Web address: http://www.champlain.edu

Founded: 1878

Accredited by: New England

Enrollment: 2,085 ◆ Adult students: 50 percent

University status: Private

Fees, Tuition, Costs
Undergraduate application fee: $25
Undergraduate cost of books: $550/yr

Financial Aid/Status
Full-time status: 12 credit hours/semester
Percentage of adult students receiving financial aid: 60 percent

Maximum Hours Awarded For
CLEP: Yes
DANTES: Yes
Prior learning portfolio: Yes
Additional information: Vermont State College Portfolio Assessment Program; PONSI

Degree	Concentration/Major	Format
A.A.	Accounting	E,CT
A.A.	Business Management	E,CT
A.A.	Computer Programming	E,CT
A.A.	General Business	E,CT
A.A.	Liberal Studies	E
A.A.	Network and PC Support Specialist	E
B.A.	Accounting	E
B.A.	Business Management	E
B.A.	Communications and Public Relations	E,CT
B.A.	Computer Programming	E,CT
B.A.	Engineering Technology	E,CT
B.A.	Legal Administrative Assistant	E,CT
B.A.	Liberal Studies	E,CT
B.A.	Marketing Management	E,CT
B.A.	Medical Administrative Assistant	E,CT
B.A.	Network & PC Support Specialist	E,CT
B.A.	Office Management	E,CT
B.A.	Paralegal/Legal Assistant	E,CT
B.A.	Radiography	E,CT
B.A.	Respiratory Therapy	E,CT
B.A.	Retailing & Fashion Merchandising	E,CT
B.A.	Speech Communication	E,CT
B.A.	Sport Management	E,CT

Features and Services

1. Is it possible to purchase books during hours most adult students attend classes? **Yes.**

2. Are the institution's administrative offices open during hours adult students attend class? **Yes.**

3. How do students taking extended classes access library resources? **Students may access the library by computer.**

4. What is the registration and payment process for adult students? **Students may register and pay by phone, walk-in, mail-in, or computer.**

5. What is the process for advising adult students? **Advising is done through the Continuing Education department by phone or by appointment.**

6. What career and placement services are available to adult students? **The Career Planning office offers career advising, workshops, and lifelong career support.**

Requirements
Residency requirement: This program offers classes and degrees through SuccessNet by computer and modem, as well as evening classes. Attendance on campus is not required for graduation. Undergraduate admissions requirements: The requirements vary for different majors, but overall no special courses or tests are required for admission. Students should contact the Continuing Education office for information.
Graduation requirements (undergraduate): Associate degree—60 credit hours; Bachelor's degree—120 credit hours.

7. What characteristics of the institution's adult degree programs are most appealing to students? **One-stop service available through Continuing Education** office, child care, single parent program, online classes.

Chapman University

333 N. Glassell Street ◆ **Orange, CA 92666**
Phone: (714) 997-6632 ◆ Fax: (714) 997-6641
Web address: http://www.chapman.edu
Program's Web address: http://www.chapman.educ/ac/index.html

Founded: 1861

Accredited by: Western Association

Enrollment: 10,000 ◆ Adult students: 65 percent

University status: Private, Church, Disciples of Christ

Degree	Concentration/Major	Format
A.A.	General Education	E,A
B.A.	Criminal Justice	E,A
B.A.	Organizational Leadership	E,A
B.A.	Psychology	E,A
B.A.	Social Science	E,A
B.A.	Sociology	E,A
B.S.	Applied Mathematics	E,A
B.S.	Computer Information Systems	E,A
B.S.	Computer Science	E,A
B.S.	Health Science	E,A
M.H.A.	Health Administration	E,A
M.A.	Counseling	E,A
M.A.	Criminal Justice	E,A
M.A.	Education	E,A
M.A.	Organizational Leadership	E,A
M.A.	Psychology	E,A
M.A.	Special Education	E,A
M.S.	Human Resources	E,A

Campus Extension Sites

Phoenix, AZ
Palm Desert, CA
Travis AFB, CA
Tucson, AZ
29 Palms, CA
Manhattan Beach, CA
Palmdale, CA
El Toro, CA
March AFB, CA

Edwards AFB, CA
Suisun, CA
Monterey, CA
Moreno Valley, CA
Modesto, CA
Merced, CA
Stockton, CA
Ontario, CA
Sacramento, CA
Diamond Springs, CA
McClellan AFB, CA
Yuba City, CA
Lemoore, CA
Visalia, CA
San Diego, CA
Vandenberg AFB, CA
Victorville, CA
Colorado Springs, CO
Peterson AFB, CO
Denver, CO
Albuquerque, NM
Kirtland AFB, NM
Syracuse, NY
Silverdale, WA
McChord AFB, WA
Ft. Lewis, WA
Oak Harbor, WA

Requirements

Residency requirement: All degree requirements may be fulfilled at the extended campus location offering that degree.
Undergraduate admissions requirements: Students should submit an admissions application; official transcripts from high school and any colleges attended; SAT, ACT, or CLEP scores; essay; and recommendations.
Graduate admissions requirements: Requirements for graduate admission vary by program.
Graduation requirements (undergraduate): Associate—62 credits; Bachelor's—124 credits

with 32 credits completed in residency at Chapman; includes General Education Breadth courses, Chapman Common Requirements, and major course work.

Graduation requirements (graduate): Requirements for graduation vary by the degree program.

Fees, Tuition, Costs

Undergraduate application fee: $30
Graduate application fee: $40
Undergraduate tuition: Varies by location/program
Graduate tuition: Varies by location/program
Undergraduate cost of books: Varies
Graduate cost of books: Varies
Other costs: Other major costs vary by program

Financial Aid/Status

Scholarship programs for adults: Adult students may qualify for federal Pell grants and loans.
Full-time status: Students taking 12 units/semester (2 consecutive terms) are full-time.

Percentage of adult students receiving financial aid: 35 percent.

Maximum Hours Awarded For

CLEP: Yes
DANTES: Yes
Additional information: Maximum of 32 credits from all examinations

Features and Services

1. Is it possible to purchase books during hours most adult students attend classes? **Yes.**

2. Are the institution's administrative offices open during hours adult students attend class? **Yes.**

3. How do students taking extended classes access library resources? **Access to the library is available by Internet or telephone. Some on-site libraries are available.**

4. What is the registration and payment process for adult students? **Registration is done on-site before each term. Payment arrangements are made at that time.**

5. What is the process for advising adult students? **Advising is done at the site by the student's program coordinator and/or the center director.**

6. What career and placement services are available to adult students? **Career and placement services are available through the Orange campus' Career/Life Planning Center.**

7. What characteristics of the institution's adult degree programs are most appealing to students? **Degree programs relevant to adults, flexibility of courses, convenience of time and location.**

Charter Oak State College

66 Cedar Street ◆ **Newington, CT 06111**
Phone: (860) 666-4595 ◆ Fax: (203) 666-4852
E-mail: pmorganti@commnet.edu
Web address: http://www.cstate.edu/charter

Founded: 1973

Accredited by: New England

Enrollment: 1,250 ◆ Adult students: 98 percent

University status: Public

Degree	Concentration/Major	Format
A.A.	General Studies	V,C,S
A.S.	General Studies	V,C,S
B.A./B.S.	Individualized Studies	V,C,S
B.A./B.S.	Liberal Studies	V,C,S
B.A./B.S.	Anthropology	V,C,S
B.A./B.S.	Applied Arts	V,C,S
B.A./B.S.	Applied Behavioral Studies	V,C,S
B.A./B.S.	Applied Science and Technology	V,C,S
B.A./B.S.	Art History	V,C,S
B.A./B.S.	Business	V,C,S
B.A./B.S.	Child Study	V,C,S
B.A./B.S.	Communication	V,C,S
B.A./B.S.	Computer Science	V,C,S
B.A./B.S.	Ecological/Environmental Studies	V,C,S
B.A./B.S.	Economics	V,C,S
B.A./B.S.	Fire Science Technology/Management	V,C,S
B.A./B.S.	Foreign Languages	V,C,S
B.A./B.S.	Health Studies	V,C,S
B.A./B.S.	History	V,C,S
B.A./B.S.	Human Services Administration	V,C,S
B.A./B.S.	Industrial Technology	V,C,S
B.A./B.S.	Literature	V,C,S
B.A./B.S.	Math	V,C,S
B.A./B.S.	Music History/Music Theory	V,C,S
B.A./B.S.	Optical Business Management	V,C,S
B.A./B.S.	Philosophy	V,C,S
B.A./B.S.	Political Science	V,C,S
B.A./B.S.	Psychology	V,C,S
B.A./B.S.	Religious Studies	V,C,S
B.A./B.S.	Sciences	V,C,S
B.A./B.S.	Sociology	V,C,S
B.A./B.S.	Technology and Management	V,C,S
B.A./B.S.	Theater History	V,C,S

Requirements

Residency requirement: Charter Oaks is an external degree program. All students can complete requirements from any location. Undergraduate admissions requirements: Admission is open to persons 16 years or older, regardless of level of formal education, who demonstrate college-level achievement. Nine college credits from any acceptable source are required.
Graduation requirements (undergraduate): Students must complete 120 semester credits, meet all core and liberal arts requirements, and complete approved concentration of study.

Fees, Tuition, Costs

Undergraduate application fee: $30
Undergraduate tuition: $54/credit (in-state), $80/credit (out-of-state); Learning Contract Credit is $125/credit (in-state), $175/credit (out-of-state)
Other costs: College fees, test fees, cost of courses through other institutions

Financial Aid/Status

Scholarship programs for adults: Waivers for basic cost fees are available based on financial need and academic promise.
Full-time status: Charter Oak State College does not participate in federal financial student aid.
Percentage of adult students receiving financial aid: 10 percent.

Maximum Hours Awarded For

CLEP: No limit
PEP: Most tests
DANTES: Most tests
Other exams: No limit
Prior learning portfolio: 50 percent/degree
Additional information: Contract

learning; American Council on Education recommendations

Features and Services

1. How do students taking extended classes access library resources? **Students may call library services to determine if a book is available. Postage will be charged.**

2. What is the registration and payment process for adult students? **Students pay an enrollment fee after being accepted as a student.**

3. What is the process for advising adult students? **Advisors, aware of adult learners' needs and specializing in specific subjects, are available.**

4. What career and placement services are available to adult students? **No placement service is available. Some literature in career areas is available.**

5. What characteristics of the institution's adult degree programs are most appealing to students? **No residency requirement; many methods of earning additional credits, degree can be completed at a distance.**

Chestnut Hill College

9601 Germantown Avenue ◆ Philadelphia, PA 19118-2695
Phone: (215) 248-7063 ◆ Fax: (215) 248-7065
E-mail: chca@aol.com

Founded: 1924

Accredited by: Middle States

Enrollment: 1,259 ◆ Adult students: 885

University status: Private, Church, Roman Catholic Church

Graduate tuition: $295-$320/credit hour
Other costs: Lab fees

Financial Aid/Status

Full-time status: Students taking 12 credit hours over 3 sessions are full-time.
Percentage of adult students receiving financial aid: 30 percent.

Maximum Hours Awarded For

CLEP: 15
Other exams: 15
Prior learning portfolio: Yes

Features and Services

1. Is it possible to purchase books during hours most adult students attend classes? **Yes.**

2. Are the institution's administrative offices open during hours adult students attend class? **Yes.**

3. What is the registration and payment process for adult students? **Registration or payment is made through walk-in, fax, mail, or deferred payment plan. Payment is due prior to first class.**

Degree	Concentration/Major	Format
B.S.	Accounting/Business	A,E
B.S.	Computer Science	A,E
B.A.	Human Services	A,E
B.A.	Management	A,E
B.S.	Marketing	A,E

Requirements

Residency requirement: All classes are student/faculty contact hours.
Undergraduate admissions requirements: Students must have completed high school or have obtained GED.
Graduation requirements (undergraduate): Students must complete 120 credit hours—40 courses with a cumulative GPA of 2.0.

Fees, Tuition, Costs

Undergraduate application fee: $35
Graduate application fee: $35
Undergraduate tuition: $220/credit hour

4. What is the process for advising adult students? **Academic advisor is available by appointment for evening hours.**

5. What career and placement services are available to adult students? **The career office on campus is available.**

6. What characteristics of the institution's adult degree programs are most appealing to students? **Accelerated classes, flexible schedule, and location.**

Chicago State University*

9501 South King Dr., Library 326 ◆ **Chicago, IL 60628**
Phone: (312) 995-2457 ◆ Fax: (312) 995-2457

Founded: 1867

Accredited by: North Central

Enrollment: 10,000 ◆ Adult students: 600

University status: Public

Degree   Concentration/Major   Format

The university did not specify the degrees and concentrations available in a format convenient for adult students.

Requirements

Residency requirement: Yes
Undergraduate admissions requirements: High school diploma or equivalent, approved prior learning

Financial Aid/Status

Full-time status: A student enrolled in 12 credit hours or more
Percentage of adult students receiving financial aid: 0 percent

Fees, Tuition, Costs

Undergraduate tuition: $79.25/ hour

Features and Services

1. Is it possible to purchase books during hours most adult students attend classes? **Yes.**

2. Are the institution's administrative offices open during hours adult students attend class? **Yes.**

3. What characteristics of the institution's adult degree programs are most appealing to students? **The prior learning option.**

Christian Brothers University
Evening Program
650 E. Parkway South ◆ **Memphis, TN 38104**
Phone: (901) 722-0291 ◆ Fax: (901) 722-0575
E-mail: eveningprog@bucs.cbu.edu
Web address: http://www.cbu.edu
Program's Web address: http://www.cbu.edu/cbuevening./tn/

Founded: 1873
Accredited by: Southern Association

Enrollment: 1,800 ◆ Adult students: 22 percent

University status: Private, Church, Roman Catholic Church

Degree	Concentration/Major	Format
B.S.	Accounting	E,A
B.S.	Business/Marketing	E,A
B.S.	Business/Management	E,A
B.S.	Business/General Business	E,A
B.S.	Business/Information Technology Management	E,A
B.S.	Business/Economics—Finance	E,A
B.S.	Psychology	E,A
M.B.A.	Business Administration	E
X M.B.A.	Executive Masters of Business Administration	E
M.S.	Engineering Management	E

Requirements
Residency requirement: All degree course work is available in the evenings or on Saturdays on campus. Some courses are available in Collierville, TN.
Undergraduate admissions requirements: High school degree with C average, upper 2/3 class, satisfactory SAT or ACT scores, or satisfactory transfer work from accredited institution, preparation in math.
Graduate admissions requirements: Undergraduate degree, official transcripts, GMAT (M.B.A./X M.B.A.); GRE for Master's of Engineering Management.
Graduation requirements (undergraduate): 130-131 credits, 35 of last 70 hours at CBU, 2.0 or better GPA, general education requirements, completion of major requirements.
Graduation requirements (graduate): M.B.A.—30 hours; X M.B.A.—51 hours; M.S. in Engineering Management—33 hours. All require 3.0 GPA.

Fees, Tuition, Costs
Undergraduate application fee: $25
Graduate application fee: $25
Undergraduate tuition: $225/semester hour
Graduate tuition: $290/semester hour
Undergraduate cost of books: $50/course
Graduate cost of books: $70/course
Other costs: $7 activity fee/term

Financial Aid/Status
Scholarship programs for adults: Scholarships are available based on financial need and academic standing (3.5 GPA).
Full-time status: Undergraduate full-time is 12 semester hours/semester; graduate full-time is 6 semester hours/semester.
Percentage of adult students receiving financial aid: 50 percent.

Maximum Hours Awarded For
CLEP: Yes
DANTES: Yes
Other exams: Yes

Features and Services
1. Is it possible to purchase books during hours most adult students attend classes? **Yes.**

2. Are the institution's administrative offices open during hours adult students attend class? **Yes.**

3. How do students taking extended classes access library resources? **Students may use other libraries through consortia arrangements.**

4. What is the registration and payment process for adult students? **Students may register and pay by phone, fax, e-mail, in person, or by mail.**

5. What is the process for advising adult students? **Each student has an extensive entrance interview. Advisors available till 8 P.M. Monday-Thursday.**

6. What career and placement services are available to adult students? **Students may use the same resources that traditional students use.**

7. What characteristics of the institution's adult degree programs are most appealing to students? **Convenience, quality, accelerated schedule.**

City College
City University of New York

160 Convent Avenue ◆ **New York, NY 10009**
Phone: (212) 925-6625 ◆ Fax: (212) 925-0963
E-mail: slebst@cwe.ccny.cuny.edu
Program's Web address: http.//www.ccny.cuny.edu

Founded: 1847

Accredited by: Middle States

University status: Public

Degree	Concentration/Major	Format
B.A.	Interdisciplinary Liberal Arts in Communications and Literature, Criminal Justice, Human Services, Labor Studies, Public Administration, Developmental Disabilities, and Urban Studies	E
B.S.	Early Childhood Education	E

Requirements

Residency requirement: Classes are held at the Center for Worker Education site in lower Manhattan. Students are required to complete 30 credits in residence to earn a City College degree.
Graduation requirements (undergraduate): Graduation requires completing 120 credits.

Fees, Tuition, Costs

Undergraduate application fee: $50

Financial Aid/Status

Full-time status: 12 or more credit hours

Maximum Hours Awarded For

Other exams: Yes
Additional information: Life experience portfolio for Center for Education

Features and Services

1. Are the institution's administrative offices open during hours adult students attend class? **Yes.**

2. How do students taking extended classes access library resources? **Students may use a computer link and access all CUNY campus libraries.**

3. What is the registration and payment process for adult students? **Students register through their counselors. Students pay by mail or in person at the Center.**

4. What is the process for advising adult students? **Each student has his or her own counselor, who handles all academic issues.**

5. What career and placement services are available to adult students? **Career Services office is open to these working adults. Students network with each other.**

6. What characteristics of the institution's adult degree programs are most appealing to students? **Flexible curriculum, peers, qualified permanent staff/faculty, evening classes, convenient services, quality program and reputation of the college, and convenient location near work and transportation.**

Clark College

Vancouver, WA 98663 ◆ Phone: (360) 992-2217
Fax: (360) 992-2870 ◆ E-mail: fultrd@ooi.clark.edu

Founded: 1932

Accredited by: Northwest Association

Enrollment: 11,000 ◆ Adult students: 80 percent

University status: Public

Degree	Concentration/Major	Format
A.A.	Comprehensive	E,V,A,T,CT,TH,S
A.A.S.	Comprehensive	E,V,A,S

Requirements

Residency requirement: Students must attend classes on campus to graduate.
Graduation requirements (undergraduate): A.A.—90 credits, with at least 60 credits in distribution requirements; A.A.S.—up to 120 credits

Fees, Tuition, Costs

Undergraduate tuition: $425/quarter; $45/credit
Undergraduate cost of books: $200/quarter (full-time)
Other costs: Class fees (miscellaneous) of $50/quarter

Financial Aid/Status

Scholarship programs for adults: Scholarships available with no restrictions for adult students
Full-time status: Being registered for 10 credits
Percentage of adult students receiving financial aid: 70 percent

Maximum Hours Awarded For

CLEP: Yes
DANTES: Yes
Other exams: Yes

Features and Services

1. Is it possible to purchase books during hours most adult students attend classes? **Yes.**

2. Are the institution's administrative offices open during hours adult students attend class? **Yes.**

3. How do students taking extended classes access library resources? **Students may access the library in person or by computer. The county library system may be used.**

4. What is the registration and payment process for adult students? **Registration may be done in person, by mail, and at off-campus sites. Payment is due at registration.**

5. What is the process for advising adult students? **Advising is the same as that for traditional students.**

6. What career and placement services are available to adult students? **Adults may use the same system that traditional students use.**

7. What characteristics of the institution's adult degree programs are most appealing to students? **Flexibility.**

Clarke College

1550 Clarke Drive ◆ Dubuque, IA 52001
Phone: (319) 588-6316 ◆ Toll-free phone: (800) 383-2345
Fax: (319) 588-6789 ◆ E-mail: bames@keller.clarke.edu
Web address: http://www.clarke.edu

Founded: 1843

Accredited by: North Central

Enrollment: 1,030 ◆ Adult students: 52 percent

University status: Private, Church, Roman Catholic Church

Degree	Concentration/Major	Format
B.A.	Business Management	E,A
B.A.	Marketing	E,A
B.A.	Accounting	E,A
B.A.	Computer Information Systems	E,A
B.A.	Advertising	E,A
B.A.	Public Relations	E,A
B.S.N.	B.S.N. Completion Program for RNs	E,A

Requirements

Residency requirement: Students must attend classes on campus. Undergraduate admissions requirements: Students must be 24 or older and have a high school diploma or the equivalent. Graduation requirements (undergraduate): Students must complete 124 credit hours with a 2.0 GPA or higher, meet individual major requirements, and complete the senior performance.

Fees, Tuition, Costs

Undergraduate application fee: $20
Undergraduate tuition: $285/credit hour
Undergraduate cost of books: $200/semester

Financial Aid/Status

Full-time status: Enrollment in 12 or more credits
Percentage of adult students receiving financial aid: 50 percent

Maximum Hours Awarded For

CLEP: 30
PEP: 31
Prior learning portfolio: 30

Features and Services

1. Is it possible to purchase books during hours most adult students attend classes? **Yes.**

2. Are the institution's administrative offices open during hours adult students attend class? **Yes.**

3. What is the registration and payment process for adult students? **New students have individual advisor appointments. Registration is done by phone or with an advisor.**

4. What is the process for advising adult students? **Faculty and 24-hour phone line allow students to set up appointments at their convenience.**

5. What career and placement services are available to adult students? **The placement office is open evenings and by appointment.**

6. What characteristics of the institution's adult degree programs are most appealing to students? **High level of service, personalized attention, social activities, faculty accommodates adult learners' time needs.**

Clarkson College

101 S. 42nd Street ◆ **Omaha, NE 68131**
Phone: (402) 552-3032 ◆ Toll-free phone: (800) 647-5500
Fax: (402) 552-6058
E-mail: ajrami@clrkcol.crhsnet.edu

Founded: 1888

Accredited by: North Central

Enrollment: 600 ◆ Adult students: 60 percent

University status: Private

Degree	Concentration/Major	Format
B.S.	Business	E,A,C
B.S.	Medical Imaging	E,V,C,CT
B.S.N.	Nursing	A,C,CT
M.S.N.	Nursing	E,C,CT
M.S.	Health Services Management	E,C,CT

Requirements

Residency requirement: All nursing students must attend clinical courses on campus. Three clinicals are offered in three-week sessions during summer semester.
Undergraduate admissions requirements: Transfer students must have a GPA of 2.0; SAT or ACT scores required; high school diploma or GED.
Graduate admissions requirements: M.S.N. programs require a B.S.N. Graduate programs: 3.0 GPA preferred, but applicants with at least a 2.0 GPA considered.
Graduation requirements (undergraduate): Students must apply for graduation one semester before anticipated graduation date.
Graduation requirements (graduate): Students must apply for graduation one semester before anticipated graduation date.

Fees, Tuition, Costs

Undergraduate application fee: $15
Graduate application fee: $15
Undergraduate tuition: $252/credit hour
Graduate tuition: $290/credit hour
Undergraduate cost of books: $150/semester (2 courses)
Graduate cost of books: $150/semester (2 courses)
Other costs: Answering machine, computer and/or modem, long-distance phone charges.

Financial Aid/Status

Scholarship programs for adults: Adult learners may apply for scholarships.
Full-time status: Full-time undergraduate students enrolled in 12 semester hours; graduate—9 semester hours.
Percentage of adult students receiving financial aid: 85 percent.

Maximum Hours Awarded For

CLEP: Yes
DANTES: Yes
Other exams: Yes

Features and Services

1. Is it possible to purchase books during hours most adult students attend classes? **Yes.**

2. Are the institution's administrative offices open during hours adult students attend class? **Yes.**

3. How do students taking extended classes access library resources? **Students may access the library by fax, BBS, and telephone.**

4. What is the registration and payment process for adult students? **Students register by phone with a staff member, are billed, and pay by mail.**

5. What is the process for advising adult students? **During the first semester of study, each student is assigned a faculty advisor.**

6. What characteristics of the institution's adult degree programs are most appealing to students? **For the graduate program, there is no campus residency requirement. For all students, the fact that the program is not site-specific.**

College Misericordia

301 Lake Street ◆ Admissions Office ◆ **Dallas, PA 18612**
Phone: (717) 674-6462 ◆ Toll-free phone: (800) 852-7675
Fax: (717) 675-2441

Founded: 1924

Accredited by: Middle States

Enrollment: 1,831

University status: Private, Church, Roman Catholic Church

Degree	Concentration/Major	Format
B.S.W.	Social Work	E,A
B.S.N.	Nursing	E,A
B.S.	Business Administration	E,A
B.S./B.A.	Liberal Studies	E,A
B.S.	Radiography	E,A
B.S.	Accounting	E,A
B.S./B.A.	General Studies	E,A
M.S.N.	Nursing	E
M.S.N.	Family Nurse Practitioner	E
M.S.	Occupational Therapy	E
M.S.	Education	E
M.S.	Organizational Management	E

Requirements

Residency requirement: Students must attend classes on campus. No distance learning or correspondence courses are available. Undergraduate admissions requirements: High school diploma or equivalent, generally 2.0-2.5 GPA for prior college work; requirements vary by the program. Graduate admissions requirements: Requirements vary depending on the graduate program. Graduation requirements (undergraduate): Graduation requirements vary with the degree. Graduation requirements (graduate): Graduation requirements vary with the degree.

Fees, Tuition, Costs

Undergraduate application fee: $15
Graduate application fee: $20
Undergraduate tuition: $280/credit hour
Graduate tuition: $325/credit hour
Undergraduate cost of books: Varies
Graduate cost of books: Varies
Other costs: Cost associated with clinical requirements in professional programs; lab fees

Financial Aid/Status

Full-time status: Undergraduates enrolled in 12-18 hours are full-time; graduate students: 9-12 hours.

Maximum Hours Awarded For

CLEP: 40
PEP: 33
Other exams: 15
Prior learning portfolio: Yes

Features and Services

1. Is it possible to purchase books during hours most adult students attend classes? **Yes.**

2. Are the institution's administrative offices open during hours adult students attend class? **Yes.**

3. What is the registration and payment process for adult students? **Registration done in the Continuing Education Office. Deferred payment/tuition reimbursement honored.**

4. What is the process for advising adult students? **A faculty advisor is assigned at admission.**

5. What career and placement services are available to adult students? **Adult learners may use the same services that traditional students use.**

6. What characteristics of the institution's adult degree programs are most appealing to students? **Flexible, predictable course scheduling.**

College for Lifelong Learning

125 N. State Street ◆ **Concord, NH 03301**
Phone: (603) 228-3000 ◆ Toll-free phone: (800) 582-7248
Fax: (603) 229-0964 ◆ E-mail: ndumont@unhf.unh.edu

Founded: 1972

Accredited by: New England

Enrollment: 2,200 ◆ Adult students: 99 percent

University status: Public

Degree	Concentration/Major	Format
A.A.	General Studies	E,S
A.S.	Business	E
A.S.	Behavioral Studies	E
A.S.	Early Childhood	E
A.S.	Microcomputer Applications	E
B.P.S.	Management	E,S
B.P.S.	Behavioral Sciences	E,S
B.P.S.	Self-Design	E,S
B.P.S.	Management	E,S
B.P.S.	Behavioral Sciences	E,S
B.P.S.	Self-Design	E,S
B.G.S.	Self-Design (Liberal Arts)	E,S

Campus Extension Sites
Portsmouth, NH
Bow, NH Rochester, NH
Lebanon, NH
Manchester, NH
Conway, NH
Nashua, NH
Berlin, NH
Littleton, NH

Requirements
Residency requirement: Students can fulfill residency requirements through course work offered in their local communities and/or by independent learning contract. Undergraduate admissions requirements: Students must have a high school diploma or GED. Graduation requirements (undergraduate): Associate degree requires minimum of 64 credits with 2.0 GPA; bachelor's degree, a minimum of 124 credits with 2.0 GPA.

Fees, Tuition, Costs
Undergraduate application fee: $35 or $135 if program is self-designed
Undergraduate tuition: $131 for New Hampshire residents; $145 for out-of-state residents
Undergraduate cost of books: $65/course

Financial Aid/Status
Full-time status: Students enrolled in 8 credit hours/term are full-time.
Percentage of adult students receiving financial aid: 60 percent.

Maximum Hours Awarded For
CLEP: 64
DANTES: 64
Prior learning portfolio: Yes
Additional information: (ACE) American Council of Education PONSI.

Features and Services
1. Is it possible to purchase books during hours most adult students attend classes? **Yes.**

2. Are the institution's administrative offices open during hours adult students attend class? **Yes.**

3. How do students taking extended classes access library resources? **Students may use libraries through the regional consortium.**

4. What is the registration and payment process for adult students? **Students must register each term and pay/course.**

5. What is the process for advising adult students? **Each student is assigned to a local advisor who helps him/her through the educational process.**

6. What career and placement services are available to adult students? **A computerized career development tool is available in each of the major regions of the college.**

7. What characteristics of the institution's adult degree programs are most appealing to students? **Opportunity to demonstrate and acquire credit for prior learning; self-designed degree option.**

College of Charleston

66 George Street ◆ Charleston, SC 29424

Phone: (803) 953-5620 ◆ Fax: (803) 953-6322

Web address: http://www.cofc.edu

Founded: 1770

Accredited by: Southern Association

Enrollment: 10,000 ◆ Adult students: 25 percent

University status: Public

Degree	Concentration/Major	Format
B.A.	Political Science	E
B.A./B.S.	Computer Science	E

Requirements

Undergraduate admissions requirements: High school (minimum state course requirements) or college (2.3 GPA or better) transcripts, SAT scores, class rank
Graduation requirements (undergraduate): 122 credit hours; 12 hours mandatory foreign language; minimum degree requirements, major requirements, and electives

Fees, Tuition, Costs

Undergraduate application fee: $35
Undergraduate tuition: $132/ semester hour
Undergraduate cost of books: $600/year
Other costs: Parking

Financial Aid/Status

Scholarship programs for adults: Scholarships are not available for part-time students. Limited grants are available for limited enrollment periods.
Full-time status: A full-time student is enrolled in 12 credit hours.

Maximum Hours Awarded For

CLEP: Yes
Other exams: 9 language

Features and Services

1. Is it possible to purchase books during hours most adult students attend classes? **Yes.**

2. Are the institution's administrative offices open during hours adult students attend class? **Yes.**

3. What is the registration and payment process for adult students? **Special registration is held for Continuing Education students. Drop boxes are used for payment.**

4. What is the process for advising adult students? **Specially trained advisors are available from 9 A.M. to 7 P.M. (M-Th).**

5. What career and placement services are available to adult students? **Adult learners may use the same services that traditional students use.**

6. What characteristics of the institution's adult degree programs are most appealing to students? **Evening hours, quality of academic programs, diversity of degrees.**

College of Mount St. Joseph

5701 Delhi Road ◆ **Cincinnati, OH 45233-1670**
Phone: (513) 244-4805 ◆ Toll-free phone: (800) 654-9314
Fax: (513) 244-4894

Founded: 1920

Accredited by: North Central

Enrollment: 2,400 ◆ Adult students: 50 percent

University status: Private, Church, Roman Catholic Church

Maximum Hours Awarded For

CLEP: Yes
Other exams: Yes
Prior learning portfolio: Yes
Additional information: No more than 1/2 of a degree earned from any combination of these sources

Features and Services

1. Is it possible to purchase books during hours most adult students attend classes? **Yes.**

2. Are the institution's administrative offices open during hours adult students attend class? **Yes.**

3. What is the registration and payment process for adult students? **Open registration begins several months prior to the semester. Payment is due before semester starts.**

4. What is the process for advising adult students? **Assigned advisors available days, evenings, and weekends. Advising before registration—recommended.**

5. What career and placement services are available to adult students? **Full career services available including resume development, counseling, and co-op.**

6. What characteristics of the institution's adult degree programs are most appealing to students? **Extended service hours including evenings and weekends, flexible time frame to earn degrees.**

Degree	Concentration/Major	Format
B.S.	Accounting	E
B.A.	Graphic Design	E
B.A.	Interior Design	E
B.S.	Business Administration	E
B.A.	Communication Arts	E
B.S.	Computer Information	E
B.A.	General Studies	E
B.A.	Gerontological Studies	E
B.S.	Management Communication	E
B.S.	Management of Healthcare Services	E
B.S.N.	RN to BSN completion	E
B.A.	Paralegal	E
B.S.	Quality Management	E
B.A.	Religious Pastoral Ministry	E
B.A.	Social Work	E

Requirements

Undergraduate admissions requirements: Open admission is used for nontraditional students (age 23 and older).
Graduation requirements (undergraduate): A bachelor's degree requires 128 credits with 48 credits in Liberal Arts and Science requirements, and the others in major requirements and electives.

Fees, Tuition, Costs

Undergraduate application fee: $25
Undergraduate tuition: $276/credit or $5,300/semester
Undergraduate cost of books: $200/semester

Financial Aid/Status

Scholarship programs for adults: Scholarships based on need, credit-hour accumulation, and academic achievement are available. The amounts vary between $500 and $2,000 a year.
Full-time status: Full-time students must be enrolled in a minimum of 12 credit hours.
Percentage of adult students receiving financial aid: 80 percent.

College of Mount Saint Vincent*

6301 Riverdale Avenue ◆ **Riverdale, NY 10471**
Phone: (718) 405-3322 ◆ Fax: (718) 601-6392

Founded: 1847

Accredited by: Middle States

Enrollment: 1,300 ◆ Adult students: 580

University status: Private

Features and Services

1. Is it possible to purchase books during hours most adult students attend classes? **Yes.**

2. Are the institution's administrative offices open during hours adult students attend class? **Yes.**

3. What characteristics of the institution's adult degree programs are most appealing to students? **Adult courses days, evenings, and Saturdays; transfer credit policies, location of campus—proximity to New York City, Westchester, Northern New Jersey—and credit for life experience.**

Degree	Concentration/Major	Format
A.A.S.	Business Career	
A.A.	Interdisciplinary/English	
A.A.	Interdisciplinary/History	
B.A.	Economics	E
B.A.	Communications	E
B.S.	Nursing (for Registered Nurses)	E
B.A.	Humanities Majors	E
B.A.	Business	E

Requirements

Residency requirement: Yes
Undergraduate admissions requirements: Application fee, official high school transcript or GED, one or more academic reference, official TOEFL scores where applicable for transfer candidate, also required official college transcripts

Fees, Tuition, Costs

Undergraduate application fee: $25
Undergraduate tuition: $11,790

Financial Aid/Status

Full-time status: Minimum of 12 credits
Percentage of adult students receiving financial aid: 70 percent

Maximum Hours Awarded For

CLEP: 18
Other exams: 18
Prior learning portfolio: 39

College of New Rochelle Graduate School

29 Castle Place ◆ **New Rochelle, NY 10850**
Phone: (914) 654-5320 ◆ Fax: (914) 654-5554

Founded: 1904

Accredited by: Middle States

Enrollment: 1,000 ◆ Adult students: 100 percent

University status: Private

Degree	Concentration/Major	Format
M.S.	Education-Elementary, Early Childhood Education, Reading, Gifted, Special Education, Teaching English as a Second Language	E
M.S.	Art-Studio Art, Art Therapy	E
M.S.	Career Development, Guidance, and Counseling, Gerontology, School Psychology	E

Requirements

Residency requirement: Students must attend classes on campus. Graduate admissions requirements: Applicants must have an undergraduate degree with 3.0 GPA in major area of study and MMR immunization. Graduation requirements (graduate): Graduates must complete graduation application, earn the minimum credits for the degree with 3.0 GPA in course work, complete a culminating experience, and complete degree work within five years.

Fees, Tuition, Costs

Graduate application fee: $35
Graduate tuition: $292/credit

Financial Aid/Status

Scholarship programs for adults: Scholarships available
Full-time status: 12 credit hours
Percentage of adult students receiving financial aid: 50 percent

Features and Services

1. Is it possible to purchase books during hours most adult students attend classes? **Yes.**

2. Are the institution's administrative offices open during hours adult students attend class? **Yes.**

3. How do students taking extended classes access library resources? **The library is open weekends and evenings.**

4. What is the registration and payment process for adult students? **Registration and payment are done by mail. Credit cards and deferral for employer reimbursement are accepted.**

5. What is the process for advising adult students? **Advising is done by faculty members, who must sign off for registration.**

6. What career and placement services are available to adult students? **Services include workshops, individual appointments, computerized career guide, placement folders.**

7. What characteristics of the institution's adult degree programs are most appealing to students? **Small class size, individual attention, and strong academic programs.**

College of Notre Dame Weekend College

4701-N. Charles Street ◆ Baltimore, MD 21210
Phone: (410) 532-5500 ◆ Toll-free phone: (800) 435-0200
Fax: (410) 435-5795 ◆ E-mail: pjablonwecdir@ndm.edu

Founded: 1873

Accredited by: Middle States

Enrollment: 3,200 ◆ Adult students: 75 percent

University status: Private, Church, Roman Catholic Church

Degree	Concentration/Major	Format
B.A.	Business/Management	E
B.A.	Business/Accounting	E
B.A.	Business/Finance	E
B.A.	Business/Human Resource Management	E
B.A.	Business/Computer Information Systems	E
B.A.	Business/Marketing	E
B.A.	Computer Information Systems	E
B.A.	Communication Arts	E
B.A.	Elementary Education	E
B.A.	Human Services	E
B.A.	Liberal Arts	E
B.A.	Religious Studies	E
B.S.N.	Nursing completion program	E

Campus Extension Site

Baltimore, MD

Requirements

Residency requirement: The program combines classroom instruction and guided independent study.
Undergraduate admissions requirements: Students must have an interview, complete admissions application, documentation of high school completion or associate degree, and review of any transfer credits.

Graduation requirements (undergraduate): Graduation requires 2.0 GPA, completion of 45 credits at the College of Notre Dame, with a total of 120 credits.

Fees, Tuition, Costs

Undergraduate application fee: $25
Undergraduate tuition: $192/credit
Undergraduate cost of books: $70-$80/course

Financial Aid/Status

Scholarship programs for adults: Scholarships include the honor society scholarship ($400) and a Continuing Studies Scholarship ($400-$1,000) based on financial need and 2.0 GPA.
Full-time status: Students taking 12 or more credits are full-time.
Percentage of adult students receiving financial aid: 25 percent.

Maximum Hours Awarded For

CLEP: 30
Prior learning portfolio: 30

Features and Services

1. Is it possible to purchase books during hours most adult students attend classes? **Yes.**

2. Are the institution's administrative offices open during hours adult students attend class? **Yes.**

3. What is the registration and payment process for adult students? **Registration by mail or walk-in. $30 registration fee. Pay by cash, credit card, check, or payment plan.**

4. What is the process for advising adult students? **New students meet with an advisor. All students have an advisor.**

5. What career and placement services are available to adult students? **The Career Center is available to adult learners.**

6. What characteristics of the institution's adult degree programs are most appealing to students? **Schedule and format of classes.**

College of Saint Mary*

1901 S. 72 Street ◆ **Omaha, NE 68124**
Phone: (402) 399-2407 ◆ Toll-free phone: (800) 926-5534
Fax: (402) 399-2341

Founded: 1923

Accredited by: North Central

Enrollment: 1,168 ◆ Adult students: 500

University status: Nonprofit, Church, Roman Catholic Church

Degree	Concentration/Major	Format
A.S.	Accounting	E
A.S.	Business	E
A.A.	Communications	E
A.A.	General Studies	E
B.S.	Accounting	E
B.S.	Business	E
B.A.	Communications	E
B.S.	Computer Information Management	E
B.A.	Computer Graphics	E
B.A.	Human Services	E
B.S.	Legal Administration	E
B.A.	Paralegal Studies	E

Requirements

Residency requirement: Yes.
Undergraduate admissions
requirements: Students must have a
2.0 GPA from previous college
work or have graduated in the top
half of the senior class with a 2.0
GPA.

Fees, Tuition, Costs

Undergraduate application fee: $20
Undergraduate tuition: $220/credit
Full-time status: 12 credit hours or
more/semester

Features and Services

1. Is it possible to purchase books during hours most adult students attend classes? **Yes.**

2. Are the institution's administrative offices open during hours adult students attend class? **Yes.**

3. What characteristics of the institution's adult degree programs are most appealing to students? **Flexibility for scheduling (three formats: day, evening, and weekend), ample free parking, convenient hours**

College of St. Francis

500 Wilcox Street ◆ **Joliet, IL 60435**
Phone: (815) 740-3455 ◆ Fax: (815) 740-4285
Web address: http://www.stfrancis.edu

Founded: 1920

Accredited by: North Central

University status: Private, Church, Roman Catholic Church

Degree	Concentration/Major	Format
B.S.	Professional Arts/ Organizational Management	E,A
B.S.	Professional Arts/ Operations Management	E,A
B.S.	Professional Arts/ Entrepreneurship Management	E,A
B.S.	Professional Arts/ Human Resource Management	E,A
B.S.	Professional Arts/ Human Service Management	E,A
B.S.	Professional Arts/ Hospitality Management	E,A
B.S.	Professional Arts/Criminal Justice	E,A

Campus Extension Site

Oak Forest, IL

Requirements

Residency requirement: Courses are offered through long-distance learning.
Undergraduate admissions requirements: Adult students need verification of high school graduation or transferred credits from a community or four-year college.
Graduation requirements (undergraduate): Students must complete 128 credit hours to graduate.

Fees, Tuition, Costs

Undergraduate application fee: $20
Undergraduate tuition: $285/credit hour
Full-time status: Full-time students are enrolled for 12 hours.

Financial Aid/Status

Percentage of adult students receiving financial aid: 50 percent

Maximum Hours Awarded For

CLEP: 33
Prior learning portfolio: 33

Features and Services

1. Is it possible to purchase books during hours most adult students attend classes? **Yes.**

2. Are the institution's administrative offices open during hours adult students attend class? **Yes.**

3. How do students taking extended classes access library resources? **An electronic library is available.**

4. What is the registration and payment process for adult students? **Registration is done by phone, mail, or in person. Students may set up a payment plan.**

5. What is the process for advising adult students? **Each adult student is assigned an advisor, who is available evening hours.**

6. What career and placement services are available to adult students? **Career and placement services are available for adult learners.**

7. What characteristics of the institution's adult degree programs are most appealing to students? **Customer-service-oriented; designed for working adults.**

College of St. Scholastica

1200 Kenwood Avenue ◆ Duluth, MN 55811
Phone: (218) 723-6046 ◆ Toll-free phone: (800) 447-5444
Fax: (218) 723-5991 ◆ E-mail: admissions@stfl.css.edu
Program's Web address: http://www.css.edu/

Founded: 1912

Accredited by: North Central

Enrollment: 1,940 ◆ Adult students: 35 percent

University status: Private, Church, Roman Catholic Church

Degree	Concentration/Major	Format
B.A.	Behavioral Arts and Sciences	E,S
B.A.	Management	E
M.A.	Management	E
M.A.	Nursing	E
M.Ed.	Education	E,V
M.Ed.	Educational Media and Technology	E
M.A.	Health Information Management	A

Campus Extension Sites

Brainard, MN
Hibbing, MN
Grand Rapids, MN

Requirements

Residency requirement: The master's degree in distance learning is the only program that does not require classroom attendance. Undergraduate admissions requirements: High school diploma (class rank top 50 percent) or GED certificate (placement in top 75 percent); writing sample; interview. Graduate admissions requirements: Admission requirements vary depending on the degree. Graduation requirements (undergraduate): Graduating requires 192 credit hours with major and liberal arts requirements satisfied. Graduation requirements (graduate): Requirements for graduation vary with the program.

Fees, Tuition, Costs

Undergraduate application fee: $25
Graduate application fee: $50
Undergraduate tuition: $13,056/ year
Graduate tuition: $292/credit
Undergraduate cost of books: $450
Graduate cost of books: $450

Financial Aid/Status

Scholarship programs for adults: Encore Benedictine Scholarship is based on merit and diverse criteria. The amount varies.
Full-time status: Undergraduate full-time students are enrolled for 12 hours; graduate, 8 hours.

Percentage of adult students receiving financial aid: 90 percent.

Maximum Hours Awarded For

CLEP: Varies
PEP: Varies
DANTES: Varies
Other exams: Yes
Prior learning portfolio: 144

Features and Services

1. Is it possible to purchase books during hours most adult students attend classes? **Yes.**

2. Are the institution's administrative offices open during hours adult students attend class? **Yes.**

3. How do students taking extended classes access library resources? **Students may use libraries in their communities.**

4. What is the registration and payment process for adult students? **Students register with their advisors. Payment is due on billing.**

5. What is the process for advising adult students? **Students are assigned advisors, who meet with them once each quarter.**

6. What career and placement services are available to adult students? **The Student Development Center is staffed to provide these services.**

7. What characteristics of the institution's adult degree programs are most appealing to students? **Flexibility, professional orientation of the program.**

The College of Santa Fe

1600 St. Michael's Drive - T-43 ◆ **Santa Fe, NM 87505**
Phone: (505) 473-6176 ◆ Toll-free phone: (800) 456-2673
Fax: (505) 473-6172 ◆ E-mail: smarcus@fogelson.csf.edu

Founded: 1874

Accredited by: North Central

Enrollment: 1,500 ◆ Adult students: 50 percent

University status: Private

Degree	Concentration/Major	Format
A.A.	Public Administration	E,A
A.A.	Business Administration	E,A
B.A.	Business Administration/Accounting	E,A
B.A.	Business Administration/Management	E,A
B.A.	Business Administration/MIS	E,A
B.A.	Humanities	E,A
B.A.	Psychology/General	E,A
B.A.	Counseling	E,A
B.A.	Hospice	E,A
B.A.	Organizational Psychology	E,A
B.A.	Public Administration	E,A
B.A.	Elementary Education	E,A
B.A.	Secondary Education	E,A
B.A.	Special Education	E,A
M.B.A.	Finance	E,A
M.B.A.	Human Resources	E,A
M.B.A.	Management	E,A
M.B.A.	MIS	E,A
M.A.	Education of At-Risk Youth	E,A

Campus Extension Site

Albuquerque, NM

Requirements

Residency requirement: Students must take 30 credits at either Santa Fe or Albuquerque.
Undergraduate admissions requirements: Students must be 21 or older; submit application, official high school transcript or GED, and any college credit transcripts; and have interview.
Graduate admissions requirements: M.B.A. requires an interview, application, GPA, GMAT score (750), recommendation. M.A. in Education requires bachelor's; teaching experience or eligibility for license, or experience working with at-risk youth.
Graduation requirements (undergraduate): Complete 128 credits including liberal arts core, 48 upper-division credits. Fewer than 18 credits of D in lower-division courses. Final GPA of 2.0 overall. Minimum of 30 credits at College of Santa Fe.
Graduation requirements (graduate): M.A. Education requires 36-48 credits, minimum GPA-3.0, master's project. M.B.A.—36 credits, 27 credits undergraduate prerequisite, GPA—3.0, fewer than 6 hours of C, 30 hours at College of Santa Fe, finish in five years.

Fees, Tuition, Costs

Undergraduate application fee: $25
Graduate application fee: $25
Undergraduate tuition: $196/credit hour
Graduate tuition: $214/credit hour
Undergraduate cost of books: $400/semester (full-time)
Graduate cost of books: $300/semester (full-time)

Financial Aid/Status

Scholarship programs for adults: Nonrenewable one-year scholarship ($500/semester) is based on need and talent. Student must be full-time undergraduate or graduate student (New Mexico resident) with GPA of 2.5.
Full-time status: Full-time undergraduates take 12 hours; graduate, 9 hours.
Percentage of adult students receiving financial aid: 27 percent.

Maximum Hours Awarded For

CLEP: 48
DANTES: 48
Other exams: 48
Prior learning portfolio: 48
Additional information: Military evaluated in accordance with American Council on Education guidelines; Advanced Placement Exams

Features and Services

1. Is it possible to purchase books during hours most adult students attend classes? **Yes.**

2. Are the institution's administrative offices open during hours adult students attend class? **Yes.**

3. How do students taking extended classes access library resources? **The library has evening and weekend hours.**

4. What is the registration and payment process for adult students? **Registration and payment take place at both campuses.**

5. What is the process for advising adult students? **Assigned advisors meet students for initial interview. Students are encouraged to meet before registering**

6. What career and placement services are available to adult students? **The Santa Fe campus has an office of career placement, whose director assists students.**

7. What characteristics of the institution's adult degree programs are most appealing to students? **Individual attention, two 9-week terms/semester, classes meet one night/week or weekends, faculty understands adults' needs, small classes.**

Colorado Christian University

180 S. Garrison Street ◆ **Lakewood, CO 80226-7499**
Phone: (303) 202-0100 ◆ Toll-free phone: (800) 44-FAITH
Fax: (303) 233-2735 ◆ E-mail: efindlay@ccu.edu
Web address: http://www.ccu.edu

Founded: 1914

Accredited by: North Central

Enrollment: 2,672 ◆ Adult students: 71 percent

University status: Private

Degree	Concentration/Major	Format
B.S.	Organizational Management/ Human Resources	E,A
B.S.	Organizational Management/ Christian Leadership	E,A
B.S.	Computer Information Systems Management	E,A
B.A.	Elementary Education	E,A
B.A.	Secondary Education	E,A
M.S.	Management	E,A
M.A.	Curriculum and Instruction	E,A
M.A.	Biblical Counseling	

Campus Extension Sites

Grand Junction, CO

Aurora, CO
Colorado Spring, CO

Requirements

Residency requirement: Students may attend classes at any of the locations.
Undergraduate admissions requirements: Students must be 25 years or older with a minimum of 32 transfer credits. Education degrees have specific requirements.
Graduate admissions requirements: M.S.M.—Bachelor's with 2.75 GPA, entrance exam (GRE, GMAT, CCU exams); M.A.C.— Bachelor's with 2.75 GPA, two years of work experience in related field.
Graduation requirements (undergraduate): Graduation requires 128 semester hours, with 30 hours at Colorado Christian University.
Graduation requirements (graduate): Graduation requires 36 semester hours in the master's program. All courses must have a grade of C or better. Three hours could be transferred as an elective.

Fees, Tuition, Costs

Undergraduate application fee: $35
Graduate application fee: $35
Undergraduate tuition: $185/hour
Graduate tuition: $280-$295
Undergraduate cost of books: $840

Graduate cost of books: $600-$840
Other costs: Additional fees $100/ semester

Financial Aid/Status
Scholarship programs for adults: Scholarships are not available.
Full-time status: Full-time students are enrolled in 12 hours/semester.
Percentage of adult students receiving financial aid: 80 percent.

Maximum Hours Awarded For
CLEP: 30
DANTES: 30
Prior learning portfolio: 34

Features and Services

1. Is it possible to purchase books during hours most adult students attend classes? **Yes.**

2. What is the registration and payment process for adult students? **Register at student's convenience. Payment options: tuition reimbursement, budget plan, financial aid.**

3. What is the process for advising adult students? **New students advised one-on-one. Advising scheduled three** times during program or when needed.

4. What career and placement services are available to adult students? **A career center is available for students. No placement service is provided.**

5. What characteristics of the institution's adult degree programs are most appealing to students? **Adult approach, one night/week (6-10 P.M.), 12 to 15 months to complete, books delivered to class, personal attention, small class size.**

Colorado State University
Division of Continuing Education ◆ Spruce Hall
Fort Collins, CO 80523-1040
Phone: (970) 491-5288 ◆ Toll-free phone: (800) 525-4950
Fax: (970) 491-7885
Web address: http://www.colostate.edu/depts/ce
Program's Web address:
http://www.colostate.edu/depts/ce/surge.html

Founded: 1870

Accredited by: North Central

Enrollment: 19,000 ◆ Adult students: 25 percent

University status: Public

Degree	Concentration/Major	Format
M.S.	Management	V
M.B.A.	Business Administration	V
M.S.	Engineering/Chemical	V
M.S.	Engineering/Civil	V
M.S.	Engineering/Mechanical	V
M.S.	Engineering/Electrical	V
M.S.	Statistics	V
M.S.	Computer Science	V
M.Ed.	Human Resource Development	V

Requirements
Residency requirement: Students are not required to attend on-campus classes.
Graduate admissions requirements: Students must hold a bachelor's degree and submit scores from the GRE or GMAT exams depending on their field.
Graduation requirements (graduate): The requirements vary by program.

Fees, Tuition, Costs
Graduate application fee: $30
Graduate tuition: $300-$350/ semester credit
Graduate cost of books: Varies

Financial Aid/Status
Full-time status: Students enrolled in 6 semester credits/semester are full-time.
Percentage of adult students receiving financial aid: 40 percent.

Maximum Hours Awarded For
CLEP: Yes
Other exams: Yes

Features and Services

1. Is it possible to purchase books during hours most adult students attend classes? **Yes.**

2. Are the institution's administrative offices open during hours adult students attend class? **Yes.**

3. How do students taking extended classes access library resources? **Students have access to the distance education librarian.**

4. What is the registration and payment process for adult students? **Payment is required at the time of registration.**

5. What is the process for advising adult students? **Advising is done through individual departments.**

6. What characteristics of the institution's adult degree programs are most appealing to students? **Flexibility of videotape programs.**

Columbia College

1001 Rogers Street ◆ **Columbia, MO 65216**
Phone: (573) 875-7352 ◆ Toll-free phone: (800) 231-2391
Fax: (573) 875-7506

Founded: 1851

Accredited by: North Central

Enrollment: 7,000 ◆ Adult students: 30-40 percent

University status: Nonprofit, Church, Disciples of Christ Church

Degree	Concentration/Major	Format
A.S.	Criminal Justice Administration	E
A.S.	Business Administration	E
A.S.	Nursing	E
A.S.	Computer Information Systems	E
B.A./B.S.	Business Administration	E
B.A./B.S.	Accounting	E
B.A./B.S.	Computer Information Systems	E
B.A./B.S.	Finance	E
B.A./B.S.	Management	E
B.A./B.S.	Marketing	E
B.A./B.S.	Criminal Justice Administration	E
B.A.	English	E
B.A.	Psychology	E
B.A.	Individualized Studies	E
M.A.	Teaching	E

Campus Extension Sites

St. Louis, MO
San Francisco, CA
Jefferson City, MO
Redstone, AL
Ft. Leonard Wood, MO
Arsenal, AL
Osage Beach, MO
Aurora, CO
Jacksonville, FL
Gurnee, IL
Crystal Lake, IL
Freeport, IL
Syracuse, NY
Grand Prairie, TX
Salt Lake City, UT
Marysville, WA

Requirements

Residency requirement: All work is done on the main campus or an extended campus, with at least 24 of the last 36 semester hours taken with Columbia College. Undergraduate admissions requirements: High school diploma or equivalency.
Graduate admissions requirements: Official transcripts, three letters of recommendation, summary of career goals, affidavit of moral character, baccalaureate in education or with background in psychology, education/curriculum, 3.0 GPA.
Graduation requirements (undergraduate): 120 semester hours, with at least 39 semester hours in 300-400 level courses, 44 semester hours of general education.
Graduation requirements (graduate): 36 semester hours.

Fees, Tuition, Costs

Undergraduate application fee: $25
Graduate application fee: $25

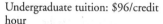

Undergraduate tuition: $96/credit hour
Graduate tuition: $180/credit hour
Undergraduate cost of books: $150-$200/semester
Graduate cost of books: $150-$200/semester

Financial Aid/Status

Full-time status: Six credits every eight weeks is considered full-time for evening and extended sites. Percentage of adult students receiving financial aid: 40 percent.

Features and Services

1. Is it possible to purchase books during hours most adult students attend classes? **Yes.**

2. Are the institution's administrative offices open during hours adult students attend class? **Yes.**

3. How do students taking extended classes access library resources? **Some facilities are available at each site and other schools in their area.**

4. What is the registration and payment process for adult students? **Registration is held at each site. Payment is at least half at registration, with the balance due four weeks later.**

5. What is the process for advising adult students? **Each student is assigned an advisor and is required to meet prior to registration for classes.**

6. What career and placement services are available to adult students? **Each site has some services, but the majority of services are through the home campus. Fax and 800 numbers are available.**

7. What characteristics of the institution's adult degree programs are most appealing to students? **Schedule (4:20 P.M.-10:00 P.M.), some Saturday classes, low tuition cost, quality program.**

Columbia College of South Carolina

1301 Columbia College Drive ◆ **Columbia, SC 29203**
Phone: (803) 786-3871 ◆ Toll-free phone: (800) 277-1301
Fax: (803) 786-3874 ◆ E-mail: belevenger@colacoll.edu

Founded: 1854

Accredited by: Southern Association

Enrollment: 1,310 ◆ Adult students: 154

University status: Private, Church, United Methodist Church

Degree	Concentration/Major	Format
B.A.	Business Administration	E
B.A.	Accounting	E
B.A.	Entrepreneurship	E
B.A.	Public Affairs	E
B.A.	Social Work	E

Requirements

Residency requirement: Students are required to attend classes on the main campus.
Undergraduate admissions requirements: Students submit transcripts from previous colleges and/or high school; admission interview; SAT scores may be required from recent high school graduates.
Graduate admissions requirements: M.Ed. in Elementary Education—certificate in Elementary Education, NTE, official transcripts.
Graduation requirements (undergraduate): 127 credits in General Education, major, and elective categories; 2.0 cumulative GPA/2.5 cumulative in major; pass math and writing proficiency tests.
Graduation requirements (graduate): Complete 32 semester hours in required areas; successfully complete the comprehensive exam.

Fees, Tuition, Costs

Undergraduate application fee: $20
Graduate application fee: $20
Undergraduate tuition: $320/semester hour
Graduate tuition: $175/semester hour
Undergraduate cost of books: Varies

Graduate cost of books: Varies
Other costs: $10 technology fee for students enrolled in six or more semester hours each semester

Financial Aid/Status
Scholarship programs for adults: Institutional grants, based on merit and need, are available for full-time undergraduate students (up to $4,380).
Full-time status: Full-time students are enrolled in 12 semester hours.
Percentage of adult students receiving financial aid: 44 percent.

Maximum Hours Awarded For
CLEP: Yes
Other exams: Yes
Prior learning portfolio: Yes
Additional information: No maximum set for credit; however,

30 hours earned at Columbia, with 12 hours in major

Features and Services
1. Is it possible to purchase books during hours most adult students attend classes? **Yes.**

2. Are the institution's administrative offices open during hours adult students attend class? **Yes.**

3. What is the registration and payment process for adult students? **Preregistration with advisor on phone or in person. Payment by mail/in person. Finalize first class.**

4. What is the process for advising adult students? **A**

full-time Director of Student Services for Evening College advises women individually.**

5. What career and placement services are available to adult students? **Services include workshops, SIGI Plus (computerized career planning system), and placement file service. Career center library is available.**

6. What characteristics of the institution's adult degree programs are most appealing to students? **Small class size, collaborative learning, all women students (under-graduate), convenient class hours, split-term classes, Saturday classes.**

Columbia Union College
Adult Evening College
7600 Flower Avenue ◆ Takoma Park, MD 20912
Phone: (301) 891-4086 ◆ Fax: (301) 891-4023
Web address: http://www.cuc.edu

Founded: 1904

Accredited by: Middle States

Enrollment: 900 ◆ Adult students: 40 percent

University status: Private, Church, Seventh-Day Adventist Church

Degree	Concentration/Major	Format
B.S.	Business Administration	E,A
B.S.	Health Care Administration	E,A
B.S.	Organizational Management	E,A
B.S.	Information Systems	E,A

Requirements
Residency requirement: Students must attend classes on the main campus.

Undergraduate admissions requirements: Students must have a minimum of 60 credits from an accredited degree-granting college

with a minimum of 2.0 GPA. Exceptions may be made on appeal. Graduation requirements (undergraduate): Graduation requires 120 hours, including 36 hours of residency in the core subjects.

Fees, Tuition, Costs
Undergraduate application fee: $25
Undergraduate tuition: $220/hour
Undergraduate cost of books: $50/course
Other costs: Information System major requires $200 lab fee. There are four labs.

Financial Aid/Status
Full-time status: Nine credit hours is 3/4 time in the Adult Evening Program.
Percentage of adult students receiving financial aid: 50 percent.

Maximum Hours Awarded For
CLEP: 24
PEP: 24

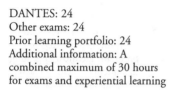

DANTES: 24
Other exams: 24
Prior learning portfolio: 24
Additional information: A combined maximum of 30 hours for exams and experiential learning

Features and Services

1. Is it possible to purchase books during hours most adult students attend classes? **Yes.**

2. Are the institution's administrative offices open during hours adult students attend class? **Yes.**

3. How do students taking extended classes access library resources? **Students may access the library by writing.**

4. What is the registration and payment process for adult students? **Complete registration form. Admission made by committee. Payment at start of course.**

5. What is the process for advising adult students? **Two** academic advisors are available 9 A.M.-7 P.M. **M-Th** and 9 A.M.-12 P.M. **F.**

6. What career and placement services are available to adult students? **Students are counseled by academic advisors.**

7. What characteristics of the institution's adult degree programs are most appealing to students? **Accelerated program, personal nature, small classes—15-25 students.**

Concord College

P.O. Box 1000 ◆ **Athens, WV 24712**

Phone: (304) 384-5248 ◆ Toll-free phone: (800) 344-6679
Fax: (304) 384-9044 ◆ E-mail: admjb@ccvms.wvnet.edu

Founded: 1872

Accredited by: North Central

Enrollment: 2,631 ◆ Adult students: 23 percent

University status: Public

Degree	Concentration/Major	Format
B.S.	Business	E

Campus Extension Site

Beckley Center, WV

Requirements

Residency requirement: Students must do 36 semester hours of resident work for any bachelor's degree.
Undergraduate admissions requirements: English—4 units, social studies—3, higher math—2, lab science—2, foreign language—2 recommended; ACT or SAT. Students out of high school five years or more may take the ASSET.
Graduation requirements (undergraduate): 128 semester hours. Some departments require a minimum GPA of 2.5.

Fees, Tuition, Costs

Undergraduate tuition: $2,150
Undergraduate cost of books: $400/year

Financial Aid/Status

Scholarship programs for adults: Ten $250 scholarships are offered to students at the Beckley Center.
Full-time status: Students must carry 12 semester hours to be considered full-time.
Percentage of adult students receiving financial aid: 90 percent.

Maximum Hours Awarded For

CLEP: 64
PEP: Yes
DANTES: Yes
Other exams: Yes
Prior learning portfolio: Yes
Additional information: Advanced Placement Exam credits

Features and Services

1. How do students taking extended classes access library resources? **Students may visit the library on campus.**

2. What is the registration and payment process for adult students? **Registration and payment are the same as for traditional students.**

3. What is the process for advising adult students?

Advising is the same as for traditional students.

4. What career and placement services are available to adult students? **Students register** by completing a form and submitting their resume. Interviews are then scheduled.

5. What characteristics of the institution's adult degree programs are most appealing to students? **Evening classes for adults in business at Beckley Center.**

Concordia University

7400 Augusta Street ◆ **River Forest, IL 60305**
Phone: (708) 209-3269 ◆ Fax: (708) 209-3176
Web address: http://www.cuis.edu.www/curf/home.html

Founded: 1913

Accredited by: North Central

Adult students: 110

University status: Private, Church, Lutheran Church-Missouri Synod

---

Degree	Concentration/Major	Format
B.A.	Organizational Management	A

Campus Extension Site
Rockford, IL

Requirements
Residency requirement: Students are not required to attend classes on the main campus to graduate. Undergraduate admissions requirements: Admission application and fee, all official transcripts, 25 years or older. (Admission committee may make exceptions.) Graduation requirements (undergraduate): 48 hours in major plus 140 quarter hours—total 188 hours. Normally, 100 hours are transferred from other schools. Complete senior project; 2.0 GPA.

Fees, Tuition, Costs
Undergraduate application fee: $25
Undergraduate tuition: $206/quarter hour
Undergraduate cost of books: Provided in adult program

Financial Aid/Status
Percentage of adult students receiving financial aid: 50 percent

Maximum Hours Awarded For
CLEP: Yes
DANTES: Yes
Prior learning portfolio: Yes

Features and Services

1. Is it possible to purchase books during hours most adult students attend classes? **Yes.**

2. Are the institution's administrative offices open during hours adult students attend class? **Yes.**

3. How do students taking extended classes access library resources? **The library is open most evenings.**

4. What is the registration and payment process for adult students? **Students are asked to attend a two-hour registration on campus prior to starting the program.**

5. What is the process for advising adult students? **An academic advisor is on staff to work just with adult learners.**

6. What career and placement services are available to adult students? **The university placement office is available for adult students.**

7. What characteristics of the institution's adult degree programs are most appealing to students? **High level of personal interest and friendly service.**

Concordia University Wisconsin

8465 Keystone Crossing, Suite 195 ◆ Indianapolis, IN 46240
Phone: (317) 259-5090 ◆ Fax: (317) 259-5095

Founded: 1881

Accredited by: North Central

Enrollment: 80 ◆ Adult students: 100 percent

University status: Private, Church,
Lutheran Church-Missouri Synod

Degree	Concentration/Major	Format
A.A.	Management and Communication	E,A,C
B.A.	Management and Communication	E,A,C
M.A.	20 Independent Master's Degrees	C,T

Campus Extension Sites

Mequon, WI
Kenosha, WI
Madison, WI
Indianapolis, IN
Fort Wayne, IN
St. Louis, MO
New Orleans, LA

Requirements

Residency requirement: Students do not have to attend classes on the main campus to graduate. Undergraduate admissions requirements: Three years of work experience and a high school diploma or GED are the minimum requirements for admission. Graduate admissions requirements: Requirements include a bachelor's degree from a regionally accredited institution with 2.75 GPA and approval of the Admissions Committee. Graduation requirements (undergraduate): A.A.—48 credits major; 3 esthetic, 3 empiric, 10 electives (64 total credits); B.A.—48 credits major; 27 core; 53 electives (128 total credits). Graduation requirements (graduate): A minimum of 36 credits must be earned, depending on the area of study.

Fees, Tuition, Costs

Undergraduate application fee: $25
Graduate application fee: $50
Undergraduate tuition: $195/credit
Graduate tuition: $300/credit
Undergraduate cost of books: Included in tuition
Graduate cost of books: Included in tuition
Other costs: Computer for e-mail access to professor for Independent Studies with master's degree

Financial Aid/Status

Full-time status: Full-time students in the accelerated program attend one night a week and earn three credits every four weeks.

Percentage of adult students receiving financial aid: 10 percent.

Maximum Hours Awarded For

CLEP: Yes
DANTES: Yes
Other exams: Yes
Prior learning portfolio: Yes
Additional information: Work/life experience possibly awarded up to 10 credits toward A.A.; up to 20 toward B.A.

Features and Services

1. Are the institution's administrative offices open during hours adult students attend class? **Yes.**

2. How do students taking extended classes access library resources? **Students may use local libraries with a Concordia I.D. card.**

3. What is the registration and payment process for adult students? **Students register for the major when they apply. Payment is made by mail to the main campus.**

4. What characteristics of the institution's adult degree programs are most appealing to students? **One night a week (four hours), accelerated courses, 12:1 ratio in class, seminar atmosphere.**

Concordia University at Austin

3400 IH35 North ◆ **Austin, TX 78705-2799**
Phone: (512) 452-7662 ◆ Fax: (512) 459-8517
E-mail: ctxdegcomp@crf.cuis.edu

Founded: 1926

Accredited by: Southern Association

Enrollment: 700 ◆ Adult students: 30 percent

University status: Private, Church,
Lutheran Church-Missouri Synod

Degree	Concentration/Major	Format
B.A.	Business Management	E,A,TH

Requirements

Residency requirement: Students must attend classes on the main campus.
Undergraduate admissions requirements: High school diploma or GED, official transcripts from any previous colleges attended, SAT or ACT; not required from students graduating from high school five years or more before application.
Graduation requirements (undergraduate): Graduation requires 128 hours, with 30 hours in residence, 39 hours upper-level courses, and 59 hours of core curriculum.

Fees, Tuition, Costs

Undergraduate application fee: $25
Undergraduate tuition: $9,750 for 40 hours, 13 modules, including books

Financial Aid/Status

Scholarship programs for adults: Scholarships are not available.
Full-time status: Full-time students are enrolled for 12 semester hours.
Percentage of adult students receiving financial aid: 85 percent.

Maximum Hours Awarded For

CLEP: Yes
PEP: Yes
DANTES: Yes
Prior learning portfolio: 18
Additional information: A total of 30 credits possible combining CLEP, PEP, and DANTES

Features and Services

1. Is it possible to purchase books during hours most adult students attend classes? **Yes.**

2. Are the institution's administrative offices open during hours adult students attend class? **Yes.**

3. How do students taking extended classes access library resources? **The library has extended hours.**

4. What is the registration and payment process for adult students? **Payment may be made by check or credit card.**

5. What is the process for advising adult students? **Students meet with the program director for advising.**

6. What characteristics of the institution's adult degree programs are most appealing to students? **Accelerated evening classes.**

Cornerstone College

1001 E. Beltline N.E. ◆ **Grand Rapids, MI 49505**
Phone: (616) 285-9448 ◆ Toll-free phone: (800) 9-GRADUATE
Fax: (616) 285-1528 ◆ E-mail: ACE@cornerstone.edu
Web address: http://www.grfn.org/~cstone

Founded: 1941

Accredited by: North Central

Enrollment: 1,000 ◆ Adult students: 20 percent

University status: Private, Church, Baptist

Degree	Concentration/Major	Format
B.A.	Organizational Leadership	E,A

Requirements

Residency requirement: All classes are currently held on campus. Students must meet an academic residency requirement to graduate. Undergraduate admissions requirements: Application, writing/essay, high school diploma or GED, interview, 60 semester hours of transferable prior college-level credit.
Graduation requirements (undergraduate): Completion of 120 semester hours, including 30 hours of general education, 30 hours of academic residency, and a maximum of 30 credits for portfolio credit. A 2.5 GPA in major area; 2.0 overall.

Fees, Tuition, Costs

Undergraduate application fee: $25
Undergraduate tuition: $7,820 for the program
Undergraduate cost of books: $650
Other costs: Registration fee of $45/semester; graduation fee of $30; prior learning credit: $75/evaluation

Financial Aid/Status

Scholarship programs for adults: Scholarships are not available.
Full-time status: Students enrolled in 12 semester hours/semester are full-time.
Percentage of adult students receiving financial aid: 80 percent.

Maximum Hours Awarded For

CLEP: 30
DANTES: 30
Prior learning portfolio: 30
Additional information: A maximum of 30 credits from a combination of all testing

Features and Services

1. Is it possible to purchase books during hours most adult students attend classes? **Yes.**

2. What is the registration and payment process for adult students? **Register the first class night. Payment is made on or before the class or other arrangements.**

3. What is the process for advising adult students? **Assessment advisors help students form an education plan. Track student up to six months after program**

4. What career and placement services are available to adult students? **Students are offered testing and assessment, resume writing, "how to" seminars, and job placement.**

5. What characteristics of the institution's adult degree programs are most appealing to students? **Location, evening/weekend class hours, the accelerated format.**

Covenant College

Quest Program

409 Chestnut Street, Suite A-110 ◆ **Chattanooga, TN 37402**

Phone: (423) 265-7784 ◆ Fax: (423) 265-2703

Founded: 1955

Accredited by: Southern Association

Enrollment: 700 ◆ Adult students: 20 percent

University status: Private, Church, Presbyterian Church in America

Degree	Concentration/Major	Format
B.S.	Organizational Management	E,A
M.Ed.	Integrated Curriculum and Instruction	E
M.Ed.	Administration and Supervision	E

Campus Extension Sites

Chattanooga, TN
Cleveland, TN
Fort Oglethorpe, GA
Dalton, GA

Requirements

Residency requirement: Students must attend a library night as part of the research module on campus. Undergraduate admissions requirements: The degree completion program, Quest, requirements include 60 semester hours (30 in core requirements), five years of work/volunteer experience, writing sample. Graduate admissions requirements: The master's education program requires B.S./B.A., two years of teaching, GRE, currently teaching or have access to school situation, writing sample, credible written profession of faith. Graduation requirements (undergraduate): Graduation requires 126 semester hours with C- or better in ALL courses and completion of ALL requirements—i.e., Portfolio, Research, and ALL core courses. Graduation requirements (graduate): Graduation requires 30 semester hours and passing comprehensive exams.

Fees, Tuition, Costs

Undergraduate application fee: $20
Graduate application fee: $35
Undergraduate tuition: $6,990/program
Graduate tuition: $202/hour
Undergraduate cost of books: $350/Quest
Graduate cost of books: $210/course
Other costs: Experiential Learning Component billed at $20/semester hour

Financial Aid/Status

Scholarship programs for adults: Students may apply for $1,000 scholarship awarded for academics, completing the most hours toward graduation, and the highest GPA. Full-time status: 20 hours seat time/course—9 courses and a research module.
Percentage of adult students receiving financial aid: 40 percent.

Maximum Hours Awarded For

CLEP: 30
Additional information: Up to 31 semester hours possibly earned after completing the portfolio development course

Features and Services

1. Is it possible to purchase books during hours most adult students attend classes? **Yes.**

2. Are the institution's administrative offices open during hours adult students attend class? **Yes.**

3. How do students taking extended classes access library resources? **Students may access the library with the assistant librarian or through ERIC.**

4. What is the registration and payment process for adult students? **Registration in class ($75 fee). Carry account at 14 percent/year. Pay first semester by end of semester.**

5. What career and placement services are available to adult students? **Career Development Office is available to all students.**

6. What characteristics of the institution's adult degree programs are most appealing to students? **The program is designed to last 14 months and meets one night a week for four hours.**

Creighton University

2500 California Plaza ◆ Omaha, NE 68178
Phone: (402) 280-2424 ◆ Toll-free phone: (800) 637-4279
Fax: (402) 280-2423 ◆ E-mail: ddaly@creighton.edu
Web address: http://www.creighton.edu

Founded: 1878

Accredited by: North Central

Enrollment: 6,000 ◆ Adult students: 9 percent

University status: Private, Church, Roman Catholic Church

Degree	Concentration/Major	Format
A.S.	Applied Computer Science	E
A.A.	Ministry	E
A.A.	Journalism/Public Relations	E
A.S.	Computer Science	E
A.S.	Emergency Medical Studies	E
A.A.	Organizational Communication	E
A.A.	Spirituality	E
A.A.	Theology	E
A.S.	Mathematics	E
B.S.	Applied Computer Science	E
B.S.	Atmospheric Science	E
B.S.	Computer Science	E
B.S.	Emergency Medical Studies	E
B.A.	Journalism/Public Relations	E
B.S.	Management	E
B.A.	Organizational Communication	E
B.A.	Physics/Nuclear Industrial Operations	E
B.A.	Psychology	E

Campus Extension Site

A certificate in Applied Computer Science can be offered at businesses willing to participate in the program.

Requirements

Residency requirement: Students must attend classes on campus. Undergraduate admissions requirements: Students must submit proof of high school graduation or GED and complete an admission application. Graduation requirements (undergraduate): Graduation requires 128 credit hours with the last 48 hours in residence at Creighton and be 300 level or above.

Fees, Tuition, Costs

Undergraduate application fee: $30
Undergraduate tuition: $232/6 hours; $348/more
Undergraduate cost of books: $650/year full-time

Financial Aid/Status

Scholarship programs for adults: Dean's Merit Scholarship ($100-$500)—must demonstrate financial need and be enrolled in University College.
Full-time status: Students enrolled 12 semester hours are full-time. Students can qualify as half-time (6 or more).
Percentage of adult students receiving financial aid: 80 percent.

Maximum Hours Awarded For

CLEP: Yes

Features and Services

1. Is it possible to purchase books during hours most adult students attend classes? **Yes.**

2. Are the institution's administrative offices open during hours adult students attend class? **Yes.**

3. What is the registration and payment process for adult students? **Tuition is due two weeks after class starts, or student may make monthly installment arrangements.**

4. What is the process for advising adult students? **Adult students meet one-on-one with an advisor each semester to assess progress and course schedule.**

5. What career and placement services are available to adult students? **Students have access to the Centralized Career Services Office on campus.**

6. What characteristics of the institution's adult degree programs are most appealing to students? **Smaller classes, excellent reputation, and individualized attention.**

Dakota Wesleyan University

1200 W. University ◆ **Mitchell, SD 57301**
Phone: (605) 995-2950 ◆ Toll-free phone: (800) 333-8506
Fax: (605) 995-2892 ◆ E-mail: tmorgan@cc.dwu.edu
Web address: http://www.dwu.edu

Founded: 1885

Accredited by: North Central

Enrollment: 700 ◆ Adult students: 128

University status: Private, Church, United Methodist Church

Degree	Concentration/Major	Format
A.A.	General Studies	E
A.A.	Criminal Justice	E
B.A.	Human Resource Management	E
B.A.	Health Service Administration	E

Requirements

Residency requirement: Students must attend classes on the main campus.
Undergraduate admissions requirements: Students must submit official high school (2.0 GPA) or college transcripts, and official certification of ACT results.
Graduation requirements (undergraduate): Students graduating with the A.A. degree must have 105 credit hours; B.A.,179 credits.

Fees, Tuition, Costs

Undergraduate application fee: $15
Undergraduate tuition: $8,475
Undergraduate cost of books: $300-$400
Other costs: Nursing program: lab fees

Financial Aid/Status

Scholarship programs for adults: Scholarships (up to $1,000) are available. Applicants must submit resume, provide two letters of recommendation, and have an interview.

Maximum Hours Awarded For

CLEP: Yes
Other exams: Yes
Prior learning portfolio: Yes
Additional information: Maximum of 63 credits of undergraduate work

Features and Services

1. What is the registration and payment process for adult students? **Students register any time after open date. Phone registration is available. Finalize in two to three weeks.**

2. What is the process for advising adult students? **The Academic Advising Office assigns advisors to adult students.**

3. What career and placement services are available to adult students? **Students use career/academic placement and planning services located in the Campus Life Department.**

4. What characteristics of the institution's adult degree programs are most appealing to students? **Flexibility.**

Dallas Baptist University

3000 Mountain Creek Parkway ◆ **Dallas, TX 75211-9299**
Phone: (214) 333-5337 ◆ Toll-free phone: (800) 460-8188
Fax: (214) 333-5558 ◆ E-mail: caed@dbu.edu
Web address: http://www.dbu.edu

Founded: 1965

Accredited by: Southern Association

Enrollment: 3,100 ◆ Adult students: 1,500

University status: Private, Church, Southern Baptist

Degree	Concentration/Major	Format
B.A.A.S.	Art	E
B.A.A.S.	Criminal Justice	E
B.A.A.S.	Interdisciplinary Studies	E
B.A.A.S.	Christian Ministries	E
B.A.A.S.	Psychology	E
B.A.A.S.	Social Services	E
B.A.B.A.	Accounting	E
B.A.B.A.	Business Administration	E
B.A.B.A.	Finance	E
B.A.B.A.	Management	E
B.A.B.A.	MIS	E
B.A.B.A.	Marketing	E
B.A.B.A.	Public Administration	E
M.B.A.	Management	E
M.B.A.	Marketing	E
M.B.A.	Finance	E
M.B.A.	International Business	E
M.B.A.	MIS	E
M.A.	Organizational Management	E
M.A.	Counseling	E
M.A.	Biblical Studies	E
M.Ed.	Higher Education	E
M.L.A.	Liberal Arts	E

Requirements

Residency requirement: If needed courses are offered at extension locations, campus classes are not required. In most cases, students will need some courses offered at the campus.
Undergraduate admissions requirements: Applied Studies Degree Program: at least four years of work experience. For maximum benefit from Academic Portfolio, person should be at least 25.
Graduate admissions requirements: Students submit an application, a statement of purpose, recommendation letters, and official transcripts. A 3.0 GPA and acceptable GMAT/GRE score are needed.
Graduation requirements (graduate): Students must complete 36-54 hours depending on the program. A final project is required. There is no thesis requirement.

Fees, Tuition, Costs

Undergraduate application fee: $25
Graduate application fee: $25
Undergraduate tuition: $238/credit hour
Graduate tuition: $248/credit hour
Undergraduate cost of books: $40/course
Graduate cost of books: $40/course
Other costs: Portfolio processing fees of $250 ($125 each)

Financial Aid/Status

Scholarship programs for adults: Available scholarships vary in requirements and amounts.
Full-time status: Full-time students are enrolled in 12 credit hours in Fall and Spring, 9 hours in the Summer.
Percentage of adult students receiving financial aid: 85 percent.

Maximum Hours Awarded For

CLEP: Yes
DANTES: Yes
Prior learning portfolio: 30
Additional information: PONSI evaluation of corporate and government training programs

Features and Services

1. Is it possible to purchase books during hours most adult students attend classes? **Yes.**

2. Are the institution's administrative offices open during hours adult students attend class? **Yes.**

3. How do students taking extended classes access library resources? **Students may visit the campus library or use a local library with Alliance for Higher Education card.**

4. What is the registration and payment process for adult students? **Student fills out form with Adult Education counselor. Student goes to registrar and business office.**

5. What is the process for advising adult students? **Student meets with academic advisor to review degree plan, consult transcripts, and course schedule.**

6. What career and placement services are available to adult students? **A placement officer is available. The**

college is a member of the Students' Work Consortium.

7. What characteristics of the institution's adult degree programs are most appealing to students? **The opportunity to earn up to 30 hours for prior learning; convenient class times and locations.**

Daniel Webster College

20 University Drive ◆ Office of Continuing Education
Nashua, NH 03063-1300
Phone: (603) 577-6506 ◆ Fax: (603) 577-6001
Web address: http://www.dwc.edu/dwc.htm/

Founded: 1965

Accredited by: New England

Enrollment: 1,000 ◆ Adult students: 50

University status: Private

Degree	Concentration/Major	Format
A.S.	Accounting	E,A
A.S.	Aeronautical Engineering	E,A
A.S.	Business Management	E,A
A.S.	Information Systems	E,A
A.S.	Engineering Sciences	E,A
A.S.	General Studies	E,A
A.S.	Marketing	E,A
B.S.	Organizational Management	A
B.S.	Computer Science	E,A
B.S.	Business Management	E,A
B.S.	Information Systems	E,A
B.S.	Accounting	E,A

Requirements

Residency requirement: At the present time students must attend classes on campus. Satellite campuses and distance learning programs are being developed.

Undergraduate admissions requirements: Degree completion program (DCP)—25 years or older, five years of work experience, 60 transferable semester hours including English composition and math, a writing sample, interview. Open admission is used in the evening program.
Graduation requirements (undergraduate): The requirements depend on the specific major of the individual.

Fees, Tuition, Costs

Undergraduate application fee: $30
Undergraduate tuition: $160-$207/credit
Undergraduate cost of books: $300/DCP; varies for evening programs
Other costs: Lab fees; cost for portfolio evaluation

Maximum Hours Awarded For

CLEP: Yes
DANTES: Yes
Other exams: Yes
Prior learning portfolio: Yes
Additional information: Maximum of 30 credits for all tests and credit for prior learning, including Advanced Placement Exams

Features and Services

1. Is it possible to purchase books during hours most adult students attend classes? **Yes.**

2. Are the institution's administrative offices open during hours adult students attend class? **Yes.**

3. What is the registration and payment process for adult students? **Payment may be** made by cash, check, credit card, and payment plans.

4. What is the process for advising adult students? **Advisors available noon-8:30 P.M. M-Th. Hours are more limited on Friday and Saturday.**

5. What career and placement services are available to adult students? **The Student Career** Placement Office is available to assist students and alumni.

6. What characteristics of the institution's adult degree programs are most appealing to students? **Terms of 8 and 16 weeks; Degree Completion Program uses a 4-5 week module, cohort-based program, interactive format, small seminar fashion, relevant major, and accelerated classes.**

Defiance College

701 North Clinton Street ◆ **Defiance, OH 43512**

Phone: (419) 783-2350 ◆ Toll-free phone: (800) 520-GODC

Fax: (419) 784-0426

Founded: 1850

Accredited by: North Central

Enrollment: 856 ◆ Adult students: 46 percent

University status: Private, Church, United Church of Christ

Degree	Concentration/Major	Format
A.A.	Business Administration	E
B.S.	Business Administration	E
B.S.	Business Management	E
B.S.	Accounting	E

Requirements

Undergraduate admissions requirements: Student accepted in good standing with GPA of 2.0 or higher. Accepted conditionally: students with poor high school record or transfer students with a GPA of 2.0 or below are limited to one class.

Graduate admissions requirements: Bachelor's degree, GPA of 2.5 or more, valid teaching license, three letters of recommendation, GRE or MAT test scores.

Graduation requirements (undergraduate): Complete 120 semester hours including general education and major requirements, 26 credits from courses above 300 level, financial obligations met, GPA of 2.0 or better.

Graduation requirements (graduate): Complete 23-36 semester hours including final project, thesis, or exam with GPA of 3.0 or better, maintain portfolio, complete degree in six years, admission to candidacy for degree, file graduation application.

Fees, Tuition, Costs

Undergraduate application fee: $25
Graduate application fee: $25
Undergraduate tuition: $245/credit hour
Graduate tuition: $245/credit hour
Undergraduate cost of books: $500-$600 full-time
Graduate cost of books: $300-$400 full-time
Other costs: Library binding fee (research project or thesis) of $25; graduation fee

Financial Aid/Status

Scholarship programs for adults: Various scholarships are available. Students must meet high school requirements. Transfer students must have 15 credits with 3.0 GPA.

Full-time status: Students enrolled in 12 credit hours are full-time.

Percentage of adult students receiving financial aid: 40 percent.

Maximum Hours Awarded For

CLEP: Yes
DANTES: Yes

Other exams: Yes
Prior learning portfolio: Yes
Additional information: Students may be awarded 30 hours total of testing and 4 hours for work experience.

Features and Services

1. Is it possible to purchase books during hours most adult students attend classes? **Yes.**

2. What is the registration and payment process for adult students? **Adult students are permitted to schedule and pay until the first day of classes.**

3. What is the process for advising adult students? **Each adult student is assigned an advisor.**

4. What career and placement services are available to adult students? **Career planning, resume writing, job leads, and graduate school information are available.**

5. What characteristics of the institution's adult degree programs are most appealing to students? **Every other weekend format of classes.**

DePaul University*

1 East Jackson ◆ **Chicago, IL 60604**
Toll-free phone: (800)4-DEPAUL ◆ Fax: (800)362-5745
Web address: http://www.depaul.edu

Founded: 1898

Accredited by: North Central

Enrollment: 16,747 ◆ Adult students: 1,981

University status: Private, Church, Roman Catholic Church

Degree	Concentration/Major	Format
B.S.	Accounting	E
B.S.	Computer Science	E
B.S.	Marketing	E
B.A.	A variety of majors are available through the School for New Learning	E
M.B.A.	Accounting	E
M.S.	Computer Science	E

Requirements

Residency requirement: Yes. Undergraduate admissions requirements: 24 years or older. Transfer students must be in good standing at their previous school and have at least 12 hours of transferable credit and GPA required for program. Special student and student-at-large status possible. Graduate admissions requirements: Bachelor's degree from regionally accredited institution and must demonstrate evidence of achievement in studies sufficient to satisfy requirements for entering a specific program. GRE required for some programs. Nondegree status possible.

Fees, Tuition, Costs

Undergraduate application fee: $25
Graduate application fee: $25
Undergraduate tuition: $11,214/ program
Graduate tuition: Varies by program

Financial Aid/Status

Full-time status: 12 or more credit hours/quarter
Percentage of adult students receiving financial aid: 50 percent

Features and Services

1. Is it possible to purchase books during hours most adult students attend classes? **Yes**

2. Are the institution's administrative offices open during hours adult students attend class? **Yes**

3. What characteristics of the institution's adult degree programs are most appealing to students? **DePaul's academic standing, multi-campus locations (five extension campuses), evening and weekend class availability, and small class size.**

DeVry Institute

250 N Arcadia ◆ **Decatur, GA 30030**
Phone: (404) 292-2645 ◆ Toll-free phone: (800) 221-4771
Fax: (404) 292-2248

Founded: 1969

Accredited by: North Central

Enrollment: 2,971 ◆ Adult students: 49 percent

University status: Private, Profit

Degree	Concentration/Major	Format
A.S.	Electronic Technology	E
B.A.	Accounting	E
B.A.	Business Operations	E
B.A.	Computer Information Systems	E
B.A.	Telecommunications Management	E
B.A.	Technical Management	E

Requirements

Residency requirement: Students must attend classes on campus. Undergraduate admissions requirements: Students must be 17, have a high school diploma or GED, and submit ACT or SAT scores or take placement tests administered by DeVry. Graduation requirements (undergraduate): Students must meet curriculum requirements, 2.0 GPA, meet financial obligations, and complete 35 percent of credits at DeVry.

Fees, Tuition, Costs

Undergraduate application fee: $25
Undergraduate tuition: $6,560/year
Undergraduate cost of books: $560/year
Other costs: Transportation and personal expenses

Financial Aid/Status

Scholarship programs for adults: Scholarships are available for students.
Full-time status: Students enrolled as regular students in eligible programs are full-time.

Maximum Hours Awarded For

CLEP: 24
DANTES: 24

Features and Services

1. Is it possible to purchase books during hours most adult students attend classes? **Yes.**

2. Are the institution's administrative offices open during hours adult students attend class? **Yes.**

3. How do students taking extended classes access library resources? **The learning resource center is available to students.**

4. What is the registration and payment process for adult students? **Payment may be made using financial aid, employer reimbursement, and DeVry's payment plan—Educard.**

5. What is the process for advising adult students? **Advisors meet with new students and throughout the program.**

6. What career and placement services are available to adult students? **DeVry has a very active and professional career service office.**

7. What characteristics of the institution's adult degree programs are most appealing to students? **High placement rate; evening and weekend hours.**

DeVry Institute of Technology

3300 N. Campbell Avenue ◆ **Chicago, IL 60618-5994**
Phone: (312) 929-6550 ◆ Toll-free phone: (800) 383-3879
Fax: (312) 348-1780

Founded: 1931

Accredited by: North Central

Enrollment: 2,915 ◆ Adult students: 47 percent

University status: Private, Profit

Degree	Concentration/Major	Format
A.S.	Electronic Technology	E,A
B.A.	Accounting	E,A
B.A.	Business Operations	E,A
B.A.	Computer Information Systems	E,A
B.A.	Electronic Engineering Technology	E,A
B.A.	Technical Management	E,A

Requirements

Residency requirement: Students must attend classes on this campus. Undergraduate admissions requirements: Students must have a high school diploma or GED, provide ACT or SAT scores, or take DeVry placement tests. Graduation requirements (undergraduate): Students must complete curriculum requirements, 2.0 GPA, meet financial obligations, complete 35 percent of credits at DeVry.
Undergraduate application fee: $25
Undergraduate tuition: $6,560/year
Undergraduate cost of books: $560/year
Other costs: Transportation and personal expenses

Financial Aid/Status

Scholarship programs for adults: Scholarships are available.
Full-time status: Students enrolled as regular students are full-time.

Maximum Hours Awarded For

CLEP: 24
DANTES: 24

Features and Services

1. Is it possible to purchase books during hours most adult students attend classes? **Yes.**

2. Are the institution's administrative offices open during hours adult students attend class? **Yes.**

3. How do students taking extended classes access library resources? **The learning resource center is available to all students.**

4. What is the registration and payment process for adult students? **Payment may be arranged using financial aid, employer reimbursement, and DeVry's Educard Plan.**

5. What is the process for advising adult students? **Advisors are available through the admissions office for new students and throughout the program.**

6. What career and placement services are available to adult students? **An active professional staff is available.**

7. What characteristics of the institution's adult degree programs are most appealing to students? **High placement rate, evening and weekend classes.**

DeVry Institute of Technology

1350 Alum Creek Drive ◆ Columbus, OH 43209-2705
Phone: (614) 253-1525 ◆ Toll-free phone: (800) 426-2206
Fax: (614) 252-4108
Web address: http://www.devrycols.edu

Founded: 1952

Accredited by: North Central

Enrollment: 2,585 ◆ Adult students: 45 percent

University status: Private, Profit

Degree	Concentration/Major	Format
A.S.	Electronic Technology	E
B.A.	Accounting	E
B.A.	Business Operations	E
B.A.	Computer Information Systems	E
B.A.	Electronic Engineering Technology	E

Requirements

Residency requirement: Students must attend classes at this campus to graduate.
Undergraduate admissions requirements: Students must be 17, have a high school diploma or GED, and provide ACT or SAT scores or take DeVry placement tests.
Graduation requirements (undergraduate): Students must complete curriculum requirements, 2.0 GPA, meet financial obligations, and complete 35 percent of credits at DeVry.

Fees, Tuition, Costs

Undergraduate application fee: $25
Undergraduate tuition: $6,560/yr
Undergraduate cost of books: $560/yr
Other costs: Transportation and personal expenses

Financial Aid/Status

Scholarship programs for adults: Students may apply for scholarships.
Full-time status: Full-time students are enrolled as regular students in eligible programs.

Maximum Hours Awarded For

CLEP: 24
DANTES: 24

Features and Services

1. Is it possible to purchase books during hours most adult students attend classes? **Yes.**

2. Are the institution's administrative offices open during hours adult students attend class? **Yes.**

3. How do students taking extended classes access library resources? **The learning resource center is available to students.**

4. What is the registration and payment process for adult students? **Students may use payment plans, such as employer reimbursement, Educard Plan, or financial aid.**

5. What is the process for advising adult students? **Advisors are available at the institute.**

6. What career and placement services are available to adult students? **The professional staff aids students in finding employment.**

7. What characteristics of the institution's adult degree programs are most appealing to students? **High placement rate and weekend and evening hours.**

DeVry Institute of Technology

4801 Regent Blvd. ◆ Irving, TX 75063-2440
Phone: (214) 929-5777 ◆ Toll-free phone: (800) 633-3879
Fax: (214) 929-6778

Founded: 1969

Accredited by: North Central

Enrollment: 2,315 ◆ Adult students: 55 percent

University status: Private, Profit

Degree	Concentration/Major	Format
A.S.	Electronic Technology	E
B.A.	Accounting	E
B.A.	Business Operations	E
B.A.	Computer Information Systems	E
B.A.	Technical Management	E

Requirements

Residency requirement: Students must attend classes on campus. Undergraduate admissions requirements: Students must be high school graduates or have a GED. ACT or SAT scores must be submitted, or placement tests will administered by DeVry. Graduation requirements (undergraduate): Students must complete curriculum requirements, GPA 2.0, meet financial obligation, complete 35 percent of credits at DeVry.

Fees, Tuition, Costs

Undergraduate application fee: $25
Undergraduate tuition: $6,560/year
Undergraduate cost of books: $560/year
Other costs: Transportation and personal expenses

Financial Aid/Status

Scholarship programs for adults: Students may apply for scholarships.
Full-time status: Regular students enrolled in eligible programs qualify.

Maximum Hours Awarded For

CLEP: 24
DANTES: 24

Features and Services

1. Is it possible to purchase books during hours most adult students attend classes? **Yes.**

2. Are the institution's administrative offices open during hours adult students attend class? **Yes.**

3. How do students taking extended classes access library resources? **The learning resource center is available for students.**

4. What is the registration and payment process for adult students? **Payment may be made using financial aid, employer reimbursement, and the Educard Plan.**

5. What is the process for advising adult students? **Advising is done through the admissions office for new students. Advising is available at all times.**

6. What career and placement services are available to adult students? **DeVry has a professional, active career service office.**

7. What characteristics of the institution's adult degree programs are most appealing to students? **High placement rate; evening and weekend hours.**

DeVry Institute of Technology

11224 Holmes Road ◆ **Kansas City, MO 64131**
Phone: (816) 941-0430 ◆ Toll-free phone: (800) 821-3766
Fax: (816) 941-0896

Founded: 1931

Accredited by: North Central

Enrollment: 1,965 ◆ Adult students: 50 percent

University status: Private, Profit

Degree	Concentration/Major	Format
A.S.	Electronic Technology	E
B.A.	Computer Information Systems	E
B.A.	Telecommunication Management	E
B.A.	Technical Management	E

Requirements

Residency requirement: Students must attend classes on campus. Undergraduate admissions requirements: Students must be high school graduates or have a GED. ACT or SAT scores must be submitted, or DeVry placement tests will be given. Graduation requirements (undergraduate): 2.0 GPA, complete all curriculum requirements, meet financial obligations, complete 35 percent of credit at DeVry.

Fees, Tuition, Costs

Undergraduate application fee: $25
Undergraduate tuition: $6,560/year
Undergraduate cost of books: $560/year
Other costs: Transportation and personal expenses

Financial Aid/Status

Scholarship programs for adults: Students may apply for scholarships.
Full-time status: Regular students enrolled in eligible programs qualify.

Maximum Hours Awarded For

CLEP: 24
DANTES: 24

Features and Services

1. Is it possible to purchase books during hours most adult students attend classes? **Yes.**

2. Are the institution's administrative offices open during hours adult students attend class? **Yes.**

3. How do students taking extended classes access library resources? **Students may use the learning resource center.**

4. What is the registration and payment process for adult students? **Students pay using Educard payment plan, employer reimbursement, and financial aid.**

5. What is the process for advising adult students? **Advising is done through the admissions office.**

6. What career and placement services are available to adult students? **A professional, active career service office is available.**

7. What characteristics of the institution's adult degree programs are most appealing to students? **High rate of placement, evening and weekend hours.**

DeVry Institute of Technology

3880 Kilroy Airport Way ◆ **Long Beach, CA 90806**
Phone: (310) 427-0861 ◆ Fax: (310) 426-6943

Founded: 1994

Accredited by: North Central

Enrollment: 971

University status: Private, Profit

Degree	Concentration/Major	Format
A.S.	Electronic Technology	E
B.A.	Computer Information Systems	E
B.A.	Telecommunications Management	E

Requirements

Residency requirement: Students must attend classes on campus. Undergraduate admissions requirements: Students must have a high school diploma or GED, submit ACT or SAT scores, or take DeVry placement tests. Graduation requirements (undergraduate): Students must complete all curriculum requirements, have a minimun GPA of 2.0, meet financial obligations, and complete 35 percent of credits at DeVry.

Fees, Tuition, Costs

Undergraduate application fee: $25
Undergraduate tuition: $6,560/year
Undergraduate cost of books: $560/year
Other costs: Transportation and personal expenses

Financial Aid/Status

Scholarship programs for adults: Scholarships are available.
Full-time status: Regular students enrolled in eligible programs qualify.

Maximum Hours Awarded For

CLEP: 24
DANTES: 24

Features and Services

1. Is it possible to purchase books during hours most adult students attend classes? **Yes.**

2. Are the institution's administrative offices open during hours adult students attend class? **Yes.**

3. How do students taking extended classes access library resources? **Students may use the learning resource center.**

4. What is the registration and payment process for adult students? **Payment may be made using employer reimbursement, financial aid, and Educard payment plan.**

5. What is the process for advising adult students? **Advising is available through the admissions office.**

6. What career and placement services are available to adult students? **A very active career service office is available.**

7. What characteristics of the institution's adult degree programs are most appealing to students? **High placement rate, evening and weekend hours.**

DeVry Institute of Technology

1221 N. Swift Road ◆ **Addison, IL 60126**

Phone: (630) 953-1300 ◆ Toll-free phone: (800) 323-2450

Fax: (630) 953-1236 ◆ E-mail: edwards@dupagedevry.edu

Founded: 1930

Accredited by: North Central

Enrollment: 3,100 ◆ Adult students: 33 percent

University status: Private, Profit

Degree	Concentration/Major	Format
A.A.S.	Electronics	E
B.S.	Computer Information Systems	E
B.S.	Telecommunications Management	E
B.S.	Technical Management (requires A.A.S. degree)	E

Requirements

Residency requirement: Students must currently attend classes at this campus.
Undergraduate admissions requirements: Students must have a high school diploma or GED. A personal interview is required as well as ACT or SAT scores, or take test administered by DeVry.
Graduation requirements (undergraduate): Students must successfully complete the prescribed courses to graduate.

Fees, Tuition, Costs

Undergraduate application fee: $25
Undergraduate tuition: $220/hour
Undergraduate cost of books: $50-$75/course
Other costs: One time parking fee of $45

Financial Aid/Status

Scholarship programs for adults: Scholarships are available to community college graduates (minimum GPA-3.3).
Full-time status: To be eligible for financial aid, students must be enrolled in six credit hours.
Percentage of adult students receiving financial aid: 75 percent.

Maximum Hours Awarded For

Other exams: Yes

Features and Services

1. Is it possible to purchase books during hours most adult students attend classes? **Yes.**

2. Are the institution's administrative offices open during hours adult students attend class? **Yes.**

3. How do students taking extended classes access library resources? **The library is available until 9 P.M. each night.**

4. What is the registration and payment process for adult students? **Tuition can be paid in installments. Arrangements for this depend on several factors.**

5. What is the process for advising adult students? **Students visit the admissions office and then the academic dean.**

6. What career and placement services are available to adult students? **Students are aided in finding jobs by professionals across the country.**

7. What characteristics of the institution's adult degree programs are most appealing to students? **Typically, DeVry students secure employment within six months of graduation.**

DeVry Institute of Technology

One Tower Lane ◆ Oakbrook Terrace, IL 60181
Phone: (708) 571-7700 ◆ Fax: (708) 571-0317
Web address: http:\\www.devry.edu

Founded: 1967

Accredited by: North Central

Enrollment: 2,915 ◆ Adult students: 47 percent

University status: Private, Profit

Degree	Concentration/Major	Format
A.S.	Electronic Technician	E
B.A.	Accounting	E
B.A.	Business Operations	E
B.A.	Computer Information Systems	E
B.A.	Electronic Engineering Technology	E
B.A.	Telecommunications Management	E
B.A.	Technical Management	E

Requirements

Residency requirement: Students attend classes on campus.
Undergraduate admissions requirements: High school graduation or GED; submit ACT or SAT scores, or take placement tests at DeVry.
Graduation requirements (undergraduate): Meet all curriculum requirements, 35 percent of credit taken at DeVry, GPA 2.0, meet all financial obligations.

Fees, Tuition, Costs

Undergraduate application fee: $25
Undergraduate tuition: $6,560/year
Undergraduate cost of books: $560/year
Other costs: Transportation and personal expenses

Financial Aid/Status

Scholarship programs for adults: Scholarships are available.
Full-time status: Regular students enrolled in eligible programs qualify.

Maximum Hours Awarded For

CLEP: 24
DANTES: 24

Features and Services

1. Is it possible to purchase books during hours most adult students attend classes? **Yes.**

2. Are the institution's administrative offices open during hours adult students attend class? **Yes.**

3. How do students taking extended classes access library resources? **Students may use the learning resource center.**

4. What is the registration and payment process for adult students? **Students may pay by using employer reimbursement, financial aid, and DeVry's payment plan—Educard.**

5. What is the process for advising adult students? **Advisors are available in the admissions office.**

6. What career and placement services are available to adult students? **Professional career services are available.**

7. What characteristics of the institution's adult degree programs are most appealing to students? **High placement rate, evening and weekend hours.**

DeVry Institute of Technology

2149 West Dunlap ◆ **Phoenix, AZ 85021-2995**
Phone: (602) 870-9222 ◆ Toll-free phone: (800) 528-0250
Fax: (602) 870-1209

Founded: 1967

Accredited by: North Central

Enrollment: 2,714 ◆ Adult students: 46 percent

University status: Private, Profit

Degree	Concentration/Major	Format
A.S.	Electronic Technology	E
B.A.	Computer Information Systems	E
B.A.	Technical Management	E

Requirements

Residency requirement: Students must attend classes on campus. Undergraduate admissions requirements: Students must have a high school diploma or GED and submit ACT or SAT scores, or take placement tests at DeVry. Graduation requirements (undergraduate): GPA 2.0, complete 35 percent credit at DeVry, complete all curriculum requirements, meet financial obligations.

Fees, Tuition, Costs

Undergraduate application fee: $25
Undergraduate tuition: $6,560/year
Undergraduate cost of books: $560/year
Other costs: Transportation and personal expenses

Financial Aid/Status

Scholarship programs for adults: Scholarships are available.
Full-time status: Regular students enrolled in eligible programs qualify.

Maximum Hours Awarded For

CLEP: 24
DANTES: 24

Features and Services

1. Is it possible to purchase books during hours most adult students attend classes? **Yes.**

2. Are the institution's administrative offices open during hours adult students attend class? **Yes.**

3. How do students taking extended classes access library resources? **The learning resource center is available.**

4. What is the registration and payment process for adult students? **Payments may be made using financial aid, employer reimbursement, and Educard Plan.**

5. What is the process for advising adult students? **The admissions office provides advice to students.**

6. What career and placement services are available to adult students? **The career service office is both active and professional.**

7. What characteristics of the institution's adult degree programs are most appealing to students? **High placement rate; evening and weekend hours.**

DeVry Institute of Technology

901 Corporate Center ◆ **Pomona, CA 91768-2642**
Phone: (909) 622-8866 ◆ Toll-free phone: (800) 882-7536
Fax: (909) 623-5666

Founded: 1983

Accredited by: North Central

Enrollment: 2,988 ◆ Adult students: 48 percent

University status: Private, Profit

Degree	Concentration/Major	Format
A.S.	Electronics Technology	E
B.A.	Accounting	E
B.A.	Computer Information Systems	E
B.A.	Telecommunications Management	E
B.A.	Technical Management	E

Requirements

Residency requirement: Students must attend classes on campus.
Undergraduate admissions requirements: High school diploma or GED; submit ACT or SAT scores or take placement tests at DeVry.
Graduation requirements (undergraduate): Students must complete all curriculum requirements, fulfill financial obligations, complete 35 percent of credit at DeVry, GPA 2.0.

Fees, Tuition, Costs

Undergraduate application fee: $25
Undergraduate tuition: $6,560/year
Undergraduate cost of books: $560/year
Other costs: Transportation and personal expenses

Financial Aid/Status

Scholarship programs for adults: Scholarships are available.
Full-time status: Regular students enrolled in eligible programs qualify.

Maximum Hours Awarded For

CLEP: 24
DANTES: 24

Features and Services

1. Is it possible to purchase books during hours most adult students attend classes? **Yes.**

2. Are the institution's administrative offices open during hours adult students attend class? **Yes.**

3. How do students taking extended classes access library resources? **Students use the learning resource center.**

4. What is the registration and payment process for adult students? **Students may pay by using financial aid, employer reimbursement, and Educard Plan.**

5. What is the process for advising adult students? **Advising is available through the admissions office.**

6. What career and placement services are available to adult students? **Active career services are available.**

7. What characteristics of the institution's adult degree programs are most appealing to students? **High placement rate; evening and weekend hours.**

Doane College

303 N. 52nd Street ◆ **Lincoln, NE 68504**
Phone: (402) 466-4774 ◆ Fax: (402) 466-4228

Founded: 1872

Accredited by: North Central

Enrollment: 2,200 ◆ Adult students: 60 percent

University status: Private

Degree	Concentration/Major	Format
B.A.	Professional Studies in Business	E,A
B.A.	Professional Studies in Accounting	E,A
B.A.	Public Administration	E,A
B.A.	Industrial Management	E,A
B.A.	Corporate Communication	E,A
B.A.	Human Relations	E,A
B.A.	Commercial Art	E,A
B.A.	Allied Health Care Professions	E,A
M.A.	Administration	E,A
M.A.	Counseling	E,A
M.Ed.	Curriculum and Instruction	E,A

Campus Extension Site

Lincoln, NE

Requirements

Residency requirement: Students may attend classes at the extended campus.
Undergraduate admissions requirements: All persons are admitted upon application.
Graduate admissions requirements: Graduate requirements vary from program to program.
Graduation requirements (undergraduate): Graduation requires completion of all course and credit requirements with a minimum GPA of 2.0 on a 4.0 point scale.
Graduation requirements (graduate): Graduation requires the completion of all course and credit requirements with a minimum of 3.0 on a 4.0 point scale.

Fees, Tuition, Costs

Undergraduate application fee: $15
Graduate application fee: $25
Undergraduate tuition: $125/ semester credit
Graduate tuition: $160/semester credit
Undergraduate cost of books: $35
Graduate cost of books: $60

Financial Aid/Status

Full-time status: 6 semester credits/ term
Percentage of adult students receiving financial aid: 38 percent

Maximum Hours Awarded For

CLEP: 36
DANTES: 36
Prior learning portfolio: 36
Additional information: A maximum of 36 credits through CLEP, DANTES, and experience portfolio

Features and Services

1. Is it possible to purchase books during hours most adult students attend classes? **Yes.**

2. Are the institution's administrative offices open during hours adult students attend class? **Yes.**

3. How do students taking extended classes access library resources? **Access to University of Nebraska library, Internet, and other electronic means 24 hours, seven days a week.**

4. What is the registration and payment process for adult students? **Registration is painless—no lines. Students may use phone or fax or appear in person.**

5. What is the process for advising adult students? **Professional advisors are available any time at student's convenience.**

6. What career and placement services are available to adult students? **Full placement and career services are offered.**

7. What characteristics of the institution's adult degree programs are most appealing to students? **Degree of customer service; absolute commitment to the highest-quality learning experiences, small classes, course delivery format.**

Dordt College

498 4th Avenue, N.E. ◆ **Sioux Center, IA 51250**
Phone: (712) 722-6236 ◆ Toll-free phone: (800) 343-6738
Fax: (712) 722-1198 ◆ E-mail: jfennema@dordt.edu
Web address: http://www.dordt.edu

Founded: 1954

Accredited by: North Central

University status: Private, Church, Protestant

Degree	Concentration/Major	Format
M.Ed.	Curriculum and Instruction	C

Requirements

Residency requirement: Students average one week on campus in the summer for each course.
Graduate admissions requirements: Requirements include an undergraduate degree and a teacher's certificate or the equivalent.
Graduation requirements (graduate): Graduation requires the completion of a 10-course program.

Fees, Tuition, Costs

Graduate application fee: $25
Graduate tuition: $540/course
Graduate cost of books: $75/course

Financial Aid/Status

Full-time status: Full-time students are enrolled in three courses in a term.
Percentage of adult students receiving financial aid: 5 percent.

Features and Services

1. Is it possible to purchase books during hours most adult students attend classes? **Yes.**

2. Are the institution's administrative offices open during hours adult students attend class? **Yes.**

3. How do students taking extended classes access library resources? **Students may access the library in person, by mail, through interlibrary loan, and ERIC.**

4. What is the registration and payment process for adult students? **Registration may be done through the mail.**

5. What is the process for advising adult students? **Advising may be done in person, by mail, and by telephone.**

6. What career and placement services are available to adult students? **Adult students may use the same services that undergraduate students use.**

7. What characteristics of the institution's adult degree programs are most appealing to students? **Much of the work can be done off campus.**

Drake University

2507 University ◆ **Des Moines, IA 50311**
Phone: (515) 271-3181 ◆ Toll-free phone: (800) 44-DRAKE
Fax: (515) 271-2831 ◆ E-mail: admitinfo@acad.drake.edu
Web address: http://www.drake.edu

Founded: 1881

Accredited by: North Central

Enrollment: 5,639 ◆ Adult students: 10 percent

University status: Private

Degree	Concentration/Major	Format
B.A./B.S.	Economics	E
B.A./B.S.	Psychology	E
B.A./B.S.	Sociology	E
B.S.	Accounting	E
B.S.	Finance	E
B.S.	General Business	E
B.S.	Information Systems	E
B.S.	Insurance	E
B.S.	International Business	E
B.S.	Management	E
B.S.	Marketing	E
B.S.N.	Nursing (completion only)	E
M.A.T.	Effective Teaching	E
M.S.E.	Educational Administration	E
M.S.E.	Special Education	E

Requirements

Residency requirement: Off-site course offerings are limited. To complete all degree requirements, students must take some courses on campus.
Undergraduate admissions requirements: Students must submit official transcripts from high school and any colleges attended or GED, SAT or ACT (MSAT if out of high school four or more years), recommendations, essay (encouraged).

Graduate admissions requirements: Students must submit an application and GRE, MAT, or GMAT scores, have a bachelor's degree, and meet department requirements depending on the program.
Graduation requirements (undergraduate): Graduates must complete 124 or more credits with last 30 hours at Drake, meet the requirements of major department with 2.0 GPA.
Graduation requirements (graduate): Graduates must have a

3.0 GPA, complete the requirements of their major area, and complete any graduate project requirements.

Fees, Tuition, Costs

Undergraduate application fee: $25
Graduate application fee: $25
Undergraduate tuition: $345/ semester hour
Graduate tuition: $395/semester hour
Undergraduate cost of books: $300
Graduate cost of books: $300

Financial Aid/Status

Scholarship programs for adults: Scholarships are available for students transferring from a two-year community college with 45 or more semester hours.
Full-time status: Full-time students enrolled for 12 hours are eligible for aid programs and 10 hours for University financial aid programs.

Maximum Hours Awarded For

CLEP: Yes
PEP: Yes
Other exams: Yes

Features and Services

1. How do students taking extended classes access library resources? **All Drake students have equal access to all university resources.**

2. What is the registration and payment process for adult students? **Students may register on Saturday at the beginning of each term or by appointment.**

3. What is the process for advising adult students? **Students are assigned advisors for planning their academic programs.**

4. What career and placement services are available to adult

students? **Services available include resource library, resume assistance, testing, annual events, job board.**

5. What characteristics of the institution's adult degree programs are most appealing

to students? 24-hour computer lab, evening and weekend course offerings.

Drexel University Evening College

32nd and Chestnut Streets ◆ **Philadelphia, PA 19104**
Phone: (215) 895-2159 ◆ Toll-free phone: (800) 2-DREXEL
Fax: (215) 895-4988 ◆ E-mail: ketterra@duvm.ocs.drexel.edu
Web address: http://www.drexel.edu

Founded: 1891

Accredited by: Middle States

Enrollment: 12,000 ◆ Adult students: 1,800

University status: Private

Degree	Concentration/Major	Format
B.S.	Chemistry	E
B.S.	Computer Science	E
B.S.	Mathematics	E
B.S.	Physics and Atmospheric Science	E
B.S.	Teacher Preparation	E
B.S.	Business and Administration/Accounting	E
B.S.	Business and Administration/General Business	E
B.S.	Business and Administration/Management Information Systems	E
B.S.	Business and Administration/Management Operations	E
B.S.	Business and Administration/Marketing	E
B.S.	Construction Management-Certificate	E
B.Arch.	Architecture	E
B.S.	Hotel and Restaurant Management	E
B.S.	Chemical Engineering	E
B.S.	Civil Engineering	E
B.S.	Industrial Engineering	E
B.S.	Materials Engineering	E
B.S.	Mechanical Engineering	E
B.S.	Electrical Engineering	E
B.S.	Corporate Communication	E

Requirements

Residency requirement: Students must attend classes on the main campus.
Undergraduate admissions requirements: Students must submit proof of high school graduation or equivalent and official transcripts from any colleges attended. An admissions interview and possibly placement tests are required.
Graduation requirements (undergraduate): Student must file Application for Degree, earn minimum of 180 credits (GPA-2.0 or better), 45 credits completed at Drexel, meet program course requirements and all financial obligations.

Fees, Tuition, Costs

Undergraduate application fee: $35
Undergraduate tuition: $177/evening
Undergraduate cost of books: $50-$100/course
Other costs: Lab fees of $88.50/hr.

Financial Aid/Status

Scholarship programs for adults: A variety of scholarships are presented by the Evening College at the annual Honor Night convocation.
Full-time status: Full-time students are those taking 12 or more credits.
Percentage of adult students receiving financial aid: 33 percent.

Maximum Hours Awarded For

CLEP: 30
Other exams: Yes
Prior learning portfolio: Yes

Features and Services

1. Is it possible to purchase books during hours most adult students attend classes? **Yes.**

2. Are the institution's administrative offices open during hours adult students attend class? **Yes.**

3. How do students taking extended classes access library resources? **The university library may be used in** addition to elec-tronic access to numerous other libraries.

4. What is the registration and payment process for adult students? **Registration is done in the Evening College. Payment plan, credit card, tuition reimbursement plan accepted.**

5. What is the process for advising adult students? **Academic advisors available during the Evening College office hours M-Th 8:45 A.M.-8 P.M.; F 8:45 A.M.-6 P.M.**

6. What career and placement services are available to adult students? **Applications for employment may be filed at the Office of Student Services.**

7. What characteristics of the institution's adult degree programs are most appealing to students? **Evening office hours; discounted tuition for after-5 P.M. classes; full student services for part-time and evening college students.**

Drury College

900 N. Benton ◆ **Springfield, MO 65802**
Phone: (417) 873-7301 ◆ Fax: (417) 873-7529
E-mail: srollins@lib.drury.edu

Founded: 1874

Accredited by: North Central

Enrollment: 3,500 ◆ Adult students: 66 percent

University status: Private, Church,
United Church of Christ and Christian Church

Campus Extension Site

Ft. Leonard Wood, MO

Requirements

Residency requirement: Students are not required to attend classes on the main campus.
Undergraduate admissions requirements: Submit an application, high school transcript or GED scores, transcripts of any college work, military separation forms if applicable, and complete three hours of college-level English composition.
Graduation requirements (undergraduate): Complete 124 credits (GPA—2.0) including 36 hours in courses 300 or above; English, math, distribution, and major requirements; 30 hours earned at Drury; meet financial obligations; attend commencement.

Fees, Tuition, Costs

Undergraduate application fee: $15
Undergraduate tuition: $113/credit hour
Undergraduate cost of books: $50/book

Degree	Concentration/Major	Format
B.S.	Accounting	E
B.S.	Art	E
B.S.	Biology	E
B.S.	Business Administration	E
B.S.	Communication	E
B.S.	Criminal Justice	E
B.S.	Elementary Education	E
B.S.	English	E
B.S.	History	E
B.S.	Nursing	E
B.S.	Psychology	E
B.S.	Sociology	E

Financial Aid/Status

Scholarship programs for adults: Scholarships are available to on-campus students with 2.75 GPA or better.

Full-time status: Full-time students are enrolled for 12 credit hours. Percentage of adult students receiving financial aid: 80 percent.

Maximum Hours Awarded For

CLEP: 30
DANTES: 30
Other exams: 30
Prior learning portfolio: 30

Features and Services

1. Is it possible to purchase books during hours most adult students attend classes? **Yes.**

2. Are the institution's administrative offices open during hours adult students attend class? **Yes.**

3. How do students taking extended classes access library resources? **Students may use the library on campus.**

4. What is the registration and payment process for adult students? **Students must complete all registration procedures before attending class.**

5. What is the process for advising adult students? **Advisors are available during regular office hours and by appointment.**

6. What career and placement services are available to adult students? **The Career Center on campus offers services such as testing, SIGI Plus (computer-based career planning system), job fairs, and resources.**

7. What characteristics of the institution's adult degree programs are most appealing to students? **Quality faculty, small classes, personalized education.**

Eastern College*

10 Fairview Drive ◆ **St. Davids, PA 19087**

Phone: (610) 341-1398 ◆ Toll-free phone: (800) 732-7669

Fax: (610) 341-1468

Founded: 1952

Accredited by: Middle States

Enrollment: 2,000 ◆ Adult students: 550

University status: Private, Church, American Baptist Church

Features and Services

1. Is it possible to purchase books during hours most adult students attend classes? **Yes.**

2. Are the institution's administrative offices open during hours adult students attend class? **Yes.**

3. What characteristics of the institution's adult degree programs are most appealing to students? **Fifteen-month completion format, cohort learning model.**

Degree	Concentration/Major	Format
B.A.	Organization Management	E,A
M.B.A.	Business Administration	E
B.S.	Nursing	E, CT

Requirements

Residency requirement: Yes
Undergraduate admissions requirements: Age 25 or older, 60 or more transferable college credits, GPA of 2.0 or better, writing assessment
Graduate admissions requirements: Three to five years of professional or supervisory experience, undergraduate degree GPA of 2.5 or better, writing assessment

Fees, Tuition, Costs

Undergraduate application fee: $15
Graduate application fee: $25
Undergraduate tuition: $310/credit
Graduate tuition: $480/credit

Financial Aid/Status

Percentage of adult students receiving financial aid: 30 percent

Maximum Hours Awarded For

CLEP: 30
Prior learning portfolio: 30

Eastern Ilinois University

205 Blair Hall ◆ **Charleston, IL 61920**
Phone: (217) 581-5618 ◆ Fax: (217) 581-6697
E-mail: cflkw@eiu.edu ◆ Web address: http://www.eiu.edu

Founded: 1895

Accredited by: North Central

Enrollment: 11,000

University status: Public

Degree	Concentration/Major	Format
B.O.G./B.A	No major. Student determines concentration. Minor possible.	E,T,CT,V,C, TH
C.O.S.	Career Occupations. Undergraduate major in area of work experience. Minor permitted.	E,T

Campus Extension Sites
Champaign, IL
Olney, IL Urbana, IL
Centralia, IL
Danville, IL
Effingham, IL
Decatur, IL

Requirements
Residency requirement: Students are required to complete 15 hours from the institution. Hours delivered to extension sites count toward the 15.
Undergraduate admissions requirements: Students must be mature adults (25 years or older) with significant work/life experience. Students with some college credits prior to admission are preferred.
Graduation requirements (undergraduate): 120 hours required, including 40 upper-division; 15 BOG institute, 12 math/science, 12 social sciences, 12 humanities; pass constitution and writing exams, complete Cultural Experiences course.

Fees, Tuition, Costs
Undergraduate application fee: $25
Undergraduate tuition: $82/hour and $15-$27 fee
Undergraduate cost of books: $5 rental fee

Financial Aid/Status
Scholarship programs for adults: Some scholarships ($250-$2,000) are awarded based on need and academics.
Full-time status: Students taking 12 hours are full-time.
Percentage of adult students receiving financial aid: 80 percent.

Maximum Hours Awarded For
CLEP: Unlimited
PEP: Unlimited
DANTES: Unlimited
Other exams: Unlimited
Prior learning portfolio: Unlimited
Additional information: Scores on the CLEP and PEP must be 50 percent or more to earn credit.

Features and Services
1. How do students taking extended classes access library resources? **Students may access the library by computer from the community college or their home.**

2. What is the registration and payment process for adult students? **Off campus: mail, may use credit card, fee waiver, cash, scholarship. On campus: register by phone.**

3. What is the process for advising adult students? **Advisors available at all sites and by phone. Student gets copy of record each time it is updated.**

4. What career and placement services are available to adult students? **Services include resumes, registration, interviews, career days, notices of job openings, and newsletter.**

5. What characteristics of the institution's adult degree programs are most appealing to students? **Flexibility in meeting degree requirements, assessment of prior learning, firmly established criteria but no specific classes required.**

Eastern Mennonite University

1200 Park Road ◆ **Harrisburg, VA 22801**
Phone: (540) 432-4980 ◆ Fax: (540) 432-4444
E-mail: brownins@emu.edu ◆ Web address: http://www.emu.edu

Founded: 1917

Accredited by: Southern Association

Enrollment: 1,200 ◆ Adult students: 7 percent

University status: Private, Church, Mennonite

Degree	Concentration/Major	Format
B.S.	Management and Organizational Development	E,A

Requirements

Residency requirement: Students must complete the basic 38-semester-hour curriculum on campus.
Undergraduate admissions requirements: Students must have 60 transferable semester hours with a 2.0 GPA, complete a writing sample, have life experience (i.e., be 25 years old), and work experience.
Graduation requirements (undergraduate): Students must complete 124 hours of credit meeting general education requirements and requirements for the major in Management and Organizational Development.

Fees, Tuition, Costs

Undergraduate application fee: $15
Undergraduate tuition: Students pay for entire program, including books and 38 semester hours of credit.
Other costs: Since the curriculum is writing-intensive, a computer helps a great deal.

Financial Aid/Status

Full-time status: Our students qualify for federal grants and loans.
Percentage of adult students receiving financial aid: 50 percent.

Maximum Hours Awarded For

CLEP: Yes
DANTES: Yes
Other exams: 15
Prior learning portfolio: 30

Features and Services

1. What is the registration and payment process for adult students? **Registration and payment are handled by the ADCP staff.**

2. What is the process for advising adult students? **Students are assigned an assessment advisor, who helps with course selection and additional courses.**

3. What career and placement services are available to adult students? **Students have access to the services provided by the Career Services Office.**

4. What characteristics of the institution's adult degree programs are most appealing to students? **Accelerated format, one-night-per-week class commitment, completed degree in 15 months.**

Eastern Nazarene College*

LEAD Program
2 Adams Place ◆ **Quincy, MA 02169**
Phone: (617) 849-0225 ◆ Toll-free phone: (800) 439-LEAD
Fax: (617) 849-2911 ◆ Web address: http://www.enc.edu

Founded: 1910

Accredited by: New England

Enrollment: 1,300 ◆ Adult students: 600

University status: Private, Church, Church of the Nazarene

Features and Services

1. Are the institution's administrative offices open during hours adult students attend class? **Yes.**

2. What characteristics of the institution's adult degree programs are most appealing to students? **Accessibility, convenience, structure, adult-learner-oriented, accelerated.**

Degree	Concentration/Major	Format
B.S.	Business Administration	E,A

Requirements

Residency requirement: No
Undergraduate admissions requirements: High school; GED; 2.0 GPA; two years of full-time work experience; two years of college-level credits
Graduate admissions requirements: 130 semester hours of credit with a 2.5 GPA; 43 general education credits, completion of B.S.B.A., and completion of research project

Fees, Tuition, Costs

Undergraduate application fee: $20
Undergraduate tuition: $15,525 for program

Financial Aid/Status

Full-time status: 12 credits/term
Percentage of adult students receiving financial aid: 75 percent

Maximum Hours Awarded For

CLEP: 40
DANTES: 40
Prior learning portfolio: 40

Eastern Oregon State College

1410 L Avenue ◆ La Grande, OR 77850-2899
Phone: (541) 962-3378 ◆ Fax: (541) 962-3627
E-mail: dep@eosc.osshe.edu
Web address: http://www.eosc.osshe.edu/
Program's Web address: http://www.eosc.osshe.edu/major/det.html

Founded: 1929

Accredited by: Northwest Association

Enrollment: 2,800 ◆ Adult students: 35-40 percent

University status: Public

Degree	Concentration/Major	Format
B.A./B.S.	Liberal Studies	E,C,CT,S,A
A.A.	Office Administration	C,E,CT
B.S.	Nursing	E,C,CT,S,A
M.T.E.	Teacher Education	E,T,CT
B.S.	Business/Economics	C,E,CT

Campus Extension Sites
Portland, OR
Bitcer City, OR
Bend, OR
Pendleton, OR
Ontario, OR
Enterprise, OR
Burns, OR
John Day, OR

Requirements
Residency requirement: Students are not required to attend classes on the main campus. Undergraduate admissions requirements: Students must have a high school diploma or GED. Graduate admissions requirements: Students must have a bachelor's degree. Students in the education program must have a teaching certificate.

Graduation requirements (undergraduate): Students must earn 186 hours overall.
Graduation requirements (graduate): The graduate requirements vary.

Fees, Tuition, Costs
Undergraduate application fee: $50
Graduate application fee: $50
Undergraduate tuition: $80/credit
Graduate tuition: $125/credit
Undergraduate—Cost of books: $300-$400/year
Graduate—Cost of books: $500/year
Other costs: $80/year for computer account

Financial Aid/Status
Scholarship programs for adults: Scholarships are available for students.
Full-time status: Students enrolled in 12 hours are considered full-time.
Percentage of adult students receiving financial aid: 40 percent.

Maximum Hours Awarded For
CLEP: Yes
PEP: Yes
DANTES: Yes
Other exams: Yes
Prior learning portfolio: 46

Features and Services
1. Is it possible to purchase books during hours most adult students attend classes? **Yes.**

2. Are the institution's administrative offices open during hours adult students attend class? **Yes.**

3. How do students taking extended classes access library resources? **Students may access the library with a computer. The library has extended hours.**

4. What is the registration and payment process for adult students? **Students may register and pay using mail and fax. Credit cards are accepted.**

5. What is the process for advising adult students? **Regional advisors are available. Advising may be done by phone and e-mail.**

6. What career and placement services are available to adult students? **Students may use the services of the Career Center.**

7. What characteristics of the institution's adult degree programs are most appealing to students? **Quality of courses, variety of degree paths, support services.**

Eastern Washington University

209 Hargreaves Hall ◆ MS #14 ◆ **Cheney, WA 99004**
Phone: (509) 359-6524 ◆ Fax: (509) 359-7869
E-mail: jneace@ewu.edu ◆ Web address: http://www.ewu.edu

Founded: 1889

Accredited by: Northwest Association

Enrollment: 8,500 ◆ Adult students: 45 percent

University status: Public

Degree	Concentration/Major	Format
B.A.	Liberal Studies	E,A,C
B.A./B.S.	Communication Studies	E
B.A.	Business	E
B.A.	Journalism	E
M.A.	Public Administration	E,A
M.B.A.	Business	E

Campus Extension Sites

Spokane, WA
River Point, WA

Requirements

Residency requirement: Students do not have to attend classes on the main campus.
Undergraduate admissions requirements: Students must provide SAT or ACT test scores and have a GPA of 2.5 or better. Graduate admissions requirements: Students must have a bachelor's degree with a minimum GPA of 2.5 and provide GRE scores. Graduation requirements (undergraduate): Students must earn 180 credits including 60 credits of 300-499 level courses, language, and 45 credits in residency. GPA of 2.0 is required.

Fees, Tuition, Costs

Undergraduate application fee: $35
Graduate application fee: $35
Undergraduate tuition: $78/credit
Graduate tuition: $125/credit
Undergraduate cost of books: $60/book
Graduate cost of books: $60/book
Other costs: Transportation, parking, health fee ($45)

Financial Aid/Status

Full-time status: Students enrolled in 12 hours are full-time.
Percentage of adult students receiving financial aid: 50 percent.

Maximum Hours Awarded For

Other exams: 45
Prior learning portfolio: 45

Features and Services

1. Is it possible to purchase books during hours most adult students attend classes? **Yes.**

2. How do students taking extended classes access library resources? **The library is open at night and on weekends.**

3. What is the registration and payment process for adult students? **The students may pay at the Spokane Center.**

4. What is the process for advising adult students? **Evening appointments with advisors can be arranged.**

5. What characteristics of the institution's adult degree programs are most appealing to students? **Prior learning credit, self-directed program, night delivery of courses.**

Edinboro University of Pennsylvania*

Office of Adult Information Services (OASIS)
Advising and Career Services ◆ **Edinboro, PA 16444**
Phone: (814) 732-2701
Web address: http://www.edinboro.edu

Founded: 1857

Accredited by: Middle States

Enrollment: 7,484 ◆ Adult students: 1,391

University status: Public

Features and Services

1. Is it possible to purchase books during hours most adult students attend classes? **Yes.**

2. What characteristics of the institution's adult degree programs are most appealing to students? **Priority prescheduling, life experience credit, CLEP examinations, special weekend courses geared for adults (e.g., bowling, golf, marketing).**

Degree	Concentration/Major	Format
AS	Preschool Education	
BS	Business Administration/Accounting	
BS	Elementary Education	
AS	Computer Science	
BA	Sociology	
BS	Mentally Physically Handicapped	
BA	Psychology	
BS	Industrial Trades Leadership	

There was no indication of the format used so that adults could conveniently obtain these degrees. A comment was made that many adults can attend classes only during the day. It was included because of the number of adult students, the fact that credit is awarded for prior learning experience, and because of comments made about the appeal to adult students.

Requirements

Residency requirement: Yes
Undergraduate admissions requirements: SAT or ACT

Fees, Tuition, Costs

Undergraduate application fee: $25
Graduate application fee: $25
Undergraduate tuition: $3,685
Graduate tuition: $3,685

Financial Aid/Status

Full-time status: Undergraduate—12 credits/semester
Percentage of adult students receiving financial aid: 80 percent

Maximum Hours Awarded For

CLEP: 30
Other exams: 30
Prior learning portfolio: 30

Electronic University Network

1977 Colestin Road ◆ **Hornbrook, CA 96044**
Phone: (541) 482-5871 ◆ Toll-free phone: (800) 225-3276
Fax: (541) 482-7544 ◆ E-mail: eunhello@aol.com

Founded: 1984

Accredited by: Each institution is accredited.

Enrollment: 12,000 ◆ Adult students: 90 percent

University status: Private, Profit

Degree	Concentration/Major	Format
A.A.	General Studies	E,V,A,C,T
A.S.	Radio/Television Technology	E,V,A,C,T
A.S.	Legal Assisting	E,V,A,C,T
A.S.	Criminal Justice	E,V,A,C,T
A.S.	Solar Energy Technology	CT,E,V,A
A.S.	Drafting Design	E,V,A,C,T
A.S.	Hazardous Materials Technology	E,V,A,C,T
A.S.	International Business	E,V,A,C,T
A.S.	Marketing Management	E,V,A,C,T
A.A.	Liberal Arts	CT,E,V,A
A.A.	Humanities	CT,E,V,A
A.S.	Computer Science	CT,E,V,A
A.S.	Business Administration	CT,E,V,A
B.A.	Humanities, Social Science Quantitative Science, Commerce General Studies	CT,E,V,A
B.S.	Accounting, Business Administration, Computer Systems, Energy and Environmental Quality Management, General Studies, Law Enforcement Administration, Management Specialty, Marketing	CT,E,V,A
M.B.A.	Business Administration	CT,E,V,A
M.S.	Educational Technologies	CT,E,V,A
M.A.	International Relations	CT,E,V,A
Ph.D.	Integral Studies	CT,E,V,A

EUN is an online service available through America Online. It doesn't offer degrees but, rather, coordinates computer-based programs for a variety of institutions. The associate degrees are awarded through Brevard Community College and Rogers State College, the bachelor's degrees through City University, the M.B.A. through Heriot-Watt University, the M.S. through Walden University, the M.A. through Salve Regina University, and the Ph.D. through California Institute of Integral Studies. All of these institutions have regional accreditation.

Requirements

Residency requirement: Full degrees can be completed by computer and modem interface even outside the United States. Undergraduate admissions requirements: Students provide ACT or SAT scores or take placement exams in math, English, and science.
Graduate admissions requirements: The M.B.A. has no entrance requirements. The M.A. at Salve Regina University requires scores from either the GRE or MAT.
Graduation requirements (undergraduate): The associate degree requires 60-64 credits. Bachelor's degrees require 120 semester credits or 180 quarter credits.
Graduation requirements (graduate): These vary by institution.

Fees, Tuition, Costs

Undergraduate application fee: Varies
Graduate application fee: $75
Undergraduate tuition: Varies
Graduate tuition: Varies
Undergraduate cost of books: $60
Graduate cost of books: $80
Other costs: Computer monthly fee of $9.95 for America Online

Financial Aid/Status

Scholarship programs for adults: Scholarships depend on individual college's policies.
Full-time status: Individual college's policies apply.
Percentage of adult students receiving financial aid: 5 percent.

Maximum Hours Awarded For

CLEP: Yes
PEP: Yes
DANTES: Yes
Other exams: Yes
Prior learning portfolio: Yes
Additional information: Portfolio

assessment policies governed by individual schools

Features and Services

1. Is it possible to purchase books during hours most adult students attend classes? **Yes.**

2. Are the institution's administrative offices open during hours adult students attend class? **Yes.**

3. How do students taking extended classes access library resources? **Students may use interlibrary loans, the Internet, FTP, Telnet, etc.**

4. What is the registration and payment process for adult students? **Students may pay by credit card, check, company voucher, or purchase order.**

5. What is the process for advising adult students? **Free admissions counseling and advising are provided by the school staff by phone, online, or e-mail.**

6. What career and placement services are available to adult students? **Individual school's policies apply.**

7. What characteristics of the institution's adult degree programs are most appealing to students? **Flexibility of time; ability to start any month; not having to be at the campus; and direct access to online instructors, services, and other adult learners.**

Elizabethtown College

One Alpha Drive ◆ **Elizabethtown, PA 17022**
Phone: (717) 361-1291 ◆ Toll-free phone: (800) 877-2694
Fax: (717) 361-1466 ◆ Web address: http://www.etown.edu

Founded: 1899

Accredited by: Middle States

Enrollment: 1,450 ◆ Adult students: 6 percent

University status: Private, Church, Church of the Brethren

Degree	Concentration/Major	Format
B.S.	Accounting	E
B.S.	Business Administration	E
B.P.S.	Business Administration	S
B.P.S.	Communications	S
B.P.S.	Criminal Justice	S
B.P.S.	Early Childhood Education	S
B.P.S.	Human Services	S
B.P.S.	Medical Technology	S
B.P.S.	Public Administration	S

Requirements

Residency requirement: Students are required to attend classes on campus.

Undergraduate admissions requirements: The B.S. program is open enrollment. The B.P.S. program requires seven years of professional work experience, 50 completed college credits, and students must live within 400 miles of the college.

Graduation requirements (undergraduate): 125 credits with a minimum 2.0 overall GPA and a minimum 2.5 GPA in major.

Fees, Tuition, Costs

Undergraduate application fee: $35 for B.S.; $50 for B.P.S.
Undergraduate tuition: $195/credit
Undergraduate cost of books: $150

Financial Aid/Status

Full-time status: Students taking 12 or more credits are full-time.
Percentage of adult students receiving financial aid: 1 percent.

Maximum Hours Awarded For

CLEP: 30
DANTES: 30
Prior learning portfolio: 32
Additional information: A maximum of 30 combined credit hours from CLEP and DANTES

Features and Services

1. Is it possible to purchase books during hours most adult students attend classes? **Yes.**

2. Are the institution's administrative offices open during hours adult students attend class? **Yes.**

3. How do students taking extended classes access library resources? **Students will soon be able to access the library by modem.**

4. What is the registration and payment process for adult students? **Students use the Continuing Education office in person or by phone.**

5. What is the process for advising adult students? **Two advisors are available in the** Continuing Education office.

6. What career and placement services are available to adult students? **A career counselor is available in the Continuing Education office and through the Career Center.**

7. What characteristics of the institution's adult degree programs are most appealing to students? **Small school environment, affordable program, not treated as a "cash cow."**

Embry-Riddle Aeronautical University

600 S. Clyde Morris Blvd. ◆ **Daytona Beach, FL 32114-3900**
Phone: (904) 226-6909 ◆ Toll-free phone: (800) 5CAMPUS
Fax: (904) 226-6984 ◆ E-mail: ecinfo@db.erau.edu
Web address: http://ec.db.erau.edu/

Founded: 1926

Accredited by: Southern Association

Enrollment: 7,000 ◆ Adult students: 100 percent

University status: Private

Degree	Concentration/Major	Format
A.S.	Professional Aeronautics	E,S,A
B.S.	Professional Aeronautics	E,S,A
A.S.	Abytion Business Administration	E,S,A
B.S.	Abytion Business Administration	E,S,A
B.S.	Abytion Maintenance Management	E,S,A
A.S.	Aircraft Maintenance	E,S,A
B.S.	Management of Technical Operations	E,S,A
M.A.S.	Master of Aeronautical Science	E,A,S,V,CT
M.B.A.A.	Master of Business Administration	E,A
M.S.T.M.	Master of Science in Technical Management	E,A

Campus Extension Sites

Burlington, VT
Chico, CA
Cincinnati, OH
Colorado Springs, CO
Columbus, OH
Concord Airport, CA
Dallas, TX
Denver, CO
Atlantic City, NJ
Fort Lauderdale, FL
Hayward Airport, CA
High Desert, CA
Indianapolis, IN
Long Beach, CA
Livermore Airport, CA
Los Angeles, CA
Memphis, TN
Mesa, AZ
Miami, FL
Moses Lake, FL
Oakland Airport, CA
Ontario, CA
Phoenix, AZ
Louisville, KY
Wilmington, OH
Atlanta, GA
Ft. Worth, TX

Requirements

Residency requirement: Residency hour requirement (30) may be met at any resident center location. Undergraduate admissions requirements: Application made at Resident Center or Department of Independent Studies; high school or college transcripts, GED, or military educational records; CLEP or DANTES test scores, proof of professional training/experience. Graduate admissions requirements: Application made at Resident Center or the Graduate Admissions Office, undergraduate degree, recommendations, statement of objectives, official transcripts of all college work, test scores as required.

Graduation requirements (undergraduate): Application, complete required courses and hours for degree, meet any residency requirement, 40 credits in upper-division courses, minimum GPA 2.0, debts satisfied, behavior in good standing. Graduation requirements (graduate): Application, meet graduate residency requirement, if needed complete thesis/graduate research project, cumulative minimum GPA 3.0, all debts paid, behavior in good standing.

Fees, Tuition, Costs

Undergraduate application fee: $15
Graduate application fee: $15
Undergraduate tuition: $112-$140/credit hour
Graduate tuition: $191-$285/credit hour
Undergraduate cost of books: $40-$50
Graduate cost of books: $40-$50

Financial Aid/Status

Scholarship programs for adults: A limited number of scholarships are available.
Full-time status: Six semester hours are the minimum for full-time students. Independent study students are part-time.

Maximum Hours Awarded For

CLEP: Yes
PEP: Yes
DANTES: Yes
Other exams: Yes
Prior learning portfolio: Yes
Additional information: No maximums established for specific programs

Features and Services

1. Is it possible to purchase books during hours most adult students attend classes? **Yes.**

2. How do students taking extended classes access library resources? **Call in library support and online service, videos, research projects, and book support available.**

3. What is the registration and payment process for adult students? **Services vary at different sites. Students must sign the registration form.**

4. What is the process for advising adult students? **Counseling and evaluation available at sites. Center directors are education counselors.**

5. What career and placement services are available to adult students? **ERAU's Career Center sends to each site lists of job openings, companies that hire, and digests.**

6. What characteristics of the institution's adult degree programs are most appealing to students? **Excellent reputation in military and aviation fields, flexibility to adults' schedules, adjunct faculty understanding of adult students' needs.**

Emmanuel College

400 The Fenway ◆ Boston, MA 02115
Phone: (617) 735-9700 ◆ Toll-free phone: (800) 331-3227
Fax: (617) 735-9797
Web address: http//:www.emmanuel.edu

Founded: 1919

Accredited by: New England

Enrollment: 1,350 ◆ Adult students: 65 percent

University status: Private, Church, Roman Catholic Church

Graduate tuition: $1,230/3-hour credit course

Financial Aid/Status
Full-time status: Full-time undergraduate students are enrolled for 12 credit hours; graduate students—9 credit hours.

Maximum Hours Awarded For
CLEP: 80
PEP: 30
DANTES: 80
Prior learning portfolio: 36
Additional information: Combined maximum of 80 credits from these programs; possible credit from transfer courses

Features and Services

1. Is it possible to purchase books during hours most adult students attend classes? **Yes.**

2. How do students taking extended classes access library resources? **Students are offered extended library hours and may use the Internet.**

3. What is the registration and payment process for adult students? **Registration and payment may be done by mail, fax, phone, or in person.**

4. What is the process for advising adult students? **Preenrollment and continual advising are available by phone and in person.**

5. What career and placement services are available to adult students? **Placement service is not available.**

6. What characteristics of the institution's adult degree programs are most appealing to students? **Support services including college success seminar.**

Degree	Concentration/Major	Format
B.S.	Health Care Administration	E
B.S.	Management	E
B.S.	Business Administration	E,A
B.S.N.	Nursing	E
B.S./B.A.	Psychology	E
B.A.	Interdepartmental	E
B.A.	Art	E
B.A.	Biology	E
B.A.	Chemistry	E
B.A.	Economics	E
B.A.	Education	E
B.A.	English	E
B.A.	Math	E
B.A.	Political Science	E
B.A.	Religious Studies	E
B.A.	Sociology	E
B.A.	Speech Communication	E
B.A.	Women's Studies	E
B.A.	Interdepartmental	

Campus Extension Sites
Business Administration program available at the following campuses:
Medford, MA
Andover, MA
South Shore, MA
Framington, MA
Woburn, MA
Leominster, MA

Requirements
Residency requirement: Students must attend classes on campus, except those in the Business Administration program.

Fees, Tuition, Costs
Undergraduate application fee: $40
Graduate application fee: $40
Undergraduate tuition: $815/4-hour credit course

Empire State College—SUNY

2 Union Avenue ◆ **Saratoga Springs, NY 12866**
Phone: (518) 587-2100

Founded: 1971

Accredited by: Middle States

Enrollment: 7,213 ◆ Adult students: 7,213

University status: Public

Features and Services

1. What characteristics of the institution's adult degree programs are most appealing to students? **Flexibility, individualized degree program.**

Degree	Concentration/Major	Format
A.A.	Business	C,T
A.A.	Community	C,T
A.A.	Human Services	C,T
A.A.	Interdisciplinary	C,T
B.A.	Business	C,T
B.A.	Community	C,T
B.A.	Human Services	C,T
B.A.	Interdisciplinary	C,T
B.A.	Several areas of liberal arts	S
M.A.	Liberal Studies	S
M.A.	Business and Policy Studies	S
M.A.	Labor and Policy Studies	S

Requirements

Residency requirement: No
Undergraduate admissions requirements: High school diploma or GED, ability of the college to meet the applicant's explicit and implicit educational needs and objectives
Graduate admissions requirements: Bachelor's degree from regionally accredited institution

Fees, Tuition, Costs

Undergraduate application fee: $50
Graduate application fee: $50
Undergraduate tuition: $1,350/per 16 weeks
Graduate tuition: $2,022/per 16 weeks

Financial Aid/Status

Full-time status: Matriculated and taking 12 or more credits
Percentage of adult students receiving financial aid: 50 percent

Maximum Hours Awarded For

CLEP: 96
PEP: 96
DANTES: 96

Evergreen State College

Olympia, WA 98505 ◆ Phone: (360) 866-6000
Fax: (360) 866-6680 ◆ E-mail: admissions@elwha.evergreen.edu
Web address: http://www.evergreen.edu

Founded: 1971

Accredited by: Northwest Association

Enrollment: 3,400

University status: Public

Degree	Concentration/Major	Format
B.A.	Liberal Arts	E,S
M.P.A.	Public Administration	E
M.E.S.	Environmental Studies	E

Requirements

Residency requirement: Students must attend classes on campus. Undergraduate admissions requirements: Students over 25 with fewer than 40 transferable quarter credits may be evaluated using alternative criteria. Transfers must have 40 credits, a minimum 2.0 GPA, and be in good standing at last school attended. Graduate admissions requirements: M.P.A.—bachelor's degree; majors vary; minimum 3.0 GPA recommended. M.E.S.—B.A./B.S.; major in biology, physical, or social science recommended; math, writing, analytical, and communication skills required. Graduation requirements (undergraduate): Graduates must complete a minimum of 180 quarter credits; 45 of the last 90 credits must be earned at Evergreen.

Fees, Tuition, Costs

Undergraduate application fee: $35
Graduate application fee: $35
Undergraduate tuition: $814/quarter
Graduate tuition: $1,280/quarter
Undergraduate cost of books: $732/full-time
Graduate cost of books: $780/full-time

Financial Aid/Status

Full-time status: Undergraduates enrolled in 12 quarter credits; graduate-10 quarter credits

Maximum Hours Awarded For

CLEP: Yes
PEP: Yes
DANTES: Yes
Prior learning portfolio: 48
Additional information: Evaluation of certificated learning; military course work

Features and Services

1. Is it possible to purchase books during hours most adult students attend classes? **Yes.**

2. What is the registration and payment process for adult students? **Phone, mail, or walk-in registration depends on admission status/program. Cash, check, credit cards.**

3. What is the process for advising adult students? **Advising Center is open until 6 P.M. M-T; 7 P.M. W-Th.**

4. What career and placement services are available to adult students? **All services available at office open until 6 P.M. M-Th. Other hours possible if prearranged.**

5. What characteristics of the institution's adult degree programs are most appealing to students? **Evening hours; small classes (22-24 students/faculty member); faculty who enjoy working with adults; interdisciplinary, team-taught programs.**

Fairleigh Dickinson University*

1000 River Road ◆ Dickinson Hall (H311) ◆ **Teaneck, NJ 07666**
Phone: (201) 692-6500 ◆ Toll-free phone: (800) 338-3887
Fax: (201) 692-6505 ◆ Web address: http://www.fdu.edu

Founded: 1942

Accredited by: Middle States

Enrollment: 11,000

Status: Private

Degree	Concentration/Major	Format
B.A.	General Studies (Student designs the major)	E,T,A,V,S

Requirements

Residency requirement: No
Undergraduate admissions
requirements: Must hold a high
school diploma and have a strong
desire to learn

Fees, Tuition, Costs

Undergraduate application fee: $35
Undergraduate tuition: $367

Financial Aid/Status

Full-time status: 12 credits or
more/term

Maximum Hours Awarded For

CLEP: 33
Prior learning portfolio: 30

Features and Services

1. Is it possible to purchase
   books during hours most
   adult students attend classes?
   Yes.

2. Are the institution's
   administrative offices open
   during hours adult students
   attend class? **Yes.**

3. What characteristics of the
   institution's adult degree
   programs are most appealing
   to students? **Students have
   flexibility to design the
   program. Minimum of 120
   credits for degree, a variety
   of delivery formats on and
   off campus.**

Fairmont State College

1201 Locust Avenue ◆ **Fairmont, WV 26554-2491**
Phone: (304) 367-4000 ◆ Toll-free phone: (800) 641-5678
Fax: (304) 366-4870
Web address: http://www.fairmont.wvnet.edu:80

Founded: 1865

Accredited by: North Central

Enrollment: 6,547 ◆ Adult students: 41 percent

University status: Public

Degree	Concentration/Major	Format
A.A.	General Studies	E
A.A.S.	General Studies	E

Campus Extension Site

Clarksburg, WV

Requirements

Undergraduate admissions requirements: Application, high school graduate or GED, proof of immunity.
Graduation requirements (undergraduate): Students must complete 128 semester hours with a 2.0 GPA.

Fees, Tuition, Costs

Undergraduate tuition: $1,858 for West Virginia residents; $4,328 for nonresidents
Undergraduate cost of books: Approximately $600

Financial Aid/Status

Scholarship programs for adults: Scholarships available
Full-time status: 12 semester hours
Percentage of adult students receiving financial aid: 60 percent

Maximum Hours Awarded For

CLEP: Yes
Other exams: Yes
Prior learning portfolio: Yes
Additional information: Use of the Portfolio to earn credit in the Regents' Bachelor of Arts degree

Features and Services

1. Is it possible to purchase books during hours most adult students attend classes? **Yes.**

2. Are the institution's administrative offices open during hours adult students attend class? **Yes.**

3. How do students taking extended classes access library resources? **The library is open in the evening and weekends.**

4. What is the registration and payment process for adult students? **Evening registration is offered. Students may pay fee by mail.**

5. What is the process for advising adult students? **The advising center is open some evenings.**

Ferris State University

410 Oak Street ◆ Alumni 113 ◆ **Big Rapids, MI 49307-2022**
Phone: (616) 592-3811 ◆ Toll-free phone: (800) 562-9130
Fax: (616) 592-3539
Web address: http://about.ferris.edu/homepage.htm

Founded: 1886

Accredited by: North Central

Enrollment: 10,200 ◆ Adult students: 34 percent

University status: Public

Degree	Concentration/Major	Format
A.A.S.	Health Information Technology	E,T
B.S.	Health Care Systems Administration	E,T
B.S.	Health Information Management	E,T
B.S.	Nursing	E,T
M.S.	Information Systems Management	E
B.S.	Business Administration	E,T
B.S.	Accounting	E
M.S.	Career and Technical Education	E
B.S.	Marketing	E
B.S.	Secondary Teacher Education	E
B.S.	Computer Information Systems	E
B.S.	Social Work	E,T
B.S.	Numerous technology degrees	E,T

Campus Extension Sites

Flint, MI
Mt. Clemens, MI
Traverse City, MI
Grand Rapids, MI
Midland, MI
Dowagiac, MI
Garden City, MI
Muskegon, MI
Jackson, MI

Requirements

Residency requirement: Students are not required to attend classes on campus.
Undergraduate admissions requirements: Students submit official high school or prior college transcripts and ACT scores (not required if English and Algebra or higher math completed).
Individual assessment of skills used for admission.
Graduate admissions requirements: Students should contact the university for the specific program requirements.
Graduation requirements (undergraduate): Students must complete degree requirements with a minimum 2.0 GPA, meet general education requirements, and file formal graduation application.
Graduation requirements (graduate): Students must file formal graduation application and meet degree requirements for the specific degree.

Fees, Tuition, Costs

Undergraduate application fee: $20
Undergraduate tuition: $148/semester hour
Graduate tuition: $190/semester hr
Undergraduate cost of books: Varies
Graduate cost of books: Varies

Financial Aid/Status

Scholarship programs for adults: Various scholarships are available.
Full-time status: Full-time students are enrolled in 12 credit hours or more.

Maximum Hours Awarded For

CLEP: Yes
Other exams: Yes
Additional information: Advanced Placement Program available for earning credits

Features and Services

1. Is it possible to purchase books during hours most adult students attend classes? **Yes.**

2. How do students taking extended classes access library resources? **The library may be used with a Ferris State University ID. Electronic access is available.**

3. What is the registration and payment process for adult students? **Registration and payment are offered by mail, fax, phone, and credit card.**

4. What career and placement services are available to adult students? **Nontraditional students may use the same campus facilities that other students use.**

5. What characteristics of the institution's adult degree programs are most appealing to students? **Evening and weekend classes.**

The Fielding Institute*

2112 Santa Barbara St. ◆ **Santa Barbara, CA 93105**
Phone: (805) 687-1099 ◆ Fax: (805) 687-9793
Web address: http://www.fielding.edu

Founded: 1974

Accredited by: Western Association

Enrollment: 850

University status: Private

Features and Services

1. What characteristics of the institution's adult degree programs are most appealing to students? **They do not have to leave their communities and personal and professional responsibilities.**

Degree	Concentration/Major	Format
Ph.D.	Psychology The degree is earned through a combination of residential events and distance learning activities.	C,S
Ph.D.	Human Organization and Development The degree is earned through a combination of residential events and distance learning activities.	C,S

Requirements

Residential Requirements: Limited residential activities

Fees, Tuition, Costs

Graduate application fee: $60
Graduate tuition: $9,600/year

Financial Aid/Status

Full-time status: All of our students are considered full-time.
Percentage of adult students receiving financial aid: 33 percent.

Florida Institute of Technology

School of Extended Graduate Studies
150 W. University Blvd. ◆ **Melbourne, FL 32901**
Phone: (407) 768-8000 ◆ Fax: (407) 951-7694
E-mail: rmarshal@fit.edu ◆ Web address: http://www.fit.edu

Founded: 1958

Accredited by: Southern Association

Enrollment: 1,500 ◆ Adult students: 100 percent

University status: Private

Degree	Concentration/Major	Format
M.B.A.	General Business Administration	E
M.B.A.	Contract and Acquisitions Management Health Administration, Human Resource Management, Management of Technology	E
M.S.	Management, Accounting, Contract Management, Health Services Management, Human Resources Management, Information Systems, Logistical Management, Transportation Management	E
M.H.A.	Health Administration	E
M.S.	Aerospace Engineering, Computer Science, Computer Information Systems, Contract and Acquisitions Management, Contract Management, Electrical Engineering, Engineering Management, Mechanical Engineering, Space Systems, Systems Management	E

Campus Extension Sites

Fort Lee, VA
Patuxent, MD
Aberdeen, MD
Alexandria, VA
Fort Eustis, VA
Picatinny, NJ
Norfolk, VA
Lakehurst, NJ
Huntsville, AL
White Sands, NM
St. Petersburg, FL
Patrick AFB, FL

Requirements

Residency requirement: Students are not required to attend classes on the main campuses. Course requirements can be completed at each graduate center.
Graduate admissions requirements: Students must have bachelor's degree or equivalent, academic and professional record indicating probable success in program, references, and meet admissions requirements of specific program.
Graduation requirements (graduate): Students must meet degree requirements, complete a final program exam or a thesis if required, submit a graduation petition and fee, and complete degree within seven years.

Fees, Tuition, Costs

Graduate application fee: $50
Graduate tuition: Varies with degree
Graduate cost of books: $750 estimated

Financial Aid/Status

Scholarship programs for adults: Institutional scholarships are awarded only to undergraduate students.
Full-time status: Graduate students must be enrolled for five semester hours/term.
Percentage of adult students receiving financial aid: 95 percent.

Features and Services

1. Is it possible to purchase books during hours most adult students attend classes? **Yes.**

2. How do students taking extended classes access library resources? **Library services available through local libraries, electronic access, interlibrary loan access to campus library.**

3. What is the registration and payment process for adult

students? **Off-campus graduate students register and pay at center site. Main campus processes information.**

4. What is the process for advising adult students?

Each off-campus student has a faculty advisor at the center where class is held.

5. What career and placement services are available to adult students? **Students may request services from the campus-based Career Services.**

6. What characteristics of the institution's adult degree programs are most appealing to students? **Quality programs, convenient locations and times for class attendance in the area where students work or reside.**

Fontbonne College*

6800 Wydonn Boulevard ◆ **St. Louis, MO 63105**
Phone: (314) 889-4587 ◆ Fax: (314) 863-0917
Web address: http://www.fontbonne.edu

Founded: 1923

Accredited by: North Central

Enrollment: 1,900 ◆ Adult students: 900

University status: Private, Church, Roman Catholic Church

Degree	Concentration/Major	Format
M.B.A.	Business Administration	E,CT,A
B.B.A.	Business Administration	E,A
M.A.	Education—Reading	E,A
M.A.	Education—Early Childhood Administration	E

Requirements

Residency requirement: Yes
Undergraduate admissions requirements: 54 semester hours completed; 2.5 GPA; two years of full-time work experience; minimum 23 years of age; letter of recommendation
Graduate admissions requirements: Bachelor's degree; 2.5 GPA; three years of work experience; 23 years of age; letters of recommendation

Fees, Tuition, Costs

Undergraduate application fee: $20
Graduate application fee: $20
Undergraduate tuition: $215
Graduate tuition: $270

Financial Aid/Status

Full-time status: 12 semester hours in 6 months
Percentage of adult students receiving financial aid: 60 percent

Features and Services

1. Is it possible to purchase books during hours most adult students attend classes? **Yes.**

2. What characteristics of the institution's adult degree programs are most appealing to students? **Less than two-year guaranteed degree sequence on same nights/ weekly. Guaranteed tuition and fee level for entire two-year sequence. Approximately eight degree-program start dates/ calendar year. Faculty are full-time professionals in areas they teach.**

Fordham University
Ignatius College

Dealy Hall Room 101 ◆ Bronx, NY 10458
Phone: (718) 817-3720 ◆ Toll-free phone: (800) FORDHAM
Fax: (718) 367-9404 ◆ E-mail: ad-caltagiro@lars.fordham.edu
Web address: http://www.fordham.edu

Founded: 1966

Accredited by: Middle States

Enrollment: 500 ◆ Adult students: 95 percent

University status: Private, Church, Roman Catholic Church

Degree	Concentration/Major	Format
B.A.	Economics	E
B.A.	English	E
B.A.	Fine Arts	E
B.A.	History	E
B.A.	Political Science	E
B.A.	Psychology	E
B.A.	Social Science	E
B.A.	Sociology	E
B.S.	Biology	E
B.S.	Computer Systems	E
B.S.	General Science	E
B.S.	Accounting	E
B.S.	Finance	E
B.S.	Marketing	E
B.S.	Management	E

Requirements

Residency requirement: Students must attend classes on campus. Undergraduate admissions requirements: Applicants are reviewed individually. Students submit application, high school/college transcripts, official SAT/ACT scores if taken, and other relevant information. An interview is required.
Graduate admissions requirements: Admission requirements vary with each school.
Graduation requirements (undergraduate): Graduation requires 120 credits (63 core credits, 30 major credits, 27 electives). A cumulative GPA of 2.0 or more is required.

Fees, Tuition, Costs

Undergraduate application fee: $40
Undergraduate tuition: $350/credit hour
Undergraduate cost of books: $175/semester

Financial Aid/Status

Scholarship programs for adults: Scholarships offered include the Evening Scholar Award, the Dean's Recognition Awards, and the University grant-in-aid.
Full-time status: Full-time students are enrolled in 12 semester hours.
Percentage of adult students receiving financial aid: 70 percent.

Maximum Hours Awarded For

CLEP: 18
DANTES: 18
Other exams: 18
Additional information: Noncollegiate sponsored courses recommended by the ACE accepted

Features and Services

1. Is it possible to purchase books during hours most adult students attend classes? Yes.

2. Are the institution's administrative offices open during hours adult students attend class? Yes.

3. What is the registration and payment process for adult students? Students register on designated days. Payment must be made before the due date.

4. What is the process for advising adult students? New students meet with advisor for first registration. Then forms and progress reports are mailed.

5. What career and placement services are available to adult students? Full placement services and evening appointments are available.

6. What characteristics of the institution's adult degree programs are most appealing to students? Interaction with the faculty; sense of tradition at Fordham; availability of services during evening and Saturday hours.

Framington State College
Framington, MA 01701
Phone: (508) 626-4550 ◆ Fax: (508) 626-4030

Founded: 1839

Accredited by: New England

Enrollment: 3,000 ◆ Adult students: 25 percent

University status: Public

Features and Services

1. Is it possible to purchase books during hours most adult students attend classes? **Yes.**

2. Are the institution's administrative offices open during hours adult students attend class? **Yes.**

3. What is the registration and payment process for adult students? **Registration and payment are processed in the traditional manner.**

4. What is the process for advising adult students? **Students use the Adults Returning to College Program.**

5. What characteristics of the institution's adult degree programs are most appealing to students? **The Adults Returning to College Program.**

Degree / Concentration/Major / Format

Degree	Concentration/Major	Format
Undergraduate Degrees	Liberal Arts and Science	E
	Business Administration	E
	Nursing	E
	Nutrition Science	E
Graduate Degrees	Museum Science	E
	Food Science	E

Requirements

Residency requirement: Students must attend classes on campus. Undergraduate admissions requirements: Students must have acceptable GPA and SAT scores. Graduate admissions requirements: Students must have acceptable GPA and SAT scores. Graduation requirements (undergraduate): Students must complete 128 credit hours. Graduation requirements (graduate): Students must complete 12 courses.

Fees, Tuition, Costs

Undergraduate application fee: $25
Graduate application fee: $25
Undergraduate tuition: $482/course
Graduate tuition: $505/course
Undergraduate cost of books: $80
Graduate cost of books: $80

Financial Aid/Status

Full-time status: Students taking four courses are considered full-time.
Percentage of adult students receiving financial aid: 50 percent.

Franklin Pierce College*

20 Cotton Road ◆ Nashua, NH 03063
Phone: (603) 889-6146 ◆ Toll-free phone: (800) 325-1090
Fax: (603) 889-3795 ◆ Web address: http://www.fplc.edu

Founded: 1962

Accredited by: New England

Enrollment: 1,200 ◆ Adult students: 2,000

University status: Private

Features and Services

1. Is it possible to purchase books during hours most adult students attend classes? **Yes.**

2. Are the institution's administrative offices open during hours adult students attend class? **Yes.**

Degree	Concentration/Major	Format
B.S.	Accounting	E,CT,A
B.S.	Management	E
B.S.	General Studies	E,CT,A

Requirements

Residency requirement: No
Undergraduate admissions requirements: Open

Financial Aid/Status

Full-time status: 2 courses/term
Percentage of adult students receiving financial aid: 50 percent

Fees, Tuition, Costs

Undergraduate tuition: $399/course

Fresno Pacific College

1717 S. Chestnut Avenue ◆ **Fresno, CA 93702**
Phone: (209) 453-2280 ◆ Fax: (209) 453-2003

Founded: 1944

Accredited by: Western Association

Enrollment: 1,600 ◆ Adult students: 50 percent

University status: Private, Church, Mennonite Brethren

Degree	Concentration/Major	Format
B.A.	Management and Organizational Development	E,A
M.A.	Master of Arts in Administrative Leadership	E

Requirements

Residency requirement: Classes are held within 25 miles of the campus. Students do not have to attend classes on the campus. Undergraduate admissions requirements: Students must have seven years of work experience and 60 transferable units. Graduate admissions requirements: Students must have a bachelor's degree from an accredited institution, submit graduate test scores, and have an interview. Graduation requirements (undergraduate): Students must complete 124 units including classroom courses, personal portfolio credits, and an applied research project. Graduation requirements (graduate): The Master of Arts in Administrative Leadership requires 37 units for graduation, including 25 core units and 12 additional units in a preapproved concentration.

Fees, Tuition, Costs

Undergraduate application fee: $100
Graduate application fee: $75
Undergraduate tuition: $11,000/program
Graduate tuition: $15,500/program
Undergraduate cost of books: $650
Graduate cost of books: $750
Other costs: Access to a computer required for both programs

Financial Aid/Status

Scholarship programs for adults: Scholarships are not available.
Full-time status: Full-time students must be enrolled for 12 units/semester.
Percentage of adult students receiving financial aid: 75 percent.

Maximum Hours Awarded For

CLEP: 30
Other exams: Yes
Prior learning portfolio: 30

Features and Services

1. Is it possible to purchase books during hours most adult students attend classes? **Yes.**

2. How do students taking extended classes access library resources? **Students may access the library by modem or by visiting the library.**

3. What is the registration and payment process for adult students? **Registration may be done in class. Payment by credit card or prior arrangement is acceptable.**

4. What is the process for advising adult students? **Each person works with several personal guidance counselors.**

5. What career and placement services are available to adult students? **A placement service is available through student services.**

6. What characteristics of the institution's adult degree programs are most appealing to students? **Cohort model with defined program and predetermined finish dates.**

Gannon University

University Square ◆ Erie, PA 16541
Phone: (814) 871-7474 ◆ Toll-free phone: (800) GANNON-U
Fax: (814) 871-5827 ◆ E-mail: admissions@cluster.gannon,edu
Web address: http://www.gannon.edu

Founded: 1925

Accredited by: Middle States

Enrollment: 3,528 ◆ Adult students: 13.7 percent

University status: Private, Church, Roman Catholic Church

Degree	Concentration/Major	Format
A.A.	Paralegal	E
A.D.N.	Nursing	E
A.S.	Accounting	E
A.S.	Business Administration	E
A.S.	Electrical Engineering Technology	E
A.S.	Industrial Management	E
A.S.	Mechanical Engineering Technology	E
B.A.	Paralegal	E
B.S.	Accounting	E
B.S.	Industrial Distribution	E
B.S.	Business Administration	E
B.S.	Industrial Management	E
B.S.	Management	E
B.S.	Management Information System	E
B.S.	Marketing	E
B.S.E.E.	Electrical Engineering	E
B.S.E.T.	Electrical Engineering Technology	E
B.S.E.T.	Mechanical Engineering Technology	E
B.S.M.E.	Mechanical Engineering	E
Graduate	Business Administration	E
Degrees	Counseling, Psychology, Early Intervention, Education, Engineering, English, Health Services Administration, Natural and Environmental Sciences, Nursing, Pastoral Studies, Public Administration, Religious Education, Social Services	

Campus Extension Sites

Warren, PA
Sharon, PA

Requirements

Residency requirement: Students are not required to attend on-campus classes.

Undergraduate admissions requirements: High school transcript with 4 units English, 4 social studies/foreign language, math and science vary by major; standardized test scores or alternative test; letters of recommendation are helpful. Graduate admissions requirements: Bachelor's degree from regionally accredited institution; standardized test scores if applicable; letters of recommendation; college transcripts; an interview may be required.
Graduation requirements (undergraduate): 128 credits of academic work including 3 writing-intensive courses; overall and major GPA of at least 2.0.
Graduation requirements (graduate): Requirements vary by major; most majors require thesis or research project; most require a passing score on a comprehensive exam.

Fees, Tuition, Costs

Undergraduate application fee: $25
Graduate application fee: $25-$50
Undergraduate tuition: $365-$385/credit
Graduate tuition: $385-$420/credit
Undergraduate cost of books: $700
Graduate cost of books: $750
Other costs: University fee of $200/academic year or $8/credit; SGA fee of $84/year; various lab fees depending on major

Financial Aid/Status

Scholarship programs for adults: Type and amounts of scholarships vary.
Full-time status: Full-time undergraduate students are enrolled for 12 semester hours/semester; full-time graduate students are enrolled 9 hours.
Percentage of adult students receiving financial aid: 85 percent.

Maximum Hours Awarded For

CLEP: Yes
Additional information: Advanced Placement credits possible

Features and Services

1. Is it possible to purchase books during hours most adult students attend classes? **Yes.**

2. Are the institution's administrative offices open during hours adult students attend class? **Yes.**

3. How do students taking extended classes access library resources? **Students may use main campus facilities. Extended locations have on-site library resources.**

4. What is the registration and payment process for adult students? **Registration/ payment can be completed in the Office of Part-Time Studies, which has extended hours.**

5. What is the process for advising adult students? **By department advisor, Office of Part-Time Students, and Returning to Education Adult Program.**

6. What career and placement services are available to adult students? **Career development workshops, employment service, SIGI career software, individual assessment, other helps.**

7. What characteristics of the institution's adult degree programs are most appealing to students? **Flexible-day, evening, and weekend courses, diverse programs/ degrees; supportive in advising and help programs (math center, writing center).**

George Fox College*

414 North Meridian, Box #6099 ◆ **Newberg, OR 97132**
Phone: (503) 538-8383 ◆ Toll-free phone: (800) 632-0921
Fax: (503) 537-3834 ◆ Web address: http://www.gfc.edu

Founded: 1891

Accredited by: Northwest Association

Enrollment: 1,650 ◆ Adult students: 300

University status: Private, Church, Evangelical Quaker Church

better) from accredited institution. General education courses totaling 35 credits.
Graduate admissions requirements: Three recommendations, official transcripts, writing sample, 3.0 GPA, a baccalaureate degree from a regionally accredited college or university, two years of professional work experience, and an interview.

Fees, Tuition, Costs

Undergraduate application fee: $25
Graduate application fee: $25
Undergraduate tuition: $9,150
Graduate tuition: $17,900

Financial Aid/Status

Full-time status: 12 credit hours/ semester
Percentage of adult students receiving financial aid: 65 percent

Maximum Hours Awarded For

CLEP: 32
PEP: 32
DANTES: 32
Other exams: 32
Prior learning portfolio: 30

Degree	Concentration/Major	Format
B.A.	Management of Human Resources 15-month, degree-completion program (Junior or Senior year); Up to 30 semester hours of life experience credit granted toward B.A. degree	E,A
M.B.A.	Business Administration	E

Requirements

Residency requirement: Yes.
Undergraduate admissions requirements: Personal and professional recommendation, writing sample, official transcripts. Have a minimum of 62 semester hours of prior college work (C or

Features and Services

1. Is it possible to purchase books during hours most adult students attend classes? **Yes.**

2. What characteristics of the institution's adult degree programs are most appealing to students? **Graduate degree uses a 24-month format, cohort model, work** teams, full-time faculty, convenience of location, and M.B.A. with a management focus.

Georgian Court College

900 Lakewood Avenue ◆ **Lakewood, NJ 08701-2697**
Phone: (908) 364-8218 ◆ Fax: (908) 905-8571
E-mail: lazarick@georgian.edu
Web address: http://www.georgian.edu

Founded: 1924

Accredited by: Middle States

Enrollment: 2,500 ◆ Adult students: 25 percent

University status: Private, Church, Roman Catholic Church

Undergraduate cost of books: Varies
Other costs: Fees of $40/semester

Financial Aid/Status

Scholarship programs for adults: Scholarships are based on FAF form filed and academic profile. Full-time status: Individuals must be taking 12 or more credits. Percentage of adult students receiving financial aid: 41 percent.

Maximum Hours Awarded For

CLEP: 30
PEP: Yes
DANTES: Yes

Degree	Concentration/Major	Format
B.A.	Art	E
B.A./B.S.	Biology	E
B.S.	Business Administration/Accounting	E
B.A.	Special Education	E
ART	Education	E
B.A.	English	E
B.A.	History	E
B.A.	Humanities	E
B.A.	Mathematics	E
B.A./B.S.	Physics	E
B.A.	Psychology	E
B.A.	Religious Studies	E
B.A.	Sociology	E

Requirements

Residency requirement: Students must attend classes on campus. Undergraduate admissions requirements: Students must have a high school diploma or GED. Transfer students need a minimum 2.0 average from a two-year college program.

Graduation requirements (undergraduate): Students must have an overall cumulative minimum GPA of 2.0; 2.5 in major; and a total of 132 credits.

Fees, Tuition, Costs

Undergraduate application fee: $30
Undergraduate tuition: $271/credit

Features and Services

1. Is it possible to purchase books during hours most adult students attend classes? **Yes.**

2. Are the institution's administrative offices open during hours adult students attend class? **Yes.**

3. What is the registration and payment process for adult students? **Students register with department chairs and are billed.**

4. What is the process for advising adult students? **Advising appointments are made with department chairpersons or the Director of Evening Division.**

5. What career and placement services are available to adult

students? **An active Career Office offers day and evening workshops on Interviewing, Writing a Resume, etc.**

6. What characteristics of the institution's adult degree programs are most appealing to students? **Students enjoy taking classes with other**

adults (median age-34); caring campus.

Glenville State College

200 High Street ◆ **Glenville, WV 26351**
Phone: (304) 462-7361 ◆ Toll-free phone: (800) 924-2010
Fax: (304) 462-8619 ◆ E-mail: cottrill@wvgsc.wvnet.edu
Web address: http://www.glenville.wvnet.edu

Founded: 1872

Accredited by: North Central

Enrollment: 2,416 ◆ Adult students: 42.3 percent

University status: Public

Degree	Concentration/Major	Format
All	Board of Regents Degree	E

Campus Extension Sites
Lewis County, WV
Nicolas County, WV

Requirements
Residency requirement: Students must attend classes on campus to complete their degrees. Upper-level courses are offered only at the main campus.
Undergraduate admissions requirements: Students must be graduates of accredited high school with a 2.0 GPA and a 17 ACT or 710 SAT score.
Graduation requirements (undergraduate): The requirements vary with the degree. A bachelor's degree requires 128 hours; 47 hours of General Studies.

Fees, Tuition, Costs
Undergraduate tuition: $900/ resident/semester
Undergraduate cost of books: $200-$400
Other costs: A goal of the West Virginia Board of Colleges and Universities is "that all incoming freshmen for the Fall of 1996 will have a computer."

Financial Aid/Status
Scholarship programs for adults: No specific adult scholarships are offered; however, adults are eligible for tuition waivers and the entire list of scholarships.
Full-time status: Students carrying 12 or more semester hours are full-time.
Percentage of adult students receiving financial aid: 40 percent.

Maximum Hours Awarded For
CLEP: 16
Prior learning portfolio: Varies
Additional information: Board of Regents Degree—Only 15 of 128 hours taken at a West Virginia college

Features and Services
1. Is it possible to purchase books during hours most adult students attend classes? **Yes.**

2. How do students taking extended classes access library resources? **Students have access to the library services.**

3. What is the registration and payment process for adult students? **All students register and pay fees according to the college calendar.**

4. What is the process for advising adult students? **Every student is assigned an advisor.**

5. What career and placement services are available to adult students? **The Career and Placement Office provides its services to all students.**

6. What characteristics of the institution's adult degree programs are most appealing to students? **Glenville State College is known as the friendly campus.**

Goddard College

Route 214 ◆ Plainfield, VT 05667
Phone: (802) 454-8311 ◆ Toll-free phone: (800) 468-4888
Fax: (802) 454-8017 ◆ E-mail: beckyb@earth.goddard.edu
Program's Web address: http://sun.goddard.edu

Founded: 1938

Accredited by: New England

Enrollment: 466 ◆ Adult students: 320

University status: Private

Degree	Concentration/Major	Format
B.A.	One-week residency/semester; work done by "packet" process	S
M.A.	One-week residency/semester; work done by "packet" process	S
M.A.	Social ecology, psychology and counseling, teacher education	S
M.F.A.	Creative Writing	S

Requirements

Residency requirement: Students must attend some classes on campus. In some cases a residency waiver may be given, but this is very infrequent.
Undergraduate admissions requirements: Students must submit a written essay, high school transcripts, and two letters of recommendation, and have an interview.
Graduate admissions requirements: Students must submit three letters of recommendation (if possible, one from an academic setting), college transcripts, a personal statement, and a preliminary study plan.
Graduation requirements (undergraduate): All students must complete a senior study in the last semester of enrollment.
Graduation requirements (graduate): Requirements vary. Students are expected to do professional-level preparations for their work, apply their work to the field, and either complete a final product or thesis or acquire teaching experience.

Fees, Tuition, Costs

Undergraduate application fee: $40
Graduate application fee: $40
Undergraduate tuition: $7,520/year
Graduate tuition: $8,580/year
Undergraduate cost of books: $556
Graduate cost of books: $556
Other costs: $524/year for room and board for mandatory short-term campus residencies

Financial Aid/Status

Full-time status: B.A. students enrolled for 15 credits are full-time; M.A.—12 credits.

Maximum Hours Awarded For

CLEP: 30
Prior learning portfolio: 45

Features and Services

1. Is it possible to purchase books during hours most adult students attend classes? **Yes.**

2. Are the institution's administrative offices open during hours adult students attend class? **Yes.**

3. How do students taking extended classes access library resources? **The library is available to students during all residencies.**

4. What is the registration and payment process for adult students? **Much of the registration is done with forms by mail. The financial aid office is available.**

5. What is the process for advising adult students? **Faculty mentors help plan semester program, supervise study every three weeks, and meet with student.**

6. What career and placement services are available to adult students? **Students are helped with career planning, internships and volunteer work, and job application.**

7. What characteristics of the institution's adult degree programs are most appealing to students? **Low residency; self-designed programs.**

Goldey-Beacom College

4701 Limestone Road ◆ **Wilmington, DE 19808**
Phone: (302) 998-8814 ◆ Toll-free phone: (800) 833-4877
Fax: (302) 998-8631 ◆ E-mail: gallowaym@goldey.gbc.edu
Web address: http://goldey.gbc.edu

Founded: 1896

Accredited by: Middle States

Enrollment: 1,530 ◆ Adult students: 45 percent

University status: Private

Degree	Concentration/Major	Format
A.S.	Accounting	E,A
A.S.	Computer and Information Systems	E,A
A.S.	Administrative Office Management	E,A
A.S.	Management	E,A
A.S.	Business Administration	E,A
B.S.	Accounting	E,A
B.S.	Finance	E,A
B.S.	Computer and Information Systems	E,A
B.S.	Administrative Office Management	E,A
B.S.	International Business	E,A
B.S.	Management	E,A
B.S.	Management Information Systems	E,A
B.S.	Marketing Management	E,A
B.S.	Business Administration	E,A

Requirements

Residency requirement: Students must attend classes on the main campus.
Undergraduate admissions requirements: Students must have a high school diploma or the equivalent.
Graduation requirements (undergraduate): Graduation requires the completion of all curricular requirements with a minimum GPA of 2.0.

Fees, Tuition, Costs

Undergraduate application fee: $30
Undergraduate tuition: $6,780/year; $226/credit
Undergraduate cost of books: $500/year

Financial Aid/Status

Full-time status: Full-time students are enrolled in 9 or more credits/semester or 24 credits/year with a minimum 2.0 GPA.

Maximum Hours Awarded For

CLEP: Yes
Other exams: Yes

Features and Services

1. Is it possible to purchase books during hours most adult students attend classes? **Yes.**

2. Are the institution's administrative offices open during hours adult students attend class? **Yes.**

3. What is the registration and payment process for adult students? **All new adult students are advised and registered through admissions office.**

4. What is the process for advising adult students? **All students are assigned an academic advisor.**

5. What career and placement services are available to adult students? **The career and placement office is open from 8:00 A.M. to 8:00 P.M. (M-Th).**

6. What characteristics of the institution's adult degree programs are most appealing to students? **Personal attention, flexibility of transfer credits, and accelerated courses.**

Goshen College

1700 S. Main Street ◆ **Goshen, IN 46526**
Phone: (219) 535-7464 ◆ Fax: (219) 535-7293
E-mail: lindagg@goshen.edu
Web address: http://www.goshen.edu

Founded: 1895

Accredited by: North Central

Enrollment: 1,000 ◆ Adult students: 10-15 percent

University status: Private, Church, Mennonite Church

Degree	Concentration/Major	Format
B.S.N.	Nursing	E,A
B.S.	Organizational Management	E,A

Requirements

Residency requirement: Students must attend classes on the main campus.
Undergraduate admissions requirements: Students must be 25 years or older with 60 college credits (minimum GPA of 2.0). B.S.N. students are required to have two years of work experience as a registered nurse.
Graduation requirements (undergraduate): The B.A. in Organizational Management requires 120 credit hours (GPA of 2.0). The B.S.N. requires 124 credit hours (GPA of 2.0).

Fees, Tuition, Costs

Undergraduate application fee: $15
Undergraduate tuition: $3,120/term
Undergraduate cost of books: $200/term

Financial Aid/Status

Full-time status: Students enrolled in 12 credit hours are full-time.
Percentage of adult students receiving financial aid: 66 percent.

Maximum Hours Awarded For

CLEP: No limit
Other exams: No limit
Prior learning portfolio: 21

Features and Services

1. Is it possible to purchase books during hours most adult students attend classes? **Yes.**

2. Are the institution's administrative offices open during hours adult students attend class? **Yes.**

3. What is the registration and payment process for adult students? **Registration and payment are done at class orientation two weeks before the first class.**

4. What is the process for advising adult students? **Students make appointments with either program assistant directors or other academic advisors.**

5. What career and placement services are available to adult students? **Students may sign up for job opening mailings.**

6. What characteristics of the institution's adult degree programs are most appealing to students? **Moderate price, convenient location and parking, accelerated program, good customer service, and quality program taught by quality faculty.**

Governors State University

University Park, IL 60466

Phone: (708) 534-4490 ◆ Fax: (708) 534-8950

Web address: http://www.ecnet.net/users/gsunow/gsu

Founded: 1969

Accredited by: North Central

Enrollment: 6,100 ◆ Adult students: 80 percent

University status: Public

Degree	Concentration/Major	Format
B.A.	Board of Governors Bachelor of Arts Program	E,V,A,C,T, TH,S

Requirements

Residency requirement: Students could complete the Board of Governors Bachelor of Arts program in their own homes. Students must complete at least 15 credits at one or a combination of the Board of Governors Universities.
Undergraduate admissions requirements: Undergraduates are admitted as juniors only. Requirements include the equivalent of 60 semester hours of college credit, minimum GPA of 2.0, and good standing at the institution last attended.
Graduation requirements (undergraduate): Most undergraduate degrees require 120 hours.

Fees, Tuition, Costs

Undergraduate application fee: 0
Undergraduate tuition: $82/credit hour
Undergraduate cost of books: $350/semester

Financial Aid/Status

Scholarship programs for adults: Most scholarships require a 3.5 GPA of transferred credits.
Full-time status: Full-time students are enrolled in 12 semester hours or more.
Percentage of adult students receiving financial aid: 36 percent.

Maximum Hours Awarded For

CLEP: 60
PEP: 28
DANTES: No limit
Prior learning portfolio: No limit
Additional information: USAFI—no limit

Features and Services

1. Is it possible to purchase books during hours most adult students attend classes? **Yes.**

2. Are the institution's administrative offices open during hours adult students attend class? **Yes.**

3. What is the registration and payment process for adult students? **Payment can be made by mail or by credit card by phone.**

4. What is the process for advising adult students? **Full advising service is provided by faculty members.**

5. What career and placement services are available to adult students? **A full career services office is available.**

6. What characteristics of the institution's adult degree programs are most appealing to students? **Average age of students at Governors State University is 34.**

Grand Canyon University

3300 W. Camelback Road ◆ Phoenix, AZ 85017
Phone: (602) 274-1404 ◆ Fax: (602) 274-7993

Founded: 1949

Accredited by: North Central

Enrollment: 3,000 ◆ Adult students: 30

University status: Private

Degree	Concentration/Major	Format
B.S.	Applied Management	E,A

Campus Extension Site

Phoenix, AZ

Requirements

Residency requirement: Students must attend classes on the main campus.
Undergraduate admissions requirements: Students must be 25 years or older and have 60 transferable credits from a regionally accredited institution.
Graduation requirements (undergraduate): Students must earn 128 credit hours, including 41 general education requirements, 36 core requirements, and 51 electives.

Fees, Tuition, Costs

Undergraduate application fee: $50
Undergraduate tuition: $175/credit hour
Undergraduate cost of books: $400

Financial Aid/Status

CLEP: 10
PEP: 10
DANTES: 10
Other exams: 6
Prior learning portfolio: 30

Features and Services

1. Is it possible to purchase books during hours most adult students attend classes? **Yes.**

2. What is the registration and payment process for adult students? **Orientation night is set up to handle all administrative issues.**

3. What is the process for advising adult students? **Advising is available by appointment.**

4. What characteristics of the institution's adult degree programs are most appealing to students? **Cost, convenience, small classes, and university reputation.**

Grand Rapids Baptist Seminary

1001 E. Beltline NE ◆ **Grand Rapids, MI 49505**

Phone: (616) 285-9422 ◆ Toll-free phone: (800) 697-1133

Fax: (616) 949-4154 ◆ E-mail: jverberkmoes@cornerstone.edu

Founded: 1941

Accredited by: North Central

Enrollment: 203 ◆ Adult students: 100 percent

University status: Private, Church,
General Association of Regular Baptists

Degree	Concentration/Major	Format
D.Min.	Pastoral	A,C,S
D.Min.	Education/Management	A,C,S
D.Min.	Missions/Cross-Cultural	A,C,S
M.R.Ed.	Pastoral—In ministry degree	A,C,S
M.R.Ed.	Christian Education—In ministry degree	A,C,S
M.R.Ed.	Missions—In ministry degree	A,C,S
M.R.Ed.	School Administration—In ministry degree	A,C,S

Requirements

Graduate admissions requirements: Admission to the seminary requires minimum 2.5 cumulative undergraduate GPA, two reference letters, affirmation of basic faith statement, and complete application documentation.

Fees, Tuition, Costs

Graduate application fee: $25
Graduate tuition: $219/semester hour

Financial Aid/Status

Full-time status: Students enrolled in nine hours/semester are considered full-time for federal aid.

Features and Services

1. Is it possible to purchase books during hours most adult students attend classes? **Yes.**

2. Are the institution's administrative offices open during hours adult students attend class? **Yes.**

3. What is the registration and payment process for adult students? **Registration and payment may be done by mail.**

4. What is the process for advising adult students? **Advising is done by personal appointment or phone. Faculty advisors assist through entire program.**

5. What career and placement services are available to adult students? **Assistance is provided in preparing and distributing resumes.**

6. What characteristics of the institution's adult degree programs are most appealing to students? **Administrative and academic sensitivity to student needs as adult learners.**

Greenville College*

315 East College Avenue ◆ **Greenville, IL 62246**
Phone: (618) 664-1840

Founded: 1892

Accredited by: North Central

Enrollment: 850

University status: Private, Church, Free Methodist Church

Degree	Concentration/Major	Format
B.A.	Business Leadership Adult degree completion program.	E, A

Requirements
Residency requirement: No
Undergraduate admissions
requirements: Two years of college
work

Fees, Tuition, Costs
Undergraduate application fee: $10
Undergraduate tuition: To be
determined

Financial Aid/Status
Full-time status: 12 or more
credits/term

Features and Services
1. Is it possible to purchase
   books during hours most
   adult students attend classes?
   Yes.

Griggs University
Home Study International

P.O. Box 4437 ◆ **Silver Spring, MD 20914**
Phone: (301) 680-6570 ◆ Toll-free phone: (800) 394-GROW
Fax: (301) 680-6577 ◆ E-mail: 74617,74

Founded: 1990

Accredited by: Distance Education

Enrollment: 500

University status: Private, Church, Seventh-Day Adventist Church

Degree	Concentration/Major	Format
A.A.	Religion—Personal Ministries	C
B.A.	Religion	C
B.A.	Theology	C

Requirements

Residency requirement: Students do not have to attend classes on the main campus.
Undergraduate admissions requirements: Students must have a high school diploma or its equivalent; GED total score 224 with no score below 40. Students must have the ability to benefit from university study.
Graduation requirements (undergraduate): Students must complete 120 semester credits and a senior project.

Fees, Tuition, Costs

Undergraduate application fee: $30
Undergraduate tuition: $150/ semester hour
Undergraduate cost of books: $60- $100

Diploma fee: $50
Other costs: $60 enrollment fee when courses are requested

Maximum Hours Awarded For

CLEP: Yes
Other exams: Yes
Prior learning portfolio: Yes
Additional information: 24 credits must be completed before application for life experience.
Maximum credit: B.A.—24 hours; A.A—12 hours.

Features and Services

1. What is the registration and payment process for adult students? **$60 fee, book cost, shipping, and 20 percent of tuition due at enrollment. Balance in three monthly payments.**

2. What is the process for advising adult students? **Advising may be done by voice mail (student/teacher boxes) or by fax.**

3. What characteristics of the institution's adult degree programs are most appealing to students? **Correspondence school; allows students to get degrees in privacy of their own home and while continuing their present job.**

Hamline University*

Graduate School ◆ 1536 Hewitt Avenue ◆ **St. Paul, MN 55104**

Phone: (612) 641-2900 ◆ Toll-free phone: (800) 888-2182

Fax: (612) 641-2987 ◆ Web address: http://www.hamline.edu

Founded: 1854

Accredited by: North Central

Enrollment: 2,500 ◆ Adult students: 900

University status: Private, Church, United Methodist Church

Degree	Concentration/Major	Format
M.A.	Liberal Arts	E
M.A.	Fine Arts in Writing	E
M.A.	Public Administration	E
M.A.	Education	E

Requirements

Residency requirement: Yes
Graduate admissions requirements:
Official undergraduate/graduate
transcripts, letters of
recommendation, written
statement, supplemental materials

Fees, Tuition, Costs

Graduate tuition: $840/course

Financial Aid/Status

Full-time status: Two graduate
courses/term

Features and Services

1. Is it possible to purchase books during hours most adult students attend classes? **Yes.**

2. Are the institution's administrative offices open during hours adult students attend class? **Yes.**

3. What characteristics of the institution's adult degree programs are most appealing to students? **Quality programs aimed at the working adult; practitioner-based programs; no standardized testing required for admission.**

Hawaii Pacific University

1164 Bishop Street ◆ Suite 207 ◆ **Honolulu, HI 96813**
Phone: (808) 544-9300 ◆ Toll-free phone: (800) 669-4724
Fax: (808) 544-1136 ◆ E-mail: adulted@hpu.edu
Program's Web address: http://www.hpu.edu/

Founded: 1965

Accredited by: Western Association

Enrollment: 8,000 ◆ Adult students: 36 percent

University status: Private

Financial Aid/Status

Scholarship programs for adults: Scholarships are available through the scholarship office.
Full-time status: 12 semester hours during fall and spring sessions.
Percentage of adult students receiving financial aid: 50 percent.

Maximum Hours Awarded For

CLEP: 36
DANTES: Yes
Other exams: Yes
Additional information: 36 credits allowed by exam; documented workplace training eligible if compares to HPU course

Degree	Concentration/Major	Format
B.S.	Business Administration—13 majors	E,A
B.A.	18 fields of study	E,A
B.S.	Computer Science	E,A
B.S.	Environmental Sciences	
B.S	Marine Biology	
B.S.	Nursing	E
B.S.	Oceanography	
B.S.	Pre-Medical Studies	
M.B.A.	Business Administration—9 concentrations	E,A
M.S.I.S.	Information Systems	E,A
M.A.	Three management concentrations	E,A

Features and Services

1. Is it possible to purchase books during hours most adult students attend classes? **Yes.**

2. How do students taking extended classes access library resources? **Students have no problems using the two university libraries, which are open seven days a week.**

3. What is the registration and payment process for adult students? **Registration is handled by appointment in the ACE office. Installment payments are permitted.**

4. What is the process for advising adult students? **Advising and evaluation of transfer credit are done by appointment in the ACE office (M-F 7:30 A.M.-6:00 P.M.).**

5. What career and placement services are available to adult students? **Current job listings are available. Counseling provided by the Career Planning and Placement office.**

Requirements

Residency requirement: Students must attend classes on the main campus.
Undergraduate admissions requirements: Students must submit a high school diploma (minimum 2.5 GPA in college prep), or GED, or 24 college credits (minimum GPA of 2.00). Students out of high school 10 years or more may submit a resume for consideration.
Graduate admissions requirements: Students must have a baccalaureate degree with a minimum 2.7 GPA.
Graduation requirements (undergraduate): Generally graduation requires 124 semester credit hours and a minimum cumulative GPA of 2.0 or higher.
Graduation requirements (graduate): Graduation requires 39-45 credits depending on the degree. A minimum GPA of 3.0 is needed.

Fees, Tuition, Costs

Undergraduate application fee: $50
Graduate application fee: $50
Undergraduate tuition: $130-$460/credit
Graduate tuition: $296/credit
Undergraduate cost of books: $50/class
Graduate cost of books: $50/class
Other costs: Parking fee for those commuting by car

6. What characteristics of the institution's adult degree programs are most appealing to students? **Convenient schedule (evening/Saturday) classes; seven semesters in year, many accelerated sessions; most degrees in day or evening format.**

Hebrew College*
43 Hawes Street ◆ Brookline, MA 02146
Phone: (617) 232-8710 ◆ Fax: (617) 734-9769

Founded: 1921

Accredited by: New England

Enrollment: 150 ◆ Adult students: 80

University status: Private

Degree	Concentration/Major	Format
M.A.	Judaic Studies	E
M.A.	Jewish Education	E
B.A.	Jewish Education	E
B.A.	Hebrew Literature—Judaic Studies	E

Requirements
Residency requirement: Yes

Fees, Tuition, Costs
Undergraduate application fee: $25
Graduate application fee: $25
Undergraduate tuition: $265/credit
Graduate tuition: $265/credit

Financial Aid/Status
Full-time status: 12 credits undergraduate; 9 credits graduate

Features and Services

1. Is it possible to purchase books during hours most adult students attend classes? **Yes.**

2. Are the institution's administrative offices open during hours adult students attend class? **Yes.**

3. What characteristics of the institution's adult degree programs are most appealing to students? **Flexible hours and programs tailored to needs of individual students.**

Hofstra University
New College

130 Hofstra University ◆ Hempstead, NY 11550-1090
Phone: (516) 463-5820 ◆ Fax: (516) 463-4832
Web address: http://www.hofstra.edu

Founded: 1959

Accredited by: Middle States

Enrollment: 584 ◆ Adult students: 5 percent

University status: Private

Degree	Concentration/Major	Format
B.A./B.S.	Social Science	S
B.A./B.S.	Humanities	S
B.A./B.S.	Creative Studies	S
B.A./B.S.	Natural Science	S
B.A./B.S.	Interdisciplinary	S
M.A.	Interdisciplinary	S

Requirements

Residency requirement: One class on campus is required for the master's degree, none for the undergraduate degrees; however, students may attend on-campus classes. All students must have access to campus resources. Undergraduate admissions requirements: High school graduates with a preferred SAT or ACT score above national average, 17 transfer credits with GPA of B or better. Graduate admissions requirements: Students should have a bachelor's degree with GPA of B or better and submit a satisfactory admissions proposal useable with independent study. Graduation requirements (undergraduate): Graduation requires 120 credit hours including 1/3 breadth courses, 1/3 depth (area, theme) courses, and 1/3 electives. Graduation requirements (graduate): Graduation requires an initial study seminar, three independent study contracts (interdisciplinary), and a master's thesis proposal and thesis.

Fees, Tuition, Costs

Undergraduate application fee: $25
Graduate application fee: $25
Undergraduate tuition: $3,064 + fees/term
Graduate tuition: $12,830 + fees/program
Undergraduate cost of books: Varies—$100+
Graduate cost of books: Varies—$100+
Other costs: Transportation to campus

Financial Aid/Status

Scholarship programs for adults: Scholarships available
Full-time status: 12 credits/semester

Maximum Hours Awarded For

CLEP: 90
Other exams: 90
Prior learning portfolio: 90
Additional information: A combination of these

1. Is it possible to purchase books during hours most adult students attend classes? **Yes.**

2. Are the institution's administrative offices open during hours adult students attend class? **Yes.**

3. How do students taking extended classes access library resources? **Students must use the on-campus library.**

4. What is the registration and payment process for adult students? **Registration and payment are done through the program office at the beginning of the semester.**

5. What is the process for advising adult students? **Advising is done through the program office and with faculty.**

6. What career and placement services are available to adult students? **The university placement office and faculty help students with career counseling.**

7. What characteristics of the institution's adult degree programs are most appealing to students? **Independent study and opportunity for self-designed programs of study.**

Houghton College

910 Union Road ◆ **West Seneca, NY 14224**
Phone: (716) 674-6363 ◆ Toll-free phone: (800) 777-2556
Fax: (716) 674-6363 ◆ E-mail: nwilson@houghton.edu

Founded: 1883

Accredited by: Middle States

Enrollment: 1,380 ◆ Adult students: 10 percent

University status: Private, Church, Wesleyan Church

Degree	Concentration/Major	Format
B.S.	Organizational Management	E,A

Campus Extension Sites

West Seneca, NY
Olean, NY

Requirements

Residency requirement: Students must attend classes on the main campus.
Undergraduate admissions requirements: Students must be 25 years or older and have 64 prior college-level credits.
Graduation requirements (undergraduate): Students must complete 124 hours, including all program required courses.

Fees, Tuition, Costs

Undergraduate application fee: $25
Undergraduate tuition: $11,000/year
Undergraduate cost of books: $390
Other costs: May vary from none to $1,000

Financial Aid/Status

Scholarship programs for adults: A minimal amount of scholarship money is available by need.
Full-time status: 12 hours/semester.
Percentage of adult students receiving financial aid: 10 percent.

Maximum Hours Awarded For

CLEP: 24
DANTES: 24
Other exams: No limit
Prior learning portfolio: 24

Features and Services

1. Is it possible to purchase books during hours most adult students attend classes? **Yes.**

2. Are the institution's administrative offices open during hours adult students attend class? **Yes.**

3. How do students taking extended classes access library resources? **Students may use the on-site library and the libraries at Houghton and affiliated area colleges.**

4. What is the registration and payment process for adult students? **Registration and payment are streamlined on-site.**

5. What is the process for advising adult students? **Advising is streamlined on-site.**

6. What career and placement services are available to adult students? **Students may use networking.**

7. What characteristics of the institution's adult degree programs are most appealing to students? **The personal one-on-one touch.**

Huntingdon College

1500 E. Fairview Avenue ◆ **Montgomery, AL 36106-2148**
Phone: (334) 833-4430 ◆ Fax: (334) 833-4505
Web address: http://www.huntingdon.edu

Founded: 1854

Accredited by: Southern Association

Enrollment: 645 ◆ Adult students: 11 percent

University status: Private, Church, United Methodist Church

Degree	Concentration/Major	Format
A.A.	Business Administration	E
A.A.	General Studies	E
A.A.	Paralegal Studies	E
B.A.	Business Administration	E
B.A.	General Studies/Business Administration & Community Service	E
B.A.	General Studies/Humanities	E
B.A.	General Studies/Science	E
B.A.	General Studies/Social Science	E

Requirements

Residency requirement: Students must attend classes on campus. Undergraduate admissions requirements: Students must have a high school diploma with 2.0 GPA or GED (35 on each subtest; 45 as average standard score). Transfer students with a 2.0 GPA are accepted.
Graduation requirements (undergraduate): Graduation requires a minimum of 124 semester hours. Only one course of the last 30 hours may be taken outside Huntingdon.

Fees, Tuition, Costs

Undergraduate application fee: $25
Undergraduate tuition: $90/semester hour
Undergraduate cost of books: Varies—$500/freshman

Financial Aid/Status

Full-time status: 12 semester hours
Percentage of adult students receiving financial aid: 80 percent

Maximum Hours Awarded For

CLEP: 30
Prior learning portfolio: 30

Features and Services

1. Is it possible to purchase books during hours most adult students attend classes? **Yes.**

2. How do students taking extended classes access library resources? **The library has evening hours.**

3. What is the registration and payment process for adult students? **Registration is done by appointment with the registrar's office. Payment is made through the business office.**

4. What is the process for advising adult students? **Students are advised by the director of the Adult Studies division.**

5. What career and placement services are available to adult students? **CCDC counsels students for employment or graduate school and offer various other services.**

6. What characteristics of the institution's adult degree programs are most appealing to students? **Individual attention and small classes.**

Huntington College

2303 College Avenue ◆ **Huntington, IN 46750**
Phone: (219) 356-6000 ◆ Fax: (219) 356-9448
E-mail: jsherloc@huntcol.edu
Web address: http://www.huntcol.edu

Founded: 1897

Accredited by: North Central

Enrollment: 689 ◆ Adult students: 15 percent

University status: Private, Church, United Brethren in Christ Church

Degree	Concentration/Major	Format
B.S.	Organizational Management	E,A
M.A.	Christian Ministry	Th/F 8 A.M.-4 P.M.
M.A.	Educational Ministry	Th/F 8 A.M.-4 P.M.
M.A.	Youth Ministry	Th/F 8 A.M.-4 P.M.

Requirements

Residency requirement: All courses are offered on campus at this time. Undergraduate admissions requirements: Students must be 25 years or older, have 64 hours of transferable credit from accredited institutions, and a GPA of 2.0 or more.
Graduation requirements (undergraduate): Students must earn 128 semester hours including approximately 30 general education hours, have a GPA of 2.0+, and complete all major requirements.

Fees, Tuition, Costs

Undergraduate application fee: $15
Undergraduate tuition: $175/credit hour
Undergraduate cost of books: $235/semester

Financial Aid/Status

Full-time status: 12 or more hours/semester
Percentage of adult students receiving financial aid: 25 percent

Maximum Hours Awarded For

CLEP: No limit
PEP: No limit
DANTES: No limit
Prior learning portfolio: 25
Additional information: American Council on Education approved training courses (e.g., military awarded credits)

Features and Services

1. Is it possible to purchase books during hours most adult students attend classes? **Yes.**

2. How do students taking extended classes access library resources? **The library has extended evening and weekend hours.**

3. What is the registration and payment process for adult students? **Registration and payment are two weeks before cohort program. Deferred payment with employer reimbursement.**

4. What is the process for advising adult students? **Advisor helps form graduation plan early in program. Consulting is done at intervals during program.**

5. What career and placement services are available to adult students? **The career and placement office is available to all students.**

6. What characteristics of the institution's adult degree programs are most appealing to students? **Once-a-week class, 18-month program, oriented to adults, credit for life learning, meet with same students throughout the program.**

Huron University

333 9th Street S.W. ◆ Huron, SD 57350

Phone: (605) 352-8721 ◆ Toll-free phone: (800) 942-5826

Fax: (605) 352-7421

Founded: 1883

Accredited by: North Central

Enrollment: 500 ◆ Adult students: 50 percent

University status: Private, Profit

Degree	Concentration/Major	Format
B.S.	Accounting	E
B.S.	Business Administration	E
B.S.	Criminal Justice	E
B.S.	Applied Management	E
M.B.A.	Business Administration	E,A

Campus Extension Sites

Sioux Falls, SD
Tokyo, Japan
London, England

Requirements

Residency requirement: Students must attend classes on campus. Graduation requirements (undergraduate): Students must complete 120-128 semester hours as defined for the given major. Graduation requirements (graduate): Students must complete a minimum of 36 semester hours and foundation prerequisites as needed for each individual.

Fees, Tuition, Costs

Undergraduate application fee: $15
Graduate application fee: $100
Undergraduate tuition: $3,939/semester

Graduate tuition: $215/semester hour
Undergraduate cost of books: $600/year
Graduate cost of books: $600/year

Financial Aid/Status

Scholarship programs for adults: Scholarships are available. Full-time and half-time can apply for financial aid.
Full-time status: 12 semester hours/semester.

Maximum Hours Awarded For

CLEP: Yes
DANTES: Yes
Other exams: Yes
Prior learning portfolio: Yes
Additional information: 21 semester hours allowed by exam; 21 for the A.S. or 39 for the B.S. for credit for prior learning

Features and Services

1. Is it possible to purchase books during hours most adult students attend classes? **Yes.**

2. Are the institution's administrative offices open during hours adult students attend class? **Yes.**

3. How do students taking extended classes access library resources? **The library is open evenings.**

4. What is the registration and payment process for adult students? **Offices are open late the first night of each evening class to allow students to finish business.**

5. What is the process for advising adult students? **Advising is available by appointment.**

6. What career and placement services are available to adult students? **The placement office is available 8-5. Job listings are mailed on request.**

Indiana Institute of Technology

1600 E. Washington Blvd. ◆ **Fort Wayne, IN 46803**
Phone: (219) 422-5561 ◆ Toll-free phone: (800) 288-1766
Fax: (219) 422-1518 ◆ Web address: http://www.indtech.edu/
Program's Web address: http://www.indtech.edu/academia/
esdhome.html

Founded: 1930

Accredited by: North Central

Enrollment: 1,400 ◆ Adult students: 700

University status: Private

Degree	Concentration/Major	Format
A.S.	Management	A,C
A.S.	Finance	A,C
B.S.	Management	A,C
B.S.	Finance	A,C
B.S.	Marketing	A,C
B.S.	Human Resources	A,C
B.S.	Quality Management	A

Campus Extension Sites

Indianapolis, IN
South Bend, IN

Requirements

Residency requirement: Students in the accelerated programs must attend classes on campus. Students in the correspondence programs do not have to attend classes on campus.
Undergraduate admissions requirements: Students must have three years of professional work experience or permission from the Extended Studies Director, submit an application, official transcripts/ GED, or documentation of any transfer credit.
Graduation requirements (undergraduate): Students must have credit hours required for degree (30 hours for a B.A./B.S. at Indiana Tech, or 15 hours for an A.A.), including major requirements, have a minimum GPA of 2.0, and meet all financial obligations.

Fees, Tuition, Costs

Undergraduate application fee: $50
Undergraduate tuition: $173/hour
Undergraduate cost of books: Included in tuition

Maximum Hours Awarded For

CLEP: Yes
DANTES: Yes
Other exams: Yes
Prior learning portfolio: Yes

Features and Services

1. Are the institution's administrative offices open during hours adult students attend class? **Yes.**

2. How do students taking extended classes access library resources? **Students may use the campus library and local libraries. They may access the library by Internet.**

3. What is the registration and payment process for adult students? **ADP students may use the Deferment of Tuition Policy. Independent Study students pay in full.**

4. What is the process for advising adult students? **Admission directors advise new students. Academic counseling continues for present students.**

5. What career and placement services are available to adult students? **The main campus placement director visits off-campus sites.**

6. What characteristics of the institution's adult degree programs are most appealing to students? **Accelerated program, deferred tuition, books shipped to each student and cost included in tuition, and life experience credit.**

Indiana State University

Continuing Education ◆ Reeve Hall Room 316
Terre Haute, IN 46809
Phone: (812) 237-2336 ◆ Toll-free phone: (800) 234-1639
Fax: (812) 237-3495 ◆ E-mail: varner@quad.indstate.edu
Web address: http://www.indstate.educ

Founded: 1865

Accredited by: North Central

Enrollment: 12,181 ◆ Adult students: 15 percent

University status: Public

Degree	Concentration/Major	Format
A.S.	Drafting Technology	E
A.S.	Electronics Instrumentation	E
A.S.	Electronics—Industrial Control	E
A.S.	Secretarial Administration	E
B.S./A.S./M.S.	Vocational Trade—Industrial Technology	E
B.S./A.S./M.S.	Vocational Trade—Industrial Technology Education	E
B.A./M.B.A.	Business Administration	E
B.S.	Computer Technology	E
B.S.	Electronics Technology	E
B.S.	General Industrial Supervision	E
B.S.	General Industrial Technology	E
B.S./M.S.	Human Resource Development	E
B.S.	Mechanical Technology	E
B.S./M.S.	Recreational and Sport Management	E
B.S.	Therapeutic Recreation	E
M.S.	Business Instructional Systems	E
M.A.	Early Childhood Education	E
M.A.	Educational Administration	E
M.A.	Elementary Education	E
M.S.	Industrial Technology	E
M.P.A.	Public Administration	E
M.S.	Technology Education	E

Requirements

Residency requirement: There is an on-campus requirement but no formal class-attendance requirement.
Undergraduate admissions requirements: The top 50 percent of a high school class with college preparation classes are typically admitted. Adult learners are considered individually, with special attention given to employment and motivation.
Graduate admissions requirements: Students seeking graduate admission must meet all requirements of the School of Graduate Studies. Students should contact the Dean of Graduate Studies.
Graduation requirements (undergraduate): Students completing the undergraduate curricula and meeting all university and departmental requirements for graduation will receive the baccalaureate degree.
Graduation requirements (graduate): Graduate programs require a research component, a major, and often study outside the major. Half of the courses are 600 or above. A culminating experience or thesis/dissertation is required.

Fees, Tuition, Costs

Undergraduate application fee: $20
Graduate application fee: $20
Undergraduate tuition: $104.50/credit hour
Graduate tuition: $125.50/credit hour
Undergraduate cost of books: $500/year

Financial Aid/Status

Scholarship programs for adults: Scholarships are available. The Office of Student Financial Aid has information on various scholarships.
Full-time status: Students enrolled in 12 hours are full-time.

Maximum Hours Awarded For

CLEP: 31
Prior learning portfolio: Varies
Additional information: Military credit

Features and Services

1. Is it possible to purchase books during hours most adult students attend classes? **Yes.**

2. Are the institution's administrative offices open during hours adult students attend class? **Yes.**

3. How do students taking extended classes access library resources? **Students may use library services by mail or e-mail.**

4. What is the process for advising adult students? **When a student chooses an area of specialization, a faculty member is assigned as academic advisor.**

5. What career and placement services are available to adult students? **The Career Center** is a campus agency offering all students career services.

6. What characteristics of the institution's adult degree programs are most appealing to students? **Variety of degrees; programs respond to economic, social, and intellectual needs of students; and belief in the benefits of continuing education.**

Indiana University

General Studies Degrees ◆ Owen Hall 001
Bloomington, IN 47405-5201
Phone: (812) 855-3639 ◆ Toll-free phone: (800) 822-4792
Fax: (812) 855-8680 ◆ E-mail: extend@indiana.edu
Web address: http://www.indiana.edu/
Program's Web address: http://www.extend.indiana.edu/

Founded: 1820

Accredited by: North Central

Enrollment: 94,000 ◆ Adult students: 51 percent

University status: Public

Degree	Concentration/Major	Format
B.G.S.	General Studies—Individualized	E,V,A,C,T, CT,TH,S
A.G.S.	General Studies—Individualized	E,V,A,C,T, CT,TH,S

Campus Extension Sites
Columbus, IN
Kokomo, IN
Fort Wayne, IN
New Albany, IN
Gary, IN Richmond, IN
Indianapolis, IN
South Bend, IN

Requirements
Residency requirement: Students do not have to attend classes on the main campus. Classes at extended campus locations, media-delivered courses, and Independent Study count as "residence."
Undergraduate admissions requirements: For the General Studies degrees, adult students should be 21 or older and have a high school diploma or GED. Provisional admission may be given to adults not meeting these requirements.
Graduation requirements (undergraduate): B.G.S. requires 120 credits including 69 arts/science; remaining 51 can be professional, elective credits. A.G.S. requires 60 credits.

Fees, Tuition, Costs
Undergraduate application fee: $25
Undergraduate tuition: $82.25/hr.
Undergraduate cost of books: $60-$75
Other costs: Learning guide—$9

Financial Aid/Status
Scholarship programs for adults: Scholarship information is available through the financial aid office on campus.
Full-time status: 12 semester hours.

Maximum Hours Awarded For
CLEP: Yes
DANTES: Yes
Other exams: Yes
Prior learning portfolio: Yes

Additional information: Credit for prior learning—30/B.G.S., 15/ A.G.S.; ACE-evaluated military and company training programs

Features and Services

1. Is it possible to purchase books during hours most adult students attend classes? **Yes.**

2. Are the institution's administrative offices open during hours adult students attend class? **Yes.**

3. How do students taking extended classes access library resources? **Students may use local libraries and the Internet.**

4. What is the registration and payment process for adult students? **Registration and payment can be done by telephone (touch-tone), fax, or mail or in person.**

5. What is the process for advising adult students? **Adults are assigned to an advisor in each General Studies Degree office.**

6. What career and placement services are available to adult students? **University career and placement services are available at all eight campus sites.**

7. What characteristics of the institution's adult degree programs are most appealing to students? **An academically solid, flexible adult degree program offered by a traditional university.**

Indiana University-Purdue University-Fort Wayne

2101 Coliseum Blvd. E. ◆ **Fort Wayne, IN 46805**
Phone: (219) 481-6812 ◆ Toll-free phone: (800) 324-IPFW
Fax: (219) 481-6880
Web address: http://www.ipfw.indiana.edu

Founded: 1964

Accredited by: North Central

Enrollment: 11,011

University status: Public

Degree	Concentration/Major	Format
A.S.	A wide variety of degrees are offered.	E
A.A.	A wide variety of degrees are offered.	E
B.S.	A wide variety of degrees are offered.	E
B.A.	A wide variety of degrees are offered.	E
M.B.A.	Business Administration	E
M.P.A.	Public Administration	E
M.S.Ed.	Several areas of study	E
M.S.	Several areas of study	E

Requirements

Residency requirement: Students may need to attend classes on campus for some required courses. Some courses are available through correspondence and over public cable television.
Undergraduate admissions requirements: Students graduating from high school more than two years before the semester may have general admission requirements waived. Particular degree requirements will not be waived.
Graduate admissions requirements: Students must have an earned baccalaureate degree comparable to an IU or Purdue degree with a B or better average.
Graduation requirements (undergraduate): The bachelor's degree requires 120-135 semester credits depending on the major. The associate degree requires 60-68 semester credits depending on the major.
Graduation requirements (graduate): Graduate requirements vary by the major.

Fees, Tuition, Costs

Undergraduate application fee: $30
Graduate application fee: $30
Undergraduate tuition: $89.40/hr.
Graduate tuition: $115.25/hr.
Undergraduate cost of books:
$520/year
Graduate cost of books: $400/year
Other costs: Technology and
student services fee of $6.05/hour;
parking permit of $22/year

Financial Aid/Status

Scholarship programs for adults:
Very few scholarships are available.
Full-time status: 12 hours/semester.

Features and Services

1. Is it possible to purchase books during hours most adult students attend classes? **Yes.**

2. Are the institution's administrative offices open during hours adult students attend class? **Yes.**

3. How do students taking extended classes access library resources? **The library may be accessed by the Internet or in person.**

4. What is the registration and payment process for adult students? **Students register by class rank. Fees due before first class. Cash, check or credit card accepted.**

5. What is the process for advising adult students? **Students may make an appointment with their academic advisor on receipt of letter of admission.**

6. What career and placement services are available to adult students? **Services include career counseling, aptitude assessment, workshops, and lifetime job placement service.**

7. What characteristics of the institution's adult degree programs are most appealing to students? **The quality of degrees earned through Purdue University and Indiana University.**

Indiana University-Purdue University-Indianapolis

425 University Boulevard ◆ CA 129
Indianapolis, IN 46202-5143
Phone: (317) 274-4591 ◆ Fax: (317) 278-1862
E-mail: apply@ses.iupui.edu ◆ Web address: http://www.iupui.edu

Founded: 1969

Accredited by: North Central

Enrollment: 27,000 ◆ Adult students: 53.5 percent

University status: Public

Degree	Concentration/Major	Format
A.G.S.	Associate of General Studies	E,A,T,TH,C,V
B.G.S.	Bachelor of General Studies	E,A,T,TH,C,V
A.S./B.S.	Labor Studies	E
A.A.	Arts and Humanities	E
A.A.	Social and Behavioral Sciences	E
A.S.	Architectural Technology	E
A.S.	Biomedical Electronics Technology	E
A.S.	Civil Engineering Technology	E
A.S.	Mechanical Drafting Design Technology	E
A.A.S.	Food Service and Lodging Supervision	E
B.S./A.S.	Criminal Justice	E
A.S.	Public Affairs	E
B.S./A.S.	Electrical Engineering Technology	E
B.S./A.S.	Mechanical Engineering Technology	E
A.S.	Organizational Leadership and Supervision	E
B.S./A.S.	Computer Integrated Manufacturing Technology	E
B.S.	Construction Technology	E
B.S.	Electrical Engineering	E
B.S.	Engineering	E
B.S.	Physical Education	E
B.S.	Hospitality Management	E
M.A.	Economics, English, History Philanthropic Studies, Journalism	E
M.B.A.	Business Administration	E
M.S.W.	Social Work	E
M.P.A.	Public Administration	E
M.H.A.	Health Administration	E
M.L.S.	Library Science	E
M.S.	Engineering, Electrical Engineering Industrial Engineering, Mechanical Engineering, Education	E
J.D.	Jurisprudence, Law	E
Ph.D.	Education	

Campus Extension Sites

Classes are offered in a variety of shopping malls, businesses, and high schools around the city.

Requirements

Residency requirement: The Associate of General Studies can be earned off campus. Other degrees may be earned partially off campus. Undergraduate admissions requirements: For General Studies admissions the student must be over 21 and a high school graduate. Other programs have specific requirements. A preparatory program aids anyone not able to meet the requirements.
Graduate admissions requirements: Requirements for graduate degrees vary greatly, depending on the program.
Graduation requirements (undergraduate): The requirements vary with the program.
Graduation requirements (graduate): The requirements vary with the program.

Fees, Tuition, Costs

Undergraduate application fee: $25
Graduate application fee: $25
Undergraduate tuition: $97.75/ credit
Undergraduate cost of books: $25 to $100/course
Graduate cost of books: Varies greatly
Other costs: Include technology fee of $25 to $75; student activity fee of $12.95 to $21.85; parking fee of $25.75; athletic development fee of $15

Financial Aid/Status

Scholarship programs for adults: Scholarships are available to adult students.
Full-time status: Full-time undergraduate students are

enrolled for 12 credits. Percentage of adult students receiving financial aid: 80 percent.

Maximum Hours Awarded For

CLEP: Yes
DANTES: Yes
Other exams: Yes
Prior learning portfolio: Yes
Additional information: ACE Guide recommendations for government and business training considered for credit

Features and Services

1. Is it possible to purchase books during hours most adult students attend classes? **Yes.**

2. Are the institution's administrative offices open during hours adult students attend class? **Yes.**

3. How do students taking extended classes access library resources? **Electronic access to the library is available.**

4. What is the registration and payment process for adult students? **All registration and payment can be done by mail, phone, or computer.**

5. What is the process for advising adult students? Advising can be done by phone, e-mail, or mail or in person.

6. What career and placement services are available to adult students? **An active Career Center serves the campus. Some schools have their own placement service.**

7. What characteristics of the institution's adult degree programs are most appealing to students? **General Studies is a program only for adults, but the average undergraduate's age is 27. One-third of classes offered in the evening or on weekend.**

Indiana Wesleyan University

4406 South Harmon ◆ **Marion, IN 46953**
Phone: (317) 677-2350 ◆ Toll-free phone: (800) 621-8667
Fax: (317) 677-2380 ◆ Web address: http://www.indwes.edu

Founded: 1920

Accredited by: North Central

Enrollment: 5,060 ◆ Adult students: 77 percent

University status: Private, Church, Wesleyan Church

Degree	Concentration/Major	Format
A.S.	Business	E,A
A.S.	Christian Studies	V
B.S.	Business Administration	E,A
B.S.	Management	E,A
B.S.	Nursing	E,A
B.S.	Addiction Counseling	E,A
M.B.A.	Business Administration	E,A
M.Ed.	Education	E,A
M.S.	Management	E,A
M.S.	Community Health Nursing	E
M.S.	Primary Care Nursing	E
M.A.	Counseling	E
M.A.	Ministerial Education	Weeklong

Campus Extension Sites

Indianapolis, IN
Terre Haute, IN
Kokomo, IN
Fort Wayne, IN
Columbus, IN
Lafayette, IN
Richmond, IN
Bloomington, IN
Warsaw/Plymouth, IN
Shelbyville, IN
South Bend, IN
Mooresville, IN
Batesville/Greensburg, IN

Requirements

Residency requirement: Students do not have to attend classes on the main campus.
Undergraduate admissions requirements: Admission requires proof of high school graduation or GED, transcripts of any prior college credit, two years of work experience, and two recommendations. Some programs have additional requirements.
Graduate admissions requirements:

Graduate admission requires an undergraduate degree with minimum GPA, three years of work experience, and two recommendations. Some programs have additional requirements.

Graduation requirements (undergraduate): Students must complete 124 semester hours including core courses, cumulative minimum GPA of 2.0 or more, payment of all tuition and fees. Other requirements depend on the program.

Graduation requirements (graduate): Graduation requires completion of all credits in the curriculum sequence, minimum GPA of 3.0, payment of all tuition and fees. Other requirements vary by the degree.

Fees, Tuition, Costs

Undergraduate application fee: $15
Graduate application fee: $15

Financial Aid/Status

Scholarship programs for adults: Not available.
Full-time status: A full-time student is enrolled in the degree completion program.
Percentage of adult students receiving financial aid: 33 percent.

Maximum Hours Awarded For

CLEP: Yes
PEP: Yes
DANTES: Yes
Prior learning portfolio: Yes
Additional information: 18 prior learning credits/associate; 40/bachelors; correspondence study—12 hours

Features and Services

1. How do students taking extended classes access library resources? **Students have access to off-campus**

library services by an 800 number, online, and at various campuses.

2. What is the registration and payment process for adult students? **Registration for whole core program at first class. First payment made, then installment payments are scheduled.**

3. What is the process for advising adult students? **Assigned advisors meet one-on-one at regional location. Phone advising is available daily.**

4. What characteristics of the institution's adult degree programs are most appealing to students? **Development and support from the cohort group, convenient class location, and accelerated natural of program.**

InterAmerican University of Puerto Rico

Call Box 10004 ◆ Guayama, PR 00785
Phone: (787) 864-2222 ◆ Fax: (787) 864-8232
E-mail: njtorres@ns.inter.edu

Founded: 1957

Accredited by: Middle States

Enrollment: 2,063 ◆ Adult students: 743

University status: Private

Degree	Concentration/Major	Format
A.A.S.	Install and Repair of Computerized Systems	E
A.A.S.	Accounting	E
A.A.	Secretarial Science	E
A.A.S.	Chemical Technology	E
B.B.A.	Accounting	E
B.S.	Biology	E
B.A.	Chemical Technology	E
B.A.	Criminal Justice	E
B.A.	Secretarial Science	E

Campus Extension Site

Guayama, PR

Requirements

Residency requirement: Students must attend classes on campus.

Financial Aid/Status

Full-time status: Students enrolled in 12 credit hours are full-time.

Features and Services

1. Is it possible to purchase books during hours most adult students attend classes? **Yes.**

2. Are the institution's administrative offices open during hours adult students attend class? **Yes.**

3. How do students taking extended classes access library resources? **The library offers extended service in the evening and Saturday.**

4. What is the registration and payment process for adult students? **Registration and payment may be made during extended evening and Saturday services.**

5. What is the process for advising adult students? **The institution offers two counselors and three professors to assist adult students.**

6. What career and placement services are available to adult students? **Institution has a career center. Job placement available through the Job Department of Puerto Rico.**

7. What characteristics of the institution's adult degree programs are most appealing to students? **Nontraditional calendar.**

InterAmerican University of Puerto Rico

P.O. Box 4050 ◆ **Arecibo, PR 00614**
Phone: (800) 878-5475 ◆ Toll-free phone: (800) 878-5475
Fax: (809) 880-1624

Founded: 1912

Accredited by: Middle States

Enrollment: 5,500 ◆ Adult students: 945

University status: Private

Degree	Concentration/Major	Format
B.A.	Business Administration	E
B.A.	Education (Elementary, Secondary, Special Education)	E
N.R.S.	Nursing	E
B.A.	Criminal Justice	E
B.B.A.	Marketing	E
B.S.W.	Social Work	E
B.S.	Natural Science (Biology, Chemistry)	E
B.S.	Computer Science	E
B.A.	Secretarial Science	E

Campus Extension Sites

Arecibo, PR
Fajardo, PR
Aguadilla, PR
San German, PR
San Juan, PR

Requirements

Residency requirement: Students must attend classes on campus to graduate.
Undergraduate admissions requirements: Students must be 21 years or older with a high school degree with a minimum GPA of 1.70. Students transferring college credit must have a GPA of 2.0 or better.

Graduation requirements (undergraduate): Students must complete all the credits required for the particular academic program with a 2.0 minimum GPA.

Fees, Tuition, Costs

Undergraduate application fee: $15
Undergraduate tuition: $90/credit
Undergraduate cost of books: $25-$200
Other costs: Lab fee of $30; activities fee; medical insurance; infrastructure; other fees by academic program

Financial Aid/Status

Scholarship programs for adults: Scholarships offered have different requirements.
Full-time status: 12 credit hours/semester.
Percentage of adult students receiving financial aid: 90 percent.

Features and Services

1. Is it possible to purchase books during hours most adult students attend classes? **Yes.**

2. Are the institution's administrative offices open during hours adult students attend class? **Yes.**

3. What career and placement services are available to adult students? **Students receive individual attention through career, academic, and personal counseling.**

4. What characteristics of the institution's adult degree programs are most appealing to students? **Students are not required to take the College Board Entrance Examination.**

International School of Information Management

501 S. Cherry Street, Suite 350 ◆ **Denver, CO 80222**
Phone: (303) 333-4224 ◆ Toll-free phone: (800) 441-ISIM
Fax: (303) 336-1144 ◆ E-mail: admin@isim.com
Web address: http://www.caso.com

Founded: 1989

Accredited by: Distance Education

Enrollment: 70 ◆ Adult students: 100 percent

University status: Private, Profit

Features and Services

1. What is the registration and payment process for adult students? **Students enroll in each course. Payment plans, tuition reimbursement, and installments are offered.**

2. What is the process for advising adult students? **Advising is available.**

3. What characteristics of the institution's adult degree programs are most appealing to students? **Flexibility; accelerated; accredited; expert instructors; afford-able (flexible payment plans, financial aid available to U.S. residents.**

Degree	Concentration/Major	Format
M.B.A.	Business Administration	CT, C
M.S.	Information Management	CT, C

Requirements

Residency requirement: ISIM is a distance learning university. Students do not attend classes on campus.
Graduate admissions requirements: Students must submit a completed application with application fee, three letters of recommendation, and copies of college transcripts as proof of B.A./B.S.
Graduation requirements (graduate): Online program—completion of 9 courses and capstone project; Guided self-study program—completion of 11 courses and capstone project.

Fees, Tuition, Costs

Graduate application fee: $35
Graduate tuition: Online—$14,900; Self—$10,750
Graduate cost of books: $500-$1000
Other costs: Shipping costs, online communication charges, software charges for online program

Maximum Hours Awarded For

CLEP: Yes
PEP: Yes
DANTES: Yes
Other exams: Yes
Prior learning portfolio: Yes

Iona College
The Columba School:
College for Adults

715 North Avenue ◆ New Rochelle, NY 10801
Phone: (914) 637-2786 ◆ Toll-free phone: (800) 231-IONA
Fax: (914) 633-2277 ◆ Web address: http://www.iona.edu

Founded: 1940

Accredited by: Middle States

Enrollment: 5,588 ◆ Adult students: 25 percent

University status: Private, Church, Roman Catholic Church

Degree	Concentration/Major	Format
A.A.S.	Business Administration	E
A.A.S.	Nursing	E
A.A.	Liberal Arts, Social Science, Humanities	E
B.S.	Behavioral Science	E
B.S.	Communication Arts	E
B.S.	Computer Applications and Information Systems	E
B.S.	Criminal Justice	E
B.S.	Facilities and Property Management	E
B.S.	General Business Administration	E
B.S.	Health Care Administration	E
B.S.	Health Counseling	E
B.S.	Humanities	E
B.S.	Psychology	E
B.S.	Social Science	E
B.S.	Social Work	E
B.S.	Computer and Information Science	E
B.A.	English	E
B.B.A.	Accounting	E
M.S.	Health Services Administration	E

Campus Extension Sites

Manhattan, NY
New York, NY

Requirements

Residency requirement: Students must attend classes on campus to graduate; 30 credits must be earned at Iona.
Undergraduate admissions requirements: Students must have a high school transcript with a class standing of 75 percent or higher. Transfer students must have a minimum 2.0 GPA.
Graduate admissions requirements: Students must provide evidence of completing a bachelor's degree (GPA—2.75). Students are admitted as nonmatriculated until completion of 12 credits (GPA—3.0).
Graduation requirements (undergraduate): Associate—60 credits (70/nursing); GPA—2.0; complete liberal arts, degree, and major requirements; file candidate form B.S/B.A.—120 credits; complete all requirements; GPA—2.0; file candidate form.
Graduation requirements (graduate): 36 credits; completion of program requirements including appropriate distribution of credits; minimum GPA of 3.0; complete degree within five years.

Fees, Tuition, Costs

Undergraduate application fee: $25
Graduate application fee: $25
Undergraduate tuition: $300/credit
Graduate tuition: $375/credit
Other costs: Registration fee of $15; computer fee of $20; program fees for nursing; lab fees for some courses

Financial Aid/Status

Scholarship programs for adults: Limited scholarship money is available. The financial aid office has details.
Full-time status: Weekend students—8 credits; evening—12 credits for full-time aid; 6 credits for Pell and loans.
Percentage of adult students receiving financial aid: 80 percent.

Maximum Hours Awarded For

CLEP: Yes
DANTES: Yes
Prior learning portfolio: 40

Features and Services

1. Is it possible to purchase books during hours most adult students attend classes? **Yes.**

2. Are the institution's administrative offices open during hours adult students attend class? **Yes.**

3. How do students taking extended classes access library resources? **The library has evening and weekend hours.**

4. What is the registration and payment process for adult students? **Register by appointment. Payment due by certain date. Deferred payment for tuition reimbursement.**

5. What is the process for advising adult students? **Adult student advising is available.**

6. What career and placement services are available to adult students? **The Career Placement office is available in the evening by appointment only.**

7. What characteristics of the institution's adult degree programs are most appealing to students? **Flexible scheduling; video courses; independent study courses; the every-third-weekend format; adult student advisor availability.**

James Madison University

Office of Continuing Education ◆ Harrisburg, VA 22807
Phone: (540) 568-6824 ◆ Fax: (540) 568-7860
E-mail: currycw@jmu.edu ◆ Web address: http://www.jmu.edu
Program's Web address: http://www.jmu.edu/bgs

Founded: 1908

Accredited by: Southern Association

Enrollment: 11,927 ◆ Adult students: 20.1 percent

University status: Public

Degree	Concentration/Major	Format
B.G.S.	General Studies—Various Concentrations	E,S

Requirements

Residency requirement: Students are required to take a minimum of 32 credits through James Madison University. The 32 credits include various nontraditional mechanisms for earning credit.
Undergraduate admissions requirements: Students must have a three-year lapse in education with 30 semester hours of credit.
Graduation requirements (undergraduate): Graduation requirements include completion of an approved program, earning 120 credits with 32 JMU credits and 60 credits from a four-year school, and a GPA of 2.0.

Fees, Tuition, Costs

Undergraduate application fee: $25
Undergraduate tuition: $264/3 credit hours
Undergraduate cost of books: Market price
Other costs: Experimental Learning Assessment fee of $75/learning component for evaluation

Financial Aid/Status

Scholarship programs for adults: Like any student, adults may apply for scholarships.
Full-time status: The student is enrolled in six credit hours.

Maximum Hours Awarded For

CLEP: No limit
DANTES: No limit
Other exams: Yes
Prior learning portfolio: Yes

Features and Services

1. Is it possible to purchase books during hours most adult students attend classes? **Yes.**

2. Are the institution's administrative offices open during hours adult students attend class? **Yes.**

3. How do students taking extended classes access library resources? **Students may use the library in person or by computer.**

4. What is the registration and payment process for adult students? **Telephone registration is used. Payment may be made by credit card or check.**

5. What is the process for advising adult students? **Advisor chosen by student. Courses in career and life planning, orientation, and portfolio are held.**

6. What career and placement services are available to adult students? **Students have full career and placement services through the Office of Career Services.**

7. What characteristics of the institution's adult degree programs are most appealing to students? **Individualized, interdisciplinary curriculum, open admissions, nontraditional methods of earning credit, and prior learning assessment.**

John Brown University

2000 W. University Street ◆ Siloam Springs, AR 72761
Phone: (501) 524-7100 ◆ Toll-free phone: (800) 528-4723
Fax: (501) 524-9548 ◆ E-mail: advance@acc.jbu.edu
Web address: http://www.jbu.edu

Founded: 1919

Accredited by: North Central

Enrollment: 1,400 ◆ Adult students: 14 percent

University status: Private, Church, Nondenominational

Degree	Concentration/Major	Format
B.S.	Organizational Management	A

Campus Extension Site

Fort Smith, AR

Requirements

Residency requirement: Students are required to attend classes on campus to graduate.
Undergraduate admissions requirements: Students are 25 years or older with two years of relevant work experience; have 60 hours of transferable college credit (GPA—2.0); and submit official transcripts, application, and two recommendations.
Graduation requirements (undergraduate): Graduation requires 124 total hours with completion of both the major and General Education requirements; 2.0 GPA for overall work; and 2.25 GPA in major area.

Fees, Tuition, Costs

Undergraduate application fee: $25
Undergraduate tuition: $3,140/term
Undergraduate cost of books: $225/term

Financial Aid/Status

Full-time status: 12 or more semester hours/term

Maximum Hours Awarded For

CLEP: Yes
PEP: Yes
DANTES: Yes
Prior learning portfolio: 16
Additional information: Military training and experience

Features and Services

1. Is it possible to purchase books during hours most adult students attend classes? **Yes.**

2. Are the institution's administrative offices open during hours adult students attend class? **Yes.**

3. How do students taking extended classes access library resources? **Students have access to the library through computer modem and the Internet.**

4. What is the registration and payment process for adult students? **Registration is conducted in the evenings. A payment plan is available.**

5. What is the process for advising adult students? **Students are individually advised.**

6. What career and placement services are available to adult students? **The Career Development Center is available to all students.**

7. What characteristics of the institution's adult degree programs are most appealing to students? **Group dynamics, accelerated program, many convenient instructional sites in the community, and good academic reputation of the university.**

John F. Kennedy University

12 Altarinda Road ◆ **Orinda, CA 94563**
Phone: (510) 254-0200 ◆ Fax: (510) 254-6964
Web address: http://www.jfku.edu

Founded: 1964

Accredited by: Western Association

Enrollment: 1,829 ◆ Adult students: 100 percent

University status: Private

Degree	Concentration/Major	Format
B.A.	Liberal Arts	E
B.S.	Business Administration	E
M.B.A.	Concentrations in Organizational Leadership, Management, Financial Management, International Business	E
M.A.	Management	E
M.A.	Counseling Psychology—Marriage Family and Child Counseling	E
M.A.	Career Development	E,C
M.A.	Arts and Consciousness	E
M.A.	Interdisciplinary Consciousness Studies	E
M.A.	Holistic Health	E
M.A.	Transpersonal Psychology	E
M.A.	Consulting Psychology	E
M.A.	Sport Psychology	E
M.A.	Museum Studies	E
M.A.T.	Teaching	E
PSY.D.	Psychology	E
J.D.	Law	E

Campus Extension Sites

Walnut Creek, CA
Orinda, CA
Campbell, CA

Requirements

Residency requirement: All degree programs except M.A. in Career Development require on-campus class attendance. Career Development has a two-week summer residency requirement. Undergraduate admissions requirements: Students must have a personal interview and submit a personal statement and official transcripts of high school and prior college attendance.
Graduate admissions requirements: Students must submit a personal statement and all official transcripts of college credits and have a personal interview. Some programs may require recommendations, resumes, or testing.
Graduation requirements (undergraduate): Students must earn 180 quarter units and complete the General Education,

major, and university requirements.
Graduation requirements (graduate): The number of quarter units required for graduation depends on the program. Students must complete a master's project, thesis, final integrative project, or comprehensive examination.

Fees, Tuition, Costs

Undergraduate application fee: $50
Graduate application fee: $50
Undergraduate tuition: $187/ quarter unit
Graduate tuition: Varies—$251/ quarter unit

Financial Aid/Status

Scholarship programs for adults: Scholarships available
Full-time status: Undergraduate— 12 units/quarter; graduate—9 units/quarter
Percentage of adult students receiving financial aid: 44 percent

Maximum Hours Awarded For

CLEP: Yes
PEP: Yes
DANTES: Yes
Prior learning portfolio: 30
Additional information: Maximum of 105 quarter units of CLEP in combination with transfer from two-year college

Features and Services

1. Is it possible to purchase books during hours most adult students attend classes? **Yes.**

2. Are the institution's administrative offices open during hours adult students attend class? **Yes.**

3. What is the registration and payment process for adult students? **Generally registration is done in person. Some programs use mail registration.**

4. What career and placement services are available to adult students? **The Career Center may be used by adult students.**

5. What characteristics of the institution's adult degree programs are most appealing to students? **Convenient schedule (late afternoon, evening, weekend classes) and the ability to integrate education with family, civic, and job responsibilities.**

Johnson State College

R.R. #2 Box 75 ◆ **Johnson, VT 05656**

Phone: (802) 635-2356 ◆ Toll-free phone: (800) 635-2356

Fax: (802) 635-2145 ◆ E-mail: jscapply@jscals.vsc.edu

Web address: http://www.genghis.com/vt/html/johnson.htm

Founded: 1828

Accredited by: New England

Enrollment: 1,618 ◆ Adult students: 30 percent

University status: Public

Degree	Concentration/Major	Format
B.A.	Anthropology and Sociology	E,C,T,S
B.A.	Art	E,C,T,S
B.A.	Biology	E,C,T,S
B.A.	Business Management	E,C,T,S
B.A.	Elementary Education	E,C,T,S
B.A.	English	E,C,T,S
B.A.	History	E,C,T,S
B.A.	Hotel/Hospitality Management	E,C,T,S
B.A.	Liberal Arts	E,C,T,S
B.A.	Music	E,C,T,S
B.A.	Performing Arts	E,C,T,S
B.A.	Political Science	E,C,T,S
B.A.	Psychology	E,C,T,S
B.F.A.	Performing Arts	E,C,T,S
B.F.A.	Studio Arts	E,C,T,S
B.F.A.	Writing and Literature	E,C,T,S
B.S.	Biology	E,C,T,S
B.S.	Environmental Science	E,C,T,S
B.S.	General Studies	E,C,T,S
B.S.	Health Sciences	E,C,T,S
B.S.	Health Services Administration	E,C,T,S
B.S.	Mathematics	E,C,T,S

Campus Extension Sites
State-wide

Requirements
Residency requirement: The External Degree Program requires no campus residency. Credits may be earned through classes sponsored by Johnson State College, courses at other colleges, and independent study. Undergraduate admissions requirements: Students must have at least 60 college-level credits with C- or better. Credit may be earned in a variety of ways. Graduation requirements (undergraduate): Accumulate 120 credits including 60 transfer credits, 30 credits earned through JSC, GPA of 2.0, meet concentration and general education requirements, submit a degree plan, and pass a writing proficiency test.

Fees, Tuition, Costs
Undergraduate tuition: $143/credit
Undergraduate cost of books: $500

Financial Aid/Status
Scholarship programs for adults: Adult learners may apply for financial aid.

Maximum Hours Awarded For
Prior learning portfolio: Yes. Additional information: Students may gain advanced standing through an assessment of learning from life experience.

Features and Services

1. What is the registration and payment process for adult students? **Registration materials are mailed each semester. A mentor must approve the registration.**

2. What is the process for advising adult students? **A mentor in the student's community advises, instructs, and acts as an advocate for the student.**

3. What characteristics of the institution's adult degree programs are most appealing to students? **Flexibility, variety of course formats, and convenience of learning in one's own community.**

Joint Military Intelligence College

Joint Military Intelligence College (MCA-2)
Washington, DC 20340-5100
Phone: (202) 231-3299 ◆ Fax: (202) 231-8652

Founded: 1962

Accredited by: Middle States

Enrollment: 450

University status: Public

Degree	Concentration/Major	Format
M.S.	Strategic Intelligence	E

Campus Extension Sites

Dayton, OH
Fort Meade, MD
Washington, DC

Requirements

Residency requirement: Students are not required to attend classes on the main campus; however, they must attend classes at the home campus or an extended location. Graduate admissions requirements: Only government employees and military service members may apply. Students must pass a security clearance. The Miller Analogies Test is required. Graduation requirements (graduate): Students must complete 8 core and 6 elective courses and complete a master's thesis.

Fees, Tuition, Costs

Graduate application fee: $0
Graduate tuition: $0

Features and Services

1. Are the institution's administrative offices open during hours adult students attend class? **Yes.**

2. How do students taking extended classes access library resources? **Students have 24-hour access to the library.**

3. What is the registration and payment process for adult students? **Students preregister quarter-by-quarter and must attend lobby registration.**

4. What is the process for advising adult students? **Initial counseling is done by the enrollment staff. Follow-up advising is done by the thesis advisor.**

5. What characteristics of the institution's adult degree programs are most appealing to students? **The curriculum itself is unique. This is the only accredited graduate school teaching intelligence with access to classified materials.**

Judson College*

1151 N. State Street ◆ **Elgin, IL 60123**
Phone: (708) 695-2500 ◆ Fax: (708) 695-2500

Founded: 1964

Accredited by: North Central

Enrollment: 706 ◆ Adult students: 90

University status: Private, Church, American Baptist Church

Degree	Concentration/Major	Format
BA	Management and Leadership	E,A

Requirements

Residency requirement: Students attend classes one evening a week for 16 months in a talent-development approach. Undergraduate admissions requirements: At least 25 years of age; five years of work-related experience; minimum of 40 college credits.

Fees, Tuition, Costs

Undergraduate application fee: $30
Undergraduate tuition: $4,200

Financial Aid/Status

Full-time status: 12 or more semester hours/term
Percentage of adult students receiving financial aid: 50 percent

Maximum Hours Awarded For

CLEP: 30
PEP: 30
DANTES: 30
Other exams: 30
Prior learning portfolio: 30

Features and Services

1. Is it possible to purchase books during hours most adult students attend classes? **Yes** .

2. Are the institution's administrative offices open during hours adult students attend class? **Yes.**

3. What characteristics of the institution's adult degree programs are most appealing to students? **Customized educational plan using a talent development instructional design; Convenience and individualized attention.**

Judson College

P.O. Box 120 ◆ **Marion, AL 36756**
Phone: (334) 683-5123 ◆ Toll-free phone: (800) 447-9472
Fax: (334) 683-5147 ◆ E-mail: nchenson@future.judson.edu
Web address: http://www.judson.educ

Founded: 1838

Accredited by: Southern Association

Enrollment: 350 ◆ Adult students: 7 percent

University status: Private, Church, Alabama Baptist Church

Degree	Concentration/Major	Format
B.A.	Business	C
B.S.	Business	C
B.A.	English	C
B.A.	History	C
B.A.	Psychology	C
B.S.	Psychology	C
B.A.	Criminal Justice	C
B.A.	Religious Studies	C

Requirements

Residency requirement: Students must attend a one-day orientation as part of the education course on degree planning.
Undergraduate admissions requirements: Applicants must submit official high school and college transcripts or GED, 500-word essay, ACT/SAT scores, and references if needed. A commitment to learning is needed.
Graduation requirements (undergraduate): Students must earn at least 128 hours, complete general education core, a major, a minor, and successfully complete the English Language Usage exam.

Fees, Tuition, Costs

Undergraduate application fee: $40
Undergraduate tuition: $186/semester hour
Undergraduate cost of books: $30-$50/course
Other costs: Prior learning assessment fees

Financial Aid/Status

Full-time status: Enrollment for 12 semester hours/6 months
Percentage of adult students receiving financial aid: 80 percent

Maximum Hours Awarded For

CLEP: Yes
DANTES: Yes
Other exams: Yes
Prior learning portfolio: Yes

Features and Services

1. Is it possible to purchase books during hours most adult students attend classes? **Yes.**

2. Are the institution's administrative offices open during hours adult students attend class? **Yes.**

3. How do students taking extended classes access library resources? **Students may use the local library in their community.**

4. What is the registration and payment process for adult students? **Tuition is paid when the student signs the individual learning contract with the institution.**

5. What is the process for advising adult students? **Advising is provided through the Director of External Studies and the chair of the student's major.**

6. What characteristics of the institution's adult degree programs are most appealing to students? **Lower student-to-faculty ratio; courses taught through distance learning are taught by professors in Judson's traditional program.**

Kansas State University*

Division of Continuing Education
225 College Court ◆ **Manhattan, KS 66506**
Phone: (913) 532-5687 ◆ Toll-free phone: (800) 622-2KSU
Fax: (913) 532-5637 ◆ Web address: http://www.ksu.edu

Founded: 1863

Accredited by: North Central

Enrollment: 20,000 ◆ Adult students: 130

University status: Public

Features and Services

1. Is it possible to purchase books during hours most adult students attend classes? **Yes.**

2. Are the institution's administrative offices open during hours adult students attend class? **Yes.**

3. What characteristics of the institution's adult degree programs are most appealing to students? **The degree can be completed entirely off campus.**

Degree	Concentration/Major	Format
B.S.	Interdisciplinary Social Science	C,T,V,S
B.S.	Agriculture	C,T,V,S
B.S.	Animal Sciences	C,T,V,S
B.S.	Industry	C,T,V,S

Requirements

Residency requirement: It takes a combination of all methods to earn the degree.
Undergraduate admissions requirements: Student must have already earned a minimum of 60 semester hours of college credit and have an overall GPA of 2.0 or higher.

Fees, Tuition, Costs

Undergraduate application fee: $25
Undergraduate tuition: $465/3 hours

Financial Aid/Status

Full-time status: 12 hours or more/ semester
Percentage of adult students receiving financial aid: 20 percent

Maximum Hours Awarded For

CLEP: Yes

Keller Graduate School of Management

One Tower Lane ◆ **Oakbrook Terrace, IL 60181**
Phone: (708) 574-1957 ◆ Fax: (708) 574-1969

Founded: 1973

Accredited by: North Central

Enrollment: 3,800 ◆ Adult students: 100 percent

University status: Private, Profit

Degree	Concentration/Major	Format
M.B.A.	Accounting	E,A
M.B.A.	Project Management	E,A
M.B.A.	Health Services Management	E,A
M.B.A.	Human Resources	E,A
M.B.A.	Information Systems	E,A
M.B.A.	Marketing	E,A
M.B.A.	Finance	E,A
M.B.A.	General Management	E,A
M.P.M.	Project Management	E,A
M.H.R.	Human Resource Management	E,A

Campus Extension Sites

Mesa, AZ
Atlanta, GA
Phoenix, AZ
Decatur, GA
Long Beach, CA
Chicago, IL
Pomona, CA
Lincolnshire, IL
Schaumburg, IL
Oakland Park, IL
Downers Grove, IL
Elgin, IL
Kansas City, MO
St. Louis, MO
Milwaukee, WI
Waukesha, WI
Tysons Corner, VA

Requirements

Residency requirement: Students must attend classes on one of the campuses to graduate.

Graduate admissions requirements: Students must hold a bachelor's degree; have an acceptable score on the GRE, GMAT, or Keller's admission test; and complete a personal interview. Special admission may be possible under certain circumstances.

Graduation requirements (graduate): The M.B.A. requires completion of 16 courses, including 5 management core, 5 program-specific, and 6 elective courses. Programs may vary in specific requirements.

Fees, Tuition, Costs

Graduate tuition: $855-$1,050/4 quarter hours
Graduate cost of books: $100/course

Financial Aid/Status

Full-time status: Full-time students are enrolled in two courses/term.

Percentage of adult students receiving financial aid: 20 percent.

Features and Services

1. Is it possible to purchase books during hours most adult students attend classes? **Yes.**

2. Are the institution's administrative offices open during hours adult students attend class? **Yes.**

3. How do students taking extended classes access library resources? **Library access online to Dialog and other data bases. Information center available at each campus.**

4. What is the registration and payment process for adult students? **Registration and payment by mail, or payment can be made at first class. Payment plan, loans, and tuition reimbursement are used.**

5. What is the process for advising adult students? **Students with GPA below 2.40 should contact the center director for academic advising.**

6. What career and placement services are available to adult students? **Full career services are available including workshops, a video, and job postings.**

7. What characteristics of the institution's adult degree programs are most appealing to students? **Practitioner orientation, excellent teaching in the classroom, and service to working adults.**

King's College*

133 N. River Street ◆ **Wilkes-Barre, PA 18711**
Phone: (717) 826-5865 ◆ Fax: (717) 825-9049
Web address: http://www.kings.edu

Founded: 1946

Accredited by: Middle States

Enrollment: 2,200 ◆ Adult students: 450

University status: Private, Church, Roman Catholic Church

Features and Services

1. Is it possible to purchase books during hours most adult students attend classes? **Yes.**

2. Are the institution's administrative offices open during hours adult students attend class? **Yes.**

Degree	Concentration/Major	Format
B.S.	Business Administration	E,A
M.S.	Accounting	E
M.S.	Finance	E
M.S.	Taxation	E
M.S.	Health Care Administration	E

Requirements

Residency requirement: Yes. Undergraduate admissions requirements: Standard admissions requirements are used; however, the SAT is not required for adult learning students.
Graduate admissions requirements: Bachelor's degree from an accredited college, application, transcripts, professional resume, GMAT scores, and two letters of recommendation.

Fees, Tuition, Costs

Undergraduate application fee: $30
Graduate application fee: $35
Undergraduate tuition: $270/credit
Graduate tuition: $390/credit

Financial Aid/Status

Full-time status: 12 credits or more/semester

Maximum Hours Awarded For

CLEP: 30
Prior learning portfolio: 30

LaSierra University

Center for Lifelong Learning
4700 Pierce Street ◆ **Riverside, CA 92515**
Phone: (909) 785-2300 ◆ Fax: (909) 785-2901
E-mail: ballen@lasierra.edu
Web address: http://www.lasierra.edu

Founded: 1922

Accredited by: Western Association

Enrollment: 1,600 ◆ Adult students: 130

University status: Private, Church, Seventh-Day Adventist Church

Degree	Concentration/Major	Format
B.S.W.	Social Work	E
B.A.	Business Administration/Management	E
B.A.	Liberal Arts	E
M.B.A.	Business Administration	E
M.Ed.	Not specified	E
Ed.S.	Not specified	E
Ed.D.	Not specified	E

Requirements

Residency requirement: Students must commute to the campus to attend classes.
Undergraduate admissions requirements: Adult students must be 25 or older, have 30 semester or 44 quarter units of credit with a 2.0 GPA.
Graduate admissions requirements: The admission requirements for graduate programs depend on the particular program.
Graduation requirements (undergraduate): Students must have 190 quarter credits, including general education, major, and cognate requirements.
Graduation requirements (graduate): Varies by program.

Fees, Tuition, Costs

Undergraduate application fee: $30
Undergraduate tuition: $178/unit
Undergraduate cost of books: $50/course

Financial Aid/Status

Full-time status: 12 quarter hours
Percentage of adult students receiving financial aid: 50 percent

Maximum Hours Awarded For

CLEP: Yes
PEP: Yes
DANTES: Yes
Other exams: Yes
Prior learning portfolio: 45
Additional information: Maximum equivalency credits allowed—32 quarter units

Features and Services

1. Is it possible to purchase books during hours most adult students attend classes? **Yes.**

2. Are the institution's administrative offices open during hours adult students attend class? **Yes.**

3. What is the registration and payment process for adult students? **Students may handle this business through one stop at the office of Lifelong Learning.**

4. What is the process for advising adult students? **Personal advising is available through the Lifelong Learning office. Academic departments give support.**

5. What characteristics of the institution's adult degree programs are most appealing to students? **Quality of courses and convenience.**

Lake Erie College

391 W. Washington Street ◆ **Painesville, OH 44077**

Phone: (216) 639-7879 ◆ Toll-free phone: (800) 533-4996

Fax: (216) 352-3533

Founded: 1856

Accredited by: North Central

Enrollment: 700 ◆ Adult students: 50 percent

University status: Private

Degree	Concentration/Major	Format
B.S.	Accounting	E
B.S.	Business Administration	E
B.S.	Environmental Management	E
B.S.	International Business	E
B.S.	Legal Studies	E
M.B.A.	Business Administration	E
M.S.Ed.		E

Requirements

Residency requirement: Students must attend classes on campus to graduate.
Undergraduate admissions requirements: Entering adults submit high school transcripts, recommendation, and personal statement (500 words). Adult transfers submit college transcripts, GPA of 2.0 or more, recommendation, and personal statement.
Graduate admissions requirements: M.B.A.—college transcripts, minimum GPA of 3.0, two writing samples, recommendation, interview; M.S.Ed.—college transcripts, GPA of 2.75, teaching certificate, three references, interview.
Graduation requirements (undergraduate): Graduation requires 128 semester credits, including the completion of all general education and major requirements.
Graduation requirements (graduate): Graduation requires a 3.0 GPA and completing the requirements of the specific program.

Fees, Tuition, Costs

Undergraduate application fee: $20
Graduate application fee: $20
Undergraduate tuition: $365/credit
Graduate tuition: $380/M.B.A.; $270/M.S.Ed.
Undergraduate cost of books: $500
Graduate cost of books: $500

Financial Aid/Status

Scholarship programs for adults: Scholarships are available for undergraduates only.

Full-time status: A minimum of 12 semester hours.
Percentage of adult students receiving financial aid: 30 percent.

Maximum Hours Awarded For

CLEP: Varies
Prior learning portfolio: Varies

Features and Services

1. Is it possible to purchase books during hours most adult students attend classes? **Yes.**

2. Are the institution's administrative offices open during hours adult students attend class? **Yes.**

3. What is the registration and payment process for adult students? **Registration done in person or by mail. Payment plan, employer reimbursement, or credit cards are accepted.**

4. What is the process for advising adult students? **Each student is assigned a professor from the major field.**

5. What career and placement services are available to adult students? **Career and placement services are limited.**

6. What characteristics of the institution's adult degree programs are most appealing to students? **Small classes, flexible faculty, and safe suburban campus.**

Lakeland College

P.O. Box 359 ◆ Sheboygan, WI 53082-0359
Phone: (414) 565-1272 ◆ Toll-free phone: (800) 569-2166
Fax: (414) 565-1206

Founded: 1862

Accredited by: North Central

Enrollment: 3,640 ◆ Adult students: 66 percent

University status: Private, Church, United Church of Christ

Degree	Concentration/Major	Format
B.A.	Accounting	E
B.A.	Business Administration	E
B.A.	Computer Science	E
B.A.	Marketing	E
B.A.	Education	E
M.B.A.	Business Administration	E
M.Ed.	Education	E

Campus Extension Sites

Chippewa Falls, WI
Madison, WI
Fort McCoy, WI
Marshfield, WI
Green Bay, WI
Milwaukee, WI
Kohler, WI
Sheboygan, WI
Neenah/Menasha, WI
Wisconsin Rapids, WI

Requirements

Residency requirement: A minimum number of credits must be taken at one of the campuses. Undergraduate admissions requirements: Students must provide proof of high school graduation or GED (2.0 or better GPA), or show successful completion (2.0 or better) of course work at an accredited institution. Graduate admissions requirements: Students must provide a transcript from an accredited institution indicating completion of bachelor's degree (minimum GPA of 2.75), supply two recommendations, and meet other requirements depending on the degree.
Graduation requirements (undergraduate): Students must earn a minimum of 128 credits, complete required course work, and have a 2.0 or better GPA.
Graduation requirements (graduate): Students must complete 36 semester hours and meet the course requirements of the specific program. Up to 9 graduate semester hours from an accredited school may be accepted in transfer.

Fees, Tuition, Costs

Undergraduate application fee: $25
Graduate application fee: $25
Undergraduate tuition: $115/semester credit
Graduate tuition: $160-$215/semester credit
Undergraduate cost of books: $50/class
Graduate cost of books: $75/class

Financial Aid/Status

Full-time status: 12 semester hour credits
Percentage of adult students receiving financial aid: 15 percent

Maximum Hours Awarded For

CLEP: 12
PEP: 12
DANTES: 12

Features and Services

1. Is it possible to purchase books during hours most adult students attend classes? **Yes.**

2. How do students taking extended classes access library resources? **Students may use university, college, and pubic libraries in the area through interlibrary loan.**

3. What is the registration and payment process for adult students? **Registration may be done in person or by mail. A payment plan is available.**

4. What is the process for advising adult students? **Each student works with an individual adult education counselor at the class location.**

5. What career and placement services are available to adult students? **Central campus services may be used. Workshops and job boards are available.**

6. What characteristics of the institution's adult degree programs are most appealing to students? **Liberal credit transfer policy, high-quality instructors, low cost, class guarantee, individualized schedule planning, and student service.**

Lamar University

P.O. Box 10008 ◆ Beaumont, TX 77710
Phone: (409) 880-8431 ◆ Toll-free phone: (800) 458-7558
Fax: (409) 880-8683 ◆ E-mail: trammjd@lub002.lamar.edu
Web address: http://www.lamar.edu

Founded: 1923

Accredited by: Southern Association

Enrollment: 8,000 ◆ Adult students: 45 percent

University status: Public

Degree	Concentration/Major	Format
B.A./A.S.	Applied Arts and Sciences	E
B.B.A.	General Business	E
B.S.	Interdisciplinary Studies	E
B.S.I.T.	Industrial Technology	E
B.S.	Communication	E
B.A.	Applied Arts and Sciences	E
B.G.S.	General Studies	E

Requirements

Residency requirement: A complete degree is not available at off-campus locations.
Undergraduate admissions requirements: Students must take the SAT, but if the student is over 25 years of age, no minimum score is required. The exam is used for placement and advising.
Graduate admissions requirements: Students must submit GRE or GMAT scores. Requirements vary with each degree program.

Fees, Tuition, Costs

Undergraduate tuition: $250/3 credit hours
Graduate tuition: $250/3 credit hours
Undergraduate cost of books: $40-$50/course
Graduate cost of books: $40-50/course

Maximum Hours Awarded For

CLEP: 30
DANTES: 24
Other exams: 30
Prior learning portfolio: 24
Additional information:
Correspondence up to 18 hours

Features and Services

1. Is it possible to purchase books during hours most adult students attend classes? **Yes.**

2. Are the institution's administrative offices open during hours adult students attend class? **Yes.**

3. What characteristics of the institution's adult degree programs are most appealing to students? **Off-campus courses, evening courses, and self-designed degree program.**

Lancaster Bible College

901 Eden Road ◆ **Lancaster, PA 17601**
Phone: (717) 560-8220 ◆ Fax: (717) 560-8213

Founded: 1933

Accredited by: Middle States

Enrollment: 696 ◆ Adult students: 18 percent

University status: Private, Church, Nondenominational

Degree	Concentration/Major	Format
B.S.	Christian Life and Ministry—Bible	E,A
M.A.	Bible/Theology	E
M.A.	Christian Leadership—Ministry	E

Requirements

Residency requirement: All courses are offered only on campus. Students must complete at least 11 of the 15 courses in the program. Undergraduate admissions requirements: PLUS 20, a degree-completion program, is open to adults 25 or older with 60 college credits (GPA of 2.0). Students must meet other spiritual, personal, and academic standards.
Graduate admissions requirements: M.A. students must have a bachelor's degree (minimum GPA of 2.75) and a MAT score in the 50th percentile. Students submit application and other credentials. Ministry program requires two years in full-time ministry.
Graduation requirements (undergraduate): PLUS 20 students must complete 120 semester credits satisfying the degree and general education requirements with a minimum GPA of 2.0. 48 credits must be completed at the college.
Graduation requirements (graduate): Graduate students must complete the respective program, including General Studies, Specialized Studies, and the Directed Research Project. Students must have a GPA of 3.0 and meet financial obligations.

Fees, Tuition, Costs

Undergraduate application fee: $15
Graduate application fee: $25
Undergraduate tuition: $11,475/ PLUS 20 program
Graduate tuition: $190/credit
Undergraduate cost of books: $220/term for PLUS 20
Graduate cost of books: $100/ course
Other costs: PLUS 20—enrollment deposit (applied to tuition) of $100, portfolio evaluation fee of $20, graduation fee of $50, change-of-group fee of $50; M.A.—student service fee of $25, graduation fee of $100, transcript fee of $2

Financial Aid/Status

Scholarship programs for adults: Some scholarships may be available.

Full-time status: A full-time student is defined as taking 12 or more credit hours/term.

Maximum Hours Awarded For

CLEP: Yes
DANTES: Yes
Prior learning portfolio: 30

Features and Services

1. Is it possible to purchase books during hours most adult students attend classes? **Yes.**

2. Are the institution's administrative offices open during hours adult students attend class? **Yes.**

3. How do students taking extended classes access library resources? **The library is available in the evenings and on weekends.**

4. What is the registration and payment process for adult students? **PLUS 20 offers evening registration. Books are delivered to class.**

5. What is the process for advising adult students? **PLUS 20 is a lock-step program, with students in the group taking the same required courses in sequence.**

6. What career and placement services are available to adult students? **Adult students may use the college's placement office and its services.**

7. What characteristics of the institution's adult degree programs are most appealing to students? **Degree completion in about 20 months; attend class only one night a week; life experience credits; eligibility for graduate school or seminary.**

Lawrence Technological University

21000 W. Ten Mile Road ◆ **Southfield, MI 48075**
Phone: (810) 204-3100 ◆ Toll-free phone: (800) 225-5588
Fax: (810) 204-3727 ◆ E-mail: aml@ltu.edu

Founded: 1932

Accredited by: North Central

Enrollment: 4,153

University status: Private

Degree	Concentration/Major	Format
A.S.	Chemical Technology	E
A.S.	Construction Engineering Technology	E
A.S.	Electrical Engineering Technology	E
A.S.	Industrial Engineering Technology	E
A.S.	Industrial/Manufacturing Engineering Technology	E
A.S.	Mechanical Engineering Technology	E
B.S.	Architecture	E
B.S.	Architecture-fifth year	E
B.S.	Interior Architecture	E
B.S.	Architectural Illustration	E
B.S.	Business Administration	E
B.S.	Industrial Management	E
B.S.	Civil Engineering	E
B.S.	Mechanical Engineering	E
B.S.	Chemistry	E
B.A.	Humanities	E
B.S.	Math/Computer Science	E
B.S.	Physics	E
B.S.	Engineering Technology	E
B.S.	Administration	E
B.S.	Technical Communication	E
M.B.A.	Business Administration	E
M.S.	Engineering in Manufacturing	E
M.Arch.	Architecture	E
M.S.	Automotive Engineering	E
M.S.	Industrial Operations	E
M.S.	Architectural Engineering	E
M.S.	Information Systems	E

Requirements

Residency requirement: Students must attend classes on campus. Undergraduate admissions requirements: Student must submit an application, high school transcript showing graduation with minimum GPA of 2.5 or GED, and official copy of ACT scores. Graduate admissions requirements: Student must submit GMAT scores, GPA during third or fourth college years, proof of work or leadership experience, and capability of making future contributions in the respective field.

Graduation requirements (undergraduate): Students must complete all course requirements with GPA of 2.0, meet all financial obligations, and submit a petition for graduation.

Graduation requirements (graduate): Students must complete all course requirements with GPA of 3.0, meet all financial obligations, and submit a petition for graduation.

Fees, Tuition, Costs

Undergraduate application fee: $30
Graduate application fee: $30
Undergraduate tuition: $261-$283/course
Graduate tuition: $325/course

Financial Aid/Status

Full-time status: Undergraduate—12 credits; graduate—6 credits
Percentage of adult students receiving financial aid: 66 percent

Maximum Hours Awarded For

CLEP: 6

Features and Services

1. Is it possible to purchase books during hours most adult students attend classes? **Yes.**

2. Are the institution's administrative offices open during hours adult students attend class? **Yes.**

3. What is the registration and payment process for adult students? **Registration is available in the registrar's office or on the computer.**

4. What is the process for advising adult students? **A wide variety of academic and personal counseling opportunities are offered on campus.**

5. What career and placement services are available to adult students? **The placement office assists students and alumni in searching for full- and part-time employment.**

6. What characteristics of the institution's adult degree programs are most appealing to students? **Classes are offered in both day and evening schedules, which complement each other.**

Lebanon Valley College of Pennsylvania

101 N. College Avenue ◆ Annville, PA 17003
Phone: (717) 867-6213 ◆ Fax: (717) 867-6018
Web address: http://www.lvc.edu

Founded: 1866

Accredited by: Middle States

Enrollment: 1,884 ◆ Adult students: 721

University status: Private, Church, United Methodist Church

official transcripts of all college work, and have a personal interview.
Graduation requirements (undergraduate): Students must earn 61 credits (associate degree) or 120 credits (bachelor's degree); minimum QPI (GPA) 2.0; and meet major and general requirements.
Graduation requirements (graduate): Graduates must earn 36 credits of required courses and electives with a minimum GPA of 3.0, with no more than 2 C grades.

Degree	Concentration/Major	Format
A.A.	General Studies	E
A.A.	Accounting	E
A.A.	Management	E
B.A.	Accounting	E
B.A.	English—Communication	E
B.A.	Management	E
B.A.	Health Care Management	E
B.A.	Psychology	E
B.A.	Sociology	E
B.A.	Individualized Major	E
M.B.A.	Business Administration	E

Campus Extension Site

Lancaster, PA

Requirements

Residency requirement: Students must earn 15 credits for an associate degree; 30 credits for a bachelor's degree from LVC.

Undergraduate admissions requirements: Students must submit an application, official college transcripts, and a high school transcript if fewer than 24 transferred college credits. An interview is recommended.
Graduate admissions requirements: Students must have a bachelor's degree, submit GMAT scores and

Fees, Tuition, Costs

Undergraduate application fee: $25
Graduate application fee: $25
Undergraduate tuition: $195/ evening; $300/day
Graduate tuition: $275/credit hour
Undergraduate cost of books: $40-$60/course
Graduate cost of books: $60/course

Financial Aid/Status

Full-time status: Minimum of 12 credit hours/semester
Percentage of adult students receiving financial aid: 13.4 percent

Maximum Hours Awarded For

CLEP: Yes
PEP: Yes
DANTES: Yes
Other exams: Yes
Prior learning portfolio: Yes

Additional information: Maximum of 30 credits (bachelor's degree) or 15 (associate degree) allowed in nontraditional mode

Features and Services

1. Is it possible to purchase books during hours most adult students attend classes? **Yes.**

2. Are the institution's administrative offices open during hours adult students attend class? **Yes.**

3. What is the registration and payment process for adult students? **Registration can be by phone, fax, mail, or in person. Payment due first of semester. Installments offered.**

4. What is the process for advising adult students? **Evening appointments with faculty and continuing education; advisor signs registration form.**

5. What career and placement services are available to adult students? **Services, including computer-assisted career exploration, available by appointment evenings or weekends.**

6. What characteristics of the institution's adult degree programs are most appealing to students? **Personal attention; customer-service orientation; quality education and instructors.**

Lee College*

100 8th Street ◆ Cleveland, TN 37311

Phone: (615) 478-7456 ◆ Fax: (615) 478-7928

Founded: 1976

Accredited by: Southern Association

Enrollment: 1,000 ◆ Adult students: 1,000

University status: Private, Church, Church of God (Cleveland)

Degree	Concentration/Major	Format
B.S.	Christian Ministries	C
B.A.	Christian Ministries	C

Requirements
Residency requirement: Yes
Undergraduate admissions requirements: Application, high school diploma or GED
Graduation Requirements (undergraduate): 130 semester hours; minimum GPA of 2.0; meet other degree requirements

Fees, Tuition, Costs
Undergraduate application fee: $15
Undergraduate tuition: $180/course

Financial Aid/Status
Full-time status: 12 hours/semester

Maximum Hours Awarded For
CLEP: 32
Prior learning portfolio: Yes

Features and Services

1. Is it possible to purchase books during hours most adult students attend classes? **Yes.**

2. Are the institution's administrative offices open during hours adult students attend class? **Yes.**

3. How do students taking extended classes access library resources? **The library is available nights and weekends. Library may be accessed by mail or by on-campus visits.**

4. What is the process for advising adult students? **Advisors available from 8:00 A.M. to 5:00 P.M. Mon.-Fri. Students must have one advising session before completing the last 40 semester hours of work. This session may be by personal visit or by phone.**

5. What characteristics of the institution's adult degree programs are most appealing to students? **Distance learning.**

Lehman College
City University of New York
Bedford Park Blvd., W. ◆ **Bronx, NY 10468**
Phone: (718) 960-8666 ◆ Fax: (718) 733-3254

Founded: 1968

Accredited by: Middle States

Enrollment: 10,000

University status: Public

Degree	Concentration/Major	Format
B.A.	Liberal Arts and Individualized Interdisciplinary Majors	E

Requirements

Residency requirement: Yes.
Undergraduate admissions
requirements: Students must be
high school graduates with an
acceptable high school average or
have a GED.
Graduation requirements
(undergraduate): Students must
complete 128 credits, including a
major and 36 additional credits
outside the major; take a skills-
assessment test; and meet the
college's written English
requirements.

Fees, Tuition, Costs

Undergraduate application fee: $40
Undergraduate tuition: $135/
credit; $1,600/full load
Undergraduate cost of books:
Varies
Other costs: Student activities fee
of $40 (part-time); $55 (full-time)

Financial Aid/Status

Full-time status: Full-time students
are enrolled in 12 or more credit
hours.

Maximum Hours Awarded For

CLEP: 30
Other exams: Varies
Prior learning portfolio: 15

Features and Services

1. Is it possible to purchase
   books during hours most
   adult students attend classes?
   Yes.

2. Are the institution's
   administrative offices open
   during hours adult students
   attend class? **Yes.**

3. What is the registration and
   payment process for adult
   students? **Registration hours
   run until 6:30 P.M. on most
   registration days.**

4. What is the process for
   advising adult students?
   **Adult students may see
   special counselors in the
   Adult Degree Program for
   individual and group help.**

5. What career and placement
   services are available to adult
   students? **Services are
   available through the
   college's Career Counseling
   Services.**

6. What characteristics of the
   institution's adult degree
   programs are most appealing
   to students? **Individual
   counseling services and life
   experience credits for prior
   learning.**

Lesley College*

29 Everett Street ◆ **Cambridge, MA 02138**
Phone: (617) 349-8482 ◆ Toll-free phone: (800) 999-1959

Founded: 1930

Accredited by: New England

Enrollment: 5,600 ◆ Adult students: 700

University status: Private

Features and Services

1. Is it possible to purchase books during hours most adult students attend classes? **Yes.**

2. What characteristics of the institution's adult degree programs are most appealing to students? **Small classes; individualized programs; caring, excellent teaching faculty; and faculty advising.**

Degree	Concentration/Major	Format
B.A.L.	Intensive residency option Use of life experience portfolio	E,C,A
B.A.L.	American Studies	E
B.A.L.	Human Development	E
B.A.L.	Individualized	E

Requirements

Undergraduate admissions requirements: Three- to five-page application essay, three references, transcripts

Maximum Hours Awarded For

CLEP: 16
Prior learning portfolio: 48

Fees, Tuition, Costs

Undergraduate application fee: $45
Undergraduate tuition: $220

Financial Aid/Status

Full-time status: 12 credits/semester
Percentage of adult students receiving financial aid: 30 percent

LeTourneau University

P.O. Box 7668 ◆ Longview, TX 75607
Phone: (903) 233-3250 ◆ Toll-free phone: (800) 388-5327
Fax: (903) 233-3227 ◆ Web address: http://www.letu.edu

Founded: 1946

Accredited by: Southern Association

University status: Private, Church, Nondenominational

Degree	Concentration/Major	Format
B.S./B.M.	Business Management	E,A
M.B.A.	Business	E,A

Campus Extension Sites

Dallas, TX
Bedford, TX
Tyler, Tx
Houston, TX

Requirements

Residency requirement: Students are not required to attend classes on the main campus. Undergraduate admissions requirements: Students submit proof of high school graduation/GED, 60 college credits, minimum GPA of 2.0, four years of degree-related experience, and two recommendations. An openness to the mission of the school is needed. Graduate admissions requirements: Students need a bachelor's degree (minimum GPA of 2.8), three years of relevant work experience, three recommendations, and an entrance essay. They should support integration of learning and Christian faith. Graduation requirements (undergraduate): Students must complete course requirements. Graduation requirements (graduate): Students must complete the core curriculum with a minimum GPA of 3.0, with no more than two grades of C; pay all tuition and fees; return computer; and be approved by faculty and board of trustees to graduate.

Fees, Tuition, Costs

Undergraduate application fee: $25
Graduate application fee: $50
Undergraduate tuition: $8,901/program
Graduate tuition: $11,076/program
Undergraduate cost of books: $1,200/program
Graduate cost of books: $1,950/program
Other costs: Computer deposit (M.B.A.) of $250 (refundable)

Financial Aid/Status

Percentage of adult students receiving financial aid: 80 percent

Maximum Hours Awarded For

CLEP: Yes
PEP: Yes
DANTES: Yes
Prior learning portfolio: Yes
Additional information: Maximum of 30 credits using these programs

Features and Services

1. Is it possible to purchase books during hours most adult students attend classes? **Yes.**

2. What is the registration and payment process for adult students? **Registration is held once for all courses.**

3. What is the process for advising adult students? **Assessment is done at the time of application. A degree completion plan is developed.**

4. What career and placement services are available to adult students? **Students may receive help in resume development and may participate in on-campus interviews.**

5. What characteristics of the institution's adult degree programs are most appealing to students? **LeTourneau strives to remove as many barriers as possible for adult learners.**

Life Bible College

1100 Covina Boulevard ◆ **San Dimas, CA 91773**
Phone: (909) 599-5433 ◆ Toll-free phone: (800) 356-0001
Fax: (909) 599-6690

Founded: 1923

Accredited by: Accrediting Association

Enrollment: 410

Features and Services

1. Is it possible to purchase books during hours most adult students attend classes? **Yes.**

2. What is the registration and payment process for adult students? **Registration is offered day and evening hours. A payment plan is available.**

3. What is the process for advising adult students? **Every student has an academic advisor.**

University status: Private, Church, Foursquare Church

Degree	Concentration/Major	Format
A.A.	Bible	E,C
B.A.	Bible	E,C

Requirements

Residency requirement: Except for the associate degree, can be done totally through correspondence

Maximum Hours Awarded For

CLEP: Yes

Fees, Tuition, Costs

Undergraduate application fee: $35
Undergraduate tuition: $4,560/year
Undergraduate cost of books: $300/year
Other costs: $100/semester ASB fees

Lincoln Memorial University

Cumberland Gap Parkway ◆ Harrogate, TN 37752

Phone: (423) 869-6280 ◆ Toll-free phone: (800) 325-0900

Fax: (423) 869-6370

Founded: 1897

Accredited by: Southern Association

Enrollment: 2,000 ◆ Adult students: 40 percent

University status: Private

Degree	Concentration/Major	Format
M.Ed.	Education—Counseling	E
Ed.S.	Education	E

Campus Extension Sites

Knoxville, TN
Maryville, TN
Corbin, KY
Cumberland, KY
Madisonville, TN

Requirements

Residency requirement: Students do not have to attend classes on the main campus.
Undergraduate admissions requirements: Students must have a minimum high school GPA of 2.5 or an ACT score of 19 or higher.
Graduate admissions requirements: Students must have an undergraduate degree in the appropriate field and submit scores from the GRE, NTE, or MAT.
Graduation requirements (undergraduate): Graduates must earn a minimum of 128 semester hours.
Graduation requirements (graduate): Graduates must earn a minimum of 33 semester hours.

Fees, Tuition, Costs

Undergraduate application fee: $25
Graduate application fee: $25
Undergraduate tuition: $280/credit hour
Graduate tuition: $290/credit hour
Undergraduate cost of books: $300/year
Graduate cost of books: $300/year
Other costs: Vary with the program

Financial Aid/Status

Scholarship programs for adults: Depend on the student's qualifications
Full-time status: Undergraduate—12 or more hours; graduate—9 hours
Percentage of adult students receiving financial aid: 70 percent

Maximum Hours Awarded For

CLEP: 30
Prior learning portfolio: 30

Features and Services

1. Is it possible to purchase books during hours most adult students attend classes? **Yes.**

2. Are the institution's administrative offices open during hours adult students attend class? **Yes.**

3. How do students taking extended classes access library resources? **The library is available nights and weekends.**

4. What is the registration and payment process for adult students? **Evening registration and mail-in payment plans are available.**

5. What is the process for advising adult students? **Advising is available through assigned faculty advisors.**

6. What career and placement services are available to adult students? **Services are provided by appointment as needed.**

7. What characteristics of the institution's adult degree programs are most appealing to students? **Availability.**

Lincoln University

820 Chestnut ◆ Jefferson City, MO 65102

Phone: (573) 681-5206 ◆ Web address: http://www.lincoln.edu

Founded: 1866

Accredited by: North Central

Enrollment: 3,454

University status: Public

Features and Services

1. Is it possible to purchase books during hours most adult students attend classes? **Yes.**

2. Are the institution's administrative offices open during hours adult students attend class? **Yes.**

3. How do students taking extended classes access library resources? **Library hours are extended into evenings and weekends.**

4. What is the registration and payment process for adult students? **Registration is available during the evening and on weekends.**

5. What is the process for advising adult students? **Academic advisors are available for all students.**

6. What career and placement services are available to adult students? **Services are available through the Office of Career Advisement, Planning, and Placement.**

7. What characteristics of the institution's adult degree programs are most appealing to students? **The Liberal Arts program allows students to design their own program.**

Degree	Concentration/Major	Format
B.L.S.	Liberal Studies Program	

Campus Extension Site

Ft. Leonard Wood, MO

Requirements

Residency requirement: Students must attend classes on campus. Undergraduate admissions requirements: Open admissions; 2.0 minimum GPA required for out-of-state students. Graduate admissions requirements: Students submit application; official transcripts; scores from GRE, MAT, GMAT, TOEFL, OR MELAB if English is not native language; and three letters of reference. Graduation requirements (undergraduate): Students must earn a total of 121, credits with 40 credits in upper-division courses and 30 credits in the major.

Fees, Tuition, Costs

Undergraduate application fee: $17
Graduate application fee: $17
Undergraduate tuition: $84/credit hour

Graduate tuition: $168/credit hour
Undergraduate cost of books: $500
Graduate cost of books: $500

Financial Aid/Status

Scholarship programs for adults: Scholarships vary. Several are available.
Full-time status: To be considered full-time, a student must be enrolled in at least 12 credit hours a semester.

Maximum Hours Awarded For

CLEP: 30
Additional information: Cooperative education, dual credit, Advanced Placement, experiential learning—any combination up to 30 hours

Lindenwood College

209 S. Kingshighway ◆ St. Charles, MO 63301
Phone: (314) 949-4933 ◆ Fax: (314) 949-4910
E-mail: info@lc.lindenwood.edu

Founded: 1827

Accredited by: North Central

Enrollment: 5,500 ◆ Adult students: 51 percent

University status: Private, Church, Presbyterian Church

Degree	Concentration/Major	Format
B.A.	Business Administration	E,A
B.A.	Communications	E,A
B.A.	Gerontology	E,A
B.A.	Health Management	E,A
B.A.	Human Resource Management	E,A
B.A.	Valuation Science	E,A
M.S.	Human Resource Management	E,A
M.S.	Gerontology	E,A
M.S.	Health Management	E,A
M.S.	Communications	E,A
M.B.A.	Business Administration	E,A
M.S.	Valuation Science	E,A
M.S.	Human Service Agency Management	E,A
M.A.	Professional and School Counseling	E,A

Campus Extension Sites

St. Louis, MO
St. Peters, MO
Marshall, MO

Requirements

Residency requirement: Students may take classes at any of the sites. Graduation requirements (undergraduate): Requirements vary with the degree. Graduation requirements (graduate): Students must complete the course requirements and write a thesis.

Fees, Tuition, Costs

Undergraduate application fee: $25
Graduate application fee: $25
Undergraduate tuition: $180/credit hour
Graduate tuition: $215/credit hour
Undergraduate cost of books: $200/quarter
Graduate cost of books: $250/quarter

Financial Aid/Status

Scholarship programs for adults: Scholarships vary depending on need and eligibility.
Full-time status: 9 hours/quarter.

Percentage of adult students receiving financial aid: 68 percent.

Maximum Hours Awarded For

CLEP: Yes
DANTES: Yes
Other exams: Yes
Prior learning portfolio: Yes

Features and Services

1. Is it possible to purchase books during hours most adult students attend classes? **Yes.**

2. Are the institution's administrative offices open during hours adult students attend class? **Yes.**

3. How do students taking extended classes access library resources? **Students may use the library from 8:00 A.M. to 12 midnight.**

4. What is the registration and payment process for adult students? **Rolling registration is offered. The payment process is variable.**

5. What is the process for advising adult students? **Students are required to meet with their advisors twice each quarter.**

6. What career and placement services are available to adult students? **The Career Development department assists students with resumes and job placement.**

7. What characteristics of the institution's adult degree programs are most appealing to students? **The accelerated format allows students to complete nine hours per quarter while attending class only one night per week.**

Linfield College*

900 S. Baker ◆ McMinnville, OR 97128
Phone: (503) 434-2447 ◆ Toll-free phone: (800) 452-4176
Fax: (503) 434-2215 ◆ Web address: http://www.linfield.edu

Founded: 1849

Accredited by: Northwest Association

Enrollment: 2,000 ◆ Adult students: 900

University status: Private, Church, American Baptist Church

Features and Services

1. Is it possible to purchase books during hours most adult students attend classes? **Yes.**

2. What characteristics of the institution's adult degree programs are most appealing to students? **Local advisors, evening and weekend classes, and high educational quality.**

Degree	Concentration/Major	Format
B.A.	Management	E,CT,T
B.A.	Arts and Humanities	E,CT,T
B.A.	International Business	E,CT,T
B.A.	Accounting	E,CT,T
B.A.	Social and Behavior	E,CT,T
B.A.	Business Information System	E,CT,T

Requirements

Residency requirement: Yes
Undergraduate admissions requirements: GPA of 2.0 or higher in recent college work

Fees, Tuition, Costs

Undergraduate application fee: $65
Undergraduate tuition: $140

Financial Aid/Status

Full-time status: 12 credits/semester
Percentage of adult students receiving financial aid: 33 percent

Maximum Hours Awarded For

CLEP: 30
DANTES: 30
Prior learning portfolio: 31

Loma Linda University
School of Allied Health Professions
Loma Linda, CA 92350
Phone: (909) 824-4792 ◆ Toll-free phone: (800) 422-4558
Fax: (909) 824-4291 ◆ E-mail: tvalenzuela@ccmail.llu.edu
Web address: http://www.llu.edu

Founded: 1905

Accredited by: Western Association

Enrollment: 3,300 ◆ Adult students: 75 percent

University status: Private, Church, Seventh-day Adventist Church

Degree	Concentration/Major	Format
B.S.	ART-RRA B.S. in Health Information Administration	T
post-B.S.	Certification in Occupational Therapy	E
post-B.S.	Certification in Nutrition and Dietetics	E
post-B.S.	Certification in Health Information Administration	E

Requirements

Residency requirement: The programs require a certain number of units to be in residence on campus. The distance learning program is an exception. Undergraduate admissions requirements: Requirements vary depending on the program. Graduate admissions requirements: Requirements vary depending on the program. Graduation requirements (undergraduate): Students must complete program/general education requirements, earn minimum quarter credits with a GPA of 2.0+, show evidence of moral character in response to university's aims, and meet financial obligations. Graduation requirements (graduate): Students must complete all program requirements, earn minimum quarter credits, show evidence of moral character in response to university's aims, and meet financial obligations.

Fees, Tuition, Costs

Undergraduate application fee: $100
Graduate application fee: $200
Undergraduate tuition: Varies
Graduate tuition: Increase 7/01/96

Financial Aid/Status

Scholarship programs for adults: Scholarships are available through the university's Financial Aid Office.
Full-time status: Undergraduate is 12 units per quarter; graduate is 8.

Maximum Hours Awarded For

CLEP: Yes
Other exams: Yes

Features and Services

1. Is it possible to purchase books during hours most adult students attend classes? **Yes.**

2. Are the institution's administrative offices open during hours adult students attend class? **Yes.**

3. How do students taking extended classes access library resources? **Students may access the library by Internet.**

4. What is the registration and payment process for adult students? **Students may handle these processes by mail or telephone or in person.**

5. What is the process for advising adult students? **Advising is done by program-specific advisors and the Admissions & Records Office of the school and university.**

6. What career and placement services are available to adult students? **Career and placement services are available through the Annual Job Fair and the Alumni Association.**

7. What characteristics of the institution's adult degree programs are most appealing to students? **Career opportunities, job market, and wage scale.**

Louisiana College

P.O. Box 560 ◆ **Pineville, LA 71359**

Phone: (318) 487-7259 ◆ Toll-free phone: (800) 487-1906

Fax: (318) 487-7550 ◆ Web address: http://www.lacollege.edu

Founded: 1906

Accredited by: Southern Association

Enrollment: 1,153

University status: Private, Church, Baptist Church

Degree	Concentration/Major	Format
A.S.	Criminal Justice	E
B.A.	General Studies	C,T
B.A.	Criminal Justice	E

Requirements

Residency requirement: Normally students must take classes on campus. Students who are unable to attend classes on campus may take classes through LC online. Undergraduate admissions requirements: Students must have a high school diploma or GED. Acceptable test scores are ACT (20) or SAT (930-960). Graduation requirements (undergraduate): Students must earn approximately 127 hours—including the completion of core curriculum and major courses, minimum GPA of 2.0, last 30 hours at LC—and meet financial obligations.

Fees, Tuition, Costs

Undergraduate application fee: $25
Undergraduate tuition: $177/hour
Undergraduate cost of books: $250
Other costs: Some course fees

Financial Aid/Status

Scholarship programs for adults: Discretionary and academic scholarships are available.
Full-time status: Full-time students are enrolled in 12 or more hours.
Percentage of adult students receiving financial aid: 90 percent.

Maximum Hours Awarded For

CLEP: 30
Other exams: 30
Additional information: Advanced Placement Test; a maximum of 60 credits may be applied toward a LC degree.

Features and Services

1. Is it possible to purchase books during hours most adult students attend classes? **Yes.**

2. Are the institution's administrative offices open during hours adult students attend class? **Yes.**

3. What is the registration and payment process for adult students? **Adults use the same process that traditional students use.**

4. What is the process for advising adult students? **Adults may use the college counseling center.**

5. What career and placement services are available to adult students? **The college placement and career services are available.**

6. What characteristics of the institution's adult degree programs are most appealing to students? **Flexible hours.**

Louisiana State University at Shreveport

One University Place ◆ **Shreveport, LA 71115**
Phone: (318) 797-5061 ◆ Toll-free phone: (800) 229-5959
Fax: (318) 797-5286 ◆ E-mail: admissions@pilot.lsus.edu
Web address: http://www.lsus.edu

Founded: 1967

Accredited by: Southern Association

Enrollment: 4,233

University status: Public

Degree	Concentration/Major	Format
	A variety of courses are offered	E,V,TH

Requirements

Residency requirement: Students must earn 30 of the last 40 credits in residence.
Undergraduate admissions requirements: Students must submit applications, transcripts, and ACT scores. ACT scores are not required from students graduating five years prior to application at the university. Placement tests may be required.
Graduate admissions requirements: Students must submit applications, all supporting credentials, two official transcripts, proof of MMR immunization. Various programs may have additional requirements.
Graduation requirements (undergraduate): Students must earn 128 credits with a GPA of 2.0, meet the general education and degree requirements, make application, and meet financial obligations.
Graduation requirements (graduate): Students must make application, complete all degree requirements, and meet financial obligations. Attendance at commencement is required unless permission is granted to receive diploma in absentia.

Fees, Tuition, Costs

Undergraduate application fee: $10
Graduate application fee: $10
Undergraduate tuition: $75/hour
Graduate tuition: $95/hour

Financial Aid/Status

Scholarship programs for adults: Scholarships are available; however, there are no special "adult" scholarships.
Full-time status: Undergraduate is 12 hours in the fall; 6 hours in summer.

Maximum Hours Awarded For

CLEP: Yes
DANTES: Yes
Other exams: Yes

Features and Services

1. Is it possible to purchase books during hours most adult students attend classes? **Yes.**

2. Are the institution's administrative offices open during hours adult students attend class? **Yes.**

3. What is the registration and payment process for adult students? **Registration and payment may be handled by phone, mail, fax, or in person.**

4. What is the process for advising adult students? **Advising is available to all students. Some students are required to use advising. Some don't use it.**

5. What career and placement services are available to adult students? **Career Counseling and Placement Division resources are available.**

Lourdes College

6832 Convent Boulevard ◆ Sylvania, OH 43560

Phone: (419) 885-5291 ◆ Toll-free phone: (800) 878-3210

Fax: (419) 882-3987

Founded: 1958

Accredited by: North Central

Enrollment: 1,600 ◆ Adult students: 80 percent

University status: Private, Church, Roman Catholic Church

Degree	Concentration/Major	Format
	All degree programs are available except OTA (Occupational Therapy Assisting). Accelerated classes are available and more are being developed.	E,A
B.I.S.	Students develop a customized, self-designed degree program.	S

Requirements

Undergraduate admissions requirements: All applicants submit an application and transcripts (high school/any college attended), GPA-2.0. LC offers a five-year forgiveness policy. English and math placement tests may be required.

Graduation requirements (undergraduate): Students must complete 128 credits, including 32 hours from LC; general education and major requirements.

Fees, Tuition, Costs

Undergraduate application fee: $20
Undergraduate tuition: $247/credit hour
Undergraduate cost of books: $550/year full-time

Financial Aid/Status

Scholarship programs for adults: Scholarships ($100-$2,500) based on financial need and academic performance are available.
Full-time status: Enrollment in 12 credit hours per semester.
Percentage of adult students receiving financial aid: 99 percent.

Maximum Hours Awarded For

CLEP: 30
DANTES: Yes
Prior learning portfolio: 45

Features and Services

1. Is it possible to purchase books during hours most adult students attend classes? **Yes.**

2. Are the institution's administrative offices open during hours adult students attend class? **Yes.**

3. What is the registration and payment process for adult students? **Registration through college offices; $50 down payment. Payment plan and employer reimbursement are accepted.**

4. What career and placement services are available to adult students? **Career Services offers workshops, career counseling, self-assessment, and job search skills.**

5. What characteristics of the institution's adult degree programs are most appealing to students? **2 1/2 hour class one day a week; morning, evening, weekend classes; life experience credit; small class (35); payment plan; quality education.**

Loyola College in Maryland

4501 N. Charles Street ◆ Baltimore, MD 21210
Phone: (410) 617-5012 ◆ Toll-free phone: (800) 221-9107
Fax: (410) 617-2176 ◆ Web address: http://www.loyola.edu

Founded: 1852

Accredited by: Middle States

Enrollment: 6,264

University status: Private, Church, Roman Catholic Church

Degree	Concentration/Major	Format
B.B.A.	General Business	E
B.B.A.	Accounting	E

Requirements

Residency requirement: Students must attend class on campus. Undergraduate admissions requirements: Applicants are evaluated on academic qualifications, successful completion of secondary school, and SAT-I Reasoning Test. Transfer students submit secondary and college transcripts and SAT scores. Graduation requirements (undergraduate): Students must earn 120 credits, completing 40 courses, with a minimum GPA of 2.0. At least 20 courses must be taken at Loyola. The curriculum includes a liberal arts core.

Fees, Tuition, Costs

Undergraduate application fee: $30
Undergraduate tuition: $15,200/year; $300/credit
Undergraduate cost of books: $650/year

Financial Aid/Status

Scholarship programs for adults: Scholarships are available but not specifically for adults.
Full-time status: 12 credit hours/semester.

Maximum Hours Awarded For

CLEP: 30
Other exams: Yes
Additional information: Advanced Placement Examinations

Features and Services

1. Is it possible to purchase books during hours most adult students attend classes? **Yes.**

2. How do students taking extended classes access library resources? **Library services accessed by modem (Oracle online catalog), dial-in access number (CARL system).**

3. What is the registration and payment process for adult students? **Full-time: meet with advisor by appointment; Part-time: mail in registration or appointment with advisor.**

4. What is the process for advising adult students? **Every full-time student has a core or major advisor.**

5. What career and placement services are available to adult students? **The Career Development and Placement Center is available to students and alumni.**

Loyola University for Ministry*

6363 St. Chandler Avenue ◆ Campus Box 67
New Orleans, LA 70118 ◆ Phone: (504)865-3728
Toll-free phone: (800)777-LIMX
Fax: (504)865-3883

Founded: 1912

Accredited by: Southern Association

Enrollment: 5,400 ◆ Adult students: 900

University status: Private, Church, Roman Catholic Church

Features and Services

1. Is it possible to purchase books during hours most adult students attend classes? **Yes.**

2. Are the institution's administrative offices open during hours adult students attend class? **Yes.**

3. What characteristics of the institution's adult degree programs are most appealing to students? **Intentional learning community in home location, flexible, center areas.**

Degree	Concentration/Major	Format
M.A.	Pastoral Studies on-site print and video.	Learning group; local This course is off campus.
M.A.	Religious Education on-site print and video.	Learning group; local This course is off campus.
M.A.	Pastoral Studies	E, Special summer sessions. This course is on campus.
M.A.	Religious Education	E, Special summer sessions. This class is on campus.

Requirements

Residency requirement: No
Graduate admissions requirements: Bachelor's degree with minimum 2.5 GPA, resume, statement of educational purpose, two recommendations

Fees, Tuition, Costs

Graduate application fee: $20
Graduate tuition: $212/credit

Financial Aid/Status

Full-time status: 9 credit hours/term

Lynn University

3601 N. Military Trail ♦ Boca Raton, FL 33431-5598
Phone: (407) 994-0770 ♦ Fax: (407) 997-9541
Founded: 1962

Accredited by: Southern Association

Enrollment: 1,500 ♦ Adult students: 33 percent

University status: Private

Degree	Concentration/Major	Format
A.S.	Physical Therapist Assistant	E,A
A.S.	Occupational Therapist Assistant	E,A
A.S.	Funeral Service	E,A
B.P.S.	Business, Marketing, Behavioral Science concentrations	E,A
B.S.	Interior Design	E,A
B.S.	Health Care Administration	E,A
B.S.	Elementary Education	E,A
B.S.N.	Nursing degree completion for RNs	E,A
M.Ed.	Varying Exceptionalities	E,A
M.P.S.	International Management	E,A
M.P.S.	Hospitality Administration	E,A
M.P.S.	Health Care Administration	E,A
M.P.S.	Geriatric Care Management	E,A
M.P.S.	Health Care Administration (Nursing Home License)	E,A
M.P.S.	Sports and Athletics Administration	E,A
M.P.S.	Biomechanical Trauma	E,A
M.S.	Criminal Justice Administration	E,A
M.S.W.	Social Work	E,A

Requirements

Residency requirement: Students must attend classes on campus.
Undergraduate admissions requirements: Students are required to have a high school diploma and five years of work experience, or an associate degree and three years of work experience.
Graduate admissions requirements: Students are required to have a bachelor's degree and satisfactory completion of appropriate graduate examination.

Graduation requirements (undergraduate): Graduation requires completing all course requirements with a minimum 2.0 GPA.
Graduation requirements (graduate): Students must satisfactorily complete all course requirements with a minimum 2.0 GPA.

Fees, Tuition, Costs

Undergraduate application fee: $35
Graduate application fee: $35

Undergraduate tuition: $175/credit
Graduate tuition: $350/credit
Undergraduate cost of books: $150/term
Graduate cost of books: $150/term
Other costs: Lab fees for computer and science classes; additional fees depending on degree

Financial Aid/Status

Scholarship programs for adults: Need-based scholarships are available throughout the year from community and national organizations. Each scholarship has its own eligibility requirements.
Full-time status: 12 credits completed between September-December; January-June.
Percentage of adult students receiving financial aid: 45 percent.

Maximum Hours Awarded For

CLEP: 30
PEP: 30
DANTES: 30
Prior learning portfolio: 30
Additional information: Transfer credit from other institutions

Features and Services

1. Is it possible to purchase books during hours most adult students attend classes? **Yes.**

2. Are the institution's administrative offices open during hours adult students attend class? **Yes.**

3. What is the registration and payment process for adult students? **Registration is individualized. A tuition-deferment option for company tuition reimbursement is available.**

4. What is the process for advising adult students? **Individual advising takes place each term. Counseling is available as needed.**

5. What career and placement services are available to adult students? **The Career Center provides assistance. A computerized job search system may be used.**

6. What characteristics of the institution's adult degree programs are most appealing to students? **Small classes, very personalized service, and numerous start times per year allow credits to be accumulated rapidly.**

Malone College

515 25th Street N.W. ◆ **Canton, OH 44709**
Phone: (330) 471-8244 ◆ Toll-free phone: (800) 867-6267
Fax: (330) 471-8478 ◆ E-mail: dmurray@malone.malone.edu
Web address: http://www.malone.edu

Founded: 1892

Accredited by: North Central

Enrollment: 2,000 ◆ Adult students: 25 percent

University status: Private, Church, Evangelical Friends Church

Degree	Concentration/Major	Format
B.A.	Management	E,A
B.S.N.	Nursing	E,A
M.A.	Education	E,A
M.A.	Christian Ministries	E
M.B.A.	Business Administration	E,A

Campus Extension Site
Brecksville, OH

Requirements
Residency requirement: The full management program is offered at the Brecksville site.
Undergraduate admissions requirements: Documented experience. B.A. Management requires 60 transferable credits, 25 or more years old, working full-time. B.S.N. requires current Ohio RN license, A.A., or diploma from NLN-accredited nursing program and six months of work experience.
Graduate admissions requirements: Applicants with a B.A. degree submit official transcripts and recommendations, meet the particular program requirements, and be interviewed by the appropriate Graduate Program Director.

Graduation requirements (undergraduate): Students must complete 124 semester credits; meet the general education requirements; and meet the residency requirement, with a minimum GPA of 2.75 in major and 2.5 overall.
Graduation requirements (graduate): Students must complete 36 hours of course work, apply for graduation, and be present for conferring of degree. Research practicum or thesis may be required.

Fees, Tuition, Costs
Undergraduate application fee: $20
Graduate application fee: $20
Undergraduate tuition: $282/ semester hour
Graduate tuition: $200-$265/ semester hour
Undergraduate cost of books: $350
Graduate cost of books: $150

Financial Aid/Status
Full-time status: 12 hours for undergraduates; 9 hours for graduates
Percentage of adult students receiving financial aid: 25 percent

Maximum Hours Awarded For
CLEP: Yes
PEP: Yes
DANTES: Yes
Other exams: Yes
Prior learning portfolio: Yes

Features and Services
1. Is it possible to purchase books during hours most adult students attend classes? **Yes.**

2. How do students taking extended classes access library resources? **Books and articles are delivered to students.**

3. What is the registration and payment process for adult students? **Registration and payment process are handled in the classroom.**

4. What is the process for advising adult students? **Advising is done by appointment with an advisor or faculty member.**

5. What career and placement services are available to adult students? **Individual advising and services are available by appointment.**

6. What characteristics of the institution's adult degree programs are most appealing to students? **Accelerated program's completion time and lock-step courses.**

Manhattanville College

2900 Purchase Street ◆ **Purchase, NY 10577**
Phone: (914) 694-3425 ◆ Fax: (914) 694-3488

Founded: 1841

Accredited by: Middle States

Enrollment: 1,500 ◆ Adult students: 50 percent

University status: Private

Degree	Concentration/Major	Format
B.S.	Organizational Management	E,A
M.S.	Organizational Management and Human Resource Development	E
M.A.W.	Creative Writing	E
M.A.L.S.	Liberal Studies	E
M.A.T.	Elementary and Secondary Education	E
M.P.S.	Elementary/Special Education, Secondary/Special Education	E
M.P.S.	Special Education/Reading, Reading/Writing	E
M.P.S.	ESL, Second Language Instruction	E

Requirements

Residency requirement: Students must attend classes on campus.
Undergraduate admissions requirements: Bachelor's students must be at least 23 years old and have two years of work experience. Transfer students must have a minimum 2.5 GPA.
Graduate admissions requirements: M.A.L.S./M.A.W.—bachelor's degree, writing sample; M.S.—bachelor's degree, work experience, two letters of recommendation; Education degrees—personal statement, bachelor's degree, recommendations.
Graduation requirements (undergraduate): Students must complete 120 credits and the major requirements.

Graduation requirements (graduate): Graduates must complete all course work. Education students take comprehensive exams.

Fees, Tuition, Costs

Undergraduate application fee: $40
Graduate application fee: $40
Undergraduate tuition: $345/credit
Graduate tuition: $369/credit
Undergraduate cost of books: Varies
Graduate cost of books: Varies
Other costs: Fee for education field experience—$400

Financial Aid/Status

Scholarship programs for adults: Tuition benefits for recently involuntarily unemployed persons are available. This is 20 percent discount for up to two years.

Full-time status: 12 undergraduate credits; 9 graduate credits.
Percentage of adult students receiving financial aid: 25 percent.

Maximum Hours Awarded For

CLEP: 30

Features and Services

1. Is it possible to purchase books during hours most adult students attend classes? **Yes.**

2. Are the institution's administrative offices open during hours adult students attend class? **Yes.**

3. How do students taking extended classes access library resources? **The library is open evenings and weekends.**

4. What is the registration and payment process for adult students? **Mail in registration or appear in person; payment by check, credit card, or installment payments are possible.**

5. What is the process for advising adult students? **Student has an entry interview and is assigned an advisor. Appointments are made for advising.**

6. What career and placement services are available to adult students? **The college's Career Services office is available to all students.**

7. What characteristics of the institution's adult degree programs are most appealing to students? **Personal attention, convenient scheduling, excellent faculty, and college's reputation for excellence.**

Marian College of Fond Du Lac

45 S. National Avenue ◆ **Fond Du Lac, WI 54935**
Phone: (414) 923-7632 ◆ Toll-free phone: (800) 262-7426
Fax: (414) 923-7167

Founded: 1936

Accredited by: North Central

Enrollment: 2,000 ◆ Adult students: 50 percent

University status: Private, Church, Roman Catholic Church

Degree	Concentration/Major	Format
B.B.A.	Business Administration	E,A
B.S.O.M.	Operation Management	E,A
B.S.N.	Nursing	E,A
B.S.R.T.	Radilogic Technology	E,A
B.S.A.J.	Administration of Justice	E,A
M.S.Q.V.L.	Quality Values and Leadership	E,A
M.S.E.	Professional Teacher Development, Education Leadership	E,A

Campus Extension Sites

West Allis, WI
Appleton, WI
Fond Du Lac, WI

Requirements

Residency requirement: Students may attend classes at any of the locations.
Undergraduate admissions requirements: Students must be at least 23 years old; have 40 transferable college credits, including CLEP, CPL; and have three years of work experience.
Graduate admissions requirements: Students must have a bachelor's degree and three years of work experience, preferably with supervisory responsibilities. An essay and two professional references are required.
Graduation requirements (undergraduate): Students must complete 128 credits, including major—44; liberal arts—30; electives or transfer—54; and complete an individual empirical project.
Graduation requirements (graduate): Students must complete 36 credit hours and a major group research project.

Fees, Tuition, Costs

Undergraduate application fee: $15
Graduate application fee: $25
Undergraduate tuition: $210/credit hour
Graduate tuition: $255/credit hour
Undergraduate cost of books: $60
Graduate cost of books: $70

Financial Aid/Status

Full-time status: 12 credit hours/term
Percentage of adult students receiving financial aid: 10 percent

Maximum Hours Awarded For

CLEP: Yes
Prior learning portfolio: 36

Features and Services

1. Is it possible to purchase books during hours most adult students attend classes? **Yes.**

2. What is the registration and payment process for adult students? **Registration is two weeks before first class. Payment is due the first day of class.**

3. What is the process for advising adult students? **Advising is done by individual appointment.**

4. What career and placement services are available to adult students? **Career and placement services are the same as those for traditional students.**

5. What characteristics of the institution's adult degree programs are most appealing to students? **Quality of teaching, accelerated program, and supportive staff.**

Marietta College*

Marietta, OH 45750 ◆ Phone: (614) 376-4723
Web address: http://www.marietta.edu

Founded: 1835

Accredited by: North Central

Enrollment: 1,050 ◆ Adult students: 250

University status: Private

Features and Services

1. Is it possible to purchase books during hours most adult students attend classes? **Yes.**

2. Are the institution's administrative offices open during hours adult students attend class? **Yes.**

3. What characteristics of the institution's adult degree programs are most appealing to students? **Small discussion classes and highly qualified faculty.**

Degree	Concentration/Major	Format
A.A.	Variety of majors—not specified	E
B.A.	Variety of majors—not specified	E
M.A.	Education	E
M.A.	Liberal Learning	E

Requirements

Residency requirement: Yes
Undergraduate admissions requirements: High school diploma or equivalent
Graduate admissions requirements: Bachelor's degree

Fees, Tuition, Costs

Undergraduate application fee: $25
Graduate application fee: $25
Undergraduate tuition: $165
Graduate tuition: $240

Financial Aid/Status

Full-time status: 12 or more semester credit hours

Maximum Hours Awarded For

CLEP: Yes
DANTES: Yes
Other exams: Yes
Prior learning portfolio: Yes

Marist College

290 North Road ◆ **Poughkeepsie, NY 12601**
Phone: (914) 575-3800 ◆ Fax: (914) 575-3640
Web address: http://www.marist.edu

Founded: 1929

Accredited by: Middle States

Enrollment: 4,500 ◆ Adult students: 1,200

University status: Private

Degree	Concentration/Major	Format
B.S.W.	Social Work	E,A
B.S.	Integrative Paralegal/Business	E,A

Requirements

Residency requirement: Students must attend classes on campus.
Undergraduate admissions requirements: Transfer students are required to have a 2.5 GPA. Those without prior college credits must take writing and math placement tests.
Graduate admissions requirements: Applicants must submit scores from the GRE or GMAT and letters of recommendation.
Graduation requirements (undergraduate): Graduates must successfully complete 120 credits; have a minimum 2.0 cumulative index; and have a minimum 3.0 index in major field.
Graduation requirements (graduate): Graduation requirements vary with the program.

Fees, Tuition, Costs

Undergraduate application fee: $25
Graduate application fee: $30
Undergraduate tuition: $323/credit
Graduate tuition: $367/credit
Undergraduate cost of books: $300
Graduate cost of books: $350

Financial Aid/Status

Scholarship programs for adults: Adult Learner Scholarships for full- and part-time students range from $300 to $500. A minimum GPA of 2.5 is required. The Miller Scholarship is based on merit and awards up to $1,000.
Full-time status: 12-16 credits.
Percentage of adult students receiving financial aid: 30-40 percent.

Maximum Hours Awarded For

CLEP: Yes
DANTES: Yes
Other exams: Yes
Prior learning portfolio: Yes

Features and Services

1. Is it possible to purchase books during hours most adult students attend classes? **Yes.**

2. Are the institution's administrative offices open during hours adult students attend class? **Yes.**

3. How do students taking extended classes access library resources? **Students may use a computer to access the library.**

4. What is the registration and payment process for adult students? **Registration and payment are handled by the School of Adult Education and faculty advisors.**

5. What is the process for advising adult students? **Advising is handled by the School of Adult Education and faculty advisors.**

6. What career and placement services are available to adult students? **The Career Services office aids students in this area.**

7. What characteristics of the institution's adult degree programs are most appealing to students? **Flexibility, maximum use of transfer credit, and a large elective field for the degree.**

Marquette University

1212 Building Room 103
Wisconsin Avenue P.O. Box 1881 ◆ **Milwaukee, WI 53208-1881**
Phone: (414) 288-3153 ◆ Fax: (414) 288-3298
Web address: http://www.mu.edu

Founded: 1864

Accredited by: North Central

Enrollment: 10,651

University status: Private, Church, Roman Catholic Church

Degree	Concentration/Major	Format
B.S.	Organization and Leadership Program—Saturday only	E,A
B.A.	Arts and Sciences—Psychology, Math, Criminology	E
B.S.	General Business Administration	E
B.A.	Communication—Advertising, Public Relations, Communication Studies, Journalism	E
B.S.	Engineering—Civil, Mechanical, Computer, Electrical	E

Requirements

Residency requirement: Students must attend classes on campus. Undergraduate admissions requirements: Students submit an application, writing sample, high school transcripts, and advanced standing transcripts. Graduation requirements (undergraduate): Students must complete 128 credits.

Fees, Tuition, Costs

Undergraduate application fee: $30
Undergraduate tuition: $315/credit hour
Undergraduate cost of books: $50-$100

Financial Aid/Status

Scholarship programs for adults: Part-Time Studies/Organization and Leadership Scholarships are available twice at $600 each. Full-time status: Students taking 24 credits per year are full-time.

Maximum Hours Awarded For

CLEP: Yes

Features and Services

1. Is it possible to purchase books during hours most adult students attend classes? **Yes.**

2. Are the institution's administrative offices open during hours adult students attend class? **Yes.**

3. What is the registration and payment process for adult students? **Organization and Leadership Program advises students in person. Part-Time Studies students may phone registration.**

4. What is the process for advising adult students? **Organization and Leadership Program students receive much advising. Part-Time students use extended hours.**

5. What career and placement services are available to adult students? **Students use traditional career services program on campus. It is open one evening during the week.**

6. What characteristics of the institution's adult degree programs are most appealing to students? **Saturday classes, accelerated learning, faculty who meet adult learners' needs, and advising available later three days a week and Saturdays.**

Mars Hill College*

Marshbanks Hall ◆ **Mars Hill, NC 28754**
Phone: (704) 688-1166 ◆ Toll-free phone: (800) 582-3047
Fax: (704) 688-1474

Founded: 1856

Accredited by: Southern Association

Enrollment: 1,350 ◆ Adult students: 300

University status: Private, Church, Baptist Church

Features and Services

1. Is it possible to purchase books during hours most adult students attend classes? **Yes.**

2. Are the institution's administrative offices open during hours adult students attend class? **Yes.**

3. What characteristics of the institution's adult degree programs are most appealing to students? **Degrees available, cost, and convenience of locations.**

Degree	Concentration/Major	Format
B.S.W.	Social Work Accredited by American Council of Social Work Education	E
B.S.	Elementary Education Accredited by NCATF	E
B.S.	Business Administration	E
B.A.	Religion	E
B.S.	Allied Health	E

Campus Extension Sites

Asheville, NC
Burnsville, NC

Requirements

Residency requirement: Yes
Undergraduate admissions requirements: Open admission for persons 21 years of age and older who have a high school diploma or equivalent

Fees, Tuition, Costs

Undergraduate application fee: $15
Undergraduate tuition: $80/credit

Financial Aid/Status

Full-time status: 12 semester hours
Percentage of adult students receiving financial aid: 100 percent

Maximum Hours Awarded For

CLEP: Yes
PEP: Yes
DANTES: Yes
Prior learning portfolio: 7

Martin University

2171 Avondale Place ◆ **Indianapolis, IN 46218**
Phone: (317) 543-3237

Founded: 1977

Accredited by: North Central

Enrollment: 530 ◆ Adult students: 100 percent

University status: Private

Degree	Concentration/Major	Format
B.A.	Business Administration	E
B.A.	Marketing	E
B.A.	Communication	E
B.S.	Biology	E
B.S.	Mathematics	E
B.A.	Psychology	E
B.A.	Religious Studies	E
B.A.	Criminal Justice/Pre-law	E
B.A.	African American Studies	E
B.S.	Chemistry	E
B.S.	Computer Technology	E
B.A.	Fine Arts	E
B.A.	Finance	E
B.A.	Addictions Counseling	E
M.A.	Community Psychology	E
M.A.	Urban Ministries Studies	E

Requirements

Residency requirement: Students must attend classes on campus. Undergraduate admissions requirements: Martin University has a liberal admissions policy. Anyone with a high school diploma/GED and the ability and maturity to perform at the college level is welcome to apply. Graduate admissions requirements: Applicants must have an undergraduate degree. Graduation requirements (undergraduate): A minimum of 134 credit hours is required. A final project demonstrating a comprehensive knowledge in the major area is required. Graduation requirements (graduate): Graduates must complete 48 credit hours.

Fees, Tuition, Costs

Undergraduate application fee: $15
Graduate application fee: $15
Undergraduate tuition: $230/credit hour
Graduate tuition: $230/credit hour
Undergraduate cost of books: $200
Other costs: Computer lab fee of $20; student activity fee of $20/semester

Financial Aid/Status

Scholarship programs for adults: Scholarships are available.

Maximum Hours Awarded For

Prior learning portfolio: 6

Features and Services

1. Are the institution's administrative offices open during hours adult students attend class? **Yes.**

2. How do students taking extended classes access library resources? **Students may use the IUPUI or Marion County libraries and the Internet.**

3. What is the registration and payment process for adult students? **Consult advisor. Complete forms at Enrollment Office. Receive clearance from Bursar. Pay tuition.**

4. What is the process for advising adult students? **Students are encouraged to meet with their assigned advisors once each semester.**

5. What career and placement services are available to adult students? **Counselors are available for most situations encountered by students.**

Mary Baldwin College

Staunton, VA 24401

Phone: (540) 887-7003 ◆ Toll-free phone: (800) 822-2460
Fax: (540) 887-7265 ◆ E-mail: adp@cit.mbc.edu
Web address: http://www.mbc.edu

Founded: 1842

Accredited by: Southern Association

Enrollment: 2,000 ◆ Adult students: 60 percent

University status: Private, Church, Presbyterian Church

Degree	Concentration/Major	Format
B.A.	Asian Studies	E,V,S
B.A.	Business	E,V,S
B.A.	Communications	E,V,S
B.A.	Economics	E,V,S
B.A.	English	E,V,S
B.A.	Health Care Administration	E,V,S
B.A.	History	E,V,S
B.A.	Marketing Communications	E,V,S
B.A.	Philosophy	E,V,S
B.A.	Political Science	E,V,S
B.A.	Psychology	E,V,S
B.A.	Sociology	E,V,S

Campus Extension Sites

Richmond, VA
Roanoke, VA
Charlottesville, VA
Weyers Cave, VA

Requirements

Residency requirement: Students do not have to attend classes on the main campus. They are required to attend an all-day orientation on the main campus.
Undergraduate admissions requirements: Students must be at least 21 years old, have completed high school or GED, had some prior college experience

(recommended, with a minimum GPA of 2.0), have basic reading and writing skills, and be within driving distance of a campus site.
Graduation requirements (undergraduate): Students must complete 132 total semester hours, including 33 hours earned at Mary Baldwin College. Additional general education and major requirements must be met.

Fees, Tuition, Costs

Undergraduate application fee: $25
Undergraduate tuition: $258/semester hour
Undergraduate cost of books: $40/course

Other costs: Orientation fee of $25; portfolio evaluation fee of $200; graduation fee of $35

Financial Aid/Status

Scholarship programs for adults: The Adult Degree Program grants $1,000 annual scholarships to outstanding students with high GPAs.
Full-time status: 12 semester hours per semester.
Percentage of adult students receiving financial aid: 80 percent.

Maximum Hours Awarded For

CLEP: Varies
Prior learning portfolio: Varies

1. Is it possible to purchase books during hours most adult students attend classes? **Yes.**

2. Are the institution's administrative offices open during hours adult students attend class? **Yes.**

3. How do students taking extended classes access library resources? **Students may use local libraries, interlibrary loan, and dial-up access to the campus library.**

4. What is the registration and payment process for adult students? **After consulting with an advisor by phone or in person, the process can be handled by mail.**

5. What is the process for advising adult students? **A full-time faculty advisor is assigned to the student at the local regional center.**

6. What career and placement services are available to adult students? **A full-service career center is available by phone or in person.**

7. What characteristics of the institution's adult degree programs are most appealing to students? **Flexibility, an independent tutorial study** option, a large thriving program with good students and faculty, and rigorous academic program.

Marylhurst College for Lifelong Learning*

PO Box 261 ◆ Marylhurst, OR 97036

Phone: (503) 636-8141 ◆ Toll-free phone: (800) 634-9982

Fax: (503) 636-9526

Founded: 1893

Accredited by: Northwest Association

Enrollment: 1,500 ◆ Adult students: 1,500

University status: Private

Degree	Concentration/Major	Format
	All majors are designed for adults.	E,A

Requirements

Residency requirement: Yes. Undergraduate admissions requirements: Admission at the undergraduate level is open. Graduate admissions requirements: Admission requirements vary. Students should refer to the college catalog for details.

Fees, Tuition, Costs

Undergraduate application fee: $81
Graduate application fee: $81
Undergraduate tuition: $189/credit
Graduate tuition: $212/credit

Financial Aid/Status

Full-time status: Graduate—6 credits; undergraduate—12 credits
Percentage of adult students receiving financial aid: 65 percent

Maximum Hours Awarded For

CLEP: 45
DANTES: 45
Prior learning portfolio: 45

Features and Services

1. Is it possible to purchase books during hours most adult students attend classes? **Yes.**

2. Are the institution's administrative offices open during hours adult students attend class? **Yes.**

3. What characteristics of the institution's adult degree programs are most appealing to students? **Flexible hours of course scheduling, ability to design majors around areas of specific interest, and credit for prior learning experiences.**

Marymount College

Webster Weekend College Program
30800 Palos Verdes Drive E. ◆ **Rancho Palos Verdes, CA 90275**
Phone: (310) 377-7742 ◆ Fax: (310) 377-6223
E-mail: marymount@earthlink.net

Founded: 1932

Accredited by: Western Association

Enrollment: 850 ◆ Adult students: 200

University status: Private, Church, Roman Catholic Church

Degree	Concentration/Major	Format
A.A.	Associate in Arts—Weekends	E
A.S.	Associate in Science—Weekends	E
B.A.	Business/Management	E

Campus Extension Site

Irvine, CA

Requirements

Residency requirement: Students must attend classes on campus. Undergraduate admissions requirements: Students must be over 18 years of age. An admissions application must be submitted. Graduation requirements (undergraduate): Associate degree requires 60 units; minimum GPA-2.0; 30 units at Marymount; core and general education courses completed. B.A. requires 128 credits; major, general education, and elective courses.

Fees, Tuition, Costs

Undergraduate application fee: $25
Undergraduate tuition: $239/unit
Other costs: Computer and book expenses

Financial Aid/Status

Scholarship programs for adults: Students should contact the financial aid office for scholarship information.
Full-time status: 12 units in day school; 9 units in weekend colleges. Some aid available for 6 units.
Percentage of adult students receiving financial aid: 40 percent.

Maximum Hours Awarded For

CLEP: Yes
DANTES: Yes
Other exams: Yes
Prior learning portfolio: Yes
Additional information: Military and business experience evaluated using American Council for Education guidelines by petition

Features and Services

1. Is it possible to purchase books during hours most adult students attend classes? **Yes.**

2. Are the institution's administrative offices open during hours adult students attend class? **Yes.**

3. How do students taking extended classes access library resources? **The library is open on Teaching Weekends.**

4. What is the registration and payment process for adult students? **Credit cards over phone or by fax. Business office is open limited hours on Teaching Weekends.**

5. What is the process for advising adult students? **Weekend College has four advisors. Students have access to the transfer center for advisement.**

6. What career and placement services are available to adult students? **Students may use the transfer center.**

7. What characteristics of the institution's adult degree programs are most appealing to students? **Course requires only six nonconsecutive weekends each four-month term. This is one of the few—if not the only—weekend-only programs in L.A.**

Marymount Manhattan College

221 E. 71st Street ◆ New York, NY 10021
Phone: (212) 517-0555 ◆ Toll-free phone: (800) MARYMOUNT
Fax: (212) 517-0413

Founded: 1961

Accredited by: Middle States

Enrollment: 1,876 ◆ Adult students: 40 percent

University status: Private

Degree	Concentration/Major	Format
B.S.	Accounting	E
B.A.	Art	E
B.A.	Business Management	E
B.A.	Communication Arts	E
B.A.	Education	E
B.A.	Political Science	E
B.A.	Psychology	E
B.A.	Sociology	E
B.A.	English	E
B.A.	History	E
B.A.	International Studies	E
B.A.	Liberal Arts	E
B.A.	Theater Arts	E

Requirements

Residency requirement: Students must attend classes on campus. Undergraduate admissions requirements: Students must have a high school diploma and submit scores from a college placement test.
Graduation requirements (undergraduate): Graduates must complete 120 credits plus specific department requirements.

Fees, Tuition, Costs

Undergraduate application fee: $30
Undergraduate tuition: $325/credit
Undergraduate cost of books: $250

Financial Aid/Status

Scholarship programs for adults: Scholarships are available.
Full-time status: 12 credits or more.
Percentage of adult students receiving financial aid: 80 percent.

Maximum Hours Awarded For

CLEP: 30
Prior learning portfolio: 30

Features and Services

1. Is it possible to purchase books during hours most adult students attend classes? **Yes.**

2. Are the institution's administrative offices open during hours adult students attend class? **Yes.**

3. What is the registration and payment process for adult students? **The school offers a one-stop enrollment center.**

4. What is the process for advising adult students? **One-to-one counseling is available with either a general advisor or a faculty member.**

5. What career and placement services are available to adult students? **Individual service is available through faculty in the department. Periodic workshops are offered.**

6. What characteristics of the institution's adult degree programs are most appealing to students? **Individualized attention.**

Maryville University of Saint Louis*

13550 Conway Road ◆ St. Louis, MO 63141
Phone: (314)529-9466 ◆ Fax: (314)542-9918

Founded: 1872

Accredited by: North Central

Enrollment: 3,425 ◆ Adult students: 2,070

University status: Private

Degree	Concentration/Major	Format
B.A.	Communication	E
B.A.	Liberal Studies	E
B.A.	Psychology	E
B.A.	Sociology	E
B.S.	Accounting	E
B.S.	Information Systems	E
B.S.	Management	E
B.S.	Marketing	E
B.S.	Healthcare Management	E
M.B.A.	Business Administration	E
M.A.	Education	E

Course work is offered in late afternoon-early evening, which accommodates teacher's schedules

Requirements

Residency requirement: Yes
Undergraduate admissions requirements: Application and fee, high school transcript or GED score, transcripts from previously attended schools
Graduate admissions requirements: Application and fee, personal letter, transcripts from previously attended schools

Fees, Tuition, Costs

Undergraduate application fee: $20
Graduate application fee: $20

Undergraduate tuition: $9,250/yr
Graduate tuition: $9,250/year

Financial Aid/Status

Full-time status: 12 credit hours/term
Percentage of adult students receiving financial aid: 26 percent

Maximum Hours Awarded For

CLEP: 30
PEP: 30
DANTES: 30
Prior learning portfolio: 60

Features and Services

1. Is it possible to purchase books during hours most adult students attend classes? **Yes.**

2. Are the institution's administrative offices open during hours adult students attend class? **Yes.**

3. What characteristics of the institution's adult degree programs are most appealing to students? **Graduate courses offered at times convenient to students' professional schedules. Weekend college has alternate weekend option, plus desirable degree programs offered.**

Marywood College

2300 Adams Avenue ◆ **Scranton, PA 18509-1598**
Phone: (717) 348-6235 ◆ Toll-free phone: (800) 836-6940
Fax: (717) 961-4751 ◆ E-mail: pmunk@ac.marywood.edu
Web address: http://www.marywood.edu

Founded: 1915

Accredited by: Middle States

Enrollment: 3,100 ◆ Adult students: 60 percent

University status: Private, Church, Roman Catholic Church

Degree	Concentration/Major	Format
B.S.	Business Administration	C
B.S.	Accounting	C

Requirements

Residency requirement: Students must earn 12 credits in residence. This is done in one- and/or two-week increments.
Undergraduate admissions requirements: Students must have a high school diploma or GED (score 235+) and reside within 25 miles of Scranton, PA. Transfer students need a 2.25+ QPA.
Graduation requirements (undergraduate): Students must earn 126 credits with a 2.5 GPA. Four weeks in residence must be completed.

Fees, Tuition, Costs

Undergraduate application fee: $40
Undergraduate tuition: $237/credit
Undergraduate cost of books: $80/credit
Other costs: Semester registration fee; summer registration of $40/3 credits; $70/6+ credits.

Financial Aid/Status

Full-time status: All the students in this program are considered part-time.
Percentage of adult students receiving financial aid: 20 percent.

Maximum Hours Awarded For

CLEP: Yes
PEP: Yes
DANTES: Yes
Other exams: Yes
Prior learning portfolio: Yes
Additional information: maximum of 66 transfer credits allowed

Features and Services

1. Is it possible to purchase books during hours most adult students attend classes? **Yes.**

2. Are the institution's administrative offices open during hours adult students attend class? **Yes.**

3. How do students taking extended classes access library resources? **Students may use local libraries in person and by the Internet.**

4. What is the registration and payment process for adult students? **Open registration is available. Year-round registration by fax and mail is offered.**

5. What is the process for advising adult students? **Personal advising is done by phone or e-mail. Advisement is done in person during residency.**

6. What career and placement services are available to adult students? **Career/placement service is done through advising and reciprocal agreements with other institutions.**

7. What characteristics of the institution's adult degree programs are most appealing to students? **Open enrollment, home study, accredited regionally, and personalized service.**

The Master's College and Seminary*

21726 Placerita Canyon Rd. ◆ **Santa Clarita, CA 91321**
Phone: (805) 259-3540 ◆ Toll-free phone: (800) 229-XCEL
Fax: (805) 254-1998

Founded: 1927

Accredited by: Western Association

Enrollment: 914 ◆ Adult students: 64

University status: Private

Degree	Concentration/Major	Format
B.A.	Organizational Leadership	E,A
B.A.	Christian Ministries	E,A
	Video courses offered to complete general education requirements	

Requirements

Residency requirement: No.
Undergraduate admissions requirements: Applicants must be at least 27 years old, have 60 semester hours of college-level course work in an accredited institution, and make testimony of personal faith in Jesus Christ.

Fees, Tuition, Costs

Undergraduate application fee: $35
Undergraduate tuition: $10,450/program
Undergraduate cost of books: $500

Financial Aid/Status

Full-time status: Enrolled in organizational leadership or Christian ministries programs
Percentage of adult students receiving financial aid: 30 percent

Maximum Hours Awarded For

CLEP: Yes
Prior learning portfolio: Yes
Additional information: Directed studies can be used to earn credits.

Features and Services

1. Is it possible to purchase books during hours most adult students attend classes? **Yes.**

2. Are the institution's administrative offices open during hours adult students attend class? **Yes.**

3. What characteristics of the institution's adult degree programs are most appealing to students? **Discussion-oriented teaching format, application-focused, and equipping emphasis.**

Medaille College

18 Agassiz Circle ◆ Buffalo, NY 14214

Phone: (716) 884-3281 ◆ Toll-free phone: (800) 292-1582

Fax: (716) 884-0291

Founded: 1937

Accredited by: Middle States

Enrollment: 842 ◆ Adult students: 69 percent

University status: Private

$800/term

Other costs: Fees depend on major and full- or part-time status

Financial Aid/Status

Scholarship programs for adults: A variety of scholarships are available. Full-time status: 12 or more credits per semester.

Percentage of adult students receiving financial aid: 74 percent.

Maximum Hours Awarded For

CLEP: 60

PEP: 60

DANTES: 60

Other exams: 60

Prior learning portfolio: Varies

Additional information: Maximum combined credit of 60 hours; Prior Learning Credit—45 toward an A.S., 90 toward a B.A.

Degree	Concentration/Major	Format
A.S.	Government Service	E
A.S.	Liberal Studies	E
B.S.	Business Administration	E
B.S.	Child and Youth Services	E
B.S.	Computer Information Systems	E
B.S.	Financial Services	E
B.S.	Government Service	E
B.S.	Human Resource Development	E
B.S.	Human Services	E
B.S.	Liberal Studies	E
B.S.	Management of Nonprofit Organizations	E
B.S.	Media/Communications	E
B.S./B.A.	Social Sciences	E
B.S.	Sports Management	E
B.A.	Humanities	E
B.S.	Elementary Education	E

Features and Services

1. Is it possible to purchase books during hours most adult students attend classes? **Yes.**

2. Are the institution's administrative offices open during hours adult students attend class? **Yes.**

3. How do students taking extended classes access library resources? **The library is open days, evenings, and weekends. Computer access is also available.**

4. What is the registration and payment process for adult students? **Registration—day, evening, weekend; on-campus courses—in person. Several payment options offered.**

Requirements

Residency requirement: Students may take courses off campus (e.g., at employment location), but to date there is usually a combination of on- and off-campus classes. Undergraduate admissions requirements: Students must submit an application, transcripts from high school or any colleges attended, and proof of immunization. A personal interview is required. Graduation requirements (undergraduate): Students must complete all required courses in the program and electives, earning the required credit hours for the degree, have a GPA of 2.0-2.5, and earn 15 credits (A.S.) or 30 credits (B.A.) at Medaille.

Fees, Tuition, Costs

Undergraduate application fee: Varies

Undergraduate tuition: $9,560/term

Undergraduate cost of books:

5. What is the process for advising adult students? **Student meets with advisor at least twice a year. Evening and Saturday advising available.**

6. What career and placement services are available to adult students? **Services include the Career Library, career planning, workshops, job listings, and placement folders.**

7. What characteristics of the institution's adult degree programs are most appealing to students? **Evening modular format (2+2=12); free, convenient parking; weekend option; small class size fosters camaraderie and individual treatment.**

Mercy College

555 Broadway ◆ **Dobbs Ferry, NY 10522**

Phone: (914) 674-7434 ◆ Toll-free phone: (800) MERCY NY

Fax: (914) 693-9455

Founded: 1950

Accredited by: Middle States

Enrollment: 7,200 ◆ Adult students: 65 percent

University status: Private

Degree	Concentration/Major	Format
B.S./B.A.	All 56 majors offered by Mercy College	E,CT,C,S
B.S./B.A.	Criminal Justice	TH,T
B.S./B.A.	Business Leadership	E,A
M.S.	Human Resource Management	E
M.S.	Physical Therapy	E,CT
M.S.	Occupational Therapy	E,CT
M.S.	Learning Technologies	E,CT

Campus Extension Sites

Yorktown Heights, NY
White Plains, NY
Bronx, NY

Requirements

Residency requirement: Students can take their degrees through a combination of Distance Learning, correspondence, CLEP, and life experience while never placing a foot on campus.
Undergraduate admissions requirements: Students must score a passing grade on the college placement/entrance exam, or transfer 24 college credits with a 2.0 or higher GPA.
Graduate admissions requirements: Students have an interview with the program director and meet the various program prerequisites.
Graduation requirements (undergraduate): Students must earn 120 credits (minimum GPA of 2.0 and major GPA of 2.0) and complete exit competency exams.
Graduation requirements (graduate): Students must have a 3.0+ index and complete a thesis or internship if required.

Fees, Tuition, Costs

Undergraduate application fee: $35
Graduate application fee: $60
Undergraduate tuition: $275/ credit; $6,600/year
Graduate tuition: $355/credit
Undergraduate cost of books: $500/semester
Graduate cost of books: $300-$600/semester
Other costs: International student fee of $500; laboratory fees

Financial Aid/Status

Scholarship programs for adults: Scholarships are available based on need, academics, and community contributions. The maximum scholarship is $6,600 per year. Percentage of adult students receiving financial aid: 70 percent.

Maximum Hours Awarded For

CLEP: 30
PEP: 30

DANTES: 30
Prior learning portfolio: 30

Features and Services

1. Is it possible to purchase books during hours most adult students attend classes? **Yes.**

2. Are the institution's administrative offices open during hours adult students attend class? **Yes.**

3. How do students taking extended classes access library resources? **Students** may access the library by computer and modem from any extension or their homes.

4. What is the registration and payment process for adult students? **The process can be handled by phone or through an admissions counselor catering to students' needs.**

5. What is the process for advising adult students? **Campuses offer weekly evening/weekend information sessions about college demands and career.**

6. What career and placement services are available to adult students? **Six career fairs are held at school annually. The school has an 84 percent placement rate.**

7. What characteristics of the institution's adult degree programs are most appealing to students? **Course schedule for adults using the accelerated program allows courses to be completed in one month by attending two nights a week for three credits.**

Mercyhurst College

501 E. 38th Street ◆ Erie, PA 16506

Phone: (814) 824-2294 ◆ Toll-free phone: (800) 825-1926

Fax: (814) 824-2055

Web address: http://www.utopia.mercy.edu

Founded: 1926

Accredited by: Middle States

Enrollment: 2,500 ◆ Adult students: 25 percent

University status: Private, Church, Roman Catholic Church

Degree	Concentration/Major	Format
B.A.	Management	E,A
B.A.	Accounting	E
B.A.	Marketing	E,A
B.A.	Finance	E
B.A.	Computer Management Information Systems	E,CT
M.S.	Special Education	E
M.S.	Criminal Justice	E

Requirements

Residency requirement: The school uses a portfolio for life experience. In certain situations, tutorials and independent study may be used to earn a degree.
Undergraduate admissions requirements: Students submit application, two letters of recommendation, and high school and college transcripts. Accelerated students must be 25, employed, have three years of work experience, and 30 transferable credits.
Graduate admissions requirements: Students must have completed 120 credits, including both the liberal arts and major cores.
Graduation requirements (undergraduate): Students must earn 120 credits meeting the course requirements.

Fees, Tuition, Costs

Undergraduate application fee: $25
Graduate application fee: $25
Undergraduate tuition: $936/

course/3 credits
Graduate tuition: $750/course
Undergraduate cost of books: $75/class
Graduate cost of books: $75/class
Other costs: Parking fee of $17.50/term; registration fee of $20; building assessment fee of $45/course; computer fee of $25/term

Financial Aid/Status

Scholarship programs for adults: Scholarships are available. Postbaccalaureates receive a significant tuition discount. Adult courses are reduced $100 from traditional tuition.
Full-time status: 3 courses/term. This is a trimester school.
Percentage of adult students receiving financial aid: 80 percent.

Maximum Hours Awarded For

CLEP: Yes
DANTES: Yes

Other exams: Yes
Prior learning portfolio: 15
Additional information: Military courses; maximum of 15 credits allowed

Features and Services

1. Is it possible to purchase books during hours most adult students attend classes? **Yes.**

2. Are the institution's administrative offices open during hours adult students attend class? **Yes.**

3. How do students taking extended classes access library resources? **The library has extended hours.**

4. What is the registration and payment process for adult students? **Tuition is due three weeks before term;** three-part payment plan. Registration by phone, fax, or in person.

5. What is the process for advising adult students? **Initial advising is through the Adult College Center. Faculty advisor is assigned to each student.**

6. What career and placement services are available to adult students? **The career service department coordinates internships, resume writing, and placement.**

7. What characteristics of the institution's adult degree programs are most appealing to students? **Trimester; evening/weekend format; accelerated degree with convenient and quick completion.**

Messiah College*

Grantham, PA 17027

Phone: (717) 691-6054 ◆ Fax: (717) 691-6057

Web address: http://www.messiah.edu

Founded: 1909

Accredited by: Middle States

Enrollment: 2,400 ◆ Adult students: 40

University status: Private, Church, Brethren in Christ Church

Features and Services

1. Is it possible to purchase books during hours most adult students attend classes? **Yes.**

2. What characteristics of the institution's adult degree programs are most appealing to students? **Accelerated classes, reduced tuition rates, and credit for life-learning.**

Degree	Concentration/Major	Format
B.S.	Nursing	E,A
B.S.	Business Administration	E,A

Requirements

Residency requirement: Yes
Undergraduate admissions requirements: 57 credit hours of college credit, including specific general education and prerequisite courses

Fees, Tuition, Costs

Undergraduate application fee: $20
Undergraduate tuition: $180

Financial Aid/Status

Full-time status: 12 hours/semester

Maximum Hours Awarded For

CLEP: 32
Prior learning portfolio: 15

Metropolitan State University*

700 E. Seventh Street ◆ **St. Paul, MN 55106**
Phone: (612) 772-7600 ◆ Fax: (612) 772-7738
Web address: http://www.metro.msus.edu

Founded: 1971

Accredited by: North Central

Enrollment: 4,982 ◆ Adult students: 4,484

University status: Public

Features and Services

1. Is it possible to purchase books during hours most adult students attend classes? **Yes.**

2. What characteristics of the institution's adult degree programs are most appealing to students? **Flexible.**

Degree	Concentration/Major	Format
	All degree programs can be completed at night. Only portions are in other formats.	E

Requirements

Residency requirement: Yes
Undergraduate admissions requirements: High school or GED diploma; high school rank in the upper one-half of graduating class or score above 21 on ACT exam
Graduate admissions requirements: Bachelor's degree, meet prerequisite undergraduate requirements

Fees, Tuition, Costs

Undergraduate application fee: $15
Graduate application fee: $15
Undergraduate tuition: $186/credit
Graduate tuition: $277/credit

Financial Aid/Status

Full-time status: 12 quarter credits/ quarter
Percentage of adult students receiving financial aid: 19 percent

Maximum Hours Awarded For

CLEP: 90
Prior learning portfolio: 90

Mid-America Bible College

3500 S.W. 119th ◆ Oklahoma City, OK 73170
Phone: (405) 692-3161 ◆ Fax: (405) 692-3165

Founded: 1953

Accredited by: North Central

Enrollment: 450 ◆ Adult students: 25 percent

University status: Private, Church, Church of God, Anderson, IN

Degree	Concentration/Major	Format
B.S.	Business—Management and Ethics	E,A
B.S.	Pastoral Ministry	C,S

Requirements

Residency requirement:
Management and ethics students
must attend class on campus.
Pastoral ministry students do not
have to attend class on campus.
Undergraduate admissions
requirements: Students must be 25
years or older and have completed
two years of college.
Graduation requirements
(undergraduate): Graduates must
complete 124 college hours.

Fees, Tuition, Costs

Undergraduate application fee: $20
Undergraduate tuition: $150/
semester hour
Undergraduate cost of books:
$300/semester

Financial Aid/Status

Full-time status: 12 hours or more
Percentage of adult students
receiving financial aid: 50 percent

Maximum Hours Awarded For

CLEP: Yes
DANTES: Yes
Other exams: Yes
Prior learning portfolio: Yes
Additional information: Credit for
demonstrating competency/life
experience

Features and Services

1. Is it possible to purchase
   books during hours most
   adult students attend classes?
   Yes.

2. Are the institution's
   administrative offices open
   during hours adult students
   attend class? **Yes.**

3. How do students taking
   extended classes access
   library resources? **The
   library is accessed through
   library exchange or the
   scholar program.**

4. What is the registration and
   payment process for adult
   students? **Students may
   register at class time or
   through the mail.**

5. What is the process for
   advising adult students?
   **Students may make
   individual appointments
   with an advisor.**

6. What career and placement
   services are available to adult
   students? **Students are told
   of employers who look
   favorably at the degree.**

7. What characteristics of the
   institution's adult degree
   programs are most appealing
   to students? **Individual
   attention, low student-to-
   instructor ratio, curriculum
   relevant to the work
   situation, and excellent
   pace.**

MidAmerica Nazarene College

2030 E. College Way ◆ Olathe, KS 66062

Phone: (913) 782-3750 ◆ Web address: http://www.manc.edu

Founded: 1966

Accredited by: North Central

Enrollment: 1,453 ◆ Adult students: 48 percent

University status: Private, Church, Church of the Nazarene

Features and Services

1. How do students taking extended classes access library resources? **The library is open evenings.**

2. What characteristics of the institution's adult degree programs are most appealing to students? **Small classes, personal contact, faculty interest in students, and emphasis on ethics.**

Degree	Concentration/Major	Format
B.A.	Management and Human Relations	E,A
M.B.A.	Business Administration	E,A
M.Ed.	Education	E,A

Requirements

Residency requirement: Yes.
Undergraduate admissions requirements: Students must be at least 25 years old and have 60 semester hours of transferable credit with a 2.0 GPA.
Graduate admissions requirements: Students must have a baccalaureate degree.
Graduation requirements (undergraduate): Students must complete the prescribed 32 hours major program.
Graduation requirements (graduate): M.Ed. students must complete the 14-month program. M.B.A. students complete the structured 43-semester hour program.

Fees, Tuition, Costs

Undergraduate application fee: $15
Graduate application fee: $75
Undergraduate tuition: $7,634/ program
Graduate tuition: M.Ed.—$5,540; M.B.A.—$11,692

Undergraduate cost of books: Included in program cost
Graduate cost of books: Included in program cost

Financial Aid/Status

Full-time status: Undergraduate is 12 hours or more per term; graduate is 9 hours or more per term.

Maximum Hours Awarded For

CLEP: 25
PEP: Yes
DANTES: Yes
Other exams: Yes
Prior learning portfolio: Yes
Additional information: Maximum 25 credits allowed for all advanced placement credit

Millersville University

P.O. Box 182 ◆ Millersville, PA 17551-0302
Phone: (717) 872-3030 ◆ Fax: (717) 871-2022
E-mail: rlabriol@mu3.millersv.edu
Web address: http://marauder.millersv.edu/

Founded: 1850

Accredited by: Middle States

Enrollment: 7,500 ◆ Adult students: 2,500

University status: Public

Degree	Concentration/Major	Format
B.A.	Business Administration	E
	Accounting, Management, Marketing	
B.S.	Computer Science	E
B.A.	English	E
B.A.	History	E
B.S.	Industry and Technology	E
O.S.H.M.	Occupational Safety Health Management	E
M.Ed.	Elementary Education	E
M.Ed.R.	Education—Reading	E
M.Ed.G.	Education—Gifted	E

Campus Extension Site
Dallastown, PA

Requirements
Residency requirement: All undergraduate students must attend some classes on the main campus. The master's degrees in education are available off campus.
Undergraduate admissions requirements: Students must submit SAT scores, class standing, and individual recommendations.
Graduate admissions requirements: Students must submit scores of GRE or MAT, three letters of recommendation, a goal statement, and proof of 2.75 undergraduate record.
Graduation requirements (undergraduate): Students must earn at least 120 credits; 54 credits must be in general education.
Graduation requirements (graduate): Students must complete 36 credits with 3.0 GPA.

Fees, Tuition, Costs
Undergraduate application fee: $25
Graduate application fee: $25
Undergraduate tuition: $134/credit; $2,954/year
Graduate tuition: $179/credit; $4,000/year
Undergraduate cost of books: $200-$300/year
Graduate cost of books: $150/year
Other costs: Undergraduate and graduate students pay a general fee.

Financial Aid/Status
Scholarship programs for adults: Scholarships are available. The amount depends on the needs of the student.
Full-time status: Students must take 6 or more credits in the summer.
Percentage of adult students receiving financial aid: 72 percent.

Maximum Hours Awarded For
CLEP: 30
PEP: 30

Features and Services

1. Is it possible to purchase books during hours most adult students attend classes? **Yes.**

2. Are the institution's administrative offices open during hours adult students attend class? **Yes.**

3. How do students taking extended classes access library resources? **The library has extended hours to accommodate students.**

4. What is the registration and payment process for adult students? **Registration is done by mail, fax, or in person.**

5. What is the process for advising adult students? **Departments offer degrees and assume all responsibility for advising.**

6. What career and placement services are available to adult students? **Special seminars and workshops for adult students are offered. Extended office hours are provided.**

7. What characteristics of the institution's adult degree programs are most appealing to students? **Courses are offered at convenient, nontraditional hours.**

Millsaps College

P.O. Box 150035 ◆ Jackson, MS 39210-0001
Phone: (601) 974-1132 ◆ Toll-free phone: (800) 352-1050
Fax: (601) 974-1119 ◆ E-mail: sallihg@kra.millsaps.edu
Web address: http://www.millsaps.edu

Founded: 1890

Accredited by: Southern Association

Enrollment: 1,400 ◆ Adult students: 24.7 percent

University status: Private, Church, United Methodist Church

Degree	Concentration/Major	Format
B.L.S.	Bachelor of Liberal Studies All majors available	E,S
B.B.A.	Business Administration—Economics	E
M.L.S.	Interdisciplinary	E
M.B.A.	Business Administration	E
M.Acc.	Accounting	E

Requirements

Residency requirement: None of the degrees can be delivered exclusively without residency. Distance Education is not yet available.
Undergraduate admissions requirements: Applicants to the adult degree program must submit an application, official transcripts of all previous academic work, two letters of recommendation, and an introductory essay.
Graduate admissions requirements: Applicants must submit all academic transcripts. M.L.S.—essay and interview; M.B.A./M.Acc.—GMAT score.
Graduation requirements (undergraduate): Students must complete 32 course units including core requirements and a major area of study. A comprehensive exam must be passed to graduate.

Graduation requirements (graduate): M.L.S.—complete 8 graduate-level courses and project. The ELSE School administers the M.B.A. and M.Acc. degrees.

Fees, Tuition, Costs

Undergraduate application fee: $25
Graduate application fee: $25
Undergraduate tuition: $398/semester hour
Graduate tuition: $1,150/4-hour course
Undergraduate cost of books: $2,800
Graduate cost of books: $600
Other costs: Comprehensive fee of $80

Financial Aid/Status

Scholarship programs for adults: Scholarships are available.
Full-time status: 3-4 courses.
Students taking 1.5 (6-hour) or 2 (8-hour) units are eligible for aid. Percentage of adult students receiving financial aid: 85 percent.

Maximum Hours Awarded For

CLEP: Yes
Other exams: Yes
Prior learning portfolio: Yes
Additional information: ADP allowed 3 courses in a single discipline; 8 course maximum

Features and Services

1. Is it possible to purchase books during hours most adult students attend classes? **Yes.**

2. Are the institution's administrative offices open during hours adult students attend class? **Yes.**

3. What is the registration and payment process for adult students? **The Adult Learning staff will do work if student cannot get to campus. Phone and credit card used.**

4. What is the process for advising adult students? **Three academic advisors work only with ADP students.**

5. What career and placement services are available to adult students? **The office serves all students.**

6. What characteristics of the institution's adult degree programs are most appealing to students? **Individual counseling from recruitment through graduation; Adult Learning Office serves adults and removes barriers to their progress.**

Milwaukee School of Engineering

1025 N. Broadway ◆ **Milwaukee, WI 53202**
Phone: (414) 277-7155 ◆ Toll-free phone: (800) 321-6763
Fax: (414) 277-7475 ◆ E-mail: psicihulis@admin.msoe.edu
Web address: http://www.msoe.edu

Founded: 1903

Accredited by: North Central

Enrollment: 3,200 ◆ Adult students: 1,450

University status: Private

Degree	Concentration/Major	Format
A.A.S.	Electrical Engineering Technology	E
A.A.S.	Management Systems	E
A.A.S.	Mechanical Engineering Technology	E
B.S.	Business and Computer Systems	E
B.S.	Construction Management	E
B.S.	Electrical Engineering Technology	E
B.S.	Management Systems	E
B.S.	Manufacturing Engineering Technology	E
B.S.	Mechanical Engineering Technology	E
M.S.	Engineering	E
M.S.	Engineering Management	E
M.S.	Environmental Engineering	E

Campus Extension Site
Appleton, WI

Requirements
Residency requirement: Because of laboratory requirements with the B.S. program, a student may need to be on campus. In this case, transportation is provided for the student. This occurs rarely. Undergraduate admissions requirements: Applicants must be high school graduates or have GED. ACT scores must be submitted. Adult students may enroll temporarily, allowing them to register before being accepted. Graduate admissions requirements: Applicants must have a degree with an academic record indicating potential success; submit recommendations, application, and official transcripts; and meet program requirements. Graduation requirements (undergraduate): A.A.—complete all courses, minimum GPA of 2.0, residency of 1/2 courses. B.A.—complete all courses, minimum GPA of 2.0 (2.0 in major), residency 1/2 courses, participate in graduation ceremony. Graduation requirements (graduate): Graduates must complete all courses for area of study with a minimum GPA of 3.0; all courses at MSOE; complete project or thesis; participate in graduation ceremony.

Fees, Tuition, Costs
Undergraduate application fee: $25
Graduate application fee: $30
Undergraduate tuition: $250/credit; $12,375/year
Graduate tuition: $310/credit
Undergraduate cost of books: $330/quarter
Graduate cost of books: $330/quarter

Financial Aid/Status
Scholarship programs for adults: Part-time students are considered for scholarships granted through MSDE.
Full-time status: Minimum of 6 credits in any quarter. In some cases, a Pell Grant may be given for 3 credits.
Percentage of adult students receiving financial aid: 10 percent.

Maximum Hours Awarded For
Other exams: Varies
Prior learning portfolio: Varies

Features and Services
1. Is it possible to purchase books during hours most adult students attend classes? **Yes.**

2. How do students taking extended classes access library resources? **Students may use interlibrary loan.**

3. What is the registration and payment process for adult students? **New students register in person and pay 1/2 tuition. Others use mail or fax; may register without paying.**

4. What is the process for advising adult students? **Advisors available in evening by appointment.**

Counselors in Continuing Education available till 7 P.M.

5. What career and placement services are available to adult students? **The college**

placement services are available.

6. What characteristics of the institution's adult degree programs are most appealing to students? **Strong**

academic reputation, tuition reimbursement program, transfer credit, excellent instructors, flexible class schedule, and hands-on methods.

Mind Extension University

9697 E. Mineral Avenue ◆ Englewood, CO 80112

Phone: (303) 792-3111 ◆ Toll-free phone: (800) 777-MIND

Fax: (303) 799-0966 ◆ E-mail: jgietl@meu.edu

Web address: http://www.meu.edu

Founded: 1987

Accredited by: Varies by cooperative school

University status: Private

Degree	Concentration/Major	Format
A.A.	General	E,V,T,TH
B.S.	Animal Sciences and Industry (Degree completion program)	E,V,T,TH,CT
B.S.	Interdisciplinary Social Science (Degree completion program)	E,V,T,TH
B.A.	Social Sciences (Degree completion program)	E,V,T,TH
B.S.	Hotel, Restaurant, Institutional Management (Degree completion program)	E,V,T,TH
B.S./B.A.	Management (Degree completion program)	E,V,T,CT,TH
B.S.	Nursing (Degree completion program)	E,V,A,T,CT,TH
B.S.	Business Administration (Degree completion program)	E,V,A,T,TH
M.A.	Business Communication	E,V,T,CT,TH
M.A.	Educational Technology Leadership	E,V,T,CT,TH

Requirements

Residency requirement: Mind Extension University offers degrees through affiliate institutions. Degrees are offered through distance education (i.e., videotape or cable). Each affiliate regionally accredited instituion actually awards the degree.

Undergraduate admissions requirements: Requirements depend on the institution in which the student enrolls.
Graduate admissions requirements: Requirements depend on the institution in which the student enrolls.
Graduation requirements

(undergraduate): Vary
Graduation requirements (graduate): Vary

Fees, Tuition, Costs

Undergraduate application fee: Varies
Graduate application fee: Varies
Undergraduate tuition: Varies
Graduate tuition: Varies
Undergraduate cost of books: Varies
Graduate cost of books: Varies
Other costs: Videotapes if using the view method; computer if applicable

Financial Aid/Status

Full-time status: 12 or more hours/semester
Percentage of adult students receiving financial aid: 20 percent

Maximum Hours Awarded For

CLEP: Varies
PEP: Varies
DANTES: Varies
Other exams: 18/nursing
Prior learning portfolio: 45
Additional information: All cooperative institutions allow at least 45 credits for prior learning.

Features and Services

1. Is it possible to purchase books during hours most adult students attend classes? **Books may be ordered by phone.**

2. Are the institution's administrative offices open during hours adult students attend class? **Contact by phone or computer.**

3. How do students taking extended classes access library resources? **Students use the library locally or by computer.**

4. What is the registration and payment process for adult students? **Students call 800 number to register and make payment arrangements.**

5. What is the process for advising adult students? **Advising is available by calling an 800 number.**

6. What career and placement services are available to adult students? **Career planning and placement services are handled through the individual institutions.**

7. What characteristics of the institution's adult degree programs are most appealing to students? **Courses are available to anyone, anytime, and anywhere. Courses are taken in the comfort of the home and viewed at student's convenience.**

Montana State University—Billings

1500 N. 30th Street ◆ Billings, MT 59101-0298
Phone: (406) 657-2038 ◆ Fax: (406) 657-2299
Web address: http://www.msu.billings

Founded: 1927

Accredited by: Northwest Association

Enrollment: 6,400 ◆ Adult students:

University status: Public

Graduate tuition: $2,656
Undergraduate cost of books: $500
Graduate cost of books: $500

Financial Aid/Status

Scholarship programs for adults: Scholarships are available.

Maximum Hours Awarded For

CLEP: Yes
DANTES: Yes
Other exams: Yes
Additional information: Advanced Placement Credit

Degree	Concentration/Major	Format
N/S	Not Specified	A,S

Requirements

Undergraduate admissions requirements: Applicants must have a high school GPA of 2.5, be in the upper half of their graduating class, and have acceptable ACT/SAT scores. Graduate admissions requirements: Applicants must submit all college transcripts, MAT/GRE scores, and three letters of recommendation, and be approved.
Graduation requirements (undergraduate): Graduates must meet the requirements of the university and major department. Graduation requirements (graduate): Graduates must meet the requirements of the university and degree program.

Fees, Tuition, Costs

Undergraduate application fee: $30
Undergraduate tuition: $2,304

Mount Olive College

2131 S. Glenburnie Road, Suite 6 ◆ New Bern, NC 28562
Phone: (919) 633-4464 ◆ Toll-free phone: (800) 868-8479
Fax: (919) 633-6365

Founded: 1951

Accredited by: Southern Association

Enrollment: 1,200 ◆ Adult students: 25 percent

University status: Private, Church, Original Freewill Baptist Church

Degree	Concentration/Major	Format
A.A.	Degrees offered at campus	E
B.S.	Business Administration—Management/Organizational Development	E,A
B.S./B.A.	Degrees offered at campus	E

Campus Extension Sites

New Bern, NC
Wilmington, NC
Salemburg, NC
Goldsboro, NC

Requirements

Residency requirement: Attending classes at any of the four centers is equivalent to residency. The centers have full-time staff and faculty of Mount Olive College.
Undergraduate admissions requirements: Alternative Education Program requires 60 semester hours of transferable credit; submit application, writing sample, autobiographical outline; and have an interview/information meeting with program representative
Graduation requirements (undergraduate): Graduates must complete 126 semester hours, including general education and degree program requirements (minimum GPA of 2.0). Students must complete test, meet residency requirement, and file graduation application.

Fees, Tuition, Costs

Undergraduate application fee: $20
Undergraduate tuition: $7,450/evening college
Undergraduate cost of books: $500
Other costs: Assessment of Prior Learning for credit—$20/credit hours; maximum of $400

Financial Aid/Status

Full-time status: 12 semester hours per term/semester
Percentage of adult students receiving financial aid: 99 percent

Maximum Hours Awarded For

CLEP: 30
DANTES: 30
Other exams: Yes
Prior learning portfolio: 30

Features and Services

1. Is it possible to purchase books during hours most adult students attend classes? **Yes.**

2. Are the institution's administrative offices open during hours adult students attend class? **Yes.**

3. How do students taking extended classes access library resources? **Students visit campus library, use Internet, e-mail, fax, college courier, mail, and interlibrary loan.**

4. What is the registration and payment process for adult students? **The program representative helps with registering and gives information for other procedures.**

5. What is the process for advising adult students? **Student has an assessment counselor, major professor, thesis advisor, and program representative.**

6. What career and placement services are available to adult students? **All campus services are available including workshops, job fairs, and referrals.**

7. What characteristics of the institution's adult degree programs are most appealing to students? **Personal attention, affordable, classes one night a week, complete in slightly more than one year, and credit for prior learning.**

Mount Vernon Nazarene College

2000 Polaris Parkway ◆ **Columbus, OH 43240**
Phone: (800) 839-2355 ◆ Toll-free phone: (800) 839-2355
Fax: (614) 888-5675

Founded: 1968

Accredited by: North Central

Enrollment: 1,450 ◆ Adult students: 250

University status: Private, Church, Church of the Nazarene

Degree	Concentration/Major	Format
B.B.A.	Business Administration	E,A,CT

Campus Extension Sites

Mount Vernon, OH
Columbus, OH

Requirements

Residency requirement: Each campus offers all courses with the exception of a one-hour Executive Senior course, which is held on the main campus.
Undergraduate admissions requirements: EXCELL applicants must be at least 25, with two years of work experience, have completed 3 semester hours of English Composition, 60 semester credit hours from accredited institution with 2.0+ GPA.
Graduation requirements (undergraduate): Graduates must complete 124 semester hours with a GPA of 2.0 for all college work, and 2.5 for the 51 credit hours in the B.B.A. curriculum.

Fees, Tuition, Costs

Undergraduate application fee: $25
Undergraduate tuition: $260/credit hour
Undergraduate cost of books: $1,500
Other costs: Computer provided at no additional cost

Financial Aid/Status

Full-time status: EXCELL students are full-time since they are taking at least 12 semester hours.
Percentage of adult students receiving financial aid: 75 percent.

Maximum Hours Awarded For

CLEP: 30
DANTES: 30
Other exams: 30
Prior learning portfolio: 40
Additional information: Correspondence, Independent Studies, Military ACE, Professional Licensures, Sponsored Learning Petitions

Features and Services

1. Is it possible to purchase books during hours most adult students attend classes? **Yes.**

2. Are the institution's administrative offices open during hours adult students attend class? **Yes.**

3. How do students taking extended classes access library resources? **Students have access to all Ohio State main and branch libraries.**

4. What is the registration and payment process for adult students? **Registration/payment through the mail. Students preregister for entire program, a seat is guaranteed.**

5. What is the process for advising adult students? **An education specialist works with the student throughout the program.**

6. What career and placement services are available to adult students? **Career and placement services are available at the Mount Vernon campus.**

7. What characteristics of the institution's adult degree programs are most appealing to students? **Laptop computers for each student give access to World Wide Web, classes one night per week, 22-month program, books delivered to class, and adults over 25 only.**

Muhlenberg College

2400 Chew Street ♦ Allentown, PA 18104
Phone: (610) 821-3300 ♦ Fax: (610) 821-3532

Founded: 1848

Accredited by: Middle States

Enrollment: 1,700 ♦ Adult students: 500

University status: Private, Church, Evangelical
Lutheran Church in America

Degree	Concentration/Major	Format
A.A.	Accounting	E,A
A.A.	Computer Science	E,A
B.A.	Accounting	E,A
A.A.	Business Administration	E,A
A.A.	Information Science	E,A
A.A.	Religion	E
A.A.	Psychology	E
B.A.	Business Administration	E,A
B.A.	Management (Degree completion program)	E,A
B.S.	Computer Science	E,A
B.A.	Information Science	E,A
B.A.	Economics—Finance Track	E,A
B.A.	Psychology	E
B.A.	Social Science	E,A
B.A.	English	E

Requirements

Residency requirement: Students must attend classes on campus.
Undergraduate admissions requirements: Open admission is offered to adults who have the ability to benefit.
Graduation requirements (undergraduate): Graduates must complete 34 course units in a major and general education requirements.

Fees, Tuition, Costs

Undergraduate application fee: $25
Undergraduate tuition: $625/unit of 4 credits
Undergraduate cost of books: $50-$75

Financial Aid/Status

Scholarship programs for adults: The Incentive Scholarship equal to tuition for one course is offered to adults returning after an interruption in their education.

Maximum Hours Awarded For

CLEP: Yes
DANTES: Yes

Prior learning portfolio: Yes
Additional information: Use PONSI to evaluate other learning experiences for credit

Features and Services

1. Is it possible to purchase books during hours most adult students attend classes? **Yes.**

2. Are the institution's administrative offices open during hours adult students attend class? **Yes.**

3. What is the registration and payment process for adult students? **Register by mail, fax, phone, or in person. Payment by check, credit card, or deferred payment plan.**

4. What is the process for advising adult students? **Advising in person or phone by counselors or major faculty advisor.**

5. What career and placement services are available to adult students? **Special career/job issue seminars held in evening. College services are available.**

6. What characteristics of the institution's adult degree programs are most appealing to students? **Acceleration, quality of instruction, attractive campus, and commitment of college departments to evening program.**

National Technological University

700 Centre Avenue ◆ Fort Collins, CO 80526-1842
Phone: (970) 495-6400 ◆ Fax: (970) 498-0601
E-mail: gerryj@mail.ntu.edu
Web address: http://www.ntu.edu

Founded: 1984

Accredited by: North Central

Enrollment: 1,350 ◆ Adult students: 1,350

University status: Private

Degree	Concentration/Major	Format
M.S.	Chemical Engineering	T
M.S.	Computer Engineering	T
M.S.	Electrical Engineering	T
M.S.	Computer Science	T
M.S.	Engineering Management	T
M.S.	Hazardous Waste Management	T
M.S.	Health Physics	T
M.S.	Management of Technology	T
M.S.	Manufacturing Systems Engineering	T
M.S.	Software Engineering	T
M.S.	Materials Sciences	T
M.S.	Transportation Systems Engineering	T

Requirements

Residency requirement: Students do not attend classes on a campus. Graduate admissions requirements: Students must be employed by a sponsoring organization. An undergraduate degree in engineering or science with a GPA of 2.5 or more is required. Graduation requirements (graduate): Students must complete 30-33 credits. A nonthesis option is offered.

Fees, Tuition, Costs

Graduate application fee: $50
Graduate tuition: $560/credit
Graduate cost of books: $100/course

Financial Aid/Status

Scholarship programs for adults: No scholarships are available. Many organizations provide tuition reimbursement.

Features and Services

1. Are the institution's administrative offices open during hours adult students attend class? **Yes.**

2. How do students taking extended classes access library resources? **Students use organization libraries.**

3. What is the registration and payment process for adult students? **Electronic registration and admission are used. Students are billed. Books are ordered electronically.**

4. What is the process for advising adult students? **Each student has an advisor from one of the 45 participating universities.**

5. What career and placement services are available to adult students? **The advisor provides career and placement information.**

6. What characteristics of the institution's adult degree programs are most appealing to students? **Televised courses delivered to place of employment and broad offerings.**

National-Louis University

2840 Sheridan Road ♦ **Evanston, IL 60201-1796**
Phone: (847) 475-1100 ♦ Toll-free phone: (800) 443-5522
Web address: http://nlu.nl.edu

Founded: 1886

Accredited by: North Central

Enrollment: 7,955 ♦ Adult students: 78 percent

University status: Private

Degree	Concentration/Major	Format
B.A.	Health Care Leadership	E
B.A.	Applied Behavioral Science	E
B.S.	Management	E
M.Ed.	Interdisciplinary Studies in Curriculum and Instruction	E
M.S.	Management	E
M.S.	Human Resource Management and Development	E

Other undergraduate and graduate degrees are offered in the evenings.

Campus Extension Sites

Atlanta, GA
McLean, VA
Milwaukee, WI
Washington, DC
St. Louis, MO
Tampa, FL
Elgin, IL

Requirements

Residency requirement: Students are not required to attend classes at the main campus.
Undergraduate admissions requirements: Freshmen: Official high school transcript (top 50 percent of class); two letters of recommendation; ACT/SAT scores (waived if 21+). Transfer: Official high school and college transcripts; two recommendations.

Graduate admissions requirements: Official college transcripts with degree (3.0 GPA); recommendations; writing sample; test scores depending on program; interview possible.
Graduation requirements (undergraduate): Students complete 180 quarter hours with 2.0 GPA or higher; 45-hour residency; 45-hour concentration requirements; 25 hours of upper-level courses.
Graduation requirements (graduate): Graduates need a 3.0 GPA and must fulfill all residency, concentration, thesis/dissertation, and specific program requirements.

Fees, Tuition, Costs

Undergraduate application fee: $25
Graduate application fee: $25

Undergraduate tuition: $212-$240/quarter hour
Graduate tuition: $305-$360/quarter hour
Undergraduate cost of books: $225/term
Graduate cost of books: $225/term
Other costs: Other fees possible

Financial Aid/Status

Scholarship programs for adults: All scholarships are open to adults, although none is specifically for adults.
Full-time status: Undergraduates taking 12 quarter hours per term are full-time; graduate is 8 quarter hours per term.

Maximum Hours Awarded For

CLEP: Yes
PEP: Yes
DANTES: Yes
Other exams: Yes
Prior learning portfolio: Yes
Additional information: Testing, Portfolio, AP, DSSTs, ACE; 60-credit maximum allowed

Features and Services

1. Is it possible to purchase books during hours most adult students attend classes? **Yes.**

2. Are the institution's administrative offices open during hours adult students attend class? **Yes.**

3. How do students taking extended classes access library resources? **Students have toll-free access by modem or phone. Evening and weekend library hours are offered.**

4. What is the registration and payment process for adult students? **Field programs have one-time program**

registration, payment scheduling, and book buying at the site.

5. What is the process for advising adult students? **All campus centers have advisors. Support staff visit the field program classrooms.**

6. What career and placement services are available to adult students? **Career and placement services are available at the center.**

7. What characteristics of the institution's adult degree programs are most appealing to students? **Regular classes, evening and weekend hours, many locations, field programs, cohort group, accelerated, one-time registration, and geared to adults.**

Nazareth College

4245 East Avenue ◆ **Rochester, NY 14618**

Phone: (716) 586-2525 ◆ Fax: (716) 586-2452

Web address: http://www.naz.edu

Founded: 1924

Accredited by: Middle States

Enrollment: 1,350 ◆ Adult students: 30 percent

University status: Private, Church, Nondenominational

Degree	Concentration/Major	Format
B.S.	Nursing	E
B.S.	Social Science	E
B.S.	Accounting	E
B.S.	Business Administration	E
B.A.	Psychology	E

Requirements

Residency requirement: Students must attend classes on campus. Undergraduate admissions requirements: Students must submit an application, transcripts, two essays, a letter of recommendation, and SAT/ACT scores. Graduate admissions requirements: Students must submit all transcripts for undergraduate work. Graduation requirements (undergraduate): Students must earn 120 credits with a minimum 2.0 GPA. At least 90 credits in liberal arts for B.A.; 60 for B.S.; 42-45 for Mus.B. A minimum of 30 credits must be earned at Nazareth. Graduation requirements (graduate): Students must file an application for graduation, complete a comprehensive exam, and meet program requirements.

Fees, Tuition, Costs

Undergraduate application fee: $30
Graduate application fee: $30
Undergraduate tuition: $11,926/ year

Graduate tuition: $379/credit
Undergraduate cost of books: $550
Other costs: Lab fees

Financial Aid/Status

Full-time status: 12 credit hours

Maximum Hours Awarded For

CLEP: Yes
PEP: Yes
DANTES: Yes
Other exams: Yes
Prior learning portfolio: Yes
Additional information: Military experience

Features and Services

1. Is it possible to purchase books during hours most adult students attend classes? **Yes.**

2. Are the institution's administrative offices open during hours adult students attend class? **Yes.**

3. What is the registration and payment process for adult students? **Register with no lines using phone, fax, mail, or in person. Prompt, courteous service is given.**

4. What is the process for advising adult students? **Students have an initial interview. Appointments are made for planning and registering.**

5. What career and placement services are available to adult students? **Students have the same access that full-time day students have.**

6. What characteristics of the institution's adult degree programs are most appealing to students? **Very personal,** small, supportive environment, and friendly campus.

Nebraska Wesleyan University

5000 St. Paul Avenue ◆ **Lincoln, NE 68504-2796**

Phone: (402) 465-2330 ◆ Toll-free phone: (800) 541-3818

Fax: (402) 465-2179 ◆ E-mail: gwb@nebrwesleyan.edu

Founded: 1887

Accredited by: North Central

Enrollment: 1,610

University status: Private, Church, United Methodist Church

Degree	Concentration/Major	Format
B.S./B.A.	Business Administration	E
B.S.	Nursing	E
B.S./B.A.	Paralegal Studies	E
B.S./B.A.	Social Work	E

Requirements

Residency requirement: Students are required to attend classes on campus.
Undergraduate admissions requirements: Wesleyan PM program: 25 or older; adults with multiple roles. Admission requirements are the same as for traditional students. Special student status may be granted to persons not meeting requirements. Graduation requirements (undergraduate): Graduates must earn 126 credits (last 30 hours at NWU), complete major and general education requirements, have a minimum GPA of 2.0, and complete a senior comprehensive.

Fees, Tuition, Costs

Undergraduate application fee: $20
Undergraduate tuition: $142/credit hour
Undergraduate cost of books: $50/course

Financial Aid/Status

Full-time status: 12 credit hours
Percentage of adult students receiving financial aid: 50 percent

Maximum Hours Awarded For

CLEP: 16
PEP: 42
Other exams: No limit

Prior learning portfolio: 32
Additional information: Credit for prior learning using ACE recommendations

Features and Services

1. Is it possible to purchase books during hours most adult students attend classes? **Yes.**

2. What is the registration and payment process for adult students? **Registration is done by phone, fax, or e-mail. Payment is due first week. Deferment can be arranged.**

3. What is the process for advising adult students? **Evening appointments with the department or continuing education advisors are available.**

4. What career and placement services are available to adult students? **Daytime services are available.**

5. What characteristics of the institution's adult degree programs are most appealing to students? **Students determine the pace; small and personal classes; and best faculty teach classes.**

New College of California*

50 Fell Street ◆ San Francisco, CA 94102

Phone: (415) 241-1364 ◆ Toll-free phone: (800) 335-6262

Fax: (415) 626-5171 ◆ Web address: http://www.newcollege.edu

Founded: 1971

Accredited by: Western Association

Enrollment: 850 ◆ Adult students: 157

University status: Private

Degree	Concentration/Major	Format
B.A.	Humanities—Choose Own Emphasis Degree-completion program: must be able to transfer at least 45 credits	E,A
M.A.	Psychology—Emphasis in Social Work or Feminist Psychology Classes start at 4:30 P.M.; B.A. required; leads to licensure for MFCC—Marriage, Family, Child Counselor	E

Requirements

Residency requirement: Yes
Undergraduate admissions
requirements: Transcripts of
previous college work, application
Graduate admissions requirements:
B.A., transcripts, two letters of
recommendation, no GRE,
application

Fees, Tuition, Costs

Undergraduate application fee: $40
Graduate application fee: $45
Undergraduate tuition: $7,500/two
terms
Graduate tuition: $8,200/year

Financial Aid/Status

Full-time status: 8 units/trimester
Percentage of adult students
receiving financial aid: 70 percent

Maximum Hours Awarded For

CLEP: Yes
Prior learning portfolio: Yes

Features and Services

1. Is it possible to purchase books during hours most adult students attend classes? **Yes.**

2. Are the institution's administrative offices open during hours adult students attend class? **Yes.**

3. What characteristics of the institution's adult degree programs are most appealing to students? **Alternative, humanities-based, faculty/advisor and student relationships.**

New Mexico Highlands University

Las Vegas, NM 87701

Phone: (505) 454-3233 ◆ Toll-free phone: (800) 338-NMHU
Fax: (505) 454-3552 ◆ Web address: http://www.nmhu

Founded: 1893

Accredited by: North Central

Enrollment: 2,991 ◆ Adult students: 30 percent

University status: Public

Degree	Concentration/Major	Format
M.A.	Special Education	E
M.Ed.	Education Administration	E
M.A.	Counseling	E
M.A.	Curriculum and Instructions	E
M.S.W.	Social Work	E

Requirements

Residency requirement: Students must attend classes on campus. The residency requirement is the final 16 hours.
Undergraduate admissions requirements: Students need a minimum 2.0 GPA. A sensitive admission policy allows students to appeal the grade point requirement.
Graduate admissions requirements: Students need a minimum 3.0 GPA. An appeal process may be used if the student has a lower GPA.
Graduation requirements (undergraduate): Students must earn 128 semester hours, including the 32-hour residency requirement.
Graduation requirements (graduate): Programs require from 32 to 64 hours.

Fees, Tuition, Costs

Undergraduate application fee: $15
Graduate application fee: $15
Undergraduate tuition: $62.75/hour
Graduate tuition: $67/hour
Undergraduate cost of books: $300
Graduate cost of books: $350
Other costs: Vary with program

Financial Aid/Status

Full-time status: Undergraduate enrolled 12 hours; graduate enrolled 9
Percentage of adult students receiving financial aid: 75 percent

Maximum Hours Awarded For

CLEP: 24
DANTES: Yes
Other exams: Yes
Additional information: ACT

Features and Services

1. Is it possible to purchase books during hours most adult students attend classes? **Yes.**

2. Are the institution's administrative offices open during hours adult students attend class? **Yes.**

3. How do students taking extended classes access library resources? **The library may be accessed through online services.**

4. What is the registration and payment process for adult students? **Students may mail or phone in registration and payment.**

5. What is the process for advising adult students? **Advising is done evenings and weekends.**

6. What career and placement services are available to adult students? **The placement services are available in the evening.**

7. What characteristics of the institution's adult degree programs are most appealing to students? **Convenience.**

New Mexico Institute of Mining and Technology

801 Leroy Place ◆ Socorro, NM 87801

Phone: (505) 835-5424 ◆ Toll-free phone: (800) 428-TECH

Fax: (505) 835-5989 ◆ E-mail: admission@admin.nmt.edu

Web address: http://www.nmt.edu

Founded: 1889

Accredited by: North Central

Enrollment: 1,500 ◆ Adult students: 31 percent

University status: Public

Maximum Hours Awarded For

Other exams: Yes

Degree	Concentration/Major	Format
M.S.T.	Science Teaching—Secondary Math/Science Teachers	S

Requirements

Residency requirement: Students must attend classes on campus. The M.S.T. classes can be taken in the summer and can be completed as independent studies.
Undergraduate admissions requirements: Students must be high school graduates (2.0 GPA) or have GED (50) and ACT score of 21. Students must submit an application, official transcripts, and ACT report.
Graduate admissions requirements: Students with bachelor's degrees must submit an application, official transcripts, three references, and GRE scores. M.S.T. must have teaching certificate or one year of teaching experience; 30 hours of credit.
Graduation requirements (undergraduate): Students must meet all requirements of the institution and their individual department.

Graduation requirements (graduate): Students must meet the requirements for the degree. M.S.T. may choose a thesis or nonthesis program.

Fees, Tuition, Costs

Undergraduate application fee: $15
Graduate application fee: $25
Undergraduate tuition: $57/credit hour
Graduate tuition: $80.50/credit hour
Undergraduate cost of books: $600/year
Graduate cost of books: $600/year

Financial Aid/Status

Scholarship programs for adults: Academic scholarships are available for incoming freshmen and transfer students.
Full-time status: 12 credit hours/ semester.

New School for Social Research*

66 West 12 Street, Room 401 ◆ New York, NY 10011
Phone: (212) 229-5630 ◆ Fax: (212) 989-3887

Founded: 1919

Accredited by: Middle States

Enrollment: 20,000 ◆ Adult students: 7,000

University status: Private

Degree	Concentration/Major	Format
B.A.	Humanities and Social Sciences	E

Requirements

Residency requirement: Yes
Undergraduate admissions
requirements: Students should have
completed a year of college work or
be over 24 years old. Students need
to submit official transcripts and
essays and have a personal
interview.

Fees, Tuition, Costs

Undergraduate application fee: $30
Undergraduate tuition: $375/credit

Financial Aid/Status

Full-time status: 12 credits/
semester
Percentage of adult students
receiving financial aid: 30 percent

Features and Services

1. Is it possible to purchase
   books during hours most
   adult students attend classes?
   Yes.

2. Are the institution's
   administrative offices open
   during hours adult students
   attend class? **Yes.**

3. What characteristics of the
   institution's adult degree
   programs are most appealing
   to students? **Flexibility of
   program, wide course
   selection, close advising
   through all course selection,
   other adult students, and
   part-time nature of
   program.**

New York Institute of Technology

Bldg. 66, Room 322 ◆ Box 9029 ◆ Central Islip, NY 11722
Phone: (516) 348-3059 ◆ Fax: (516) 348-0299
E-mail: mlehmann@acl.nyit.ed
Web address: http://www.nyit.edu

Founded: 1955

Accredited by: Middle States

Enrollment: 1,100 ◆ Adult students: 300

University status: Private

Degree	Concentration/Major	Format
B.S.	Interdisciplinary Studies	CT
B.A.	Interdisciplinary Studies	CT
B.S.	Business Administration	CT
B.S.	Behavioral Sciences: psychology, sociology	CT
B.S.	Behavioral Sciences: community mental health	CT
B.S.	Behavioral Sciences: criminal justice	CT
B.P.S.	Interdisciplinary Studies	

Requirements

Residency requirement: No
Undergraduate admissions
requirements: Application form;
$30 fee, H.S. diploma, transcripts
from previous colleges, proficiency
exam results
Graduation requirements
(undergraduate): Behavioral
sciences—128 credits;
Interdisciplinary Studies—120
credits; Business—120 credits

Fees, Tuition, Costs

Undergraduate application fee: $30
Undergraduate tuition: $295/credit
Undergraduate cost of books:
Varies
Other costs: Need computer with
modem or access to a NYIT
campus

Financial Aid/Status

Scholarship programs for adults:
Yes
Full-time status: 12 credits or more

Maximum Hours Awarded For

CLEP: Yes
DANTES: Yes
Other exams: Yes
Prior learning portfolio: Yes

Features and Services

1. Is it possible to purchase books during hours most adult students attend classes? **Yes.**

2. Are the institution's administrative offices open during hours adult students attend class? **Yes.**

3. How do students taking extended classes access library resources? **Students need a computer with a modem or access to a New York Institute of Technology campus.**

4. What is the registration and payment process for adult students? **Varies: MasterCard, VISA, loans.**

5. What is the process for advising adult students? **Personal advisor, business days 9-5.**

6. What career and placement services are available to adult students? **Office of career development available to students and alumni.**

7. What characteristics of the institution's adult degree programs are most appealing to students? **Personal service, small classes, and friendly and helpful staff.**

New York University Gallatin School of Individualized Study

715 Broadway ◆ New York, NY 10003
Phone: (212) 998-7310 ◆ Toll-free phone: (800) FIND NYU
Fax: (212) 995-4150 ◆ E-mail: gallatin@nyu.edu
Web address: http://www.nyu.edu
Program's Web address: http://www.nyu.edu/pages/gallatin

Founded: 1972

Accredited by: Middle States

Enrollment: 46,000 ◆ Adult students: 53 percent

University status: Private

Degree	Concentration/Major	Format
B.A.	Individualized Study	S
M.A.	Individualized Study	S

Requirements

Residency requirement: Students must take the final 32 credits on campus. Study abroad outside New York City should be done before completing 96 credits.
Undergraduate admissions requirements: Students need a high school diploma or GED, demonstrated record of academic and/or professional achievement.
Graduate admissions requirements: Admissions are competitive. A bachelor's degree is required with a demonstrated record of academic or professional achievement. The GRE is not required.
Graduation requirements (undergraduate): Students must complete 128 total credits—32 in liberal arts, 32 in Gallatin program—and present colloquium (two-hour oral presentation).
Graduation requirements (graduate): Students must complete 40 credits for the M.A., including a three-credit thesis that may be a research, performance, or project thesis.

Fees, Tuition, Costs

Undergraduate application fee: $45
Graduate application fee: $45
Undergraduate tuition: $577/credit
Graduate tuition: $548/credit
Undergraduate cost of books: $200
Graduate cost of books: $200
Other costs: No other costs, but computer recommended

Financial Aid/Status

Scholarship programs for adults: Scholarships ($500/year part-time; $1000/year full-time) based on need/merit are available equally to adults. All adult students accepted are eligible. Other larger scholarships are offered.
Full-time status: Students taking 12-18 semester credits are full-time. 16 credits/semester needed for Academic Progress.
Percentage of adult students receiving financial aid: 33 percent.

Maximum Hours Awarded For

CLEP: Yes

Prior learning portfolio: Yes
Additional information: Course Equivalency credit for life experience

Features and Services

1. Is it possible to purchase books during hours most adult students attend classes? **Yes.**

2. Are the institution's administrative offices open during hours adult students attend class? **Yes.**

3. How do students taking extended classes access library resources? **Students access the university libraries using an I.D. card.**

4. What is the registration and payment process for adult students? **Registration is the same as for traditional students. Part-payment plans are offered.**

5. What is the process for advising adult students? **Individual attention is given to student's needs. An advisor is assigned based on a student's concentration.**

6. What career and placement services are available to adult students? **All NYU students have access to all career services, including special career counseling for adults.**

7. What characteristics of the institution's adult degree programs are most appealing to students? **Individual attention, flexibility of independent study, mixed group classrooms, faculty trained in adult education, and Returning Student Office.**

Norfolk State University

Department of Interdisciplinary Studies ◆ **Norfolk, VA 23504**
Phone: (804) 683-8881 ◆ Fax: (804) 683-8602
E-mail: dadams@vger.nsu,.edu
Web address: http://cyclops.nsu.edu

Founded: 1935

Accredited by: Southern Association

Enrollment: 8,600 ◆ Adult students: 25 percent

University status: Public

Features and Services

1. Is it possible to purchase books during hours most adult students attend classes? **Yes.**

2. What is the process for advising adult students? **Each student is assigned a regular advisor.**

3. What characteristics of the institution's adult degree programs are most appealing to students? **Flexible, open, individualized, and student-paced decisions.**

Degree	Concentration/Major	Format
B.A.	Interdisciplinary Studies (Various Concentrations)	E,T
B.S.	Interdisciplinary Studies (Various Concentrations)	E,T

Requirements

Residency requirement: Students must attend classes on campus. Undergraduate admissions requirements: Students must have a GPA of C or 2.0 on a 4.0 scale. Graduation requirements (undergraduate): Students must complete 120 credit hours with a C or 2.0 minimum on a 4.0 scale.

Fees, Tuition, Costs

Undergraduate application fee: $20
Undergraduate tuition: $126/hour

Financial Aid/Status

Scholarship programs for adults: The G. W. Brown scholarship is available. The amount varies depending on the individual situation.
Full-time status: 12 credit hours.
Percentage of adult students receiving financial aid: 20 percent.

Maximum Hours Awarded For

CLEP: Yes
PEP: Yes
DANTES: Yes

North Adams State College

North Adams, MA 01247
Phone: (413) 662-5410 ◆ Toll-free phone: (800) 292-6632
Fax: (413) 662-5179 ◆ E-mail: mlavalle@nasc.mass.edu
Web address: http://www.nasc.mass.edu

Founded: 1894

Accredited by: New England

Enrollment: 1,500 ◆ Adult students: 20 percent

University status: Public

Degree	Concentration/Major	Format
B.S.	Business Administration	E
B.A.	Sociology	E

Requirements

Residency requirement: Students are required to attend classes on campus.
Undergraduate admissions requirements: Students must submit high school and/or college transcripts and SAT scores (not required if out of high school more than three years). A student with a GED must schedule an interview.
Graduation requirements (undergraduate): Graduates must complete 120 credits.

Fees, Tuition, Costs

Undergraduate application fee: $10
Undergraduate tuition: $3,555/ full-time
Undergraduate cost of books: $500

Financial Aid/Status

Scholarship programs for adults: Academic Recognition Scholarships are available to transfer students with at least a 3.0 GPA.
Full-time status: Full-time students must be enrolled in at least 9 credits.

Maximum Hours Awarded For

CLEP: Yes
Prior learning portfolio: 12
Additional information: Military Service, Advanced Placement Exams

Features and Services

1. Is it possible to purchase books during hours most adult students attend classes? **Yes.**

2. Are the institution's administrative offices open during hours adult students attend class? **Yes.**

3. What is the process for advising adult students? **Students meet with the advising center.**

4. What career and placement services are available to adult students? **Students may use the Career Development Center.**

5. What characteristics of the institution's adult degree programs are most appealing to students? **Small class size and caring faculty.**

North Carolina Wesleyan College

3400 N. Wesleyan Boulevard ◆ **Rocky Mount, NC 27804**
Phone: (919) 985-5128 ◆ Toll-free phone: (800) 488-6292
Fax: (919) 977-3701 ◆ E-mail: rtrullinger@ncwc.edu
Web address: http://www.ncwc.edu

Founded: 1956

Accredited by: Southern Association

Enrollment: 1,690 ◆ Adult students: 64 percent

University status: Private, Church, United Methodist Church

Degree	Concentration/Major	Format
B.S.	Accounting	E
B.S.	Business Administration	E,A
B.S.	Computer Information Systems	E
B.A.	Justice Studies	E
B.A.	Psychology	E

Campus Extension Sites

Goldsboro, NC
Raleigh, NC

Requirements

Residency requirement: Students may attend classes on campus or at an off-site location.
Undergraduate admissions requirements: Applicants must submit an application, nonrefundable application fee, and all postsecondary transcripts for transfer evaluation.
Graduation requirements (undergraduate): All students must satisfy basic and general education requirements with a minimum GPA of 2.0, complete 30 semester hours at Wesleyan (9 in major), math and English proficiency, 124 semester hours.

Fees, Tuition, Costs

Undergraduate application fee: $25
Undergraduate tuition: $75-$175 range/semester
Undergraduate cost of books: $200

Financial Aid/Status

Full-time status: A full-time student must take a minimum of 12 hours per semester.
Percentage of adult students receiving financial aid: 21 percent.

Maximum Hours Awarded For

CLEP: Yes
PEP: Yes
DANTES: Yes
Other exams: Yes
Prior learning portfolio: 30

Features and Services

1. Is it possible to purchase books during hours most adult students attend classes? **Yes.**

2. How do students taking extended classes access library resources? **Staff send resources (three-week loan) to off-campus students. Interlibrary loan; reciprocal agreements.**

3. What is the registration and payment process for adult students? **Registration available for two to three weeks. Payment in advance unless using employer tuition reimbursement.**

4. What is the process for advising adult students? **Academic advisor helps in course selection and scheduling throughout the entire program.**

5. What career and placement services are available to adult students? **A resource library is available. Workshops and seminars on resume writing, interviewing skills, etc.**

6. What characteristics of the institution's adult degree programs are most appealing to students? **Points of pride are personalized service and a small student-to-teacher ratio.**

North Central College

P.O. Box 3036 ◆ 30 N. Brainard Street
Naperville, IL 60566-7063
Phone: (630) 637-5556 ◆ Toll-free phone: (800) 411-1861
Fax: (630) 637-5561
E-mail: cdb@noctrl.edu

Founded: 1861

Accredited by: North Central

Enrollment: 2,500 ◆ Adult students: 45 percent

University status: Private, Church, United Methodist Church

Degree	Concentration/Major	Format
B.A.	Management	E
B.A.	Marketing	E
B.A.	Computer Science	E
B.A.	Accounting	E
B.A.	Management Information Systems	E
B.A.	Organizational Communication	E
B.A.	Psychology	E
B.A.	Finance	E

Campus Extension Sites

St. Charles, IL
Schaumburg, IL

Requirements

Residency requirement: Students are not required to attend classes on the main campus. Undergraduate admissions requirements: Applicants must have a high school diploma or GED and a minimum cumulative GPA of 2.0 on a 4.0 scale. Graduation requirements (undergraduate): Graduates must complete 36 course credits (180 quarter hours; 120 semester hours); have a minimum cumulative GPA of 2.0 (minimum 2.0 GPA in

major/minor); and complete all major and liberal arts requirements.

Fees, Tuition, Costs

Undergraduate application fee: $20
Undergraduate tuition: $1,246/ course
Undergraduate cost of books: $75/ course

Financial Aid/Status

Scholarship programs for adults: Special Needs Scholarship is available to students indicating need. Approximately $200 per course is awarded.
Full-time status: 2.5-3.5 course credits (12-15 quarter hours).
Percentage of adult students receiving financial aid: 15 percent.

Maximum Hours Awarded For

CLEP: Yes
Prior learning portfolio: Yes
Additional information: Maximum of 12 credits awarded through CLEP and prior learning

Features and Services

1. Is it possible to purchase books during hours most adult students attend classes? **Yes.**

2. Are the institution's administrative offices open during hours adult students attend class? **Yes.**

3. How do students taking extended classes access library resources? **A librarian is on duty to assist students.**

4. What is the registration and payment process for adult students? **After the first registration, students register by phone or mail. Deferred payment plans offered.**

5. What is the process for advising adult students? **Each student is assigned an advisor, who is available weekends and evenings.**

6. What career and placement services are available to adult students? **North Central College's Career Center offers a full range of services to adult students.**

7. What characteristics of the institution's adult degree programs are most appealing to students? **Small classes, three locations, flexible formats, highly personalized educational environment, and individualized advising for each student.**

North Park College

3225 W. Foster Avenue ◆ **Chicago, IL 60625**
Phone: (312) 244-5500 ◆ Toll-free phone: (800) 888-6728
Fax: (312) 244-4953 ◆ E-mail: std@npcts.edu
Web address: http://www.npcts.edu

Founded: 1891

Accredited by: North Central

Enrollment: 1,745 ◆ Adult students: 166

University status: Private, Church, Evangelical Covenant Church

Degree	Concentration/Major	Format
B.A.	Organizational Management	E,A
B.A.	Human Development	E,A
B.G.S.	Organizational Management	E,A
B.G.S.	Human Development	E,A
B.S.	Nursing Completion	E

Requirements

Residency requirement: At least 32 credits must be taken at North Park. Normally these hours are in the major.
Undergraduate admissions requirements: Applicants for the accelerated programs must be 25 years or older and have 30 completed credits and a minimum GPA of 2.0.
Graduation requirements (undergraduate): Graduates must complete 120 credit hours with a minimum 2.0 GPA.

Fees, Tuition, Costs

Undergraduate tuition: $275-$300/credit hour
Undergraduate cost of books: $200/semester
Other costs: Credit for prior learning fee of $35; change of group fee of $100

Financial Aid/Status

Full-time status: 12 semester hours

Maximum Hours Awarded For

CLEP: Yes
Other exams: Yes
Prior learning portfolio: 20

Features and Services

1. Is it possible to purchase books during hours most adult students attend classes? **Yes.**

2. Are the institution's administrative offices open during hours adult students attend class? **Yes.**

3. What is the registration and payment process for adult students? **Registration takes place through the adult program (GOAL) office.**

4. What is the process for advising adult students? **Students are assigned to a specific academic advisor for adult students in the accelerated program.**

5. What career and placement services are available to adult students? **Services include computerized guidance program (SIGI Plus), career planning, and alumni network.**

6. What characteristics of the institution's adult degree programs are most appealing to students? **Accelerated courses, credit for prior learning, evening and Saturday classes, portfolio advisor, and academic advisor.**

Northeastern Illinois University

5500 N. St. Louis ◆ **Chicago, IL 60625-4699**
Phone: (312) 794-6684 ◆ Fax: (312) 794-6243

Founded: 1867

Accredited by: North Central

Enrollment: 10,000 ◆ Adult students: 9.5+ percent

University status: Public

Degree	Concentration/Major	Format
B.A.	Board of Governors	E,A
B.A./B.S.	University Without Walls	E,A,S

Campus Extension Site

Chicago, IL

Requirements

Residency requirement: Some course work is required on campus. Undergraduate admissions requirements: Board of Governor applicants attend a student meeting and complete application. University Without Walls applicants submit transcripts, autobiographical statement, and explanation of prior learning. Graduation requirements (undergraduate): Graduates must complete 120 semester hours (GPA—2.0) meeting course requirements, pass Constitution/proficiency exams, submit all forms, and make all payments to the institution.

Fees, Tuition, Costs

Undergraduate tuition: $82/credit hour
Undergraduate cost of books: $250
Other costs: Mandatory student fees; portfolio assessment fee

Financial Aid/Status

Scholarship programs for adults: Program-specific scholarships are available.
Full-time status: A student enrolled for 12 credit hours or more is considered full-time.

Maximum Hours Awarded For

CLEP: Yes
PEP: Yes
DANTES: Yes
Prior learning portfolio: Yes

Features and Services

1. Is it possible to purchase books during hours most adult students attend classes? **Yes.**

2. How do students taking extended classes access library resources? **Students access the library by Internet.**

3. What is the registration and payment process for adult students? **Students may register using the phone. Bills may be mailed.**

4. What is the process for advising adult students? **Advising is done by appointment.**

5. What career and placement services are available to adult students? **Counseling is available days and selected evenings by appointment or walk-in.**

6. What characteristics of the institution's adult degree programs are most appealing to students? **Portfolio assessment and time frame.**

Northeastern University
University College

180 Ryder, 360 Huntington Avenue ◆ **Boston, MA 02115-9959**
Phone: (617) 373-2400 ◆ Fax: (617) 373-2325
Web address: http://ww.neu.edu/uc/catalog/welcome/html

Founded: 1957

Accredited by: New England

Enrollment: 10,000 ◆ Adult students: 100 percent

University status: Private

Degree	Concentration/Major	Format
A.S.	Accounting	E
A.A.	Arts & Sciences	E
A.S.	Biotechnology	E
A.S.	Business Administration	E
A.A.	Graphic Design and Visual Communication	E
A.A.	Human Resource Management	E
A.S.	Medical Laboratory Science	E
A.S.	Operations Management	E
B.S.B.A.	Accounting	E
B.S.	Biological Science	E
B.S.	Corrections	E
B.A.	English	E
B.S.	Graphic Design	E
B.A.	History	E
B.A.	Liberal Studies	E
ACCEL	Liberal Arts	E,A
ACCEL	Management Information Systems	E,A
ACCEL	Management	E,A
B.S.	Nursing	E,A
B.S.	Psychology	E,A
B.S.	Technical Communications	E,A

Campus Extension Sites
Burlington, MA
Milford, MA
Dedham, MA
Westwood, MA
Framington, MA
Weymouth, MA
Marshfield, MA

Requirements
Residency requirement: The residency for undergraduate degree programs is 24 quarter hours for an A.S.; 45 quarter hours for a B.S. Undergraduate admissions requirements: Open enrollment; then student must submit proof of high school or GED completion; completion of at least 18 quarter hours, including 9 quarter hours of English; and a minimum 2.0 GPA. Graduation requirements (undergraduate): Graduates must complete all required courses, plus have a 2.0 GPA in major concentration and 2.0 overall GPA.

Fees, Tuition, Costs
Undergraduate tuition: $157/ quarter hour
Undergraduate cost of books: Varies
Other costs: Commuting, parking, laboratory or studio fees

Financial Aid/Status
Scholarship programs for adults: A variety of scholarships with specified eligibility requirements are available. Awards range from $500 to $1,000.
Full-time status: Students admitted to a degree program taking two courses per term qualify. Full-time status is 12 quarter hours.

Maximum Hours Awarded For
CLEP: Yes
PEP: Yes
DANTES: Yes
Prior learning portfolio: 18 quarter hours
Additional information: Maximum of 128 quarter hours of transfer credit allowed for B.S. degree from all sources

Features and Services
1. Is it possible to purchase books during hours most adult students attend classes? **Yes.**

2. Are the institution's administrative offices open during hours adult students attend class? **Yes.**

3. How do students taking extended classes access

library resources? **Main library has extended hours. Computer access from labs at four campuses. Satellite library available.**

4. What is the registration and payment process for adult students? **Registration by mail, fax, phone, or in person. Billing by mail. Credit cards accepted.**

5. What is the process for advising adult students? **Advising available during the day or evening by appointment, phone, or walk-in. Extra aid at sites at peak times.**

6. What career and placement services are available to adult students? **Full career services for adult students, includ-**

ing **workshops, resource center, networking, and counseling.**

7. What characteristics of the institution's adult degree programs are most appealing to students? **Access, convenience, wide choice of courses and programs, and courses designed for adult learners.**

Northwest Christian College

828 E. 11th Avenue ◆ **Eugene, OR 97405**

Phone: (541) 687-0397 ◆ Toll-free phone: (800) 888-6927

Fax: (541) 343-9159

Founded: 1895

Accredited by: Northwest Association

Enrollment: 410 ◆ Adult students: 40 percent

University status: Private, Church, Christian Church Disciples of Christ

---

Degree	Concentration/Major	Format
B.A.	Management	E,A

Campus Extension Sites

Roseburg, OR
Grants Pass, OR
Medford, OR

Requirements

Residency requirement: Students are not required to attend classes on the main campus.
Undergraduate admissions requirements: Applicants must have an Oregon A.A. degree or 93 transferable quarter credit hours, a minimum 2.0 GPA, and significant

supervisory or management work experience.
Graduation requirements (undergraduate): Graduates must have minimum 2.5 cumulative GPA, 186 quarter hour credits, 110 credits graded, 45 quarter hours in residence, and 30 quarter hours in upper-division credits for major.

Fees, Tuition, Costs

Undergraduate application fee: $25
Undergraduate tuition: $193/ quarter hour
Undergraduate cost of books:

$812/program
Other costs: Fees of approximately $280 total (student body fees, academic fees, and graduation fees)

Financial Aid/Status

Full-time status: Full-time students are enrolled in a minimum of 12 quarter credit hours per term. Percentage of adult students receiving financial aid: 90+ percent.

Maximum Hours Awarded For

CLEP: 46
DANTES: 46
Prior learning portfolio: 46
Additional information: Maximum 75 quarter hour credits accepted from CLEP, DANTES, and prior learning

Features and Services

1. Is it possible to purchase books during hours most adult students attend classes? **Yes.**

2. How do students taking extended classes access library resources? **Through arrangements students use local area libraries, the NCC and University of Oregon libraries.**

3. What is the registration and payment process for adult students? **All registration and payment procedures are done by mail and phone.**

4. What is the process for advising adult students? **Each student is assigned an** advisor. **The area coordinator provides advising at Medford/Grants Pass.**

5. What career and placement services are available to adult students? **All NCC students have access to the career placement services at the University of Oregon.**

6. What characteristics of the institution's adult degree programs are most appealing to students? **The cohort model for classes and convenient evening and Saturday schedule.**

Northwest College

P.O. Box 579 ◆ **Kirkland, WA 98083**
Phone: (206) 889-7799 ◆ Fax: (206) 827-0148

Founded: 1934

Accredited by: Northwest Association

Enrollment: 824 ◆ Adult students: 20 percent

University status: Private, Church, Assemblies of God Church

Degree	Concentration/Major	Format
B.A.	Organizational Management	E,A

Requirements

Residency requirement: The degree-completion program classes are located on the campus. Graduation requirements (undergraduate): Graduates must earn at least 30 credits from the institution and satisfy all degree requirements.

Fees, Tuition, Costs

Undergraduate application fee: $20
Undergraduate tuition: $3,570/12-17 hours

Undergraduate cost of books: $250/semester

Financial Aid/Status

Percentage of adult students receiving financial aid: 50 percent

Maximum Hours Awarded For

CLEP: 30
DANTES: No limit
Other exams: No limit
Prior learning portfolio: 30

Features and Services

1. Is it possible to purchase books during hours most adult students attend classes? **Yes.**

2. Are the institution's administrative offices open during hours adult students attend class? **Yes.**

3. How do students taking extended classes access library resources? **All courses are on the campus. The library is open late into the evening.**

4. What is the registration and payment process for adult students? **Evening registration is two weeks prior to the first class.**

5. What is the process for advising adult students? **Advising is handled by the Center for Adult Leadership Studies and faculty advisors.**

6. What characteristics of the institution's adult degree programs are most appealing to students? **Evening classes and accelerated format.**

Northwest Graduate/ Undergraduate School of Ministry

9051 132nd Avenue N.E. ◆ **Kirkland, WA 98033**

Phone: (206) 828-7431 ◆ Toll-free phone: (800) 935-4723

Fax: (206) 889-0652 ◆ E-mail: ministers@nw.com

Founded: 1990

Accredited by: TRACS

Enrollment: 400 ◆ Adult students: 100 percent

University status: Private, Church, Christian Church

Degree	Concentration/Major	Format
A.A.	Christian Ministry	E
M.A.	Christian Ministry	A
D.Min.	Christian Ministry	A

Requirements

Residency requirement: A.A. students attend evening classes on campus for 10 weeks. One-week modular classes on campus are offered for M.A. and D.Min. students.

Undergraduate admissions requirements: Students must have a high school diploma.

Graduate admissions requirements: Students must have a B.A. in Bible or related subjects or 30 units of Bible and 15 units of theology and be involved in professional Christian ministry work.

Graduation requirements (undergraduate): Graduates must complete 96 quarter hours.

Graduation requirements (graduate): M.A. requires 65 semester hours and thesis; D.Min. requires 65 semester hours and dissertation (entrance degree— M.A.); D.Min. requires 45 semester hours and dissertation

(entrance degree—M.Div.)

Fees, Tuition, Costs

Undergraduate application fee: $30

Graduate application fee: $30

Undergraduate tuition: $35/ quarter hour credit

Graduate tuition: $99/semester hour credit

Undergraduate cost of books: $50/ quarter

Graduate cost of books: $200/ semester

Other costs: Travel and motel if student lives out of the area

Financial Aid/Status

Scholarship programs for adults: A need scholarship of one half of the tuition may be granted at the graduate level.

Full-time status: Undergraduate level is 9 quarter hours per quarter; graduate is 15 semester hours per year.

Percentage of adult students receiving financial aid: 20 percent.

Features and Services

1. Is it possible to purchase books during hours most adult students attend classes? **Yes.**

2. How do students taking extended classes access library resources? **Library services are available by mail.**

3. What is the registration and payment process for adult students? **Students mail application and fee. The admissions committee reviews and notifies each student.**

4. What is the process for advising adult students? **Advising is available through the college and graduate school offices by appointment.**

5. What career and placement services are available to adult students? **Files regarding church-related jobs are accumulated.**

6. What characteristics of the institution's adult degree programs are most appealing to students? **Emphasis on practical skills for church leadership, convenient schedules, and affordable.**

Northwestern College

3003 Snelling Avenue N. ◆ **St. Paul, MN 55113**
Phone: (612) 631-5364 ◆ Fax: (612) 631-5124
E-mail: naf@nwc.edu

Founded: 1902

Accredited by: North Central

Enrollment: 1,269

University status: Private

Degree	Concentration/Major	Format
B.S.	Business Administration	E,A
B.S.	Organizational Administration	E,A
B.S.	Psychology	E,A

Campus Extension Sites

Anoka, MN
Bloomington, MN
Golden Valley, MN

Requirements

Residency requirement: Off-campus B.S./B.A. students are required to complete computer applications on campus. All other majors may be completed off campus.
Undergraduate admissions requirements: Applicants must be at least 25, have 75 transferable quarter hour credits with C- or better (86 quarter credits for graduation), and a profession of faith in Jesus Christ as personal Savior.
Graduation requirements (undergraduate): Graduates must earn 180 credits and successfully complete the FOCUS 15 curriculum.

Fees, Tuition, Costs

Undergraduate application fee: $15
Undergraduate tuition: Approximately $2,000/term
Undergraduate cost of books: Approximately $500
Other costs: Enrollment fee of $100; computer lab fee (required for B.S./B.A.) of $150; graduation fee of $30

Financial Aid/Status

Full-time status: Approximately 12 credits/term
Percentage of adult students receiving financial aid: 50 percent

Maximum Hours Awarded For

CLEP: 45
DANTES: 45
Prior learning portfolio: 33

Features and Services

1. Is it possible to purchase books during hours most adult students attend classes? **Yes.**

2. Are the institution's administrative offices open during hours adult students attend class? **Yes.**

3. How do students taking extended classes access library resources? **Resource librarians are available. Some extended hours are available to use the library.**

4. What is the process for advising adult students? **Students have individual contact with professors. The FOCUS 15 Student Affairs Coordinator advises.**

5. What career and placement services are available to adult students? **The Career Development office provides assessment tests, job listings, and resume referral.**

6. What characteristics of the institution's adult degree programs are most appealing to students? **Off-campus locations, learning in Christian environment, classes in adult setting, and instructors trained in teaching adults.**

Northwestern University
University College

2115 N. Campus Drive ◆ Evanston, IL 60208-2660
Phone: (847) 491-5611 ◆ Toll-free phone: (800) FINDS NU
Fax: (847) 491-3660 ◆ E-mail: fmiller@nwu.edu
Web address: http://nuinfo.acns.nwu.edu/
Program's Web address: http://nuinfo.nwu.edu/

Founded: 1851

Accredited by: North Central

Enrollment: 14,000 ◆ Adult students: 2,500

University status: Private

Degree	Concentration/Major	Format
B.Phil.	Anthropology	E
B.S.G.S.	Art History	E
B.S.G.S.	Computer Studies	E
B.S.G.S.	Economics	E
B.S.G.S.	English	E
B.S.G.S.	Environmental Studies	E
B.S.G.S.	Fine and Performing Arts	E
B.S.G.S.	History	E
B.S.G.S.	Mathematics	E
B.S.G.S.	Organization Behavior	E
B.S.G.S.	Philosophy	E
B.S.G.S.	Political Science	E
B.S.G.S.	Psychology	E
B.S.G.S.	Sociology	E

Campus Extension Site
Chicago, IL

Requirements
Residency requirement: Students attend classes one night a week or Saturday mornings for 2 1/2 hours on the Evanston or Chicago campus. The semester is 14 weeks. Undergraduate admissions requirements: The open enrollment system gives provisional admission until four courses are completed. Grades in these courses determine students' eligibility.

Graduate admissions requirements: Applicants submit an application, college transcripts, two letters of recommendation, a statement of purpose, and a writing sample. The M.A. in English requires GRE scores. Graduation requirements (undergraduate): Graduates satisfactorily complete 120 semester hours and fulfill the required courses as listed in the graduate bulletin. Graduation requirements (graduate): Graduates complete 9 courses and the graduate essay with a B average.

Fees, Tuition, Costs
Undergraduate application fee: None
Graduate application fee: $40
Undergraduate tuition: $240/semester hour
Graduate tuition: $1,273/course
Undergraduate cost of books: Varies
Graduate cost of books: Varies
Other costs: $40 lab fee for computer, art, R/TW/F production courses, chemistry, and physics lab courses

Financial Aid/Status
Scholarship programs for adults: A one-time award of tuition for one course is granted by the university to matriculate students who demonstrate need.
Full-time status: 4 courses or 12 semester hours/semester.
Percentage of adult students receiving financial aid: 12 percent.

Maximum Hours Awarded For
CLEP: 60
DANTES: 60

Features and Services
1. Is it possible to purchase books during hours most adult students attend classes? **Yes.**

2. Are the institution's administrative offices open during hours adult students attend class? **Yes.**

3. What is the registration and payment process for adult students? **The registration period is three weeks before the beginning of each semester. New students meet with an advisor and may register then. Returning students are sent preprinted forms and may**

register by mail. Tuition may be paid in two installments by check or money order. Sixty percent plus fees is paid at registration, and balance is due eight weeks after the term begins.

4. What is the process for advising adult students? **New students are required to meet with advisor. Students** may request an advisor who maintains their files.

5. What career and placement services are available to adult students? **Career and placement materials available. Students with 12 hours may use the university's office.**

6. What characteristics of the institution's adult degree programs are most appealing to students? **The open enrollment policy allows new students who left their last institution in good standing to enroll without formal application. The admission decision is made after four courses have been completed. If a B average is achieved and the writing requirement is satisfied, students are officially admitted into the program.**

Northwood University University College

3225 Cook Road ◆ Midland, MI 48640

Phone: (517) 837-4411 ◆ Toll-free phone: (800) 445-5873

Founded: 1957

Accredited by: North Central Association

Enrollment: 6,000

University status: Private

Undergraduate tuition: $50-$195/credit
Graduate tuition: $195/credit

Financial Aid/Status

Full-time status: 12 quarter hours/term
Percentage of adult students receiving financial aid: 10 percent

Maximum Hours Awarded For

CLEP: Yes
Other exams: Yes
Prior learning portfolio: Yes

Degree	Concentration/Major	Format
A.A.	Management	E,C,T,CT,A,V,S
B.B.A.	Management	E,C,T,CT,A,V,S

Campus Extension Sites

Dallas, TX
Livonia, MI
Sheldon, MI
Van Dyke, MI
Indianapolis, IN
New Orleans, LA
Cedar Hills, TX
West Palm Beach, FL
Showhegan, ME

Requirements

Residency requirement: Yes
Undergraduate admissions requirements: 25 years of age, 2.0 GPA
Graduate admissions requirements: Five years of administration experience

Fees, Tuition, Costs

Undergraduate application fee: $15
Graduate application fee: $15

Features and Services

1. Is it possible to purchase books during hours most adult students attend classes? **Yes.**

2. Are the institution's administrative offices open during hours adult students attend class? **Yes.**

3. What characteristics of the institution's adult degree programs are most appealing to students? **Many course formats.**

Nova Southeastern University

3100 S.W. Ninth Avenue ◆ **Ft. Lauderdale, FL 33315**

Phone: (954) 475-7533 ◆ Toll-free phone: (800) 672-7223

Fax: (954) 476-4865 ◆ E-mail: sbeinfo@sbe.nova.edu

Web address: http://www.sbe.nova.edu

Founded: 1967

Accredited by: Southern Association

Enrollment: 15,000 ◆ Adult students: 100 percent

University status: Private

Degree	Concentration/Major	Format
M.B.A.	Business Administration	E,A
	Nine concentrations available	
M.I.B.A.	International Business Administration	E,A
M.S.	Human Resource Management	E,A
M.S.	Health Services Administration	E,A
M.P.A.	Public Administration	E,A
M.Acc.	Accounting	E,A
M.S.	Medical Management	E,A
D.B.A.	Business Administration	E
	Eight concentrations available	
D.P.A.	Public Administration	E
D.I.B.A.	International Business Administration	E

Campus Extension Sites

Cluster locations exist throughout the United States. Clusters are groups of students assigned to a cluster, who are coordinated by a professional from the university, and take classes at the cluster area closest to their home.

Requirements

Residency requirement: All students are required to attend either the main campus or some other predetermined national site for workshops.

Graduate admissions requirements:

Applicants must have either a bachelor's or master's degree, provide the required documentation and written information requested by the university, and attain the minimum test score required.

Graduation requirements (graduate): Graduates must complete all admission requirements for full acceptance and all course work/seminars.

Fees, Tuition, Costs

Graduate application fee: $40

Graduate tuition: $370/master's; $450/doctoral

Graduate cost of books: $900-$1200

Financial Aid/Status

Full-time status: Graduate students must enroll in 6 credit hours of study to receive financial aid.

Features and Services

1. How do students taking extended classes access library resources? **Students may obtain information from local libraries or request information from the NSU library.**

2. What is the registration and payment process for adult students? **Students pay for classes at registration using check, credit card, or cash.**

3. What is the process for advising adult students? **Advisors are available from 8:30 A.M. to 5:00 P.M.**

4. What career and placement services are available to adult students? **A career placement office is available to all NSU alumni.**

5. What characteristics of the institution's adult degree programs are most appealing to students? **Weekend format, convenience of class location, and doctorally qualified faculty.**

Nyack College*

1 South Boulevard ◆ **Nyack, NY 10960**
Phone: (914) 358-5360 ◆ Toll-free phone: (800) 876-9225
Fax: (914) 358-4771

Founded: 1882

Accredited by: Middle States

Enrollment: 813 ◆ Adult students: 236

University status: Private, Church,
Christian and Missionary Alliance

Features and Services

1. Is it possible to purchase books during hours most adult students attend classes? **Yes.**

2. What characteristics of the institution's adult degree programs are most appealing to students? **Length of program (14 months) and evening classes.**

Degree	Concentration/Major	Format
B.S.	Organizational Management	E,A

Requirements

Residency requirement: Yes
Undergraduate admissions requirements: 60 transferable college credits, five years of work experience, and writing proficiency

Fees, Tuition, Costs

Undergraduate application fee: $25
Undergraduate tuition: $9,360/ year

Financial Aid/Status

Full-time status: 16 credits/ semester
Percentage of adult students receiving financial aid: 25 percent

Maximum Hours Awarded For

CLEP: 28
PEP: 28
DANTES: 28
Other exams: 28
Prior learning portfolio: 28

Oakland University

101 N. Foundation Hall ◆ **Rochester, MI 48309-4401**
Phone: (810) 370-3360 ◆ Toll-free phone: (800) OAK UNIV
Fax: (810) 370-4462 ◆ E-mail: ouinfo@oakland.edu
Web address: http://www.acs.oakland.edu

Founded: 1957

Accredited by: North Central

Enrollment: 13,600 ◆ Adult students: 46 percent

University status: Public

Degree	Concentration/Major	Format
B.A./B.S.	Human Resource Development	E
B.A./B.S.	General Studies	E
	Degrees offered in 15 majors not specified by the university.	E

Campus Extension Sites

Rochester Hills, MI
Warren, MI
Royal Oak, MI
Madison Heights, MI
Birmingham, MI

Requirements

Residency requirement: Students must attend classes on campus except for the off-campus programs. Undergraduate admissions requirements: Admission for high school graduates whose formal education has been interrupted for three or more years is based on employment record, recommendations, and standardized test results. An interview is required. Graduate admissions requirements: Applicants must hold a baccalaureate degree and submit official transcripts, recommendations, and GRE scores. Graduation requirements (undergraduate): Students must meet requirements in general education, writing proficiency, ethnic diversity, the degree program, and upper-level credit; have a minimum 2.0 GPA; and file an application. Graduation requirements (graduate): Requirements vary with each program.

Fees, Tuition, Costs

Undergraduate application fee: $25
Graduate application fee: $30
Undergraduate tuition: $118.50/credit
Graduate tuition: $200.25/credit
Undergraduate cost of books: $450/semester
Graduate cost of books: $450/semester

Financial Aid/Status

Scholarship programs for adults: Scholarships supporting nontraditional female students and State of Michigan Adult Part-Time Student Grants are available. Full-time status: Undergraduate full-time status is 12 credit hours per semester; graduate is 8 credit hours per semester.

Maximum Hours Awarded For

CLEP: Yes
Other exams: Yes
Additional information: Maximum 60 credits allowed based on nonclassroom experience

Features and Services

1. Is it possible to purchase books during hours most adult students attend classes? **Yes.**

2. Are the institution's administrative offices open during hours adult students attend class? **Yes.**

3. How do students taking extended classes access library resources? **The library offers online resources. Special arrangements can be made with the library.**

4. What is the registration and payment process for adult students? **Registration by Touch-Tone phone. Payment about one week before class by mail or in person.**

5. What is the process for advising adult students? **Advising by appointment or walk-in through department of major.**

6. What career and placement services are available to adult students? **The Adult Career Counseling Center and the Department of Placement and Career Services are available.**

7. What characteristics of the institution's adult degree programs are most appealing to students? **Ninety-eight percent of classes are taught by senior faculty members demonstrating the emphasis on academic quality.**

Oakwood College

Blake Administration Building ◆ Oakwood Road
Huntsville, AL 35896
Phone: (205) 726-7098 ◆ Fax: (205) 726-7409

Founded: 1896

Accredited by: Southern Association

Enrollment: 1,700 ◆ Adult students: 7 percent

University status: Private, Church, Seventh-Day Adventist

Degree	Concentration/Major	Format
B.S.	Organizational Management	E,A

Requirements

Residency requirement: All classes are held on campus.
Undergraduate admissions requirements: Applicants must be at least 25 years old, have earned 60 or more college credit hours (GPA—2.0), and have two years of work experience. Official transcripts must be submitted.
Graduation requirements (undergraduate): Graduates must complete 128 semester hours, with 44 received through the LEAP program.

Fees, Tuition, Costs

Undergraduate application fee: $15
Undergraduate tuition: $2,900/term
Undergraduate cost of books: $300/term
Other costs: Graduation fee of $50; Credit for prior learning papers fee of $25/semester credit earned; Drop/add fee of $10; Transfer fee of $25

Financial Aid/Status

Scholarship programs for adults: Academic and other scholarships are applicable to adults.
Full-time status: Requires being enrolled in 6 semester hours or more.
Percentage of adult students receiving financial aid: 75 percent.

Maximum Hours Awarded For

CLEP: Yes
DANTES: Yes
Other exams: Yes
Prior learning portfolio: 30
Additional information: Maximum 30 credits from CLEP, DANTES, and departmental exam

Features and Services

1. Is it possible to purchase books during hours most adult students attend classes? **Yes.**

2. How do students taking extended classes access library resources? **The library is open weekends and evenings.**

3. What is the registration and payment process for adult students? **Accommodations are made for students registering in the evening.**

4. What is the process for advising adult students? **Advising is available M-Th evenings.**

5. What career and placement services are available to adult students? **Job positions and resume services are available if needed.**

6. What characteristics of the institution's adult degree programs are most appealing to students? **One-night-per-week class and one class at a time.**

Oglethorpe University
University College

4484 Peachtree Road ◆ Atlanta, GA 30319
Phone: (404) 364-8383 ◆ Fax: (404) 364-8347

Founded: 1835

Accredited by: Southern Association

Enrollment: 1,300 ◆ Adult students: 25 percent

University status: Private

Degree	Concentration/Major	Format
B.B.A.	Business Administration	E
B.B.A.	Accounting	E
B.A.L.S.	Organizational Management	E
B.A.L.S.	Psychology	E
B.A.L.S.	Humanities	E
B.A.L.S.	Social Science	E
B.A.L.S.	Communications	E
B.A.L.S.	Administration	E
M.B.A.	Business Administration	E

Requirements

Residency requirement: Students must meet a 45-semester-hour residency requirement.
Undergraduate admissions requirements: Applicants must be at least 21 years old, have graduated from high school or passed GED, and have a minimum 2.3 cumulative GPA on all college work attempted in the last two years.
Graduate admissions requirements: M.B.A. program requires a bachelor's degree—including Accounting I & II, Management, Marketing, Finance, Micro & Macro Economics, and Management Science—and the GMAT.
Graduation requirements (undergraduate): Graduates must complete 120 semester hours, the general education and major requirements with a minimum 2.0 GPA.
Graduation requirements (graduate): M.B.A. graduates must complete 10 required courses.

Fees, Tuition, Costs

Undergraduate application fee: $25
Graduate application fee: $30
Undergraduate tuition: $805/3-hour class
Graduate tuition: $1,400/4-hour class
Undergraduate cost of books: $100/class
Graduate cost of books: $100/class
Other costs: Graduation fee of $100

Financial Aid/Status

Scholarship programs for adults: Harold Hirsch Scholarship ($500/semester) based on financial need and grades and Hope Scholarship (currently $1,250/semester) for full-time students are offered.
Full-time status: 12 semester hours/term.
Percentage of adult students receiving financial aid: 40 percent.

Maximum Hours Awarded For

CLEP: 30
Additional information: PONSI credit up to 30 semester hours

Features and Services

1. Is it possible to purchase books during hours most adult students attend classes? **Yes.**

2. How do students taking extended classes access library resources? **The library is open weekends and evenings.**

3. What is the registration and payment process for adult students? **Registration and payment are done in the evening or Saturdays through the Continuing Education Office.**

4. What is the process for advising adult students? **Advising is available by appointment or drop in with the dean and associate dean of University College.**

5. What career and placement services are available to adult students? **Services are available through the Office of Career Services.**

6. What characteristics of the institution's adult degree programs are most appealing to students? **Personal attention, well-trained faculty, convenience, and flexibility of schedule.**

Ohio State University at Newark

1179 University Drive ◆ Newark, OH 43055

Phone: (614) 366-9309 ◆ Toll-free phone: (800) 9NEWARK

Fax: (614) 366-5047 ◆ E-mail: bruner.4@osu.edu

Founded: 1957

Accredited by: North Central

Enrollment: 1,550 ◆ Adult students: 50 percent

University status: Public,

Maximum Hours Awarded For

CLEP: 97
DANTES: Yes
Other exams: Varies
Additional information: Advanced Placement Program

Features and Services

1. Is it possible to purchase books during hours most adult students attend classes? **Yes.**

2. Are the institution's administrative offices open during hours adult students attend class? **Yes.**

3. How do students taking extended classes access library resources? **Students may use the library computer system.**

4. What is the registration and payment process for adult students? **After the initial orientation, the process can be done by mail or phone.**

5. What is the process for advising adult students? **Students will have advisors in their field. Advisors were all adult students themselves.**

6. What career and placement services are available to adult students? **Career and placement services are handled through the Columbus campus.**

7. What characteristics of the institution's adult degree programs are most appealing to students? **Pathways office support for ADC students, extended classroom and library hours, on-campus child care, personal counselor, and free tutoring and study help.**

Degree	Concentration/Major	Format
A.S./A.A.	Many degrees available	E
B.S./B.A.	Many degrees available	E
B.A.	Education	E
B.A.	Psychology	E
B.A.	English	E
B.A.	Accounting	E
B.S.	Economics	E
M.Ed.	Elementary Education	E

Requirements

Residency requirement: This campus is an extended campus. Degrees can be completed on campus or may require one or two courses at the Columbus campus. Classes are held from 8 A.M. to 10 P.M. daily and Saturday from 9 A.M. to 1 P.M.

Undergraduate admissions requirements: Open admission is available to Ohio residents who are graduates of a chartered Ohio high school, passed 9th grade proficiency test, or have a GED. Graduate admissions requirements: M.A. in elementary education requires a minimum 2.7 GPA, GRE scores, references, letter of intent, and application. Graduation requirements (undergraduate): Graduates must complete degree requirements—normally 180-200 credit hours.

Fees, Tuition, Costs

Undergraduate application fee: $30 or fee waiver
Graduate application fee: $30
Undergraduate tuition: $1,052/quarter
Graduate tuition: $1,530/quarter
Undergraduate cost of books: $150/quarter
Graduate cost of books: $200/quarter
Other costs: Transportation costs (90 percent of students are commuters)

Financial Aid/Status

Full-time status: 12 credit hours or more
Percentage of adult students receiving financial aid: 60 percent

Ohio University—Chillicothe

571 W. Fifth Street ◆ P.O. Box 629 ◆ Chillicothe, OH 45601
Phone: (614) 774-7200 ◆ Fax: (614) 774-7214

Founded: 1946

Accredited by: North Central

Enrollment: 1,388 ◆ Adult students: 40 percent

University status: Public

Degree	Concentration/Major	Format
A.A.B.	Business Management Technology	E
A.A.B.	Office Administration Technology	E
A.A.S.	Human Services Technology	E
A.A.S.	Law Enforcement Technology	E
A.A.S.	Security Safety Technology	E
A.A.S.	Hazardous Materials Technology	E
A.A.S.	Nursing	E
A.I.S.	Individualized Studies	E
B.S.S.	Specialized Studies	E
B.S.N.	Nursing	E
B.C.J.	Criminal Justice	E
B.S.	Elementary Education	E
M.A.	Graduate programs available in selected areas	E

Campus Extension Sites

Athens, OH
Zanesville, OH
Lancaster, OH
Clairsville, OH
Ironton, OH

Requirements

Undergraduate admissions requirements: Applicants must be high school graduates or have completed requirements for the GED.
Graduate admissions requirements: Admission to graduate study is based on the possession of a bachelor's degree from an accredited college or university.
Graduation requirements (undergraduate): Ohio University has two sets of requirements to meet: (1) university-wide requirements and (2) specific college-level requirements.
Graduation requirements (graduate): Ohio University has specific college-level requirements.

Fees, Tuition, Costs

Undergraduate application fee: $15
Graduate application fee: $25
Undergraduate tuition: $89/credit hour
Graduate tuition: $184/credit hour
Undergraduate cost of books: $300/quarter
Graduate cost of books: $150/quarter

Financial Aid/Status

Scholarship programs for adults: Scholarships ($250-$1000/year) are available.
Full-time status: Full-time students carry a normal load of 16-20 quarter hours.
Percentage of adult students receiving financial aid: 85 percent.

Maximum Hours Awarded For

Other exams: Yes
Prior learning portfolio: Yes

Features and Services

1. Is it possible to purchase books during hours most adult students attend classes? **Yes.**

2. Are the institution's administrative offices open during hours adult students attend class? **Yes.**

3. How do students taking extended classes access library resources? **Quinn Library is open day, evening, and weekend hours to meet the needs of adult students.**

4. What is the registration and payment process for adult students? **New students register during posted hours. Others register through TRIPS, a Touch-Tone process.**

5. What is the process for advising adult students? **Advisors are available by appointment at convenient times for adult students.**

6. What career and placement services are available to adult students? **Career counseling with computer-assisted programs and follow-up assistance are available.**

7. What characteristics of the institution's adult degree programs are most appealing to students? **OUC offers a small college atmosphere, day and evening classes, credit for work and life experiences, and a flexible curriculum.**

Ohio University*

External Student Program ◆ 301 Tupper Hall
Athens, OH 45701
Phone: (614) 593-2150 ◆ Toll-free phone: (800) 444-2420
Fax: (614) 593-2901 ◆ Web address: http://www.ohiou.edu

Founded: 1804

Accredited by: North Central

Enrollment: 17,000 ◆ Adult students: 1,100

University status: Public

Degree	Concentration/Major	Format
A.S.	This degree focuses on Natural Sciences, Applied Sciences, and Quantitative Skills.	C
A.A.	Social Sciences or Arts and Humanities Students may choose to focus their studies on either the Social Sciences or Arts and Humanities.	C
A.A.B.	Business Management Technology	C
A.S.	Self-designed. Students design their own degree based on career goals and interests.	S
B.S.S.	Self-designed This degree provides students the opportunity to design an individualized four-year plan.	S

Requirements

Residency requirement: Credits toward the degree may be earned through a variety of methods, including correspondence courses, credit by examination, independent study projects, independent study media courses, on-campus classes, classes at other universities, and credits at Institutes for Adult Learners (one- or two-week intensive on-campus classes). Undergraduate admissions requirements: High school transcript or GED; transfer students must have a 2.0 GPA.

Fees, Tuition, Costs

Undergraduate application fee: $100
Undergraduate tuition: $53/credit

Financial Aid/Status

Full-time status: On-campus students must attend 12-19 hours of classes to be considered full-time students.

Maximum Hours Awarded For

CLEP: Yes
Other exams: No limit

Prior learning portfolio: 25 percent of the credits required for a degree
Additional information: Credit for professional training in accordance with the American Council on Education guidelines, transferring prior college credits, and military courses

Features and Services

1. Is it possible to purchase books during hours most adult students attend classes? **Books are purchased through the mail.**

2. What characteristics of the institution's adult degree programs are most appealing to students? **Flexible hours; affordable tuition; work at own pace; no on-campus attendance required; can enroll in Ohio University Independent Studies course work from anywhere in the country, or even out of the country.**

Oklahoma City University

2501 N. Blackwelder ◆ Oklahoma City, OK 73106
Phone: (405) 521-5288 ◆ Toll-free phone: (800) 633-7242
Fax: (405) 521-5447 ◆ E-mail: dshort@frodo.ocu.edu
Colleges Web address: http://frodo.okcu.edu/

Founded: 1904

Accredited by: North Central

Enrollment: 4,000 ◆ Adult students: 15 percent

University status: Private, Church, United Methodist Church

Degree	Concentration/Major	Format
B.S.	Business Administration	E,A,C
B.S.	Technical Management	E,A,C
B.A.	Liberal Arts	E,A,C
B.S.	Health Services Administration	E,A,S

Campus Extension Site

Tulsa, OK

Requirements

Residency requirement: Students must attend a weekend Foundations of Adult Learning course on campus.
Undergraduate admissions requirements: Applicants must be high school graduates or have GED, be 22 years or older, and have an initial evaluation.
Graduation requirements (undergraduate): Graduates must fulfill general education and concentration requirements and electives to equal a minimum of 124 credit hours.

Fees, Tuition, Costs

Undergraduate application fee: $25
Undergraduate tuition: $135-

$270/credit hour
Undergraduate cost of books: $200/6-10 credit hours

Financial Aid/Status

Scholarship programs for adults: Scholarships are not usually available. One $500 scholarship for a student involved with a public service, nonprofit organization is offered.
Full-time status: 12 semester hours.
Percentage of adult students receiving financial aid: 20 percent.

Maximum Hours Awarded For

CLEP: 30
PEP: 30
DANTES: 30
Prior learning portfolio: 31
Additional information: Maximum 30 credits awarded for all standardized tests

Features and Services

1. How do students taking extended classes access library resources? **Students may access the library through library loan.**

2. What is the process for advising adult students? **The PLUS office is available by appointment for evaluation and degree planning.**

3. What career and placement services are available to adult students? **Services include the Strong/Campbell inventory, resume help, and job listings.**

4. What characteristics of the institution's adult degree programs are most appealing to students? **The PLUS office service, accelerated courses, self-directed studies, and reputation of the university.**

Oklahoma State University

470 Student Union ◆ **Stillwater, OK 74078**
Phone: (405) 744-6606 ◆ Toll-free phone: (800) 803-8455
Fax: (405) 744-7923 ◆ E-mail: nivens@okway.okstate.edu
Web address: http://www.okstate.edu

Founded: 1890

Accredited by: North Central

Enrollment: 19,500 ◆ Adult students: 25 percent

University status: Public

Degree	Concentration/Major	Format
M.S.	Chemical Engineering	T
M.S.	Mechanical Engineering	T
M.S.	Electrical Engineering	T
M.S.	Computer Science	T
M.B.A.	Corporate Masters in Business Administration	T
M.S.	Telecommunications Management	T

Campus Extension Sites

Corporate sites in Oklahoma

Requirements

Residency requirement: Corporate M.B.A. students come to campus for six Saturday seminars.
Graduate admissions requirements: The requirements vary depending on the degree program.
Graduation requirements (graduate): The number of credit hours required to graduate varies by the degree.

Fees, Tuition, Costs

Graduate application fee: $25
Graduate tuition: $175-$195/ credit hour
Graduate cost of books: $125

Financial Aid/Status

Scholarship programs for adults: Scholarships offered on the same basis as other students: i.e., full load, need-based, performance-based.
Full-time status: 12 hours undergraduate; 9 hours graduate.

Features and Services

1. Is it possible to purchase books during hours most adult students attend classes? **Yes.**

2. How do students taking extended classes access library resources? **Students may use the local library. Online access is also available.**

3. What is the registration and payment process for adult students? **Registration is on-site. Payment is through the corporate contractor or by mail.**

4. What is the process for advising adult students? **Advising is provided by phone or computer.**

5. What characteristics of the institution's adult degree programs are most appealing to students? **Availability at remote locations.**

Oklahoma State University—Okmulgee

1801 E. 4th Street ◆ **Okmulgee, OK 74447**
Phone: (918) 756-6211 ◆ Toll-free phone: (800) 722-4471
Fax: (918) 756-4157 ◆ E-mail: shill@okway.okstate.edu

Founded: 1946

Accredited by: North Central

Enrollment: 2,200 ◆ Adult students: 69 percent

University status: Public

Degree	Concentration/Major	Format
A.A.S.	Air Conditioning and Refrigeration	
A.A.S.	Automotive Technology	
A.A.S.	Business Technology	
A.A.S.	Construction Technology	
A.A.S.	Electrical and Electronics Technology	
A.A.S.	Engineering Graphics Technology	
A.A.S.	Heavy Equipment and Vehicle Institute	
A.A.S.	Hospitality Services	
A.A.S.	Small Business Occupations	
A.A.S.	Visual Communications	

Requirements

Residency requirement: Lab classes must be attended to allow for training in the latest technology. Graduation requirements (undergraduate): Graduates must complete the degree plan with a minimum 2.0 GPA.

Fees, Tuition, Costs

Undergraduate application fee: None
Undergraduate tuition: $46/credit hour
Undergraduate cost of books: $600
Other costs: Tools specific to the technical trade

Financial Aid/Status

Scholarship programs for adults: Scholarships are available.
Full-time status: Students carrying 12 or more credit hours are full-time.
Percentage of adult students receiving financial aid: 75 percent.

Maximum Hours Awarded For

CLEP: Yes
Other exams: Yes
Additional information: Military credit

Features and Services

1. Is it possible to purchase books during hours most adult students attend classes? **Yes.**

2. Are the institution's administrative offices open during hours adult students attend class? **Yes.**

3. How do students taking extended classes access library resources? **The library hours are from 7 A.M. to 9 P.M.**

4. What is the registration and payment process for adult students? **Schedule set by academic department; 1/3 tuition paid at registration, billed for rest over semester.**

5. What is the process for advising adult students? **Advisement is handled through the academic department.**

6. What career and placement services are available to adult students? **The Multiplex offers testing and exploration. Placement is available from the academic department.**

7. What characteristics of the institution's adult degree programs are most appealing to students? **Uniqueness of programs and high job placement of graduates.**

Old Dominion University

217 New Administration Building ◆ **Norfolk, VA 23529**
Phone: (804) 683-5314 ◆ Toll-free phone: (800) 968-2638
Fax: (804) 683-3004 ◆ E-mail: arrloou@jefferson.na.odu.edu
Web address: http://www.odu.edu

Founded: 1939

Accredited by: Southern Association

Enrollment: 17,000 ◆ Adult students: 50 percent

University status: Public

Degree	Concentration/Major	Format
B.S.	Business Administration Management	T,E,CT
B.S.	Civil Engineering Technology	T,E,CT
B.S.	Computer Engineering Technology	T,E,CT
B.S.	Criminal Justice	T,E.CT
B.S.	Electrical Engineering Technology	T,E,CT
B.S.	Health Sciences Health Care Management	T,E,CT
B.S.	Human Services Counseling	T,E,CT
B.S.	Interdisciplinary Studies Professional Communications	T,E,CT
B.S.	Nursing (RN to BSN)	T,E,CT
B.S.	Mechanical Engineering Technology	T,E,CT
M.S.	Special Education	T,E,CT
M.S.	Nursing	T,E,CT
M.S.	Engineering Management	T,E,CT
M.S.	Electrical Engineering	T,E,CT
M.S.	Civil Engineering	T,E,CT
M.S.	Mechanical Engineering	T,E,CT
M.S.	Aerospace Engineering	T,E,CT

Campus Extension Sites

Weyers Cave, VA
Melfa, VA
Lynchburg, VA
Locust Grove, VA
Clifton Forge, VA
Richmond, VA
Danville, VA
Middletown, VA
Dublin, VA
Annandale, VA
Martinsville, VA
Charlottesville, VA
Alberta, VA
Keysville, VA

Richlands, VA
Roanoke, VA
Wythevill, VA
Virginia Beach, VA
Portsmouth, VA
Hampton, VA

Requirements

Residency requirement: Students are not required to attend class on the main campus.
Undergraduate admissions requirements: Applicants must complete an associate degree or have at least 45 credit hours at a lower-division school.
Graduate admissions requirements: Applicants must have earned a baccalaureate degree.
Graduation requirements (undergraduate): Graduates must earn 120 credit hours, fulfill the general education and degree requirements, and pass the writing exit exam.
Graduation requirements (graduate): Graduation requirements vary.

Fees, Tuition, Costs

Undergraduate application fee: $30
Undergraduate tuition: $129/credit hour
Graduate tuition: $153/credit hour
Undergraduate cost of books: $800/2 years
Graduate cost of books: $600

Financial Aid/Status

Scholarship programs for adults: Scholarships are available.
Full-time status: 12 hours for undergraduates; 9 hours for graduate.
Percentage of adult students receiving financial aid: 30 percent.

Maximum Hours Awarded For

CLEP: Yes
Other exams: Yes

Features and Services

1. Is it possible to purchase books during hours most adult students attend classes? **Yes.**

2. Are the institution's administrative offices open during hours adult students attend class? **Yes.**

3. How do students taking extended classes access library resources? **Students may request materials online for distant delivery.**

4. What is the registration and payment process for adult students? **Online registration and payment by phone and credit card may be used.**

5. What is the process for advising adult students? **Advising is available in person, by phone, and by television.**

6. What career and placement services are available to adult students? **Televised services available, and every undergraduate is guaranteed a practicum if wanted.**

7. What characteristics of the institution's adult degree programs are most appealing to students? **Student support services, scheduling classes, and quality of instruction.**

Olivet Nazarene University

P.O. Box 592 ◆ **Kankakee, IL 60901-0592**

Phone: (815) 939-5291 ◆ Toll-free phone: (800) 7-OLIVET
Fax: (815) 935-4991 ◆ Web address: http://www.olivet.edu
Program's Web address: http://www.olivet.edu.departments/
grad/gradindx.html

Founded: 1907

Accredited by: North Central

Enrollment: 2,269 ◆ Adult students: 464

University Status: Private, Church, Church of the Nazarene

Degree	Concentration/Major	Format
B.A.S.	Management	E,A
B.S.	Management	E,A
B.S.	Nursing	E,A
M.A.E.	Curriculum and Instruction	E,A
M.B.A.	Business Administration	E,A
M.A.T.	Teaching	E,A
M.C.M.	Church Management	
M.P.C.	Pastoral Counseling	
M.A.	Religion	

Campus Extension Sites

Homewood, IL
Woodfield, IL
Joliet, IL
Arlington Heights, IL
Barrington, IL
Elk Grove Village, IL
Schaumburg, IL
Chicago, IL
Lisle, IL

Requirements

Residency requirement: Students enrolled in graduate programs for church, pastoral, and religion degrees attend week-long seminars on campus at scheduled times convenient for full-time church pastors and staff.
Undergraduate admissions requirements: 60 hours of college credit, minimum 2.0 GPA, two letters of recommendation, moral character consistent with attendance at a Christian university, and some additional departmental requirements.
Graduate admissions requirements: Bachelor's degree from accredited college, ability to pursue graduate work successfully, moral character consistent with attendance at a Christian university, and some departmental requirements.
Graduation requirements (undergraduate): Requirements vary by program.
Graduation requirements (graduate): Requirements vary by program.

Fees, Tuition, Costs

Undergraduate application fee: $20
Graduate application fee: $20
Undergraduate tuition: $290/hour, 4 terms, 2 years
Graduate tuition: $300/hour, 4 terms, 2 years
Undergraduate cost of books: $1,080 average
Graduate cost of books: $1,188 average
Other costs: Nursing mobility lab fee of $124/term; computer fee built into tuition

Financial Aid/Status

Scholarship programs for adults: Departmental selection—graduate assistants. University Foundation awards scholarships from $400 to $1,000.

Full-time status: A student is considered full-time if he or she carries the number of hours called for in a "packaged program" during a given term.
Percentage of adult students receiving financial aid: 27 percent.

Maximum Hours Awarded For

CLEP: 50 hours
PEP: 50 hours

DANTES: 50 hours
Other exams: 50 hours
Prior learning portfolio: 50 hours

Features and Services

1. How do students taking extended classes access library resources? **Extended library hours, "network" of libraries, ONU electronic library access.**

2. What is the registration and payment process for adult students? **A coupon booklet is used for payment of tuition. Registration is done course by course or by term.**

3. What characteristics of the institution's adult degree programs are most appealing to students? **Evening classes and convenient off-campus locations.**

Oral Roberts University

7777 S. Lewis Avenue ◆ Tulsa, OK 74171
Phone: (918) 495-6236 ◆ Toll-free phone: (800) 678-8876
Fax: (918) 495-6033 ◆ E-mail: slle@oru.edu
Web address: http://www.oru.edu

Founded: 1965

Accredited by: North Central

Enrollment: 4,000 ◆ Adult students: 400+

University status: Private, Church, Nondenominational

Degree	Concentration/Major	Format
B.S.	Church Ministries	C
B.S.	Business Administration	C
B.S.	Elementary Christian School Education	C
B.S.	Christian Care and Counseling	C
B.S.	Liberal Studies	C

Requirements

Residency requirement: Students must meet a 12-hour residential requirement.
Undergraduate admissions requirements: Applicants must have a minimum 2.0 GPA and complete the full application process.
Graduation requirements (undergraduate): Graduation requires successful completion of 129 hours of study in a specific degree program.

Fees, Tuition, Costs

Undergraduate application fee: $25
Undergraduate tuition: $105/hour
Undergraduate cost of books: $90/course
Other costs: Postage for assignments

Financial Aid/Status

Full-time status: 9 hours of correspondence study/semester
Percentage of adult students receiving financial aid: 85 percent

Maximum Hours Awarded For

CLEP: Yes
DANTES: Yes
Other exams: 30
Prior learning portfolio: 30

Features and Services

1. Is it possible to purchase books during hours most adult students attend classes? **Yes.**

2. Are the institution's administrative offices open during hours adult students attend class? **Yes.**

3. What is the registration and payment process for adult students? **Phone registration using credit cards is available.**

4. What is the process for advising adult students? **Advising may be done by phone.**

5. What characteristics of the institution's adult degree programs are most appealing to students? **Very flexible.**

Oregon Institute of Technology

3201 Campus Drive ◆ **Klamath Falls, OR 97601-8801**
Phone: (541) 885-1525 ◆ Fax: (541) 885-1923
E-mail: harrisc@mail.oit.osshe.edu
Web address: http://www.oit.osshe.edu

Founded: 1947

Accredited by: Northwest Association

Enrollment: 2,100 ◆ Adult students: 2 percent

University status: Public

Degree   Concentration/Major   Format

Not specified: The institute indicated that it has just received approval for both undergraduate and graduate degrees and that they are in development. Currently courses are offered through teleconferencing. Check with institute officials on the status of these degrees.

Requirements

Residency requirement: Students must meet a residency requirement with the last 15 hours taken on campus.
Undergraduate admissions requirements: Applicants must submit an application, official transcripts, scores from ACT or SAT, and a health form.
Graduation requirements (undergraduate): Graduates must meet all university and department requirements.

Fees, Tuition, Costs

Undergraduate application fee: $50
Undergraduate tuition: $2,904/3 terms
Undergraduate cost of books: $750/3 terms

Financial Aid/Status

Scholarship programs for adults: Scholarships are available.
Full-time status: Full-time students must complete 36 credits per year.

Maximum Hours Awarded For

CLEP: Yes
Other exams: Yes

Features and Services

1. How do students taking extended classes access library resources? **Students may use the Learning Resources Center.**

2. What is the registration and payment process for adult students? **Registration and payment are the same for all students.**

3. What is the process for advising adult students? **Students are required to meet with advisors before registering.**

4. What career and placement services are available to adult students? **The Career Services Office is available to all students.**

5. What characteristics of the institution's adult degree programs are most appealing to students? **Adult students enjoy being mainstreamed with traditional students.**

Ottawa University

2340 W. Mission Lane ◆ Phoenix, AZ 85021

Phone: (602) 371-1188 ◆ Toll-free phone: (800) 235-9586

Fax: (602) 371-0035

Founded: 1865

Accredited by: North Central

Enrollment: Varies ◆ Adult students: 100 percent

University status: Private, Church, American Baptist Church

Degree	Concentration/Major	Format
B.A.	Education	E,A
B.A.	Psychology	E,A
B.A.	Business Administration	E,A
B.A.	Human Services	E,A
B.A.	Human Resources	E,A
B.A.	Health Management	E,A
B.A.	Computer Science	CT
B.A.	Fire Service Management	E,A
B.A.	Sociology	E,A
M.A.	Education	E,A
M.A.	Human Resources	E,A
M.A.	Counseling	E,A

Campus Extension Sites

Overland Park, KS
Brookfield, WI
Phoenix, AZ

Requirements

Residency requirement: Students must attend classes on campus. Undergraduate admissions requirements: Applicants must be high school graduates or have GED certificate. An application and all previous transcripts should be submitted. A preadmission interview is held.
Graduate admissions requirements: Applicants must have at least a 3.0 Jr./Sr. GPA with 60 semester hours completed and submit official transcripts. Preference is given to applicants with at least two years of relevant experience.
Graduation requirements (undergraduate): Graduates must complete 128 semester hours, 48 upper-division hours, 28-40 semester hours in major; minimum 2.0 GPA. A minimum of 24 semester hours must be completed from OU.

Fees, Tuition, Costs

Undergraduate application fee: $30
Graduate application fee: $40
Undergraduate tuition: $170-$200/credit
Graduate tuition: $190-$220/credit
Undergraduate cost of books: $100/semester; $400/year

Financial Aid/Status

Full-time status: 8 credits/term
Percentage of adult students receiving financial aid: 50 percent

Maximum Hours Awarded For

CLEP: Yes
PEP: Yes
DANTES: Yes
Prior learning portfolio: Yes

Features and Services

1. Is it possible to purchase books during hours most adult students attend classes? **Yes.**

2. Are the institution's administrative offices open during hours adult students attend class? **Yes.**

3. How do students taking extended classes access library resources? **Internet connections to large university libraries are available for students.**

4. What is the registration and payment process for adult students? **Tuition is paid at registration. A registration appointment is provided each semester.**

5. What is the process for advising adult students? **Each student is assigned a personal advisor.**

6. What career and placement services are available to adult students? **Career advising seminars and meetings are provided in the Education Program.**

7. What characteristics of the institution's adult degree programs are most appealing to students? **Flexibility, convenient hours for working adults, and easily accessible location.**

Our Lady of the Lake University

411 S.W. 24th Street ◆ San Antonio, TX 78207-4689
Phone: (210) 431-3949 ◆ Fax: (210) 431-3945
E-mail: sarvc@lake.ollusa.edu
Web address: http://www.ollusa.edu

Founded: 1895

Accredited by: Southern Association

Enrollment: 3,100 ◆ Adult students: 1,500

University status: Private, Church, Roman Catholic Church

Degree	Concentration/Major	Format
B.B.A.	Management, Accounting, Computer Science, Human Resources, Marketing	E
B.S.	Computer Science	E
B.A.	Liberal Studies/Management, Human Resources Development	E
B.A.S.	Liberal Studies/Management	E
M.A.	Human Sciences	E
M.B.A.	Management/Health Care Management	E
M.Ed.	Education/State Certification	E

Campus Extension Sites
Dallas, TX
Houston, TX

Requirements
Residency requirement: Students must meet a 30-hour residency requirement.
Undergraduate admissions requirements: Applicant must be a high school graduate or have GED, and submit all transcripts and application. An admissions test is required if applicant has not taken Freshman Composition I & II.
Graduate admissions requirements: Applicant must have a bachelor's degree and an acceptable score on the GRE, GMAT, or MAT. A completed application and transcripts must be submitted.

Graduation requirements (undergraduate): Graduates must complete at least 128 hours with minimum 2.0 overall GPA.
Graduation requirements (graduate): Graduation requirements vary with the degree—usually 36 hours with at least a 3.0 GPA.

Fees, Tuition, Costs
Undergraduate application fee: $15
Graduate application fee: $15
Undergraduate tuition: $297/hour
Graduate tuition: $314/hour
Undergraduate cost of books: $100/trimester
Graduate cost of books: $150/trimester

Financial Aid/Status
Scholarship programs for adults: Scholarships are available.

Full-time status: 12 hours.
Percentage of adult students receiving financial aid: 50 percent.

Maximum Hours Awarded For
CLEP: Yes
DANTES: Yes
Other exams: Yes
Prior learning portfolio: 30

Features and Services
1. Is it possible to purchase books during hours most adult students attend classes? **Yes.**

2. Are the institution's administrative offices open during hours adult students attend class? **Yes.**

3. How do students taking extended classes access library resources? **The library is open for adults and may be accessed by computer.**

4. What is the registration and payment process for adult students? **Registration and payment are the same for all students.**

5. What is the process for advising adult students? **A team of advisors is available for Weekend College students.**

6. What career and placement services are available to adult students? **A special counselor is available in the Career Placement and Counseling Office.**

7. What characteristics of the institution's adult degree programs are most appealing to students? **Weekend format.**

Palm Beach Atlantic College*

901 S. Flagler Dr., Box 24708 ◆ **West Palm Beach, FL 33416**
Phone: (407) 835-4305 ◆ Fax: (407) 835-4341
Web address: http://www.pbac.edu

Founded: 1968

Accredited by: Southern Association

Enrollment: 2,000 ◆ Adult students: 400

University status: Private, Church, Baptist Church

Features and Services

1. Is it possible to purchase books during hours most adult students attend classes? **Yes.**

2. Are the institution's administrative offices open during hours adult students attend class? **Yes.**

3. What characteristics of the institution's adult degree programs are most appealing to students? **Convenient locations and accelerated classes.**

Degree	Concentration/Major	Format
B.S.	Management of Human Resources Classes meet once a week for four hours. Degree-completion program. Students who transfer 60 credits may possibly finish in one year.	E,A
M.S.	Human Resource Development Classes meet either one night a week or one weekend a month. Both formats take 18 months to complete.	E,A

Requirements

Residency requirement: No
Undergraduate admissions requirements: 60 hours of undergraduate work
Graduate admissions requirements: GRE score, three recommendations, essay, and last 60-hour GPA must be 3.0 or higher

Fees, Tuition, Costs

Undergraduate application fee: $25
Graduate application fee: $35
Undergraduate tuition: $215
Graduate tuition: $240

Financial Aid/Status

Full-time status: 12 hours/semester

Maximum Hours Awarded For

CLEP: 30
DANTES: 30
Prior learning portfolio: 30

Paul Quinn College

3837 Simpson Stuart Road ◆ Dallas, TX 75241

Phone: (214) 302-3611 ◆ Toll-free phone: (800) 300-5125

Fax: (214) 302-3559

Founded: 1872

Accredited by: Southern Association

Enrollment: 700 ◆ Adult students: 200

University status: Private, Church,
African Methodist Episcopal Church

Degree	Concentration/Major	Format
B.S.	Organizational Management	E

Campus Extension Sites

Waco, TX
Fort Worth, TX

Requirements

Residency requirement: Students must attend classes at the college or an extension.
Undergraduate admissions requirements: Applicants must be 25 years or older and have earned 60 credit hours or more with a 2.0 GPA or better.
Graduation requirements (undergraduate): Graduates must complete 124 semester hours and secure financial and academic clearance from all departments.

Fees, Tuition, Costs

Undergraduate application fee: $15
Undergraduate tuition: $150/credit hour
Undergraduate cost of books: $300/semester
Other costs: Credit for Life Learning paper fee of $35/credit hour

Financial Aid/Status

Scholarship programs for adults: The Orville Redenbacher Second Chance Scholarship is available.
Full-time status: 14 semester hours/semester.
Percentage of adult students receiving financial aid: 10 percent.

Maximum Hours Awarded For

CLEP: 30
DANTES: 30
Other exams: 30
Prior learning portfolio: 30
Additional information: Seminar, licensing, workshop 30 contact hours = 1 semester

Features and Services

1. How do students taking extended classes access library resources? **Library hours are extended. Adult learners use a student ID card.**

2. What is the registration and payment process for adult students? **Students register, get books and homework assignment before business office closes.**

3. What is the process for advising adult students? **Learners are advised before entering the program. Advising is available one-on-one as needed.**

4. What career and placement services are available to adult students? **Learners may contact the career and placement services center between 9 and 6.**

5. What characteristics of the institution's adult degree programs are most appealing to students? **The most appealing feature is the hours: 6 to 10 P.M. one night each week.**

Pennsylvania State University

Delaware County Campus ◆ 25 Yearsley Mill Road
Media, PA 19063
Phone: (610) 892-1200 ◆ Fax: (610) 892-1357
E-mail: dje4@psu.edu
Web address: http://www.de.psu.edu

Founded: 1966

Accredited by: Middle States

University status: Public

Degree	Concentration/Major	Format
A.A.	Business Administration	E
A.A.	Letters, Arts, Sciences	E,C
B.A.	Letters, Arts, Sciences	E,C
B.A.	Speech Communication	E,C
B.S.	Urban Education	N/specified
B.A.	American Studies	E,C

Requirements

Residency requirement: Some required courses are offered only on campus.
Undergraduate admissions requirements: Applicant must have a high school diploma or GED and submit SAT/ACT scores. If high school graduation is five years beyond requested date of entrance, no standardized tests are required.
Graduation requirements (undergraduate): Students must meet university and department requirements.

Fees, Tuition, Costs

Undergraduate application fee: $40
Undergraduate tuition: $5,024/year
Undergraduate cost of books: $400
Other costs: Computer fee of $70

Financial Aid/Status

Scholarship programs for adults: Scholarships are available.
Full-time status: 12 credits/semester.

Maximum Hours Awarded For

CLEP: Yes
Other exams: Yes

Features and Services

1. How do students taking extended classes access library resources? **The library is available to students.**

2. What is the registration and payment process for adult students? **Registration is offered by mail, phone, or in person till 8 P.M. M-Th.**

3. What is the process for advising adult students? **Counselors are available in the evening.**

4. What career and placement services are available to adult students? **The Career Center is open in the evening.**

Philadelphia College of Bible*

200 Manor Avenue ◆ **Langhorne, PA 19047-2990**

Phone: (215) 752-5800 ◆ Toll-free phone: (800) 4-ADVANCE

Fax: (215) 752-5812

Founded: 1913

Accredited by: Middle States

Enrollment: 1,050

University status: Private, Church, Nondenominational

Degree	Concentration/Major	Format
B.S.	Bible	E,A
M.S.	Bible	E
M.S.	Education	E
M.S.	Counseling	E

Requirements

Residency requirement: Yes
Undergraduate admissions requirements: Completion of 60+ credits from an accredited postsecondary institution, minimum GPA of 2.0, completion of application, official copies of transcripts from all colleges and universities attended, two personal references, Christian commitment, 550 TOFEL
Graduate admissions requirements: Bachelor's degree from an accredited college or university, official copies of transcripts from every college or university attended, letters of recommendation, GPA of 2.5, 550 TOFEL for international students

Fees, Tuition, Costs

Undergraduate application fee: $30
Graduate application fee: $25
Undergraduate tuition: $220/credit
Graduate tuition: $235/credit

Financial Aid/Status

Full-time status: 12 credits/ semester undergraduate; 6 credits/ semester graduate
Percentage of adult students receiving financial aid: 44 percent

Maximum Hours Awarded For

CLEP: 30
DANTES: 24
Prior learning portfolio: 24

Features and Services

1. Is it possible to purchase books during hours most adult students attend classes? **Yes.**

2. Are the institution's administrative offices open during hours adult students attend class? **Yes.**

3. What characteristics of the institution's adult degree programs are most appealing to students? **Undergraduate: module format, group structure, one session per week on campus, and faculty skilled in adult learning. Graduate: practicality of curriculum, flexible scheduling, and outstanding faculty.**

Philadelphia College of Textiles and Science*

School House Lane & Henry Avenue ◆ Philadelphia, PA 19144
Phone: (215) 951-2902 ◆ Fax: (215) 951-2615

Founded: 1876

Accredited by: North Central Association

Enrollment: 3,220 ◆ Adult students: 1,550

University status: Private

Features and Services

1. Is it possible to purchase books during hours most adult students attend classes? **Yes.**

2. Are the institution's administrative offices open during hours adult students attend class? **Yes.**

3. What characteristics of the institution's adult degree programs are most appealing to students? **Three campuses allow 89 credits in transfer from a two-year school.**

Degree	Concentration/Major	Format
B.S.	All degrees offered by college are available through evening courses.	E

Requirements

Residency requirement: Yes
Undergraduate admissions requirements: Open admissions

Fees, Tuition, Costs

Undergraduate application fee: $25
Undergraduate tuition: $230/credit

Financial Aid/Status

Full-time status: 12 or more credits/term
Percentage of adult students receiving financial aid: 5 percent

Maximum Hours Awarded For

CLEP: 30
PEP: 30
DANTES: 30
Additional information: Maximum 30 credit hours from CLEP, PEP, and DANTES

Point Park College

201 Wood Street ◆ **Pittsburgh, PA 15222**
Phone: (412) 392-3809 ◆ Fax: (412) 391-1980
E-mail: orrisje@westol.com
Web address: http://www.lm.com/~markv20/ppc.html

Founded: 1960

Accredited by: Middle States

Enrollment: 2,133 ◆ Adult students: 1,094

University status: Private

Full-time status: 12 credits or more.
Percentage of adult students receiving financial aid: 65 percent.

Maximum Hours Awarded For

CLEP: 30
DANTES: 30
Other exams: 18
Additional information: Transfer—70 credits plus 20 credits at the junior/senior level

Degree	Concentration/Major	Format
B.S.	Accounting	E
B.S.	Business Management	E
B.S.	Computer Science	E
B.S.	Public Administration	E
B.S.	Civil Engineering Technology	E
B.S.	Electrical Engineering Technology	E
B.S.	Mechanical Engineering Technology	E
B.S.	Business	E,A
B.S.	Biological Sciences	E
B.S.	Environmental Protection Science	E
B.S.	Health Services (Capstone)	E
B.S.	Human Resources Management (Capstone)	E

Requirements

Residency requirement: Students attend classes on campus; however, classes are offered at education and corporate centers, allowing students to take classes closer to their homes. Undergraduate admissions requirements: Part-time students: high school or college transcripts (12 credits or 6 months). Saturday Fast Accelerated Program: associate degree or 60 credits or bachelor's degree and English/math proficiency. Graduate admissions requirements: Applicants with bachelor's degree submit an application, official transcripts, recommendations, statement of purpose, and any test scores required. Graduation requirements (undergraduate): Graduation requires a cumulative and major QPA of 2.0 and 30 credits in residence. Graduation requirements (graduate): Graduation requires a cumulative QPA of 3.0 and completion of all courses, including undergraduate prerequisites.

Fees, Tuition, Costs

Undergraduate application fee: $20
Graduate application fee: $30
Undergraduate tuition: $275/credit
Graduate tuition: $329/credit
Undergraduate cost of books: $120/semester
Graduate cost of books: $200/semester
Other costs: $450/year

Financial Aid/Status

Scholarship programs for adults: A part-time grant based on financial need is available.

Features and Services

1. Is it possible to purchase books during hours most adult students attend classes? **Yes.**

2. Are the institution's administrative offices open during hours adult students attend class? **Yes.**

3. What is the registration and payment process for adult students? **The Office of Continuing, Corporate, and Part-Time Studies is open day, evening, and Saturday hours.**

4. What is the process for advising adult students? **Students should meet with advisors at least once a year. Office is available six days a week.**

5. What career and placement services are available to adult students? **A fully equipped Career Development Office is available in the evenings.**

6. What characteristics of the institution's adult degree programs are most appealing to students? **Equitable transfer of credits; availability of classes; convenient services through Office of Continuing, Corporate, and Part-Time Studies.**

Prescott College

283 S. Scott Avenue ◆ Tucson, AZ 85701

Phone: (520) 622-8334

Founded: 1966

Accredited by: North Central

Enrollment: 870 ◆ Adult students: 172

University status: Private

Degree	Concentration/Major	Format
B.A.	Elementary Education	S
B.A.	Psychology	S
B.A.	Counseling	S
B.A.	Management	S
B.A.	Environmental Studies	S
B.A.	Human Services	S
B.A.	Secondary Education	S
B.A.	Photography	S
B.A.	Liberal Arts	S

Campus Extension Sites

Tuscon, AZ
Phoenix, AZ

Requirements

Residency requirement: Students can complete their work anywhere in the United States.
Undergraduate admissions requirements: Students must have 30 semester credits of college work and show an ability to complete independent study, communicate goals, find mentors, and show prior success in college and/or employment.
Graduation requirements (undergraduate): Students attend three residential sessions, be enrolled at least 12 months, have college-level math and writing skills, show learning in a competence and two breadth areas, and complete a graduation project.

Fees, Tuition, Costs

Undergraduate application fee: $25
Undergraduate tuition: $3,140/18-23 quarter hours
Undergraduate cost of books: Very little
Other costs: Travel and accommodations for two weekend residencies. Since no required texts are used in the program, students use libraries and mentor resources and have very few book expenses.

Financial Aid/Status

Full-time status: 18 credits/term
Percentage of adult students receiving financial aid: 61 percent

Maximum Hours Awarded For

CLEP: Yes
DANTES: Yes

Prior learning portfolio: Yes
Additional information: Conversion portfolio for nonaccredited courses

Features and Services

1. Is it possible to purchase books during hours most adult students attend classes? **Yes.**

2. Are the institution's administrative offices open during hours adult students attend class? **Yes.**

3. How do students taking extended classes access library resources? **Students may use Internet and World Wide Web consortium agreement with county libraries.**

4. What is the registration and payment process for adult students? **New students register and pay at orientation. Continuing students are billed.**

5. What is the process for advising adult students? **The advising process allows students to direct their own program within their study area.**

6. What career and placement services are available to adult students? **Services include placement files, job listings, resume development, and job search workshops.**

7. What characteristics of the institution's adult degree programs are most appealing to students? **Flexibility, independent design of course work, recognition of prior learning, and experiential components.**

Purchase College—State University of New York

735 Anderson Hill Road ◆ Purchase, NY 10577-1400
Phone: (914) 251-6500 ◆ Fax: (914) 251-6515
Web address: http://www.purchase.edu

Founded: 1967

Accredited by: Middle States

Enrollment: 3,500 ◆ Adult students: 25 percent

University status: Public

Degree	Concentration/Major	Format
B.A.L.A.	Liberal Studies	E

Requirements

Residency requirement: Students must meet a residency requirement for last 15 credits. A maximum of 90 credits are accepted in transfer. Undergraduate admissions requirements: Applicants must have a minimum 2.0 GPA or 80 percent for high school average and 1100 combined SAT score. Individual consideration is given for returning adults with poor high school or college records. Graduation requirements (undergraduate): Liberal studies students must complete 120 credits with a minimum 2.0 QPA, meet the course requirements from various areas of study, and show writing proficiency. Application for graduation is required.

Fees, Tuition, Costs

Undergraduate application fee: $30
Undergraduate tuition: $137.85/ credit; $1,700 for 12 or more credits

Undergraduate cost of books: $550/year
Other costs: No student activity, athletic, health, or orientation fees for liberal studies students

Financial Aid/Status

Scholarship programs for adults: Very limited scholarships are offered. This is a new program in 1995-96.
Full-time status: 12 credits/ semester.

Maximum Hours Awarded For

CLEP: 30
PEP: 30
Additional information: Maximum of 45 credits by examination

Features and Services

1. Is it possible to purchase books during hours most adult students attend classes? **Yes.**

2. Are the institution's administrative offices open during hours adult students attend class? **Yes.**

3. What is the registration and payment process for adult students? **Registration and payment may be done by mail, fax, or in person.**

4. What is the process for advising adult students? **Two advisors are available: one for non-liberal studies students and one for liberal studies students.**

5. What career and placement services are available to adult students? **Services include individual and group counseling, workshops, assessment, and credential files.**

6. What characteristics of the institution's adult degree programs are most appealing to students? **Flexible degree requirements allow a variety of concentrations, and students complete the degree at their own pace.**

Purdue University

Schleman Hall ◆ **West Lafayette, IN 47907-1080**
Phone: (317) 494-1776 ◆ Fax: (317) 494-0544
E-mail: admissions@adms.purdue.edu
Web address: http://www.purdue.edu/

Founded: 1869

Accredited by: North Central

Enrollment: 35,000 ◆ Adult students: 15 percent

University status: Public

Degree	Concentration/Major	Format
	All programs available to adults/ limited evening classes	E

Campus Extension Sites

Anderson, IN
Muncie, IN
Columbus, IN
New Albany, IN
Kokomo, IN
Richmond, IN
South Bend, IN
Indianapolis, IN
Versailles, IN

Requirements

Residency requirement: Students must attend classes on campus. Most technology programs (A.A.S.) can be completed at the statewide sites.
Undergraduate admissions requirements: Applicants submit an application, official high school/college transcripts, SAT-1/ACT scores, and must meet minimum English, math, and science requirements.
Graduate admissions requirements: Applicants are expected to hold a baccalaureate degree. Official transcripts showing at least a B average are required. Many departments have special requirements.
Graduation requirements (undergraduate): The requirements vary depending on the school. Generally 124-130 semester hours, according to the program.
Graduation requirements (graduate): Requirements vary depending on the plan of study recommended by the student's advisory committee. Master's degree students have a thesis or nonthesis option.

Fees, Tuition, Costs

Undergraduate application fee: $30
Graduate application fee: $30
Undergraduate tuition: $3,056/year
Graduate tuition: $3,056/year
Undergraduate cost of books: $600
Graduate cost of books: $600

Financial Aid/Status

Scholarship programs for adults: Scholarships vary depending on the school. Span Plan Grants are available to part-time students needing financial help.

Maximum Hours Awarded For

CLEP: Yes
Other exams: Yes

Features and Services

1. Is it possible to purchase books during hours most adult students attend classes? **Yes.**

2. What is the process for advising adult students? **The Span Plan offers special counseling and other services to returning adults.**

3. What career and placement services are available to adult students? **The Span Plan Program counselors offer career services.**

4. What characteristics of the institution's adult degree programs are most appealing to students? **Adult Students' Association, child-care program, and orientation seminar.**

Queens College
City University of New York

Adult Collegiate Education Program (ACE)

65-30 Kissena Boulevard ◆ **Flushing, NY 11367**

Phone: (718) 997-5717 ◆ Fax: (718) 997-5723

Founded: 1937

Accredited by: Middle States

Enrollment: 1,500 ◆ Adult students: 100 percent

University status: Public

Degree	Concentration/Major	Format
B.A.	Approximately 100 liberal arts majors are available.	E (also Days)

Requirements

Residency requirement: Students must attend classes on campus. No correspondence courses are offered. Undergraduate admissions requirements: Students must be 25 or older and have a high school diploma or GED in the English language.
Graduation requirements (undergraduate): Total of 120 credit hours, including distribution requirements, foreign language, academic major.

Fees, Tuition, Costs

Undergraduate application fee: $40 for freshman; $50 for transfer students
Undergraduate tuition: $135/credit
Undergraduate cost of books: $50-$100/semester

Financial Aid/Status

Scholarship programs for adults: A whole range of endowments provide various scholarships per semester.
Full-time status: A student taking a 12-hour credit load.
Percentage of adult students receiving financial aid: 50 percent.

Maximum Hours Awarded For

Prior learning portfolio: 36
Additional information: Prior learning credit ("life experience") up to 36 tuition-free credits

Features and Services

1. Is it possible to purchase books during hours most adult students attend classes? **Yes.**

2. Are the institution's administrative offices open during hours adult students attend class? **Yes.**

3. What is the registration and payment process for adult students? **Students register and pay on campus or through computerized registration by telephone.**

4. What is the process for advising adult students? **Advisors are available by appointment and on a walk-in basis.**

5. What career and placement services are available to adult students? **The Career Development Center is available on campus.**

6. What characteristics of the institution's adult degree programs are most appealing to students? **User-friendly, courses heavily credited, convenient schedules, counseling, and *esprit de corps*.**

Quincy University

1800 College Avenue ◆ **Quincy, IL 62307**
Phone: (217) 228-5215 ◆ Fax: (217) 228-5479
E-mail: admissions@quincy.edu
Web address: http://www.quincy.edu

Founded: 1860

Accredited by: North Central

Enrollment: 1,200

University status: Private, Church, Roman Catholic Church

Features and Services

1. Is it possible to purchase books during hours most adult students attend classes? **Yes.**

2. What is the registration and payment process for adult students? **Telephone registration is available.**

3. What characteristics of the institution's adult degree programs are most appealing to students? **Program designed for working adults.**

Degree	Concentration/Major	Format
B.S.	Business Administration	E
M.B.A.	Business Administration	E
M.S.Ed.	Education	E

Requirements

Residency requirement: Students must attend classes on campus. Undergraduate admissions requirements: Applicants must have a high school diploma or GED. Graduate admissions requirements: M.B.A.—application, all official college transcripts, two letters of recommendation, GMAT; M.S.Ed.—application, all official college transcripts, two recommendation forms, MAT, personal statement. Graduation requirements (undergraduate): Graduates must meet general, major, and support course requirements. A 2.0 GPA is required. Graduation requirements (graduate): M.B.A. graduates must complete 10 required courses with a minimum 3.0 GPA. M.S.Ed. graduates must complete 36 semester hours with a thesis, practicum, or comprehensive exams.

Fees, Tuition, Costs

Undergraduate application fee: $20
Graduate application fee: $25
Undergraduate tuition: $10,700/year
Graduate tuition: $325/semester hour

Financial Aid/Status

Full-time status: 12 hours

Maximum Hours Awarded For

CLEP: Yes
Prior learning portfolio: Yes

Quinnipiac College

Mt. Carmel Avenue ◆ **Hamden, CT 06518**
Phone: (203) 281-8612 ◆ Fax: (203) 281-8749
Web address: http://www.quinnipiac.edu

Founded: 1929

Accredited by: New England

Enrollment: 4,800 ◆ Adult students: 60 percent

University status: Private

Degree	Concentration/Major	Format
A.S.	Business Administration	A,E,S
A.S.	Science	E
A.A.	Arts	E
B.S.	Business Studies	S,E
B.S.	Health and Science Studies	S,E
B.A.	Liberal Studies	S,E
B.S.	Accounting	E
B.S.	Computer Science	E
B.S.	Management	E
B.S.	Marketing	E
B.S.	International Business	E
B.S.	Health Management	E
B.S.	Financial Management	E
B.S.	Accounting and Computer Science	E
B.S.	Computer Science and Management	E
B.S.	Computer Science and Financial Management	E
B.A.	Gerontology	E
M.S.P.T.	Physical Therapy	E
M.H.A.	Health Administration	E
M.H.S.	Medical Laboratory Science	E
M.B.A.	Business Administration	E
J.D.	Law	E

Requirements

Residency requirement: Students must meet a 45-credit residence requirement.
Undergraduate admissions requirements: A high school diploma or equivalent, transcripts, SAT/ACT scores, and an application are required. Test scores are not required from applicants graduating five years ago or having 30 college credits.
Graduate admissions requirements: An application, official transcripts of all college work completed, an autobiography or resume, and two letters of recommendation must be submitted.

Graduation requirements (undergraduate): A.S.—completion of at least 60 semester hours meeting major and all course requirements, minimum QPA of 2.0, and faculty recommendation. B.A.—completion of at least 120 semester hours meeting all college and major requirements. Graduation requirements (graduate): Major requirements, minimum QPA of 2.0, and faculty recommendation.

Fees, Tuition, Costs

Undergraduate application fee: $40
Graduate application fee: $40
Undergraduate tuition: $255/credit
Graduate tuition: $345/credit
Undergraduate cost of books: $200
Graduate cost of books: $200

Financial Aid/Status

Scholarship programs for adults: Endowment scholarships ($100-$150) are available. Eligibility is based on a 3.5 GPA and senior standing.
Full-time status: Enrollment in 12 credits per semester.
Percentage of adult students receiving financial aid: 15 percent.

Maximum Hours Awarded For

CLEP: 33
Other exams: Up to 1/2 of credits for major
Prior learning portfolio: 60
Additional information: Up to 1/2 major requirements through exam

Features and Services

1. Is it possible to purchase books during hours most adult students attend classes? **Yes.**

2. Are the institution's administrative offices open during hours adult students attend class? **Yes.**

3. What is the registration and payment process for adult students? **Registration is done in person. Payment may be done in person, by mail, or by fax if using credit card.**

4. What is the process for advising adult students? **Students meet with the associate dean and/or departmental advisors.**

5. What career and placement services are available to adult students? **Career Counseling Services are available to adult as well as traditional-aged students.**

6. What characteristics of the institution's adult degree programs are most appealing to students? **Accelerated, weekend format, and credit for prior learning.**

Ramapo College of New Jersey

505 Ramapo Valley Road ♦ **Mahwah, NJ 07430**
Phone: (201) 529-7617 ♦ Fax: (201) 529-7658
E-mail: ktalbird@ramapo.edu
Web address: http://www.ramapo.edu

Founded: 1971

Accredited by: Middle States

Enrollment: 4,543 ♦ Adult students: 41 percent

University status: Public

Degree	Concentration/Major	Format
B.S.	Biology	E
B.S.	Business Administration	E
B.S.	Chemistry	E
B.S.	Computer Science	E
B.A.	Economics	E
B.S./B.A.	Environmental Studies	E
B.S./B.A.	Psychology	E
B.S.	Accounting	E
B.S.	Information Systems	E
B.A.	International Business	E

Requirements

Residency requirement: Students must attend classes on campus. Undergraduate admissions requirements: Applicants must submit an application; provide a high school transcript or transfer 60 college credits; and supply SAT/ACT scores for first-time, full-time students.
Graduate admissions requirements: Applicants must have bachelor's degree with a 3.0 GPA and submit an application. Students not meeting the GPA requirement may ask for an interview for special consideration.
Graduation requirements (undergraduate): Graduates must complete 128 credits.
Graduation requirements (graduate): Graduates must complete 30 credits and a master's essay or project.

Fees, Tuition, Costs

Undergraduate application fee: $35
Graduate application fee: $55
Undergraduate tuition: $2,707.50/30 credits
Graduate tuition: $210/credit
Undergraduate cost of books: $500
Graduate cost of books: $350
Other costs: Admission deposit of $100; late registration fee of $100; Ramapo monthly payment plan application of $50

Financial Aid/Status

Scholarship programs for adults: Institutional scholarships are based on merit and are given in the form of waivers and/or cash.
Full-time status: Full-time students take 12-18 credits per semester. Percentage of adult students receiving financial aid: 10 percent.

Maximum Hours Awarded For

CLEP: Yes
PEP: Yes
DANTES: Yes
Prior learning portfolio: Yes
Additional information: Up to 83 credits for any combination of these programs

Features and Services

1. Is it possible to purchase books during hours most adult students attend classes? **Yes.**

2. What is the registration and payment process for adult students? **At the beginning of the term, extended office hours are available. Payment may be made by mail.**

3. What is the process for advising adult students? **The Advisement Center assists students. The Center operates days and some evenings.**

4. What career and placement services are available to adult students? **Services include career counseling, resumes, job search, a career library, and others.**

5. What characteristics of the institution's adult degree programs are most appealing to students? **Courses offered evenings and weekends for degree completion, small class size, and classes with other returning adults (not exclusively, but primarily).**

Regent University

1000 Regent Drive ◆ **Virginia Beach, VA 23464**
Phone: (804) 579-4014 ◆ Fax: (804) 579-4317
E-mail: johnmah@beacon.regent.edu
Web address: http://www.regentuniv.edu
Program's Web address: www.regent.edu

Founded: 1977

Accredited by: Southern Association

Enrollment: 1,400 ◆ Adult students: 100 percent

University status: Private

Degree	Concentration/Major	Format
M.B.A./M.A	Business Administration	E,CT,S
M.A.	Communication	E,CT,S
M.A.	Counseling	E,CT,S
M.A.	Education	E,CT,S
M.A.	Government and Public Policy	E,CT,S
M.A.	Divinity	E,CT,S
M.Div.	Divinity	E,CT,S
Ph.D.	Business Administration	E,CT,S
Ph.D.	Communication	E,CT,S
Psy.D.	Counseling	E,CT,S
Ph.D.	Education	E,CT,S
J.D.	Law	E,CT,S
D.Min.	Divinity	E,CT,S
Ph.D.	Divinity	E,CT,S

Campus Extension Site

Washington, DC

Requirements

Residency requirement: Residency in summer is the only requirement for distance education curriculum. Graduate admissions requirements: GRE, GMAT, MAT, OR LSAT test scores must be submitted, depending on the school. Graduation requirements (graduate): A thesis or culminative experience is required.

Fees, Tuition, Costs

Graduate application fee: $20-$50
Graduate tuition: Approximately $10,000/year
Graduate cost of books: $70/3-credit course
Other costs: Computers required in fall 1997

Financial Aid/Status

Scholarship programs for adults: Scholarships available
Full-time status: 9 credits or more/semester
Percentage of adult students receiving financial aid: 25 percent

Features and Services

1. Is it possible to purchase books during hours most adult students attend classes? **Yes.**

2. How do students taking extended classes access library resources? **Students may use consortiums, reciprocal agreements, and electronic libraries on the Internet.**

3. What is the registration and payment process for adult students? **Regent is moving toward an electronic process on the Internet.**

4. What is the process for advising adult students? **Each school has faculty and staff acting as advisors.**

5. What career and placement services are available to adult students? **Each school has a career development program built into the curriculum.**

6. What characteristics of the institution's adult degree programs are most appealing to students? **Ease of use and completion by Internet curriculum.**

Regents College
University of the State of New York

7 Columbia Circle ◆ Albany, NY 12203-5159
Phone: (518) 464-8500 ◆ Fax: (518) 464-8777
Web address: http://www.regents.edu

Founded: 1970

Accredited by: Middle States

Enrollment: 18,048 ◆ Adult students: 100 percent

University status: Public

Degree	Concentration/Major	Format
A.A.N.	Applied Science—Nursing	S
A.S.N.	Science—Nursing	S
A.A./A.S.	Arts (Liberal Arts)	S
B.S.N.	Science—Nursing	S
A.S.B.	Science—Business	S
A.C.S.	Science in Computer Science	S
A.E.T.	Science in Electronics Technology	S
A.N.T.	Science in Nuclear Technology	S
A.S.T.	Science in Technology	S
B.C.I.	Science in Computer Information Systems	S
B.C.T.	Science in Computer Technology	S
B.E.T.	Science in Electronics Technology	S
B.N.T.	Science in Nuclear Technology	S
B.S.T.	Science in Technology (with specialty)	S
B.G.B.	Science in General Business	S
B.A.G.	Science in Accounting—General	S
B.A.C.	Science in Accounting— New York State CPA track	S
B.F.I.	Science in Finance	S
B.I.B.	Science in International Business	S
B.M.H.	Science in Management of Human Resources	S
B.M.I.	Science in Management Information Systems	S
B.M.K.	Science Marketing	S
B.O.M.	Science in Operations Management	S
B.A.	Arts (Liberal Arts, with concentration)	S
B.A.L.	Arts in Liberal Studies	S
B.S.	Science (with concentration)	S
B.S.L.	Science in Liberal Studies	S

Requirements

Residency requirement: Regents College is located wherever students seek a degree. Because its programming is totally portable, the college moves with students wherever and whenever they move. Undergraduate admissions requirements: Open admissions; nursing enrollment is limited to students with certain health care backgrounds.

Graduation requirements (undergraduate): Associate degrees require the completion of 60 credits. Baccalaureate degrees require the completion of 120 credits; Nuclear Technology B.S. requires 124 credits. Each program has specific requirements.

Fees, Tuition, Costs

Other costs: Enrollment/initial evaluation fee of $565; Credit review fee of $115; Annual advisement and evaluation fee of $270; Program completion and graduation fee or $340 (associate) or $370 (baccalaureate)

Financial Aid/Status

Scholarship programs for adults: Access to Learning Scholarships are available.
Full-time status: 12 or more credits/term.
Percentage of adult students receiving financial aid: 2 percent.

Maximum Hours Awarded For

CLEP: No limit.
PEP: No limit.
DANTES: No limit.
Other exams: No limit.
Prior learning portfolio: No limit.
Additional information: GRE, AP, DLI, ACE-NYS, and ACE-PONSI can be used to accumulate credits.

Features and Services

1. Is it possible to purchase books during hours most adult students attend classes? **Yes.**

2. Are the institution's administrative offices open during hours adult students attend class? **Yes.**

3. What is the registration and payment process for adult students? **Registration and payment are handled by mail, phone, or fax.**

4. What is the process for advising adult students? **Phone, mail, and e-mail used for program planning, course approval, and finding learning resources.**

5. What characteristics of the institution's adult degree programs are most appealing to students? **Flexibility of methods of earning credits and comprehensive series of examinations offered by Regents College.**

Regis University

3333 Regis Boulevard ◆ **Denver, CO 80221**

Phone: (303) 458-3530 ◆ Toll-free phone: (800) 967-3237

Fax: (303) 964-5539 ◆ Web address: http://www.regis.edu

Founded: 1877 ◆ Accredited by: North Central

Enrollment: 9,500 ◆ Adult students: 85 percent

University status: Private, Church, Roman Catholic Church

Degree	Concentration/Major	Format
B.S.	Computer Information Systems	E,A,T,TH,V,C
B.S.	Computer Science	E,A,T,TH,V,C
B.S.	Accounting	E,A,T,TH,V,C,S
B.S.	Business Administration	E,A,T,TH,V,C,S
B.S.	Community Organization	E,A,T,TH,V,C,S
B.S.	Economics	E,A,T,TH,V,C,S
B.S.	Environmental Management	E,A,T,TH,V,C,S
B.S.	Gerontology	E,A,T,TH,V,C,S
B.S.	Human Resource Development	E,A,T,TH,V,C,S
B.S.	Labor Relations	E,A,T,TH,V,C,S
B.S.	Public Administration	E,A,T,TH,V,C,S
B.S.	Small Business Administration	E,A,T,TH,V,C,S
B.A.	Adult Education	E,A,T,TH,V,C,S
B.A.	Art	E,A,T,TH,V,C,S
B.A.	Behavioral Science	E,A,T,TH,V,C,S
B.A.	Communication	E,A,T,TH,V,C,S
B.A.	English	E,A,T,TH,V,C,S
B.A.	Fine Arts	E,A,T,TH,V,C,S
B.A.	History	E,A,T,TH,V,C,S
B.A.	Journalism	E,A,T,TH,V,C,S
B.A.	Language Arts	E,A,T,TH,V,C,S
B.A.	Mass Communications	E,A,T,TH,V,C,S
B.A.	Organizational Development	E,A,T,TH,V,C,S
B.A.	Philosophy	E,A,T,TH,V,C,S
B.A.	Spanish	E,A,T,TH,V,C,S
B.A.	Women's Studies	E,A,T,TH,V,C,S
M.B.A.	Business Administration	E,A
M.L.S.	Liberal Studies	E,S
M.S.M.	Management	E,A
M.S.C.I.S.	Computer Information Systems	E,A
M.A.C.L.	Community Leadership	E,S
M.N.M.	Nonprofit Management	E,A

The university has several other majors available.

Campus Extension Sites

Boulder, CO
Loveland, CO
Colorado Springs, CO
Steamboat Spring, CO
Denver, CO
Sterling, CO
Glenwood Springs, CO
Cheyenne, WY
Gillette, WY

Requirements

Residency requirement: Students completing degrees under the Guided Independent Study Format have to come to campus only once for orientation. Graduate programs that are self-study may require periodic attendance at intensive workshops on campus.

Undergraduate admissions requirements: Students must have three years of full-time work experience and submit an admissions essay and application. Graduate admissions requirements: Students must have a baccalaureate degree. Other requirements vary by the degree.

Graduation requirements (undergraduate): Graduates must complete 128 semester hours. Graduation requirements (graduate): Graduates must complete 30-48 semester hours, depending on the degree.

Fees, Tuition, Costs

Undergraduate application fee: $60
Graduate application fee: $75
Undergraduate tuition: $192-$247/credit hour
Graduate tuition: $242-$247/credit hour

Undergraduate cost of books: $150/semester
Graduate cost of books: $150/semester

Financial Aid/Status

Full-time status: 12 semester hours for undergraduates; 6 semester hours for graduates
Percentage of adult students receiving financial aid: 27 percent

Maximum Hours Awarded For

CLEP: 98
PEP: 98
DANTES: 98
Other exams: Yes
Prior learning portfolio: 45
Additional information: Maximum 98 credits awarded using CLEP, PEP, and DANTES; 30 hours must be accumulated from courses through Regis

Features and Services

1. Is it possible to purchase books during hours most adult students attend classes? **Yes.**

2. Are the institution's administrative offices open during hours adult students attend class? **Yes.**

3. How do students taking extended classes access library resources? **Students access libraries through cooperative agreements with local libraries and interlibrary loan programs.**

4. What is the registration and payment process for adult students? **Registration and payment options can be made by phone, fax, mail, or walk-in. Tuition is due at the end of the first class week.**

5. What is the process for advising adult students? **After completing admissions file, students meet with advisors to sign degree plans and get advising services.**

6. What career and placement services are available to adult students? **No formal placement center is available. Career Services can be used for career assistance.**

7. What characteristics of the institution's adult degree programs are most appealing to students? **Accelerated programs; flexibility; liberal transfer credit policy; and deferment option, with tuition due 55 days after end of class.**

Rider University

2083 Lawrenceville Road ◆ **Lawrenceville, NJ 08648**
Phone: (609) 896-5033 ◆ Fax: (609) 896-5261
Web address: http://www.rider.edu

Founded: 1865

Accredited by: Middle States

Enrollment: 3,700 ◆ Adult students: 30 percent

University status: Private

Degree	Concentration/Major	Format
A.A.	Business Administration	E
A.A.	General Studies	E
B.S./B.A.	Accounting	E
B.S./B.A.	Advertising	E
B.S./B.A.	Computer Information Systems	E
B.S./B.A.	Finance	E
B.S./B.A.	Human Resource Management	E
B.S./B.A.	Marketing	E
B.S./B.A.	Business Administration	E
B.S./B.A.	Management	E
B.A.	Liberal Studies	E
B.S.	Chemistry	E

Requirements

Residency requirement: Weekend College requires less attendance at formal classroom meetings. Undergraduate admissions requirements: Applicants must submit an application, high school/college transcripts, and a student statement or essay. Adult students are not required to submit test scores.
Graduate admissions requirements: M.B.A. applicants submit GMAT score, transcripts, application, and recommendations. M.A. applicants submit NTE, GRE, or MAT score; transcripts; application; and recommendations.
Graduation requirements (undergraduate): Graduates must complete 120 credits and all course requirements.
Graduation requirements (graduate): Requirements vary by program.

Fees, Tuition, Costs

Undergraduate application fee: $35
Graduate application fee: $35
Undergraduate tuition: $236/credit; $7,200/semester
Graduate tuition: $305-$375/credit
Undergraduate cost of books: Varies
Graduate cost of books: Varies

Financial Aid/Status

Scholarship programs for adults: Scholarships are available.

Full-time status: Undergraduate full-time status is 12 or more credits per semester.

Maximum Hours Awarded For

CLEP: No limit
DANTES: No limit
Other exams: Some
Prior learning portfolio: Some

Features and Services

1. Is it possible to purchase books during hours most adult students attend classes? **Yes.**

2. Are the institution's administrative offices open during hours adult students attend class? **Yes.**

3. What is the registration and payment process for adult students? **Initial registration is done in person. Most is done by mail.**

4. What is the process for advising adult students? **Extensive, accessible advising is provided by the College of Continuing Education staff.**

5. What career and placement services are available to adult students? **All services are available to adults. The office is open till 8 P.M. three nights each week.**

6. What characteristics of the institution's adult degree programs are most appealing to students? **Support and help of the CCS office, excellent faculty, location of university, and availability of courses and programs at desired times.**

Rochester Institute of Technology

Part-Time Enrollment Services
58 Lomb Memorial Drive ◆ **Rochester, NY 14623-5604**
Phone: (716) 475-2229 ◆ Toll-free phone: (800) CALL RIT
Fax: (716) 475-5476 ◆ E-mail: opes@rit.edu
Web address: http://www.rit.edu/

Founded: 1829 ◆ Accredited by: Middle States

Enrollment: 12,600 ◆ Adult students: 34 percent

University status: Private

Degree	Concentration/Major	Format
A.S.	Computer Science	E
A.A.S.	Computer Engineering Technology	E
A.A.S.	Electrical Technology	E
A.A.S.	Manufacturing Technology	E
A.A.S.	Applied Arts and Sciences	E,TH,CT,S
A.A.S.	Logistics and Transportation Management	E
B.S.	Computer Science	E
B.S.	Computer Engineering Technology	E
B.S.	Electrical Engineering Technology	E
B.S.	Electrical/Mechanical Technology	E,T
B.S.	Manufacturing Engineering Technology	E
B.S.	Applied Arts and Sciences	E,TH,CT,S
B.S.	Accounting	E
B.S.	Information Systems	E
B.S.	Finance	E
B.S.	Management	E
B.S.	Marketing	E
B.S.	Criminal Justice	E
B.S.	Chemistry	E
B.S.	Physics	E
M.S.	Computer Science	E
M.S.	Computer Integrated Manufacturing	E
M.S.	Software Development and Management	E
M.S.	Packaging Science	E
M.S.	Telecommunications	E
M.S.	Telecommunications Software Technology	E
M.S.	Career and Human Resource Development	E
M.S.	Health Systems Administration	E,TH,CT
M.S.	International Business	E
M.S.	Finance	E
M.B.A.	Business Administration	E
M.S.	Applied and Mathematical Statistics	E
M.S./M.E.	Computer Engineering	E
M.S./M.E.	Electrical Engineering	E
M.E.	Engineering Management	E
M.E.	Industrial Engineering	E
M.S.	Materials Science and Engineering	E
M.S.	Mechanical Engineering	E
M.E.	Systems Engineering	E

Requirements

Residency requirement: RIT offers distance learning options.
Undergraduate admissions requirements: Applicants must file an application, official high school or college transcripts, ACT/SAT scores, and MMR health form.
Graduate admissions requirements: Applicants must hold a baccalaureate degree. Other requirements depend on the degree program.
Graduation requirements (undergraduate): Graduates must earn at least 180 credits, meet course requirements, have a minimum QPA of 2.0, demonstrate writing skills, and make full payment of all financial obligations to RIT.
Graduation requirements (graduate): Graduates must earn at least 45 quarter credit hours. A research and thesis or project may be required.

Fees, Tuition, Costs

Undergraduate application fee: $40
Graduate application fee: $40
Undergraduate tuition: $211-$231/credit
Graduate tuition: $458/credit

Financial Aid/Status

Scholarship programs for adults: Scholarships available
Full-time status: 12 or more credits/quarter
Percentage of adult students receiving financial aid: 20 percent

Maximum Hours Awarded For

CLEP: Yes
PEP: Yes
DANTES: Varies
Other exams: Yes
Additional information: Maximum 36 quarter hours awarded for CLEP, PEP, and/or exam

Features and Services

1. Is it possible to purchase books during hours most adult students attend classes? **Yes.**

2. Are the institution's administrative offices open during hours adult students attend class? **Yes.**

3. How do students taking extended classes access library resources? **The library can be accessed through a computer connection (VAX) by PC or Macintosh.**

4. What is the registration and payment process for adult students? **Registration may be done by phone, fax, VAX, or in person. Payment plans are available.**

5. What is the process for advising adult students? **Students may start with the Part-Time Enrollment Office. Department advisors are also available.**

6. What career and placement services are available to adult students? **A cooperative education program is available for students.**

7. What characteristics of the institution's adult degree programs are most appealing to students? **Quality, accredited degree programs that can be completed at night, part-time, or through distance learning.**

Rockhurst College

1100 Rockhurst Road ◆ **Kansas City, MO 64110**
Phone: (816) 501-4100 ◆ Fax: (816) 501-4588
E-mail: tonjes@vax2.rockhurst.edu
Web address: http://vaxl.rockhurst.edu/

Founded: 1910 ◆ Accredited by: North Central

Enrollment: 2,880 ◆ Adult students: 31.7 percent

University status: Private, Church, Roman Catholic Church

Degree	Concentration/Major	Format
B.S.	Computer Science	E
B.S.	Computer Information Systems	E
B.A.	Philosophy	E
B.A.	English	E
B.A.	Sociology	E
B.A.	Political Science	E
M.B.A.	Business Administration—Various concentrations available	E

Requirements

Residency requirement: Students attend classes on campus. Undergraduate admissions requirements: Students must submit an application and high school transcript and/or transcripts of any prior college work. Transfer credits must be at least 2.25 GPA. ACT/SAT scores may be required.

Graduate admissions requirements: M.B.A. applicants must have a bachelor's degree and submit an application, GMAT scores, and official transcripts of all prior college work. M.O.T./M.P.T. degrees have other requirements.
Graduation requirements (undergraduate): Students must have 128 semester credits, 2.0 GPA,

complete liberal core and concentration courses, and pass the required senior comprehensive exam. The final 30 credits must be earned at Rockhurst.
Graduation requirements (graduate): Graduates must complete a minimum of 30 graduate credits with a minimum 3.0 QPA. Each program has specific requirements, which may be higher than this minimum.

Fees, Tuition, Costs

Undergraduate application fee: $20
Undergraduate tuition: $195-$320/semester hour
Graduate tuition: $280/semester hour
Undergraduate cost of books: Varies
Graduate cost of books: Varies
Other costs: Laboratory fees; other fees depending on course work

Financial Aid/Status

Full-time status: Undergraduates—12 credit hours; graduates-9 credit hours

Features and Services

1. What is the registration and payment process for adult students? **Rockhurst College has mail-in registration. Evening hours are available for on-campus registration.**

2. What career and placement services are available to adult students? **The Career Center works with all students.**

3. What characteristics of the institution's adult degree programs are most appealing to students? **The M.B.A.**

classes are generally offered entirely in the early evenings and on Saturdays for the dual roles of employee-student.

Roger Williams University
University College
Bristol, RI 02809

Phone: (401) 254-3530 ◆ Toll-free phone: (800) 458-7144
Fax: (401) 254-3560 ◆ E-mail: jws@alpha.rwu.edu
Web address: http://www.rwu.edu
Program's Web address: http://www.rwu.edu:80/uni.html

Founded: 1956 ◆ Accredited by: New England

Enrollment: 3,630 ◆ Adult students: 40 percent

University status: Private

Degree	Concentration/Major	Format
A.A./A.S.	Administration of Justice	E,A,C
A.A./A.S.	Business Management	E,A,C
A.A./A.S.	Engineering	E,A,C
A.A./A.S.	Industrial Technology	E,A,C
B.A.	Social Science	E,A,C,S
B.S.	Industrial Technology	E,A,C,S
B.S.	Administration of Justice	E,A,C,S
B.S.	Engineering	E,A,C,S
B.S.	Business Management	E,A,C,S
B.S.	Computer Information Systems	E,A,C,S
B.S.	Accounting	E,A,C,S
B.S.	Paralegal Studies	E,A,C
B.S.	Social and Health Service	C,S,A
B.S.	Public Administration	E,A,C
B.S.	Historic Preservation	A,C,S
B.S.	Construction Science	A,C,S
B.S.	Computer Science	A,C,S
B.S.	Individualized Majors	A,C,S
B.A.	Art	A,C,S
B.A.	Creative Writing	A,C,S
B.A.	Theatre	A,C,S
B.A.	History	A,C,S
B.A.	Philosophy	A,C,S
B.A.	Literature	A,C,S
B.A.	Communications	A,C,S
B.A.	Mathematics	A,C,S
B.A.	Political Science	A,C,S
B.A.	Individualized Majors	A,C,S

Requirements
Residency requirement: The university enrollment requirement is 30 credits; however, this is not necessarily in the classroom or on campus. Several degrees are available through distance learning. Undergraduate admissions requirements: Applicants need a high school diploma or GED. The external program recommends prior college work. The distance program requires "advanced standing" of two years of college credit or the equivalent. Graduation requirements (undergraduate): B.A./B.S. graduates must earn 120 credits, with a minimum of 30 credits from Roger Williams; complete a major program and general education requirements; and have a 2.0 GPA.

Fees, Tuition, Costs
Undergraduate application fee: $35
Undergraduate tuition: $130-
$325/credit
Undergraduate cost of books: $40-
$60/course
Other costs: Computer and science lab fees

Financial Aid/Status
Scholarship programs for adults: The number of scholarships available varies each year. Eligibility of adult students is based on academic performance and financial need. Full-time status: Full-time designation is either 6 or 12 credits, depending on the grant or loan. Percentage of adult students receiving financial aid: 35 percent.

Maximum Hours Awarded For

CLEP: 60
PEP: 60
DANTES: 60
Other exams: 60
Prior learning portfolio: 60
Additional information: Military credits—90

Features and Services

1. Is it possible to purchase books during hours most adult students attend classes? **Yes.**

2. Are the institution's administrative offices open during hours adult students attend class? **Yes.**

3. How do students taking extended classes access library resources? **Students use interlibrary loan, local library, Internet, and other computer access.**

4. What is the registration and payment process for adult students? **Registration is assisted by advisors. Payment is at registration or by installment plans or loans.**

5. What is the process for advising adult students? **A** faculty advisor assists each student throughout the program from planning to credit documentation.

6. What career and placement services are available to adult students? **The university operates a full career counseling and placement service for all students.**

7. What characteristics of the institution's adult degree programs are most appealing to students? **Credit for prior and nontraditional learning, external and nonclassroom courses, and ability to design individualized majors.**

Rollins College*
Hamilton Holt School

1000 Holt Avenue Box 2725 ◆ **Winter Park, FL 32789**
Phone: (407) 646-2232 ◆ Fax: (407) 646-1551
Web address: http://www.rollins.edu

Founded: 1885

Accredited by: Southern Association

Enrollment: 4,500 ◆ Adult students: 1,200

University status: Private

Degree	Concentration/Major	Format
B.A.	Anthropology/Sociology	E
B.A.	Economics	E
B.A.	English	E
B.A.	Environmental Studies	E
B.A.	Humanities	E
B.A.	International Affairs	E
B.A.	Organizational Behavior	E
B.A.	Organizational Communication	E
B.A.	Psychology	E
B.A.	Urban/Public Affairs	E
M.L.S.	Master of Liberal Studies	E
M.A.	Human Resource Development	E
M.A.	Counseling	E

Requirements

Residency requirement: Yes.
Undergraduate admissions requirements: Admission to a degree program is based on the performance of a student at Rollins College.
Graduate admissions requirements: Vary by program.

Fees, Tuition, Costs

Undergraduate application fee: $50
Graduate application fee: $50
Undergraduate tuition: $470/ course
Graduate tuition: $660-$750/ course

Financial Aid/Status

Full-time status: 4 credit courses/ term
Percentage of adult students receiving financial aid: 70 percent

Maximum Hours Awarded For

CLEP: 30
DANTES: 30

Features and Services

1. Is it possible to purchase books during hours most adult students attend classes? **Yes.**

2. Are the institution's administrative offices open during hours adult students attend class? **Yes.**

3. What characteristics of the institution's adult degree programs are most appealing to students? **Performance-based admissions; mail-in registration; personal advisor; and small, discussion-oriented classes.**

Rutgers University College— Camden* University College

Armitage Hall ◆ 5th and Penn Streets ◆ **Camden, NJ 08102**
Phone: (609) 225-6060 ◆ Fax: (609) 225-6495
Web address: http://camden-www.rutgers.edu

Founded: 1766

Accredited by: Middle States

Enrollment: 5,000 ◆ Adult students: 900

University status: Public

Financial Aid/Status

Full-time status: 12 or more credits/term
Percentage of adult students receiving financial aid: 25 percent

Maximum Hours Awarded For

CLEP: Yes
Other exams: Yes

Features and Services

1. Is it possible to purchase books during hours most adult students attend classes? **Yes.**

2. Are the institution's administrative offices open during hours adult students attend class? **Yes.**

3. What is the process for advising adult students? **Newly admitted students receive an evaluation/ curriculum worksheet. For new students this is done by the faculty and Academic Advising Center. Once students declare a major, they are assigned faculty advisors in their major department.**

4. What characteristics of the institution's adult degree programs are most appealing to students? **The quality of the faculty, same require- ments for day and evening students, and flexible scheduling.**

Degree	Concentration/Major	Format
B.A.	Computer Science Information Systems Track	E,CT
B.A.	English	E
B.A.	History	E
B.A.	Physics—Microelectronics Track	E
B.S.	Finance	E
B.S.	Management	E
B.S.	Marketing	E
B.A.	Political Science	E
B.A.	Psychology	E
B.A.	Social Work	E
B.S.	Accounting	E

Requirements

Residency requirement: Yes. Undergraduate admissions requirements: High school transcript or GED, transcripts from other colleges. SAT not required for students who have been out of high school for two or more years. Factors such as work experience, involvement in community organizations, and other personal qualifications are considered along with previous academic records.

Fees, Tuition, Costs

Undergraduate application fee: $50
Undergraduate tuition: $118-$240/ credit

Rutgers University
University College

14 College Avenue ◆ Miller Hall ◆ New Brunswick, NJ 08903
Phone: (908) 932-7276 ◆ Fax: (908) 932-1174
E-mail: ucnb@rci.rutgers.edu
Web address: http://www.rutgers.edu

Founded: 1934

Accredited by: Middle States

Enrollment: 3,000 ◆ Adult students: 3,000

University status: Public

Degree	Concentration/Major	Format
B.S.	Accounting	E
B.S.	Administration of Justice	E
B.A.	Biological Sciences	E
B.A.	Chemistry	E
B.A.	Communication	E
B.S./B.A.	Computer Science	E
B.A.	Economics	E
B.A.	English	E
B.S.	Finance	E
B.S.	Food Science	E
B.A.	French	E
B.A.	History	E
B.A.	Journalism and Mass Media	E
B.A.	Labor Studies	E
B.A.	Latin American Studies	E
B.S.	Management	E
B.S.	Marketing	E
B.A.	Nutritional Sciences	E
B.A.	Philosophy	E
B.A./B.S.	Psychology	E
B.A.	Sociology	E
B.A.	Spanish	E
B.A.	Statistics	E

Campus Extension Sites

Camden, NJ
Newark, NJ

Requirements

Residency requirement: 30 credits must be in residence at our college. Undergraduate admissions requirements: All students must be high school graduates or have GED. Applicants should be in the upper 50 percent in high school or, if transferring, have a 2.5 or above cumulative average.
Graduation requirements (undergraduate): Graduates must complete at least 120 credits; show proficiency in English, math, and foreign language; meet liberal arts and science, and major requirements; and have a 2.0 GPA.

Fees, Tuition, Costs

Undergraduate application fee: $50
Undergraduate tuition: $122.50-$126/credit
Other costs: Student fee of $101.75/term

Financial Aid/Status

Scholarship programs for adults: Special scholarships are available through University College. Eligibility and amounts vary.
Full-time status: 12 credits/term.

Maximum Hours Awarded For

CLEP: Yes
Other exams: Yes

Features and Services

1. Is it possible to purchase books during hours most adult students attend classes? **Yes.**

2. Are the institution's administrative offices open during hours adult students attend class? **Yes.**

3. How do students taking extended classes access library resources? **Students may access the library by computer, World Wide Web browser, or in person.**

4. What is the registration and payment process for adult students? **Registration is done by phone, mail, or in person; payment by mail or in person; credit cards accepted.**

5. What is the process for advising adult students? **Newly admitted students receive an evaluation/ curriculum worksheet. Advising available evenings.**

6. What career and placement services are available to adult students? **Recruiters come to campus. Some advisors available on-site. Career resource center is available.**

7. What characteristics of the institution's adult degree programs are most appealing to students? **Ability to study part-time, as few as 1-3 credits/semester. Commencement ceremonies at 8 P.M.**

Sacred Heart University*

Continuing Education ◆ 5151 Park Avenue
Fairfield, CT 06432
Phone: (203) 371-7830 ◆ Toll-free phone: (800) 288-2498
Fax: (203) 365-7500

Founded: 1963

Accredited by: New England

Enrollment: 5,600 ◆ Adult students: 3,300

University status: Private

Degree	Concentration/Major	Format
Not Specified	Ahead Program—Business and Finance	E,A
Not Specified	General Studies—Humanities, Science, Social Science	E
Not Specified	Professional Studies	E
Not Specified	Weekend UMV—Business of Finance	E,A

Requirements

Residency requirement: Yes
Undergraduate admissions requirements: Completion of a high school degree program
Graduate admissions requirements: Completion of appropriate undergraduate degree program or appropriate undergraduate preparation

Fees, Tuition, Costs

Undergraduate application fee: $20
Graduate application fee: $35
Undergraduate tuition: $245/credit
Graduate tuition: $285-$320/credit

Financial Aid/Status

Full-time status: 12 credits or more/term
Percentage of adult students receiving financial aid: 10 percent

Maximum Hours Awarded For

CLEP: 60
Prior learning portfolio: 60

Features and Services

1. Is it possible to purchase books during hours most adult students attend classes? **Yes.**

2. Are the institution's administrative offices open during hours adult students attend class? **Yes.**

3. What characteristics of the institution's adult degree programs are most appealing to students? **Accelerated models at convenient times, credit for prior learning and CLEP exams.**

Sage Colleges*
Sage Evening College

140 New Scotland Avenue ◆ Albany, NY 12110
Phone: (518) 445-1717 ◆ Fax: (518) 270-1728
Web address: http://www.sage.edu

Founded: 1916

Accredited by: Middle States

Enrollment: 4,000 ◆ Adult students: 800

University status: Private

Campus Extension Site
Troy, NY

Requirements
Residency requirement: Yes
Undergraduate admissions requirements: Application, high school transcript, or GED
Graduate admissions requirements: Varies by program

Fees, Tuition, Costs
Undergraduate application fee: $20
Undergraduate tuition: $245/credit

Financial Aid/Status
Full-time status: 12 credits/semester

Maximum Hours Awarded For
CLEP: Yes
DANTES: Yes
Other exams: Yes
Prior learning portfolio: 30

Features and Services
1. Is it possible to purchase books during hours most adult students attend classes? **Yes.**

2. What characteristics of the institution's adult degree programs are most appealing to students? **Flexibility, location, and understanding of adult needs.**

Degree	Concentration/Major	Format
A.S./A.A.S.	Accounting	E
A.S./A.A.S.	Chemical Dependency Studies	E
A.A.S.	Computer Information Systems	E
A.A.	Elementary Education Preparation	E
A.A.S.	Fine Arts	E
A.A.S.	Graphic Designs	E
A.A.	Individual Studies	E
A.A.S.	Interior Design	E
A.A.S.	Legal Assistant	E
A.A.	Liberal Arts	E
A.S.	Marketing and Management	E
A.A.S.	Math/Science	E
A.A.	Studies in Social Science	E
B.A.	Biology	E
B.A.	English	E
B.A.	History	E
B.A.	Psychology	E
B.A.	Psychology with Human Services	E
B.A.	Sociology	E
B.A.	Interdisciplinary Studies	E
B.S.	Accounting	E
B.S.	Computer Science	E
B.S.	Computer Information Systems	E
B.S.	Criminal Justice	E
B.S.	Health Education	E
B.S.	Business Administration	E
B.S.	Marketing	E
B.S.	Medical Technology	E
B.S.	Nursing	E
B.S.	Occupational Therapy	E
B.S.	Public Administration	E
B.S.	Interdisciplinary Studies	E
M.B.A.	Business Administration	E
M.P.A.	Public Administration	E
M.S.	Occupational Therapy	E

St. Ambrose University*

518 W. Locust Street ◆ Cosgrove Hall
Davenport, IA 52803
Phone: (319) 383-8758 ◆ Fax: (319) 383-8791
Web address: http://www.sau.edu/sau.html

Founded: 1882

Accredited by: North Central

Enrollment: 2,584 ◆ Adult students: 645

University status: Private, Church, Roman Catholic Church

Maximum Hours Awarded For

CLEP: 60
DANTES: 60
Other exams: 60
Prior learning portfolio: 60

Features and Services

1. Is it possible to purchase books during hours most adult students attend classes? **Yes.**

2. Are the institution's administrative offices open during hours adult students attend class? **Yes.**

3. What characteristics of the institution's adult degree programs are most appealing to students? **Flexibility: Students may attend days, evenings, and weekends to complete a degree.**

Degree	Concentration/Major	Format
B.A.	Business Administration	E,A
B.A.	Computer Science	E,A
B.S.	Computer Science	E,A
B.A.M.	Applied Management Technology	E
B.S.I.E.	Industrial Engineering	E
B.E.S.	Elected Studies	E
B.A.	Psychology	E
M.C.J.	Criminal Justice	E
M.H.C.A.	Health Care Administration	E
M.B.A.	Business Administration	E
M.Ed.	Special Education	E,A
M.A.	Criminal Justice	E

Requirements

Residency requirement: Yes. Undergraduate admissions requirements: Graduation from accredited high school with GPA of 2.5, or a high school equivalency certificate with a minimum score of 45 in each of the areas. Transfer students (12 semester hours or more) must have a minimum GPA of 2.0.
Graduate admissions requirements: M.H.C.A. & M.B.A.—undergraduate degree in any field; minimum score of 950 on GMAT. M.C.J.—undergraduate degree with major in criminal justice or related major with two years of professional experience. M.Ed.—degree, license, and 1000 on GRE or 20 on MAT.

Fees, Tuition, Costs

Undergraduate application fee: $15
Graduate application fee: $25
Undergraduate tuition: $5,225 for program
Graduate tuition: $325/credit

Financial Aid/Status

Full-time status: Any student enrolled in 12 semester credits or more
Percentage of adult students receiving financial aid: 45 percent

Saint Francis College

2701 Spring Street ◆ **Fort Wayne, IN 46808**
Phone: (219) 434-3279 ◆ Toll-free phone: (800) 729-4732
Fax: (219) 434-3183

Founded: 1890

Accredited by: North Central

Enrollment: 1,000 ◆ Adult students: 45 percent

University status: Private, Church, Roman Catholic

Degree	Concentration/Major	Format
A.A.	Art—Commercial	E
A.A.	Business Administration	E
A.S.	Human Services	E
A.A.	Human Resource Management	E
A.S.	Liberal Studies	E
B.S.	Business Administration	E
B.S.	Liberal Studies	E
B.S.	Psychology	E
M.S.N.	Nursing	T

Campus Extension Site

Beech Grove, IN

Requirements

Residency requirement: Students are not required to attend classes on the main campus.
Undergraduate admissions requirements: Weekend applicants are 25+ years. They must have a minimum 2.0 GPA from high school or college; on GED a composite score of 50 required for automatic acceptance. Others are reviewed and tested for acceptance. Graduate admissions requirements: Applicants must have a bachelor's degree with a minimum 2.5 GPA from an accredited college or university and meet specific program requirements.

Graduation requirements (undergraduate): Graduates must have a minimum 2.0 GPA and complete general education, major, and individual program requirements.
Graduation requirements (graduate): Graduates must have a minimum 3.5 GPA and complete individual program requirements.

Fees, Tuition, Costs

Undergraduate application fee: $20
Graduate application fee: $20
Undergraduate tuition: $295/credit $4,675/sem.
Graduate tuition: $305/credit hour
Undergraduate cost of books: $50/book
Graduate cost of books: $100/book

Financial Aid/Status

Scholarship programs for adults: Scholarships available include Adult Student Grant, Agnes Hake Seyfert Scholarship, and Transfer Scholarships.
Full-time status: 12 credit hours.
Percentage of adult students receiving financial aid: 85 percent.

Maximum Hours Awarded For

CLEP: 32
PEP: 32
DANTES: 32
Other exams: 32
Prior learning portfolio: 32

Features and Services

1. Is it possible to purchase books during hours most adult students attend classes? **Yes.**

2. Are the institution's administrative offices open during hours adult students attend class? **Yes.**

3. What is the registration and payment process for adult students? **Registration for classes is handled by an Adult Services Counselor.**

4. What is the process for advising adult students? **An appointment can be scheduled with an Adult Service Counselor.**

5. What characteristics of the institution's adult degree programs are most appealing to students? **Services through Adult Student Resource Center are run by adult students.**

St. John's College*

1160 Camino Cruz Blanco ◆ **Santa Fe, NM 87501-4599**
Phone: (505) 984-6082
Web address: http://www.sjcsf.edu

Founded: 1964

Accredited by: North Central

Enrollment: 505 ◆ Adult students: 105

University status: Private

Degree	Concentration/Major	Format
M.A.	Liberal Arts	E
M.A.	Eastern Classics	E

Requirements

Residency requirement: Yes
Graduate admissions requirements:
four-year college degree,
application form, two references,
transcripts, two essays

Fees, Tuition, Costs

Graduate application fee: None
Graduate tuition: $3,480/4
semesters

Financial Aid/Status

Full-time status: 9 credit hours
Percentage of adult students
receiving financial aid: 60 percent

Features and Services

1. Is it possible to purchase books during hours most adult students attend classes? **Yes.**

2. Are the institution's administrative offices open during hours adult students attend class? **Yes.**

3. What characteristics of the institution's adult degree programs are most appealing to students? **Students can take classes two evenings a week and get a master's degree at an accelerated rate.**

Saint Joseph's College*

External Degree Programs ◆ **Windham, ME 04062**
Phone: (207) 892-6766 ◆ Toll-free phone: (800) 343-5498
Fax: (207) 892-7423
Web address: http://www.sjcme.edu

Founded: 1912

Accredited by: New England

Adult students: 5,150

University status: Private, Church, Roman Catholic Church

Degree	Concentration/Major	Format
A.S.M.	Management	C
B.S.H.C.A.	Health Care Administration	C
B.S.R.T.	Radiologic technology	C
	Degree-completion program for licensed health professionals	
B.S.P.A.	Health Care	C
	Degree-completion program for licensed health professionals	
B.S.B.A.	Business Administration	C
B.S.N.	RN to B.S.N.	C
M.H.S.	Health Services Administration	C

Requirements

Residency requirement: Nine semester hours must be completed during a three-week residential summer session.
Undergraduate admissions requirements: High school diploma, licensure as noted for B.S.R.T. and B.S.P.A.
Graduate admissions requirements: Bachelor's degree from accredited institution, two years of health-care experience, accounting, and statistics.

Fees, Tuition, Costs

Undergraduate application fee: $50
Graduate application fee: $50

Undergraduate tuition: $160/credit
Graduate tuition: $195/credit

Financial Aid/Status

Full-time status: Doesn't apply to adult students unless on campus, then 12 hours per term
Percentage of adult students receiving financial aid: 4 percent

Maximum Hours Awarded For

CLEP: 30
PEP: 30
DANTES: 30
Prior learning portfolio: 18

Features and Services

1. Is it possible to purchase books during hours most adult students attend classes? **Books and course materials are sent to students.**

2. Are the institution's administrative offices open during hours adult students attend class? **Students can communicate with offices through the telephone.**

3. What characteristics of the institution's adult degree programs are most appealing to students? **Strong student focus and beautiful campus.**

Saint Leo College*

Center for Distance Learning ◆ St. Francis Hall
St. Leo, FL 33574
Phone: (904) 588-8084 ◆ Fax: (904) 588-8207

Founded: 1889

Accredited by: Southern Association

Enrollment: 8,000 ◆ Adult students: 7,000

University status: Private, Church, Roman Catholic Church

Features and Services

1. Is it possible to purchase books during hours most adult students attend classes? **Yes.**

2. Are the institution's administrative offices open during hours adult students attend class? **Yes.**

3. What characteristics of the institution's adult degree programs are most appealing to students? **Excellent faculty and supportive administrators.**

Degree	Concentration/Major	Format
B.A.	Business Administration Specializations in Accounting, Marketing, Management, and Health Care	E
B.A.	Criminology Specialization in Human Services and Administration	E
B.A.	Education Elementary, Secondary, and Recertification programs	E
B.Sc.	Health Care Administration	E

Requirements

Residency requirement: Yes
Undergraduate admissions requirements: High school diploma or GED; Form 214 and DD 2586 for veterans; SAT or ACT for Elementary Education

Maximum Hours Awarded For

CLEP: Yes
DANTES: Yes

Saint Martin's College

5300 Pacific Avenue S.E. ◆ **Lacey, WA 98503**
Phone: (360) 438-4311 ◆ Toll-free phone: (800) 368-8803
Fax: (360) 459-4124
E-mail: admissions@stmartin.edu
Web address: http://www.stmartin.edu

Founded: 1895

Accredited by: Northwest Association

Enrollment: 924 ◆ Adult students: 60 percent

University status: Private, Church, Roman Catholic Church

Degree	Concentration/Major	Format
Not Specified	Accounting	E
Not Specified	Business	E
Not Specified	Computer Science	E
Not Specified	Criminal Justice	E
Not Specified	Political Science	E
Not Specified	Psychology	E

Campus Extension Sites

Fort Lewis, WA
McChord, AFB, WA

Requirements

Residency requirement: Students are required to attend classes at extension education center sites. Undergraduate admissions requirements: Extension campus students must submit an application, military forms, or college transcripts; possibly high school or GED documents; and USAFI or CLEP scores.
Graduate admissions requirements: Applicants must have a bachelor's degree. Each program has specific requirements.
Graduation requirements (undergraduate): An associate degree requires 64 semester hours with a 2.0 GPA. A bachelor's degree requires 128 semester hours with 2.0 GPA. Graduates must meet all college and degree requirements.
Graduation requirements (graduate): Graduation requirements vary with the degree program.

Fees, Tuition, Costs

Undergraduate application fee: $25
Graduate application fee: $25
Undergraduate tuition: $12,360/year; $412/semester hour
Graduate tuition: $412/semester hour
Undergraduate cost of books: $500
Graduate cost of books: $500

Financial Aid/Status

Scholarship programs for adults: Scholarships are available.
Full-time status: 12-18 semester hours.
Percentage of adult students receiving financial aid: 100 percent.

Maximum Hours Awarded For

CLEP: Yes
DANTES: Yes
Other exams: Yes
Prior learning portfolio: Yes
Additional information: Credit for prior learning available to students in FOCUS program

Features and Services

1. Is it possible to purchase books during hours most adult students attend classes? **Yes.**

2. Are the institution's administrative offices open during hours adult students attend class? **Yes.**

3. What is the registration and payment process for adult students? **Extension students should contact the extension center about registration and payment.**

4. What is the process for advising adult students? **Extension students should contact the extension center about advisement.**

5. What career and placement services are available to adult students? **The Career Center is available on campus.**

6. What characteristics of the institution's adult degree programs are most appealing to students? **Evening availability and five eight-week terms per year.**

Saint Mary College

10000 W. 75th ◆ Shawnee Mission, KS 66204
Phone: (913) 384-6279 ◆ Fax: (913) 384-6914

Founded: 1923

Accredited by: North Central

Enrollment: 800 ◆ Adult students: 60 percent

University status: Private, Church, Roman Catholic Church

Degree	Concentration/Major	Format
B.A.	Liberal Studies	E,A
B.A.	Human Development	E,A
B.S.	Organizational Management	E,A
B.S.	Elementary Education	E,A
B.A.	Communication Studies	E,A
M.A.	Psychology	E,A
M.A.	Education	E,A
M.S.	Management	E,A

Campus Extension Site

Leavenworth, KS

Requirements

Residency requirement: Students are not required to attend classes on the main campus.
Undergraduate admissions requirements: Applicants need a minimum 2.0 GPA, must meet ACT/SAT score requirements, and must have 60 transferable credit hours.
Graduate admissions requirements: Applicants need a degree from an accredited institution, have a minimum 2.75 GPA, and must submit three letters of recommendation and a personal essay.
Graduation requirements (undergraduate): Graduation requires completing a writing portfolio, all courses completed, and a 2.0 GPA minimum.
Graduation requirements (graduate): Graduation requires the completion of all course work with a B average or better, a summary paper, and an oral presentation.

Fees, Tuition, Costs

Undergraduate application fee: $20
Graduate application fee: $20
Undergraduate tuition: $236/credit hour
Graduate tuition: $198/credit hour
Undergraduate cost of books: $150
Graduate cost of books: $100

Financial Aid/Status

Scholarship programs for adults: Scholarships are available.
Full-time status: 12 credits for undergraduates; 6 credits for graduates.
Percentage of adult students receiving financial aid: 80 percent.

Maximum Hours Awarded For

CLEP: Yes
Other exams: Yes
Prior learning portfolio: Yes

Features and Services

1. Is it possible to purchase books during hours most adult students attend classes? **Yes.**

2. Are the institution's administrative offices open during hours adult students attend class? **Yes.**

3. How do students taking extended classes access library resources? **Library services are available to adult students.**

4. What is the registration and payment process for adult students? **One-stop registration and payment are available for adult students.**

5. What is the process for advising adult students? **Advisors are assigned and available to students.**

6. What characteristics of the institution's adult degree programs are most appealing to students? **Accelerated schedule, time schedule, personal attention, faculty, and convenience of location.**

Saint Mary's College of California

School of Extended Education
P.O. Box 5219, 1925 St. Mary's Road
Moraga, CA 94575-5219
Phone: (510) 631-4900 ◆ Toll-free phone: (800) 538-9999
Fax: (510) 631-9869
Program's Web address: http://www.gaelnet.stmarys~ca.edu

Founded: 1863

Accredited by: Western Association

Enrollment: 4,000 ◆ Adult students: 25 percent

University status: Private, Church, Roman Catholic Church

Degree	Concentration/Major	Format
B.A.	Management	E,A
B.A.	Health Services Administration	E,A
M.S.	Health Services Administration	E

Campus Extension Sites

Livermore, CA
Moraga, CA
Oakland, CA
Walnut Creek, CA
Newark, CA
San Ramon, CA
Pleasanton, CA
Novato, CA
Sacramento, CA
San Francisco, CA
Stockton, CA
Redwood City, CA
San Jose, CA
Pleasant Hill, CA
Benicia, CA
Fairfield, CA
Vallejo, CA
Santa Rosa, CA

Requirements

Residency requirement: Students do not have to come to the main campus, but they must attend class at their chosen site once a week for four hours. Graduate classes meet two nights for three hours each. Undergraduate admissions requirements: Applicants have 60 transferable college credits, minimum 2.0 GPA, work experience in the degree area, adequate writing skills, and life experience learning that indicates an ability to attain senior standing. Graduate admissions requirements: Applicants must have a bachelor's degree, two years of experience in a health-related setting, and show satisfactory skills in written and oral communications and elementary accounting. Graduation requirements (undergraduate): Some students complete the degree at the end of the 10-course curriculum. To meet degree requirements, students may submit additional portfolio material, take more course work, or earn CLEP credit.

Graduation requirements (graduate): Graduates must successfully complete the curriculum and the final research project.

Fees, Tuition, Costs

Undergraduate application fee: $35
Graduate application fee: $35
Undergraduate tuition: $10,678/program
Graduate tuition: $10,941/program
Undergraduate cost of books: $700
Graduate cost of books: $700
Other costs: Undergraduate students need computer, modem, and server

Financial Aid/Status

Full-time status: The undergraduate program is considered half-time for financial aid.
Percentage of adult students receiving financial aid: 50 percent.

Maximum Hours Awarded For

CLEP: 30
DANTES: 30
Prior learning portfolio: 30
Additional information: ACE, PONSI; credit assessed for diploma nurses

Features and Services

1. Is it possible to purchase books during hours most adult students attend classes? **Books may be ordered by phone or mail.**

2. How do students taking extended classes access library resources? **The library may be accessed by computer, mail, and personal visits.**

3. What is the registration and payment process for adult students? **Students enroll, complete an admission**

application, and pay the application fee.

4. What is the process for advising adult students? **Admission counselors work in person or by phone with each student to pre-evaluate transcripts.**

5. What career and placement services are available to adult students? **Saint Mary's College has a career development center.**

6. What characteristics of the institution's adult degree programs are most appealing to students? **Convenient class locations, accelerated program, evening classes, excellent reputation of college, affordable tuition, and tuition assistance.**

Saint Mary-of-the-Woods College

Guerin Hall ◆ **Saint Mary-of-the-Woods, IN 47876**

Phone: (812) 535-5106 ◆ Toll-free phone: (800) 926-SMWC

Fax: (812) 535-5212 ◆ E-mail: smwcadms.woods.smwc.edu

Founded: 1840

Accredited by: North Central

Enrollment: 1,292 ◆ Adult students: 65 percent

University status: Private, Church, Roman Catholic Church

Requirements

Residency requirement: Students must come to campus to begin classes each semester. New student orientation/residency is 2 1/2 days, or 1/2 day on campus each semester.

Undergraduate admissions requirements: Women's External Degree applicants must submit an application, essay, resume, official high school/college transcripts or GED scores, and a letter of recommendation. Admission is limited to women.

Graduate admissions requirements: M.A. applicants must have a baccalaureate degree and submit an application including the student's goals, three letters of recommendation, and all collegiate transcripts. Admission is limited to women.

Graduation requirements (undergraduate): Associate degrees require at least 62 credit hours and a minimum 2.0 GPA; bachelor's degrees require at least 125 credit hours and a 2.0 GPA, and 30 credits must be earned at Saint Mary-of-the-Woods College.

Graduation requirements (graduate): M.A. requirements include the completion of 36 graduate credit hours, with a minimum 3.0 cumulative GPA, and successfully completing the written qualifying examination.

Degree	Concentration/Major	Format
A.A.	Humanities	C
A.A.	Early Childhood Education	C
A.A.	Paralegal Studies	C
A.S.	Gerontology	C
A.S.	General Business	C
B.A./B.S.	Accounting	C
B.A./B.S.	Business Administration	C
B.A./B.S.	Human Resource Management	C
B.A./B.S.	Marketing	C
B.A./B.S.	Early Childhood, Kindergarten-Primary (K-3)	C
B.A./B.S.	Elementary Education (1-6, 7-8 nondepartmentalized)	C
B.A./B.S.	All Grade Education (K-12)	C
B.A./B.S.	Special Education	C
B.A.	English	C
B.A.	Journalism	C
B.A.	Humanities	C
B.A./B.S.	Computer Information Systems	C
B.A./B.S.	Mathematics	C
B.A./B.S.	Human Services	C
B.A./B.S.	Paralegal Studies	C
B.A./B.S.	Psychology	C
B.S.	Gerontology	C
B.S.	Theology	C
M.A.	Pastoral Theology	E,C

Fees, Tuition, Costs

Undergraduate application fee: $30
Graduate application fee: $35
Undergraduate tuition: $229/credit hour
Graduate tuition: $252/credit hour
Undergraduate cost of books: $100/course
Graduate cost of books: $100/course

Financial Aid/Status

Full-time status: 12 credit hours
Percentage of adult students receiving financial aid: 45 percent

Maximum Hours Awarded For

CLEP: Yes
PEP: Yes
DANTES: Yes
Prior learning portfolio: Yes

Features and Services

1. Is it possible to purchase books during hours most adult students attend classes? **Yes.**

2. Are the institution's administrative offices open during hours adult students attend class? **Yes.**

3. How do students taking extended classes access library resources? **The library is open evenings and weekends.**

4. What is the registration and payment process for adult students? **Students can pay with either full payment, payment plan, tuition reimbursement, scholarships, or financial aid.**

5. What is the process for advising adult students? **Students meet with their advisors each semester during the half day they are on campus.**

6. What career and placement services are available to adult students? **On-campus and phone counseling are available. The Alumnae Resource Center provides a helpful network.**

7. What characteristics of the institution's adult degree programs are most appealing to students? **The flexibility of semesters and assignments; due dates within a structured, guided independent study format.**

Saint Michael's College
The Prevel School

Box 273, Winooski Park ◆ **Colchester, VT 05439**
Phone: (802) 654-2100 ◆ Fax: (802) 654-2664
Web address: http://www.waldo.smcvt.edu

Founded: 1904

Accredited by: New England

Enrollment: 2,500 ◆ Adult students: 40 percent

University status: Private, Church, Roman Catholic Church

Degree	Concentration/Major	Format
B.A.	Human Development	E
B.A.	Management and Leadership	E
M.S.	Administration	E
M.A.	Clinical Psychology	E
M.A.	Teaching English as a Second Language	E
M.A.	Theology	E
M.Ed.	Education	E

Requirements

Residency requirement: Students must attend classes on campus. Undergraduate admissions requirements: Applicants must be 21 years or older, high school graduates, and complete the entrance assessment.
Graduate admissions requirements: Applicants must hold a bachelor's degree with a minimum 2.8 GPA (3.0—M.A. in Clinical Psychology and Teaching English as a Second Language). All prerequisites must be met.
Graduation requirements (undergraduate): Graduates must earn 124 credit hours with a minimum of 34 courses. A minimum 2.0 GPA in major courses is required.
Graduation requirements (graduate): Graduates must complete all requirements depending on the degree program. An overall 3.0 GPA is required.

Fees, Tuition, Costs

Undergraduate application fee: $50
Graduate application fee: $25
Undergraduate tuition: $275/credit
Graduate tuition: $245/credit

Financial Aid/Status

Full-time status: Undergraduates taking 12 credits are full-time; graduates taking 9 credits are full-time.
Percentage of adult students receiving financial aid: 40 percent.

Maximum Hours Awarded For

CLEP: Yes
Prior learning portfolio: 30
Additional information: Transfer credits

Features and Services

1. Is it possible to purchase books during hours most adult students attend classes? **Yes.**

2. Are the institution's administrative offices open during hours adult students attend class? **Yes.**

3. What is the registration and payment process for adult students? **Registration is done by mail, fax, or in person. Students must make a $50 deposit, with full payment due by the first class. Employer deferment is available.**

4. What is the process for advising adult students? **Advisors available when needed.**

5. What characteristics of the institution's adult degree programs are most appealing to students? **Convenience (near parking and the interstate), comfort, individual attention, practical. SMC is among the top 10 schools listed in** *U.S. News and World Report.*

Saint Peter's College*

2641 Kennedy Boulevard ◆ **Jersey City, NJ 07306**
Phone: (201) 915-9009 ◆ Fax: (201) 451-0036

Founded: 1872

Accredited by: Middle States

Enrollment: 4,000 ◆ Adult students: 1,600

University status: Private, Church, Roman Catholic

Degree	Concentration/Major	Format
A.S.	Marketing	E,A
A.S.	Social Sciences	E,A
A.S.	Banking	E,A
A.S.	Management	E,A
A.S.	Finance	E,A
A.S.	Humanities	E,A
A.S.	Information Systems	E,A
A.S.	International Business and Trade	E,A
A.A.S.	Public Policy	E
	Semester with three intensive weeks (day and night) spaced throughout the academic year	
B.S.	Accounting	E,A
B.S.	Management	E,A
B.A./B.S.	Economics	E,A
B.S.	Health Care Management	E,A
B.S.	Computer Science	E,A
B.S.	International Business and Trade	E,A
B.S.	Marketing	E,A
B.S.	Natural Sciences	E,A
B.S.	Psychology	E,A
B.A.	Elementary Education	E,A
B.A.	English	E,A
B.A.	History	E,A
B.A.	Humanities	E,A
B.A.	Philosophy	E,A
B.A.	Social Sciences	E,A
B.A.	Urban Studies	E,A

Requirements

Residency requirement: Yes.
Undergraduate admissions requirements: Minimum requirement is high school degree or GED equivalent. SAT scores preferred if high school graduation or equivalent is less than five years prior to application.

Fees, Tuition, Costs

Undergraduate tuition: $336/credit

Financial Aid/Status

Full-time status: 24 credits between September and May over three trimesters
Percentage of adult students receiving financial aid: 50 percent

Maximum Hours Awarded For

CLEP: Yes
PEP: Yes
DANTES: Yes
Other exams: Yes
Additional information: Practicum and cooperative education

Features and Services

1. Is it possible to purchase books during hours most adult students attend classes? **Yes.**

2. Are the institution's administrative offices open during hours adult students attend class? **Yes.**

3. What characteristics of the institution's adult degree programs are most appealing to students? **Trimester schedule, small class size, class hours, summer terms.**

Saint Xavier University

3700 W. 103rd Street ◆ **Chicago, IL 60655**
Phone: (312) 298-3156 ◆ Fax: (312) 779-9061
E-mail: catellanos@sxu.edu
Web address: http://www.sxu.edu

Founded: 1847

Accredited by: North Central

Enrollment: 3,500 ◆ Adult students: 1,750

University status: Private, Church, Roman Catholic Church

Degree	Concentration/Major	Format
B.S.	Business Administration	
B.S.	Accounting	
B.A.	Nursing	
B.A.	Criminal Justice	
B.A.	Liberal Studies	
B.A.	English	
B.A.	Psychology	
M.B.A.	Business	
M.A.	Education	
M.A.	Speech Pathology	
M.A.	Counseling	

Campus Extension Sites

Chicago Area: 18 locations for the field-based master's degree in education.

Requirements

Residency requirement: None for the field-based Master's Program. All courses taught on location. Undergraduate admissions requirements: Formula used; ACT/SAT tests are not required for adults. "Forgiveness" of early academic record.
Graduate admissions requirements: Varies by school. GRE, MAT, or GMAT required, and good scholarship at required level.
Graduation requirements (undergraduate): 120 credit hours
Graduation requirements (graduate): 36-39 credit hours

Fees, Tuition, Costs

Undergraduate application fee: $25
Graduate application fee: $25
Undergraduate tuition: $383/hour
Graduate tuition: $408/hour
Undergraduate cost of books: $150-$300
Graduate cost of books: $150- depends on major
Other costs: Lab fees

Financial Aid/Status

Scholarship programs for adults: Need-based and academic scholarships; amount varies
Full-time status: 12 credit hours/ semester for undergraduates; 9 credit hours for graduates
Percentage of adult students receiving financial aid: 85 percent

Maximum Hours Awarded For

CLEP: Yes
PEP: Yes
Other exams: Yes
Prior learning portfolio: Yes

Features and Services

1. Is it possible to purchase books during hours most adult students attend classes? **Yes.**

2. Are the institution's administrative offices open during hours adult students attend class? **Yes.**

3. How do students taking extended classes access library resources? **Computer access and delivery on-site.**

4. What is the process for advising adult students? **All students are assigned a faculty or professional advisor.**

5. What career and placement services are available to adult students? **All services are available to adult students.**

6. What characteristics of the institution's adult degree programs are most appealing to students? **Academic programs; use of independent study; time frames include weekend courses and accelerated courses; small classes; and personalized attention.**

Salem College

Winston-Salem, NC 27108 ◆ Phone: (910) 721-2669
Fax: (910) 717-5432

Founded: 1772

Accredited by: Southern Association

Enrollment: 932 ◆ Adult students: 481

University status: Private, Church, Moravian Church

Degree	Concentration/Major	Format
B.S.B.A.	Business Administration	E,S
B.A.B.S.	Accounting	E,S
B.S.	Chemistry	E,S
B.A.	Arts Management	E,S
B.A.	Communication	E,S
B.A.	Interior Design	E,S
B.A.	Sociology	E,S
B.A.	American Studies	S
B.A.	Art	S
B.A./B.S.	Biology	S
B.A.	Chemistry	S
B.A.	Economics	S
B.A.	English	S
B.A.	Foreign Language	S
B.A.	Management	S
B.A.	French	S
B.A.	German	S
B.A.	History	S
B.A.	International Relations	S
B.A./B.S.	Mathematics	S
B.A.	Music	S
B.A.	Philosophy	S
B.A.	Psychology	S
B.A.	Religion	S
B.S.	Medical Technology	S
B.S.	Physician Assistant	S
M.A.T.	Elementary Education	E
M.A.T.	Learning Disabilities	E
M.A.T.	Early Childhood Education and Leadership	E
M.Ed.	Language and Literacy	E
M.Ed.	Music Performance	E

Requirements

Residency requirement: Students must take at least nine courses at Salem; however, many of these may be done through learning contracts with instructors (independent study).

Undergraduate admissions requirements: The adult program requires an application and fee, all transcripts of prior college work, proof of high school completion, two letters of recommendation, and a one-page autobiographical essay. Graduate admissions requirements: Applicants must submit transcripts showing a baccalaureate degree and graduating GPA, GRE test scores, two letters of recommendation, and have an interview with the graduate studies director. Graduation requirements (undergraduate): Adult students must meet all of the traditional degree requirements with the exception of physical education and the Salem Signature. Requirements vary depending on the degree program. Graduation requirements (graduate): Graduates must meet all course requirements including practicum with GPA 3.0; complete the degree audit, a comprehensive exam, and a graduation application.

Fees, Tuition, Costs

Undergraduate application fee: $30
Graduate application fee: $30
Undergraduate tuition: $600/course
Graduate tuition: $165/credit hour
Undergraduate cost of books: $550/year

Financial Aid/Status

Scholarship programs for adults: Scholarships for adult students are available.
Full-time status: Undergraduate full-time—3 courses (1 course = 4 semester hours); graduate—3 courses (1 course = 3 semester hours).

Maximum Hours Awarded For

CLEP: Yes
Prior learning portfolio: 3 courses

Features and Services

1. Is it possible to purchase books during hours most adult students attend classes? **Yes.**

2. Are the institution's administrative offices open during hours adult students attend class? **Yes.**

3. What is the registration and payment process for adult students? **Students preregister through the Continuing Studies office and are billed after registration.**

4. What is the process for advising adult students? **Adult students have advisors in the Continuing Studies office.**

5. What career and placement services are available to adult students? **Student Developmental Services offer many** no-cost services. Fees are charged for some services.

6. What characteristics of the institution's adult degree programs are most appealing to students? **Flexibility, opportunity to study independently, and small classes.**

Sarah Lawrence College

1 Mead Way ◆ Bronxville, NY 10708
Phone: (914) 395-2205 ◆ Fax: (914) 395-2664
E-mail: aolson@mail.slc.edu
Web address: http://www.slc.edu

Founded: 1927

Accredited by: Middle States

Enrollment: 900 ◆ Adult students: 10 percent

University status: Private

Degree	Concentration/Major	Format
B.A.	Concentrations in liberal arts areas	S

Requirements

Residency requirement: Of the required minimum of 45 credits earned from Sarah Lawrence College, a minimum of 25 credits must be earned in residence. Undergraduate admissions requirements: Adult admissions requirements include a personal interview, a written application with three essay questions, two references/recommendations, and transcripts from all prior college-level study.
Graduation requirements (undergraduate): Graduation requires 120 credits spread across at least three of four general curriculum divisions (natural science/math, literature/languages, history/social sciences, and the creative arts).

Fees, Tuition, Costs

Undergraduate application fee: $45
Undergraduate tuition: $681/credit
Undergraduate cost of books: $75/course
Other costs: General college fee—$200; Parking—$100; Computer account—$185

Financial Aid/Status

Scholarship programs for adults: The federal method of determining need is used. Offer institutional aid of approximately 45 percent of direct costs to adult B.A. candidates. Full-time status: 12 credits per term. Percentage of adult students receiving financial aid: 30 percent.

Maximum Hours Awarded For

Prior learning portfolio: 20

Features and Services

1. Is it possible to purchase books during hours most adult students attend classes? **Yes.**

2. Are the institution's administrative offices open during hours adult students attend class? **Yes.**

3. What is the registration and payment process for adult students? **The process is the same for all students except at the beginning, which is much simpler.**

4. What is the process for advising adult students? **A "don" from the faculty is the primary student service contact for guiding and advising the student**

5. What career and placement services are available to adult students? **Excellent career services and internship and fieldwork program using alumnae are available.**

6. What characteristics of the institution's adult degree programs are most appealing to students? **Unusual degree of individual attention and** support, absence of competition among students, and freedom to design individual courses of study.

Saybrook Institute Graduate School

450 Pacific ◆ **San Francisco, CA 94133-4640**
Phone: (415) 433-9200 ◆ Toll-free phone: (800) 825-4480
Fax: (415) 433-9271 ◆ E-mail: rhesseling@igc.apc.org

Founded: 1971

Accredited by: Western Association

Enrollment: 350

University status: Private

Degree	Concentration/Major	Format
M.A.	Psychology	C,CT,T
M.A.	Human Science	C,CT,T
Ph.D.	Psychology	C,CT,T
Ph.D.	Human Science	C,CT,T

Requirements

Residency requirement: Students are required to attend two week-long conferences each year in San Francisco.
Graduate admissions requirements: Applicants must hold a bachelor's degree from a regionally accredited institution with a major closely related to the degree being sought.
Graduation requirements (graduate): Graduation requirements vary with the degree program.

Fees, Tuition, Costs

Graduate application fee: $55
Graduate tuition: $10,500/year
Graduate cost of books: $1,500/year
Other costs: Cost for two residential conferences—$600 per conference and travel expenses

Financial Aid/Status

Percentage of adult students receiving financial aid: 70 percent

Features and Services

1. How do students taking extended classes access library resources? **Saybrook assists students in library research and electronic access to library services.**

2. What career and placement services are available to adult students? **The Alumni Association provides an informal professional network.**

3. What characteristics of the institution's adult degree programs are most appealing to students? **Saybrook is a regionally accredited, dispensed residency, at-a-distance graduate school.**

School for International Training

Brattleboro, VT 05302-0676 ◆ Phone: (802) 257-7751
Toll-free phone: (800) 451-4465 ◆ Fax: (802) 258-3500
E-mail: 6261427@mcimail.com

Founded: 1964

Accredited by: North Central

Enrollment: 1,018 ◆ Adult students: 20 percent

University status: Private

Degree	Concentration/Major	Format
B.I.S.	International Studies Community, Society, and Development	A,S
B.I.S.	International Studies Economic Analysis and Development	A,S
B.I.S.	International Studies Peace and Conflict Studies	A,S
B.I.S.	International Studies Environmental Studies	A,S
B.I.S.	International Studies Human Ecology	A,S
B.I.S.	International Studies Population Studies	A,S
M.I.I.M.	International & Intercultural Management—International Education	A,S
M.I.I.M.	International & Intercultural Management—Sustainable Development	A,S
M.I.I.M.	International & Intercultural Management—Training and Human Resource Development	A,S
M.A.T.	Teaching/English as a Foreign Language	A,S
M.A.T.	Teaching/Spanish	A,S
M.A.T.	Teaching/French	A,S

Requirements

Residency requirement: Each program requires a short period on campus followed by off-campus course work.

Undergraduate admissions requirements: Applicants need a minimum number of transferable credits, show academic ability, have volunteer or work experience, and international/intercultural experience. TOEFL score 550 for non-native speakers of English. Graduate admissions requirements: Students need a bachelor's degree or equivalent, professional and intercultural experience, ability to analyze experiences, understanding of the program. TOEFL score 550 for non-native speakers of English.

Graduation requirements (undergraduate): Graduates must complete course, credit, and learning contract requirements, a field study/internship, and the Senior Paper/Oral Presentation. Competency in a foreign language must be demonstrated.

Graduation requirements (graduate): Graduates must complete course and credit requirements, a professional practicum, and a capstone paper and seminar or Independent Professional Project. Competency in a foreign language must be demonstrated.

Fees, Tuition, Costs

Undergraduate application fee: $35
Graduate application fee: $35
Undergraduate tuition: $12,200/yr
Graduate tuition: $16,000/program
Undergraduate cost of books: $500/term
Graduate cost of books: $500/term

Financial Aid/Status

Scholarship programs for adults: Scholarships are available.
Full-time status: 9 graduate credits or 12 undergraduate credits.

Maximum Hours Awarded For

CLEP: 30
PEP: 30
DANTES: 30
Prior learning portfolio: 60
Additional information: Military—30; International Baccalaureate—30

Features and Services

1. Is it possible to purchase books during hours most adult students attend classes? **Yes.**

2. Are the institution's administrative offices open during hours adult students attend class? **Yes.**

3. What is the registration and payment process for adult students? **On-campus**

registration takes place after billing by mail or in person. Payment options vary.

4. What is the process for advising adult students? Faculty advisors are matched with student interest at each phase of the program.

5. What career and placement services are available to adult students? **The Professional Development Resource Center provides in-person and electronic guidance without cost.**

6. What characteristics of the institution's adult degree programs are most appealing to students? **Brief on-campus course work, integration with career calendar, career opportunity and advancement, low relative cost.**

Seattle Pacific University

3307 Third Avenue W. ◆ Division of Continuing Studies
Seattle, WA 98119
Phone: (206) 281-2121 ◆ Toll-free phone: (800) 648-7898
Fax: (206) 281-2662 ◆ E-mail: dcsmkt@spu.edu
Web address: http://paul.spu.edu/dcs

Founded: 1891

Accredited by: Northwest Association

Enrollment: 2,474 ◆ Adult students: 38 percent

University status: Private, Church, Free Methodist Church

Degree	Concentration/Major	Format
B.A.	Business Administration	E,V
B.S.	Computer Engineering	E,V
B.S.	Electrical Engineering	E,V
B.A.	Computer Science	E,V
B.A.	General Studies	E,V
M.A.	Teaching English to Speakers of Other Languages	E
M.S.	Marriage and Family Therapy	E
M.B.A.	Business Administration	E
M.A.T.	Secondary Education	E
M.Ed.	Curriculum and Instruction	E
M.Ed.	Reading/Language Arts	E
M.Ed.	School Administration	E
M.Ed.	School Counseling	E
M.S.N.	Nursing	E
Ed.D.	Instructional Leadership	E
Psy.D.	Clinical Family Psychology	E

Requirements

Undergraduate admissions requirements: Admission requirements vary with the degree. Graduate admissions requirements: Admission requirements vary with the program.
Graduation requirements (undergraduate): Students must meet general education and major requirements.
Graduation requirements (graduate): Graduation requirements vary with the degree program.

Fees, Tuition, Costs

Undergraduate application fee: $35
Graduate application fee: Vary
Undergraduate tuition: $4,493/quarter full-time
Graduate tuition: Varies

Financial Aid/Status

Scholarship programs for adults: Scholarships are available.
Full-time status: Students taking 9 or more credits each quarter are full-time.

Maximum Hours Awarded For

CLEP: Yes
Other exams: Yes

Features and Services

1. Is it possible to purchase books during hours most adult students attend classes? **Yes.**

2. Are the institution's administrative offices open during hours adult students attend class? **Yes.**

3. What is the registration and payment process for adult students? **Registration and payment are handled by mail, fax, or in person.**

4. What is the process for advising adult students? **Students have faculty advisors in their majors.**

5. What career and placement services are available to adult students? **All students use the college career and placement services.**

6. What characteristics of the institution's adult degree programs are most appealing to students? **Flexible program and course hours and reputation of excellence.**

Seattle University*

School of Education All Loyola
401 Loyola, Broadway and Madison ◆ **Seattle, WA 98501**
Phone: (206)296-5696 ◆ Fax: (206)296-2053
Web address: http://www.seattleu.edu

Founded: 1891

Accredited by: Northwest Association

Enrollment: 6,000 ◆ Adult students: 100

University status: Private, Church, Roman Catholic Church

Features and Services

1. Is it possible to purchase books during hours most adult students attend classes? **Yes.**

2. Are the institution's administrative offices open during hours adult students attend class? **Yes.**

3. What characteristics of the institution's adult degree programs are most appealing to students? **Practical orientation, evening courses, and Jesuit/ethical focus.**

Degree	Concentration/Major	Format
M.A./M.Ed.	Adult Education and Training	E

Requirements
Residency requirement: An internship that provides work experience
Graduate admissions requirements: BA degree, 2.75 or higher GPA or Millers or GRE test scores, one year of work experience, TOFEL scores if international applicant

Fees, Tuition, Costs
Graduate application fee: $45
Graduate tuition: $285/credit

Financial Aid/Status
Full-time status: 5 credit hours

Shasta Bible College

2980 Hawthorne Avenue ◆ **Redding, CA 96002**

Phone: (916) 221-4275 ◆ Toll-free phone: (800) (800) 4722

Fax: (916) 221-6929

Founded: 1971

Accredited by: TRACS

Enrollment: 200 ◆ Adult students: 100 percent

University status: Private, Church, Nondenominational

Degree	Concentration/Major	Format
A.A.	Biblical Studies	E,A
A.A.	Christian Preschool Administration	E,A
B.A.	Christian Teacher Education	E
B.A.	Bible and Theology	E
B.A.	Christian Professional Studies	E,A

Requirements

Undergraduate admissions requirements: Students in the adult Biblical Studies program must be 25 years or older, have 60 units of completed college credit or an A.A. degree, and personally express faith in Jesus Christ.

Graduation requirements (undergraduate): Adult students in the Biblical Studies Completion Program must complete a total of 128 units of study including general education, biblical studies, and elective course work.

Fees, Tuition, Costs

Undergraduate application fee: $25
Undergraduate tuition: $5,000/ program
Undergraduate cost of books: $200

Financial Aid/Status

Scholarship programs for adults: Scholarships are available.
Full-time status: 12 units/semester.
Percentage of adult students receiving financial aid: 10 percent.

Maximum Hours Awarded For

CLEP: 15
Other exams: 15
Prior learning portfolio: 15

Features and Services

1. Is it possible to purchase books during hours most adult students attend classes? **Yes.**

2. Are the institution's administrative offices open during hours adult students attend class? **Yes.**

3. How do students taking extended classes access library resources? **The library is open from 5 to 9 P.M. on weekdays.**

4. What is the registration and payment process for adult students? **Students may pay at the beginning of each course, prepay for the entire program, or make four payments.**

5. What is the process for advising adult students? **Advising is done through the deans.**

6. What career and placement services are available to adult students? **Career and placement services is done with the deans.**

7. What characteristics of the institution's adult degree programs are most appealing to students? **Evening and accelerated program.**

Sheldon Jackson College

801 Lincoln Street ◆ **Sitka, AK 99835**
Phone: (907) 747-5221 ◆ Toll-free phone: (800) 478-4556
Fax: (907) 747-6366 ◆ E-mail: tndac@acadl.alaska.edu

Founded: 1878

Accredited by: Northwest Association

Enrollment: 175 ◆ Adult students: 6 percent

University status: Private, Church, Presbyterian Church, U.S.A.

Degree	Concentration/Major	Format
B.A./B.S.	Aquatic Resources	E
B.A./B.S.	Natural Resources	E
B.A./B.S.	Business Administration	E
B.A./B.S.	Elementary Education	E
B.A./B.S.	Secondary Education	E
B.A./B.S.	Liberal Studies	E
B.A./B.S.	Interdisciplinary Studies	S,E

Requirements

Residency requirement: Students must attend classes on campus. Undergraduate admissions requirements: Students must submit a copy of all transcripts. Graduation requirements (undergraduate): Students must earn 130 credits to receive a bachelor's degree.

Fees, Tuition, Costs

Undergraduate application fee: None
Undergraduate tuition: $9,000/year
Undergraduate cost of books: $350
Other costs: Travel expenses—$1,000/year

Financial Aid/Status

Scholarship programs for adults: The types, amounts, and eligibility of scholarships vary.
Full-time status: A full-time student takes 12 or more credits.
Percentage of adult students receiving financial aid: 98 percent.

Features and Services

1. Is it possible to purchase books during hours most adult students attend classes? **Yes.**

2. Are the institution's administrative offices open during hours adult students attend class? **Yes.**

3. How do students taking extended classes access library resources? **The library is open late for student accessibility.**

4. What is the registration and payment process for adult students? **Registration/payment is the same for all students.**

5. What is the process for advising adult students? **Advising is the same for all students.**

6. What career and placement services are available to adult students? **Career and placement service is the same for all students.**

7. What characteristics of the institution's adult degree programs are most appealing to students? **Evening and late afternoon classes are appealing to students.**

Shimer College

P.O. Box 500 ◆ **Waukegan, IL 60079**

Phone: (847) 623-8400 ◆ Toll-free phone: (800) 215-7173

Fax: (847) 249-7171

Founded: 1853

Accredited by: North Central

Enrollment: 120 ◆ Adult students: 30 percent

University status: Private

Degree	Concentration/Major	Format
B.A.	Humanities	E
B.A.	Social Sciences	E
B.A.	Natural Sciences	E
B.S.	Social Sciences	E
B.S.	Natural Sciences	E

Requirements

Residency requirement: Students must attend classes on campus. Undergraduate admissions requirements: Students must complete an application form, provide a writing sample, and submit transcripts of all academic work.
Graduation requirements (undergraduate): Graduates must complete 125 credit hours and an undergraduate thesis.

Fees, Tuition, Costs

Undergraduate application fee: $10
Undergraduate tuition: $13,000/year
Undergraduate cost of books: $700/year

Financial Aid/Status

Scholarship programs for adults: Need-based scholarships are available.
Full-time status: Full-time students take 12 1/2 to 17 1/2 credits.
Percentage of adult students receiving financial aid: 90 percent.

Features and Services

1. Is it possible to purchase books during hours most adult students attend classes? **Yes.**

2. Are the institution's administrative offices open during hours adult students attend class? **Yes.**

3. What is the registration and payment process for adult students? **Registration takes place on campus three weeks before the semester.**

4. What is the process for advising adult students? **All applicants are urged to visit the college to answer questions and get financial assistance.**

5. What characteristics of the institution's adult degree programs are most appealing to students? **The scheduling (every third weekend) and small discussion classes (12 or fewer per class).**

Shorter College

School of Professional Programs

1950 Spectrum Circle, A305 ◆ **Marietta, GA 30067**
Phone: (770) 989-5673 ◆ Fax: (770) 980-3413
E-mail: woolfp@mindspring.com
Web address: http://www.shortercollege.edu

Founded: 1873

Accredited by: Southern Association

Enrollment: 1,300 ◆ Adult students: 50 percent

University status: Private, Church, Southern Baptist Church

Degree	Concentration/Major	Format
B.S.	Business Administration	E,A
B.S.	Business Management	E,A
M.B.A.	Business Administration	E,A

Campus Extension Sites

Lawrenceville, GA
Rome, GA

Requirements

Residency requirement: Students must attend classes on campus. Undergraduate admissions requirements: Students in the adult program must be 23 years or older and have two years of work experience. A high school diploma or GED certificate and three letters of reference must be submitted. Graduate admissions requirements: Students must be 23 years or older and have a bachelor's degree from an accredited institution (2.75 GPA). Two letters of reference must be submitted.
Graduation requirements (undergraduate): Graduation requires the completion of 126 undergraduate hours and an applied business project. All fees and tuition must be paid.
Graduation requirements (graduate): Graduation requires the completion of 43 semester hours, and an oral and written business project. All fees and tuition must be paid.

Fees, Tuition, Costs

Undergraduate application fee: $40
Graduate application fee: $50
Undergraduate tuition: $225/semester hours
Graduate tuition: $285/semester hours
Undergraduate cost of books: $70/course
Graduate cost of books: $100/course

Financial Aid/Status

Scholarship programs for adults: Scholarships include the HOPE state scholarship ($1,500/year) and GTEG ($1,000/year). Various financial packages are available.

The M.B.A. program provides a laptop computer as part of the tuition.
Full-time status: Based on total credits taken per year as stipulated by federal guidelines.
Percentage of adult students receiving financial aid: 85 percent.

Maximum Hours Awarded For

CLEP: 30
PEP: 30
DANTES: 30
Other exams: 30
Prior learning portfolio: 30
Additional information: Up to 30 semester hours can be earned by noncollegiate means.

Features and Services

1. Is it possible to purchase books during hours most adult students attend classes? **Yes.**

2. Are the institution's administrative offices open during hours adult students attend class? **Yes.**

3. How do students taking extended classes access library resources? **Students may use CD-ROM and the Internet. Interlibrary loans are also available.**

4. What is the registration and payment process for adult students? **Registration is done only once at the beginning of the degree program. Payment is discussed individually.**

5. What is the process for advising adult students? **Undergraduate advising is done by student service office. Graduate advising is done by graduate faculty.**

6. What career and placement services are available to adult students? **Computerized job**

bank—recently created as a project by Students in a Free Enterprise—is available.

7. What characteristics of the institution's adult degree programs are most appealing to students? **Accelerated program, study team**

groups, class one night a week, computer-enhanced MBA program, and degreed instructors with business experience.

Siena Heights College

1247 E. Siena Heights Drive ◆ **Adrian, MI 49221**

Phone: (517) 263-0731 ◆ Toll-free phone: (800) 521-0009

Fax: (517) 265-3380

Founded: 1919

Accredited by: North Central

Enrollment: 1,895 ◆ Adult students: 50 percent

University status: Private, Church, Roman Catholic Church

Degree	Concentration/Major	Format
A.A.	Computer and Information Systems	E
A.A.	Business Administration	E
A.A.	General Studies	E
A.A.	Humanities	E
B.A.	Business Administration	E
B.A.	Computer and Information Systems	E
B.A.	General Studies	E
B.A.	Humanities	E
B.A.S.	Inverted Major	E
M.A.	Human Resource Development	E
M.A.	Counselor Education	E
M.A.	Teacher Education	E

Campus Extension Sites

Battle Creek, MI
Benton Harbor, MI
Monroe, MI
Southfield, MI

Requirements

Residency requirement: Students must attend classes on campus. Undergraduate admissions requirements: Students must submit high school and/or college transcripts, or GED, and an application. SAT/ACT scores may be needed.
Graduate admissions requirements: Students must have a bachelor's degree (3.0 GPA) or 9 hours of graduate work (minimum 3.5 GPA). A resume or vita, an application, and three letters of recommendation must be submitted. An interview is required.
Graduation requirements (undergraduate): Graduates must earn 120 semester hours, meeting all degree requirements; have at least a 2.0 GPA; and be approved by the Office of the Registrar.
Graduation requirements (graduate): Graduates must complete all course work (3.0 GPA), the selected readings from the Graduate Reading List, and a thesis/research project, including a public presentation.

Fees, Tuition, Costs

Undergraduate application fee: $15
Graduate application fee: $15
Undergraduate tuition: $250/ semester hour
Graduate tuition: $250/semester hr
Undergraduate cost of books: $180
Graduate cost of books: $150
Other costs: Approximate $30 fee for computer class

Financial Aid/Status

Scholarship programs for adults: Scholarships are available.
Full-time status: A full-time student carries an academic load of 12 or more credit hours.

Maximum Hours Awarded For

CLEP: 36.
Prior learning portfolio: Yes.
Additional information: Cooperative Internships—24 semester hours. Credit for prior learning is limited to 9 hours (A.A.) or 18 hours (B.A.).

Features and Services

1. Is it possible to purchase books during hours most adult students attend classes? **Yes.**

2. What is the registration and payment process for adult students? **New students set up degree plans and register with an academic advisor. Current students use phone.**

3. What is the process for advising adult students? **Initial advising is done with Nontraditional Program director or faculty member.**

4. What career and placement services are available to adult students? **Placement services include resume writing, job referral service, job fairs, and credential files.**

5. What characteristics of the institution's adult degree programs are most appealing to students? **An office devoted to serving adult students, individual attention, and personal advising by competent and empathetic staff.**

Silver Lake College

2406 S. Alverno Road ◆ **Manitowoc, WI 54220**
Phone: (414) 584-5955 ◆ Toll-free phone: (800) 236-4752
Fax: (414) 684-7082 ◆ E-mail: admslc@sl.edu
Web address: http://www.sl.edu

Founded: 1935

Accredited by: North Central

Enrollment: 1,300 ◆ Adult students: 80 percent

University status: Private, Church, Roman Catholic Church

Degree	Concentration/Major	Format
B.S.	Management	E,A
B.S.	Specialized Administration Concentrations in Leadership in Public Service, Healthcare Management, Human Resource Management	E,A
B.S.	Accounting	E,A
B.S.	Manufacturing Systems Engineering Technology	E,A
M.S.	Management and Organizational Behavior Concentrations in Training and Development, General Management, International Business, Quality in Business Management, Vocational, Technical, and Adult Education, Health Service Management	E,A

Campus Extension Sites

Appleton, WI
Fond du Lac
Green Bay, WI
Madison, WI
Milwaukee, WI
Tomah, WI
Wausau, WI

Requirements

Residency requirement: Students are not required to attend classes on the main campus.
Undergraduate admissions requirements: Students must submit an application, all high school and/or college transcripts, and ACT/SAT scores. GED/HSE applicants are eligible for provisional admission. Graduate admissions requirements: Applicants must have a bachelor's degree (minimum 3.0 GPA). A writing sample and an interview with the program director are required. Graduation requirements (undergraduate): A.A.—complete core requirements, required semester hours (GPA—2.0); B.A.—complete 128 semester hours (GPA—2.0), the liberal arts, major, and minor requirements. At least 30 hours must be earned at Silver Lake. Graduation requirements (graduate): Graduates must earn the minimum credits for the degree (GPA—3.0), make an oral presentation of the thesis/project, and pass a comprehensive exam on the course work.

Fees, Tuition, Costs

Undergraduate application fee: $20
Graduate application fee: $30
Undergraduate tuition: $555/3-credit course

Graduate tuition: $675/3-credit course
Undergraduate cost of books: $60/course
Graduate cost of books: $75/course

Financial Aid/Status

Scholarship programs for adults: Scholarships ($100-$1,000) available
Full-time status: 12 credits
Percentage of adult students receiving financial aid: 50 percent

Maximum Hours Awarded For

CLEP: 60
PEP: 60
DANTES: 60
Prior learning portfolio: 60
Additional information: 60-credit maximum through all forms of prior learning

Features and Services

1. Is it possible to purchase books during hours most adult students attend classes? **Yes.**

2. Are the institution's administrative offices open during hours adult students attend class? **Yes.**

3. How do students taking extended classes access library resources? **Access to the library is limited.**

4. What is the registration and payment process for adult students? **Registration/**payment may be done by mail or phone with a credit card.

5. What is the process for advising adult students? **Phone counseling and individual appointments are available at the class site.**

6. What career and placement services are available to adult students? **Services include free placement listings, individual appointments, workshops, and resume service.**

7. What characteristics of the institution's adult degree programs are most appealing to students? **Convenience, service, quality of the programs, and cost.**

Simpson College

701 N. C Street ◆ Indianola, IA 50125-1299
Phone: (515) 961-1614 ◆ Toll-free phone: (800) 362-2454
Fax: (515) 961-1498 ◆ Web address: http://www.simpson.edu

Founded: 1860

Accredited by: North Central

Enrollment: 1,760 ◆ Adult students: 33 percent

University status: Private, Church, United Methodist Church

Campus Extension Site

West Des Moines, IA

Requirements

Residency requirement: Students can attain the B.A. degree in total at the West Des Moines site. Undergraduate admissions requirements: Students must submit a part-time application for admission and official transcripts of high school and any previous college work. ACT/SAT scores may be requested.
Graduation requirements (undergraduate): Requirements include 128 semester hours (GPA—2.0), including required liberal arts, major, and May Term courses; math and English competency; completion of required hours beyond transferred credits.

Degree	Concentration/Major	Format
B.A.	Accounting	E,A
B.A.	Management	E,A
B.A.	Communication Studies	E,A
B.A.	Computer Science	E
B.A.	Computer Information Systems	E
B.A.	Elementary Education	E
B.A.	English	E
B.A.	Social Science	E

Fees, Tuition, Costs

Undergraduate application fee: $50
Undergraduate tuition: $170/
semester hour
Undergraduate cost of books: $50/
class

Financial Aid/Status

Full-time status: 12-16 semester hrs
Percentage of adult students
receiving financial aid: 35 percent

Maximum Hours Awarded For

CLEP: 24
DANTES: 16
Other exams: Yes
Prior learning portfolio: 24
Additional information: Vo-tech,
LOMA, CPCU (unaccredited
organizations)/16 credit maximum;
maximum of 32 nontraditional
credits

Features and Services

1. Is it possible to purchase books during hours most adult students attend classes? **Yes.**

2. Are the institution's administrative offices open during hours adult students attend class? **Yes.**

3. How do students taking extended classes access library resources? **The library may be accessed by computer or personal visit.**

4. What is the registration and payment process for adult students? **Students may register and pay by phone, FAX, or in person at either location.**

5. What is the process for advising adult students? **Adult academic advisors are available evenings until 8 P.M. Monday through Thursday at either location.**

6. What career and placement services are available to adult students? **Counseling and Career Services are available at either location by appointment.**

7. What characteristics of the institution's adult degree programs are most appealing to students? **Attaining total degree in evening classes, flexible schedule, access to advisors, and ease of registration and book purchase.**

Simpson College*

2211 College View Drive ◆ **Redding, CA 96003**

Phone: (916) 224-5600 ◆ Toll-free phone: (800) 598-2493
Fax: (916) 224-5608

Founded: 1921

Accredited by: Western Association

Enrollment: 840 ◆ Adult students: 265

University status: Private, Church,
Christian and Missionary Alliance Church

Degree	Concentration/Major	Format
B.A.	Business and Human Resources Management	E,A
B.A.	Psychology	E,A
B.A.	Liberal Arts	E,A

Requirements

Residency requirement: Yes
Undergraduate admissions
requirements: Minimum of 60
undergraduate credits in specific
areas and at least five years of work
experience

Fees, Tuition, Costs

Undergraduate application fee: $25
Undergraduate tuition: $6,800 for
program

Financial Aid/Status

Full-time status: 9 credits/15-week
term
Percentage of adult students
receiving financial aid: 95 percent

Maximum Hours Awarded For

CLEP: 25
Other exams: 12

Features and Services

1. Is it possible to purchase books during hours most adult students attend classes? **Yes.**

2. Are the institution's administrative offices open during hours adult students attend class? **Yes.**

3. What characteristics of the institution's adult degree programs are most appealing to students? **Accelerated courses in established schedule.**

Skidmore College*
University Without Walls

Sarasota Springs, NY 12866 ◆ Phone: (518) 584-5000
Fax: (518) 581-7400
Web address: http://www.skidmore.edu

Founded: 1971

Accredited by: Middle States

Enrollment: 230 ◆ Adult students: 230

University status: Private

Features and Services

1. Is it possible to purchase books during hours most adult students attend classes? **Yes.**

2. What characteristics of the institution's adult degree programs are most appealing to students? **Flexible degree plan, no residency, and quality liberal arts education.**

Degree	Concentration/Major	Format
B.A.	Liberal Arts Field (Most areas)	E,C,T,A,S
B.S.	Studio Art	E,C,T,A,S
B.S.	Music	E,C,T,A,S
B.S.	Theatre	E,C,T,A,S
B.S.	Business	E,C,T,A,S
B.S.	Human Services	E,C,T,A,S
B.A./B.S.	Self-Determined	E,C,T,A,S

Requirements

Residency requirement: None. The format for classes includes many of the different formats but must be used in combination to complete the degree.
Undergraduate admissions requirements: High school diploma, ability to succeed at college work.

Fees, Tuition, Costs

Undergraduate application fee: $30

Financial Aid/Status

Full-time status: 8 courses (24 credits) per year
Percentage of adult students receiving financial aid: 20 percent

Maximum Hours Awarded For

CLEP: No limit
PEP: No limit
DANTES: No limit
Other exams: No limit
Prior learning portfolio: No limit

Southeastern Bible College

3001 Highway 280 E. ◆ Birmingham, AL 35243
Phone: (205) 970-9220 ◆ Toll-free phone: (800) 749-8878
Fax: (205) 970-9207

Founded: 1935

Accredited by: Accrediting Association

Enrollment: 490 ◆ Adult students: 90 percent

University status: Private, Church, Nondenominational

Degree	Concentration/Major	Format
B.S.	Biblical Studies	C

Requirements

Residency requirement: The B.S. program may be completed by correspondence.
Undergraduate admissions requirements: The B.S. applicant must be 25 or have completed the Southeastern Associate of Arts program or have 32 semester hours of transferable work. Official transcripts and an application must be submitted.
Graduation requirements (undergraduate): Graduates must earn 128 credit hours, including 32 hours through Southeastern.

Fees, Tuition, Costs

Undergraduate application fee: $20
Undergraduate tuition: $90-$145/semester hour
Undergraduate cost of books: $30-40/3-hour course

Financial Aid/Status

Full-time status: External degree students cannot receive federal aid.

Maximum Hours Awarded For

CLEP: 30
PEP: 30
DANTES: 30
Other exams: 30
Prior learning portfolio: 30
Additional information: Maximum combination of 30 credit hours

Features and Services

1. Is it possible to purchase books during hours most adult students attend classes? **Yes.**

2. Are the institution's administrative offices open during hours adult students attend class? **Yes.**

3. How do students taking extended classes access library resources? **Students may access the library by mail from the college library, by interlibrary loan, and the Internet.**

4. What is the registration and payment process for adult students? **The B.S. program has a time payment plan with four monthly payments.**

5. What is the process for advising adult students? **A faculty advisor is available.**

6. What characteristics of the institution's adult degree programs are most appealing to students? **The ability to take courses at home.**

Southeastern College of the Assemblies of God

1000 Longfellow Boulevard ◆ Lakeland, FL 33801
Phone: (941) 665-4404 ◆ Fax: (941) 665-0486
E-mail: spongc@mail.firn.edu

Founded: 1935

Accredited by: Southern Association

Enrollment: 992 ◆ Adult students: 75 percent

University status: Private, Church, Assemblies of God Church

Degree	Concentration/Major	Format
B.A.	Pastoral Ministries	C
B.A.	Pastoral Ministries—Counseling	C
B.A.	Pastoral Ministries—Urban Ministry	C
B.A.	Bible	C
B.A.	Christian Education—Children's Ministry	C
B.A.	Christian Education—Youth Ministry	C
B.A.	Christian Education—Teacher K-6	C
B.A.	Christian Education—Teacher: English 6-12	C
B.A.	Christian Education—Teacher: Math 6-12	C
B.A.	Christian Education—Teacher: Social Science 6-12	C
B.A.	Missions	C

Requirements

Residency requirement: Course work is completed by mail. Communication is done by mail, phone, FAX, and e-mail. Undergraduate admissions requirements: Applicant must be 22, have a high school or GED diploma, and be active in a local church. A pastoral recommendation; scores of SAT, ACT, or TOEFL exams; and writing/reading competencies are needed.
Graduation requirements (undergraduate): B.A. candidates must complete a minimum of 130 semester hours with a 2.0 GPA, including general education requirements, core requirements in Bible and theology, and the major program.

Fees, Tuition, Costs

Undergraduate application fee: $40
Undergraduate tuition: $176/hour
Undergraduate cost of books: $20/hour

Financial Aid/Status

Full-time status: 12 hours
Percentage of adult students receiving financial aid: 5 percent

Maximum Hours Awarded For

CLEP: 45
DANTES: Yes

Other exams: Yes
Prior learning portfolio: Yes

Features and Services

1. Is it possible to purchase books during hours most adult students attend classes? **Yes.**

2. Are the institution's administrative offices open during hours adult students attend class? **Yes.**

3. How do students taking extended classes access library resources? **Students may make library requests by phone, FAX, and e-mail.**

4. What is the registration and payment process for adult students? **Students mail a one-page registration form. Payment can be made by check or credit card.**

5. What is the process for advising adult students? **Orientation includes handbook, audio, phone seminar. Faculty contact students after each 15 hours of work.**

6. What career and placement services are available to adult students? **A placement file of graduates and prospective openings is maintained.**

7. What characteristics of the institution's adult degree programs are most appealing to students? **Study any time, any place, at own pace; reduced cost; course content; and support of college.**

Southeastern University

501 I Street, S.W. ◆ **Washington, DC 20024**
Phone: (202) 265-5343 ◆ Fax: (202) 488-8093
E-mail: jackf@admin.sev.edu

Founded: 1879

Accredited by: Middle States

Enrollment: 488 ◆ Adult students: 90 percent

University status: Private

Degree	Concentration/Major	Format
A.S.	Legal Studies	E,A
A.S.	Management	E,A,C
B.S.	Management	E,A,C
B.S.	Marketing	E,A
B.S.	Accounting	E,A,C
B.S.	Information Systems	E,A
B.S.	Government Management	E,A
B.S.	Health Administration	E,A
B.S.	Computer Science	E,A
B.S.	General Studies	E,A
B.S.	Finance	E,A
M.B.A.	Business Administration	E,A,C
M.P.A.	Public Administration	E,A
M.S.	Taxation	E,A
M.S.	Computer Science	E,A

Requirements

Residency requirement: Students must attend class on campus. Undergraduate admissions requirements: Official high school or certified transcript; all undergraduate transcripts; university placement tests if required; immunization if under 26. Graduate admissions requirements: Two letters of recommendation; letter of intent, all official undergraduate transcripts; GRE of 1200 (computer science program only). Graduation requirements (undergraduate): B.S. degree requires 120 credits; A.S. requires 60 credits. Graduation requirements (graduate): M.B.A./M.P.A. degrees require 45 credits; M.S. taxation requires 30-36 credits; M.S. computer science requires 45 credits.

Fees, Tuition, Costs

Undergraduate application fee: $45
Graduate application fee: $45
Undergraduate tuition: $185/credit
Graduate tuition: $228/credit
Undergraduate cost of books: $75
Graduate cost of books: $90
Other costs: University fee—$75 during preregistration; $150 during regular registration

Financial Aid/Status

Full-time status: Undergraduate—12 credit hours; graduate—9 credit hours
Percentage of adult students receiving financial aid: 75 percent

Maximum Hours Awarded For

CLEP: 12
DANTES: 60
Other exams: 12
Prior learning portfolio: 60
Additional information: Up to 30 credits toward A.S. degree through DANTES and prior learning

Features and Services

1. Is it possible to purchase books during hours most adult students attend classes? **Yes.**

2. Are the institution's administrative offices open during hours adult students attend class? **Yes.**

3. How do students taking extended classes access library resources? **The library may be accessed by the Internet.**

4. What is the registration and payment process for adult students? **Students pay for classes at registration or use a payment plan. Financial aid students need SARs.**

5. What is the process for advising adult students? **Academic advisors and department heads are available.**

6. What career and placement services are available to adult students? **Students may obtain information in the Career Services office.**

7. What characteristics of the institution's adult degree programs are most appealing to students? **Full evening schedule; a quadmester allowing students to complete degrees in two years (full-time) or four years (part-time).**

Southern Arkansas University

100 E. University ◆ **Magnolia, AR 71753**
Phone: (501) 235-4040

Founded: 1909

Accredited by: North Central

Enrollment: 2,745 ◆ Adult students: 52 percent

University status: Public

Degree	Concentration/Major	Format
Not Specific	Counseling, Education, and Agency	E

Requirements

Residency requirement: Students must attend class on campus. Undergraduate admissions requirements: Students must submit application, ACT scores (19), high school transcript, and other requirements as requested. Medical immunization is required. Graduate admissions requirements: Students must have an undergraduate degree; 3.0 GPA last 60 hours; and be certified or certifiable (i.e., NTE). Other department requirements must be met.
Graduation requirements (undergraduate): Graduates must have a minimum of 124 semester hours with 15 hours in residence and 2.0 GPA.
Graduation requirements (graduate): Graduates must have a minimum of 33 hours; minimum 3.0 GPA. Other requirements as stated must be met.

Fees, Tuition, Costs

Undergraduate tuition: $840/ semester 12-18 hours
Graduate tuition: $85/hour
Undergraduate cost of books: $250
Graduate cost of books: $150

Financial Aid/Status

Scholarship programs for adults: Scholarships available
Full-time status: 12 or more credits

Maximum Hours Awarded For

CLEP: Yes

Features and Services

1. Is it possible to purchase books during hours most adult students attend classes? **Yes.**

2. Are the institution's administrative offices open during hours adult students attend class? **Yes.**

3. How do students taking extended classes access library resources? **The library may be accessed by computer.**

4. What is the registration and payment process for adult students? **Registration can be done by appointment.**

5. What is the process for advising adult students? **Advising is available by appointment.**

6. What career and placement services are available to adult students? **All students receive the same services.**

Southern California College

55 Fair Drive ◆ **Costa Mesa, CA 92626**
Phone: (714) 668-6130 ◆ Fax: (714) 668-6194

Founded: 1920

Accredited by: Western Association

Enrollment: 1,200 ◆ Adult students: 20 percent

University status: Private, Church, Assemblies of God Church

Degree / Concentration/Major / Format

Degree	Concentration/Major	Format
B.A.	Business—Organizational Management	E,A
B.A.	Religion—Ministry and Leadership	E,A
M.A.	Education	E
M.A.	Religion	E

Requirements

Residency requirement: This is a residential program available only at campus.
Undergraduate admissions requirements: Applicants must be 25, have 40 semester college credits (2.0 GPA), and have two years of work experience. They must submit an application, provide college transcripts, and complete a Credit for Prior Learning interview.
Graduation requirements (undergraduate): Graduates earn 124 semester units, including 55 units of general education courses.

Fees, Tuition, Costs

Undergraduate tuition: $3,417-$3,917/semester
Undergraduate cost of books: $300/semester
Other costs: Computer

Financial Aid/Status

Scholarship programs for adults: Some aid available through special church program
Full-time status: 12 semester hours
Percentage of adult students receiving financial aid: 90 percent

Maximum Hours Awarded For

CLEP: Yes
DANTES: Yes
Other exams: Yes
Prior learning portfolio: Yes

Features and Services

1. Is it possible to purchase books during hours most adult students attend classes? **Yes.**

2. Are the institution's administrative offices open during hours adult students attend class? **Yes.**

3. How do students taking extended classes access library resources? **The library is open evenings.**

4. What is the registration and payment process for adult students? **Evening registration and payment are convenient for students.**

5. What is the process for advising adult students? **Counselors are on-site for admission and assessment.**

6. What career and placement services are available to adult students? **Career and placement services are limited.**

7. What characteristics of the institution's adult degree programs are most appealing to students? **On campus, small class size (14-18 students), faculty, and overall student services to the adult learner.**

Southern Illinois University at Edwardsville

Campus Box 1080 ◆ **Edwardsville, IL 62026**
Phone: (618) 692-3775 ◆ Toll-free phone: (800) 447-SIUE
Fax: (618) 692-2081 ◆ E-mail: admis@siue.edu
Web address: http://www.siue.edu

Founded: 1957 ◆ Accredited by: North Central

Enrollment: 11,047 ◆ Adult students: 44 percent

University status: Public

Degree	Concentration/Major	Format
B.S.A.	Accountancy	E
B.S.	Business Administration	E
B.S.	Business Economics	E
B.A./B.S.	Computer Science	E
B.A./B.S.	Economics	E
B.S.	Electrical Engineering	E
B.A./B.S.	History	E
B.A./B.S.	Geography	E
B.L.S.	Liberal Studies	E
B.A./B.S.	Mathematics	E
B.A./B.S.	Political Science	E
B.A.	Philosophy	E
B.A./B.S.	Speech Communication	E
M.S.A.	Accountancy	E
M.A.	Art Therapy	E
M.B.A.	Business Administration	E
M.S.	Chemistry	E
M.S.	Computing and Information Systems	E
M.A./M.S.	Economics	E
M.S. Ed.	Education—Educational Administration and Instructional Technology	E
M.S. Ed.	Education—Elementary Education and Secondary Education	E
M.S. Ed.	Education—Physical Education	E
M.S. Ed.	Special Education	E
M.A.	English—Teaching of English as a Second Language	E
M.S.	Engineering—Civil Engineering	E
M.S.	Engineering—Electrical Engineering	E
M.S.	Environmental Studies—General and Science	E
M.A./M.S.	Geographical Studies	E
M.A.	History	E
M.M.R.	Marketing Research	E
M.S.	Mass Communications	E
M.S.	Mathematics	E
M.M.	Music	E
M.S.	Nursing—Community Health, Medical-Surgical and Psychiatric-Mental Health	E
M.S.	Physics	E
M.P.A.	Public Administration	E
M.A.	Psychology—Industrial-Organizational	E
M.A.	Sociology	E
M.A.	Speech—Specialization in Speech Communication	E

Campus Extension Sites

Belleville, IL
Olney, IL
St. Louis, MO
Hillsboro, IL
Ina, IL
Carlyle, IL
Ullin, IL
Columbia, IL
Jerseyville, IL

Requirements

Residency requirement: It is common for students to make their first visit to campus for commencement.

Undergraduate admissions requirements: If high school graduation was five years before application, student must have been in upper half of class or scored in 50th percentile (ACT/SAT). GED applicants may have to take additional courses.

Graduate admissions requirements: Applicants must hold a baccalaureate degree. Other requirements vary depending on the degree program.

Graduation requirements (undergraduate): Students must earn a minimum of 124 hours (2.0 GPA) and meet all degree and university course requirements; 30 semester hours must be earned through SIUE.

Graduation requirements (graduate): Graduation requirements vary with the degree. A minimum of 30 semester hours is required for a master's degree. Some programs require additional hours.

Fees, Tuition, Costs

Undergraduate application fee: None
Graduate application fee: $20
Undergraduate tuition: $1,928/yr
Graduate tuition: $2,066/year
Undergraduate cost of books:

Included in tuition
Graduate cost of books: $656/year

Financial Aid/Status
Scholarship programs for adults: Awards are given regardless of age. Adult students are encouraged to apply for all types of financial aid using the FAFSA application. Full-time status: A full-time student is anyone taking 12 undergraduate semester hours or 9 graduate hours.

Maximum Hours Awarded For
CLEP: 32

Features and Services
1. Is it possible to purchase books during hours most adult students attend classes? **Yes.**

2. Are the institution's administrative offices open during hours adult students attend class? **Yes.**

3. How do students taking extended classes access library resources? **Student ID cards can be used at SIUE's library and other university libraries in the St. Louis area.**

4. What is the registration and payment process for adult students? **Students must pay by due date or registration may be canceled. Process is the same for all students.**

5. What is the process for advising adult students? **Advising by Academic Counseling & Advising or major department is required before registration.**

6. What career and placement services are available to adult students? **Career Development Center services are available for all students.**

7. What characteristics of the institution's adult degree programs are most appealing to students? **Convenient evening and weekend course offerings, helpful staff, and dynamic classmates and instructors.**

Southern Methodist University
6410 Airline Road ◆ **Dallas, TX 75275**
Phone: (214) 768-6483 ◆ Fax: (214) 768-1445
E-mail: evening@smu.edu ◆ Web address: http://www.smu.edu/
Program's Web address: http://www.smu.edu/sp-acadc.html

Founded: 1911 ◆ Accredited by: Southern Association

Enrollment: 9,200 ◆ Adult students: 10 percent

University status: Private, Church, United Methodist Church

Degree	Concentration/Major	Format
B.Hum.	Humanities	E
B.Soc.Sci.	Social Sciences	E
M.L.A.	Liberal Arts	E

Requirements
Residency requirement: Students must attend classes on the Dallas campus.
Undergraduate admissions requirements: Applicants must have a high school or equivalent degree and at least 45 transferable semester credit hours from accredited institution (2.5 GPA). Credit more than 10 years old will be reviewed.
Graduate admissions requirements: M.L.A. degree is open to persons with a bachelor's or higher professional degree. An admission application, official transcripts, and a Social Security number are required.
Graduation requirements (undergraduate): Graduates must have 120 credits (minimum 2.0 GPA); 60 credits at SMU. Common requirements, major, minor, and elective courses must be completed. Common requirements should be part of the transfer credit hours.
Graduation requirements (graduate): M.L.A. graduates must earn 36 credits within six years of beginning work. HUMN 6370 & HUMN 7104 are required in the first 12 hours of course work. Six graduate credits may be transferred with approval.

Fees, Tuition, Costs
Undergraduate application fee: $35
Graduate application fee: $35
Undergraduate tuition: $220/credit
Graduate tuition: $220/credit
Undergraduate cost of books: $20/book
Graduate cost of books: $20/book

Financial Aid/Status

Full-time status: 12 credit hours/semester

Maximum Hours Awarded For

CLEP: 12
Other exams: 12
Additional information: Advanced Placement scores up to 12 hours

Features and Services

1. Is it possible to purchase books during hours most adult students attend classes? **Yes.**

2. Are the institution's administrative offices open during hours adult students attend class? **Yes.**

3. What is the registration and payment process for adult students? **One-stop shopping available; register and pay in Evening Studies office.**

4. What is the process for advising adult students? **A student may spend as much time as needed with a staff advisor.**

5. What career and placement services are available to adult students? **The Career Center on campus is available to students.**

6. What characteristics of the institution's adult degree programs are most appealing to students? **Reduced tuition, evening hours, and prestigious university.**

Southern Nazarene University

6729 N.W. 39th Expressway ◆ Bethany, OK 73008
Phone: (405) 491-6060 ◆ Fax: (405) 491-6302
E-mail: wmurrown@icon.net ◆ Web address: http://www.snu.edu

Founded: 1899 ◆ Accredited by: North Central

Enrollment: 1,800 ◆ Adult students: 35 percent

University status: Private, Church, Church of the Nazarene

Degree	Concentration/Major	Format
B.S.	Family Studies and Gerontology	E,A
B.S.	Organizational Leadership	E,A
M.S.	Management	E,A
M.B.A.	Business Administration	E,A
M.S.	Counseling Psychology	E,A
M.A.	Education - Curriculum, Instruction, Reading	E

Campus Extension Site

Tulsa, OK

Requirements

Residency requirement: Students may complete major at the Tulsa, OK, center.
Undergraduate admissions requirements: Applicants must be 25 years of age or, if 23, have two years of full-time employment. They must have 62 accredited transferable hours and pass a writing exam.
Graduate admissions requirements: Applicants must have a degree from an accredited undergraduate institution (2.70 GPA). A goals essay and scores from an appropriate admissions test must be submitted.
Graduation requirements (undergraduate): Students must earn 124 credit hours; 36 hours must be earned at SNU.
Graduation requirements (graduate): Students must complete at least 32 hours of graduate studies with a grade average of B.

Fees, Tuition, Costs

Undergraduate application fee: $25
Graduate application fee: $25
Undergraduate tuition: $9,500/program
Graduate tuition: $8,458-$12,500/program
Undergraduate cost of books: Included in tuition
Graduate cost of books: Included in tuition

Maximum Hours Awarded For

CLEP: Yes
Other exams: Yes
Prior learning portfolio: Yes
Additional information: Practicum

Features and Services

1. Is it possible to purchase books during hours most adult students attend classes? **Yes.**

2. Are the institution's administrative offices open during hours adult students attend class? **Yes.**

3. What characteristics of the institution's adult degree programs are most appealing to students? **Service orientation geared to adult schedules.**

Southern University at New Orleans

6400 Press Drive ◆ **New Orleans, LA 70126**
Phone: (504) 286-5367 ◆ Fax: (504) 286-5260
Web address: http://www.subr.edu

Founded: 1959 ◆ Accredited by: Southern Association

Enrollment: 4,700 ◆ Adult students: 50 percent

University status: Public

Degree	Concentration/Major	Format
A.A.	Substance Abuse	E
A.A.	Real Estate	E
A.S.	Computer Information Systems	E
B.A.	Art	E
B.A.	Art Education	E
B.A.	Elementary Education	E
B.A.	English	E
B.A.	English Education	E
B.A.	French Education	E
B.A.	History	E
B.A.	Instructional Music	E
B.A.	Political Science	E
B.A.	Psychology	E
B.A.	Social Studies Education	E
B.A.	Sociology	E
B.A.	Spanish	E
B.S.	Accounting	E
B.S.	Biology	E
B.S.	Business Administration	E
B.S.	Chemistry	E
B.S.	Computer Information Systems	E
B.S.	Criminal Justice	E
B.S.	Economics	E
B.S.	Mathematics	E
B.S.	Physics	E
B.S.	Science Education	E
B.S.	Substance Abuse	E
B.S.	Technology	E
B.S.W.	Social Work	E
M.S.W.	Social Work	E

Requirements

Residency requirements: At least two semesters (or four summer sessions) at the university, and at least 31 semester hours of credit and 62 quality points in courses passed. Undergraduate admissions requirements: Open admission to applicants who have a high school diploma from an accredited school or GED. Transcripts must be submitted. Graduate admissions requirements: Applicants must have a bachelor's degree (minimum 2.5-3.0 GPA). Other requirements depend on the degree program.
Graduation requirements (undergraduate): Associate degree: minimum 62 semester hours/124 quality points (C average); B.A. degree: minimum 124 semester hours/248 quality points (C average), complete required tests.
Graduation requirements (graduate): Graduates must meet the course requirements for the degree program. A practicum may be required.

Fees, Tuition, Costs

Undergraduate application fee: $5
Graduate application fee: $5
Undergraduate tuition: $831
Graduate tuition: $1,200
Undergraduate cost of books: $375
Graduate cost of books: $500
Other costs: Lab fees

Financial Aid/Status

Scholarship programs for adults: Academic scholarships are based on ACT scores, high school GPA, and high school rank.
Full-time status: Full-time students take a minimum of 12 credit hours.

Percentage of adult students receiving financial aid: 50 percent.

Maximum Hours Awarded For
CLEP: Yes
Other exams: Yes

Features and Services
1. Is it possible to purchase books during hours most adult students attend classes? **Yes.**

2. Are the institution's administrative offices open during hours adult students attend class? **Yes.**

3. How do students taking extended classes access library resources? **Library resources in the area are utilized. Computer access is also used.**

4. What is the registration and payment process for adult students? **Students may pay cash in full or defer up to 40 percent of the student fees until mid-semester.**

5. What is the process for advising adult students? **Advisors and counselors are assigned to all students.**

6. What career and placement services are available to adult students? **All students use the same placement services.**

7. What characteristics of the institution's adult degree programs are most appealing to students? **Variety of courses available, convenient hours, and an excellent group of adjunct evening instructors.**

Southern Utah University
351 W. Center Street ◆ **Cedar City, UT 84720**
Phone: (801) 586-7740 ◆ Fax: (801) 865-8223
E-mail: adminfo@suu.edu ◆ Web address: http://www.suu.edu

Founded: 1897

Accredited by: Northwest Association

Enrollment: 5,160

University status: Public

Degree	Concentration/Major	Format
B.A./B.S.	Elementary Education	T
B.A./B.S.	Business Administration	T

Campus Extension Sites
St. George, UT
Richfield, UT

Requirements
Residency requirement: Students do not have to attend classes on the main campus.
Undergraduate admissions requirements: Students must submit an application, transcripts from high school and all colleges attended, and ACT/SAT scores.
Graduation requirements (undergraduate): Graduates must have minimum of 183 credit hours covering general education requirements as well as meeting specified major/minor requirements.

Fees, Tuition, Costs
Undergraduate application fee: $25
Undergraduate tuition: $1,386/3 quarters
Undergraduate cost of books: $576/year
Other costs: Student fees—$393/yr

Financial Aid/Status
Scholarship programs for adults: Scholarships are available, including Utah tuition and academic scholarships (3.85 GPA; 26+ ACT).
Full-time status: Full-time students attend 12 or more credits per quarter.

Maximum Hours Awarded For
CLEP: 48
Other exams: 48

Features and Services
1. Is it possible to purchase books during hours most adult students attend classes? **Yes.**

2. Are the institution's administrative offices open during hours adult students attend class? **Yes.**

3. How do students taking extended classes access library resources? **The library is open late at night and on weekends. Phone requests for materials are considered.**

4. What is the registration and payment process for adult students? **Registration can be completed in person or** by phone. Payment is made by mail or in person. Credit cards are accepted.

5. What is the process for advising adult students? **The office of Student Development will assist students with advisement.**

6. What career and placement services are available to adult students? **Placement office** provides help with resume preparation, employment interviews, interest testing.

7. What characteristics of the institution's adult degree programs are most appealing to students? **Individualized attention, small class size, and quality education.**

Southern Vermont College*

Bennington, VT 05201 ◆ Phone: (802) 442-5427
Toll-free phone: (800) 378-2782 ◆ Fax: (802) 442-5527

Founded: 1926

Accredited by: New England

Enrollment: 750 ◆ Adult students: 325

University status: Private

Degree	Concentration/Major	Format
A.S.	Accounting	E
A.A.	Child Development	E
A.S.	Business	E
A.S.	Environmental Studies	E
A.S.	Criminal Justice	E
A.S.	Gerontology	E
A.A./A.S.	Liberal Arts	E
A.S.	Nursing (for L.P.N.s)	E
A.S.	Human Services	E
B.S.	Business Management	E
B.S.	Child Care Management	E
B.S.	Communications	E
B.S.	Criminal Justice	E
B.A.	English	E
B.S.	Environmental Studies	E
B.S.	Gerontology Management	E
B.S.	Hospitality/Resort Management	E
B.A./B.S.	Liberal Arts	E
B.S.	Accounting	E
B.S.	Social Work	E
B.S.	Private Security Management	E
B.S.	Nursing for RNs	E

Requirements

Residency requirement: Yes
Undergraduate admissions requirements: Application and fee, high school transcripts, two letters of recommendation, transcripts from previously attended schools

Fees, Tuition, Costs

Undergraduate application fee: $25
Undergraduate tuition: $298/credit

Features and Services

1. Are the institution's administrative offices open during hours adult students attend class? **Yes.**

2. What characteristics of the institution's adult degree programs are most appealing to students? **Evening and Saturday classes, life experience credit for adults, and classes in session from 4 P.M. to 8 P.M.**

Southern Wesleyan University*

CWC Box 497 ◆ **Central, SC 29630**
Phone: (803) 639-2453 ◆ Fax: (803) 639-1956

Founded: 1906

Accredited by: Southern Association

Enrollment: 1,100 ◆ Adult students: 700

University status: Private, Church, Wesleyan Church

Features and Services

1. Is it possible to purchase books during hours most adult students attend classes? **Yes.**

2. What characteristics of the institution's adult degree programs are most appealing to students? **Lock step, one night per week (plus study group).**

Degree	Concentration/Major	Format
A.S.B.	Business	E
B.S.	Management of Human Resources	E,A
B.B.A.	Business	E
B.S.	Elementary Education	E
B.S.	Special Education	E
M.A.	Management of Organizations	E
M.A.	Christian Ministry	E

Requirements

Residential Requirement: Students do not have to attend classes on campus.
Undergraduate admissions requirements: Bachelor's degrees: 60 hours transfer credit, writing proficiency.
Graduate admissions requirements: Bachelor's degree, MAT (or equivalent), 2.7 GPA.

Fees, Tuition, Costs

Undergraduate application fee: $25
Graduate application fee: $25
Undergraduate tuition: $185/credit
Graduate tuition: $225/credit

Financial Aid/Status

Full-time status: Enrolled in a core program
Percentage of adult students receiving financial aid: 70 percent

Maximum Hours Awarded For

CLEP: 30
PEP: 30
DANTES: 30
Other exams: 30
Prior learning portfolio: 30

Southwest Texas State University

San Marcos, TX 78666
Phone: (512) 245-2115 ◆ Fax: (512) 245-3047
E-mail: ssol@swt.edu ◆ Web address: http://www.swt.edu

Founded: 1899

Accredited by: Southern Association

Enrollment: 21,000 ◆ Adult students: 500+

University status: Public

Degree	Concentration/Major	Format
B.A.A.S.	Applied Arts/Sciences	E,C,A
M.S.I.S.	Interdisciplinary Studies	E,A

Campus Extension Site

San Antonio, TX

Requirements

Residency requirement: Students must attend classes on campus for 1/3 of the B.A.A.S. and 1/3 of the master's degree.
Undergraduate admissions requirements: Students must submit an application, all high school or college transcripts, and SAT/ACT scores if required, and meet minimum GPA requirements.
Graduate admissions requirements: Students must have a minimum GPA of 2.75 or meet GPA/GRE requirements.
Graduation requirements (undergraduate): Graduates must earn 128 credit hours; 30 hours must be at SWT.
Graduation requirements (graduate): Graduates must earn 36-45 hours. Up to 6 hours may be in transfer credit.

Fees, Tuition, Costs

Undergraduate application fee: $25
Graduate application fee: $25
Undergraduate tuition: $100/credit
Graduate tuition: $100/credit
Other costs: Normal state fees

Financial Aid/Status

Scholarship programs for adults: Two scholarships specifically for adults are offered. Other scholarships are not earmarked.
Full-time status: Full-time undergraduate status is 12 hours; 9 hours graduate.

Maximum Hours Awarded For

CLEP: Yes
PEP: Yes
DANTES: Yes
Other exams: Yes
Prior learning portfolio: 24

Features and Services

1. Is it possible to purchase books during hours most adult students attend classes? **Yes.**

2. How do students taking extended classes access library resources? **The library may be accessed by computer. The library is open seven days a week.**

3. What is the registration and payment process for adult students? **Registration and payment may be done by phone and mail.**

4. What is the process for advising adult students? **Counselors are available at extended times and locations.**

5. What career and placement services are available to adult students? **Complete career guidance and placement are available.**

6. What characteristics of the institution's adult degree programs are most appealing to students? **Credit for prior learning, individualized plans, and credit by examination.**

Southwestern Adventist College*

Keene, TX 76059

Phone: (817) 645-3921 ◆ Toll-free phone: (800) 433-2240
Fax: (817) 556-4742 ◆ Web address: http://www.swac.edu

Founded: 1893

Accredited by: Southern Association

Enrollment: 970 ◆ Adult students: 220

University status: Private, Church, Seventh-Day Adventist

Features and Services

1. Is it possible to purchase books during hours most adult students attend classes? **Yes.**

2. What characteristics of the institution's adult degree programs are most appealing to students? **Flexibility of study and class time, no on-campus class requirement, videotapes of classes.**

Degree	Concentration/Major	Format
B.A.	Business Administration	S
B.A.	Communication	S
B.A.	Education	S
B.A.	English	S
B.A.	Office Administration	S
B.A.	Office Information Systems	S
B.A.	Psychology	S
B.A.	Religion	S
B.A.	Social Science	S

Requirements

Residency requirement: No, this is a University Without Walls program. There is an outline for the class. There are on-campus and off-campus classes. The course is taken by correspondence with instructor communication. Undergraduate admissions requirements: Application form, high school transcripts, high school diploma or GED, photo, any copies of tests (i.e., SAT, ACT).

Fees, Tuition, Costs

Undergraduate application fee: None
Undergraduate tuition: $251/credit

Financial Aid/Status

Full-time status: 12 hours or more

Maximum Hours Awarded For

CLEP: Yes
Other exams: Yes
Prior learning portfolio: 32

Southwestern College

123 E. 9th ♦ Winfield, KS 67156
Phone: (316) 221-7999 ♦ Toll-free phone: (800) 846-1543
Fax: (316) 221-0808 ♦ E-mail: mali@jinx.sckans.edu
Web address: http://www.sckans.edu/psc
Program's Web address: http://www.sckans.edu

Founded: 1885

Accredited by: North Central

Enrollment: 700 ♦ Adult students: 110

University status: Private, Church, United Methodist Church

Degree	Concentration/Major	Format
B.S.	Manufacturing Technology	E,A
B.S.	Business Quality Management	E,A
B.A.	Organizational Resource Management	E,A

Campus Extension Sites

Winfield, KS
Wichita, KS

Requirements

Residency requirement: Students are not required to attend classes on the main campus. Undergraduate admissions requirements: Applicants must have a minimum of 48 transferable hours; GPA greater than 2.0; general education requirements completed in Composition I & II, algebra, and science.
Graduation requirements (undergraduate): Students must complete 124 total hours: 60 hours from a four-year college; 30 hours from Southwestern College; 2.0 GPA.

Fees, Tuition, Costs

Undergraduate application fee: None
Undergraduate tuition: $150-$170/credit hour
Undergraduate cost of books: $70

Financial Aid/Status

Full-time status: 12 hours fall and spring; 6 hours summer
Percentage of adult students receiving financial aid: 30 percent

Maximum Hours Awarded For

Prior learning portfolio: 30

Features and Services

1. Is it possible to purchase books during hours most adult students attend classes? **Yes.**

2. Are the institution's administrative offices open during hours adult students attend class? **Yes.**

3. How do students taking extended classes access library resources? **Students may use the library on campus or the Internet.**

4. What is the registration and payment process for adult students? **Registration forms are completed to enroll in class. Payment by company voucher for each class.**

5. What is the process for advising adult students? **Two full-time staff advisors work with students.**

6. What characteristics of the institution's adult degree programs are most appealing to students? **Evening classes, flexible schedule, and off campus for all student needs; a one-center, one-process system.**

Spaulding University

851 S. Fourth Street ◆ **Louisville, KY 40203**
Phone: (502) 585-7115 ◆ Toll-free phone: (800) 896-8941
Fax: (502) 585-7158

Founded: 1814

Accredited by: Southern Association

Enrollment: 1,342 ◆ Adult students: 64 percent

University status: Private, Church, Roman Catholic Church

Degree	Concentration/Major	Format
B.S.	Business Administration	E
B.S.	Communication	E
B.A.	Liberal Arts	E
B.S.N.	RN to B.S.N.	E
B.A.	Psychology	E

Campus Extension Site

Bardstown, KY

Requirements

Residency requirement: Students must attend class on campus. Students may complete degrees by attending classes only on weekends. Undergraduate admissions requirements: Weekend College has a flexible admission policy. To apply a student has an interview, completes math and writing placement tests, and submits high school/any college transcripts and an application.
Graduation requirements (undergraduate): B.A. graduates must earn 128 semester hours; minimum 2.0 GPA. A.S. graduates must earn 63 semester hours; 2.0 GPA.

Fees, Tuition, Costs

Undergraduate application fee: $20
Undergraduate tuition: $300/credit hour

Financial Aid/Status

Scholarship programs for adults: All students, whether traditional age or adult, are eligible to apply for scholarships.
Full-time status: Weekend College students are full-time if enrolled for 9 hours each term (27 hours per year).
Percentage of adult students receiving financial aid: 47 percent.

Maximum Hours Awarded For

CLEP: 30
PEP: Yes
Other exams: 30
Prior learning portfolio: 60
Additional information: Portfolio development—30 hours. No more than 60 credit hours required for graduation are awarded for extra-institutional or experiential learning.

Features and Services

1. Is it possible to purchase books during hours most adult students attend classes? **Yes.**

2. Are the institution's administrative offices open during hours adult students attend class? **Yes.**

3. How do students taking extended classes access library resources? **The library is open additional hours on Weekend College weekends.**

4. What is the registration and payment process for adult students? **Registration and payment may be handled by phone, mail, or in person.**

5. What is the process for advising adult students? **Each student has an academic advisor, who can be reached by phone or in person.**

6. What career and placement services are available to adult students? **Services are available through the office of Career Planning and Placement.**

7. What characteristics of the institution's adult degree programs are most appealing to students? **Getting an entire degree on weekends; classes do not meet every weekend or for a full day; the entire program is geared to working adults.**

Spring Arbor College

106 E. Main Street ◆ **Spring Arbor, MI 49283**
Phone: (517) 750-6343 ◆ Toll-free phone: (800) 968-9103
Fax: (517) 750-6602 ◆ E-mail: gianetti@admin.cougar.edu
Web address: http://www.arbor.edu

Founded: 1873

Accredited by: North Central

Enrollment: 2,247 ◆ Adult students: 1,584

University status: Private, Church, Free Methodist Church

Degree	Concentration/Major	Format
B.A.	Business Administration	E
B.A.	Management and Organizational Development	E,A
B.A.	Management of Health Services	E,A
B.A.	Family Life Education	E,A
B.A.	Management of Health Promotions	E,A

Campus Extension Sites

Jackson, MI
Troy, MI
Lambertville, MI
Flint, MI
Dearborn, MI
Port Huron, MI
Detroit, MI
Bay City, MI
Lansing, MI
Traverse City, MI
Battle Creek, MI
Grand Rapids, MI
Gaylord, MI

Requirements

Residency requirement: All classes are held at the extended campus locations.
Undergraduate admissions requirements: Applicants must have 60 semester hours of transferable credit and pass a writing evaluation.

Fees, Tuition, Costs

Undergraduate application fee: $15
Undergraduate tuition: $8,550
(1995-96 year only)
Undergraduate cost of books: $700 average
Other costs: Prior learning credit (portfolio) up to $400, depending on credits requested

Financial Aid/Status

Full-time status: Anyone carrying 12 semester credits per 15 weeks has full-time status.
Percentage of adult students receiving financial aid: 80 percent.

Maximum Hours Awarded For

CLEP: 60
DANTES: 60
Prior learning portfolio: 30
Additional information: TECEP-60; total of 60 combined credits allowed for any testing

Features and Services

1. Is it possible to purchase books during hours most adult students attend classes? **Yes.**

2. How do students taking extended classes access library resources? **The library may be accessed by computer and modem or phone.**

3. What is the registration and payment process for adult students? **Registration takes place where classes are held. Payment can be spread out over the program.**

4. What is the process for advising adult students? **Advisors are available at the site. Cohort groups have two counselors assigned to them.**

5. What career and placement services are available to adult students? **Career and placement services are very limited.**

6. What characteristics of the institution's adult degree programs are most appealing to students? **Accelerated format, cohort groups, locations close to students, evening class meetings one night each week, and convenient registration.**

State University of New York College at Potsdam

Raymond Hall 206 ◆ 44 Pierrepont Avenue
Potsdam, NY 13676
Phone: (315) 267-2166 ◆ Toll-free phone: (800) 458-1142
Fax: (315) 267-3088 ◆ E-mail: zelinscg@potsdam.edu
Web address: http://www.potsdam.edu/

Founded: 1816

Accredited by: Middle States

Enrollment: 4,000 ◆ Adult students: 849

University status: Public

Degree   Concentration/Major   Format

Degrees not specified.

Requirements

Residency requirement: Students must attend classes on campus. Many degrees require experiential segments. Home faculty wish to supervise these segments as well as teaching methods courses. Undergraduate admissions requirements: Nontraditional students are admitted based on current potential, not high school records/test scores. Applicants must have a high school diploma or the equivalent. Official transcripts are needed.
Graduate admissions requirements: Applicants must hold a bachelor's degree. Other requirements vary with the degree program.
Graduation requirements (undergraduate): Students must earn 120-124 semester hours for the bachelor's degree and complete the degree program.
Graduation requirements (graduate): Graduates must

satisfactorily complete the degree program.

Fees, Tuition, Costs

Undergraduate application fee: $30
Graduate application fee: $50
Undergraduate tuition: $137/credit hour
Graduate tuition: $213/credit hour
Undergraduate cost of books: $250-$300/semester
Graduate cost of books: $300-$350/semester

Financial Aid/Status

Scholarship programs for adults: Scholarships available
Full-time status: 12 credit hours/semester
Percentage of adult students receiving financial aid: 80 percent

Maximum Hours Awarded For

CLEP: Unlimited

DANTES: Unlimited
Other exams: Limited
Prior learning portfolio: Yes
Additional information: Correspondence courses, ACE credits (MOS), and DANTES-subject

Features and Services

1. Is it possible to purchase books during hours most adult students attend classes? **Yes.**

2. How do students taking extended classes access library resources? **The library may be accessed by links with services.**

3. What is the registration and payment process for adult students? **Payment may be done by credit card or three-time payment plan.**

4. What is the process for advising adult students? **Transfer counselor, adult counselor, and faculty members are available.**

5. What career and placement services are available to adult students? **The office of career services is open days and evenings by appointment for students and the community.**

6. What characteristics of the institution's adult degree programs are most appealing to students? **Individualized, personal service to support adults; a total evening degree will be offered** *soon*; **student can use the Internet somewhat.**

Stephens College

Campus Box 2083 ◆ School of Continuing Education
Columbia, MO 65215
Phone: (573) 876-7125 ◆ Toll-free phone: (800) 388-7579
Fax: (573) 876-7248 ◆ E-mail: sce@womenscol.stephens.edu
Web address: http://www.stephens.edu

Founded: 1833 ◆ Accredited by: North Central

Enrollment: 1,000 ◆ Adult students: 30 percent

University status: Private

Degree	Concentration/Major	Format
B.A.	Business Administration	E,C
B.S.	Marketing—Public Relations/Advertising	E
B.A.	Psychology	C
B.S.	Early Childhood/Elementary Education	C
B.S.	Health Information Management	C
B.A.	Philosophy, Law, and Rhetoric	C
B.A.	English	C
B.A.	Health Care/2nd area (build on previous RN training)	C
B.A.	Health Science/2nd area (build on allied health training)	C
B.A./B.S.	Student-initiated major (combine two disciplines available)	C

Requirements

Residency requirement: External degree students must take an introductory course on the campus. A C or better must be earned to enter the program. The course is offered many times a year in seven-day or double-weekend format.

Undergraduate admissions requirements: Students must provide an application, official transcripts from high school/GED, professional programs, and any accredited institutions attended, and standardized test scores. TOEFL score, if needed. Graduation requirements (undergraduate): Minimum 120 semester hours; communication skills; lower- and upper-level general education area; major requirements; 12 upper-level courses; minimum GPA-2.0; 36 hours taken with Stephens.

Fees, Tuition, Costs

Undergraduate application fee: $50
Undergraduate tuition: $650/3 semester hours
Undergraduate cost of books: Varies
Other costs: Travel and room and board for external degree students who come to campus for introductory course

Financial Aid/Status

Full-time status: Weekend College students enroll in three 3-semester-hour courses per 10-week term.
Percentage of adult students receiving financial aid: Available to Weekend College students only.

Maximum Hours Awarded For

CLEP: 30
PEP: Yes
DANTES: Yes
Other exams: Yes
Prior learning portfolio: 30
Additional information: American Council on Education evaluated credit

Features and Services

1. Is it possible to purchase books during hours most adult students attend classes? **Yes.**

2. How do students taking extended classes access library resources? **Library services by mail, phone, interlibrary loan, and local libraries.**

3. What is the registration and payment process for adult students? **Students are billed up-front. Tuition may be paid by credit card or on a monthly payment plan.**

4. What is the process for advising adult students? **Each student has an advisor who helps plan the degree program and guides the student through the program.**

5. What career and placement services are available to adult students? **The Career Services office is available to local and long-distance students.**

6. What characteristics of the institution's adult degree programs are most appealing to students? **Individualized advising and attention, collaborative faculty, one office registration, small classes, peer mentors, and academic support services.**

Strayer College

1025 15th Street, N.W. ◆ **Washington, DC 20005**
Phone: (202) 408-2400 ◆ Fax: (202) 289-1831
Web address: http://www.strayer.edu

Founded: 1892 ◆ Accredited by: Middle States

Enrollment: 7,419 ◆ Adult students: 78 percent

University status: Private, Profit

Degree	Concentration/Major	Format
A.A.	Accounting	E
A.A.	Business Administration	E
A.A.	Computer Information Systems	E
A.A.	Economics	E
A.A.	General Studies	E
A.A.	Marketing	E
B.S.	Accounting	E
B.S.	Business Administration	E
B.S.	Computer Information Systems	E
B.S.	Economics	E
M.S.	Professional Accounting	E
M.S.	Business Administration	E
M.S.	Information Systems	E

Campus Extension Sites

Alexandria, VA
Manassas, VA
Arlington, VA
Washington, DC
Fredericksburg, VA
Woodbridge, VA
Ashburn, VA
Fort Belvoir, VA
Quantico, VA
Dahlgren, VA
Falls Church, VA

Requirements

Residency requirement: Students must declare a "home campus" for registration and advisement purposes. They are free to attend classes at any Strayer branch campus in order to complete the necessary degree requirements. Undergraduate admissions requirements: Certificate of high school graduation/GED; math/English skills proved by SAT 400 or more, college-level transfer credit in each subject, or score on Strayer's math and/or English placement exams.

Graduate admissions requirements: College transcripts for each undergraduate/graduate institution attended; one of the following: GMAT of 450, GRE of 1000, 2.75 cumulative GPA, or demonstrated evidence of graduate potential. Graduation requirements (undergraduate): Students must complete all courses in their major area with a grade of C or better. A minimum 2.0 GPA is required for all degree course requirements. Graduation requirements (graduate): Students must complete at least 54 quarter hours with a 3.0 GPA and meet specified graduation requirements.

Fees, Tuition, Costs

Undergraduate application fee: $25
Graduate application fee: $25
Undergraduate tuition: $160-$170/credit hour
Graduate tuition: $230/credit hour
Undergraduate cost of books: $65/course
Graduate cost of books: $65/course

Financial Aid/Status

Scholarship programs for adults: Scholarships available
Full-time status: 13.5 quarter hour credits (three classes per quarter); graduate—9 hours (two classes)

Maximum Hours Awarded For

CLEP: Yes
DANTES: Yes
Other exams: Yes
Prior learning portfolio: Yes
Additional information: Military service school credits; credits not to exceed 63 quarter credit for A.A. degree or 126 for bachelor's

Features and Services

1. Is it possible to purchase books during hours most adult students attend classes? **Varies by campus. Many have extended hours during first week of quarter and have weekend hours.**

2. Are the institution's administrative offices open during hours adult students attend class? **Varies by campus. All have extended hours during registration and first week of classes. Some have weekend hours.**

3. How do students taking extended classes access library resources? **Learning Resource Center open during scheduled class hours at branch. Main campus library available.**

4. What is the registration and payment process for adult students? **Registration for continuing students is by phone. Payment and first-time registration are in person.**

5. What is the process for advising adult students? **Students are assigned academic advisors and meet once a quarter to register and as needed.**

6. What career and placement services are available to adult students? **Career Development offices on each campus offer free help. Alumni may participate in this service.**

7. What characteristics of the institution's adult degree programs are most appealing to students? **Degree completion available through day, evening, weekend classes attended at most convenient location, and fast, convenient phone registration.**

Suffolk University*

8 Ashburton Place ◆ **Boston, MA 02108**

Phone: (617) 573-8070 ◆ Toll-free phone: (800) 6SUFFOLK
Fax: (617) 742-4291 ◆ Web address: http://www.suffolk.edu

Founded: 1906 ◆ Accredited by: New England

Enrollment: 6,600 ◆ Adult students: 6,600

University status: Private

Degree	Concentration/Major	Format
M.B.A.	Business Administration	E,A
M.P.A.	Public Administration	E,A
M.S.F.	Finance	E
M.S.A.	Accounting	E
M.S.T.	Taxation	E
M.S.I.E.	International Economics	E
M.C.	Communications	E
M.S.	Human Resource Development	E
M.S.	Business Education	E
M.S.	Adult/Continuing Education	E
M.Ed.	Higher Education Administration	E
M.Ed.	School Counseling	E
M.Ed.	Foundations of Education	E
M.Ed.	Mental Health Counseling	E
M.S.	Business Education	E
M.S.	Political Science	E
M.Ed.	School Counseling	E

Requirements

Residency requirement: Yes
Graduate admissions requirements: Varies by program

Fees, Tuition, Costs

Graduate application fee: Varies by program
Undergraduate tuition: $12,046 (1996-97)

Graduate tuition: Varies by program

Financial Aid/Status

Full-time status: Four or more courses per term
Percentage of adult students receiving financial aid: 91 percent

Features and Services

1. Is it possible to purchase books during hours most adult students attend classes? **Yes.**

2. Are the institution's administrative offices open during hours adult students attend class? **Yes.**

3. What characteristics of the institution's adult degree programs are most appealing to students? **Convenience of location, cost, flexibility (can take courses day or evening), all classes taught by professors/faculty.**

Syracuse University

610 Fayette Street
Continuing Education and Summer Sessions
Syracuse, NY 13244-6020
Phone: (315) 443-3273 ◆ Fax: (315) 443-4174
E-mail: parttime@uc.syr.edu ◆ Web address: http://www.syr.edu

Founded: 1870 ◆ Accredited by: Middle States

Enrollment: 15,000 ◆ Adult students: 20 percent

University status: Private

Maximum Hours Awarded For

CLEP: Yes
DANTES: Yes
Other exams: Yes
Additional information: Regents College Exam, College Board Advanced Placement Exams, International Baccalaureate Course Equivalency, Credit, Military Service, Academic Credit

Degree	Concentration/Major	Format
B.A.	English	E
B.A.	Psychology	E
B.A.	Political Science	E
B.S.	Engineering and Computer Science	E
B.S.	Human Development/Child and Family Studies	E
B.S.	Information Studies	E
B.S.	Management	E
B.S.	Nursing	E
B.S.	Social Work	E
B.S.	Visual and Performing Arts/Speech Communications	E
M.S.	Education	E
M.S.	Engineering and Computer Science	E
M.S.	Information Studies	E
M.L.S.	Information Studies/Library Science	E
M.B.A.	Management/Business Administration	E
M.S.	Social Work	E

Requirements

Undergraduate admissions requirements: Admissions requirements vary by the program. Graduate admissions requirements: Admissions requirements vary by the program. Graduation requirements (undergraduate): Graduation requirements vary by the program. Graduation requirements (graduate): Graduation requirements vary by the program.

Fees, Tuition, Costs

Undergraduate application fee: $40
Graduate application fee: $40
Undergraduate tuition: $305/credit hour

Graduate tuition: $503/credit hour
Undergraduate cost of books: $150/course
Graduate cost of books: $150/course
Other costs: Travel and online computer access

Financial Aid/Status

Scholarship programs for adults: Scholarships are available.
Full-time status: Undergraduate students must carry 12 credit hours per term.
Percentage of adult students receiving financial aid: 15 percent.

Features and Services

1. Is it possible to purchase books during hours most adult students attend classes? **Yes.**

2. Are the institution's administrative offices open during hours adult students attend class? **Yes.**

3. How do students taking extended classes access library resources? **The library closes at midnight. It is open on weekends. Online access is available.**

4. What is the registration and payment process for adult students? **Students may register by mail or in person.**

5. What is the process for advising adult students? **Advising is available 8:30 A.M.-8:00 P.M. Monday through Thursday; 8:30 A.M.-5:00 P.M. Friday.**

6. What career and placement services are available to adult students? **Students have access to the University Career Services Center.**

7. What characteristics of the institution's adult degree programs are most appealing to students? **Flexibility, discounted tuition, and access to all university resources and degree programs.**

Tabor College of Wichita

8100 E. 22nd N. ◆ Tallgrass Executive Park
Wichita, KS 67226
Phone: (316) 681-8616 ◆ Toll-free phone: (800) 546-8616
Fax: (316) 689-0996

Founded: 1908

Accredited by: North Central

Enrollment: 100 ◆ Adult students: 100 percent

University status: Private, Church, Mennonite Brethren Church

Degree	Concentration/Major	Format
B.A.	Management	E,A

Requirements

Residency requirement: Students are not required to attend classes on campus.
Undergraduate admissions requirements: Applicants must have 60 transferable hours and be approved by the college administration. A writing sample and all admissions forms need to be completed.
Graduation requirements (undergraduate): Students must complete 124 required hours to graduate from the program. Students must have a C or above to receive credit for management classes.

Fees, Tuition, Costs

Undergraduate application fee: $10
Undergraduate tuition: $8,500-$9,000
Undergraduate cost of books: Included in tuition cost

Financial Aid/Status

Full-time status: Students in this program are considered part-time for federal grants.
Percentage of adult students receiving financial aid: 90 percent.

Maximum Hours Awarded For

CLEP: Yes
DANTES: Yes
Other exams: Yes
Prior learning portfolio: Yes

Features and Services

1. Is it possible to purchase books during hours most adult students attend classes? **Yes.**

2. How do students taking extended classes access library resources? **Students use the Wichita state library.**

3. What is the registration and payment process for adult students? **Registration and payment are completed by the office staff and students before the first night of class.**

4. What is the process for advising adult students? **Students receive advising before they enter the program and during the time in the program.**

5. What characteristics of the institution's adult degree programs are most appealing to students? **Quality education, Christian environment, excellent faculty, and low professor-to-student ratio.**

Teikyo Marycrest University

1607 W. 12th Street ◆ **Davenport, IA 52804**
Phone: (319) 326-9562 ◆ Toll-free phone: (800) 728-9705
Fax: (319) 326-9356 ◆ E-mail: venhourst@tmu1.mcrest.edu
Web address: http://geraldine.mcrest.edu

Founded: 1939

Accredited by: North Central

Enrollment: 1,052 ◆ Adult students: 526

University status: Private

Degree	Concentration/Major	Format
B.A.	Business Administration	E,A
B.S.N.	Nursing degree for RNs	E,T
B.A.	Social and Behavioral Science	E,A
B.A.	Psychology	E,A
M.S.	Computer Science	E
M.A.	Education	E

Requirements

Residency requirement: Some classes (nursing) are televised to Clinton, Muscatine, and Ottumwa, Iowa.
Undergraduate admissions requirements: Applicants must submit an admissions application and transcripts of all colleges attended. Students need at least a 2.3 GPA on a 4.0 scale.
Graduate admissions requirements: Applicants must provide evidence of a baccalaureate degree (minimum 2.8 GPA on 4.0 scale) and three letters of recommendation.
Graduation requirements (undergraduate): Students must complete at least 124 semester hours for B.A./B.S., including general education and major.
Graduation requirements (graduate): Students must complete specific requirements with a minimum cumulative GPA of 3.0, with no grade below C, earn 30-36 semester hours, and complete a comprehensive exam or thesis if required.

Fees, Tuition, Costs

Undergraduate application fee: $25
Graduate application fee: $25
Undergraduate tuition: $345/semester hour
Graduate tuition: $360/semester hour
Undergraduate cost of books: $250/semester
Graduate cost of books: $300/semester
Other costs: Computer recommended but not required

Financial Aid/Status

Scholarship programs for adults: Students must apply for scholarships. Students should check with the admissions office for more information.
Full-time status: Full-time is a minimum of 12 semester hours completed between Jan. 1 and June 30 or July 1 and Dec. 31.
Percentage of adult students receiving financial aid: 25 percent.

Maximum Hours Awarded For

CLEP: 30
DANTES: 30
Prior learning portfolio: 30

Features and Services

1. Is it possible to purchase books during hours most adult students attend classes? **Yes.**

2. Are the institution's administrative offices open during hours adult students attend class? **Yes.**

3. How do students taking extended classes access library resources? **Students may access the library through library loan.**

4. What is the registration and payment process for adult students? **Registration and payment must be completed before the first class.**

5. What is the process for advising adult students? **The faculty serve as advisors.**

6. What career and placement services are available to adult students? **A placement office is available.**

7. What characteristics of the institution's adult degree programs are most appealing to students? **Reduced time format.**

Tennessee Wesleyan College

P.O. Box 40 ◆ **Athens, TN 37303**
Phone: (423) 745-7504 ◆ Toll-free phone: (800) PICK TWC
Fax: (423) 744-9968

Founded: 1857

Accredited by: Southern Association

Enrollment: 633 ◆ Adult students: 241

University status: Private, Church, United Methodist Church

Degree	Concentration/Major	Format
B.S.	Business Administration—General Management	E,A
B.S.	Business Administration—Human Resource Management	E
B.S.	Business Administration—Computer Information Systems	E
B.S.	Business Administration—Accounting	E
B.S.	Business Administration—Economics/Finance	E
B.A.S.	Business Administration—General Management	E,A
B.A.S.	Business Administration—Health Care Management	E,A
B.A.S.	Business—Human Resource Management	E
B.A.S.	Business Administration—Computer Information	E
B.A.S.	Business Administration—Economics/Finance	E
B.A.S.	Business Administration—Accounting	E

Campus Extension Sites
Knoxville, TN
Oak Ridge, TN
Chattanooga, TN
Cleveland, TN

Requirements
Residency requirement: Students are not required to attend classes on campus. Graduation ceremonies are jointly held in the spring on the Athens campus.
Undergraduate admissions requirements: Applicants must have a minimum of 60 semester hours or an associate degree from an accredited institution with a 2.0 GPA.
Graduation requirements (undergraduate): Students must complete 128 semester hours with 2.0 minimum GPA; the TWC/major/core requirements, and the last 30 hours in residency; and pass the English proficiency requirement.

Fees, Tuition, Costs
Undergraduate application fee: $25
Undergraduate tuition: $175/credit hour
Undergraduate cost of books: $225/semester

Financial Aid/Status
Full-time status: 12 semester hours
Percentage of adult students receiving financial aid: 85 percent

Maximum Hours Awarded For
CLEP: 12
Other exams: 12
Additional information: Advanced Placement; maximum of 12 semester hours allowed for all combined

Features and Services
1. Is it possible to purchase books during hours most adult students attend classes? **Yes.**

2. How do students taking extended classes access library resources? **Students may use library resources through an agreement with colleges in off-campus sites.**

3. What is the registration and payment process for adult students? **Registration is on-site. Payment: full cash or credit card, three equal payments, employer reimbursement.**

4. What is the process for advising adult students? **Site coordinators are available for advising.**

5. What career and placement services are available to adult students? **Students use the main campus career placement services, and a college fair provides access to prospective employers.**

6. What characteristics of the institution's adult degree programs are most appealing to students? **Accelerated program, traditional curriculum, quality and institutional reputation, and convenience of branch campus location.**

Texas Christian University

TCU Box 297026 ◆ Fort Worth, TX 76129
Phone: (817) 921-7130 ◆ Toll-free phone: (800) 828-7134
Fax: (817) 921-7134 ◆ Web address: http://www.tcu.edu

Founded: 1869

Accredited by: Southern Association

Enrollment: 6,500 ◆ Adult students: 10-14 percent

University status: Private, Church,
Christian Church–Disciples of Christ

Degree	Concentration/Major	Format
B.G.S.	General Studies	E

Requirements

Residency requirement: Students must attend classes on campus. Undergraduate admissions requirements: Applicants must be at least 23 years old. Students must not have been enrolled as a full-time student at an institution within two years of entering the program.
Graduation requirements (undergraduate): Students complete 124 semester hours; at least 45 hours at TCU; 36 upper-level hours; last 30 hours taken at TCU, and meet curriculum requirements. Degree plan developed after completing 60 hours.

Fees, Tuition, Costs

Undergraduate tuition: $300/hour

Financial Aid/Status

Scholarship programs for adults: Scholarships are available.

Maximum Hours Awarded For

CLEP: Yes
Prior learning portfolio: 18

Features and Services

1. Is it possible to purchase books during hours most adult students attend classes? **Yes.**

2. Are the institution's administrative offices open during hours adult students attend class? **Yes.**

3. What is the registration and payment process for adult students? **Registration and payment are the same for all students.**

4. What is the process for advising adult students? **Advising is the same for all students.**

5. What career and placement services are available to adult students? **Placement and career services are the same for all students.**

6. What characteristics of the institution's adult degree programs are most appealing to students? **Wider variety of courses accepted.**

Texas Tech University

Box 45005 ◆ Office of New Student Relations
Lubbock, TX 79409-5005
Phone: (806) 742-1480 ◆ Fax: (806) 742-0980
Web address: http://www.ttu.edu/

Founded: 1923

Accredited by: Southern Association

Enrollment: 24,185

University status: Public

Degree   Concentration/Major   Format

A wide variety of degrees and courses are available through the Seniors' Academy. This is a program especially designed for adults over 55 who want to take classes to earn a degree or for personal enrichment. Seniors' Academy provides special services to support the educational efforts of older students.

Requirements

Undergraduate admissions requirements: Seniors' Academy: Flexible entrance procedures—no transcripts, SAT/ACT scores. Transfer of credits of D if approved by academic dean. Information available through Texas Tech Visitor Center.
Graduate admissions requirements: Formal application, college transcripts, GRE or GMAT score. Students should contact the appropriate department for admissions requirements for a specific degree.
Graduation requirements (undergraduate): Graduates must meet requirements of the university, the college, and the particular degree program.
Graduation requirements (graduate): Varies by degree

Fees, Tuition, Costs

Undergraduate application fee: $25
Graduate application fee: $25
Undergraduate tuition: $2,200/year in-state; $7,960 out-of-state
Graduate tuition: $2,264/year in-state; $6,872 out-of-state
Undergraduate cost of books: $350
Graduate cost of books: $250

Financial Aid/Status

Scholarship programs for adults: Yes
Full-time status: 12 or more hours/semester

Maximum Hours Awarded For

CLEP: Yes
Other exams: Yes
Additional information: Acceptable hours from two-year college for up to 1/2 of total hours for degree program; maximum of 66 hours

Features and Services

1. Is it possible to purchase books during hours most adult students attend classes? **Yes.**

2. Are the institution's administrative offices open during hours adult students attend class? **Yes.**

3. How do students taking extended classes access library resources? **The library can be accessed through various online services and interlibrary loan.**

4. What is the registration and payment process for adult students? **Simplified registration is available for the Seniors' Academy.**

5. What is the process for advising adult students? **Orientation, counseling by adult learning experts, academic counseling, and tutoring**

6. What career and placement services are available to adult students? **Career planning and placement center provides services to all students.**

Thiel College

75 College Avenue ◆ **Greenville, PA 16125**
Phone: (412) 589-2215 ◆ Toll-free phone: (800) 588-4435
Fax: (412) 589-2021

Founded: 1866

Accredited by: Middle States

Enrollment: 1,025 ◆ Adult students: 25 percent

University status: Private, Church, E.I.C.A. Lutheran Church

Degree	Concentration/Major	Format
A.A.	Accounting	E
B.A.	Accounting	E
B.A.	Business Administration	E

Requirements

Residency requirement: Not all classes are offered at off-campus sites. These classes must be taken on campus.
Undergraduate admissions requirements: Applicants must have a 2.0 high school GPA.
Graduation requirements (undergraduate): Graduates must earn 124 credit hours with approximately 1/3 in integrative subjects, 1/3 in major, and 1/3 electives.

Fees, Tuition, Costs

Undergraduate application fee: $25
Undergraduate tuition: $186/credit hour
Undergraduate cost of books: $150-$200

Financial Aid/Status

Scholarship programs for adults: Requirements vary. Students are required to be admitted to the college and taking at least 6 credit hours.
Full-time status: Full-time students are matriculated and taking 12 or more credit hours.

Maximum Hours Awarded For

CLEP: 30
Prior learning portfolio: 30

Features and Services

1. Is it possible to purchase books during hours most adult students attend classes? **Yes.**

2. Are the institution's administrative offices open during hours adult students attend class? **The college provides special services for adult students.**

3. How do students taking extended classes access library resources? **Students use the college library and other area libraries.**

4. What is the registration and payment process for adult students? **Registration and payment may be done through the mail.**

5. What is the process for advising adult students? **Advising is available by appointment with Lifelong Learning Center staff, over the phone, and at class site.**

6. What career and placement services are available to adult students? **Students may use the services at the college.**

7. What characteristics of the institution's adult degree programs are most appealing to students? **Staff continually monitor students' progress for their class and course needs to try to offer what students need—when they need it, and where they need it.**

Thomas Edison State College

101 W. State Street ◆ Trenton, NJ 08608-1176
Phone: (609) 633-6472 ◆ Fax: (609) 984-8447
E-mail: info@call.tesc.edu ◆ Web address: http://www.tesc.edu

Founded: 1972

Accredited by: Middle States

Enrollment: 8,549 ◆ Adult students: 100 percent

University status: Public

Percentage of adult students receiving financial aid: 1 percent

Maximum Hours Awarded For

CLEP: Yes
PEP: Yes
DANTES: Yes
Other exams: Yes
Prior learning portfolio: Yes
Additional information: Portfolio Assessment; Guided Study

Features and Services

1. What is the registration and payment process for adult students? **Enrollment is continual. Students may mail applications and pay by cash, check, or credit card.**

2. What is the process for advising adult students? **Each student is assigned an advisor. Appointments may be handled in person or by phone.**

3. What characteristics of the institution's adult degree programs are most appealing to students? **Students work at their pace, flexible—no time or location barriers, many ways to earn degrees, and large number of degree programs and specializations.**

Degree	Concentration/Major	Format
A.S.M.	Data Processing, Banking, and others	E,V,C,T,CT,S
A.A.	Liberal Arts	E,V,C,T,CT,S
A.S.N.S.M.	Biology, Computer Science, and others	E,V,C,T,CT,S
A.S.A.S.T.	Forestry, Environmental Studies, and others	E,V,C,T,CT,S
A.A.S.R.T.	Radilogic Technology	E,V,C,T,CT,S
A.S.P.S.S.	Social Services, Recreation Services, and others	E,V,C,T,CT,S
B.A.	American Studies, Anthropology, Art, and others	E,V,C,T,CT,S
B.S.B.A.	Accounting, Chemistry, and others	E,V,C,T,CT,S
B.S.A.S.T.	Horticulture, Engineering Graphics, and others	E,V,C,T,CT,S
B.S.H.S.	Community Services, Legal Services, and others	E,V,C,T,CT,S
B.S.N.	Nursing	E,V,C,T,CT,S
M.S.M.	Management	E,V,C,T,CT,S

Requirements

Residency requirement: Students are not required to attend classes on campus. Credits can be earned through a variety of methods and can be transferred to the college. Undergraduate admissions requirements: Students must complete an application form and provide official documentation of all degrees, certificates, college-level exams, and any other courses earned.
Graduate admissions requirements: Contact Director of Graduate Studies, Master of Science in Management.

Graduation requirements (undergraduate): Graduates must complete the degree. All fees must be paid in full.

Fees, Tuition, Costs

Undergraduate application fee: $75
Undergraduate tuition: $490/year in-state; $843/year out-of-state
Other costs: Fees associated with credit options pursued and credit transfer evaluation

Financial Aid/Status

Full-time status: A student who is taking at least 12 or more approved credits per semester

Thomas More College

333 Thomas More Parkway ◆ **Crestview Hills, KY 41017**
Phone: (606) 344-3333 ◆ Fax: (606) 344-3345
E-mail: emeryj@thomasmore.edu
Web address: http://www.thomasmore.edu/welcome.html

Founded: 1921

Accredited by: Southern Association

Enrollment: 1,300 ◆ Adult students: 40 percent

University status: Private, Church, Roman Catholic Church

Degree / Concentration/Major / Format

Degree	Concentration/Major	Format
A.A.	Accounting	E
A.A.	Business Administration	E,A
A.A.	Computer Information Systems	E
A.A.	Sociology	E
A.A.	Theology	E
A.A.	Individualized Program	E
A.A.	Microcomputer Applications Systems	E
B.A.	Accounting	E
B.A.	Business Administration	E,A
B.A.	Computer Information Systems	E
B.A.	Sociology	E
B.A.	Theology	E
B.A.	Individualized Program	E

Requirements

Residency requirement: Thomas More has a residency requirement of 38 credits.
Undergraduate admissions requirements: Applicants need a high school average of 80 or above, or GED in top 50 percent, or 2.0 GPA or above for previous college work. An essay and an interview are required. Conditional admission may be given.
Graduation requirements (undergraduate): Graduates must earn 128 credits with 2.0 GPA.

Fees, Tuition, Costs

Undergraduate application fee: None
Undergraduate tuition: $268/credit

Financial Aid/Status

Scholarship programs for adults: Academic scholarships are available to part-time adults who have completed 12 credits with 3.5 or better. Awards of $1,000 per year are also given.
Full-time status: 12 or more credits.

Maximum Hours Awarded For

CLEP: Yes
Other exams: Yes
Prior learning portfolio: 32

Features and Services

1. Is it possible to purchase books during hours most adult students attend classes? **Yes.**

2. Are the institution's administrative offices open during hours adult students attend class? **Yes.**

3. What is the registration and payment process for adult students? **Registration and payment are made by mail, phone, fax, or in person; tuition deferment offered for employer tuition reimbursement.**

4. What is the process for advising adult students? **Advising is available through continuing education and/or faculty advisors.**

5. What characteristics of the institution's adult degree programs are most appealing to students? **Courses available in evening format, services of continuing education, individual attention, and 13:1 student:faculty ratio.**

Tougaloo College

500 W. County Line Road ◆ Tougaloo, MS 39174
Phone: (601) 977-6157

Founded: 1869

Accredited by: Southern Association

Enrollment: 974 ◆ Adult students: 6 percent

University status: Private, Church, United Church of Christ

Degree	Concentration/Major	Format
A.A.	Early Childhood Education	E

Requirements

Residency requirement: Some courses can be taken off campus. Undergraduate admissions requirements: Applicants must submit proof of high school completion with minimum 2.0 GPA. Any college transcripts should be submitted if applicable. Graduation requirements (undergraduate): Graduates must complete the requirements for the major.

Fees, Tuition, Costs

Undergraduate tuition: $8,484/ year for tuition and room and board.
Undergraduate cost of books: $500

Financial Aid/Status

Scholarship programs for adults: Scholarships are not available. Adults receive reduced tuition. Full-time status: 12 hours.

Maximum Hours Awarded For

CLEP: Yes
Other exams: Yes

Features and Services

1. Is it possible to purchase books during hours most adult students attend classes? **Yes.**

2. How do students taking extended classes access library resources? **Students use the on-campus library and libraries located near off-site locations.**

3. What is the registration and payment process for adult students? **Adults register during evening hours.**

4. What career and placement services are available to adult students? **Students have advisors in their major area. Advisors are available during evening hours.**

Towson State University*

College of Continuing Studies ◆ 8000 York Road
Towson, MD 21204
Phone: (410) 830-2028 ◆ Toll-free phone: (800) CALL-TSU
Fax: (410) 830-2006

Founded: 1866

Accredited by: Middle States

Enrollment: 14,551 ◆ Adult students: 1,829

University status: Public

Features and Services

1. Is it possible to purchase books during hours most adult students attend classes? **Yes.**

Degree	Concentration/Major	Format
B.A.	Accounting	E
B.A.	Art—Studio	E
B.S.	Biology	E
B.S.	Business Administration	E
B.S.	Economics	E
B.S.	Early Childhood Education	E
B.S.	Elementary Education	E
B.S.	General and Secondary Education	E
B.S.	Geography	E
B.S.	Environmental Planning	E
B.A.	History	E
B.A.	Law Enforcement	E
B.A.	Mass Communication	E
B.S.	Mathematics	E
B.S.	Physics	E
B.S.	Psychology	E
B.S.	Social Sciences	E
B.S.	Sociology	E

Requirements

Residency requirement: Yes
Undergraduate admissions requirements: High school diploma or GED, application form and fee

Fees, Tuition, Costs

Undergraduate application fee: $25
Undergraduate tuition: $127/credit for Maryland residents; $163 for out-of-state residents
Full-time status: 12 credit hours

Maximum Hours Awarded For

CLEP: Yes
PEP: Yes
Other exams: Yes
Prior learning portfolio: Yes
Additional information: Portfolio and individualized assessment

Trevecca Nazarene University

333 Murfreesboro Road ◆ **Nashville, TN 37210**
Phone: (615) 248-1529 ◆ Fax: (615) 248-1700
E-mail: kbowman@trevecca.edu

Founded: 1901

Accredited by: Southern Association

Enrollment: 1,537 ◆ Adult students: 54 percent

University status: Private, Church, Church of the Nazarene

Degree	Concentration/Major	Format
B.A.	Management and Relations	E,A
M.A.	Organizational Management	E,A

Requirements

Residency requirement: Students must attend classes on campus. Undergraduate admissions requirements: Transcripts, high school and college; must have 62 college semester credits (30 hours general education); minimum 2.0 GPA; must be 25 or over; provide recommendations, health history; pass math and writing skills test; assessment interview.
Graduate admissions requirements: Application; official college transcripts; bachelor's degree; minimum 2.5 GPA; GMAT scores; employer's recommendation, two other recommendations; resume; essay; and pass quantitative skills proficiency exam.
Graduation requirements (undergraduate): Graduates must earn 128 semester hours (minimum GPA of 2.0); 34 semester hours of the major must be taken at Trevecca (C- grade or better); meet other requirements as stated.

Graduation requirements (graduate): Graduates must complete 37 semester hours at Trevecca; 3.0 GPA; no grade below C-; and complete graduate project. Requirements must be met within six years of entrance into program.

Fees, Tuition, Costs

Undergraduate application fee: $25
Graduate application fee: $25
Undergraduate tuition: $8,772/program
Graduate tuition: $8,917/program
Undergraduate cost of books: Included in tuition
Graduate cost of books: $1,050
Other costs: Evaluation of prior learning up to $38/hour for a maximum of 32 hours

Financial Aid/Status

Scholarship programs for adults: Dean's scholarships available
Full-time status: 12 hours/semester
Percentage of adult students receiving financial aid: 80 percent

Maximum Hours Awarded For

CLEP: 30
PEP: 30
DANTES: 30
Other exams: 32
Prior learning portfolio: 32

Features and Services

1. What is the registration and payment process for adult students? **Students register and pay for classes in their classroom the first night of each semester.**

2. What is the process for advising adult students? **Advising is done before applying. Prior learning assessment advising at admission and throughout the program.**

3. What career and placement services are available to adult students? **These services are available through the university placement office.**

4. What characteristics of the institution's adult degree programs are most appealing to students? **Shortness of program. It takes 57 weeks to complete work on a B.A.; 20 months for the M.A.; classes are held one night per week; modular format; and use of adult learning classroom and assessment methods.**

Trinity College

300 Summit Street ◆ Hartford, CT 06112
Phone: (860) 297-2150 ◆ Fax: (860) 297-5362
Web address: http://www.trincoll.edu

Founded: 1823

Accredited by: New England

Enrollment: 2,000 ◆ Adult students: 10 percent

University status: Private

Degree	Concentration/Major	Format
B.A.	Art History, American Studies, Classical Civilization, Classics, Comparative Literature, History, International Studies, Modern Languages, Music, Philosophy, Public Policy Studies, Religion, Studio Arts, Theater and Dance, Women's Studies	S
B.S.	Anthropology, Biochemistry, Biology, Chemistry Computer Coordinate, Computer Science, Economics, Educational Studies Coordinate, Engineering, Mathematics, Neuroscience, Physics, Political Science Psychology, Sociology	S

Requirements

Residency requirement: Depending on the major, students may be required to attend some classes on campus.
Undergraduate admissions requirements: Applicants must have a B or above average in previous college work, exhibit excellent writing skills, have two strong recommendations, and be highly motivated.
Graduation requirements (undergraduate): Graduates must earn 36 course credits (at least 16 credits at Trinity) and complete all general education and major requirements with average of C- or better.

Fees, Tuition, Costs

Undergraduate application fee: $50
Undergraduate tuition: $1,750/ credit on contractual basis
Undergraduate cost of books: $60-$75/course
Other costs: Computer (approximately $2,000) recommended

Financial Aid/Status

Scholarship programs for adults: Students may be eligible for a Trinity grant depending on their financial need.
Full-time status: Full-time students are enrolled in two courses per semester.

Percentage of adult students receiving financial aid: 55 percent.

Maximum Hours Awarded For

Other exams: Yes

Features and Services

1. Is it possible to purchase books during hours most adult students attend classes? **Yes.**

2. Are the institution's administrative offices open during hours adult students attend class? **Yes.**

3. What is the registration and payment process for adult students? **Students register with a faculty advisor. Payments are made contractually.**

4. What is the process for advising adult students? **Students have program/ academic, major, integration of knowledge, and peer advisors.**

5. What career and placement services are available to adult students? **Services are rendered through college counseling offices.**

6. What characteristics of the institution's adult degree programs are most appealing to students? **Flexibility of part-time work, 10-year time frame to complete degree, option of independent work, and extended payment plan.**

Trinity College of Vermont*

PACE Program

208 Colchester Avenue ◆ **Burlington, VT 05401**

Phone: (802)658-0337 ◆ Fax: (802)658-5446

Founded: 1925

Accredited by: New England Association

Enrollment: 973 ◆ Adult students: 587

University status: Private, Church, Roman Catholic Church

Degree	Concentration/Major	Format
B.A.	Accounting	E
B.S.	Business	E
B.A.	Liberal Arts	E

Requirements

Residency requirement: Yes
Undergraduate admissions
requirements: Completed
application with $30 fee; high
school transcript or GED unless
completed a college degree; all
college transcripts and military
transcripts (if applicable)

Fees, Tuition, Costs

Undergraduate application fee: $30
Undergraduate tuition: $367

Financial Aid/Status

Full-time status: A minimum of 12
credits per term
Percentage of adult students
receiving financial aid: 70 percent

Maximum Hours Awarded For

CLEP: 90
DANTES: 90
Prior learning portfolio: 90

Features and Services

1. Is it possible to purchase books during hours most adult students attend classes? **Yes.**

2. Are the institution's administrative offices open during hours adult students attend class? **Yes.**

3. What characteristics of the institution's adult degree programs are most appealing to students? **Flexibility in scheduling and availability of majors. For example, Business Administration or Accounting degrees entirely in the evenings or on the weekends.**

Trinity International University

2065 Half Day Road ◆ Deerfield, IL 60015
Phone: (847) 317-6500 ◆ Toll-free phone: (800) 417-9999
Fax: (847) 317-6509

Founded: 1897

Accredited by: North Central

Enrollment: 660

University status: Private

Degree	Concentration/Major	Format
B.A.	Interpersonal and Group Communications	E, A
B.A.	Business Administration	E, A, CT

Campus Extension Site

Brookfield, WI

Requirements

Residency requirement: It is not a correspondence program. Students must attend class on campus or at the Milwaukee location.
Undergraduate admissions requirements: Applicants must be 25 years of age, have proof of high school graduation or GED, and successful demonstration of thinking, organization, and writing abilities.
Graduation requirements (undergraduate): Graduates must complete 126 credit hours, including the school's general education requirements.

Fees, Tuition, Costs

Undergraduate application fee: $20
Undergraduate tuition: $260/hour
Undergraduate cost of books: $75/course

Financial Aid/Status

Full-time status: Any student enrolled in the degree-completion program is considered full-time.

Features and Services

1. Is it possible to purchase books during hours most adult students attend classes? **Yes.**

2. How do students taking extended classes access library resources? **The library is available to all students daily till 11 P.M.**

3. What is the registration and payment process for adult students? **Register by mail; semester payment using financial aid, loans, payment plan, or tuition reimbursement.**

4. What is the process for advising adult students? **The advisor on staff is available to students at their convenience.**

5. What career and placement services are available to adult students? **A campus career services department is available to students. Information and contacts are offered.**

Trinity University*

715 Stadium Drive ◆ **San Antonio, TX 78212**
Phone: (210) 736-7206 ◆ Fax: (210) 736-7202
Web address: http://www.trinity.edu

Founded: 1869

Accredited by: Southern Association

Enrollment: 2,479 ◆ Adult students: 46

University status: Private

Degree	Concentration/Major	Format
M.S.	Health Care Administration	TH

Requirements

Residency requirement: The program requires on-campus sessions at beginning and end of each term.

Fees, Tuition, Costs

Graduate application fee: $25
Graduate tuition: $510/credit

Financial Aid/Status

Full-time status: 12 semester hours/term

Union Institute

440 E. McMillan Street ◆ **Cincinnati, OH 45206-1947**
Phone: (513) 861-6400 ◆ Toll-free phone: (800) 486-3116
Fax: (513) 861-0779 ◆ E-mail: mrobertson@tui.edu
Web address: http://www.tui.edu

Founded: 1964

Accredited by: North Central

Enrollment: 1,740 ◆ Adult students: 1,740

University status: Private

Degree	Concentration/Major	Format
B.A.	Arts and Sciences curriculum	S,E,CT
B.S.	Arts and Sciences curriculum	S,E,CT
Ph.D.	Interdisciplinary Studies	S,E,CT
Ph.D.	Professional Psychology	S,E,CT

Campus Extension Sites

North Miami Beach, FL
San Diego, CA
Los Angeles, CA
Sacramento, CA

Requirements

Residency requirement: Distant learning (undergraduate) and graduate school programs have brief residency at various locations. Undergraduate admissions requirements: Applicants must submit an application, transcripts of all previous college work, three references, and a structured essay. An interview is usually required. Graduate admissions requirements: Applicants are expected to have an earned bachelor's and master's degrees from accredited institutions. No standardized test scores are required. Individual consideration may be offered if requested.
Graduation requirements (undergraduate): Graduates must complete a minimum of 128 semester credits and a senior project.
Graduation requirements (graduate): Graduates must complete a minimum active enrollment of 24 months, a dissertation, and a program summary.

Fees, Tuition, Costs

Undergraduate application fee: $50
Graduate application fee: $50
Undergraduate tuition: $216/semester credit hour
Graduate tuition: $3,660/semester
Undergraduate cost of books: Varies
Graduate cost of books: Varies
Other costs: Travel and room and board for undergraduate distant learning program and graduate school program

Financial Aid/Status

Scholarship programs for adults: Some limited institutional scholarships of varying amounts are available. Generally these are available to students who are already enrolled.
Full-time status: Full-time undergraduate status is 12 hours per semester. All graduate students are full-time.
Percentage of adult students receiving financial aid: 76 percent.

Maximum Hours Awarded For

CLEP: 32
Other exams: 32
Prior learning portfolio: 32
Additional information: ACE credit for training programs and military credit

Features and Services

1. Is it possible to purchase books during hours most adult students attend classes? **Yes.**

2. Are the institution's administrative offices open during hours adult students attend class? **Yes.**

3. How do students taking extended classes access library resources? **Library access by Internet and library agreements. Information (research) specialist is available.**

4. What is the registration and payment process for adult students? **Students must register whether active or not. Tuition is due each semester.**

5. What is the process for advising adult students? **Faculty advisors serve as mentors. A 1:12 faculty-to-student ratio allows faculty guidance.**

6. What career and placement services are available to adult students? **No career or placement services are available. Most students are working adults.**

7. What characteristics of the institution's adult degree programs are most appealing to students? **Individually designed programs, tutorial based, flexible scheduling, self-paced, and geared to adult students.**

Union University

2447 Highway 45 Bypass ◆ **Jackson, TN 38305**
Phone: (901) 668-1818 ◆ Toll-free phone: (800) 33-UNION
Fax: (901) 661-5187 ◆ E-mail: info@buster.uu.edu
Web address: http://www.uu.edu/

Founded: 1823

Accredited by: Southern Association

Enrollment: 1,845

University status: Private, Church, Southern Baptist Church

Degree	Concentration/Major	Format
B.S.B.A.	Accounting	E,A
B.S.B.A.	Management	E,A
B.S.B.A.	Marketing	E,A
B.S.B.A.	Finance	E,A
M.Ed.	Education	S,A
M.B.A.	Business Administration	E,A

Requirements

Residency requirement: Students must attend classes on campus. Undergraduate admissions requirements: Applicants must submit an application, ACT/SAT scores, proof of high school graduation or at least 12 transferable college credits (GPA-2.0). An Academic Forgiveness Program is available.
Graduate admissions requirements: Applicants must submit an application, official transcripts of all college work, references, and test scores as required.
Graduation requirements (undergraduate): Graduates must earn 128 semester hours completing the common core, specific degree core, and major courses.
Graduation requirements (graduate): Graduates must complete common core and elective courses. M.Ed. degree has two tracks: thesis and nonthesis. M.B.A. degree is nonthesis.

Fees, Tuition, Costs

Undergraduate application fee: $10
Graduate application fee: $25
Undergraduate tuition: $6,950/yr
Graduate tuition: M.Ed.—$145/ semester hour; M.B.A.—$250/ semester hour
Undergraduate cost of books: $500/year
Other costs: Computer fee of $55/ semester; lab fees

Financial Aid/Status

Scholarship programs for adults: Junior college transfer scholarships are available.
Full-time status: 12-16 hours per semester.

Maximum Hours Awarded For

CLEP: 32
PEP: 32
DANTES: 32
Additional information: CEEB; credit for U.S. military training

Features and Services

1. Is it possible to purchase books during hours most adult students attend classes? **Yes.**

2. Are the institution's administrative offices open during hours adult students attend class? **Yes.**

3. What is the registration and payment process for adult students? **Mail/evening registration done in three steps: advising, business office, and classes entered by computer.**

4. What is the process for advising adult students? **Advising at registration or by appointment with faculty/evaluators. Self-advising is an option.**

5. What characteristics of the institution's adult degree programs are most appealing to students? **Accelerated calendar and flexibility of M.Ed. degree.**

United States Sports Academy*

One Academy Drive ◆ **Daphne, AL 36526**
Phone: (205) 626-3303 ◆ Toll-free phone: (800) 223-2668
Fax: (205) 626-1149 ◆ Web address: http://www.sport.ussa.edu

Founded: 1972

Accredited by: Southern Association

Enrollment: 250 ◆ Adult students: 250

University status: Private

Features and Services

1. Are the institution's administrative offices open during hours adult students attend class? **Yes.**

2. What characteristics of the institution's adult degree programs are most appealing to students? **Credit for hands-on experience and flexibility to earn degree with on-campus and off-campus course work.**

Degree	Concentration/Major	Format
M.S.S.	Various	C,A
Ed.D.	Sport Management	S,A

Requirements

Residency requirement: No
Graduate admissions requirements: B.A. or B.S. from regionally accredited college or university, 2.75 GPA, three letters of recommendation, GRE or MAT test score, resume and personal statement, proof of health insurance

Fees, Tuition, Costs

Graduate application fee: $25 for M.S.; $100 for Ed.D.
Graduate tuition: $9,000 for M.S.; $16,800 for Ed.D.

Financial Aid/Status

Full-time status: A student enrolled for 8 hours a quarter
Percentage of adult students receiving financial aid: 52 percent

University of Alabama

Adult Student Office ◆ P.O. Box 870388
Tuscaloosa, AL 35487
Phone: (205) 348-8490 ◆ Fax: (205) 348-6614
Web address: http://www.ua.edu

Founded: 1831

Accredited by: Southern Association

Enrollment: 20,000 ◆ Adult students: 5,000

University status: Public

Fees, Tuition, Costs

Undergraduate application fee: $25
Graduate application fee: $25
Undergraduate tuition: $1,187/semester
Graduate tuition: $1,187/semester
Undergraduate cost of books: $200/semester
Graduate cost of books: $250/semester

Financial Aid/Status

Scholarship programs for adults: 16 Adult Student Scholarships are administered yearly through the adult student office.
Full-time status: A full-time student is enrolled in 12 semester hours (undergraduate) or 9 semester hours (graduate).

Maximum Hours Awarded For

CLEP: 30
DANTES: Yes
Other exams: Yes
Prior learning portfolio: Yes
Additional information: Foreign language credit, Advanced Placement, ACE, and USAFI used to evaluate experience for credit

Degree	Concentration/Major	Format
B.S.	Commerce and Business Administration-Management	E
B.S./B.A.	External Degree Program	E,C,S
M.A.	Human Resource Management	E
M.S.	Aerospace Engineering	V,T
M.S.E.	Environmental Engineering	V,T
M.S.	Electrical Engineering	V,T
M.S.	Mechanical Engineering	V,T
M.A.	Military History	E
M.A.	Criminal Justice	E,C,S
M.S.W.	Social Work	E
D.P.A.	Public Administration	E

Campus Extension Sites

Montgomery, AL
Gadsden, AL

Requirements

Residency requirement: Students do not have to attend classes on campus. M.A. in Criminal Justice requires short periods of time on campus each semester. Undergraduate admissions requirements: Adults graduating from high school four years prior to application are not required to submit ACT/SAT scores if high school GPA is 2.5 or more. External degree applicants must be 22 or older.

Graduate admissions requirements: Applicants must hold a bachelor's degree. Transcripts, required test scores, and letters of recommendation are required as well as evidence of good health. Graduation requirements (undergraduate): Graduates must complete 128 semester hours, including 48-51 "core curriculum" requirements. Other requirements vary depending on the individual college.
Graduation requirements (graduate): Graduates must complete 30 graduate hours and a thesis or 36 graduate hours without a thesis. Other requirements depend on the specialty.

Features and Services

1. Is it possible to purchase books during hours most adult students attend classes? **Yes.**

2. Are the institution's administrative offices open during hours adult students attend class? **Yes.**

3. How do students taking extended classes access library resources? **The library hours are flexible.**

4. What is the registration and payment process for adult students? **Registration is flexible to fit any schedule.**

5. What is the process for advising adult students? **Advising is the same for all students, except for support services from the Adult Student Office.**

6. What career and placement services are available to adult students? **Adults have access to the career center including a specialized adult career exploration program.**

7. What characteristics of the institution's adult degree programs are most appealing to students? **Flexibility in scope, variety of offerings, organization of support services, prior learning credit, and individualized curriculum.**

University of Baltimore

1420 N. Charles Street ◆ **Baltimore, MD 21201-5779**
Phone: (410) 837-4777 ◆ Fax: (410) 837-4820
E-mail: jcorcorane@ubmail.ubalt.edu

Founded: 1925

Accredited by: Middle States

Enrollment: 5,000

University status: Public

Degree	Concentration/Major	Format
B.S.	Business Administration: Concentrations in Accounting, Computer Information Systems, Economics, Finance, Management, Marketing, and International Business	E,V
B.S.	Corporate Communication	E,V
B.S.	Criminal Justice	E,V
B.A.	English	E,V
B.A.	History	E,V
B.A.	Interdisciplinary Studies	E,V
B.A.	Jurisprudence	E,V
B.A.	Psychology	E,V
M.B.A.	Business Administration	E,V
M.S.	Accounting	E,V
M.S.	Business	E,V
M.S.	Finance	E,V
M.S.	Management Information Systems	E,V
M.S.	Taxation	E,V
M.S.	Applied Psychology	E,V
M.S.	Criminal Justice	E,V
M.A.	Legal and Ethical Studies	E,V
M.A.	Publications Design	E,V
M.P.A.	Public Administration	E,V
J.D./M.P.A.	Law and Public Administration	E,V

Campus Extension Site
Harford County, MD

Requirements
Residency requirement: Students must attend classes on campus except for Corporate Communication and Criminal Justice degrees at Heat Center.
Undergraduate admissions requirements: Applicants must have a minimum of 56 college credits (minimum 2.0 GPA). This upper-division university offers classes for students in their third to fourth year (community college graduates). Average student age is 29.
Graduate admissions requirements: Applicants must meet the admission requirements for the particular degree program.
Graduation requirements (undergraduate): Graduates must fulfill all entrance requirements and earn 120 credit hours (minimum 2.0 GPA).
Graduation requirements (graduate): Graduates must meet the requirements of the particular degree program as specified.

Fees, Tuition, Costs
Undergraduate application fee: $20
Graduate application fee: $30
Undergraduate tuition: $145/hour for Maryland residents
Graduate tuition: $176-$192/hour for Maryland residents
Undergraduate cost of books: $75/class

Financial Aid/Status
Scholarship programs for adults:
Merit scholarships provided
Full-time status: 12 credits or more
Percentage of adult students
receiving financial aid: 80 percent

Maximum Hours Awarded For
CLEP: Yes
DANTES: Yes
Additional information: Credit for
prior learning in transfer

Features and Services
1. Is it possible to purchase books during hours most adult students attend classes? **Yes.**

2. Are the institution's administrative offices open during hours adult students attend class? **Yes.**

3. How do students taking extended classes access library resources? **The library may be accessed by Internet or in person.**

4. What is the registration and payment process for adult students? **Offices are open for students' use.**

5. What is the process for advising adult students? **All students are required to meet with an advisor before registering.**

6. What career and placement services are available to adult students? **Coop and career services are available.**

7. What characteristics of the institution's adult degree programs are most appealing to students? **Large selection of evening courses; evening classes meet just one night per week.**

University of Bridgeport*
380 University Avenue ◆ **Bridgeport, CT 06601**
Phone: (203) 576-4552 ◆ Toll-free phone: (800) 972-9488
Fax: (203) 576-4941

Founded: 1927

Accredited by: New England

Enrollment: 1,939 ◆ Adult students: 900

University status: Private

Requirements
Residency requirement: Yes
Undergraduate admissions
requirements: High school
graduate or GED; 16 acceptable
units of academic work—4
English, 3 Math, 1 lab science, 1
social science, 7 electives
Graduate admissions requirements:
Vary by program

Fees, Tuition, Costs
Undergraduate application fee: $35
Graduate application fee: $35
Undergraduate tuition: $235/credit
Graduate tuition: $290/credit

Financial Aid/Status
Full-time status: Undergraduate—
12 or more credits; graduate—9 or
more credits

Maximum Hours Awarded For
CLEP: 30
Maximum hours for prior learning:
Yes

Degree	Concentration/Major	Format
M.S.	Human Nutrition	E
	Classes meet each weekend for 18 months.	
M.S.	Electrical Engineering	E
M.S.	Computer Engineering	E
M.S.	Computer Science	E
M.S.	Mechanical Engineering	E
M.S.	Management Engineering	E
M.S.	Education	E
M.S.	Counseling	E
B.S.	Business Administration	E,A
B.E.S.	Elective Studies	E,A
M.B.A.	Business Administration	E
M.S.	Counseling Human Resource Development Concentration	E
Ed.D.	Educational Leadership	E

Features and Services

1. Is it possible to purchase books during hours most adult students attend classes? **Yes.**

2. Are the institution's administrative offices open during hours adult students attend class? **Yes.**

3. What characteristics of the institution's adult degree programs are most appealing to students? **Small class size, accelerated format, weekend format, and specialized services.**

University of California, Santa Barbara

Off Campus Studies Department ◆ **Santa Barbara, CA 93106**
Phone: (805) 893-8841 ◆ Fax: (805) 893-4943
E-mail: hadamson@serf.xlrn.ucsb.edu
Web address: http://www.ucsb.edu

Founded: 1865

Accredited by: Western Association

Enrollment: 17,834 ◆ Adult students: 100

University status: Public

Degree	Concentration/Major	Format
B.A.	Anthropology	E,T,V
B.A.	English	E,T,V
B.A.	History	E,T,V
B.A.	Interdisciplinary Studies	E,T,V
B.A.	Law and Society	E,T,V
B.A.	Political Science	E,T,V
B.A.	Psychology	E,T,V
B.A.	Sociology	E,T,V
M.S.	Electrical and Computer Engineering	E,T,V,CT
M.S.	Computer Science	E,T,V,CT

Campus Extension Site

Ventura, CA

Requirements

Residency requirement: Undergraduate students may complete all requirements at the UCSB Ventura Center. Graduate students must go to the main campus for final exams.
Undergraduate admissions requirements: Requirements vary depending on the major. Applicants must meet all lower division requirements with a minimum 2.5 GPA.
Graduate admissions requirements: Applicants must score in the top 15 percent on the GRE and have an undergraduate GPA of 3.5.
Graduation requirements (undergraduate): Graduates must complete 180 quarter units with 35 of the last 45 units in residence.
Graduation requirements (graduate): Requirements vary by department. Generally graduates must complete 30 quarter units and either a thesis or a comprehensive exam.

Fees, Tuition, Costs

Undergraduate application fee: $40
Graduate application fee: $40
Undergraduate tuition: $1,459/ California
Graduate tuition: $1,703.85/ California
Undergraduate cost of books: $200
Graduate cost of books: $350
Other costs: $255 of graduate fees may be saved with proof of health insurance.

Financial Aid/Status

Scholarship programs for adults: Scholarships up to full tuition based on financial need are available.
Full-time status: 10 quarter units.
Percentage of adult students receiving financial aid: 20 percent.

Features and Services

1. Are the institution's administrative offices open during hours adult students attend class? **Yes.**

2. How do students taking extended classes access

library resources? **The library may be accessed by computer terminal and courier service.**

3. What is the registration and payment process for adult students? **Registration and payment are the same for all students.**

4. What is the process for advising adult students? **Special advisors are available by drop-in during day hours or evenings by appointment.**

5. What career and placement services are available to adult students? **All fully matricu-**

lated students may use the same services.

6. What characteristics of the institution's adult degree programs are most appealing to students? **Convenience of schedule and location, access to faculty, and prestige of institution.**

University of Central Texas*

PO Box 1416 ◆ **Killeen, TX 76540**

Phone: (817) 526-8262 ◆ Fax: (817) 526-8403

Founded: 1973

Accredited by: Southern Association

Enrollment: 900 ◆
Adult students: 702

University status: Private

Graduate application fee: None
Undergraduate tuition: $126/credit
Graduate tuition: $141/credit

Financial Aid/Status

Full-time status: Undergrad—12+ hours; graduate—9+ hours

Maximum Hours Awarded For

CLEP: Yes
PEP: Yes
DANTES: Yes
Prior learning portfolio: Yes

Features and Services

1. Is it possible to purchase books during hours most adult students attend classes? **Yes.**

2. Are the institution's administrative offices open during hours adult students attend class? **Yes.**

Degree	Concentration/Major	Format
B.S.	Business Administration	E,A
B.S.	Psychology	E,A
B.S.	Interdisciplinary	E,A
B.S.W.	Social Work	E,A
B.S	Criminal Justice	E,A
M.S.	Management	E
M.S.	Counseling	E
M.S.	Psychology	E
M.S.	Educational Psychology	E

Requirements

Residency requirement: Yes
Undergraduate admissions requirements: Minimum 2.0 GPA on course work accepted. At least 51 transcripted semester hours from regionally accredited college or university.

Graduate admissions requirements: Earned bachelor's degree from regionally accredited college or university. Minimum 2.5 upper-level GPA.

Fees, Tuition, Costs

Undergraduate application fee: None

University of Connecticut*

U-56c, One Bishop Circle ◆ **Storrs, CT 06269-4056**
Phone: (203) 486-3832 ◆ Toll-free phone: (800) 622-9907
Fax: (203) 486-3845 ◆ Web address: http://www.uconn.edu

Founded: 1881

Accredited by: New England

Enrollment: 25,000 ◆ Adult students: 900

University status: Public

Features and Services

1. Is it possible to purchase books during hours most adult students attend classes? **Yes.**

2. What characteristics of the institution's adult degree programs are most appealing to students? **Flexible curriculum, individualized major, price, convenience, and liberal transfer policies.**

Degree	Concentration/Major	Format
B.G.S.	Individualized Day and night classes during the week	E

Requirements

Residency requirement: Yes
Undergraduate admissions requirements: Associate degree or at least 60 semester credits from regionally accredited college and special application.

Fees, Tuition, Costs

Undergraduate application fee: $95
Undergraduate tuition: $580/3 credits

Financial Aid/Status

Full-time status: 12 credits or more per semester

Maximum Hours Awarded For

CLEP: Varies
DANTES: Varies
Other exams: Varies
Prior learning portfolio: Varies

University of Delaware*

Room 205 John M. Clayton Hall
Newark, DE 19716
Phone: (302) 831-1119 ◆ Fax: (302) 831-1077
Web address: http://www.udel.edu

Founded: 1743

Accredited by: Middle States

Enrollment: 21,700 ◆ Adult students: 300

University status: Public

Features and Services

1. Is it possible to purchase books during hours most adult students attend classes? **Yes.**

2. Are the institution's administrative offices open during hours adult students attend class? **Yes.**

3. What characteristics of the institution's adult degree programs are most appealing to students? **Evening format and discipline.**

Degree	Concentration/Major	Format
B.A.	English	E
B.A.	History	E
B.A.	Computer and Information Science	E
B.S.	Accounting	E
B.A.	Psychology	E
B.A.	Women's Studies	E
B.S.N.	Nursing for the R.N.	E
B.A.	Criminal Justice	E
B.A./B.S.	Chemistry	E
B.A.S.	Engineering Technology	E
B.A.	Sociology	E
B.S.	Human Resources	E

Requirements

Residency requirement: No
Undergraduate admissions requirements: SAT scores and high school record for traditional students; SCRU for older students or transfer grades, credits, or successful completion of 9-18 credits as nonmatriculation

Fees, Tuition, Costs

Undergraduate application fee: $50
Undergraduate tuition: $154

Financial Aid/Status

Full-time status: 12 to 15 hours/ semester

Maximum Hours Awarded For

Other exams: Yes

University of Denver
University College

2211 S. Josephine ◆ **Denver, CO 80208**
Phone: (303) 871-3354 ◆ Fax: (303) 871-3303
E-mail: kaharvey@circe.cair.du.edu
Web address: http://www.du.edu
Program's Web address: http://www.du.edu/~aserdl|dept.html

Founded: 1864

Accredited by: North Central

Enrollment: 8,710 ◆ Adult students: 1,728

University status: Private

Degree	Concentration/Major	Format
B.A.	Environmental Sciences	E,A
M.C.I.S.	Computer Information Systems	E,A
M.S.S.	Applied Communication	E,A
M.E.P.M.	Environmental Policy and Management	E,A,CT
M.H.S.	Health Care Systems	E,A
M.L.S.	Liberal Studies	E,A
M.O.T.	Management of Technology	E,A
M.L.I.S.	Library and Information Services	E,A
M.T.E.L.	Telecommunications	E,A

Requirements

Residency requirement: Students must attend classes on campus; however, the new distance initiative program (M.E.P.M.) requires only one weekend each quarter. *Note: This is distance education only.* Undergraduate admissions requirements: Nontraditional program requirements: high school diploma or GED, passing foundation seminars (English, math), completion of admission packet (essays, recommendations, etc.), and work experience. Graduate admissions requirements: Applicants must have a baccalaureate degree (minimum 3.0 GPA), complete admission packet, and receive recommendation of the program director and approval of committee.
Graduation requirements (undergraduate): Graduates must earn 180 quarter hours with a strong liberal arts core. Graduation requirements (graduate): Graduates must earn 53-58 quarter hours (3.0 GPA).

Fees, Tuition, Costs

Undergraduate application fee: $25
Graduate application fee: $25
Undergraduate tuition: $220/ quarter hour
Graduate tuition: $150-$215/ quarter hour
Undergraduate cost of books: $60/ course
Graduate cost of books: $60-$100/ course
Other costs: Personal computer

Financial Aid/Status

Scholarship programs for adults: Limited scholarships offered
Full-time status: 8 quarter hours
Percentage of adult students receiving financial aid: 80 percent

Features and Services

1. Is it possible to purchase books during hours most adult students attend classes? **Yes.**

2. Are the institution's administrative offices open during hours adult students attend class? **Yes.**

3. How do students taking extended classes access library resources? **The library is available for all students.**

4. What is the registration and payment process for adult students? **Registration/ payment may be done by phone, fax, e-mail, and in person.**

5. What is the process for advising adult students? **Four highly qualified academic advisors are available.**

6. What career and placement services are available to adult students? **The university career services are available to all students.**

7. What characteristics of the institution's adult degree programs are most appealing to students? **Quality, flexibility, relevance, convenience, accelerated, and evening and weekend classes.**

University of Evansville

1800 Lincoln Avenue ♦ **Evansville, IN 47711**
Phone: (812) 479-2981 ♦ Fax: (812) 474-4079
E-mail: lp22@evansville.edu
Web address: http://www.evansville.edu
Program's Web address:
http://www.cedar.evansville.edu/catalog/cond_ed

Founded: 1919

Accredited by: North Central

Enrollment: 2,500

University status: Private, Church, United Methodist Church

Degree	Concentration/Major	Format
B.L.S.	Liberal Studies	E,A
B.S.	External Studies—Individualized	E,S

Requirements

Residency requirement: All three years of the Liberal Studies degrees must be completed on campus. At least 24 semester hours on campus are required for the External Studies program.
Undergraduate admissions requirements: Applicants must have a high school diploma or GED. Minimum 2.0 GPA is required for either high school or college credit.
Graduation requirements (undergraduate): Students must meet the requirements of the degree program.

Fees, Tuition, Costs

Undergraduate application fee: $30
Undergraduate tuition: $365/ semester hour

Financial Aid/Status

Scholarship programs for adults: Full-time students are eligible for various need-based scholarships. Part-time students are eligible for $500/year scholarships.
Full-time status: 12 or more hours/ semester.

Maximum Hours Awarded For

CLEP: 100
DANTES: 100
Other exams: 100
Prior learning portfolio: 100

Features and Services

1. Is it possible to purchase books during hours most adult students attend classes? **Yes.**

2. What is the registration and payment process for adult students? **Students may register through the Center for Continuing Education.**

3. What is the process for advising adult students? **Academic advising is done by advisors in the Center for Continuing Education.**

4. What career and placement services are available to adult students? **Students have access to the university Career Services Center.**

5. What characteristics of the institution's adult degree programs are most appealing to students? **Evening programs, classes with other adults, and three-year bachelor's degree.**

University of Findlay

1000 N. Main Street ◆ **Findlay, OH 45840**
Phone: (419) 424-4600 ◆ Toll-free phone: (800) 472-9502
Fax: (419) 424-4822

Founded: 1882

Accredited by: North Central

Enrollment: 3,324 ◆ Adult students: 44 percent

University status: Private, Church, Church of God,
General Conference

Degree	Concentration/Major	Format
A.A.	Business Administration	E
A.A.	Office Information Systems	E
A.A.	Legal Assisting	E
B.S.	Business Administration	E
B.S.	Marketing	E
B.S.	Business Management (degree completion)	A
B.S.	Environmental Management (degree completion)	A
B.S.	Occupational Therapy (degree completion)	E
B.S.	Physical Therapy (degree completion)	E

Campus Extension Sites

Cincinnati, OH
Lima, OH
Toledo, OH

Requirements

Residency requirement: Students do not have to attend classes on campus. The last two years of the bachelor's degree-completion programs are available at extended campuses.
Undergraduate admissions requirements: Adult students must submit a high school transcript or GED, an application, and transcripts of any previous college work.
Graduation requirements (undergraduate): B.S. degree—124 semester hours, minimum 2.0 GPA, major; A.A. degree—62 semester hours, minimum 2.0 GPA, major, general education and proficiency requirements. Program requirements must be met.

Fees, Tuition, Costs

Undergraduate tuition: $290-$321/hour
Cost of books: $300/semester
Other costs: Activity fees

Financial Aid/Status

Scholarship programs for adults: The university offers scholarships to returning undergraduate adult students.
Full-time status: Full-time status is at least 12 credits during the regular semester or 9 credits on weekends.
Percentage of adult students receiving financial aid: 60 percent.

Maximum Hours Awarded For

CLEP: No limit
Other exams: 30
Prior learning portfolio: 94
Additional information: Military credit—no limit

Features and Services

1. Is it possible to purchase books during hours most adult students attend classes? **Yes.**

2. Are the institution's administrative offices open during hours adult students attend class? **Yes.**

3. How do students taking extended classes access library resources? **Students may make library requests by phone. Access to files available through Internet or dial-in.**

4. What is the registration and payment process for adult students? **Registration is in person, mail, and phone. Billing is done after registration.**

5. What is the process for advising adult students? **Three adult student advisors are available days, evenings, and weekends.**

6. What career and placement services are available to adult students? **The Office of Career Planning and the Office of Career Placement are available by appointment.**

7. What characteristics of the institution's adult degree programs are most appealing to students? **Easy application, shorter time frame (weekends and off campus).**

University of Hawaii

College of Continuing Education and Community Services
2530 Dole Street, Sakamaki Hall D410
Honolulu, HI 96822
Phone: (808) 956-6780 ◆ Fax: (808) 956-3364
E-mail: cokinaga@hawaii.edu

Founded: 1907

Accredited by: Western Association

University status: Public

Degree	Concentration/Major	Format
B.A.	Psychology	E,A
B.A.	Liberal Studies	E,T

Campus Extension Sites

Maui, HI
Kauai, HI

Requirements

Residency requirement: Students may attend classes at extended sites for the bachelor's degrees. Undergraduate admissions requirements: 24 credits may be earned as unclassified students through College of Continuing Education/Community Service courses. Then an application to a degree program at the university at Manoa is needed.
Graduation requirements (undergraduate): Both day and evening students must meet the same graduation requirements.

Fees, Tuition, Costs

Undergraduate tuition: $64/credit in Hawaii
Other costs: Lab fees

Financial Aid/Status

Scholarship programs for adults: Board of Regents Tuition Waivers are available to students.

Features and Services

1. Are the institution's administrative offices open during hours adult students attend class? **Yes.**

2. How do students taking extended classes access library resources? **The registration receipt permits students to access library services.**

3. What is the registration and payment process for adult students? **Registration may be done in person or by mail.**

4. What is the process for advising adult students? **Two counselors are available during the evenings and weekends in the Office of Student Affairs.**

5. What characteristics of the institution's adult degree programs are most appealing to students? **Flexible hours and locations, small classes, more personal service to students, excellent instructors**

University of Houston

4242 South Mason Road ◆ **Katy, TX 77450**
Phone: (713) 395-2800 ◆ Toll Free Phone: (800) OUR-UHTV
Fax: (713) 395-2629 ◆ E-mail: sfrieden@uh.edu
Web address: http://www.uh.edu

Founded: 1927

Accredited by: Southern Association

Enrollment: 30,000 ◆ Adult students: 46 percent

University status: Public

Degree	Concentration/Major	Format
B.A.	English (preprofessional program)	TH,T
B.A./B.S.	Psychology	TH,T
B.S.	Hotel & Restaurant Management	TH,T
B.S.T.	Industrial Supervision	TH,T
B.S.T.	Computer Engineering Technology	TH,T
B.S.T.	Mechanical Technology (Computer Drafting Design)	TH,T
M.S.O.T.	Occupational Technology (Training & Development)	TH,T
M.H.M.	Hospitality Management	TH,V,CT,T
M.I.E.	Industrial Engineering (Engineering Management)	T
M.E.E.	Electrical Engineering	T

Campus Extension Sites

Katy, TX
Houston, TX
Sugarland, TX

Requirements

Residency requirement: Some programs have labs, a PE activity requirement, or other courses that require campus attendance at this time.
Undergraduate admissions requirements: Requirements vary by degree.
Graduate admissions requirements: Requirements vary by degree.
Graduation requirements (undergraduate): Requirements vary by degree.

Graduation requirements (graduate): Requirements vary by degree.

Fees, Tuition, Costs

Undergraduate application fee: $25
Graduate application fee: SEES
Undergraduate tuition: $100/credit hour for residents; $171 for nonresidents
Graduate tuition: $100/credit hour for residents; $171 for nonresidents
Undergraduate cost of books: $650
Graduate cost of books: $650
Other costs: Student service fee $20-$100/semester; computer use fee $10-$50/semester; library fee $15/semester; UC fee $15/semester; health fee $20/semester

Financial Aid/Status

Scholarship programs for adults: Yes; scholarships and amounts vary
Full-time status: 12 hours for undergraduate and graduate; 9 hours for doctoral
Percentage of adult students receiving Financial Aid: 50 percent

Maximum Hours Awarded For

CLEP: No limit
DANTES: No limit
Other exams: No limit
Additional information: Students may take as many tests as they would like for college credit.

Features and Services

1. Is it possible to purchase books during hours most adult students attend classes? **Yes.**

2. Are the institution's administrative offices open during hours adult students attend class? **Yes.**

3. How do students taking extended classes access library resources? **Students can access the library through online computer system, telephone reference services, interlibrary loan.**

4. What is the registration and payment process for adult students? **Registration is over the telephone, and if students register early enough, payments can be sent by mail.**

5. What is the process for advising adult students? **Distance education advisors can advise students at remote sites over the phone or on Internet.**

6. What career and placement services are available to adult students? **Adults have access to a wide variety of services that are available to all students.**

7. What characteristics of the institution's adult degree programs are most appealing to students? **UH provides junior, senior, and graduate level courses in a variety of** convenient methods (e.g., off-campus sites, instructional television, over the Internet, tape purchase, tape viewing).

University of Illinois at Springfield

Shephard Road ◆ **Springfield, IL 62794-9243**
Phone: (217) 786-7422 ◆ Toll-free phone: (800) 252-8533
Fax: (217) 786-7188 ◆ E-mail: ettinger@eagle.uis.edu
Web address: http://www.sangamon.edu

Founded: 1970

Accredited by: North Central

Enrollment: 4,500 ◆ Adult students: 60 percent

University status: Public

Degree	Concentration/Major	Format
B.A.	Liberal Studies	S
M.A.	Individualized Option—Interdisciplinary	S

Requirements

Residency requirement: Although much off-campus study can be incorporated into the degree program, several on-campus courses are required.
Undergraduate admissions requirements: Upper-division admission requires 45 credit hours (minimum 2.0 GPA on 4.0 scale) and at least 3 semester hours of English composition.
Graduate admissions requirements: Applicants must have an earned baccalaureate (minimum 2.5 GPA on 4.0 scale). The degree program requires separate application and an interview.

Fees, Tuition, Costs

Undergraduate tuition: $85/ semester hour
Graduate tuition: $88/semester hour

Financial Aid/Status

Scholarship programs for adults: The Office of Financial Assistance coordinates a broad range of federal, state, institutional, and private financial aid programs.
Full-time status: At least 6 semester hours.

Maximum Hours Awarded For

Prior learning portfolio: No limit

Features and Services

1. Is it possible to purchase books during hours most adult students attend classes? **Yes.**

2. Are the institution's administrative offices open during hours adult students attend class? **Yes.**

3. How do students taking extended classes access library resources? **Students may access libraries through interlibrary loan.**

4. What is the registration and payment process for adult students? **Registration may be done by phone. Payment by credit card, billing, and payment plan are available.**

5. What is the process for advising adult students? **Personal interviews with faculty advisors, an orientation course, and a degree committee are provided for each student.**

6. What career and placement services are available to adult students? **Career Services and Placement Office offer programs, interviews, interest testing, etc.**

7. What characteristics of the institution's adult degree programs are most appealing to students? **Small classes, personal contact with faculty, evening/weekend classes, and self-designed independent study options.**

University of Illinois at Urbana–Champaign

302 E. Johns Street, Suite 1405 ◆ Champaign, IL 61820
Phone: (217) 333-3061 ◆ Toll-free phone: (800) 252-1360
Fax: (217) 244-8481 ◆ E-mail: bobb@cecredit.extramural.uiuc.edu
Web address: http://www.uiuc.edu
Program's Web address: http://www.extramural.uiuc.edu

Founded: 1867

Accredited by: North Central ◆ Enrollment: 36,000

University status: Public

Degree	Concentration/Major	Format
M.S.	Agronomy	E
M.S.	Food Science	E
M.S.	Rehabilitation	E
M.Ed.	Educational Administration	E
M.Ed.	Continuing Education	E
M.Ed.	Elementary Education	E
M.Ed.	Votec/Human Resource Development	E
M.S.	Electrical Engineering	V
M.S.	General Engineering	V
M.S.	Mechanical Engineering	V
M.S.	Theoretical and Applied Mechanics	V

Campus Extension Sites
Oak Brook, IL
Arlington Hts., IL
Palos Hills, IL
River Grove, IL

Requirements
Residency requirement: Students are not required to attend classes on campus. Some video classes are taught at various public and company sites in Illinois and other states.
Graduate admissions requirements: Admission to the graduate program requires a minimum GPA of 4.0 (A = 5.0) for the last 60 hours of undergraduate work completed.

Some departments may have higher or additional requirements. Graduation requirements (graduate): Graduates complete at least 8 units (32 semester hours) of credit; at least 3 units (12 semester hours) in 400-level courses; 2 of 3 units in major; possibly a final exam, research paper, or thesis.

Fees, Tuition, Costs
Graduate application fee: $30
Graduate tuition: $119/semester hour; $189/engineering

Financial Aid/Status
Full-time status: 12 semester hours (3 units)

Features and Services

1. Is it possible to purchase books during hours most adult students attend classes? **Yes.**

2. How do students taking extended classes access library resources? **Extramural Library coordinates resources to students. University and regional libraries may be used with a library card provided for off-campus students.**

3. What is the registration and payment process for adult students? **Students complete the extramural registration form and pay tuition and fees by check or credit card.**

4. What is the process for advising adult students? **Students are assigned academic advisors. General advising is provided by the Extramural Office.**

5. What career and placement services are available to adult students? **The University Career Services Center and college and department job placement programs are open.**

6. What characteristics of the institution's adult degree programs are most appealing to students? **Ability to pursue a graduate degree near home or work, programs equal to on-campus degrees, and 90 percent of courses taught by regular campus faculty.**

University of Indianapolis

1400 E. Hanna Avenue ◆ **Indianapolis, IN 46227**
Phone: (317) 788-3389 ◆ Toll-free phone: (800) 232-8634
Fax: (317) 788-3300 ◆ E-mail: stockton@gandlf.uindy.edu
Web address: http://www.uindy.edu/
Program's Web address: http://www.uindy.edu/app.html

Founded: 1902

Accredited by: North Central

Enrollment: 4,000 ◆ Adult students: 1,000

University status: Private, Church, United Methodist Church

Degree	Concentration/Major	Format
A.S.	Banking and Finance	E
A.S.	Business Administration	E
A.S.	Computer Information Systems	E
A.S.	Corrections	E
A.S.	Law Enforcement	E
A.S.	Legal Assistant	E
A.S.	Purchasing and Procurement Management	E
B.S.	Accounting	E
B.S.	Business Administration	E
B.S.	Corrections	E
B.S.	Economics and Finance	E
B.S.	Industrial Management	E
B.S.	Information Systems	E
B.S.	International Business	E
B.S.	Marketing	E

Requirements

Undergraduate admissions requirements: Applicants must rank in the upper half of high school class, have 24 semesters of college preparatory subjects, 920 on the recentered SAT or 20 composite on the ACT. Graduation requirements (undergraduate): Graduates must earn 124 credit hours of general education and major courses.

Fees, Tuition, Costs

Undergraduate application fee: $20
Undergraduate tuition: $148/hour
Undergraduate cost of books: $535
Other costs: Fees $35/semester

Financial Aid/Status

Scholarship programs for adults: Scholarships available
Full-time status: 12 credit hours or more/semester
Percentage of adult students receiving financial aid: 53 percent

Maximum Hours Awarded For

CLEP: Varies
Other exams: Varies

Features and Services

1. Is it possible to purchase books during hours most adult students attend classes? **Yes.**

2. Are the institution's administrative offices open during hours adult students attend class? **Yes.**

3. How do students taking extended classes access library resources? **Students may use an ID card at the library. Computer search of the online catalog is available.**

4. What is the registration and payment process for adult students? **Students can preregister and pay between specified dates, or use walk-in registration and payment.**

5. What is the process for advising adult students? **Major advisor available one evening per week till 7 P.M.; Dean—four evenings till 9:00 and Saturday mornings.**

6. What characteristics of the institution's adult degree programs are most appealing to students? **Small class sizes, good faculty, helpful staff, friendly community, and secure environment.**

University of Iowa

116 International Center ◆ **Iowa City, IA 52242**
Phone: (319) 335-2575 ◆ Toll-free phone: (800) 272-6430
Fax: (319) 335-2740 ◆ E-mail: credit-programs@uiowa.edu
Web address: http://www.uiowa.edu
Program's Web address: http://www.nccp/bls

Founded: 1847

Accredited by: North Central ◆ Enrollment: 29,000

University status: Public

Degree	Concentration/Major	Format
B.L.S.	Liberal Studies	E,C,T,TH

Requirements

Residency requirement: No residency requirement is used. Students in Iowa may take courses in any of the four formats. Correspondence courses are available anywhere in the U.S. Undergraduate admissions requirements: Applicants must have an associate degree or 62 semester hours with 2.25 GPA. Graduation requirements (undergraduate): Graduates must earn 124 semester hours.

Fees, Tuition, Costs

Undergraduate application fee: $20
Undergraduate tuition: $77/ semester hour

Financial Aid/Status

Scholarship programs for adults: Limited scholarships for bachelor of liberal studies students
Full-time status: 12 semester hours

Maximum Hours Awarded For

CLEP: 32
DANTES: Yes

Features and Services

1. Is it possible to purchase books during hours most adult students attend classes? **Yes.**

2. Are the institution's administrative offices open during hours adult students attend class? **Yes.**

3. What is the registration and payment process for adult students? **Students must complete the admission form and pay $20 fee.**

4. What is the process for advising adult students? **Assigned advisors are available by phone, fax, e-mail, or in person. Office open/8-7 P.M.-WATS line.**

5. What career and placement services are available to adult students? **Students may call the WATS line free of charge and be transferred to the office.**

6. What characteristics of the institution's adult degree programs are most appealing to students? **Quality program, degree through College of Liberal Arts, no on-campus requirements, flexibility, convenience, and personal advising.**

University of Louisville*

Admissions Office, Hovchens Building
Louisville, KY 40292-0001
Phone: (502) 852-6168 ◆ Fax: (502) 852-0685
Web address: http://www.louisville.edu

Founded: 1798

Accredited by: Southern Association

Enrollment: 21,826 ◆ Adult students: 9,685

University status: Public

Degree   Concentration/Major   Format

The university indicated that a large number of degree programs were available by taking evening and weekend classes. However, they did not specify which degrees were available. Bachelor's, master's, and doctoral degrees are available.

Requirements

Residency requirement: Yes

Fees, Tuition, Costs

Undergraduate application fee: $25
Graduate application fee: $25
Undergraduate tuition: $1,195
Graduate tuition: $1,305

Financial Aid/Status

Full-time status: 12 hours—undergraduate; 9 hours—graduate
Percentage of adult students receiving financial aid: 50 percent

Maximum Hours Awarded For

CLEP: Yes
PEP: Yes
DANTES: Yes
Other exams: Yes
Prior learning portfolio: Yes
Additional information: Up to 24 credit hours accepted through exams and prior life experience assessment

Features and Services

1. Is it possible to purchase books during hours most adult students attend classes? **Yes.**

2. Are the institution's administrative offices open during hours adult students attend class? **Yes.**

3. What is the registration and payment process for adult students? **Students can register using a Touch-Tone system.**

4. What characteristics of the institution's adult degree programs are most appealing to students? **Scheduling of courses and variety of course offerings.**

University of Maine*

5713 Chadbourne Hall, Room 122
Orono, ME 04469
Phone: (207) 581-3142 ◆ Fax: (207) 581-3141
Web address: http://www.ume.maine.edu

Founded: 1862

Accredited by: New England

Enrollment: 11,000 ◆ Adult students: 150

University status: Public

Features and Services

1. Is it possible to purchase books during hours most adult students attend classes? **Yes.**

2. What characteristics of the institution's adult degree programs are most appealing to students? **Evening classes and flexibility to self-design the degree to fit individual needs.**

Degree	Concentration/Major	Format
B.A.	University Studies	E,S

Requirements

Residency requirement: Yes
Undergraduate admissions requirements: High school diploma or GED, interview, completed 18 credit hour requirement with a minimum C average.

Financial Aid/Status

Full-time status: 12 credit hours/term. Students taking at least 6 credit hours and enrolled in a degree program are eligible for student aid.

Fees, Tuition, Costs

Undergraduate application fee: $25
Undergraduate tuition: $103/credit for Maine residents; $297 for out-of-state

University of Maine at Augusta

46 University Drive ◆ Augusta, ME 04330-9410
Phone: (207) 621-3444 ◆ Toll-free phone: (800) 696-6000
Fax: (207) 621-3116 ◆ E-mail: elis@maine.maine.edu

Founded: 1965

Accredited by: New England

Enrollment: 6,100 ◆ Adult students: 60 percent

University status: Public

Degree	Concentration/Major	Format
A.S.	Business Administration	T,TH
A.S.	General Studies	T,TH
A.S./A.A.	Human Services and Social Services	T,TH
A.A.	Liberal Arts and Liberal Studies	T,TH
A.S.	Library Information Technology	T,TH
A.S.	Nursing	T
B.S.	Business Administration	T,TH
B.Mus.	Jazz and Contemporary Music	E
B.A.	English	E
B.A.	Social Sciences	E
B.A.	Math/Science	E
B.S.	Public Administration	E

Campus Extension Sites
Bangor, ME
Lewiston, ME

Requirements
Residency requirement: Students may not be required to attend classes on campus; however, this varies by the degree program. Undergraduate admissions requirements: Generally open admission is available. Some programs may have selective admissions. Graduation requirements (undergraduate): The requirements vary by the program.

Fees, Tuition, Costs
Undergraduate application fee: $25
Undergraduate tuition: $85/credit hour

Undergraduate cost of books: $200
Other costs: Fees approximately $100/semester

Financial Aid/Status
Scholarship programs for adults: Scholarships are no different for adults than for traditional students. Requirements vary depending on the scholarship.
Full-time status: 12 credit hours.
Percentage of adult students receiving financial aid: 40 percent.

Maximum Hours Awarded For
CLEP: Yes
DANTES: Yes
Other exams: Yes
Prior learning portfolio: Yes
Additional information: CLEP credit toward Associate, 45 credits;

toward bachelor's, 60 credits

Features and Services

1. Is it possible to purchase books during hours most adult students attend classes? **Yes.**

2. Are the institution's administrative offices open during hours adult students attend class? **Yes.**

3. How do students taking extended classes access library resources? **Library access available directly, by intercampus loan, local libraries, and statewide computer system.**

4. What is the registration and payment process for adult students? **Registration and payment are done by one-stop shopping approach. Interactive voice response is available.**

5. What is the process for advising adult students? **Advising is available in person and by phone both on and off campus.**

6. What career and placement services are available to adult students? **Career and placement services are available off campus and at the main campus.**

7. What characteristics of the institution's adult degree programs are most appealing to students? **Scheduling and student support services.**

University of Mary

7500 University Drive ◆ **Bismarck, ND 58504**

Phone: (701) 255-7500 ◆ Fax: (701) 255-7687

Founded: 1959

Accredited by: North Central

Enrollment: 1,800 ◆ Adult students: 30 percent

University status: Private, Church, Roman Catholic Church

Degree	Concentration/Major	Format
B.S.	Business Administration	E,TH
B.S.	Accounting	E,TH
B.S.	Social and Behavioral Science	E,TH
B.S.	Computer Information Systems	E,C

Requirements

Residency requirement: Attendance on campus depends on the student's transfer credit, prior learning potential, etc.
Undergraduate admissions requirements: Applicants must have a high school diploma or its equivalent.
Graduation requirements (undergraduate): Graduates must earn 128 semester hours.

Fees, Tuition, Costs

Undergraduate application fee: $15
Undergraduate tuition: $215/ semester hour
Undergraduate cost of books: $100/class

Financial Aid/Status

Scholarship programs for adults: Scholarships depend on enrollment status and financial need.
Full-time status: 12 semester hours; half-time is 6 semester hours.
Percentage of adult students receiving financial aid: 70 percent.

Maximum Hours Awarded For

CLEP: Yes
Prior learning portfolio: Yes
Additional information: Military (MOS) credit

Features and Services

1. Is it possible to purchase books during hours most adult students attend classes? **Yes.**

2. Are the institution's administrative offices open during hours adult students attend class? **Yes.**

3. How do students taking extended classes access library resources? **Library resources may be accessed through interlibrary loan.**

4. What is the registration and payment process for adult students? **Students use regular registration and meet payment dates, with the exception of some adult courses.**

5. What is the process for advising adult students? **Advisors are available during registration and other times by arrangement.**

6. What career and placement services are available to adult students? **The Central Career Placement Office is available.**

7. What characteristics of the institution's adult degree programs are most appealing to students? **Convenience, use of adult learning theory, credit for prior learning, quality, and hospitality.**

University of Maryland at College Park

2174 Engineering Classroom Building
College Park, MN 20742
Phone: (301) 405-5256 ◆ Fax: (301) 314-9477
Web address: http://www.umcp.umd.edu

Founded: 1856

Accredited by: Middle States

Enrollment: 32,908 ◆ Adult students: 13.2 percent

University status: Public

Degree	Concentration/Major	Format
M.Eng.	Engineering	E,T

Campus Extension Sites

Rockville, MD
Baltimore, MD
California, MD
Aberdeen, MD

Requirements

Residency requirement: Classes may be taken at any of the centers. Graduate admissions requirements: Applicants must have a degree in engineering or related field from a regionally accredited institution. Three letters of recommendation are required.
Graduation requirements (graduate): Graduates must complete 30 credits of approved course work.

Fees, Tuition, Costs

Graduate application fee: $50
Graduate tuition: $292/credit
Graduate cost of books: $70/course

Financial Aid/Status

Scholarship programs for adults: No scholarships available
Full-time status: Three courses

Features and Services

1. How do students taking extended classes access library resources? **Sites have small libraries. Books can be ordered using the courier service.**

2. What is the registration and payment process for adult students? **Students can register electronically by phone.**

3. What is the process for advising adult students? **Each student has a faculty advisor.**

4. What career and placement services are available to adult students? **Career and placement services may be used as other graduate students.**

5. What characteristics of the institution's adult degree programs are most appealing to students? **Flexibility of taking courses in the evening.**

University of Massachusetts, Dartmouth

285 Old Westport Road ◆ Division of Continuing Education
North Dartmouth, MA 02738
Phone: (508) 999-8041 ◆ Fax: (508) 999-8641
E-mail: bbrown@umassd.edu
Web address: http://www.umassd.edu

Program's Web address: http://www.umassd.edu/cybered

Founded: 1896

Accredited by: New England

Enrollment: 1,400 ◆ Adult students: 100 percent

University status: Public

Degree	Concentration/Major	Format
B.A.	Sociology	E,CT,S
B.A.	English	E,CT,S
B.S.	Psychology	E,CT,S
B.A.	Humanities/Social Science	E,CT,S
B.S.	Accounting	E,CT,S
B.S.	Management	E,CT,S

Campus Extension Sites

Attleboro, MA
Cape Cod, MA
Taunton, MA

Requirements

Residency requirement: If course requirements can be met at the satellite campus, a degree can be earned off campus; however, this is unusual.
Undergraduate admissions requirements: Applicants must submit a high school diploma or GED to the Continuing Education office. To be accepted into the major, 30 credits with 2.0 cumulative average or higher must be earned.

Graduation requirements (undergraduate): Graduates must earn 120 credits.

Fees, Tuition, Costs

Undergraduate application fee: $25
Undergraduate tuition: $365/3 credits
Undergraduate cost of books: $60-$75
Other costs: Occasional lab fees of $10-$25

Financial Aid/Status

Scholarship programs for adults: Scholarships available
Full-time status: 12 credits

Maximum Hours Awarded For

CLEP: 30
DANTES: 30
Other exams: Yes
Prior learning portfolio: 30
Additional information: Maximum of 30 credits combining CLEP and DANTES

Features and Services

1. Is it possible to purchase books during hours most adult students attend classes? **Yes.**

2. Are the institution's administrative offices open during hours adult students attend class? **Yes.**

3. How do students taking extended classes access library resources? **The library is open in the evening and on weekends.**

4. What is the registration and payment process for adult students? **Registration and payment may be done by phone or fax using check or credit card.**

5. What is the process for advising adult students? **Two full-time and one part-time Continuing Education advisors are available.**

6. What career and placement services are available to adult students? **Career and placement services are available during the day.**

University of Memphis*

J1 Johnson Hall ◆ Memphis, TN 38152
Phone: (901) 678-2716 ◆ Fax: (901) 678-4913
Web address: http://www.memphis.edu

Founded: 1912

Accredited by: Southern Association

Enrollment: 20,000 ◆ Adult students: 10,000

University status: Public

Features and Services

1. Is it possible to purchase books during hours most adult students attend classes? **Yes.**

2. Are the institution's administrative offices open during hours adult students attend class? **Yes.**

3. What characteristics of the institution's adult degree programs are most appealing to students? **Flexibility and ability to graduate in a shorter time.**

Degree	Concentration/Major	Format
B.P.S.	Individual Studies Self-designed degree programs; credit for experiential learning	E,C,S
B.L.S.	Individual Studies Self-designed degree programs; credit for experiential learning	E,C,S

Requirements

Residency requirement: Yes

Financial Aid/Status

Full-time status: 12 semester hours

Fees, Tuition, Costs

Undergraduate application fee: $15

Maximum Hours Awarded For

DANTES: Yes
Other exams: Yes
Prior learning portfolio: Yes

University of Miami

P.O. Box 248005 ◆ **Coral Gables, FL 33124**
Phone: (305) 284-2727 ◆ Fax: (305) 284-6279
E-mail: lseville@cstudies.msmail.miami.edu
Web address: http://www.ir.miami.edu

Founded: 1926

Accredited by: Southern Association

Enrollment: 8,000 ◆ Adult students: 20 percent

University status: Private

Degree	Concentration/Major	Format
B.A.	General Studies	E

Requirements

Residency requirement: Students must attend classes on campus. Undergraduate admissions requirements: Adult degree program requirements—minimum 2.0 GPA, U.S. citizen or resident, high school graduation at least four years prior to application. Graduation requirements (undergraduate): Graduates must earn 120 credits.

Fees, Tuition, Costs

Undergraduate application fee: $35
Undergraduate tuition: $217/credit for adult program

Undergraduate cost of books: $200/semester
Other costs: university fees of $200

Financial Aid/Status

Scholarship programs for adults: More than 45 scholarships ($1,000/year/renewable) available
Full-time status: 12 credits/semester
Percentage of adult students receiving financial aid: 40 percent

Maximum Hours Awarded For

CLEP: 27

Features and Services

1. Is it possible to purchase books during hours most adult students attend classes? **Yes.**

2. Are the institution's administrative offices open during hours adult students attend class? **Yes.**

3. How do students taking extended classes access library resources? **The library can be accessed by computer.**

4. What is the registration and payment process for adult students? **Easy, hassle-free, one-stop advising, registration, and payment are available (after 5:00 if needed).**

5. What is the process for advising adult students? **Advising is done two times each year. Personal, one-on-one advising is offered.**

6. What career and placement services are available to adult students? **Students have full access to two placement centers.**

7. What characteristics of the institution's adult degree programs are most appealing to students? **Tuition (2/3 less than traditional student payment), flexible areas of concentration, and easy advising and registration.**

University of Minnesota
University College/Continuing
Education and Extension

314 Nolte Center ◆ 315 Pillsbury Drive S.E.
Minneapolis, MN 55455-0197
Phone: (612) 625-2500 ◆ Fax: (612) 625-5364
E-mail: ceeadv@mail.cee.umn.edu
Web address: http://www.umn.edu/tc/

Program's Web address: http://www.cee.umn.edu

Founded: 1858

Accredited by: North Central

Enrollment: 65,000 ◆ Adult students: Vary

University status: Public

Degree	Concentration/Major	Format
B.A.	Art, Computer Science, Psychology, and others	E
B.S.	Civil Engineering	E
B.E.E.	Electrical Engineering	V,C
B.S.	Mechanical Engineering	E,T
B.A./B.S.	Individualized Program	S
B.A.B.	Applied Business	E
B.I.N.	Information Networking	E
M.S.W.	Social Work	E
M.L.S.	Liberal Studies	S
M.S.	English	E
M.F.A.	Fine Arts	E
M.B.T.	Business Taxation	E
M.Ed.	Education	E

Requirements

Residency requirement: Many distance education programs are available, including correspondence study.

Undergraduate admissions requirements: The requirements vary with the college and the degree program. Contact University College/Continuing Education and Extension.

Graduate admissions requirements: The requirements vary with the college and the degree program. Contact University College/Continuing Education and Extension.

Graduation requirements (undergraduate): Graduation requirements vary by the degree program.

Graduation requirements (graduate): Graduation requirements vary by the degree program and the college.

Fees, Tuition, Costs

Undergraduate application fee: $25
Graduate application fee: $40
Undergraduate tuition: Varies
Graduate tuition: Varies
Undergraduate cost of books: Varies
Graduate cost of books: Varies
Other costs: Cost varies between day and evening enrollment.

Financial Aid/Status

Scholarship programs for adults: Various undergraduate scholarships available for adults
Full-time status: 12 credits for federal aid, 15 for state aid

Maximum Hours Awarded For

CLEP: No limit
DANTES: No limit
Other exams: No limit
Prior learning portfolio: No limit
Additional information: Amount of credit awarded varies

Features and Services

1. Is it possible to purchase books during hours most adult students attend classes? **Yes.**

2. Are the institution's administrative offices open during hours adult students attend class? **Yes.**

3. What is the registration and payment process for adult students? **University College uses mail, fax, and in-person registration methods.**

4. What is the process for advising adult students? **Advising and career counseling services are offered by the department of Counseling, University College.**

5. What career and placement services are available to adult students? **Placement services are available to admitted students through the college career services offices.**

6. What characteristics of the institution's adult degree programs are most appealing to students? **The breadth and depth of courses and degrees available.**

University of Mississippi

117 Lyceum ◆ **University, MS 38677**
Phone: (601) 232-7226 ◆ Fax: (601) 232-5869
E-mail: a&rmail@lyceum1.reg.olemiss.edu
Web address: http://www.olemiss.edu

Founded: 1848

Accredited by: Southern Association

Enrollment: 10,181

University status: Public

Degree   Concentration/Major   Format

A wide variety of undergraduate and graduate degrees offered.
Not Specified

Campus Extension Sites

Tupelo, MS
Southaven, MS
Jackson, MS

Requirements

Residency requirement: Students are required to attend classes on campus unless they are enrolled at degree-granting centers. Undergraduate admissions requirements: A student over age 21, who does not qualify for admission, may be admitted as a "special" student. After earning 12 semester hours with a minimum

2.0 (C) GPA, regular admission status may be attained.
Graduate admissions requirements: An applicant with a bachelor's degree from an accredited institution may be admitted to a graduate program. Other requirements and procedures depend on the program. Graduation requirements (undergraduate): Graduates must complete degree and core curriculum requirements with at least a 2.0 GPA. At least 120 semester hours must be earned. Attendance at commencement is required.
Graduation requirements

(graduate): Graduates must meet the requirements for a particular degree program.

Fees, Tuition, Costs

Undergraduate tuition: $83/credit hour
Graduate tuition: $111/credit hour
Undergraduate cost of books: $275
Graduate cost of books: $300
Other costs: Required activity fee of $275 for students enrolled in more than 6 credit hours per semester

Financial Aid/Status

Full-time status: A full-time undergraduate is enrolled for 12 or more credits; graduate—9 or more credits.

Maximum Hours Awarded For

CLEP: 63
Additional information: Military experience and training

Features and Services

1. Is it possible to purchase books during hours most adult students attend classes? **Yes.**

2. How do students taking extended classes access library resources? **The library is open 24 hours M-Th and extended hours on other days.**

3. What is the registration and payment process for adult students? **Any university student may register for classes by phone and pay fees by mail.**

4. What is the process for advising adult students? **All students are required to meet with academic advisors each semester.**

5. What career and placement services are available to adult students? **A comprehensive career service area offers two career classes for credit, recruiting, workshops.**

University of Missouri— Kansas City

5100 Rockhill Rd., 101 SSB ◆ **Kansas City, MO 64110-2499**
Phone: (816)235-1111 ◆ Fax: (816)235-1717

Web address: http://www.cstp.umkc.edu

Founded: 1933

Accredited by: North Central

Enrollment: 10,209

University status: Public

Financial Aid/Status
Full-time status: Undergraduate—12 credit hours, graduate—9 credit hours

Maximum Hours Awarded For
CLEP: Yes
Other exams: Yes
Additional information: Advanced Placement Program

Features and Services

1. Is it possible to purchase books during hours most adult students attend classes? **Yes.**

2. Are the institution's administrative offices open during hours adult students attend class? **Yes.**

3. What is the registration and payment process for adult students? **Extended hours, phone registration, credit card payment.**

Degree	Concentration/Major	Format
B.L.A.	College of Arts and Sciences: Liberal Arts	E
B.S.	Accounting	E
M.A.	Counseling and Guidance	E
M.A.	Educational Administration	E
M.A.	Educational Research and Psychology	E
M.A.	Reading Education	E
M.A.	Special Education	E
M.S.	Accounting	E
M.B.A.	Business Administration	E
M.P.A.	Public Administration	E
Ph.D.	Counseling Psychology	E

Requirements

Undergraduate admissions requirements: ACT score percentile and high school rank percentile
Graduate admissions requirements: Varies
Graduation requirements (undergraduate): Minimum 120 credit hours and program requirements
Graduation requirements (graduate): Varies

Fees, Tuition, Costs

Undergraduate application fee: $25
Graduate application fee: $25
Undergraduate tuition: $121/credit hour
Graduate tuition: $153/credit hour

University of Nebraska—Lincoln

162 Hardin 33rd and Holdredge Streets
Nebraska Center for Continuing Education
Lincoln, NE 68583-9200
Phone: (402) 472-1392 ◆ Toll-free phone: (800) 742-8800
Fax: (402) 472-0591 E-mail: eversoll@unlinfo.unl.edu
Web address: http://www.unl.edu

Program's Web address: http://www.unl.edu/conted

Founded: 1869

Accredited by: North Central

Enrollment: 24,320 ◆ Adult students: 6,456

University status: Public

Degree	Concentration/Major	Format
B.S.	Business Administration	E
B.A.	Communication Studies	E
B.A./B.S.	Economics	E
B.S.	Finance	E
B.A.	Integrated Studies	E
B.S.	Management	E
B.S.	Marketing	E
B.A.	Political Science	E
B.A.	Psychology	E
B.A.	Sociology	E
M.B.A.	Business Administration	E
M.C.R.P.	Community and Regional Planning	E

Campus Extension Site

Bellevue, NE

Requirements

Residency requirement: Undergraduates must complete 30 of the final 36 hours in residence. Graduate degrees require 1/2 of master's course work in residence; doctoral degree, at least 27 hours in an 18-month period or less. Undergraduate admissions requirements: 16 high school units: English(4), math (4—including algebra I & II, geometry, advanced math), social science (3), natural science (3), foreign language (2); upper half of class; SAT (950) or ACT (20).

Graduate admissions requirements: Undergraduate degree from accredited institution; entrance exams (GRE, GMAT, etc.); three letters of recommendation; and possibly statement of goals, letter of intent, or portfolio.

Graduation requirements (undergraduate): Undergraduate degrees require at least 125 semester hours. The academic standards (GPA) and course requirements vary from program to program.

Graduation requirements (graduate): Graduates must earn at least 30 semester hours for the master's; 90 semester hours for doctoral degrees. Course requirements vary greatly from program to program; 3.0 GPA is required for the program.

Fees, Tuition, Costs

Undergraduate application fee: $25
Graduate application fee: $25
Undergraduate tuition: $72.75/semester hour
Graduate tuition: $96.25/semester hour
Undergraduate cost of books: $0-$100
Graduate cost of books: $0-$100
Other costs: Program and facilities fees (assessed every semester); special course fees; lab fees

Financial Aid/Status

Scholarship programs for adults: No special adult scholarships are offered, but all other scholarships are open to adult students who qualify.
Full-time status: At least 12 semester hours/semester; 30-33 hours/academic year.

Maximum Hours Awarded For

CLEP: Yes
PEP: Yes
DANTES: Yes
Additional information: Transfer credit from other colleges

Features and Services

1. How do students taking extended classes access library resources? **Library resources may be used through computer access or local and area college libraries.**

2. What is the registration and payment process for adult students? **Registration is the same for all students. Students are billed for tuition and fees.**

3. What is the process for advising adult students? **Major advisor assigned at admission. Prospective**

adult students are advised by Continuing Education.

4. What career and placement services are available to adult students? **Career planning for adult students is available through the division of Continuing Studies.**

5. What characteristics of the institution's adult degree programs are most appealing to students? **Quality instruction by esteemed faculty, accessibility of programs and services, part-time evenings/weekends degrees, and very reasonable tuition.**

University of Nevada—Reno

Continuing Education-048 ◆ **Reno, NV 89557**

Phone: (702) 784-4046 ◆ Toll-free phone: (800) 233-8928

Fax: (702) 784-4801 ◆ E-mail: judith@unr.edu

Web address: http://www.scs.unr.edu/unr/index/html

Program's Web address: http://www.scs.unr.edu/indstudy

Founded: 1874

Accredited by: Northwest Association

Enrollment: 12,000 ◆ Adult students: 3,555

University status: Public

Degree	Concentration/Major	Format
B.G.S.	General Studies	E,C,T
B.A.	Business Administration	E
M.B.A.	Business Administration	E

Campus Extension Site
Elko, NV

Requirements
Residency requirement: Students are not required to attend classes on campus.
Undergraduate admissions requirements: Applicants must be high school graduates (minimum 2.5 GPA). Specific high school courses are required. Degree programs may have additional requirements. Applicants over 25 are exempt from ACT/SAT requirement. Graduate admissions requirements: Applicants must hold a bachelor's degree and meet academic requirements of the degree program.
Graduation requirements (undergraduate): Graduation requirements vary from degree to degree.
Graduation requirements

(graduate): Graduation requirements vary from degree to degree.

Fees, Tuition, Costs
Undergraduate application fee: $20
Graduate application fee: $20
Undergraduate tuition: $61/credit
Graduate tuition: $84/credit
Undergraduate cost of books: Varies
Graduate cost of books: Varies

Financial Aid/Status
Scholarship programs for adults: Scholarships available
Full-time status: 12 or more credits

Maximum Hours Awarded For
CLEP: Varies
PEP: Varies
DANTES: Varies
Other exams: Varies

Features and Services
1. How do students taking extended classes access library resources? **The library is open at night and on weekends.**

2. What is the registration and payment process for adult students? **Registration and payment are the same for all students.**

---

3. What is the process for advising adult students? **Advising is the same as for regular students.**

4. What career and placement services are available to adult students? **Career and placement services are the same for all students.**

5. What characteristics of the institution's adult degree programs are most appealing to students? **Courses available at night, weekends, and by correspondence.**

University of New Hampshire*
Varrette House
6 Garrison Avenue ◆ **Durham, NH 03824**
Phone: (603) 862-1937 ◆ Fax: (603) 862-1113
Web address: http://www.unh.edu

Founded: 1866

Accredited by: New England

Enrollment: 12,500 ◆ Adult students: 233

University status: Public

Features and Services

1. Is it possible to purchase books during hours most adult students attend classes? **Yes.**

2. What characteristics of the institution's adult degree programs are most appealing to students? **Quality of instruction.**

Degree	Concentration/Major	Format
A.A.	General Studies	

Requirements

Residency requirement: Yes
Undergraduate admissions requirements: Successful academic experience, either in high school or in previous college work, plus personal and/or professional accomplishments since high school

Fees, Tuition, Costs

Undergraduate application fee: $45
Undergraduate tuition: $161

Financial Aid/Status

Full-time status: 12 semester hours or more
Percentage of adult students receiving financial aid: 58 percent

Maximum Hours Awarded For

CLEP: Yes
PEP: Yes
Other exams: Yes
Additional information: Maximum of 48 hours through exams

University of New Hampshire at Manchester

220 Hackatt Hill Road ◆ Manchester, NH 03102
Phone: (603) 668-0700 ◆ Fax: (603) 623-2745

Founded: 1967

Accredited by: New England

Enrollment: 708 ◆ Adult students: 39 percent

University status: Public

Degree	Concentration/Major	Format
A.A./A.S.	Biology	E
A.A./A.S.	Business	E
A.A./A.S.	General Studies	E
A.A./A.S.	Studio Arts	E
B.A.	Communication	E
B.A.	English	E
B.A.	History	E
B.A.	Humanities	E
B.A.	Political Science	E
B.A.	Psychology	E
B.S.	Business Administration	E
B.S.	Electrical Engineering Technology	E
B.S.	Mechanical Engineering Technology	E
B.S.	Sign Language Interpretation	E
B.S.	Nursing for RNs	E

Requirements

Residency requirement: Students must attend classes on campus. Some courses are broadcast to and received from off-campus sites by instructional television. Undergraduate admissions requirements: Applicants must have a high school diploma or GED, file an application with required documents, GPA 2.5-2.8 or better. Graduation requirements (undergraduate): Associate degree: 64 credit hours (minimum 2.0 GPA); general education and core course requirements. Bachelor's: 128 credit hours (minimum 2.0 GPA); general education, major, degree requirements.

Fees, Tuition, Costs

Undergraduate application fee: $25
Undergraduate tuition: $3,390/year
Undergraduate cost of books: $650/year

Financial Aid/Status

Full-time status: 12 credit hours

Maximum Hours Awarded For

CLEP: Yes
PEP: Yes
DANTES: Yes
Other exams: Yes

Features and Services

1. Is it possible to purchase books during hours most adult students attend classes? **Yes.**

2. Are the institution's administrative offices open during hours adult students attend class? **Yes.**

3. What is the registration and payment process for adult students? **Registration and payment may be done by phone, walk-in, mail, or fax.**

4. What is the process for advising adult students? **Advisors are assigned to each student—usually a faculty member in the student's academic area.**

5. What career and placement services are available to adult students? **Career and placement services are administered through the Academic Counseling Office.**

6. What characteristics of the institution's adult degree programs are most appealing to students? **Location, schedule, costs, and access.**

University of New Haven*

300 Orange Avenue ◆ **West Haven, CT 06516**
Phone: (203) 932-7235 ◆ Toll-free phone: (800) DIAL-UNH
Fax: (203) 933-5610
Web address: http://www.newhaven.edu

Founded: 1920

Accredited by: New England

Enrollment: 6,000 ◆ Adult students: 5,049

University status: Private

Degree Concentration/Major — Format

Degree	Concentration/Major	Format
B.A.	Art, Biology, Biomedical Computing, Chemistry, Communication, Economics, English, Environmental Science, General Studies, Graphic Design, History, Interior Design, Journalism, Mathematics, Music, Music Industry & Sound Recording, Political Science, Psychology, Sociology.	E
B.S.	Accounting, Business Administration, Business Economics, Communication, Finance, International Business, Marketing, Public Administration, Chemical Engineering, Civil Engineering, Computer Science, Electrical Engineering, Industrial Engineering, Materials Technology, Mechanical Engineering, General Dietics, Hotel & Restaurant Management, Tourism & Travel Administration, Air Transportation Management, Arson Investigation, Criminal Justice, Fire Science, Fire & Occupational Safety & Health, Paralegal Studies	E
M.B.A.	Business Administration	E
M.P.A.	Public Administration	E
E.M.B.A.	Executive M.B.A.	E
M.A.	Community Psychology	E
M.A.	Industrial/Organizational Psychology	E
M.S.I.E.	Industrial Engineering	E
M.S.E.E.	Electrical Engineering	E
M.S.M.E.	Mechanical Engineering	E
Sc.D.	Management Systems	E

Requirements

Residency requirement: Yes
Undergraduate admissions requirements: Graduates of accredited high schools or secondary schools or persons who have a state high school equivalency diploma
Graduate admissions requirements: Graduates from accredited college or university

Fees, Tuition, Costs

Undergraduate application fee: $25
Graduate application fee: $50
Undergraduate tuition: $208/credit
Graduate tuition: $1,550/course

Financial Aid/Status

Full-time status: 12 undergraduate credits, 9 graduate credits
Percentage of adult students receiving financial aid: 15 percent

Maximum Hours Awarded For

CLEP: 15
PEP: 15
DANTES: 15
Other exams: 30

Features and Services

1. Is it possible to purchase books during hours most adult students attend classes? **Yes.**

2. What characteristics of the institution's adult degree programs are most appealing to students? **Variety of program offerings.**

University of New Orleans

103 Administration Building ◆ **New Orleans, LA 70148**
Phone: (504) 286-6595 ◆ Toll-free phone: (800) 256-5866
Fax: (504) 286-5522
Web address: http://www.uno.edu

Founded: 1958

Accredited by: Southern Association

Enrollment: 15,600 ◆ Adult students: 40 percent

University status: Public

Degree	Concentration/Major	Format
B.G.S.	General Studies	S
B.S.	Engineering	E
B.S.	Business	E

Requirements

Residency requirement: The last 30 hours in residence are required. Undergraduate admissions requirements: Requirements include 2.0 cumulative GPA for transfer students; ACT 20 or SAT 950; or 2.0 GPA in 17 1/2 high school core units for freshmen. Graduation requirements (undergraduate): Graduates must earn at least 128 semester hours.

Fees, Tuition, Costs

Undergraduate application fee: $20
Undergraduate tuition: $1,181/semester
Undergraduate cost of books: $500/year

Financial Aid/Status

Scholarship programs for adults: Tuition waived for first three semester hours for first-time adult students
Full-time status: 12 undergraduate semester hours; 9 graduate semester hours
Percentage of adult students receiving financial aid: 50 percent

Maximum Hours Awarded For

CLEP: 30
PEP: 30
DANTES: 30
Other exams: 30

Features and Services

1. Is it possible to purchase books during hours most adult students attend classes? **Yes.**

2. Are the institution's administrative offices open during hours adult students attend class? **Yes.**

3. What is the registration and payment process for adult students? **Fee payment may be done by credit card. Registration/payment may be done by mail.**

4. What is the process for advising adult students? **Advising is available.**

5. What career and placement services are available to adult students? **Career and placement services are available.**

University of North Alabama

Box 5021 ◆ Florence, AL 35632-0001
Phone: (205) 760-4288 ◆ Fax: (205) 760-4329

Founded: 1830

Accredited by: Southern Association

Enrollment: 5,400 ◆ Adult students: 25 percent

University status: Public

Degree	Concentration/Major	Format
B.S.	General Studies	E

Requirements

Residency requirement: Students must attend classes on campus. Undergraduate admissions requirements: Applicants (25 years old or out of high school for five years) must demonstrate competency by having minimum 2.0 high school GPA. Transfer students must have at least 24 credits (2.0 GPA). Graduation requirements (undergraduate): Graduates must earn 128 semester hours (2.0 GPA). The last 16 hours of the 32 requires residence at UNA. Score satisfactorily in both English proficiency and general studies.

Fees, Tuition, Costs

Undergraduate application fee: $25
Undergraduate tuition: $75/credit hour
Undergraduate cost of books: $275/semester
Other costs: $3/credit hour technology fee

Financial Aid/Status

Scholarship programs for adults: Endowments are available for nontraditional students. Academic transfer scholarships are available. Transfer status is required. Other scholarships are offered for full-time students.
Full-time status: Full-time status for fall/spring is 12 hours; summer term is 6 hours.

Maximum Hours Awarded For

CLEP: Yes
DANTES: Yes
Additional information: SOC, Advanced Placement, & CPS exams; maximum of 34 hours by nontraditional subject exams

Features and Services

1. Is it possible to purchase books during hours most adult students attend classes? **Yes.**

2. Are the institution's administrative offices open during hours adult students attend class? **Yes.**

3. How do students taking extended classes access library resources? **The library has late evening hours and is open on weekends.**

4. What is the registration and payment process for adult students? **Registration hours are extended during the registration period to accommodate working adults.**

5. What is the process for advising adult students? **Advisement is mandatory. Students must meet with an assigned advisor. Appointments are made by student.**

6. What career and placement services are available to adult students? **The UNA Office of Career Services keeps students informed of job opportunities in their field.**

7. What characteristics of the institution's adult degree programs are most appealing to students? **Personal contact between students and faculty, the availability of evening and weekend classes, and library access.**

University of North Dakota

P.O. Box 8135 ◆ **Grand Forks, ND 58202-8135**
Phone: (701) 777-4463 ◆ Toll-free phone: (800) 225-5863
Web address: http://www.und.nodax.edu

Founded: 1883

Accredited by: North Central

Enrollment: 12,000 ◆ Adult students: 3,338

University status: Public

Degree	Concentration/Major	Format
B.B.A.	Management	T
M.B.A.	Business Administration	T
M.P.A.	Public Administration	T

Campus Extension Sites

Devil's Lake, ND
Williston, ND
Bismarck, ND
Dickinson, ND

Requirements

Residency requirement: Students do not have to attend classes on campus.
Undergraduate admissions requirements: Applicants must have a high school diploma or GED, immunization proof, and submit an application. Transfer students need a C average or better.
Graduate admissions requirements: Applicants must hold a bachelor's degree from a recognized institution with a minimum of 20 semester credits in the appropriate major field.
Graduation requirements (undergraduate): Graduates must earn at least 125 semester credits meeting general education, major, minor, grade point average, upper-division courses, and residence requirements.
Graduation requirements (graduate): Graduates must meet the specific requirements for the degree program.

Fees, Tuition, Costs

Undergraduate application fee: $25
Graduate application fee: $20
Undergraduate tuition: $1,214/semester
Graduate tuition: $1,319/semester
Undergraduate cost of books: $500/year full-time
Graduate cost of books: $700/year full-time
Other costs: Lab fees

Financial Aid/Status

Full-time status: 12 semester credits

Maximum Hours Awarded For

CLEP: Yes
Other exams: Yes

Features and Services

1. Is it possible to purchase books during hours most adult students attend classes? **Yes.**

2. How do students taking extended classes access library resources? **Library resources are available on ODIN, an online catalog.**

3. What is the registration and payment process for adult students? **Registration and payment are the same for all students.**

4. What is the process for advising adult students? **Advising is available.**

5. What career and placement services are available to adult students? **Career and placement services are available.**

University of Northern Colorado

College of Continuing Education
Greeley, CO 80639
Phone: (970) 351-2944 ◆ Fax: (970) 351-2519
E-mail: sdarling@cce.univnorthco.edu
Web address: http://community.univnorthco.edu/cce/index.html

Founded: 1889

Accredited by: North Central

Enrollment: 10,000

University status: Public

Degree	Concentration/Major	Format
B.S.	Human Rehabilitative Services	E
B.A.	Spanish	E
M.A.	Agency Counseling	E
M.S.	Applied Statistics and Research Methods: Operations Research	E
M.A.	Special Education: Moderate Needs, Gifted and Talented, Severe Needs	E
M.A.	Educational Technology	E
M.A.	Interdisciplinary Studies: Education	E
M.A.	Physical Education: Pedagogy	E
M.A.	Human Communication or Communication Education	E
M.A.	Physical Education: Sports Administration	E
M.A.	Communication Disorders: Speech/Language Multimedia	T
M.A.	Elementary Education: Early Childhood Education	E

Campus Extension Sites

Metro Denver, CO
Colorado Spring, CO
Pueblo, CO
Fort Lupton, CO
Grand Junction, CO
Sterling, CO
Aurora, CO
Fort Carson, CO

Requirements

Residency requirement: Students do not have to attend classes on campus. Off-campus degree programs are available at the sites. Undergraduate admissions requirements: Requirements vary by the degree. Graduate admissions requirements: Requirements vary by the degree. Contact the Graduate School (970) 351-2831 for more information. Graduation requirements (undergraduate): Requirements vary by the degree. Graduation requirements (graduate): Graduation requirements depend on the degree.

Fees, Tuition, Costs

Graduate application fee: $40
Undergraduate tuition: $146/credit hour
Graduate tuition: $169/credit hour
Undergraduate cost of books: Varies
Graduate cost of books: Varies

Financial Aid/Status

Scholarship programs for adults: No special scholarships are offered. Other scholarships use national standards for eligibility.
Full-time status: Full-time graduate status is 9 or more credits per semester.

Maximum Hours Awarded For

CLEP: Yes

Features and Services

1. How do students taking extended classes access library resources? **Off campus library services are available.**

2. What is the registration and payment process for adult students? **Registration and payment are available off-campus in person, by mail, fax, and phone.**

3. What is the process for advising adult students? **Advising is available on-site by a graduate advisor. Special meetings are held on-site.**

4. What characteristics of the institution's adult degree programs are most appealing to students? **Evening and weekend format and concentrated format.**

University of the Pacific

3601 Pacific Avenue ◆ Stockton, CA 95211
Phone: (209) 946-2427 ◆ E-mail: dduns@vmsi.uop.edu
Web address: http://www.

Founded: 1851

Accredited by: Western Association

Enrollment: 6,000 ◆ Adult students: 10-15 percent

University status: Private

Degree	Concentration/Major	Format
B.A.	Liberal Studies	S
B.A.	Organizational Communications	S
B.A.	Human Services	S

Requirements

Residency requirement: Students must attend classes on campus. Adult students are "mainstreamed" into the traditional university academic programs.
Undergraduate admissions requirements: Applicants need a high school diploma. Adult reentry students will be given special consideration for admission if needed.
Graduation requirements (undergraduate): Graduation generally requires 124 units, a major, a minimum C average in the major and all work, and a minimum of 32 units at Pacific.

Fees, Tuition, Costs

Undergraduate application fee: $50
Graduate application fee: $50
Undergraduate tuition: $591/unit
Graduate tuition: $591/unit
Undergraduate cost of books: $350-$400

Financial Aid/Status

Scholarship programs for adults: Scholarships are available.
Full-time status: Full-time students are enrolled for at least 12 units; some financial programs only require 6 units.
Percentage of adult students receiving financial aid: 65 percent.

Maximum Hours Awarded For

CLEP: Yes
Other exams: Yes
Prior learning portfolio: Yes

Features and Services

1. Is it possible to purchase books during hours most adult students attend classes? **Yes.**

2. Are the institution's administrative offices open during hours adult students attend class? **Yes.**

3. What is the registration and payment process for adult students? **The same process is used for all students. Full or installment payment must be made prior to registration.**

4. What is the process for advising adult students? **University College provides an advisor and a peer advisor. A major advisor may also be assigned.**

5. What career and placement services are available to adult students? **Full career and placement services are available.**

6. What characteristics of the institution's adult degree programs are most appealing to students? **Excellent quality, small classes, and personal attention by superior faculty members.**

University of Pennsylvania

College of General Studies

3440 Market Street, Suite 100 ◆ **Philadelphia, PA 19104**

Phone: (215) 898-7326 ◆ Fax: (215) 573-2053

E-mail: cgs@sas.upenn.edu

Web address: http://www.sas.upenn.edu/cgs

Founded: 1892

Accredited by: Middle States

Enrollment: 1,500 ◆ Adult students: 100 percent

University status: Private

Degree	Concentration/Major	Format
A.A.	Broad range of liberal arts majors	E
B.A.	Broad range of liberal arts majors	E
M.L.A.	Liberal Arts—Individualized, interdisciplinary humanities	E,S

Requirements

Residency requirement: Students must attend classes on campus. One off-site program at the CIGNA Corporation is open to their employees only. Undergraduate admissions requirements: Applicants need a strong academic record in liberal arts with a commitment to a liberal arts education; two- or four-year college experience is preferred; SAT/ACT scores are not required. Graduate admissions requirements: Applicants need a superior academic record in liberal arts, ability to work independently, and cohesive concept for the individualized program of study. Graduation requirements (undergraduate): Requirements vary depending on the major. Students must meet distribution requirements, writing requirement, four semesters of foreign language, and pass proficiency exams. Graduation requirements (graduate): M.L.A. requires completing 9 courses, a professional seminar, and a capstone project.

Fees, Tuition, Costs

Undergraduate application fee: $35
Graduate application fee: $35
Undergraduate tuition: $802/course
Graduate tuition: $1,325/course
Undergraduate cost of books: Varies
Graduate cost of books: Varies

Financial Aid/Status

Scholarship programs for adults: Scholarships available
Full-time status: 4 courses/semester

Maximum Hours Awarded For

Other exams: Yes
Prior learning portfolio: Yes

Features and Services

1. Is it possible to purchase books during hours most adult students attend classes? **Yes.**

2. Are the institution's administrative offices open during hours adult students attend class? **Yes.**

3. How do students taking extended classes access library resources? **The library is available during the evening and by computer.**

4. What is the registration and payment process for adult students? **Registration/payment may be done during the evening.**

5. What is the process for advising adult students? **Advising is available by appointment both day and evening. Walk-in hours are also available.**

6. What career and placement services are available to adult students? **A university-wide career planning and placement service is available to students.**

7. What characteristics of the institution's adult degree programs are most appealing to students? **Flexible programs, excellent advising staff, full Ivy-League degree, exactly the same program as traditional undergraduate B.A. at 1/3 cost.**

University of Phoenix

4615 E. Elwood Street ◆ **Phoenix, AZ 85040**
Phone: (602) 966-5394 ◆ Fax: (602) 894-1758
E-mail: trelisal.oramial@apollogrp.edu
Web address: http://www.uophx.edu

Founded: 1976

Accredited by: North Central

Enrollment: 27,054 ◆ Adult students: 100 percent

University status: Private, Profit

Degree	Concentration/Major	Format
B.S.B.	Administration	E,A,C,CT,S
B.S.B.	Information Systems	E,A,C,S
B.S.B.	Management	E,A,C,CT,S
B.S.	Nursing	E,A
M.B.A.	Administration	E,A,C,CT,S
M.N.	Nursing	E,A
M.C.	Counseling	E,A
M.S.C.I.S.	Information Systems	E,A
M.A.Ed.	Education	E,A

Requirements

Residency requirement: Students do not have to attend classes on campus. Self-paced/directed study options and online/computer options may be used to gain degree.
Undergraduate admissions requirements: Applicants must be at least 23 years old and be currently employed.
Graduate admissions requirements: Applicants must be at least 23 years old, have three years of work experience after high school, be currently employed, hold a bachelor's degree, and have a minimum 2.5 entry GPA.
Graduation requirements (undergraduate): Undergraduates need 120 credits (39 general education credits), complete postcognitive assessment test, a graduation form, and pay all fees.
Graduation requirements (graduate): Graduates must complete 41-51 credits, depending on the major, complete the postcognitive assessment test, a graduation form, and pay all fees.

Fees, Tuition, Costs

Undergraduate application fee: $50
Graduate application fee: $50
Undergraduate tuition: $230
Graduate tuition: $280

Financial Aid/Status

Scholarship programs for adults: Scholarships are available.
Full-time status: All students are full-time; equivalent of 24 semester credits per year.
Percentage of adult students receiving financial aid: 57 percent.

Maximum Hours Awarded For

CLEP: Yes
PEP: Yes
DANTES: Yes
Other exams: Yes
Prior learning portfolio: 39

Features and Services

1. Is it possible to purchase books during hours most adult students attend classes? **Yes.**

2. Are the institution's administrative offices open during hours adult students attend class? **Yes.**

3. What is the registration and payment process for adult students? **To register, call or visit the local campus.**

4. What is the process for advising adult students? **An enrollment representative monitors first three classes. Guidance is provided by an academic counselor.**

5. What characteristics of the institution's adult degree programs are most appealing to students? **Convenient, evening classes, and some projects are group-oriented.**

University of Pittsburgh

University External Studies Program
3804 Forbes Avenue ◆ **Pittsburgh, PA 15260**
Phone: (412) 624-7210 ◆ Fax: (412) 624-7213
Web address: http://www.pitt.edu
Program's Web address:
http://www.pitt.edu/cidde/cdde.home.html

Founded: 1787

Accredited by: Middle States

Enrollment: 33,000 ◆ Adult students: 2,400

University status: Public

Degree	Concentration/Major	Format
B.A.	Economics	E,S
B.A.	History	E,S
B.S.	Psychology	E,S

The Center for Instructional Development and Distance Education (CIDDE) was established in July 1995. One of its major thrusts is to provide assistance in developing and supporting distance education programs and courses. Plans are currently under way to provide a plethora of graduate programs.

Campus Extension Sites

Bradford, PA
Greenburg, PA
Johnstown, PA
Titusville, PA

Requirements

Residency requirement: Students attend three Saturday workshops during the term, usually on the Pittsburgh campus. Students complete most of the work independently, using specially prepared self-instructional materials.
Undergraduate admissions requirements: Admissions of adult-age students are made individually. Educational background, nonacademic activities, and academic goals are reviewed.
Graduation requirements (undergraduate): Although there are differences among majors, generally speaking, successful completion of 120 credits is required for most undergraduate degree programs.

Fees, Tuition, Costs

Undergraduate application fee: $35
Undergraduate tuition: $2,592/ semester
Undergraduate cost of books: $10-$100
Other costs: Activity fee of $30; Computing and Network Services Fee of $46; Security and Transportation Fee of $30

Financial Aid/Status

Scholarship programs for adults: Grants available for full- and part-time students
Full-time status: 12-18 credits

Maximum Hours Awarded For

CLEP: 30

Features and Services

1. Is it possible to purchase books during hours most adult students attend classes? **Yes.**

2. Are the institution's administrative offices open during hours adult students attend class? **Yes.**

3. What is the registration and payment process for adult students? **Students may register in person, through the mail, or by fax. Credit cards are accepted for tuition.**

4. What is the process for advising adult students? **Students may meet with their advisors in person or arrange a phone appointment.**

5. What career and placement services are available to adult students? **Help with resume preparation is available by individual or group appointments.**

6. What characteristics of the institution's adult degree programs are most appealing to students? **Independent study allows student flexibility in choosing time to study.**

University of Pittsburgh at Bradford

300 Campus Drive ◆ **Bradford, PA 16701**
Phone: (814) 362-0911 ◆ Fax: (814) 362-0914
E-mail: gal2t@pitt.edu

Founded: 1963

Accredited by: Middle States

Enrollment: 1,200 ◆ Adult students: 400

University status: Public

Degree	Concentration/Major	Format
B.A.	Economics	E,S
B.A.	History	E,S
B.S.	Psychology	E,S

Degrees and services are currently being reviewed/revised at this time. Contact the Continuing Education Department for current information.

Campus Extension Site

St. Mary's, PA
Warren, PA
Kane, PA
Coudersport, PA

Requirements

Residency requirement: Students must currently attend classes on campus. Adding off-campus degrees is currently being considered.
Undergraduate admissions requirements: Currently being reviewed. Contact the Continuing Education office for up-to-date information.
Graduate admissions requirements: Graduate degrees are not currently being offered. Degrees may be offered in the future. Contact the office for more information.

Fees, Tuition, Costs

Undergraduate application fee: $35
Undergraduate tuition: $181/ semester hour

Financial Aid/Status

Scholarship programs for adults: Scholarships available
Full-time status: 12 or more semester hours

Maximum Hours Awarded For

CLEP: Yes
Other exams: Yes

Features and Services

1. Is it possible to purchase books during hours most adult students attend classes? **Yes.**

2. Are the institution's administrative offices open during hours adult students attend class? **Yes.**

3. What is the registration and payment process for adult students? **One-stop service for admission, registration, payment through the Continuing Education Department.**

4. What is the process for advising adult students? **Initial undeclared major advising is done through Continuing Education. Major advisor is assigned.**

5. What career and placement services are available to adult students? **Testing and career counseling, interviewing workshops, simulated job interviewing, and placement service.**

6. What characteristics of the institution's adult degree programs are most appealing to students? **One-stop services through Continuing Education and faculty who care about and are interested in teaching and assisting adults.**

University of Redlands Whitehead College

1200 E. Colton Avenue ◆ **Redlands, CA 92373**
Phone: (909) 335-4060 ◆ Fax: (909) 335-3400
Web address: http://www.uor.edu

Founded: 1907

Accredited by: Western Association

Enrollment: 3,705 ◆ Adult students: 2,300

University status: Private

Degree	Concentration/Major	Format
B.S.	Business and Management	E
B.S.	Information Systems	E
B.A.	Liberal Studies	E
M.B.A.	Business Administration	E
M.A.	Management	E
M.A.	Counseling	E
M.A.	Education Administration	E
M.A.	Curriculum Leadership	E

Requirements

Residency requirement: Programs offered in many Southern California cities and at corporate sites. Graduate degrees and some undergraduate degrees may be completed at the sites.
Undergraduate admissions requirements: Requirements are currently being revised. Interested students should contact the university for current information.
Graduate admissions requirements: Applicants must hold a bachelor's degree, minimum 3.0 GPA in last two years of undergraduate and postbaccalaureate work. An application, essay, and two recommendations must be submitted.
Graduation requirements (undergraduate): Requirements vary depending on the program.
Graduation requirements (graduate): Requirements vary depending on the program.

Fees, Tuition, Costs

Undergraduate application fee: $40
Graduate application fee: $40
Undergraduate tuition: $341/unit
Graduate tuition: $369/unit
Undergraduate cost of books: $1,500
Graduate cost of books: $1,500

Financial Aid/Status

Scholarship programs for adults: Contact the Financial Aid office for current information.
Percentage of adult students receiving financial aid: 70 percent.

Maximum Hours Awarded For

CLEP: 24
Prior learning portfolio: 30

Features and Services

1. How do students taking extended classes access library resources? **Students may use the electronic library.**

2. What is the registration and payment process for adult students? **The process depends on the program, financial aid track, or if attending at a corporate site.**

3. What is the process for advising adult students? **Advising done by phone or appointment. Class visits are made at various points during the program.**

4. What career and placement services are available to adult students? **A career center on campus provides job fairs and other services.**

5. What characteristics of the institution's adult degree programs are most appealing to students? **Method of delivery in convenient locations; books delivered to classroom.**

University of Richmond*

School of Continuing Studies ◆ Special Programs Building
Richmond, VA 23173
Phone: (804) 289-8133 ◆ Fax: (804) 289-8138
Web address: http://www.urich.edu

Founded: 1830

Accredited by: Southern Association

Enrollment: 4,315 ◆ Adult students: 558

University status: Private, Church, Baptist

Degree	Concentration/Major	Format
B.A.S.	Humanities and Social Sciences	E
B.A.S.	Human Resource Management	E
B.A.S.	Information Processing Systems	E
B.A.S.	Paralegal Studies	E

Requirements

Residency requirement: Yes
Undergraduate admissions
requirements: Complete
application and furnish transcripts
from all schools previously
attended

Fees, Tuition, Costs

Undergraduate tuition: $152/
semester hour

Financial Aid/Status

Full-time status: Students enrolled
in 12 semester hours or more
Percentage of adult students
receiving financial aid: 27 percent

Maximum Hours Awarded For

CLEP: 60

Features and Services

1. Is it possible to purchase books during hours most adult students attend classes? **Yes.**

2. Are the institution's administrative offices open during hours adult students attend class? **Yes.**

3. What characteristics of the institution's adult degree programs are most appealing to students? **Ease of entry and counseling one-step services. Programs developed for adults.**

University of Rhode Island

712 Chafee Social Science Building
Education Department
Kingston, RI 02881
Phone: (401) 792-4159 ◆ Fax: (401) 792-5471
Web address: http://www.uri.edu

Founded: 1892

Accredited by: New England

Enrollment: 12,000 ◆ Adult students: 50

University status: Public

Features and Services

1. Is it possible to purchase books during hours most adult students attend classes? **Yes.**

2. Are the institution's administrative offices open during hours adult students attend class? **Yes.**

3. What characteristics of the institution's adult degree programs are most appealing to students? **Competency-based, evening classes, and adult-learner-oriented.**

Degree	Concentration/Major	Format
M.A.	Adult Education	E

Requirements

Residency requirement: Students are not required to attend classes on campus.
Graduate admissions requirements: Applicants must hold a baccalareate degree. MAT/GRE scores, three letters of recommendation, and official transcripts must be submitted.

Fees, Tuition, Costs

Graduate application fee: $30
Graduate tuition: $4,612/year

Financial Aid/Status

Full-time status: At least 9 credits/ semester

University of San Francisco
College of Professional Studies
2130 Fulton Street ◆ **San Francisco, CA 94117-1080**
Phone: (415) 666-2612 ◆ Fax: (415) 666-2793
E-mail: wilsonj@usfca.com
Web address: http://www.usfca.edu

Founded: 1855

Accredited by: Western Association

Enrollment: 10,000 ◆ Adult students: 60 percent

University status: Private, Church, Roman Catholic Church

Degree	Concentration/Major	Format
B.S.	Organizational Behavior	E,A
B.S.	Information Systems Management	E,A
B.S.	Applied Economics	E,A
B.P.A.	Public Administration	E,A
M.H.R.O.D.	Human Resources and Organizational Development	E,A
M.P.A.	Public Administration	E,A
M.P.A.	Public Administration: Health Services Administration	E,A
M.N.A.	Nonprofit Administration	E,A

Campus Extension Sites
San Ramon, CA
Oakland, CA
Cupertino, CA
Stockton, CA
Sacramento, CA
Orange, CA
Santa Rosa, CA

Requirements
Residency requirement: All courses are offered at extended campus locations use a lock-step, cohort model.
Undergraduate admissions requirements: Applicants must have 50 transferable semester units with 2.0 GPA.
Graduate admissions requirements: Applicants must hold an accredited bachelor's degree, have 2.7 overall/ 3.0 major GPAs, strong writing skills, and 2-5 years of experience in the field of study.
Graduation requirements (undergraduate): Graduates must complete and pass all course work with 2.0 GPA, pay all fees and tuition, and complete all GECs.
Graduation requirements (graduate): Graduates must pass all course work with 3.0 GPA, pay all tuition and fees, and complete thesis or project.

Fees, Tuition, Costs
Undergraduate application fee: $35
Graduate application fee: $35
Undergraduate tuition: $422-$437/unit
Graduate tuition: $460-$479/unit
Undergraduate cost of books: $800
Graduate cost of books: $800

Other costs: Access to computer recommended, but not required

Financial Aid/Status
Scholarship programs for adults: Graduate scholarships are based on academic achievement. The amount given is 3-6 units.
Full-time status: Students enrolled in at least 6 units per semester are considered full-time. All programs qualify.
Percentage of adult students receiving financial aid: 20 percent.

Maximum Hours Awarded For
CLEP: No limit
DANTES: No limit
Prior learning portfolio: 30
Additional information: American Council on Education—no limit

Features and Services
1. Is it possible to purchase books during hours most adult students attend classes? **Yes.**

2. Are the institution's administrative offices open during hours adult students attend class? **Yes.**

3. How do students taking extended classes access library resources? **Library services are available at the regional campus. Online service from main library is offered.**

4. What is the registration and payment process for adult students? **Registration for entire program is done at beginning. Payment is monthly.**

5. What is the process for advising adult students? **Students attend an information seminar.**

Individual meetings are held for advising and transcript evaluation.

6. What career and placement services are available to adult students? **A counselor works with only adult students.**

Classes are given on resumes, job interviews, and placement service.

7. What characteristics of the institution's adult degree programs are most appealing to students? **Cohort, lock-**step model; classes meet one evening a week for four hours; interactive, adult-centered curriculum; convenient locations; and portfolio process.

University of Sarasota

5250 17th Street ♦ **Sarasota, FL 34240**

Phone: (941) 379-0404 ♦ Toll-free phone: (800) 331-5995
Fax: (941) 379-9464

Web address: http://www.sol.sarasota.fl.us/univ.html

Founded: 1969

Accredited by: Southern Association

Enrollment: 950 ♦ Adult students: 100

University status: Private

Degree	Concentration/Major	Format
M.A.Ed.	Educational Leadership	E,A,C
M.A.	Guidance, Marriage and Family, Mental Health Management	E,A,C
M.B.A.	Human Resources, Marketing, Finance, International Trade	E
M.B.A	Health Care Administration	E
Ed.D.	Educational Leadership	E,A,C
Ed.D.	Counseling Psychology	E,A,C
D.B.A.	Management, Marketing, Information Systems	E,A,C

Requirements
Residency requirement: Students must complete a minimum of 8 courses on campus in accelerated sessions.
Graduate admissions requirements: Requirements include an under-graduate and/or graduate degrees. Other requirements depend on the individual degree program.
Graduation requirements (graduate): Graduates must meet the requirements of the degree program with a 3.2 or higher GPA.

Fees, Tuition, Costs
Graduate application fee: $50
Graduate tuition: $317/credit
Graduate cost of books: $100/course
Other costs: Travel and lodging costs for on-campus sessions

Financial Aid/Status
Scholarship programs for adults: No scholarships are available.
Percentage of adult students receiving financial aid: 20 percent.

Features and Services
1. How do students taking extended classes access library resources? **Library resources for out-of-area students are available through CompuServe.**

2. What is the registration and payment process for adult students? **Registration may be done by mail or phone.**

3. What is the process for advising adult students? **Faculty advisors are available on campus.**

4. What career and placement services are available to adult students? **All students are currently in careers.**

5. What characteristics of the institution's adult degree programs are most appealing to students? **Flexible one-week sessions allow working adults to get advanced degrees.**

University of Sioux Falls

1101 W. 22 Street ◆ Sioux Falls, SD 57105

Phone: (605) 331-6735 ◆ Toll-free phone: (800) 456-1430

Fax: (605) 331-6615 ◆ E-mail: hilda@thecoo.edu

Web address: http://www.thecoo.edu

Founded: 1883

Accredited by: North Central

Enrollment: 951 ◆ Adult students: 47 percent

University status: Private, Church, North American Baptist Church

Degree	Concentration/Major	Format
B.A.	Management	E,A
M.B.A.	Business Administration	E,A
M.Ed.	Education	E

Requirements

Residency requirement: Students must attend classes on campus.
Undergraduate admissions requirements: Applicants must be high school graduates and submit transcripts and application. Degree completion: 64 transferable hours (minimum 2.0 GPA), application, two recommendations, interview, writing sample.
Graduate admissions requirements: General requirements include a bachelor's degree, an application, official transcripts of all prior college work, personal recommendations, and supportive data.
Graduation requirements (undergraduate): Graduates must meet the university and degree requirements and apply for graduation.
Graduation requirements (graduate): Graduation requirements vary with the degree program.

Fees, Tuition, Costs

Undergraduate application fee: $25
Graduate application fee: $25
Undergraduate tuition: $9,450/year

Financial Aid/Status

Scholarship programs for adults: Scholarships available based on financial need and academic merit
Full-time status: 12 or more semester hours/semester

Maximum Hours Awarded For

CLEP: 32
DANTES: Yes
Other exams: 16
Prior learning portfolio: 16
Additional information: Workshops, internships, independent study

Features and Services

1. Is it possible to purchase books during hours most adult students attend classes? **Yes.**

2. Are the institution's administrative offices open during hours adult students attend class? **Yes.**

3. What is the registration and payment process for adult students? **Degree Completion Program has registration in the first evening class or first night of each term.**

4. What is the process for advising adult students? **Advising is individualized and by appointment.**

5. What career and placement services are available to adult students? **A full career and placement service department is available to all students.**

6. What characteristics of the institution's adult degree programs are most appealing to students? **One night a week, guaranteed schedule, and accelerated format.**

University of South Alabama

214 Alpha East U.S.A. ◆ **Mobile, AL 36688**
Phone: (334) 460-6263 ◆ Fax: (334) 460-6519
Web address: http://www.usouthal.edu

Founded: 1963

Accredited by: Southern Association

Enrollment: 12,000 ◆ Adult students: 29 percent

University status: Public

Degree	Concentration/Major	Format
B.A.	Adult Personalized Study	E,S
B.S.	Adult Personalized Study	E,S

Campus Extension Site

Fairhope, AL

Requirements

Residency requirement: Almost all work can be completed at the branch campus at Fairhope, AL. Undergraduate admissions requirements: Applicants must be at least 25 years old and/or have assumed the responsibilities and commitments of adulthood of work, family, and community and be operating independently in society.
Graduation requirements (undergraduate): Graduates must have a minimum 2.0 GPA, 48 upper-level hours from USA, and earn 192 total hours.

Fees, Tuition, Costs

Undergraduate application fee: $25
Undergraduate tuition: $2,352/year
Other costs: $189/year for basic fees

Financial Aid/Status

Scholarship programs for adults: Scholarships are available. The department offers three scholarships per year to students. Full-time status: 12 hours/quarter.

Maximum Hours Awarded For

CLEP: 48
Other exams: 48
Additional information: Military credit-6 hours; maximum of 48 hours for all credit

Features and Services

1. Is it possible to purchase books during hours most adult students attend classes? **Yes.**

2. What is the registration and payment process for adult students? **Registration and payment are the same for all students.**

3. What is the process for advising adult students? **Extensive advising provided during the academic career. Advising newsletters are sent three times a year.**

4. What career and placement services are available to adult students? **Career Services provides Senior Services, help for job search, and Cooperative Education Program.**

5. What characteristics of the institution's adult degree programs are most appealing to students? **Students design their field of study based on their goals, providing a very flexible program. Evening, weekend, and media-assisted courses are attractive to students.**

University of South Florida

B.I.S. Program HMS 443 ◆ **Tampa, FL 33620**

Phone: (813) 974-4058 ◆ Toll-free phone: (800) 635-1484

Fax: (813) 974-5101 ◆ E-mail: bis@luna.cas.usf.edu

Web address: http://www.usf.edu/

Program's Web address: http://www.cas.usf.edu/bis/index.html

Founded: 1968

Accredited by: Southern Association

Enrollment: 36,058 ◆ Adult students: 95 percent

University status: Public

Degree	Concentration/Major	Format
B.I.S.	Interdisciplinary	C,S

Requirements

Residency requirement: Students may attend tutorials and are required to attend two-week summer seminars.
Undergraduate admissions requirements: Applicants must have acceptable high school grades and ACT/SAT scores.
Graduation requirements (undergraduate): Graduates must earn 120 hours for four-area track; 60 hours for two-area track (A.A. or equivalent).

Fees, Tuition, Costs

Undergraduate application fee: $20
Undergraduate tuition: $55/ semester credit hour
Undergraduate cost of books: $50/ 15 credit hours

Financial Aid/Status

Scholarship programs for adults: Students have access to scholarship funds.
Full-time status: All students are full-time at registration, even if they study part-time.
Percentage of adult students receiving financial aid: 5 percent.

Maximum Hours Awarded For

CLEP: Yes

Features and Services

1. Are the institution's administrative offices open during hours adult students attend class? **Yes.**

2. How do students taking extended classes access library resources? **Students may use any of 10 university, community college, or local libraries.**

3. What is the registration and payment process for adult students? **Registration and payment are done through the office staff.**

4. What is the process for advising adult students? **Advising is done through the office and by faculty.**

5. What career and placement services are available to adult students? **Career and placement services are provided for all university students.**

6. What characteristics of the institution's adult degree programs are most appealing to students? **Distance learning, rigor, and valuable degree that is time efficient.**

University of Southern Colorado

2200 Bonforte Boulevard ◆ **Pueblo, CO 81001-4901**
Phone: (719) 549-2316 ◆ Toll-free phone: (800) 388-6154
Fax: (719) 549-2438 ◆ E-mail: rstubenr@uscolo.edu
Web address: http://meteor.uscolo.edu

Founded: 1933

Accredited by: North Central

Enrollment: 4,300

University status: Public

Degree	Concentration/Major	Format
B.S.	Social Science	E,V,A,C,TH

Campus Extension Sites

Colorado Spring, CO
Fort Dix, NJ
Altus AFB, OK
McGuire AFB, NJ
Peterson AFB, CO

Requirements

Residency requirement: Students do not have to attend classes on campus.
Undergraduate admissions requirements: Students must be high school graduates or have GED. An application and official transcripts must be submitted.
Graduation requirements (undergraduate): The minimum requirements for graduation are GPA 2.0; 128 semester hours; 40 semester hours junior/senior-level credits; 36 semester hours in major; 39 semester hours of general education and electives.

Fees, Tuition, Costs

Undergraduate application fee: $15
Undergraduate tuition: $822/semester
Undergraduate cost of books: $250
Other costs: Videotape costs of $50-$75; $25 refund possible

Financial Aid/Status

Scholarship programs for adults: All students eligible for designated scholarships
Full-time status: 12 semester hours
Percentage of adult students receiving financial aid: 33 percent

Maximum Hours Awarded For

CLEP: 30
PEP: 30
DANTES: 30
Other exams: 30
Additional information: DANTES credit requires department approval.

Features and Services

1. Is it possible to purchase books during hours most adult students attend classes? **Yes.**

2. Are the institution's administrative offices open during hours adult students attend class? **Yes.**

3. How do students taking extended classes access library resources? **The library resources are available through interlibrary loan, the Internet, and local libraries.**

4. What is the registration and payment process for adult students? **Registration by phone, fax, mail, and in person. Pay by credit card, mail, money order, check, and cash.**

5. What is the process for advising adult students? **Advisors are available at sites. Distant students are advised by letter and phone.**

6. What career and placement services are available to adult students? **On-campus placement services are used. Limited resume bank is offered to off-campus students.**

7. What characteristics of the institution's adult degree programs are most appealing to students? **Low tuition cost and program flexibility.**

University of Southern Indiana

8600 University Boulevard ◆ **Evansville, IN 47712**
Phone: (812) 464-1765 ◆ Toll-free phone: (800) 467-1965
Fax: (812) 465-7154 ◆ E-mail: tbuecher.ucs@smtp.usi.edu
Web address: http://www.usi.edu

Founded: 1965

Accredited by: North Central

Enrollment: 7,666 ◆ Adult students: 37 percent

University status: Public

Degree   Concentration/Major   Format

Nontraditional students may enroll in any degree programs if granted admission.

Requirements

Residency requirement: Students must attend classes on campus. Undergraduate admissions requirements: Applicants must provide a high school diploma or equivalent, high school grades, ACT/SAT scores, class rank, recommendations, personal qualifications, and proof of citizenship.
Graduate admissions requirements: Applicants must hold a bachelor's degree with a minimum 2.5 GPA, GRE, NTE, or GMAT, and adequate undergraduate preparation to begin graduate study.
Graduation requirements (undergraduate): Graduates must earn 124 semester credit hours, including general education component, 2.0 GPA, and completion of major requirements.
Graduation requirements (graduate): Graduates must earn at least 32 semester credit hours, 3.0 GPA, and degree completion within seven calendar years.

Fees, Tuition, Costs

Undergraduate application fee: $25
Graduate application fee: $25
Undergraduate tuition: $77.75/hour
Graduate tuition: $111.25/hour
Undergraduate cost of books: $350
Graduate cost of books: $400

Financial Aid/Status

Scholarship programs for adults: USI offers grants to first-time nontraditional college attendees to pay for their first three hours of college tuition (one course).
Full-time status: Any student enrolled for 12 or more semester credit hours/term.
Percentage of adult students receiving financial aid: 65 percent.

Maximum Hours Awarded For

CLEP: 94
Other exams: 6

Features and Services

1. Is it possible to purchase books during hours most adult students attend classes? **Yes.**

2. Are the institution's administrative offices open during hours adult students attend class? **Yes.**

3. How do students taking extended classes access library resources? **Nontraditional students have full access to the library and electronic information resources.**

4. What is the registration and payment process for adult students? **Nontraditional students may register either in person or by phone.**

5. What is the process for advising adult students? **All nontraditional students are advised by faculty and academic staff in the Academic Skills Center.**

6. What career and placement services are available to adult students? **Nontraditional students participate in career and placement programs, internships, and other programs.**

7. What characteristics of the institution's adult degree programs are most appealing to students? **Flexibility, student-centered attention, and value for one's educational dollars.**

University of Tampa

401 W. Kennedy Boulevard ◆ Tampa, FL 33606
Phone: (813) 253-6249
Web address: http://www.utampa.edu

Founded: 1931

Accredited by: Southern Association

Enrollment: 2,529 ◆ Adult students: 34 percent

University status: Private

Degree	Concentration/Major	Format
B.S.N.	Nursing for RNs	E
B.S.	Accounting	E
B.S.	Computer Information Systems	E
B.S.	Finance	E
B.S.	Management	E
B.S.	Marketing	E
B.A.	Psychology	E
B.L.S.	Liberal Studies—Humanities, with concentrations in Social Science or interdisciplinary studies	E
M.B.A.	Business Administration with concentrations in Accounting, Finance, Healthcare Administration, Information Systems Management, International Business, Management, Marketing	E
M.S.N.	Nursing-Nursing Administration, Family Nurse Practitioner	E

Requirements

Residency requirement: The last 31 semester credits must be in residence.
Undergraduate admissions requirements: Adult evening students must complete a one-page application and provide the school with transcripts from previous college and high school (if appropriate).
Graduate admissions requirements: Applicants must hold a degree from a regionally accredited institution with an acceptable GPA and two letters of recommendation.

Graduation requirements (undergraduate): All students must complete general distribution core and other requirements depending on the major.
Graduation requirements (graduate): Graduates must complete 39 semester hours, 30 of which are core curriculum and 9 electives.

Fees, Tuition, Costs

Undergraduate application fee: $25
Graduate application fee: $35 for M.B.A.; $25 for others
Undergraduate tuition: $195/semester hour

Undergraduate cost of books: $80-$100

Financial Aid/Status

Scholarship programs for adults: Scholarships are available. Eligibility criteria are being reviewed.
Full-time status: Most students are considered part-time.

Maximum Hours Awarded For

CLEP: 30
PEP: 24 (RNs)
DANTES: 30
Prior learning portfolio: 9
Additional information:
Military service schools—30;
correspondence—30;
extension courses—30;
advanced placement—30

Features and Services

1. Is it possible to purchase books during hours most adult students attend classes? **Yes.**

2. Are the institution's administrative offices open during hours adult students attend class? **Yes.**

3. What is the registration and payment process for adult students? **Preenroll by mail, fax, phone, or in person. Students are given ample time for course selection.**

4. What is the process for advising adult students? **Evening students work with an Advisement Director in selecting a faculty advisor in major area.**

5. What career and placement services are available to adult students? **Multiple services are available, including vocational assessment,**

computer-based career program, job search, and placement.

6. What characteristics of the institution's adult degree programs are most appealing to students? **Downtown location; accessible, adult-oriented faculty and staff; same faculty as day program; supportive career services; and strong curriculum.**

University of Texas at Arlington

UTA Station Box 1911 ◆ Arlington, TX 76019
Phone: (817) 272-2225 ◆ Fax: (817) 272-3435
E-mail: admissions@uta.edu ◆ Web address: http://www.uta.edu/

Founded: 1895

Accredited by: Southern Association

Enrollment: 22,121 ◆ Adult students: 72 percent

University status: Public

Degree	Concentration/Major	Format
B.S.	Civil Engineering	T
B.S.	Electrical Engineering	T
B.S.W.	Social Work	T
B.S.	Nursing	V
B.A.	Art History	E
B.A.	Interdisciplinary Studies	E
M.S.	Nursing	V
M.S.W.	Social Work	T
M.S.	Software Engineering	T
M.S.	Accounting	E
Ph.D.	Applied Chemistry	E

All degree programs available to adults. Evening courses offered by all schools and colleges.

Requirements

Residency requirement: No degree program is offered whereby all requirements can be met at extended campus locations. Undergraduate admissions requirements: 30 semester hours in residence; at least 24 of last 30 semester hours in residence; at least 18 semester hours in residence of advanced course work (12 hours of advanced major courses).

Graduate admissions requirements: Requirements vary according to academic unit and degree level (master's or doctorate program). Graduation requirements (undergraduate): Graduates must complete 47 hours of general education core plus 73-91 in major, minor, and elective courses. The exact number of the total varies according to the degree program.
Graduation requirements (graduate): Graduate requirements vary according to academic unit and degree level (master's or doctoral program).

Fees, Tuition, Costs

Undergraduate application fee: $25
Graduate application fee: $25
Undergraduate tuition: $906/12-hour semester
Graduate tuition: $1,290/12-hour semester
Undergraduate cost of books: $500/year
Graduate cost of books: $500/year
Other costs: Computer and laboratory fees; parking and international fee

Financial Aid/Status

Scholarship programs for adults: Adult students eligible to apply for all scholarships
Full-time status: 12 undergraduate semester hours; 9 graduate semester hours

Percentage of adult students receiving financial aid: 35 percent

Maximum Hours Awarded For

CLEP: No limit
DANTES: No limit
Additional information: Advanced Placement Program; International Baccalaureate; SAT II; CLEP; DANTES; no limit except hours in residence

Features and Services

1. Is it possible to purchase books during hours most adult students attend classes? **Yes.**

2. Are the institution's administrative offices open during hours adult students attend class? **Yes.**

3. How do students taking extended classes access library resources? **Students may access library resources through interlibrary loan and UTA's interlibrary loan and on the World Wide Web.**

4. What is the registration and payment process for adult students? **Students may register and pay in person or by phone.**

5. What is the process for advising adult students? **Students are assigned an advisor to discuss course schedule before registering. General advising offered.**

6. What career and placement services are available to adult students? **Career library, company videos, computer lab with World Wide Web access, and resume referral service available.**

7. What characteristics of the institution's adult degree programs are most appealing to students? **Comprehensive range of degrees with evening classes and metropolitan campus location allows employed adults to expand education.**

University of Texas at Dallas

P.O. Box 830688 ◆ Richardson, TX 75083-0688
Phone: (214) 883-2209 ◆ Toll-free phone: (800) 899-2443
Fax: (214) 833-2212 ◆ E-mail: csutton@utdallas.edu
Web address: http://www.utdallas.edu

Founded: 1969

Accredited by: Southern Association

Enrollment: 9,008 ◆ Adult students: 64 percent

University status: Public

Degree   Concentration/Major   Format

All of UT Dallas' degree programs are available during night classes.

Requirements

Residency requirement: Students are required to earn 30 hours in residence.
Undergraduate admissions requirements: Freshman: high school/equivalent diploma; complete core curriculum; SAT/ACT test; class rank in top 25 percent; TASP test. Sophomore: 30-54 credits of satisfactory college work; minimum C average. Graduate admissions requirements: Bachelor's degree; fluent in written and spoken English; minimum B average in upper-division courses; GRE/GMAT scores.
Graduation requirements (undergraduate): 120 semester credits; 51 upper-level; 30 credits at UT Dallas; 12 in advanced courses; 24 of last 30 hours at UT Dallas; minimum GPA 2.0; 6 hours each American history/government; enrolled at degree completion.
Graduation requirements (graduate): Graduation

requirements for master's and doctoral degrees vary by the program.

Fees, Tuition, Costs

Undergraduate application fee: $25
Graduate application fee: $25
Undergraduate tuition: $30/hour
Graduate tuition: $60/hour
Undergraduate cost of books: $664/annual
Graduate cost of books: $664/annual
Other costs: Undergraduate fees based on 12 hours/semester for two semesters—$1,022; graduate fees based on 9 hours for two semesters—$875

Financial Aid/Status

Scholarship programs for adults: Scholarships vary
Full-time status: 14 hours/semester for undergraduates

Maximum Hours Awarded For

CLEP: 30
DANTES: 30

Additional information: Maximum 30 hours credit by exam

Features and Services

1. Is it possible to purchase books during hours most adult students attend classes? **Yes.**

2. Are the institution's administrative offices open during hours adult students attend class? **Yes.**

3. How do students taking extended classes access library resources? **The library is open during class time and has extended and weekend hours.**

4. What is the registration and payment process for adult students? **Registrar and bursar's offices are open for night-time registration during regular registration.**

5. What is the process for advising adult students? **Advising is determined by the degree program.**

6. What career and placement services are available to adult students? **Office hours are 9:00 A.M.-6:30 P.M. Seminars are offered on job search, resume writing, and interviews.**

7. What characteristics of the institution's adult degree programs are most appealing to students? **Night-time availability of classes.**

University of Toledo

4140 University Hall ◆ 2801 W. Bancroft
Toledo, OH 43606
Phone: (419) 530-2051 ◆ Fax: (419) 530-6180
E-mail: gterwil@uoft02.utoledo.edu
Web address: http://www.utoledo.edu

Founded: 1872

Accredited by: North Central

Enrollment: 20,000

University status: Public

Degree	Concentration/Major	Format
B.A.	Interdisciplinary—Adult Liberal Studies	E,A,T,S
B.A./B.S.	Interdisciplinary—Individualized Program	E,A,T,S

Requirements

Residency requirement: Off-campus sites are located in the city and at businesses, but most students cannot avoid coming to campus. Courses delivered at plant sites may make off-campus degrees possible.
Undergraduate admissions requirements: Adult Liberal Studies: 25 years or older; plan program of study with advisor; written approval of study plan by director.
Graduation requirements (undergraduate): Graduates must earn 186 quarter credits; 60 hours in upper-level courses; 45 hours in residence. In planning a study program, students should be sure to include the core curriculum courses.

Fees, Tuition, Costs

Undergraduate application fee: $30
Undergraduate tuition: $78.91/credit hour
Other costs: Various other course and university fees possible

Financial Aid/Status

Scholarship programs for adults: Scholarships vary
Full-time status: 12 credit hours/quarter

Maximum Hours Awarded For

CLEP: 46
Other exams: Varies
Prior learning portfolio: Varies

Features and Services

1. Is it possible to purchase books during hours most adult students attend classes? **Yes.**

2. Are the institution's administrative offices open during hours adult students attend class? **Yes.**

3. What is the registration and payment process for adult students? **Weekend and evening registration are offered. The process is the same for all students.**

4. What is the process for advising adult students? **Various advising is used depending on the program.**

5. What career and placement services are available to adult students? **Career and placement services are the same for all students.**

6. What characteristics of the institution's adult degree programs are most appealing to students? **Accelerated and specialized degrees.**

University of Utah*

Center for Adult Development
1195 Annex Building ◆ **Salt Lake City, UT 84112**
Phone: (801) 581-3228 ◆ Fax: (801) 585-5414
Web address: http://www.utah.edu

Founded: 1850

Accredited by: Northwest Association

Enrollment: 27,000 ◆ Adult students: 90

University status: Public

Features and Services

1. Is it possible to purchase books during hours most adult students attend classes? **Yes.**

2. Are the institution's administrative offices open during hours adult students attend class? **Yes.**

3. What characteristics of the institution's adult degree programs are most appealing to students? **Evening and weekend format, ease of registration, and convenience of preparation such as book buying.**

Degree	Concentration/Major	Format
B.A./B.S.	Business Administration	E
M.B.A.	Business Administration	E
	Two-year program culminating in seminar trip usually held overseas	
M.P.A.	Public Administration	E
	Two-year program culminating with a capstone held in Washington D.C.	

Requirements

Residency requirement: Yes. Undergraduate admissions requirements: Applicants are required to have completed all Liberal Education and lower-division course work required by the university, and to have cleared all transfer credits with the College of Business Advising office. Graduate admissions requirements: EMBA: Applicants are required to have completed college algebra (or equivalent) with a grade of B or better within the last 10 years, have an undergraduate degree with at least 3.0, passed the GMAT with a score of 500, and five years of work experience.

Fees, Tuition, Costs

Undergraduate application fee: $30
Graduate application fee: $30
Graduate tuition: $18,500 for MBA; $9,170 for MPA

Financial Aid/Status

Full-time status: 12 credit hours, undergraduate; 9 credit hours, graduate

Maximum Hours Awarded For

CLEP: 46

University of Virginia
104 Midmont Lane ◆ **Charlottesville, VA 22903**
Phone: (804) 982-5208 ◆ Toll-free phone: (800) 346-3882
Fax: (804) 982-5550 ◆ E-mail: jaf6r@virginia.edu
Web address: http://www.virginia.edu
Program's Web address: http://minerva.acc.virginia.edu/~
contined/home.html

Founded: 1819

Accredited by: Southern Association

Enrollment: 18,000

University status: Public

Degree	Concentration/Major	Format
M.E.	Engineering, Chemical	T
M.E.	Engineering, Civil	T
M.E.	Engineering, Electrical	T
M.M.S.	Engineering, Materials Science	T
M.E.	Engineering, Nuclear	T
M.E.	Engineering, Systems	T
M.E.	Engineering, Mechanical and Aerospace	T
M.P.	Urban Planning	E
M.Ed.	Reading	E
M.Ed.	Instruction	E
M.Ed.	Leadership and Policy Studies	E
M.Ed.	Social Foundations of Education	E

Campus Extension Sites
Lynchburg, VA
Richmond, VA
Roanoke, VA
Hampton Roads, VA
Charlotteville, VA
Abingdon, VA
Falls Church, VA

Requirements
Residency requirement: Students are not required to attend classes on campus for the listed degrees. Graduate admissions requirements: The requirements vary from field to field. Most require strong undergraduate records, GRE exam, an application, and statements.

Off-campus requirements are the same as on-campus programs. Graduation requirements (graduate): Graduates must complete all course work and either a master's exam or a major research paper, depending on the field.

Fees, Tuition, Costs
Graduate tuition: Varies by field
Graduate cost of books: Varies; about $100-$200

Financial Aid/Status
Scholarship programs for adults: The question is not adult, but part-time. Part-time students have limited financial aid opportunities. Many are paid by employers in part

or in whole.
Full-time status: In most departments, full-time is 12 semester hours per semester. Additional information: Most master's degree programs will accept 6 hours of transfer credit.

Features and Services
1. Is it possible to purchase books during hours most adult students attend classes? **Yes.**

2. Are the institution's administrative offices open during hours adult students attend class? **Yes.**

3. How do students taking extended classes access library resources? **The library is available online, with 48-hour delivery of materials to the regional centers.**

4. What is the registration and payment process for adult students? **Registration by phone, fax, mail; payment by check, purchase order, credit card, or cash.**

5. What is the process for advising adult students? **Each master's program has a faculty director or advisor in addition to the regional center staff.**

6. What career and placement services are available to adult students? **The career and placement services on campus are available. This varies by department.**

7. What characteristics of the institution's adult degree programs are most appealing to students? **Quality of the degree and the institution; convenience of evening, weekend, and TV formats.**

University of West Los Angeles*

School of Law
1155 W. Arbor Vitae Street ◆ **Ingelwood, CA 90301**
Phone: (310) 215-3339 ◆ Fax: (310) 641-4736

Founded: 1966

Accredited by: Commission of Bar Examiners

Enrollment: 550

University status: Private

Features and Services

1. What characteristics of the institution's adult degree programs are most appealing to students? **Flexible schedule, affordable tuition, and intimate academic environment.**

Degree	Concentration/Major	Format
J.D.	Law	E

Part-time students can take classes in the day or evening.
Full-time students can take classes only during the day.

Requirements

Residency requirement: Yes
Graduate admissions requirements:
B.A. applicants considered without
LSAT

Financial Aid/Status

Full-time status: 12 units/semester
Percentage of adult students
receiving financial aid: 70 percent

Fees, Tuition, Costs

Graduate application fee: $35
Graduate tuition: $298

University of Wisconsin–Madison

432 N. Lake Street
Department of Engineering Professional Development
Madison, WI 53706
Phone: (608) 262-0133 ◆ Toll-free phone: (800) 462-0876
Fax: (608) 263-3160 ◆ E-mail: karena@epd.engr.wisc.edu
Web address: http://www.wisc.edu
Program's Web address: http://epdwww.eng.wisc.edu

Founded: 1849

Accredited by: North Central

Enrollment: 42,000 ◆ Adult students: 25 percent

University status: Public

Degree	Concentration/Major	Format
P.D.	Engineering (postbaccalaureate degree)	E,V,A,C,CT,S,T

Requirements

Residency requirement: Students are not required to take courses on campus. They may take courses on campus if it is convenient. The student chooses courses with accessible formats.
Graduate admissions requirements: For this postbaccalaureate program, most applicants have a B.S. in engineering from an ABET-accredited program or the equivalent.
Graduation requirements (graduate): Graduates earn 120 continuing education units in five years, including 100 CEU course work, 60 CEU from UW—Extension or UW—Madison, 1 graduate-level course, and an Independent Study Project.

Fees, Tuition, Costs

Graduate application fee: $20
Graduate tuition: Depends on chosen courses
Graduate cost of books: Varies

Financial Aid/Status

Scholarship programs for adults: Since P.D. degree students are not on campus full-time, they are not eligible. Some use employer reimbursement or V.A. benefits.
Full-time status: Graduate-level full-time status is 8 or more credits on campus.
Percentage of adult students receiving financial aid: 70 percent.

Features and Services

1. How do students taking extended classes access library resources? **Students are issued temporary (visiting scholar) ID allowing access to on-campus libraries.**

2. What is the registration and payment process for adult students? **Registration and payment vary.**

3. What is the process for advising adult students? **An on-campus advisor is available by phone, fax, e-mail, or in person to assist with curriculum.**

4. What career and placement services are available to adult students? **An on-campus advisor is available by phone, fax, e-mail, or in person to assist students.**

5. What characteristics of the institution's adult degree programs are most appealing to students? **Students develop their own curriculum based on their objectives; courses offered in a variety of formats; students never have to come to campus unless they want to.**

University of Wisconsin–Oshkosh

800 Algoma Boulevard ◆ **Oshkosh, WI 54901**
Phone: (414) 424-0202 ◆ Fax: (414) 424-1098
E-mail: oshadmuw@vaxa.cis.uwosh.edu
Web address: http://www.uwash.edu/

Founded: 1871

Accredited by: North Central

Enrollment: 10,472

University status: Public

Degree	Concentration/Major	Format
B.L.S.	Liberal Studies	E
B.B.A.	Business Administration	E

Requirements

Residency requirement: Most classes are on campus.
Undergraduate admissions requirements: B.L.S.—high school degree or GED; B.B.A.—2.5 GPA in all college course work and 3.5 GPA in all prebusiness courses.
Graduation requirements (undergraduate): Graduates must earn 128 credits with 30 credits taken at U.W.—Oshkah, and at least 2.0 GPA in all major course work.

Fees, Tuition, Costs

Undergraduate application fee: $28
Graduate application fee: $38
Undergraduate tuition: $2,300/year
Graduate tuition: $167/credit hour
Undergraduate cost of books: $400-$500/year

Financial Aid/Status

Scholarship programs for adults: Students should contact the financial aid office.

Maximum Hours Awarded For

CLEP: No limit

Features and Services

1. Is it possible to purchase books during hours most adult students attend classes? **Yes.**

2. What is the registration and payment process for adult students? **Registration and payment may be done by mail or in person.**

3. What is the process for advising adult students? **Advising is available during the students' nonworking hours (4-6 P.M.) by appointment.**

4. What career and placement services are available to adult students? **Career Services office is open Monday through Thursday till 7 P.M.**

5. What characteristics of the institution's adult degree programs are most appealing to students? **B.L.S.— complete one course in four weekends; four courses per semester; classes with peers. B.B.A.—nationally accredited degree in evening. Cost and quality.**

University of Wisconsin–Platteville

1 University Plaza ◆ **Platteville, WI 53818**
Phone: (608) 342-1468 ◆ Toll-free phone: (800) 362-5460
Fax: (608) 342-1466 ◆ E-mail: adams@uwplatt.edu
Web address: http://www.uwplatt.edu

Founded: 1871

Accredited by: North Central

Enrollment: 5,000 ◆ Adult students: 400

University status: Public

Degree	Concentration/Major	Format
B.S.	Business Administration	C,CT

Requirements

Undergraduate admissions requirements: High school graduate, in good standing at last college attended
Graduation requirements (undergraduate): 128 credits, 2.00 GPA

Fees, Tuition, Costs

Undergraduate application fee: $28
Undergraduate tuition: $80.25/credit
Undergraduate cost of books: $50+/course

Financial Aid/Status

Percentage of adult students receiving financial aid: 10 percent

Maximum Hours Awarded For

CLEP: Yes
PEP: Yes
DANTES: Yes
Other exams: Yes
Prior learning portfolio: Yes

Features and Services

1. Is it possible to purchase books during hours most adult students attend classes? **Yes.**

2. How do students taking extended classes access library resources? **By computer.**

3. What is the registration and payment process for adult students? **Registration and payment are made by mail.**

4. What is the process for advising adult students? **By phone.**

5. What career and placement services are available to adult students? **Access to placement office files.**

6. What characteristics of the institution's adult degree programs are most appealing to students? **Flexibility of the program.**

University of Wisconsin— River Falls

410 S. 3rd Street ◆ **River Falls, WI 54022**
Phone: (715) 425-3239 ◆ Toll-free phone: (800) 228-5421
Fax: (715) 425-3785 ◆ E-mail: katrina.larsen@uwrf.edu
Program's Web address: http://www.uwrf.edu/college-of-agriculture/ext-deg.html

Founded: 1874

Accredited by: North Central

Enrollment: 5,400 ◆ Adult students: 20 percent

University status: Public

Degree	Concentration/Major	Format
B.S.	Broad Area Agriculture	C,V,S

Requirements

Fourteen majors are offered to adults, but most degrees are offered during the day.
Undergraduate admissions requirements: Top 70 percent of high school graduating class or 22 on ACT; transfer students—at least 2.00 GPA on a 4-point scale.
Graduation requirements (undergraduate): 120 credits, 32 credits from UWRF, minimum 2.0 overall GPA, 2.25 in the major; 64 credits must be from a four-year institution.

Fees, Tuition, Costs

Undergraduate application fee: $28
Undergraduate tuition: $90/credit for Wisconsin residents; $105/credit for Minnesota residents; $150/credit for nonresidents

Undergraduate cost of books: Varies
Other costs: $50 annual enrollment fee

Financial Aid/Status

Scholarship programs for adults: Varies by scholarship; application forms available in January
Full-time status: 12 credits/annual contract
Percentage of adult students receiving financial aid: 50 percent

Maximum Hours Awarded For

CLEP: 15
Other exams: Yes
Prior learning portfolio: 45

Maximum Hours Awarded For

1. Is it possible to purchase books during hours most adult students attend classes? **Yes.**

2. Are the institution's administrative offices open during hours adult students attend class? **Yes.**

3. How do students taking extended classes access library resources? **Students may use interlibrary loan and the World Wide Web to access the library.**

4. What is the registration and payment process for adult students? **Students may register by mail. Payment of 1/2 tuition due at enrollment; other 1/2 in two months.**

5. What is the process for advising adult students? **Individualized advising by phone, mail, or in person as student's needs dictate.**

6. What career and placement services are available to adult students? **Services include career service lists of employment opportunities, interviews, personal career counseling, Discover program, resume writing assistance, and resource room.**

7. What characteristics of the institution's adult degree programs are most appealing to students? **Flexible starting date, flexible course pace, which is determined by the student.**

University of Wisconsin—Superior *

1800 Grand Avenue ◆ Superior, WI 54880
Phone: (715) 394-8487
Web address: http://www.uwsuper.edu

Founded: 1893

Accredited by: North Central

Enrollment: 2,200 ◆ Adult students: 450

University status: Public

Features and Services

1. Is it possible to purchase books during hours most adult students attend classes? **Yes.**

2. Are the institution's administrative offices open during hours adult students attend class? **Yes.**

3. What characteristics of the institution's adult degree programs are most appealing to students? **Flexibility and opportunity to design their own major.**

Degree	Concentration/Major	Format
B.S.	Individualized degree	C,TH,CT,S

Requirements

Residency requirement: None. The distance learning program incorporates print material with technology.
Undergraduate admissions requirements: Program is available only to Wisconsin residents or Minnesota students who qualify for reciprocity.

Fees, Tuition, Costs

Undergraduate application fee: $25
Undergraduate tuition: $1,000

Financial Aid/Status

Full-time status: Enrolled for 18 credits, to be completed within 12 months
Percentage of adult students receiving financial aid: 50 percent

Maximum Hours Awarded For

CLEP: 32
DANTES: 32
Other exams: 32

Upper Iowa University

P.O. Box 1861 ◆ **Fayette, IA 52142**
Phone: (319) 425-5283 ◆ Toll-free phone: (800) 553-4150
Fax: (319) 425-5353 ◆ E-mail: extdegree@uiu.edu
Web address: http://www.uiu.edu
Program's Web address: http://www.uiu.edu

Founded: 1857

Accredited by: North Central

Enrollment: 3,804 ◆ Adult students: 75 percent

University status: Public

Degree	Concentration/Major	Format
A.A.	Liberal Arts	E
A.A.	General Business	E
B.S.	Business	E
B.S.	Marketing	E
B.S.	Management	E
B.S.	Accounting	E
B.S.	Human Resources Management	E
B.S.	Human Services	E
B.S.	Social Sciences	E
M.A.	Business Leadership	E

Campus Extension Sites

Des Moines, IA
Fort Irwin, CA
Janesville, WI
Fort Polk, LA
Calmar, IA
Fort Riley, KS
Fort Benning, GA
Fayette, IA
Madison, WI
Manchester, IA
West Allis, WI
Newton, IA
Prairie du Chien, WI
Waterloo, IA
Wausau, WI

Requirements

Undergraduate admissions requirements: High school transcript or GED, minimum 2.0 GPA, transfer.
Graduate admissions requirements: Undergraduate degree from accredited school, minimum 2.5 GPA from previous college, minimum 3.00 GPA for prior graduate work.
Graduation requirements (undergraduate): Graduates normally have 10 years after initial enrollment to complete the baccalaureate program.
Graduation requirements (graduate): Meet all requirements for degree completion.

Fees, Tuition, Costs

Undergraduate application fee: $35
Graduate application fee: $50
Undergraduate tuition: $135/semester
Graduate tuition: $200/semester
Undergraduate cost of books: $65
Graduate cost of books: $65

Financial Aid/Status

Full-time status: Students must take six semester hours to be eligible for loans and Pell grants. This is only considered a part-time program through external degree. Percentage of adult students receiving financial aid: 5 percent.

Maximum Hours Awarded For

CLEP: Yes
PEP: Yes
DANTES: Yes
Prior learning portfolio: 30

Features and Services

1. Is it possible to purchase books during hours most adult students attend classes? **Yes.**

2. Are the institution's administrative offices open during hours adult students attend class? **Yes.**

3. How do students taking extended classes access library resources? **Students use local libraries or borrow books from campus library.**

4. What is the registration and payment process for adult students? **Phone registration or mail, check or credit card for payment.**

5. What is the process for advising adult students? **Advisors available at each university location. Phone access to external degree advisor is available.**

6. What career and placement services are available to adult students? **Information regarding job search and current openings, resume review, and information over the phone.**

7. What characteristics of the institution's adult degree programs are most appealing to students? **Flexibility, various delivery modes, eight-week term for extended campus on-site** **programs, independent study self-paced (six-month enrollment).**

Urbana University

579 College Way ◆ **Urbana, OH 43078**

Phone: (513) 484-1356 ◆ Toll-free phone: (800) 7URBANA
Fax: (513) 484-1322

Founded: 1850

Accredited by: North Central

Enrollment: 1,073

University status: Private, Church, Swedanborogan Church

Degree	Concentration/Major	Format
A.A.	Business Administration	E
B.S.	Business Administration	E
B.A.	Accounting	E
B.A.	General Management	E
B.A.	Human Resources Management	E
B.A.	Marketing	E

Campus Extension Sites
Columbus, OH
Dayton, OH

Requirements
Residency requirement: Last 30 hours of degree must be completed in residency.
Undergraduate admissions requirements: ACT score of 17 or SAT equivalent for students under 23, plus high school GPA of 2.25 or higher.
Graduation requirements (undergraduate): Completion of 126 or more credit hours, minimum quality point average of 2.00, completion of core curriculum, and requirements of major program.

Fees, Tuition, Costs
Undergraduate application fee: $15
Undergraduate tuition: $9,336/year
Undergraduate cost of books: $500

Financial Aid/Status
Scholarship programs for adults: The associate degree scholarship of $1,500 is available. If the student doesn't have an associate degree, scholarships are based on high school records the same as for traditional students.
Full-time status: Any student taking 12 or more credit hours per semester is considered full-time.
Percentage of adult students receiving financial aid: 95 percent.

Maximum Hours Awarded For
Other exams: Yes

Features and Services
1. Is it possible to purchase books during hours most adult students attend classes? **Yes.**

2. Are the institution's administrative offices open during hours adult students attend class? **Yes.**

3. What is the registration and payment process for adult students? **Tuition must be paid in full before semester begins.**

4. What is the process for advising adult students? **An advisor is assigned when a major is declared.**

5. What career and placement services are available to adult students? **An advisor is available.**

Valley City State University

101 College Street S.E. ◆ **Valley City, ND 58072**
Phone: (701) 845-7101 ◆ Toll-free phone: (800) 532-8641
Fax: (701) 845-7245
Web address: http://www.vcsu.nodak.edu/home.html

Founded: 1890

Accredited by: North Central

Enrollment: 1,118 ◆ Adult students: 25 percent

University status: Public

Features and Services

1. Is it possible to purchase books during hours most adult students attend classes? **Yes.**

2. Are the institution's administrative offices open during hours adult students attend class? **Yes.**

3. How do students taking extended classes access library resources? **The library is open in the evening.**

4. What is the registration and payment process for adult students? **Students may register at class.**

5. What is the process for advising adult students? **Advising is available by appointment and phone.**

6. What career and placement services are available to adult students? **The same services are available to all students.**

Degree	Concentration/Major	Format

No specific degree programs were listed.

Requirements

Residency requirement: Students must attend classes on campus. Undergraduate admissions requirements: Applicants must be high school graduates or have a GED certificate. Graduation requirements (undergraduate): Graduates must earn 128 semester hours and complete Foundation Studies and the major and minor requirements.

Fees, Tuition, Costs

Undergraduate application fee: $25
Undergraduate tuition: $1,680/year
Undergraduate cost of books: $600
Other costs: Computer rental fee of $427 per semester

Financial Aid/Status

Full-time status: 12 semester hours

Maximum Hours Awarded For

CLEP: Yes
Other exams: Yes
Prior learning portfolio: Yes

Vanderbilt University

401 21st Avenue S., Room 100 ◆ **Nashville, TN 37203**
Phone: (615) 322-2513 ◆ Fax: (615) 343-2293
E-mail: hamburtb@ctrvax.vanderbilt.edu
Web address: http://www.vanderbilt.edu

Founded: 1969

Accredited by: Southern Association, AACSB

Enrollment: 500 ◆ Adult students: 500

University status: Private

Degree	Concentration/Major	Format
M.B.A.	Business Administration	E

Requirements

Residency requirement: Students must attend classes on campus—weekends only.
Graduate admissions requirements: Applicants must submit GMAT scores, applications, official transcripts, and three letters of recommendation.
Graduation requirements (graduate): Graduates must complete the two-year program, which includes 20 courses (50 credit hours). A 2.0 GPA is required to graduate.

Fees, Tuition, Costs

Graduate application fee: $50
Graduate tuition: $23,500/year
Graduate cost of books: Included in tuition
Other costs: Lodging on class weekends

Financial Aid/Status

Percentage of adult students receiving financial aid: 50 percent

Features and Services

1. Are the institution's administrative offices open during hours adult students attend class? **Yes.**

2. How do students taking extended classes access library resources? **The library is open extended hours and on weekends.**

3. What is the registration and payment process for adult students? **Students must be admitted by the admissions committee. Payment is made by the semester.**

4. What is the process for advising adult students? **All courses are preset. No electives are chosen.**

5. What career and placement services are available to adult students? **All students should be employed while attending class.**

6. What characteristics of the institution's adult degree programs are most appealing to students? **The alternate weekend (Friday/Saturday) schedule; top-quality program; ability to work full-time while completing studies.**

Virginia Commonwealth University

812 W. Franklin Street ◆ P.O. Box 843028
Richmond, VA 23284-3028
Phone: (804) 828-2333 ◆ Fax: (804) 828-2335
Web address: http://opal.vcu.edu

Founded: 1837

Accredited by: Southern Association

Enrollment: 21,523

University status: Public

Features and Services

1. Is it possible to purchase books during hours most adult students attend classes? **Yes.**

2. Are the institution's administrative offices open during hours adult students attend class? **Yes.**

Degree   Concentration/Major   Format

No specific degrees were listed. Classes are offered 8 A.M.-10:30 P.M.

Requirements

Residency requirement: Students are required to attend classes on campus.

Fees, Tuition, Costs

Undergraduate application fee: $20
Graduate application fee: $20
Undergraduate tuition: $1,957
Graduate tuition: $2,228.50

Financial Aid/Status

Full-time status: 12 hours in a degree program

Maximum Hours Awarded For

CLEP: 54
Other exams: Yes

Virginia Wesleyan College

1584 Wesleyan Drive ◆ **Norfolk, VA 23502**
Phone: (804) 455-3263 ◆ Fax: (804) 455-5703
E-mail: kmloring@vwc.edu
Web address: http://www.vwc.edu

Founded: 1961

Accredited by: Southern Association

Enrollment: 1,569 ◆ Adult students: 34 percent

University status: Private, Church, United Methodist Church

Degree	Concentration/Major	Format
B.A.	Management	E
B.A.	Business	E
B.A.	Economics	E
B.A.	Liberal Studies	E
B.A.	Social Sciences—Human Services	E
B.A.	Social Sciences—History	E

Requirements

Residency requirement: Students must earn 30 hours in residence. Undergraduate admissions requirements: Adult Studies Program—23 years or older; high school diploma or GED; 2.0 GPA if transferring; interview; no SAT/ACT scores required.
Graduation requirements (undergraduate): Graduates must complete 120 hours, the major requirements, and the general education requirements. Other requirements depend on the degree.

Fees, Tuition, Costs

Undergraduate application fee: $10
Undergraduate tuition: $210/semester hour
Undergraduate cost of books: $60/course

Financial Aid/Status

Scholarship programs for adults: Need-based and merit scholarships available for community college transfer students with exceptional grades (3.4 or higher GPA)
Full-time status: 12 hours/semester

Maximum Hours Awarded For

CLEP: 30
Prior learning portfolio: 30

Features and Services

1. Is it possible to purchase books during hours most adult students attend classes? **Yes.**

2. Are the institution's administrative offices open during hours adult students attend class? **Yes.**

3. What is the registration and payment process for adult students? **Students register and pay in the Adult Studies Office.**

4. What is the process for advising adult students? **Extensive advising held initially. Short sessions are done prior to each registration and as needed.**

5. What career and placement services are available to adult students? **A wide range of services—such as resumes, job search, and interviewing assistance—are offered.**

6. What characteristics of the institution's adult degree programs are most appealing to students? **Individual attention and outstanding faculty.**

Walden University

801 Anchor Rode Drive ◆ **Naples, FL 33940**
Phone: (800) 444-6795 ◆ Toll-free phone: (800) 444-6795
Fax: (941) 261-7695 ◆ E-mail: request@waldenu.edu

Founded: 1970

Accredited by: North Central

Enrollment: 1,000 ◆ Adult students: 100 percent

University status: Profit

Degree	Concentration/Major	Format
M.S.	Educational Change and Technology Innovation	CT
Ph.D.	Administration/Management	S
Ph.D.	Health Services	S
Ph.D.	Human Services	S
Ph.D.	Education	S

Requirements

Residency requirement: Residency experience in a flexible format of one three-week summer session and one four-day meeting per year. Graduate admissions requirements: For the Ph.D. degrees, a master's (from accredited university) and three or more years of work experience. For the M.S., a bachelor's (from accredited university) and two or more years of work experience.

Fees, Tuition, Costs

Graduate application fee: $50
Graduate tuition: Ph.D.—$2,850/quarter
Graduate cost of books: $100/quarter
Other costs: Computer needed

Financial Aid/Status

Full-time status: All students enrolled at Walden are considered full-time
Percentage of adult students receiving financial aid: 65 percent.

Features and Services

1. How do students taking extended classes access library resources? **Students have access through the Internet and a collaborative arrangement with Indiana University.**

2. What is the registration and payment process for adult students? **Students work with a recruitment counselor.**

3. What is the process for advising adult students? **Program advisors and faculty mentors are available for students.**

4. What characteristics of the institution's adult degree programs are most appealing to students? **Flexibility; distance learning transcends time and space.**

Warner Pacific College*

2219 S.E. 68th Avenue ◆ **Portland, OR 97215**

Phone: (503) 775-4366 ◆ Toll-free phone: (800) 582-7885

Fax: (503) 775-8853

Founded: 1937

Accredited by: Northwest Association

Enrollment: 700 ◆ Adult students: 233

University status: Private, Church,
Church of God (Anderson, Indiana)

Features and Services

1. What characteristics of the institution's adult degree programs are most appealing to students? **One evening per week class schedule, modular class design, and PLE system.**

Degree	Concentration/Major	Format
B.S.	Business Administration	E,A
B.S.	Human Development	E,A

Requirements

Residency requirement: Yes
Undergraduate admissions requirements: Junior class rank (60 semester/90 quarter hours) and one semester or two quarters of college-level writing

Fees, Tuition, Costs

Undergraduate application fee: $25
Undergraduate tuition: $3,970/semester

Financial Aid/Status

Percentage of adult students receiving financial aid: 90 percent

Maximum Hours Awarded For

CLEP: Yes
DANTES: Yes
Other exams: Yes
Prior learning portfolio: 30
Additional information: Certificate and license evaluation; military evaluation

Warner Southern College

5301 U.S. Highway 27 South ◆ Lake Wales, FL 33853

Phone: (941) 638-3801 ◆ Fax: (941) 638-3702

Founded: 1967

Accredited by: Southern Association

Enrollment: 580 ◆ Adult students: 42 percent

University status: Private, Church,
Church of God (Anderson, Indiana)

Degree	Concentration/Major	Format
B.A.	Organizational Management	E,A

Campus Extension Sites

Lake Wales, FL
Leesburg, FL
Melbourne, FL
Orlando, FL
Fort Pierce, FL
Deland, FL
Plant City, FL
Titusville, FL

Requirements

Residency requirement: None
Undergraduate admissions
requirements: Application,
transcripts, 23 years old, 60
transferable hours, 2.00 GPA, 6
semester hours of English
composition, 3 semester hours of
math
Graduation requirements
(undergraduate): 2.00 GPA,
complete Organizational
Management course work, meet all
General Education requirements,
pass CLAST, complete total of 128
semester hours

Fees, Tuition, Costs

Undergraduate application fee: $20
Undergraduate tuition: $2,520/
semester
Undergraduate cost of books: $240

Financial Aid/Status

Scholarship programs for adults:
Several programs available
Full-time status: 12 credit hours/
term
Percentage of adult students
receiving financial aid: 80 percent

Maximum Hours Awarded For

CLEP: Yes
Prior learning portfolio: Yes
Additional information: Maximum
30 credit hours through CLEP and
portfolio assessment

Features and Services

1. Is it possible to purchase books during hours most adult students attend classes? **Yes.**

2. How do students taking extended classes access library resources? **Students use local public and university libraries.**

3. What is the registration and payment process for adult students? **Students may make appointments during a defined period for registration.**

4. What is the process for advising adult students? **Students are advised during the application, the registration, and the graduation processes.**

5. What characteristics of the institution's adult degree programs are most appealing to students? **Quality of instruction, service to students, and time frame to complete the degree.**

Washington Bible College

6511 Princess Garden Parkway ◆ **Lanham, MD 20706**

Phone: (301) 552-1400 ◆ Toll-free phone: (800) 787-0256

Fax: (301) 552-2775

Web address: http://www.bible.edu

Founded: 1938

Accredited by: Middle States

Enrollment: 320 ◆ Adult students: 70 percent

University status: Private, Church, Nondenominational

Degree	Concentration/Major	Format
B.A.	Counseling	E
B.A.	Pastoral Ministry	E
B.A.	Music/Music Education	E
B.A.	Teacher Education	E
B.A.	Church Education	E
B.A.	Sports and Recreation	E
B.A.	Missions	E
B.A.	Urban Ministries	E

Requirements

Residency requirement: Yes
Undergraduate admissions requirements: Application, SAT/ACT, high school/college transcripts, two references, signed doctrinal statement
Graduation requirements (undergraduate): 128 hours completed in three major areas

Fees, Tuition, Costs

Undergraduate application fee: $15
Undergraduate tuition: $195/credit hour
Undergraduate cost of books: $400/year

Financial Aid/Status

Scholarship Programs for Adults: Scholarships available based on academics, leadership, and merit
Full-time status: 12 hours in undergraduate; 9 hours in graduate
Percentage of adult students receiving financial aid: 50 percent

Maximum Hours Awarded For

CLEP:15

Features and Services

1. Is it possible to purchase books during hours most adult students attend classes? **Yes.**

2. What is the registration and payment process for adult students? **Registration may be done in person during evening registration hours. Tuition may be paid through a payment plan.**

3. What is the process for advising adult students? **Each student is assigned an academic advisor on faculty.**

4. What career and placement services are available to adult students? **Placement listings available monthly.**

5. What characteristics of the institution's adult degree programs are most appealing to students? **Hours in evening.**

Washington State University

204 Van Doren Hall ◆ Pullman, WA 99164-5220
Phone: (509) 335-3557 ◆ Toll-free phone: (800) 222-4978
Fax: (509) 335-0945 ◆ E-mail: eap@wsu.edu
Web address: http://www.wsu.edu
Program's Web address: http://www.eecs.wsu.edu/~edp

Founded: 1890

Accredited by: Northwest Association

Enrollment: 18,000

University status: Public

Degree	Concentration/Major	Format
B.A.	Social Sciences	TH,V,C,CT

Requirements

Residency requirement: None
Undergraduate admissions
requirements: Application, official
transcripts, and Extended Degree
Program admissions essay

Fees, Tuition, Costs

Undergraduate application fee: $35
Undergraduate tuition: $151/credit
for video; $90/credit for
correspondence
Undergraduate cost of books: $75
Other costs: Tape rental if
necessary

Financial Aid/Status

Scholarship programs for adults:
State and federal financial aid
grants and loans available
Full-time status: 12 semester
credits
Percentage of adult students
receiving financial aid: 50 percent

Maximum Hours Awarded For

CLEP: Yes
DANTES: Yes
Other exams: Yes
Prior learning portfolio: Yes
Additional information: Advanced
Placement credit; American
Council on Education;
international baccalaureate

Features and Services

1. Is it possible to purchase books during hours most adult students attend classes? **Yes.**

2. Are the institution's administrative offices open during hours adult students attend class? **Yes.**

3. How do students taking extended classes access library resources? **A half-time librarian is available by toll-free phone to provide reference assistance.**

4. What is the registration and payment process for adult students? **Register by mail or toll-free phone, and pay by credit card or check.**

5. What is the process for advising adult students? **Each student is assigned to an advisor who sends study plans each semester. Advisors are available by toll-free phone.**

6. What career and placement services are available to adult students? **Career advising from student's advisor is available.**

7. What characteristics of the institution's adult degree programs are most appealing to students? **Strong student and library services by toll-free phone, assigned advisor, flexible degree requirements, courses by distance learning, formats to be completed according to students' schedules.**

Wayland Baptist University

1900 W. 7th Street ◆ Plainview, TX 79072

Phone: (806) 296-5521 ◆ Fax: (806) 296-4580

Founded: 1908

Accredited by: Southern Association

University status: Private, Church, Southern Baptist Church

Degree	Concentration/Major	Format
A.A.S.	Business Administration	E
A.A.S.	Religion	E
A.A.S.	Human Services	E
A.A.S.	Occupational Education	E
B.S.O.E.	Business Administration	E
B.S.O.E.	Health Care Administration	E
B.S.O.E.	Human Services	E
B.S.O.E.	Criminal Justice	E
B.S.O.E.	Occupational Education	E
B.S.O.E.	Religion	E
B.S.O.E.	Vocational Education	E

Campus Extension Sites

Plainview, TX
Wichita Falls, TX
Amarillo, TX
Phoenix, AZ
Lubbock, TX
Honolulu, HI
San Antonio, TX
Anchorage, AK
Fairbanks, AK
Glorietta, NM

Requirements

Residency requirement: 15 resident hours for A.A.S. degree and 31 resident hours for B.S.O.E. degree
Undergraduate admissions requirements: Completed Application for Admission form and $35 fee, high school transcript or GED, all official transcripts from prior colleges
Graduation requirements (undergraduate): A.A.S.—63 hours, 15 residential hours, 30 hours in academic foundation, 33 hours in major. B.S.O.E.—124 hours, 31 residential hours, 43 hours in academic foundation, 36 hours in major, 36 in professional development, 9 hours electives

Fees, Tuition, Costs

Undergraduate application fee: $35
Undergraduate tuition: $180/hour
Undergraduate cost of books: $240
Other costs: $175/semester general fees; $25/semester computer fee; $25/semester lab fee

Financial Aid/Status

Scholarship programs for adults: Scholarships available are the Ministerial Scholarship, a minister dependent's scholarship, vocational-technical scholarships, and endowed scholarships.
Full-time status: 12 hours at Plainview campus, 9 hours at External campus.
Percentage of adult students receiving financial aid: 68 percent.

Maximum Hours Awarded For

CLEP: Yes
PEP: Yes
DANTES: Yes
Other exams: Yes
Prior learning portfolio: Yes

Features and Services

1. Is it possible to purchase books during hours most adult students attend classes? **Yes.**

2. Are the institution's administrative offices open during hours adult students attend class? **Yes.**

3. How do students taking extended classes access library resources? **Library agreements are made at all external campuses with local university, public, and military libraries.**

4. What is the registration and payment process for adult students? **Three-week registration period prior to each term. Payment is made at the local external office.**

5. What is the process for advising adult students? **Full-time counselors are available at each external campus for academic advising.**

6. What career and placement services are available to adult students? **A career and placement office is maintained at the Plainview campus and is available to each external campus.**

7. What characteristics of the institution's adult degree programs are most appealing to students? **Availability of classes, high standards, and regionally accredited degree programs.**

Wayne State College

1111 Main Street ◆ **Wayne, NE 68787**
Phone: (402) 375-7217 ◆ Toll-free phone: (800) 228-9972
Fax: (402) 375-7204 ◆ E-mail: jdinsmor@wscgate.wsc.edu
Web address: http://www.wsc.edu

Founded: 1909

Accredited by: North Central

Enrollment: 3,500 ◆ Adult students: 1,000

University status: Public

Degree	Concentration/Major	Format
B.S.	Business/Professional	E
B.S.	Business/Human Resources Management	E
B.S.	Social Science	E

Campus Extension Sites

South Sioux City, NE
Norfolk, NE

Requirements

Residency requirement: All classes are delivered to sites listed. Undergraduate admissions requirements: Complete admissions form, pay $10 matriculation fee, send transcripts. Graduation requirements (undergraduate): Varies.

Fees, Tuition, Costs

Undergraduate application fee: $10
Undergraduate tuition: $55/semester hour
Undergraduate cost of books: $40

Financial Aid/Status

Scholarship programs for adults: Contact financial aid
Full-time status: Graduate—6 hours, undergraduate—12 hours
Percentage of adult students receiving financial aid: 80 percent

Maximum Hours Awarded For

CLEP: Yes
Other exams: Yes

Features and Services

1. Is it possible to purchase books during hours most adult students attend classes? **Yes.**

2. How do students taking extended classes access library resources? **Students may use computer access or phone.**

3. What is the registration and payment process for adult students? **Payment is due by the first class meeting. Payment can be made in installments.**

4. What is the process for advising adult students? **Advising completed by phone or at site by faculty.**

5. What career and placement services are available to adult students? **All students can use all placement and career services.**

6. What characteristics of the institution's adult degree programs are most appealing to students? **Location, quality, and tuition costs.**

Wayne State University

College of Lifelong Learning
2406 Academic/Administration Building, 5700 Cass Avenue
Detroit, MI 48202
Phone: (313) 577-4627 ◆ Fax: (313) 577-8585
E-mail: isp@cll.wayne.edu
Web address: http://www.wayne.edu

Founded: 1973

Accredited by: North Central

Enrollment: 600 ◆ Adult students: 100 percent

University status: Public

Degree	Concentration/Major	Format
B.I.S.	Interdisciplinary	E,S,TH
B.T.I.S.	Interdisciplinary	E,S,TH
M.I.S.	Interdisciplinary	E,S,TH

Campus Extension Site

Clinton Township, MI

Requirements

Residency requirement: Yes for B.I.S. and M.I.S.; B.T.I.S.—some on campus; M.I.S.—some on campus.
Undergraduate admissions requirements: High school diploma or GED, must be 21 years old, complete admission documents, pay application fee, documented previous education records.
Graduate admissions requirements: Degree from an accredited school, 2.25 GPA or above, 60 semester credits.
Graduation requirements (undergraduate): Students must complete all school and degree requirements.

Graduation requirements (graduate): Graduates must earn 32 credit hours with a 3.0 minimum GPA.

Fees, Tuition, Costs

Undergraduate application fee: $20
Graduate application fee: $20
Undergraduate tuition: $102/hour
Graduate tuition: $148/hour
Undergraduate cost of books: Varies
Graduate cost of books: Varies

Financial Aid/Status

Scholarship programs for adults: Scholarships available for female ISP students
Full-time status: 12 credit hours/term
Percentage of adult students receiving financial aid: 50 percent

Maximum Hours Awarded For

CLEP: 36

Features and Services

1. Is it possible to purchase books during hours most adult students attend classes? **Yes.**

2. Are the institution's administrative offices open during hours adult students attend class? **Yes.**

3. How do students taking extended classes access library resources? **Some library materials are at the class site, but most are on campus.**

4. What is the registration and payment process for adult students? **Students register before each term. This may be done by mail. Payment must be made by the WSU schedule.**

5. What characteristics of the institution's adult degree programs are most appealing to students? **The curriculum design enables students to focus on themes and issues using interdisciplinary methods. The college makes a university education more accessible to adults with family, work, and other responsibilities.**

Wentworth Institute of Technology

550 Huntington Avenue ◆ **Boston, MA 02115**
Phone: (617) 442-9010 ◆ Toll-free phone: (800) 323-9481
Fax: (617) 427-2852 ◆ E-mail: flynnj@wit.edu
Web address: http://www.wit.edu

Founded: 1904

Accredited by: New England

Enrollment: 2,400 ◆ Adult students: 25 percent

University status: Private

Degree	Concentration/Major	Format
A.A.S.	Electronic Technology	E
A.A.S.	Building Construction Technology	E
A.A.S.	Architectural Technology	E
A.A.S.	Electromechanical Systems	E
A.A.S.	Mechanical Design Technology	E
A.A.S.	Telecommunications and Fiber Optics	E
B.S.	Computer Science Systems	E
B.S.	Construction Management	E
B.S.	Electronic Systems Engineering Technology	E
B.S.	Mechanical Systems Engineering Technology	E
B.S.	Project Management	E

Requirements

Residency requirement: Yes
Undergraduate admissions requirements: High school graduation or GED, four years of high school English, Algebra I & II, Geometry, and one laboratory science
Graduation requirements (undergraduate): Technical courses, English I & II, mathematics, physics, and social science electives; Associate degree—64 credits; Bachelor's degree—128 credits

Fees, Tuition, Costs

Undergraduate application fee: $30
Undergraduate tuition: $300/credit hour
Undergraduate cost of books: $60/course

Financial Aid/Status

Full-time status: 12 credit hours
Percentage of adult students receiving financial aid: 50 percent

Maximum Hours Awarded For

CLEP: Yes
Other exams: Yes

Features and Services

1. Is it possible to purchase books during hours most adult students attend classes? **Yes.**

2. Are the institution's administrative offices open during hours adult students attend class? **Yes.**

3. How do students taking extended classes access library resources? **An online catalog is available.**

4. What is the registration and payment process for adult students? **Payment may be made using a three-payment plan—1/3 of tuition at registration, 1/3 in 5 weeks, 1/3 in 10 weeks—or an employer reimbursement system. Registration begins one month before each semester.**

5. What is the process for advising adult students? **Continuing education provides the initial advising. Faculty advisors are assigned for ongoing assistance.**

6. What career and placement services are available to adult students? **Resume mailing service, Job Bank, resume-writing, job searching strategy development are available.**

7. What characteristics of the institution's adult degree programs are most appealing to students? **Hands-on technical training, and small classes.**

Wesley College

111 Wesley Circle, PO Box 1070 ◆ **Florence, MS 39073**
Phone: (601) 845-2265 ◆ Toll-free phone: (800) 748-9972
Fax: (601) 845-2265

Founded: 1944

Accredited by: Accrediting Association of Bible Colleges

Enrollment: 110 ◆ Adult students: 64 percent

University status: Private, Church,
Congregational Methodist Church

Degree	Concentration/Major	Format
B.S.	Christian Ministries	E,S

Requirements

Residency requirement: Specific times are designated for this.
Undergraduate admissions requirements: Minimum 17 on ACT or 700 on SAT, high school diploma or GED.
Graduation requirements (undergraduate): Complete general education core, complete major concentration core, satisfy chapel and Christian service requirements, pass Bible exam, pass English proficiency, and maintain 2.00 GPA

Fees, Tuition, Costs

Undergraduate application fee: $20
Undergraduate tuition: $80/hour, $960/12-16 hours
Undergraduate cost of books: $200/year

Financial Aid/Status

Scholarship programs for adults: The college is in the process of developing some. There is none in place at present other than those offered to everyone
Full-time status: Enrolled in 12 hours or more.
Percentage of adult students receiving financial aid: 90 percent.

Maximum Hours Awarded For

Prior learning portfolio: 24
Additional information: Challenge exam

Features and Services

1. Is it possible to purchase books during hours most adult students attend classes? **Yes.**

2. Are the institution's administrative offices open during hours adult students attend class? **Yes.**

3. How do students taking extended classes access library resources? **Students may use the fax in each class. Some computer access is available.**

4. What is the registration and payment process for adult students? **Mail or bring in application and registration form. Payment may be made using financial aid. Students must pay 1/4 of tuition at registration.**

5. What is the process for advising adult students? **Each student is assigned on individual advisor.**

6. What characteristics of the institution's adult degree programs are most appealing to students? **One week in length three times a year or four to five weekends per semester.**

West Coast University

440 Shatto Place ◆ **Los Angeles, CA 90020-1765**
Phone: (213) 427-4400 ◆ Toll-free phone: (800) 2484-WCU
Fax: (213) 380-4362 ◆ E-mail: info@katz.wcula.edu
Web address: http://katz.wcula.edu

Founded: 1909

Accredited by: Western Association

Enrollment: 1,000 ◆ Adult students: 1,000

University status: Private

Degree	Concentration/Major	Format
B.S.	Business Administration	E
B.S.	Business Administration—Management of Information Systems	E
B.S.	Business Administration—Environmental Management	E
B.S.	Industrial Technology (Environmental Applications)	E
B.S.	Industrial Technology	E
B.S.	Electrical Engineering	E
B.S.	Mechanical Engineering	E
B.S.	Computer Science	E
M.S.	Electrical Engineering	E
M.S.	Mechanical Engineering	E
M.S.	Computer Science	E
M.S.	Management Information Systems	E
M.S.	Acquisition and Contract Management	E
M.B.A.	Business Administration	E
M.S.	Engineering Management	E
M.S.	Environmental Management	E

Campus Extension Sites

Orange, CA
San Diego, CA
Vandenberg AFB, CA

Requirements

Residency requirement: At least 30 units undergraduate and 24 graduate credits must be taken at the university.
Undergraduate admissions requirements: Most students are transfer students (A.A. or A.S.), minimum 2.00 GPA.
Graduate admissions requirements: Regionally accredited B.A. or B.S. and minimum 2.5 GPA.
Graduation requirements (undergraduate): Minimum of 124 units, at least 30 at WCU.
Graduation requirements (graduate): Minimum of 33 units, at least 24 at WCU.

Fees, Tuition, Costs

Undergraduate application fee: $35
Graduate application fee: $35
Undergraduate tuition: $340/semester unit
Graduate tuition: $370/semester unit

Undergraduate cost of books: $500/year
Graduate cost of books: $700/year

Financial Aid/Status

Full-time status: 18 semester units per year for graduate students; 24 semester units per year for undergraduates
Percentage of adult students receiving financial aid: 15 percent

Maximum Hours Awarded For

CLEP: 30
PEP: 30
DANTES: 30
Other exams: 12

Features and Services

1. Is it possible to purchase books during hours most adult students attend classes? **Yes.**

2. Are the institution's administrative offices open during hours adult students attend class? **Yes.**

3. How do students taking extended classes access library resources? **Can be accessed by the Internet, fax, and modem.**

4. What is the registration and payment process for adult students? **Student pays and registers for classes six times per year; no yearly rates.**

5. What is the process for advising adult students? **All students have faculty advisors.**

6. What characteristics of the institution's adult degree programs are most appealing to students? **Evening classes; six eight-week terms per year; one to two courses per term.**

West Virginia State College

P.O. Box 1000 ◆ Institute, WV 25112
Phone: (304) 766-3221 ◆ Toll-free phone: (800) 987-2112
E-mail: greenrl@ernie.wsc.wvnet.edu

Founded: 1891

Accredited by: North Central

Enrollment: 4,486

University status: Public

Degree   Concentration/Major   Format

All majors are available.

Requirements

Residency requirement: Yes
Undergraduate admissions
requirements: High school
graduate (2.0 GPA or ACT
composite score of 17) or GED
certificate (45 on each part or 55
average score); submit ACT scores
Graduation requirements
(undergraduate): Vary with
program

Fees, Tuition, Costs

Undergraduate application fee:
None
Undergraduate tuition: $1,025/
semester
Undergraduate cost of books: $500
Other costs: Supplies

Financial Aid/Status

Full-time status: 12 credit hours/
semester

Maximum Hours Awarded For

CLEP: Yes

Features and Services

1. Is it possible to purchase
   books during hours most
   adult students attend classes?
   Yes.

2. What is the registration and
   payment process for adult
   students? **Registration can
   be done during evening
   hours.**

3. What is the process for
   advising adult students?
   **Each student is assigned a
   faculty advisor.**

4. What career and placement
   services are available to adult
   students? **Career counseling
   and placement services are
   offered.**

5. What characteristics of the
   institution's adult degree
   programs are most appealing
   to students? **Offers classes
   from 8 A.M. to 10 P.M.
   Monday through Thursday.**

West Virginia University

P.O. Box 6287
Regents Bachelor of Arts Degree Program
Morgantown, WV 26506
Phone: (304) 293-5441 ◆ Fax: (304) 293-7490
E-mail: patersa@wvnvm.wvnet.edu
Web address: http://www.wvu.edu

Founded: 1867

Accredited by: North Central

Enrollment: 22,000 ◆ Adult students: 5 percent

University status: Public

Degree	Concentration/Major	Format
B.A.	General Education	E,TH

Campus Extension Sites

West Liberty, WV
Fairmont, WV
Glenville, WV
Huntington, WV
Institute, WV
Montgomery, WV
Athens, WV
Bluefield, WV
Parkersburg, WV
Shepherdstown, WV

Requirements

Residency requirement: Students must earn 15 credits at public West Virginia institutions—these can be TV courses. Most students take on-campus courses.
Undergraduate admissions requirements: High school diploma or GED, or transferring with good academic standing. It must be at least four years since high school graduation.

Graduation requirements (undergraduate): Graduates must earn 128 hours with a minimum 2.0 GPA, 40 hours of upper-level courses, and 36 hours of general education.

Fees, Tuition, Costs

Undergraduate application fee: $15 in-state; $35 out-of-state
Undergraduate tuition: $66/credit in-state; $243/credit out-of-state
Other costs: Lab and computer fees, depending on courses

Financial Aid/Status

Scholarship programs for adults: No special scholarships for adults are available. Adults are eligible for regular WVU scholarships.
Full-time status: Students taking 12 hours per semester are considered full-time.

Maximum Hours Awarded For

CLEP: Yes
PEP: Yes
DANTES: Yes
Other exams: Yes
Prior learning portfolio: Yes
Additional information: Military credit, ACE

Features and Services

1. What is the registration and payment process for adult students? **Students may register and pay by mail. VISA may be used for a portion of tuition.**

2. What is the process for advising adult students? **An advisor is available full-time. Phone and mail advising are used.**

3. What career and placement services are available to adult students? **Both services are available for all WVU students.**

4. What characteristics of the institution's adult degree programs are most appealing to students? **No major (just distributive requirements); short residency (15 hours); possibility of portfolio credit; flexibility.**

West Virginia University at Parkersburg

Route 5 Box 130 ◆ Parkersburg, WV 26101
Phone: (304) 424-8220 ◆ Fax: (304) 424-8332

Founded: 1971

Accredited by: North Central

Enrollment: 3,747 ◆ Adult students: 43 percent

University status: Public

Degree	Concentration/Major	Format
A.A./B.A.	Business Administration	E

Campus Extension Site

Ripley, WV

Requirements

Residency requirement: Yes.
Undergraduate admissions
requirements: For the two-year
program, any student who has
graduated from high school more
than five years before submits an
application. A GED is also
accepted.
Graduation requirements
(undergraduate): Requirements
depend on the degree program.

Fees, Tuition, Costs

Undergraduate application fee: $0
Undergraduate tuition: $48.50/
semester hour
Undergraduate cost of books:
$200/semester

Financial Aid/Status

Scholarship programs for adults:
After completing 12 hours of
college credit, students can apply
for full tuition waiver for a full
year.
Full-time status: 12 semester hours.
Percentage of adult students
receiving financial aid: 47 percent.

Maximum Hours Awarded For

CLEP: Yes
Other exams: Yes

Features and Services

1. Is it possible to purchase
books during hours most
adult students attend classes?
Yes.

2. Are the institution's
administrative offices open
during hours adult students
attend class? **Yes.**

3. How do students taking
extended classes access
library resources? **The
library is available on
Saturday and during
evening hours.**

4. What is the registration and
payment process for adult
students? **Registration and
payment may be done on
campus or by mail. Evening
hours are available.**

5. What is the process for
advising adult students?
**Academic advising is
available during evening
hours.**

Westbrook College

Stevens Avenue ◆ **Portland, ME 04103**
Phone: (207) 797-7261 ◆ Fax: (207) 797-7318

Founded: 1831

Accredited by: New England

Enrollment: 300 ◆ Adult students: 20 percent

University status: Private

Features and Services

1. Are the institution's administrative offices open during hours adult students attend class? **Yes.**

2. What is the registration and payment process for adult students? **Payment is due before the start of each enrollment period.**

3. What career and placement services are available to adult students? **Full academic and career placement services are available.**

Degree	Concentration/Major	Format
A.S.	Dental Hygiene	
B.S.	Organizational Leadership	E,A
B.S.	Nursing	
B.S.	Dental Hygiene	
B.A.	American Studies	
B.A.	Business Management	
B.A.	Early Childhood Education	
B.A.	English	
B.S.	Environmental Biology	
B.A.	Human Development	
B.S.	Medical Technology	
B.A.	Psychology	

Requirements

Residency requirement: Yes
Undergraduate admissions requirements: Organizational Leadership—48 credits of previous college-level work. Other degrees—2.3 cumulative GPA in transferred credits; health science programs—2.5 average in math and lab science preparatory courses
Graduation requirements (undergraduate): 120 credits with at least 2.0 cumulative average

Fees, Tuition, Costs

Undergraduate application fee: $25
Undergraduate tuition: Organizational Leadership—$220/credit; other programs—$11,650/year

Undergraduate cost of books: $550

Financial Aid/Status

Scholarship programs for adults: Scholarships are need-based. They are varied (e.g., Phi Theta Kappa Scholarship is $2,500).
Full-time status: 12 credits/semester.

Maximum Hours Awarded For

CLEP: 15
Prior learning portfolio: 60

Western Baptist College

5000 Deer Park Drive, S.E. ◆ **Salem, OR 97301**
Phone: (503) 375-7590 ◆ Toll-free phone: (800) 764-1383
Fax: (503) 375-7583 ◆ E-mail: nmartyn@wbc.edu
Web address: http://www.wbc.ed

Founded: 1935

Accredited by: Northwest Association

Enrollment: 690 ◆ Adult students: 110

University status: Private, Church, Baptist Church

Degree	Concentration/Major	Format
B.A.	Management and Communications	E,A,CT
B.S.	Management and Communications	E,A,CT
B.A.	Family Studies	E,A
B.S.	Family Studies	E,A

Campus Extension Site
Portland, OR

Requirements
Residency requirement: Family Studies is offered at the extended location in Portland, OR. Undergraduate admissions requirements: Applicants must have 60 semester hours of transferable credit (C average), demonstrate writing skills, provide personal and professional references, and show evidence of a personal Christian faith.
Graduation requirements (undergraduate): B.S./B.A. degrees— 128 semester units with at least a 2.0 GPA in major, including 51 hours of general education and 40 hours of upper-level courses. Management and Communications curriculum includes 37 upper-level hours; Family Studies includes 44.

Fees, Tuition, Costs
Undergraduate application fee: $25
Undergraduate tuition: $8,950/

program of 15 months
Undergraduate cost of books: Included in tuition
Other costs: Computer/modem needed for distance program in Management and Communications

Financial Aid/Status
Scholarship programs for adults: "Church Scholarship" for Family Studies majors is based on a pastoral evaluation of involvement and potential for future contribution to church-family life.
Full-time status: Full-time students must complete at least 12 semester hours per semester.
Percentage of adult students receiving financial aid: 90 percent.

Maximum Hours Awarded For
CLEP: 32
DANTES: 32
Prior learning portfolio: 30
Additional information: Up to 32 hours may be awarded between CLEP and DANTES. Weekend College provides an opportunity to meet general education requirements.

Features and Services

1. Are the institution's administrative offices open during hours adult students attend class? Yes.

2. How do students taking extended classes access library resources? **The library is open seven days a week. It may be accessed by phone or computer. Online services and interlibrary loans are available.**

3. What is the registration and payment process for adult students? **Registration paperwork is completed in the Adult Studies office. The files are given to the registrar prior to the first class. Business office personnel meet with students the first class night to set up contracts.**

4. What is the process for advising adult students? **When the Initial Transcript Evaluation is completed by the registrar, students are assigned an assessment counselor, who develops an academic plan detailing requirements for graduation.**

5. What career and placement services are available to adult students? **The College Career Center is available for testing and advising.**

6. What characteristics of the institution's adult degree programs are most appealing to students? **Format of one-night-a-week class appeals to working adults; great instructors from the college faculty; adjuncts who are specialists within community; curriculum integrated with Biblical principles; credit for prior learning; Weekend College.**

Western Connecticut State University

181 White Street ◆ Danbury, CT 06810
Phone: (203) 837-8241 ◆ Fax: (203) 837-8320
E-mail: quinn@wcsu.ctstateu.edu

Founded: 1903

Accredited by: New England

Enrollment: 5,500 ◆ Adult students: 51 percent

University status: Public

Degree   Concentration/Major   Format

No degree programs were specified. The university indicated that degree programs were available in the evening.

Requirements

Residency requirement: Yes. Undergraduate admissions requirements: Admission is moderately competitive. SAT scores and an essay are required. Graduate admissions requirements: Admission is competitive. An undergraduate 2.7 GPA is needed. No testing is required. Graduation requirements (undergraduate): Graduation requires a 2.0 overall GPA; a 2.3-2.7 GPA in the major area of study. Graduation requirements (graduate): Graduation requires a 3.0 cumulative GPA.

Fees, Tuition, Costs

Undergraduate application fee: $20
Graduate application fee: $20
Undergraduate tuition: $147/credit
Graduate tuition: $170/credit
Undergraduate cost of books: $500
Graduate cost of books: $250

Financial Aid/Status

Full-time status: Full-time undergraduate status is 12 credits; graduate is 9 credits. Percentage of adult students receiving financial aid: 25 percent.

Maximum Hours Awarded For

CLEP: Yes
Other exams: Yes
Prior learning portfolio: Yes
Additional information: AP exams

Features and Services

1. Is it possible to purchase books during hours most adult students attend classes? **Yes.**

2. Are the institution's administrative offices open during hours adult students attend class? **Yes.**

3. How do students taking extended classes access library resources? **Students may use the library evenings and weekends. Computer access is also available.**

4. What is the registration and payment process for adult students? **Registration and payment may be done in person and by mail. Dropping or adding a course may be done by phone and faxing the materials.**

5. What is the process for advising adult students? **Advising is done in person. An advisor must sign off on registration.**

6. What career and placement services are available to adult students? **Services include a career library and computer, comprehensive services, workshops, and interviews both on and off campus.**

7. What characteristics of the institution's adult degree programs are most appealing to students? **Being able to attend classes for several programs at night.**

Western Evangelical Seminary

12753 S.W. 68th Avenue ◆ **Tigard, OR 97223**
Phone: (503) 639-0559 ◆ Toll-free phone: (800) 493-4937
Fax: (503) 598-4338 ◆ E-mail: wes@iclnet.org
Web address: http://wes.iclnet.org/

Founded: 1947

Accredited by: Association of Theological Studies

Enrollment: 351 ◆ Adult students: 100 percent

University status: Private

Degree	Concentration/Major	Format
M.Div.	Master of Divinity	E
M.A.	Counseling	E
M.A.	Marriage and Family Therapy	E
M.A.	Theological Studies	E
M.A.	Leadership	E
M.A.	Urban Ministry	E
M.A.	Christian Education	E

Campus Extension Site

Salem, OR

Requirements

Residency requirement: Yes. Class participation is an integral part of the program.
Graduate admissions requirements: Applicants must hold either a B.S. or B.A. degree (3.0 GPA).
Graduation requirements (graduate): Graduates must successfully complete all program courses with a 3.0 GPA.

Fees, Tuition, Costs

Graduate application fee: $25
Graduate tuition: $169/hour
Graduate cost of books: $700/annually
Other costs: Computer recommended; no campus housing available

Financial Aid/Status

Scholarship programs for adults: Scholarships available based on need
Full-time status: 12 quarter hours/term
Percentage of adult students receiving financial aid: 50 percent

Features and Services

1. Is it possible to purchase books during hours most adult students attend classes? **Yes.**

2. Are the institution's administrative offices open during hours adult students attend class? **Yes.**

3. How do students taking extended classes access library resources? **Students may use local college libraries or the main WES library.**

4. What is the registration and payment process for adult students? **On-site registration and payment are available. Times are flexible.**

5. What is the process for advising adult students? **Each student has a faculty advisor to provide assistance throughout the program.**

6. What career and placement services are available to adult students? **Job announcements are posted.**

7. What characteristics of the institution's adult degree programs are most appealing to students? **Program content and certification, scheduling, cost, accessibility.**

Western Illinois University

5 Horrabin Hall ◆ **Macomb, IL 61455**
Phone: (309) 298-1929 ◆ Fax: (309) 298-2226
Web address: http://www.wiu.edu

Founded: 1898

Accredited by: North Central

Enrollment: 12,000 ◆ Adult students: 8-9 percent

University status: Public

Degree	Concentration/Major	Format
B.A.	Board of Governors Degree Program	E,V,C,T,S

Campus Extension Site

Rock Island, IL

Requirements

Residency requirement: None.
Undergraduate admissions requirements: For the Board of Governors B.A. Degree Program, the only expectation is significant work experience.
Graduation requirements (undergraduate): Graduates must earn 120 semester hours—including 40 semester hours of upper-division work and 12 semester hours each in humanities, social science, and natural science/math—pass the university writing and constitution exams, and have an overall C average.

Fees, Tuition, Costs

Undergraduate application fee: None
Undergraduate tuition: $80/semester hour

Financial Aid/Status

Scholarship programs for adults: Scholarships available
Full-time status: 12 semester hours

Maximum Hours Awarded For

CLEP: No limit
PEP: No limit
DANTES: No limit
Other exams: No limit
Prior learning portfolio: No limit

Features and Services

1. Is it possible to purchase books during hours most adult students attend classes? **Yes.**

2. Are the institution's administrative offices open during hours adult students attend class? **Yes.**

3. How do students taking extended classes access library resources? **Students access the library on their own.**

4. What is the registration and payment process for adult students? **Students are billed. Student-designed payment plans are available.**

5. What is the process for advising adult students? **Each student is assigned an advisor. An advisor is on duty 7 A.M.-5 P.M. Monday through Friday.**

6. What career and placement services are available to adult students? **Regular university services may be used by adult students.**

7. What characteristics of the institution's adult degree programs are most appealing to students? **Flexibility; the students design their own learning.**

Western International University

9215 N. Black Canyon Highway ◆ Phoenix, AZ 85021

Phone: (602) 943-2311 ◆ Fax: (602) 371-8637

Founded: 1978

Accredited by: North Central

Enrollment: 1,100 ◆ Adult students: 100 percent

University status: Profit

Degree	Concentration/Major	Format
B.A.	Behavioral Science	E,A
B.A.	General Studies	E,A
B.A.	International Studies	E,A
B.S.	Accounting	E,A
B.S.	Abytion Management	E,A
B.S.	Finance	E,A
B.S.	General Business	E,A
B.S.	Information Systems	E,A
B.S.	International Business	E,A
B.S.	Management	E,A
B.S.	Marketing	E,A
M.B.A.	Finance	E,A
M.B.A.	Healthcare Management	E,A
M.B.A.	International Business	E,A
M.B.A.	Management	E,A
M.B.A.	Management Information Systems	E,A
M.B.A.	Marketing	E,A
M.P.A.	Public Administration	E,A
M.S.	Accounting	E,A
M.S.	Healthcare Information Resources Management	E,A
M.S.	Information Systems	E,A
M.S.	Information Systems Engineering	E,A

Campus Extension Sites

Douglas, AZ

Sierra Vista, AZ

Requirements

Residency requirement: WIU holds classes at corporate sites throughout the Valley. Undergraduate admissions requirements: High school diploma/GED with either 2.5 GPA or upper half of graduating class or SAT—950/ACT—22; college preparatory course of study. Transfer students must have at least 12 hours of college credit (2.0 GPA). Provisional admission may be granted to applicants with successful work experience, maturity, and motivation. Graduate admissions requirements: Applicants must have a bachelor's degree (2.75 GPA). GMAT is strongly recommended. Graduation requirements (undergraduate): Graduates must earn 126 credits (2.0 GPA); 36 credits must be earned at WIU.

Other course requirements must be met. Graduation requirements (graduate): Students must complete the Common Body of Knowledge requirements before continuing into higher-level courses. Graduates earn a total of 39 additional credits.

Fees, Tuition, Costs

Undergraduate application fee: $50

Graduate application fee: $50

Undergraduate tuition: $165/credit hour

Graduate tuition: $210/credit hour

Undergraduate cost of books: $700

Graduate cost of books: $700

Financial Aid/Status

Full-time status: 27 credits in 45 weeks

Percentage of adult students receiving financial aid: 45 percent

Maximum Hours Awarded For

CLEP: Yes

PEP: Yes

DANTES: Yes

Prior learning portfolio: Yes

Features and Services

1. Is it possible to purchase books during hours most adult students attend classes? **Yes.**

2. Are the institution's administrative offices open during hours adult students attend class? **Yes.**

3. What is the registration and payment process for adult students? **Students are encouraged to preregister by phone, in person, online, or by mail with the Registrar's Office. Students may register at any time during regular office hours.**

4. What is the process for advising adult students? **Students are assigned a specific advisor, who will** guide them throughout the program.

5. What characteristics of the institution's adult degree programs are most appealing to students? **Quality; an accelerated delivery system.**

Western Oregon State College*

345 N. Monmouth Avenue ◆ **Monmouth, OR 97364**
Phone: (503) 838-8483 ◆ Fax: (503) 838-8473

Founded: 1856

Accredited by: Northwest Association

Enrollment: 3,900 ◆ Adult students: 300

University status: Public

Features and Services

1. Is it possible to purchase books during hours most adult students attend classes? **Yes.**

Degree	Concentration/Major	Format
B.A./B.S.	Fire Services Administration	E,C,V

Requirements

Residency requirement: Yes. Undergraduate admissions requirements: Student must be a resident of a state in the Pacific Northwest, Hawaii, or trust territories. Must have completed a minimum of 24 quarter credits in lower-division fire science. Must have a minimum 2.0 average GPA in all transfer work.

Fees, Tuition, Costs

Undergraduate application fee: $50
Undergraduate tuition: $80/credit

Financial Aid/Status

Full-time status: 12 credits

Maximum Hours Awarded For

CLEP: Yes
DANTES: Yes
Other exams: Yes

Westfield State College
Western Avenue ◆ Westfield, MA 01086
Phone: (413) 572-5224 ◆ Fax: (413) 572-5227
Web address: http://www.wsc.mass.edu

Founded: 1839

Accredited by: New England

Enrollment: 4,721

University status: Public

Fees, Tuition, Costs
Undergraduate application fee: $30
Graduate application fee: $30
Undergraduate tuition: $120/credit
Graduate tuition: $130/credit
Other costs: $90 fee/semester

Financial Aid/Status
Full-time status: Undergraduate full-time status is 12 credits per semester; graduate is 9 credits.

Maximum Hours Awarded For
CLEP: Yes

Degree	Concentration/Major	Format
B.A.	Art, Economics, English, French, History, Liberal Studies, Mass Communication, Math, Music, Political Science, Psychology, Social Science, Spanish	E
B.S.	Applied Chemistry, Biology, Business Management, Computer Information Systems, Computer Science	E
M.A.	English, Psychology	E
M.Ed.	American History, Teacher of Reading, Early Childhood Education, Educational Administration, Elementary, Intensive Special Needs, Music, Occupational Education, Principal, Secondary, Special Needs, Technology for Educators	E
M.S.	Criminal Justice	E,T

Features and Services

1. Is it possible to purchase books during hours most adult students attend classes? **Yes.**

2. Are the institution's administrative offices open during hours adult students attend class? **Yes.**

3. What is the registration and payment process for adult students? **Registration and payment may be handled by mail, phone, or in person during registration periods. Checks and credit cards are accepted.**

4. What is the process for advising adult students? **One-on-one advising is available by appointment.**

5. What career and placement services are available to adult students? **The Career Services Office is available.**

Campus Extension Sites
Framingham, MA
Worcester, MA

Requirements
Residency requirement: Yes. Undergraduate admissions requirements: Applicants must complete a continuing education application and submit official transcripts. Transfer applicants should have 24 credits or more. Transfer applicants are admitted based on academic records and other learning experiences. SAT is not required if at least 24 credits are being transferred.

Graduate admissions requirements: Applicants must submit an application, official transcripts, three professional letters of reference, MAT/GRE scores, and other documentation, as requested by the department.
Graduation requirements (undergraduate): Graduates must earn 120 hours, including major and general education requirements.
Graduation requirements (graduate): Graduates must earn 33-36 credit hours and successfully complete a comprehensive examination or thesis.

Westminster College

West Hall ◆ New Wilmington, PA 16172-0001
Phone: (412) 946-7353 ◆ Fax: (412) 946-6314
Web address: http://www.westminster.edu

Founded: 1852

Accredited by: Middle States

Enrollment: 1,672 ◆ Adult students: 7 percent

University status: Private, Church, Presbyterian Church, U.S.A.

Degree	Concentration/Major	Format
B.A.	Business Administration	E,A
B.A.	Accounting	E,A
B.A.	English	E,A
B.A.	History	E,A
B.A.	Political Science	E,A

Requirements

Residency requirement: Day and evening students must attend classes on campus.
Undergraduate admissions requirements: The Lifelong Learning Program is an undergraduate program especially for nontraditional students. Day classes meet 14 weeks, two or three times per week. Evening classes meet one night per week for nine weeks. Interested persons should contact the director of continuing education and lifelong learning for admissions information.
Graduate admissions requirements: Students desiring graduate credit must apply for admission to graduate study. Applicants must hold a bachelor's degree (2.75 QPA). Many programs require teacher certification. Others require 12 hours of work in psychology or education.
Graduation requirements (undergraduate): Graduates must complete 35 courses, 23 courses outside their major area of study, 2.0 QPA, complete general education requirements, pass comprehensive exam if required, participate in January term as required, spend senior year at Westminster, and participate in commencement exercises.
Graduation requirements (graduate): Graduates must complete 10 courses with a B average. Oral or comprehensive written exams may be required. Students must make formal application for the degree.

Fees, Tuition, Costs

Undergraduate application fee: $20
Graduate application fee: $20
Undergraduate tuition: $765/course
Graduate tuition: $960/course
Other costs: Information technology fees of $30/course

Financial Aid/Status

Full-time status: 4 courses/semester or 2/block

Maximum Hours Awarded For

CLEP: Yes
DANTES: Yes
Prior learning portfolio: Yes

Features and Services

1. Is it possible to purchase books during hours most adult students attend classes? **Yes.**

2. How do students taking extended classes access library resources? **Students receive a library card for their personal use.**

3. What is the registration and payment process for adult students? **Students may attend regular early registration, fill out registration form, and turn it in or call to register.**

4. What is the process for advising adult students? **Declared majors see both the department chair or the department designee and the Lifelong Learning Program director.**

5. What career and placement services are available to adult students? **All students receive the same services.**

6. What characteristics of the institution's adult degree programs are most appealing to students? **One-night-a-week class for each course; opportunity to receive bachelor's degree within four years; resident faculty teaching courses; small classes.**

Westminster College

1840 South 1300 East ◆ **Salt Lake City, UT 84105-3697**
Phone: (801) 484-7651 ◆ **Toll-free phone: (800) 748-4753**
Fax: (801) 466-6916 ◆ E-mail: admispub@wcslc.edu
Web address: http://www.wcslc.edu

Founded: 1875

Accredited by: Northwest Association

Enrollment: 2,009 ◆ Adult students: 1,088

University status: Private

Degree	Concentration/Major	Format
B.S.	Accounting, Business, Economics	E
B.S.	Human Resource Management, Management	E
B.S.	Marketing, Communication	E
B.S.	Finance, Computer Science	E
M.B.A.	Business Administration	E
M.P.C.	Professional Communication	E
M.Ed.	Education	E
M.S.N..	Nursing	E

Requirements

Residency requirement: Yes.
Undergraduate admissions requirements: Applicants must have a high school diploma or GED and submit official transcripts—including any college attended or high school if transferring fewer than 60 semester hours—and completed application. Graduate admissions requirements: Applicants must submit a completed application, college transcripts, and other documents (resume, recommendations, writing samples, personal statements) as required. Test results may be required.
Graduation requirements (undergraduate): Graduates must complete 124 semester hours (40 hours in courses numbered 300 or above); major, minor, and liberal education requirements; and have a 2.0 GPA or higher.
Graduation requirements (graduate): Each graduate programs requires a 3.0 GPA or higher. The M.B.A. requires 43

semester hours; M.Ed.—32; M.P.C.—31; M.S.N.—38.

Fees, Tuition, Costs

Undergraduate application fee: $25
Graduate application fee: $25
Undergraduate tuition: $318/hour
Graduate tuition: $358/hour
Undergraduate cost of books: $600
Graduate cost of books: $300

Financial Aid/Status

Scholarship programs for adults: Full-time adult students are eligible for institutional scholarships based on their previous academic records. The amount of the merit-based aid varies. Full-time status: 12 or more semester hours for undergraduates; 7 or more semester hours for graduate students. Percentage of adult students receiving financial aid: 45 percent.

Maximum Hours Awarded For

CLEP: 40
Prior learning portfolio: 45

Features and Services

1. Is it possible to purchase books during hours most adult students attend classes? **Yes.**

2. Are the institution's administrative offices open during hours adult students attend class? **Yes.**

3. What is the registration and payment process for adult students? **Mail-in registration and payment plans are available.**

4. What is the process for advising adult students? **Following admission, adult students meet with a peer advisor from their particular school, who helps them plan their academic program and register for first semester classes. After the initial advising, a major advisor is assigned to work with them until graduation.**

5. What career and placement services are available to adult students? **The Career Resource Center offers help with career exploration, resumes, networking, interviewing, and job seeking skills. It posts more than 250 jobs with daily updating as well as internship opportunities. Information on graduate schools and graduate school test registration packets are available.**

6. What characteristics of the institution's adult degree programs are most appealing to students? **Small classes, personalized attention, flexible registration policy, flexible scheduling, high degree of interaction with the faculty.**

Wheeling Jesuit College

316 Washington Avenue ◆ **Wheeling, WV 26003-6295**
Phone: (304) 243-2250 ◆ Toll-free phone: (800) 873-7665
Fax: (304) 243-4441 ◆ E-mail: bforney@ricci.wjc.edu
Web address: http://www.wjc.edu

Founded: 1954

Accredited by: North Central

Enrollment: 1,511 ◆ Adult students: 571

University status: Private, Church, Roman Catholic Church

Degree	Concentration/Major	Format
B.S.	Business Administration—Marketing, Management, and Accounting	E
B.L.A	Liberal Arts	E
B.S.	Nursing	E
B.S.	Allied Health	E
B.A.	Human Resource Management	E,A
M.S.	Nursing/Nursing Administration	E
M.B.A.	Business Administration	E
M.S.	Accountancy	E
M.A.	Applied Theology	E,A

Campus Extension Sites

Weirton, WV
Parkersburg, WV
Clarksburg, WV
Charleston, WV

Requirements

Residency requirement: Off-campus students in the bachelor's in Human Resource Management program complete all requirements off campus.
Undergraduate admissions requirements: Applicants must provide a completed application and either an official high school transcript or GED or all previous college transcripts or nursing school transcripts. Mature men and women without high school/GED may be admitted conditionally with approval of the Dean of Adult Education.
Graduate admissions requirements: Applicants must complete an application, and provide graduate school test scores, official college transcripts, and three letters of recommendation.
Graduation requirements (undergraduate): Graduates must earn at least 120 semester hours and complete a major (at least 18 hours at Wheeling Jesuit College)and the liberal arts core with a minimum 2.0 GPA.
Graduation requirements (graduate): Graduates must complete the required number of credits for the degree (at least 24 hours at Wheeling Jesuit College) with a minimum 3.0 GPA. All requirements must be completed within seven years.

Fees, Tuition, Costs

Undergraduate application fee: $25
Graduate application fee: $25
Undergraduate tuition: $175/semester hour
Graduate tuition: $330/semester hour

Financial Aid/Status

Scholarship programs for adults: Ten $500/year scholarships awarded based on academic merit, financial need, and college/community service
Full-time status: 12 semester hours
Percentage of adult students receiving financial aid: 27 percent

Maximum Hours Awarded For

CLEP: 30
PEP: Yes
DANTES: Yes
Prior learning portfolio: 30

Features and Services

1. Is it possible to purchase books during hours most adult students attend classes? **Yes.**

2. How do students taking extended classes access library resources? **Students have access to library resources by using a modem or through arrangements with other libraries.**

3. What is the registration and payment process for adult students? **Students may register by phone, mail, or fax or in person. Payment may be made by mail or in person.**

4. What is the process for advising adult students? **Each student meets with an admissions counselor before registering for the first class. Then an academic advisor is assigned until graduation.**

5. What career and placement services are available to adult students? **Workshops, guest speakers, and counselors are available with guidance in developing career skills such as resume writing and interviewing.**

6. What characteristics of the institution's adult degree programs are most appealing to students? **Scheduling, acceleration, peers in classroom, payment plans.**

Whitworth College

300 W. Hawthorne Road ◆ **Spokane, WA 99251-1102**
Phone: (509) 466-3222 ◆ Fax: (509) 466-3251
E-mail: cvawter@whitworth.edu
Web address: http://www.whitworth.edu

Founded: 1890

Accredited by: Northwest Association

Enrollment: 1,500 ◆ Adult students: 150

University status: Private, Church, Presbyterian Church, U.S.A.

Degree	Concentration/Major	Format
B.A.	Business Management	E
B.A.	Accounting	E
B.L.S.	Humanities	E
B.L.S.	Community Leadership	E
B.L.S.	Program Management	E
B.L.S.	Upside-Down (Washington state A.A.S. degree holders)	E
B.A.	Education	E
M.Ed.	Educational Administration	E
M.Ed.	Elementary or Secondary Education	E
M.A.T.	Reading	E
M.Ed.	Guidance and Counseling/School or Social Agency	E
M.A.T.	Special Education	E
M.A.T.	English as a Second Language	E
M.A.T.	Gifted and Talented	E
M.A.T.	Physical Education	E

Requirements

Residency requirement: Yes; Whitworth has no external degree programs.
Undergraduate admissions requirements: Applicants in the Continuing Education department meet with a continuing studies advisor to review transcripts as needed. An application must be completed. Transfer students need a 2.5 GPA. Students in the Liberal Studies program must be over 25. The Upside-Down Degree requires an A.A.S. degree from a Washington state community college.
Graduate admissions requirements: Applicants must submit an application, GRE scores, four professional recommendations, and other documents as required. Students must have a bachelor's degree with a 3.0 GPA. Prerequisites may be required if applicants are lacking in preparation in a certain area.
Graduation requirements (undergraduate): Graduates must earn 130 semester hours (2.0 GPA), 36 of upper-level courses, 32 earned in a degree program at Whitworth. The general education requirements must be met.
Graduation requirements (graduate): Graduates must complete all requirements for the degree program, including any comprehensive exams or practicums, and 33-35 credits depending on the degree program.

Fees, Tuition, Costs

Undergraduate application fee: $25
Graduate application fee: $25
Undergraduate tuition: $205/ semester for the B.L.S.; $140/ semester for Continuing Studies
Graduate tuition: $195/semester credit
Undergraduate cost of books: $200/semester
Graduate cost of books: $200/ semester

Financial Aid/Status
Full-time status: Being enrolled in more than 8 credits

Maximum Hours Awarded For
CLEP: Yes

Features and Services
1. Is it possible to purchase books during hours most adult students attend classes? **Only the first week of classes.**

2. Are the institution's administrative offices open during hours adult students attend class? **Only the first week of classes.**

3. How do students taking extended classes access library resources? **Library is open until 11 P.M. Student ID cards serve as library cards.**

4. What is the registration and payment process for adult students? **Students may use the phone, mail, or come to the office for registration and payment.**

5. What is the process for advising adult students? **Students meet with the continuing studies advisor.**

6. What career and placement services are available to adult students? **"Student Life" is available to all students for advising and placement services.**

7. What characteristics of the institution's adult degree programs are most appealing to students? **Availability of general requirements in the evening; ability to complete full degree in the evening.**

Wilberforce University
Wilberforce, OH 45384-1091
Phone: (513) 376-2911 ◆ Fax: (513) 376-5598
Web address: http://www.wilberforce.edu

Founded: 1856

Accredited by: North Central

Enrollment: 900 ◆ Adult students: 10 percent

University status: Private, Church, A.M.E. Church

Degree	Concentration/Major	Format
B.S.	Organizational Management	E,A

Campus Extension Site
Columbus, OH

Requirements
Residency requirement: Students at Columbus location complete their work in Columbus.
Undergraduate admissions requirements: Applicants must be 25 years old, have at least five years of work experience, and have supervisory or program development responsibilities. They must hold an A.A. degree or have two years of college credit.
Graduation requirements (undergraduate): Graduates must earn 128 credit hours (2.0 GPA), including completing general education requirements and a major area of study. Writing competency must be achieved. At least 30 hours of residency is required during the senior year. Adult students are not required to take physical education, reading, co-op preparation, strategies, and the history of Wilberforce.

Fees, Tuition, Costs
Undergraduate application fee: $20
Undergraduate tuition: $3,470/term
Undergraduate cost of books: $300

Financial Aid/Status
Full-time status: All adult students enrolled in our degree completion program are full-time students. Percentage of adult students receiving financial aid: 95 percent.

Maximum Hours Awarded For
CLEP: 15
DANTES: 15

Prior learning portfolio: 30

Features and Services
1. How do students taking extended classes access library resources? **Students may access the library by computer and phone.**

2. What is the registration and payment process for adult students? **The Office of Adult and Continuing Education handles registration in the evening with the cooperation of the Business Office and Financial Aid.**

3. What is the process for advising adult students? **Each student meets with an advisor prior to starting the program. Periodic meetings are held throughout the program.**

4. What career and placement services are available to adult students? **They have access to the Co-op Office on campus.**

5. What characteristics of the institution's adult degree programs are most appealing to students? **Accelerated program, convenience of class time, group support from classmates.**

William Jewell College

500 College Hill ◆ Liberty, MO 64068

Phone: (816) 781-7700 ◆ Fax: (816) 415-5027

E-mail: schweglers@william.jewell.edu

Web address: http://www.jewell.edu

Founded: 1849

Accredited by: North Central

Enrollment: 2,200 ◆ Adult students: 530

University status: Private, Church, Baptist Church

Degree	Concentration/Major	Format
B.S.	Accounting	E
B.S.	Business Administration	E
B.S.	Systems: Data Processing	E
B.A.	Psychology	E
B.A.	Economics	E

Requirements

Residency requirement: Yes. Undergraduate admissions requirements: Applicants must have a high school diploma, GED, or the recommendation of their high school counselor.

Graduation requirements (undergraduate): Graduates must earn 124 credit hours. The last 30 hours must be completed with WJC.

Fees, Tuition, Costs

Undergraduate tuition: $140/credit hour

Undergraduate cost of books: $60-$80/course

Financial Aid/Status

Full-time status: 12 credit hours

Percentage of adult students receiving financial aid: 80 percent

Maximum Hours Awarded For

CLEP: Yes

Features and Services

1. Is it possible to purchase books during hours most adult students attend classes? **Yes.**

2. Are the institution's administrative offices open during hours adult students attend class? **Yes.**

3. What is the registration and payment process for adult students? **Registration can be done by phone, fax, e-mail, or in person.**

4. What is the process for advising adult students? **There are two evening division counselors available from 8:30 A.M. to 7:00 P.M.**

5. What career and placement services are available to adult students? **Students have access to the career development office.**

6. What characteristics of the institution's adult degree programs are most appealing to students? **The ease of registration, drop/add classes, no hidden fees, excellent professors.**

William Woods University

College of Graduate and Adult Studies ◆ 200 W. 12th Street
Fulton, MO 65251 ◆ Phone: (573) 592-1149
Toll-free phone: (800) 995-3199 ◆ Fax: (573) 592-1164
E-mail: cgas@iris.wmwoods.edu
Web address: http://www.wmwoods.edu

Founded: 1870

Accredited by: North Central

Enrollment: 1,138 ◆ Adult students: 369

University status: Private, Church, Disciples of Christ Church

Degree	Concentration/Major	Format
B.A.	Management	A
M.B.A.	Business Management	A
M.Ed.	Curriculum and Instruction	A
M.Ed.	Administration	A
M.Ed.	Equestrian Education	A

Campus Extension Sites

Owensville, MO
Ashland, MO
Mexico, MO
Jefferson City, MO
Columbia, MO
Moberly, MO
Kirksville, MO
Fulton, MO
Lake Ozark, MO

Requirements

Residency requirement: Students are not required to attend classes on campus.
Undergraduate admissions requirements: Applicants with at least two years of work experience must have a minimum of 50 hours of transferable credit, official transcripts, minimum GPA 2.0, minimum TOFEL for international students.
Graduate admissions requirements: Applicants must hold a bachelor's degree from an accredited college or university, 2.5 GPA, and have two years of work experience. Other requirements depend on the degree program.
Graduation requirements (undergraduate): Graduates must earn 122 hours.
Graduation requirements (graduate): M.B.A.—36 hours; M.Ed.(Equestrian)—37 hours; M.Ed. (Administration)—36 hours; M.Ed. (Curriculum and Instruction)—36 hours.

Fees, Tuition, Costs

Undergraduate application fee: $25
Graduate application fee: $25
Undergraduate tuition: $190/credit hour
Graduate tuition: $255/credit hour
Undergraduate cost of books: $75/class
Graduate cost of books: Included in tuition
Other costs: M.B.A.—$60 laptop computer fee; M.Ed. (Equestrian)—riding fees

Financial Aid/Status

Full-time status: 12 hours/semester
Percentage of adult students receiving financial aid: 50 percent

Maximum Hours Awarded For

CLEP: 30
PEP: Yes
DANTES: Yes
Prior learning portfolio: 36

Features and Services

1. Is it possible to purchase books during hours most adult students attend classes? **Yes.**

2. How do students taking extended classes access library resources? **Students have access through arrangements made with several state and private colleges.**

3. What is the registration and payment process for adult students? **Registration and payment are available by mail, phone, fax, or in person. Cash or credit card may be used.**

4. What is the process for advising adult students? **Students receive advice before entering the program. Follow-up advising is continued during the program.**

5. What career and placement services are available to adult students? **Students may use the campus services.**

6. What characteristics of the institution's adult degree programs are most appealing to students? **Convenience, acceleration, practitioner-oriented.**

Winona State University

P.O. Box 5838 ◆ Winona, MN 55987

Phone: (507) 457-5088 ◆ Fax: (507) 457-5586

E-mail: pchristensen@vax2.winona.msus.edu

Web address: http://www.winona.msus.edu

Founded: 1858

Accredited by: North Central

Enrollment: 7,200 ◆ Adult students: 20 percent

University status: Public

Degree	Concentration/Major	Format
A.A.	General	E
B.A.	Individualized Study	E,S
B.S.	Business Administration	E
M.S.	Educational Leadership	E,T
M.S.	Education	E
M.S.	Counselor Education	E
M.B.A.	Business Administration	E,T

Campus Extension Site

Rochester, MN

Requirements

Residency requirement: Students are not required to attend classes on the main campus; however, they must earn 45 credits in some way from Winona State.

Undergraduate admissions requirements: Adult Entry Program applicants must hold a high school diploma or GED and have been out of high school for five years. Graduate admissions requirements: Applicants must have a 2.5 undergraduate GPA or a GRE score of 900 (verbal and quantitative). Different departments may have additional requirements.

Graduation requirements (undergraduate): Graduates must earn a minimum of 192 credits with a minimum 2.0 GPA; at least 45 credits must be earned from WSU.

Graduation requirements (graduate): Graduates must earn 45 or more credits, depending on the program. At least 24 credits must be earned from WSU with a GPA of 3.0. Others requirements include the research writing requirement or the comprehensive exam.

Fees, Tuition, Costs

Undergraduate application fee: $20

Graduate application fee: $20

Undergraduate tuition: $52.50/credit hour

Graduate tuition: $77.90/credit hour

Undergraduate cost of books: $200

Graduate cost of books: $100

Other costs: Activity fees of $10.05/credit

Financial Aid/Status

Scholarship programs for adults: Transfer student scholarships and department scholarships available

Full-time status: 15 credits/quarter

Maximum Hours Awarded For

CLEP: 12

DANTES: Yes

Other exams: Yes

Prior learning portfolio: Yes

Features and Services

1. Is it possible to purchase books during hours most adult students attend classes? **Yes.**

2. How do students taking extended classes access library resources? **Library resources are available by computer, interlibrary loan, and cooperative arrangements in local communities.**

3. What is the registration and payment process for adult students? **All students use the same process.**

4. What is the process for advising adult students? **Extensive advising is done at admission by the Adult Entry Program. When a student declares a major, that department handles the advising.**

5. What career and placement services are available to adult students? **All students use the same services.**

6. What characteristics of the institution's adult degree programs are most appealing to students? **Advising and credit for prior learning.**

Wittenburg University

P.O. Box 720 ◆ Springfield, OH 45501
Phone: (513) 327-7012 ◆ Toll-free phone: (800) 677-7558
Fax: (513) 327-6340
Web address: http://www.wittenberg.edu

Founded: 1845

Accredited by: North Central

Enrollment: 2,150 ◆ Adult students: 110

University status: Private, Church, Lutheran Church

Degree	Concentration/Major	Format
B.A.	Organization Studies	E
B.A.	Independently Designed	S,E

Requirements

Residency requirement: Yes.
Options: internship and/or
independent study (limit: 16
credits).
Undergraduate admissions
requirements: Strong academic
preparation/ability. Transfer
students must have a GPA of 3.0 or
higher (or other significant
demonstration).
Graduation requirements
(undergraduate): Graduates must
earn 130 credits; at least 65 credits
must be earned at Wittenberg;
minimum 2.0 GPA overall and
major.

Fees, Tuition, Costs

Undergraduate application fee: $40
Undergraduate tuition: $218/
semester hour
Undergraduate cost of books: $50-
$75/course
Other costs: Travel to and from
campus

Financial Aid/Status

Scholarship programs for adults:
Two need-based programs are
available. Patmos Awards give $10-
$35 per credit for evening study;
Adult Access Awards give up to 50
percent of day tuition.
Full-time status: 12 credits/
semester.
Percentage of adult students
receiving financial aid: 90 percent.

Maximum Hours Awarded For

Other exams: Yes
Additional information: Transfer
credit includes certain nonparallel
programs such as nursing,
engineering technology

Features and Services

1. Is it possible to purchase
   books during hours most
   adult students attend classes?
   Yes.

2. Are the institution's
   administrative offices open
   during hours adult students
   attend class? **Yes.**

3. What is the registration and
   payment process for adult
   students? **Registration and
   payment are very personal
   and flexible. They may be
   handled in person or by
   phone or mail. Payment
   may be made through the
   eighth week of the semester.**

4. What is the process for
   advising adult students? **The
   dean or director reviews
   each registration and
   provides a comprehensive
   degree audit.**

5. What career and placement
   services are available to adult
   students? **Placement services
   are limited to local
   positions.**

6. What characteristics of the
   institution's adult degree
   programs are most appealing
   to students? **Nationally
   recognized academic
   quality; highly competent
   faculty; high expectations.**

Xavier University*

Center for Adult and Part-Time Students
3800 Victory Parkway ◆ **Cincinnati, OH 45207**
Phone: (513)745-3356 ◆ Toll-free phone: (800) 344-4698
Fax: (513) 745-2969

Founded: 1831

Accredited by: North Central

Enrollment: 6,180 ◆ Adult students: 3,053

University status: Private, Church, Roman Catholic Church

Degree	Concentration/Major	Format
A.A.	English, History, Modern Language, Theology, Liberal Arts, Communication Arts	E
A.S.	Pyschology, Early Childhood Education, Criminal Justice, Corrections	E
B.S.B.A.	Management, Marketing, Information Systems, General Business, Human Resources, Accounting	E
B.L.A.	Liberal Arts	E,A
B.A.	Communication Arts, Advertising, Public Relations, Organization Communication, Electronic Media	E
M.A.	Psychology—Two-year full-time program.	
M.A.	Theology	E
M.H.A.	Hospital and Health Administration	E
M.B.A.	Human Resources	E,A
M.Ed.	Agency & Community Counseling, School Counseling, Elementary Education, Physical Education, Special Education, Reading, Montessori, Sports Administration	E
M.A.	English, History, Humanities	E
M.B.A.	Business Administration	E
M.B.A.	Executive-Business Administration	E
M.S.	Criminal Justice, Nursing	E

Requirements

Residency requirement: Yes
Undergraduate admissions requirements: High school diploma or equivalent; minimum C+ average; ACT, SAT, class rank; previous college transcripts; 2.00 or better cumulative average

Graduate admissions requirements: Vary by program

Fees, Tuition, Costs

Undergraduate application fee: $25
Graduate application fee: $25
Undergraduate tuition: $298/credit
Graduate tuition: $325/credit

Financial Aid/Status

Full-time status: 12 or more hours for undergraduate; 9 or more hours for graduate
Percentage of adult students receiving financial aid: 25 percent

Maximum Hours Awarded For

CLEP: Yes
PEP: Yes

Features and Services

1. Is it possible to purchase books during hours most adult students attend classes? **Yes.**

2. Are the institution's administrative offices open during hours adult students attend class? **Yes.**

3. What characteristics of the institution's adult degree programs are most appealing to students? **Scheduling convenience and accelerated (in some cases).**

Colleges Listed by State

his appendix lists colleges by state. The name of the college is in the left-hand column. The right-hand column displays each city where the college has a campus or an extended campus site. When more than one city is listed for a college, the first city usually is the location of the main campus. Many colleges operate extended campus sites in more than one state. To verify the main campus location, refer to the address listed in the guide.

State	Cities
Alabama	
Auburn University	Auburn
Birmingham Southern College	Birmingham
Columbia College	Redstone, Arsenal
Florida Institute of Technology	Huntsville
Huntingdon College	Montgomery
Judson College	Marion
Oakwood College	Huntsville

State	Cities
Alabama (continued)	
Southeastern Bible College	Birmingham
United States Sports Academy	Daphne
University of Alabama	Tuscaloosa, Montgomery, Gadsden
University of North Alabama	Florence
University of South Alabama	Mobile, Fairhope
Alaska	
Sheldon Jackson College	Sitka
Wayland Baptist University	Anchorage, Fairbanks
Arizona	
Chapman University	Phoenix, Tucson
DeVry Institute of Technology	Phoenix
Embry-Riddle Aeronautical University	Mesa, Phoenix
Grand Canyon University	Phoenix
Keller Graduate School of Management	Mesa, Phoenix
Ottawa University	Phoenix
Prescott College	Phoenix, Tucson
University of Phoenix	Phoenix
Wayland Baptist University	Phoenix
Western International University	Phoenix, Douglas, Sierra Vista
Arkansas	
John Brown University	Siloam Springs, Fort Smith
Southern Arkansas University	Magnolia
California	
California Baptist College	Riverside, Fort Irwin, Barstow, Hesperia, San Bernardino
California Institute of Integral Studies	San Francisco
California Polytechnic State University	San Luis Obispo
California School of Professional Psychology	San Francisco
California State University, Bakersfield	Bakersfield, Lancaster, Edwards AFB, China Lake NAWC-Ridgecrest, Tulare
California State University, Chico	Chico
California State University, Dominguez Hills	Carson
California State University, Sacramento	Sacramento
Chapman University	Orange, Palm Desert, Travis AFB, 29 Palms, Manhattan Beach, Palmdale, El Toro, March AFB, Edwards AFB, Suisun, Monterey, Moreno Valley, Modesto, Merced, Stockton, Ontario, Sacramento, Diamond Springs, McClellan AFB, Yuba City, Lemoore, Visalia, San Diego, Vandenberg AFB, Victorville
Columbia College	San Francisco

State	Cities
California (continued)	
DeVry Institute of Technology	Long Beach
DeVry Institute of Technology	Pomona
Electronic University Network	Hornbrook
Embry-Riddle Aeronautical University	Chico, Concord Airport, Hayward Airport, High Desert, Long Beach, Livermore Airport, Los Angeles, Oakland Airport, Ontario
The Fielding Institute	Santa Barbara
Fresno Pacific College	Fresno
John F. Kennedy University	Orinda, Walnut Creek, Campbell
Keller Graduate School of Management	Long Beach, Pomona
LaSierra University	Riverside
Life Bible College	San Dimas
Loma Linda University	Loma Linda
Marymount College	Rancho Palos Verdes, Irvine
The Master's College and Seminary	Santa Clarita
New College of California	San Francisco
Saint Mary's College of California	Moraga, Livermore, Moraga, Oakland, Walnut Creek, Newark, San Ramon, Pleasanton, Novato, Sacramento, San Francisco, Stockton, Redwood City, San Jose, Pleasant Hill, Benicia, Fairfield, Vallejo, Santa Rosa,
Saybrook Institute Graduate School	San Francisco
Shasta Bible College	Redding
Simpson College	Redding
Southern California College	Costa Mesa
Union Institute	San Diego, Los Angeles, Sacramento
University of California, Santa Barbara	Santa Barbara, Ventura
University of the Pacific	Stockton
University of Redlands	Redlands
University of San Francisco	San Francisco, San Ramon, Oakland, Cupertino, Stockton, Sacramento, Orange, Santa Rosa
University of West Los Angeles	Ingelwood
Upper Iowa University	Fort Irwin
West Coast University	Los Angeles, Orange, San Diego, Vanderberg AFB
Colorado	
Chapman University	Colorado Springs, Peterson AFB, Denver
Colorado Christian University	Lakewood Grand Junction, Aurora, Colorado Springs
Colorado State University	Fort Collins
Columbia College	Aurora
Embry-Riddle Aeronautical University	Colorado Springs, Denver
International School of Information Management	Denver
Mind Extension University	Englewood
National Technological University	Fort Collins

State	Cities
Colorado (continued)	
Regis University	Denver, Boulder, Loveland, Colorado Springs, Steamboat Springs, Sterling, Glenwood Springs
University of Denver	Denver
University of Northern Colorado	Greeley, Metro Denver, Colorado Springs, Pueblo, Fort Lupton, Grand Junction, Sterling, Aurora, Fort Carson
University of Southern Colorado	Pueblo, Colorado Spring, Peterson AFB
Connecticut	
Albertus Magnus College	New Haven, Fairfield
Charter Oak State College	Newington
Quinnipiac College	Hamden
Sacred Heart University	Fairfield
Trinity College	Hartford
University of Bridgeport	Bridgeport
University of Connecticut	Storrs
University of New Haven	West Haven
Western Connecticut State University	Danbury
Delaware	
Goldey-Beacom College	Wilmington
University of Delaware	Newark
District of Columbia	
The American University	Washington, DC
Central Michigan University	Washington, DC
Joint Military Intelligence College	Washington, DC
National-Louis University	Washington, DC
Regent University	Washington, DC
Southeastern University	Washington, DC
Strayer College	Washington, DC
Florida	
Assemblies of God Theological Seminary	Lakeland
Barry University	Miami Shores
Central Michigan University	Jacksonville
Columbia College	Jacksonville
Embry-Riddle Aeronautical University	Daytona Beach, Fort Lauderdale, Miami, Moses Lake
Florida Institute of Technology	Melbourne, St. Petersburg, Patrick AFB
Lynn University	Boca Raton
National-Louis University	Tampa
Northwood University	West Palm Beach
Nova Southeastern University	Ft. Lauderdale
Palm Beach Atlantic College	West Palm Beach

State	Cities
Florida (continued)	
Rollins College	Winter Park
Saint Leo College	St. Leo
Southeastern College of the Assemblies of God	Lakeland
Union Institute	North Miami Beach
University of Miami	Coral Gables
University of Sarasota	Sarasota
University of South Florida	Tampa
University of Tampa	Tampa
Walden University	Naples
Warner Southern College	Lake Wales, Leesburg, Melbourne, Orlando, Fort Pierce, Deland, Plant City, Titusville
Georgia	
Central Michigan University	Atlanta
Covenant College	Fort Oglethorpe, Dalton
DeVry Institute	Decatur
Embry-Riddle Aeronautical University	Atlanta
Keller Graduate School of Management	Atlanta, Deactur
National-Louis University	Atlanta
Oglethorpe University	Atlanta
Shorter College	Marietta, Lawrenceville, Rome
Upper Iowa University	Fort Benning
Hawaii	
Central Michigan University	Honolulu
Chaminade University of Honolulu	Honolulu, Schofield Barracks, Fort Shafter, Tripler Army Medical Center, Barbers Point Naval Air Station, Pearl Harbor Naval Base, Marine Corps Base, Keneohe Bay
Hawaii Pacific University	Honolulu
University of Hawaii	Honolulu, Maui, Kauai
Wayland Baptist University	Honolulu
Idaho	
Boise State University	Boise
Illinois	
American Schools of Professional Psychology	Chicago
Aurora University	Aurora, Waukegan, Chicago
Barat College	Lake Forest
Bradley University	Peoria
Chicago State University	Chicago
College of St. Francis	Joliet, Oak Forest
Columbia College	Gurnee, Crystal Lake, Freeport
Concordia University	River Forest, Rockford

State	Cities
Illinois (continued)	
DePaul University	Chicago
DeVry Institute of Technology	Chicago, Addison, Oakbrook Terrace
Eastern Ilinois University	Charleston, Champaign, Olney, Urbana, Centralia, Danville, Effingham, Decatur
Governors State University	University Park
Greenville College	Greenville
Judson College	Elgin
Keller Graduate School of Management	Oakbrook Terrace, Chicago, Lincolnshire, Schaumburg, Oakland Park, Downers Grove, Elgin
National-Louis University	Evanston, Elgin
North Central College	Naperville, St. Charles, Schaumburg
North Park College	Chicago
Northeastern Illinois University	Chicago
Northwestern University	Evanston, Chicago
Olivet Nazarene University	Kankakee, Homewood, Woodfield, Joliet, Arlington Heights, Barrington, Elk Grove Village, Schaumburg, Chicago, Lisle
Quincy University	Quincy
Saint Xavier University	Chicago
Shimer College	Waukegan
Southern Illinois University at Edwardsville	Edwardsville, Belleville, Olney, Hillsboro, Ina, Carlyle, Ullin, Columbia, Jerseyville
Trinity International University	Deerfield
University of Illinois at Springfield	Springfield
University of Illinois at Urbana–Champaign	Champaign, Oak Brook, Arlington Hts., Palos Hills, River Grove
Western Illinois University	Macomb, Rock Island
Indiana	
Anderson University	Anderson
Ball State University	Muncie, Indianapolis, Fort Wayne, LaPorte
Bethel College	Mishawaka, Donaldson
Calumet College of St. Joseph	Whiting, Munster, Merrillville, Chesterton
Concordia University Wisconsin	Indianapolis, Fort Wayne
Embry-Riddle Aeronautical University	Indianapolis
Goshen College	Goshen
Huntington College	Huntington
Indiana Institute of Technology	Fort Wayne, Indianapolis, South Bend
Indiana State University	Terre Haute
Indiana University	Bloomington, Columbus, Kokomo, Fort Wayne, New Albany, Gary, Richmond, Indianapolis, South Bend
Indiana University-Purdue University	Fort Wayne
Indiana University-Purdue University	Indianapolis
Indiana Wesleyan University	Marion, Indianapolis, Terre Haute, Kokomo, Fort Wayne, Columbus, Lafayette, Richmond, Bloomington, Warsaw/Plymouth, Shelbyville, South Bend, Mooresville, Batesville/Greensburg

State	Cities
Indiana (continued)	
Martin University	Indianapolis
Northwood University	Indianapolis
Purdue University	West Lafayette, Anderson, Muncie, Columbus, New Albany, Kokomo, Richmond, South Bend, Indianapolis, Versailles
Saint Francis College	Fort Wayne, Beech Grove
Saint Mary-of-the-Woods College	Saint Mary-of-the-Woods
University of Indianapolis	Indianapolis
University of Southern Indiana	Evansville
Iowa	
Briar Cliff College	Sioux City
Clarke College	Dubuque
Dordt College	Sioux Center
Drake University	Des Moines
St. Ambrose University	Davenport
Simpson College	Indianola, West Des Moines
Teikyo Marycrest University	Davenport
University of Iowa	Iowa City
Upper Iowa University	Fayette, Des Moines, Calmar, Fayette, Manchester, Newton, Waterloo
Kansas	
Baker University	Overland Park, Topeka
Bethel College	N. Newton
Central Michigan University	Fort Leavenworth
Kansas State University	Manhattan
MidAmerica Nazarene College	Olathe
Ottawa University	Overland Park
Saint Mary College	Shawnee Mission, Leavenworth
Southwestern College	Winfield, Wichita
Tabor College of Wichita	Wichita
Upper Iowa University	Fort Riley
Kentucky	
Bellarmine College	Louisville, Ashland
Campbellsville College	Campbellsville, Louisville
Embry-Riddle Aeronautical University	Louisville
Lincoln Memorial University	Cumberland, Corbin
Spaulding University	Louisville, Bardstown
Thomas More College	Crestview Hills
University of Louisville	Louisville
Lousiana	
Centenary College of Louisiana	Shreveport
Central Michigan University	Fort Polk
Concordia University Wisconsin	New Orleans

State	Cities
Lousiana (continued)	
Louisiana College	Pineville
Louisiana State University at Shreveport	Shreveport
Loyola University for Ministry	New Orleans
Northwood University	New Orleans
Southern University at New Orleans	New Orleans
University of New Orleans	New Orleans
Upper Iowa University	Fort Polk
Maine	
Northwood University	Showhegan
Saint Joseph's College	Windham
University of Maine at Augusta	Augusta
University of Maine	Orono, Bangor, Lewiston
Westbrook College	Portland
Maryland	
Central Michigan University	Andrews AFB
College of Notre Dame	Baltimore
Columbia Union College	Takoma Park
Florida Institute of Technology	Aberdeen, Patuxent
Griggs University	Silver Spring
Joint Military Intelligence College	Fort Meade
Loyola College in Maryland	Baltimore
Towson State University	Towson
University of Baltimore	Baltimore
University of Maryland at College Park	College Park, Rockville, Baltimore, California, Aberdeen
Washington Bible College	Lanham
Massachusetts	
Atlantic Union College	South Lancaster
Boston College	Chestnut Hill
Cambridge College	Cambridge, Springfield
Eastern Nazarene College	Quincy
Emmanuel College	Boston, Medford, Andover, South Shore, Framington, Woburn, Leominster
Framington State College	Framington
Hebrew College	Brookline
Lesley College	Cambridge
North Adams State College	North Adams
Northeastern University	Boston, Burlington, Milford, Dedham, Westwood, Framington, Weymouth, Marshfield
Suffolk University	Boston
University of Massachusetts, Dartmouth	North Dartmouth, Attleboro, Cape Cod, Taunton
Wentworth Institute of Technology	Boston
Westfield State College	Westfield, Framingham, Worcester

State	Cities
Michigan	
Calvin College	Grand Rapids
Central Michigan University	Mount Pleasant, Detroit, Grand Rapids, Saginaw, Traverse City
Cornerstone College	Grand Rapids
Ferris State University	Big Rapids, Flint, Mt. Clemens, Traverse City, Grand Rapids, Midland, Dowagiac, Garden City, Muskegon, Jackson
Grand Rapids Baptist Seminary	Grand Rapids
Lawrence Technological University	Southfield
Northwood University	Midland, Livonia, Sheldon, Van Dyke
Oakland University	Rochester, Rochester Hills, Warren, Royal Oak, Madison Heights, Birmingham
Siena Heights College	Adrian, Battle Creek, Benton Harbor, Monroe, Southfield
Spring Arbor College	Spring Arbor, Jackson, Troy, Lambertville, Flint, Dearborn, Port Huron, Detroit, Bay City, Lansing, Traverse City, Battle Creek, Grand Rapids, Gaylord
Wayne State University	Detroit
Minnesota	
Alfred Adler Institute of Minnesota	Hopkins
Assemblies of God Theological Seminary	Minneapolis
Bemidji State University	Bemidji, Hibbing, Minneapolis/St. Paul
College of St. Scholastica	Duluth, Brainard, Hibbing, Grand Rapids
Hamline University	St. Paul
Metropolitan State University	St. Paul
Northwestern College	St. Paul, Anoka, Bloomington, Golden Valley
University of Minnesota	Minneapolis
Winona State University	Winona, Rochester
Mississippi	
Millsaps College	Jackson
Tougaloo College	Tougaloo
University of Mississippi	University, Tupelo, Southaven, Jackson
Wesley College	Florence
Missouri	
Assemblies of God Theological Seminary	Springfield
Berean University of the Assemblies of God	Springfield
Central Michigan University	Kansas City
Central Missouri State University	Warrensburg, Kansas City, St. Louis, St. Joseph
Columbia College	Columbia, St. Louis, Jefferson City, Ft. Leonard Wood, Osage Beach
Concordia University Wisconsin	St. Louis
DeVry Institute of Technology	Kansas City

State	Cities
Missouri (continued)	
Drury College	Springfield, Ft. Leonard Wood
Fontbonne College	St. Louis
Keller Graduate School of Management	Kansas City, St. Louis
Lincoln University	Jefferson City, Ft. Leonard Wood
Lindenwood College	St. Charles, St. Louis, St. Peters, Marshall
Maryville University of Saint Louis	St. Louis
National-Louis University	St. Louis
Rockhurst College	Kansas City
Southern Illinois University at Edwardsville	St. Louis
Stephens College	Columbia
University of Missouri–Kansas City	Kansas City
William Jewell College	Liberty
William Woods University	Fulton, Owensville, Ashland, Mexico, Jefferson City, Columbia, Moberly, Kirksville, Lake Ozark
Montana	
Carroll College	Helena
Central Michigan University	Great Falls
Montana State University–Billings	Billings
Nebraska	
Central Michigan University	Offut AFB, Omaha
Chadron State College	Chadron
Clarkson College	Omaha
College of Saint Mary	Omaha
Creighton University	Omaha
Doane College	Lincoln
Nebraska Wesleyan University	Lincoln
University of Nebraska	Lincoln, Bellevue
Wayne State College	Wayne, South Sioux City, Norfolk
Nevada	
University of Nevada–Reno	Reno, Elko
New Hampshire	
College for Lifelong Learning	Concord, Portsmouth, Bow, Rochester, Lebanon, Manchester, Conway, Nashua, Berlin, Littleton
Daniel Webster College	Nashua
Franklin Pierce College	Nashua
University of New Hampshire	Durham
University of New Hampshire at Manchester	Manchester
New Jersey	
Caldwell College	Caldwell

State	Cities
New Jersey (continued)	
Centenary College	Hackettstown
Central Michigan University	McGuire AFB
Embry-Riddle Aeronautical University	Atlantic City
Fairleigh Dickinson University	Teaneck
Florida Institute of Technology	Picatinny, Lakehurst
Georgian Court College	Lakewood
Ramapo College of New Jersey	Mahwah
Rider University	Lawrenceville
Rutgers University College–Camden	Camden
Rutgers University	New Brunswick, Newark
Saint Peter's College	Jersey City
Thomas Edison State College	Trenton
University of Southern Colorado	Fort Dix, McGuire AFB
New Mexico	
Central Missouri State University	Albuquerque
Chapman University	Albuquerque, Kirtland AFB
The College of Santa Fe	Santa Fe, Albuquerque
Florida Institute of Technology	White Sands
New Mexico Highlands University	Las Vegas
New Mexico Institute of Mining and Technology	Socorro
St. John's College	Santa Fe
Wayland Baptist University	Glorietta
New York	
Adelphi University	Garden City, Huntington
Audrey Cohen College	New York
Bard College	Annandale-on-Hudson
Central Michigan University	Fort Hamilton
Chapman University	Syracuse
City College, City University of New York	New York
College of Mount Saint Vincent	Riverdale
College of New Rochelle Graduate School	New Rochelle
Columbia College	Syracuse
Empire State College–SUNY	Saratoga Springs
Fordham University	Bronx
Hofstra University	Hempstead
Houghton College	West Seneca, Olean
Iona College	New Rochelle, Manhattan, New York
Lehman College, City University of New York	Bronx
Manhattanville College	Purchase
Marist College	Poughkeepsie
Marymount Manhattan College	New York
Medaille College	Buffalo
Mercy College	Dobbs Ferry, Yorktown Heights, White Plains, Bronx
Nazareth College	Rochester
New School for Social Research	New York

State	Cities

New York (continued)

New York Institute of Technology	Central Islip
New York University	New York
Nyack College	Nyack
Purchase College, State University of New York	Purchase
Queens College, City University of New York	Flushing
Regents College	Albany
Rochester Institute of Technology	Rochester
Sage Colleges	Albany, Troy
Sarah Lawrence College	Bronxville
Skidmore College	Sarasota Springs
State University of New York College at Potsdam	Potsdam
Syracuse University	Syracuse

North Carolina

Assemblies of God Theological Seminary	Dunn
Belmont Abbey College	Belmont
Campbell University	Buies Creek; Camp Lejeune Campus; Jacksonville; Ft. Bragg Campus, Fayetteville; Pope AFB Campus, Fayetteville; The Raleigh Center, Raleigh; Goldsboro; Rocky Mt.
Central Michigan University	Fort Bragg
Mars Hill College	Mars Hill, Asheville, Burnsville
Mount Olive College	New Bern, Wilmington, Salemburg, Goldsboro
North Carolina Wesleyan College	Rocky Mount, Goldsboro, Raleigh
Salem College	Winston-Salem

North Dakota

Central Michigan University	Grand Forks AFB, Minot AFB
University of Mary	Bismarck
University of North Dakota	Grand Forks, Devil's Lake, Williston, Bismarck, Dickinson
Valley City State University	Valley City

Ohio

Bluffton College	Bluffton
Central Michigan University	Dayton
College of Mount St. Joseph	Cincinnati
Defiance College	Defiance
DeVry Institute of Technology	Columbus
Embry-Riddle Aeronautical University	Cincinnati, Columbus, Wilmington
Joint Military Intelligence College	Dayton
Lake Erie College	Painesville
Lourdes College	Sylvania
Malone College	Canton, Brecksville
Marietta College	Marietta
Mount Vernon Nazarene College	Mount Vernon, Columbus

State	Cities
Ohio (continued)	
Ohio State University at Newark	Newark
Ohio University–Chillicothe	Chillicothe, Athens, Zanesville, Lancaster, Clairsville, Ironton
Ohio University	Athens
Union Institute	Cincinnati
University of Findlay	Findlay, Cincinnati, Lima, Toledo
University of Toledo	Toledo
Urbana University	Urbana, Columbus, Dayton
Wilberforce University	Wilberforce, Columbus
Wittenburg University	Springfield
Xavier University	Cincinnati
Oklahoma	
Bartlesville Wesleyan College	Bartlesville
Mid-America Bible College	Oklahoma City
Oklahoma City University	Oklahoma City, Tulsa
Oklahoma State University	Stillwater
Oklahoma State University–Okmulgee	Okmulgee
Oral Roberts University	Tulsa
Southern Nazarene University	Bethany, Tulsa
University of Southern Colorado	Altus AFB
Oregon	
Eastern Oregon State College	La Grande, Portland, Bitcer City, Bend, Pendleton, Ontario, Enterprise, Burns, John Day
George Fox College	Newberg
Linfield College	McMinnville
Marylhurst College for Lifelong Learning	Marylhurst
Northwest Christian College	Eugene, Roseburg, Grants Pass, Medford
Oregon Institute of Technology	Klamath Falls
Warner Pacific College	Portland
Western Baptist College	Salem, Portland
Western Evangelical Seminary	Tigard, Salem
Western Oregon State College	Monmouth
Pennsylvania	
Albright College	Reading
Allentown College of St. Francis de Sales	Center Valley, Easton
Assemblies of God Theological Seminary	Phoenixville
Beaver College	Glenside
Cabrini College	Radnor
Carlow College	Pittsburgh, Beaver, Cranberry, Greensburg
Cedar Crest College	Allentown
Chestnut Hill College	Philadelphia
College Misericordia	Dallas

State	Cities

Pennsylvania (continued)

Drexel University	Philadelphia
Eastern College	St. Davids
Edinboro University of Pennsylvania	Edinboro
Elizabethtown College	Elizabethtown
Gannon University	Erie, Warren, Sharon
King's College	Wilkes-Barre
Lancaster Bible College	Lancaster
Lebanon Valley College of Pennsylvania	Annville, Lancaster
Mercyhurst College	Erie
Messiah College	Grantham
Millersville University	Millersville, Dallastown
Muhlenberg College	Allentown
Pennsylvania State University	Media
Philadelphia College of Bible	Langhorne
Philadelphia College of Textiles and Science	Philadelphia
Point Park College	Pittsburgh
Thiel College	Greenville
University of Pennsylvania	Philadelphia
University of Pittsburgh	Pittsburgh, Greenburg, Johnstown, Titusville
University of Pittsburgh at Bradford	Bradford, St. Mary's, Warren, Kane, Coudersport
Westminster College	New Wilmington

Puerto Rico

American University of Puerto Rico	Bayamon, Manati
Atlantic College	Guaynabo
Caribbean University	Bayamon, Carolina, Vega Baja, Ponce
InterAmerican University of Puerto Rico	Guayama
InterAmerican University of Puerto Rico	Arecibo, Fajardo, Aguadilla, San German, San Juan

Rhode Island

Bryant College	Smithfield
Roger Williams University	Bristol
University of Rhode Island	Kingston

South Carolina

College of Charleston	Charleston
Columbia College of South Carolina	Columbia
Southern Wesleyan University	Central

South Dakota

Augustana College	Sioux Falls
Dakota Wesleyan University	Mitchell
Huron University	Huron, Sioux Falls
University of Sioux Falls	Sioux Falls

State	Cities
Tennessee	
Carson–Newman College	Jefferson City
Central Michigan University	Memphis
Christian Brothers University	Memphis
Covenant College	Chattanooga, Cleveland
Embry-Riddle Aeronautical University	Memphis
Lee College	Cleveland
Lincoln Memorial University	Harrogate, Knoxville, Maryville, Madisonville
Tennessee Wesleyan College	Athens, Knoxville, Oak Ridge, Chattanooga, Cleveland
Trevecca Nazarene University	Nashville
Union University	Jackson
University of Memphis	Memphis
Vanderbilt University	Nashville
Texas	
Assemblies of God Theological Seminary	Waxahachie
Columbia College	Grand Prairie
Concordia University at Austin	Austin
Dallas Baptist University	Dallas
DeVry Institute of Technology	Irving
Embry-Riddle Aeronautical University	Dallas, Ft. Worth
Lamar University	Beaumont
LeTourneau University	Longview, Dallas, Bedford, Tyler, Houston
Northwood University	Dallas
Our Lady of the Lake University	San Antonio, Dallas, Houston
Paul Quinn College	Dallas, Waco, Ft. Worth
Southern Methodist University	Dallas
Southwest Texas State University	San Marcos, San Antonio
Southwestern Adventist College	Keene
Texas Christian University	Fort Worth
Texas Tech University	Lubbock
Trinity University	San Antonio
University of Central Texas	Killeen
University of Houston	Katy, Houston, Sugarland
University of Texas at Arlington	Arlington
University of Texas at Dallas	Richardson
Wayland Baptist University	Plainview, Wichita Falls, Amarillo, Lubbock
Utah	
Columbia College	Salt Lake City
Southern Utah University	Cedar City, St. George, Richfield
University of Utah	Salt Lake City
Westminster College	Salt Lake City
Vermont	
Burlington College	Burlington

State	Cities
Vermont (continued)	
Champlain College	Burlington
Embry-Riddle Aeronautical University	Burlington
Goddard College	Plainfield
Johnson State College	Johnson
Saint Michael's College	Colchester
School for International Training	Brattleboro
Southern Vermont College	Bennington
Trinity College of Vermont	Burlington
Virginia	
Averett College	Danville, Vienna, Norfolk, Richmond, Hampton, Roanoke, Newport News, Lynchburg
Bluefield College	Bluefield, Blacksburg, Marion, Clifton Forge, Roanoke, Dublin, Salem, Richlands, Wytheville,
Central Michigan University	Richmond
Eastern Mennonite University	Harrisburg
Florida Institute of Technology	Fort Lee, Alexandria, Fort Eustis, Norfolk
James Madison University	Harrisburg
Keller Graduate School of Management	Tysons Corner
Mary Baldwin College	Staunton, Richmond, Roanoke, Charlottesville, Weyers Cave
National-Louis University	McLean
Norfolk State University	Norfolk
Old Dominion University	Norfolk, Weyers Cave, Melfa, Lynchburg, Locust Grove, Clifton Forge, Richmond, Danville, Middletown, Dublin, Annandale, Martinsville, Charlottesville, Alberta, Keysville, Richlands, Roanoke, Wythevill, Virginia Beach, Portsmouth, Hampton
Regent University	Virginia Beach
Strayer College	Alexandria, Manassas, Arlington, Fredericksburg, Woodbridge, Ashburn, Fort Belvoir, Quantico, Dahlgren, Falls Church
University of Richmond	Richmond
University of Virginia	Charlottesville, Lynchburg, Richmond, Roanoke, Hampton Roads, Charlotteville, Abingdon, Falls Church
Virginia Commonwealth University	Richmond
Virginia Wesleyan College	Norfolk
Washington	
Assemblies of God Theological Seminary	Kirkland
Chapman University	Silverdale, McChord AFB, Ft. Lewis, Oak Harbor
Clark College	Vancouver
Columbia College	Marysville
Eastern Washington University	Cheney, Spokane, River Point
Evergreen State College	Olympia

State	Cities
Washington (continued)	
Northwest College	Kirkland
Northwest Graduate/Undergraduate School School of Ministry	Kirkland
Saint Martin's College	Lacey, Fort Lewis, McChord AFB
Seattle Pacific University	Seattle
Seattle University	Seattle
Washington State University	Pullman
Whitworth College	Spokane
West Virginia	
Concord College	Athens, Beckley Center
Fairmont State College	Fairmont, Clarksburg
Glenville State College	Glenville
West Virginia State College	Institute
West Virginia University	Morgantown, West Liberty, Fairmont, Glenville, Huntington, Institute, Montgomery, Athens, Bluefield, Shepherdstown
West Virginia University at Parkersburg	Parkersburg, Ripley
Wheeling Jesuit College	Wheeling, Weirton, Parkersburg, Clarksburg, Charleston
Wisconsin	
Aurora University	New Berlin
Cardinal Stritch College	Milwaukee
Carthage College	Kenosha
Concordia University Wisconsin	Mequon, Kenosha, Madison
Keller Graduate School of Management	Milwaukee, Waukesha
Lakeland College	Sheboygan, Chippewa Falls, Madison, Fort McCoy, Marshfield, Green Bay, Milwaukee, Kohler, Sheboygan, Neenah/Menasha, Wisconsin Rapids
Marian College of Fond Du Lac	Fond Du Lac, West Allis, Appleton
Marquette University	Milwaukee
Milwaukee School of Engineering	Milwaukee, Appleton
National-Louis University	Milwaukee
Ottawa University	Brookfield
Silver Lake College	Manitowoc, Appleton, Fond du Lac, Wausau, Tomah, Madison, Milwaukee, Green Bay
Trinity International University	Brookfield
University of Wisconsin–Madison	Madison
University of Wisconsin–Oshkosh	Oshkosh
University of Wisconsin–Platteville	Platteville
University of Wisconsin–River Falls	River Falls
University of Wisconsin–Superior	Superior
Upper Iowa University	Janesville, Madison, West Allis, Prairie du Chien, Wausau
Wyoming	
Regis University	Cheyenne, Gillette

Colleges with External Studies and Distance Learning Degree Programs

 his appendix lists colleges and universities that have external studies and distance learning degree programs. These programs are available to students from anywhere in the nation. In some cases they involve limited travel to a campus for concentrated courses on weekends or during summer sessions.

Assemblies of God Theological
   Seminary
Atlantic Union College
Auburn University

Bemidji State University
Berean University of the
   Assemblies of God
Boise State University

Bradley University
Burlington College
Caldwell College
California Institute of Integral Studies
California State University, Dominguez Hills
Champlain College
Charter Oak State College
College for Lifelong Learning
College of St. Scholastica
Colorado State University
Concordia University Wisconsin
Electronic University Network
Empire State College–SUNY
Fairleigh Dickinson University
The Fielding Institute
Goddard College
Governor's State University
Grand Rapids Baptist Seminary
Griggs University
Hofstra University
Indiana Institute of Technology
Indiana University
International School of Information Management
John F. Kennedy University
Johnson State College
Judson College–Marion, AL
Kansas State University
Life Bible College
Louisiana College
Marywood College
Mercy College
Mid-America Bible College
Mind Extension University
National Technological University
New Mexico Institute of Mining and Technology
New York Institute of Technology
Northeastern Illinois University

Nova Southeastern University
Ohio University
Prescott College
Regent University
Regents College
Regis University
Rochester Institute of Technology
Roger Williams University
Saint Joseph's College
Saint Mary-of-the-Woods College
Salem College
Saybrook Institute Graduate School
School for International Training
Skidmore College
Southeastern Bible College
Southeastern College of the Assemblies of God
Southwestern Adventist College
Stephens College
Thomas Edison State College
Union Institute
United States Sports Academy
University of Alabama
University of Denver
University of Iowa
University of Minnesota
University of Nevada–Reno
University of Phoenix
University of Pittsburgh
University of Sarasota
University of South Florida
University of Southern Colorado
University of Wisconsin–Madison
University of Wisconsin–Plattesville
University of Wisconsin–River Falls
University of Wisconsin–Superior
Walden University
Washington State University

Universities with Doctoral Degree Programs

 large majority of the institutions listed in this guide offer graduate programs at the master's degree level. There is a much smaller number that offer degree programs at the doctoral level. This appendix lists those universities that offer Ph.D., Ed.D., D.Psy., D.Min., D.Sci., and J.D. degrees.

American Schools of Professional Psychology

The American University

Auburn University Graduate Outreach Program

Ball State University

California Institute of Integral Studies

California School of Professional Psychology

Electronic University Network

The Fielding Institute

Grand Rapids Baptist Seminary

Indiana University-Purdue University-Indianapolis

John F. Kennedy University

LaSierra University

Northwest Graduate/ Undergraduate School of Ministry

Nova Southeastern University
Quincy University
Quinnipiac College
Regent University
Saybrook Institute Graduate School
Seattle Pacific University
Union Institute
United States Sports Academy
University of Alabama

University of Baltimore
University of Bridgeport
University of Missouri–Kansas City
University of New Haven
University of Sarasota
University of Texas at Arlington
University of West Los Angeles
Walden University